Effective Teaching Methods
Third Edition

Gary D. Borich
The University of Texas at Austin

Merrill,
an imprint of
Prentice Hall
Englewood Cliffs, New Jersey   Columbus, Ohio

Library of Congress Cataloging-in-Publication Data

Borich, Gary D.
    Effective teaching methods / Gary D. Borich.—3rd ed.
       p. cm.
    Includes bibliographical references and index.
    ISBN 0-02-312461-X
     1. Teaching. 2. Lesson planning—United States.   I. Title.
  LB1025.3.B67   1996
  371.1'02—dc20   94-44812
                                            CIP

Cover photo: Susan Lapides/1990
Editor: Debra A. Stollenwerk
Production Editor: Alexandrina Benedicto Wolf
Photo Editor: Anne Vega
Design Coordinator: Julia Zonneveld Van Hook
Text Designer: STELLARViSIONs
Cover Designer: Thomas Mack
Production Manager: Deidra M. Schwartz
Electronic Text Management: Marilyn Wilson Phelps, Matthew Williams, Karen L. Bretz, Tracey Ward

This book was set in Bookman by Prentice Hall and was printed and bound by Arcata Graphics/Martinsburg. The cover was printed by Phoenix Color Corp.

 © 1996 by Prentice-Hall, Inc.
A Simon & Schuster Company
Englewood Cliffs, New Jersey 07632

Earlier editions © 1988 and 1992 by Macmillan Publishing Company.

Photo credits: pp. 1, 18, 46, 60, 79, 117, 136, 236, 325, 338, 355, 365, 402, 420, 431, 441, 458, 471, 486, and 570 by Anne Vega, Merrill/Prentice Hall; pp. 26, 106, 311, 504, 511, and 546 by Barbara Schwartz, Merrill/Prentice Hall; pp. 33, 96, 148, 176, 207, 253, 273, 382, 393, 530, 590, and 632 by Scott Cunningham, Merrill/ Prentice Hall; p. 81 by Michael Siluk, Merrill/Prentice Hall; p. 162 by Lloyd Lemmerman, Merrill/Prentice Hall; pp. 213, 596, and 622 by KS Studios, Merrill/Prentice Hall; pp. 282, 562, 636, and 659 by Todd Yarrington, Merrill/Prentice Hall; and p. 573 by Andy Brunk, Merrill/Prentice Hall

Printed in the United States of America

10 9 8 7 6 5 4 3 2 1

ISBN: 0-02-312461-X

Prentice-Hall International (UK) Limited, *London*
Prentice-Hall of Australia Pty. Limited, *Sydney*
Prentice-Hall of Canada, Inc., *Toronto*
Prentice-Hall Hispanoamericana, S. A., *Mexico*
Prentice-Hall of India Private Limited, *New Delhi*
Prentice-Hall of Japan, Inc., *Tokyo*
Simon & Schuster Asia Pte. Ltd., *Singapore*
Editora Prentice-Hall do Brasil, Ltda., *Rio de Janeiro*

Microcomputers, competency testing for students and teachers, curriculum reform, new state and federal laws, multicultural classrooms, and new teacher certification and degree requirements are but a few of the factors changing the face of American schools and creating special challenges for you, the beginning teacher. This book has been written to help you prepare to meet these challenges and to discover the opportunities for professional growth and advancement they provide.

To accomplish this, this third edition of *Effective Teaching Methods* has four simple goals. The first is to present effective teaching practices derived from a recent 25-year period of classroom research. In this research, different teaching practices were systematically studied for their effectiveness on learners. The results have made it possible to replace many age-old anecdotal suggestions for "good" teaching with modern, research-based teaching practices that are empirically related to positive outcomes in learners. How to use these teaching practices to become an effective teacher is a major focus of this book.

Second, this text describes these effective teaching practices in a friendly, conversational manner. The language of classrooms is informal, and there is no reason why a book about teachers in classrooms should not use the same language. Therefore, this book talks straight, avoiding complicated phrases, rambling discussions, or pseudoscholarly language. The idea behind each chapter is to get the point across quickly in a friendly and readable style.

The third goal of this book is practicality. Positive prescriptions for your classroom behavior show how you engage students in the learning process, manage your classroom, and increase student achievement. This book not only tells *what* to do to obtain these results; it also shows *how* to obtain them, illustrating effective teaching practices with concrete examples and entertaining classroom dialogues.

The final goal of this book is to be realistic. Some of the literature on teaching is speculative. However, this book describes what real teachers do in real classrooms and which teaching practices are and are not effective in those classrooms. Nothing in this book is pie-in-the-sky theorizing about effective teaching because most of what is presented results directly from years of research and observation of effective teaching practices in real classrooms.

These, then, are this book's four goals: to provide *research-based* effective teaching practices, presented in a *conversational style,* that are *practical* and *realistic.*

Special features of this book include the following:

- A beginning chapter on who an effective teacher is and what an effective teacher does in the classroom (Chapter 1).
- A chapter on understanding the important role of individual differences and learner diversity—prior achievement, ability, learning style, culture and ethnicity, and home and family life—on student learning needs and classroom management (Chapter 2).
- Two chapters on teaching strategies that explain how to use direct instructional methods (such as explaining, lecturing, drill and practice, and recitation—Chapter 6) and indirect instructional methods (such as group discussion, collaboration, and discovery and problem-solving activities—Chapter 7).
- A chapter on self-directed learning and how to use metacognitive techniques, teacher mediation, and the social dialogue of the classroom to help learners control, regulate, and take responsibility for their own learning (Chapter 9).
- A chapter on cooperative learning and the collaborative process for productively organizing and managing group and team activities that promote communication skills, self-esteem, and problem solving (Chapter 10).
- Two chapters on classroom management, including group development in the classroom (Chapter 11) and anticipatory management (Chapter 12).
- A chapter on teaching methods to use with special types of learners in the regular classroom—at-risk, gifted, and bilingual learners, and learners with disabilities (Chapter 13).
- A chapter on evaluation of student achievement for measuring and interpreting student progress using teacher-made and standardized tests (Chapter 14).
- A new chapter on performance assessment, which explains the concept of authentic (performance) assessment and how to construct and grade performance assessments and student portfolios (Chapter 15).

We also provide, specifically with you, the student, in mind:

- Classroom application questions and key terms at the beginning of each chapter that focus you on the key aspects of each chapter. These questions are keyed to specific sections within each chapter that answer the question.
- End-of-chapter summaries that restate key concepts in an easy-to-follow outline format.

- End-of-chapter questions for discussion and practice, and keyed answers in Appendix B.
- Annotated suggested readings at the end of each chapter that highlight or expand major concepts within the chapter.
- An observation instrument for learning how to "see" effective teaching practices in the classroom, illustrated with example dialogues in Appendix C.
- A self-report survey instrument for measuring concerns about yourself, the teaching task, and your impact on students (Chapter 3 and Appendix A).
- New procedures for organizing unit and lesson plans that lets you graphically visualize the relationship between lessons and unit (Chapter 5).

Users of the earlier editions of this book will notice that many chapters have been revised due to the rapid pace of change occurring in nearly every aspect of teaching. These changes have resulted in a text that updates and extends the content in earlier editions. High points of the new topics added to each chapter include the following:

- Family-school partnerships and the relationship of culture and ethnicity to learning (Chapter 2)
- The "thinking curriculum" and integrated bodies of knowledge (Chapter 3)
- Authentic behavior and performance objectives (Chapter 4)
- Communication and computer technologies for the classroom (Chapter 5)
- Interdisciplinary thematic units (Chapter 5)
- Direct instruction for mastery learning (Chapter 6)
- Constructivism and metacognitive strategies for learning (Chapter 7)
- Culturally responsive questioning and sociolinguistics of the classroom (Chapter 8)
- Critical thinking and problem-based learning (Chapter 9)
- Cultural diversity and cooperative learning (Chapter 10)
- Stages of group development and culturally responsive teaching (Chapter 11)
- Low-profile classroom management and natural reinforcers (Chapter 12)
- Heterogeneous grouping and normalization (Chapter 13)
- Instructional validity of teacher-made tests (Chapter 14)
- Performance assessment and student portfolios (Chapter 15)

Since publication of the earlier editions of this text, the author has prepared a new and revised edition of a companion volume, *Observa-*

tion Skills for Effective Teaching, 2nd Edition (Borich, 1994, also from Merrill/Prentice Hall). This revised companion volume is intended to be used in either a preteaching observation experience or as an applications resource to the present volume. *Observation Skills for Effective Teaching* provides extensive examples, entertaining and instructional classroom dialogues, and practical observation and recording instruments keyed to and coordinated with the effective teaching methods presented in this text. Together, these texts provide the sequence of learning for the preservice and beginning teacher illustrated in the following figure.

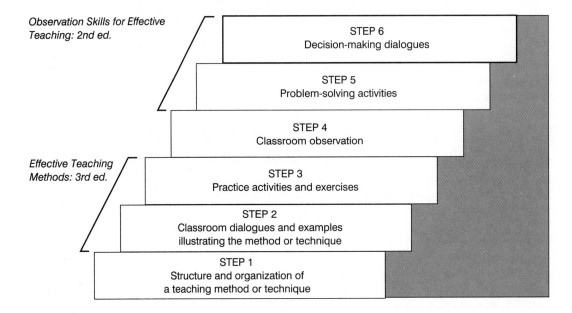

Observation Skills for Effective Teaching: 2nd ed.

STEP 6
Decision-making dialogues

STEP 5
Problem-solving activities

STEP 4
Classroom observation

Effective Teaching Methods: 3rd ed.

STEP 3
Practice activities and exercises

STEP 2
Classroom dialogues and examples illustrating the method or technique

STEP 1
Structure and organization of a teaching method or technique

ACKNOWLEDGEMENTS

Many individuals contributed to the preparation of this book. Not the least are the many professionals whose studies of classroom life have contributed to the effective teacher described in this text. The work of these professionals has made possible an integration and synthesis of effective teaching practices representing a variety of data sources and methodological perspectives. Although I accept responsibility for translations of research into practice that I have made, strengths the reader may see in this approach must be shared with the many individuals who made them possible.

I also wish to acknowledge those teachers who over the years have shared their insights about the teaching process with me.

Among these have been teachers in the Austin, Texas Independent School District, especially William B. Travis High School and Travis Heights Elementary School, who provided the opportunity to observe many of the effective teaching methods described herein. For their helpful reviews and contributions to the manuscript, I extend my gratitude to my good friend and colleague, Marty Tombari; and to Dr. George B. Belden, North Georgia College; Sister Judith Costello, Regis College; Dr. Lillian Norris-Holmes, Morgan State University; Dr. Beverly Schemmer, Taylor University; Dr. Betty Jo Simmons, Longwood College; and Dr. Patti Trietsch, Sul Ross State University.

GDB
Austin, Texas

Chapter 1

► The Effective Teacher   1

Chapter 2

► Understanding Your Students   46

Chapter 6

▶ Direct Instruction Strategies   236

Chapter 7

▶ Indirect Instruction Strategies   282

Chapter 8

▶ Questioning Strategies   338

Chapter 9

▶ Self-Directed Learning   382

Chapter 10

▶ Cooperative Learning and the Collaborative Process   420

Chapter 11

▶ Classroom Management   458

Chapter 12

▶ Classroom Order and Discipline   504

Chapter 13

▶ Teaching Special Learners in the Regular Classroom   546

Chapter 14

▶ Assessing Learners: Objective and Essay Tests   590

Chapter 15

► Assessing Learners: Performance Assessment   632

Appendix A

► Teacher Concerns Checklist   671

Appendix B

► Answers to Chapter Questions   675

Appendix C

► Formative Observation of Effective Teaching Practices Instrument   687

References   699

Author Index   I–1

Subject Index   I–5

CHAPTER 1

The Effective Teacher

Teaching is not just transmission of knowledge but but rather the interaction of teachers & learner.

 This chapter will help you answer the following questions:

1. How has effective teaching been defined?
2. How is research on effective teaching conducted?
3. What are some key effective teaching behaviors?
4. What are some behaviors that can help me perform the key teaching behaviors?
5. What are "constructivist strategies" of teaching?
6. Why are multiple definitions of "effective teaching" necessary?
7. How does effective teaching differ across socioeconomic level, culture, and ethnicity?
8. How does effective teaching differ across content areas?
9. What are some important indicators of teaching effectiveness?
10. What are "patterns" of effective teaching behavior?

This chapter will also help you learn the meaning of the following:

▶ constructivist teaching strategies
engagement in the learning process
instructional variety
key and helping teaching behaviors
lesson clarity
patterns of effective teaching behavior
psychological characteristics of teachers
student success rate
teacher task orientation
teacher-mediated dialogue

What is an effective teacher? How do I become one? How long does it take? These questions have been asked by every teacher, young or old. They are deceptively simple questions, for they have many different answers. Teaching is a complex and difficult task that demands extraordinary abilities. Despite decades of experience and research, one of the most difficult tasks in education today is defining an effective teacher.

This chapter offers no pat definitions of an "effective teacher." Instead, the goal is to introduce you to practices used by effective teachers—practices related to positive outcomes in learners. These effective teaching practices do not tell the whole story of what an effective teacher is, but they do form an important foundation to help you understand the chapters that lie ahead and to help you become an effective teacher. Subsequent chapters blend these practices with other activities, such as writing of objectives, lesson planning, teaching strategies, questioning, and classroom management. This will give you a rich and comprehensive picture of an effective teacher and, most importantly, help you become one.

>>> WHAT IS AN EFFECTIVE TEACHER? <<<

The Role-Model Definition

How has effective teaching been defined?

If you had grown up a century ago, you would have been able to answer "What is an effective teacher?" very simply: A good teacher was a good person—a role model who met the community ideal for a good citizen, good parent, and good employee. At that time, teachers were judged primarily on their goodness as people and only secondarily on their behavior in the classroom. They were expected to be honest, hardworking, generous, friendly, and considerate, and to demonstrate these qualities in their classrooms by being authoritative, organized, disciplined, insightful, and dedicated. Practically speaking, this meant that to be effective, all a beginning teacher needed was King Solomon's wisdom, Sigmund Freud's insight, Albert Einstein's knowledge, and Florence Nightingale's dedication!

It soon became evident that this definition of an ideal teacher lacked clear, objective standards of performance that could be consistently applied to all teachers and that could be used to train future teachers.

The Psychological Characteristics Definition

The early role-model approach soon gave way to another, which attempted to identify the **psychological characteristics** of a good teacher: personality characteristics (e.g., achievement-motivation, directness, and flexibility), attitude (motivation to teach, empathy toward children, and commitment), experience (years of teaching, experience in subject taught, and experience with a particular grade level), and aptitude/achievement (scores on ability tests, college grade-point average, and student teaching evaluations).

Table 1.1 lists some of these psychological characteristics. Because they have a certain intuitive appeal it is worth noting why they have *not* been useful criteria for defining good teachers.

Personality.   Over the years, only a few personality measures have been developed that relate specifically to teaching. Because most personality measures have been designed to record deviant or abnormal behavior in clinical settings, much of what they measure has been of little help in identifying the positive or "normal" behaviors that may be needed to be an effective teacher.

Consequently, the usefulness of many personality tests in predicting a teacher's classroom behavior must be inferred from their more general success in the mental health field. Although certain interpersonal, emotional, and coping behaviors are believed to be required for effective teaching (Levis, 1987), personality tests (especially clinical ones) have provided few insights into the positive social behavior that may be needed for effective teaching.

Attitude.   Attitude assessments may be either global (e.g., attitude toward the educational system and the teaching profession) or specific (e.g., attitude toward a particular task, child, or curriculum). In either case, most attempts to measure teacher attitude generally have failed to forecast what a teacher having a particular attitude *actually does in the classroom.* Research generally has shown a low and nonsignificant correspondence between teacher attitude and classroom performance (Walberg, 1986; Jackson, 1968).

Positive behavior

Table 1.1
Commonly studied teacher characteristics

Personality	Attitude	Experience	Aptitude/Achievement
Permissiveness	Motivation to teach	Years of teaching experience	National Teachers Exam
Dogmatism	Attitude toward children	Experience in subject taught	Graduate Record Exam
Authoritarianism	Attitude toward teaching	Experience in grade level taught	Scholastic Aptitude Test
Achievement-motivation	Attitude toward authority	Workshops attended	1. verbal
Introversion-extroversion	Vocational interest	Graduate courses taken	2. quantitative
Abstractness-concreteness	Attitude toward self (self-concept)	Degrees held	Special ability tests,
Directness-indirectness	Attitude toward subject taught	Professional papers written	(e.g., reasoning ability, logical
Locus of control			ability, verbal fluency)
Anxiety			Grade-point average
1. general			1. overall
2. teaching			2. in major subject
			Professional recommendations
			Student evaluations of teaching
			effectiveness
			Student teaching evaluations

Therefore, the use of attitude data for measuring teacher effectiveness has had to rest on the *assumption* that attitudes (such as positive feelings about teaching) are related to other desirable behaviors that are one or more steps removed from the actual teaching process (such as more organized lesson plans or better subject-matter preparation) (Clark & Peterson, 1986). However, defining effective teaching in this manner always will be less direct and credible than observing the actual classroom practices that good teaching is supposed to represent.

Experience.   You probably, at one time or another, provided biographical data about yourself when applying for a job. A listing of a teacher's work experience however, such as that requested on a standard job application form, defines an individual's experience so broadly as not to be very predictive of their effectiveness in the classroom. Such descriptions typically do not describe experience relevant to performing the *day-to-day* tasks required in a specific classroom, grade level, or subject area.

A teacher's experience with a *specific* curriculum or type of learner, if requested, would be more relevant to performance than nonspecific data, such as years of experience, graduate credits earned, or hours of inservice training (Barnes, 1987). The correspondence of such general biographical data to actual classroom performance has been low and nonsignificant because, by themselves, they represent only a small portion of a teacher's experience relevant to a particular teaching assignment.

Aptitude and Achievement.   Like experience variables, most aptitude and achievement data do not accurately predict classroom performance. This may be surprising, given our society's emphasis on achievement and intelligence. However, regardless of the fact that these measures often are used to predict student performance, a teacher's prior achievement seldom has correlated strongly with classroom performance—and here is why.

As an example of prior achievement, consider a teacher's college grades. Achieving good grades might indicate a positive attitude and promise good classroom performance. But a relatively narrow spread of scores in course grades and college GPAs typically characterizes the achievement of teachers. Standards set by training institutions usually require teachers to meet some minimum level of achievement. This is usually sufficient to make the small variations in grades among beginning teachers irrelevant to actual performance in the classroom.

To summarize, using psychological characteristics to define a good teacher represented an attempt to measure teacher behavior objectively. But these characteristics often were too remote from the teacher's day-to-day work in the classroom to meaningfully contribute to a definition of a good teacher. Most notably, these definitions excluded the most important and obvious measure of all for determining good teaching: *the performance of the students who are being taught.*

A New Direction

In the last two decades a revolution has occurred in the definitions of good teaching. We have seen that defining good teachers by community ideals proved unrealistic on the job and in the preparation of teachers. We also have seen how teachers' psychological characteristics proved to be poorly related to what teachers actually did in the classroom. This directed researchers to study the impact that specific teacher behaviors had on the specific cognitive and affective behaviors of their students. The term *good teaching* changed to *effective teaching,* and the research focus shifted from exclusively studying teachers to include their effects on students.

These changes have influenced the profession of teaching so dramatically that their effects now are felt in the reform of teacher training curricula, in the competency testing of teachers, in the education of teacher trainers, and in textbooks (like this one) on teaching methods. Perhaps most responsible for this change are the new ways in which classroom researchers have come to study the nature of teaching. These new ways of studying classroom behavior have made the student and teacher–student interaction in the classroom the focus of modern definitions of effective teaching.

Linking Teacher Behavior with Student Performance. During the 1970s and 1980s, researchers developed new methods for studying the interactive patterns of teachers and students. The goal was to discover which teacher behaviors promote desirable student performance, such as good grades on classroom tests, higher standardized test scores, better attitudes toward school, and improved problem-solving and thinking skills. But before unveiling the findings of this research and their implications for effective teaching, let's see how the research was performed.

How is research on effective teaching conducted?

The Research Process. To collect data on the classroom interaction of teachers and students, researchers often used instruments like those shown in Figures 1.1a, 1.1b, and 1.2. These particular instruments, devised by Good and Brophy (1987b) for their research on effective teaching in elementary school classrooms, record observations of various student–teacher behaviors. Using the response form in Figure 1.1b, the observer codes both student responses to questions and the teacher's reaction and feedback. For example, in the tenth interchange recorded on this form, a male student fails to answer a question (0), is criticized by the teacher for not answering (– –), and then is given the answer by the teacher (Gives Ans.). Numbers for the interchanges are assigned as they occur, allowing the pattern of question-answer-feedback to be recorded over an entire class period.

In Figure 1.2 the observer codes the student performance being praised by the teacher (perseverance, progress, success, good thinking, etc.). Individual students are identified by assigning each a unique number. This form records not only the praise behavior of the teacher *in relation to* individual student behavior, but also the overall pattern or sequence of action. For example, student "8" is praised three times in a row for "perseverance or effort."

With instruments such as these, a rich and varied picture of classroom activity can be captured over the course of a research study. Obviously, a single observation of a single class would produce too little data to reveal a consistent behavior pattern. However, multiple observation periods extending across different teachers, schools, and school districts can reveal consistent patterns of teacher–student interactions. These patterns of classroom behavior then can be related to student behaviors, such as performance on end-of-year standardized achievement tests, specially prepared classroom tests and performance and portfolio assessments to determine the effects of teacher–student interaction on student performance.

It was in this manner that **patterns of effective teaching** began to emerge in studies conducted by different researchers. As in all research, some studies provided contradictory results or found no relationships among certain types of classroom interactions and student outcomes. But many studies found patterns of interaction that consistently produced desirable student outcomes in the form of higher test scores, increased problem-solving skills, and improved learning skills.

Now that you know how the research was conducted, let's look at the teaching behaviors that researchers generally agree contribute to effective teaching, regardless of context. Afterward, we will modify these behaviors and add to them to describe effective teaching at various levels of schooling, in different content areas, and with different student populations.

Researchers now look at teaching behaviors that may contribute to effective teaching-learning

Symbol Label		Definition
Student Sex		**Definition**
M Male		The student answering the question is male.
F Female		The student answering the question is female.
Student Response		
+ Right		The teacher accepts the student's response as correct or satisfactory.
± Part right		The teacher considers the student's response to be only partially correct or to be correct but incomplete.
− Wrong		The teacher considers the student's response to be incorrect.
0 No answer		The student makes no response or says he doesn't know (code student's answer here if teacher gives feedback reaction before he is able to respond).
Teacher Feedback Reaction		
++ Praise		Teacher praises student either in words ("fine," "good," "wonderful," "good thinking") or by expressing verbal affirmation in a notably warm, joyous, or excited manner.
+ Affirm		Teacher simply affirms that the student's response is correct (nods, repeats answer, says "Yes," "OK," etc.).
0 No reaction		Teacher makes no response whatever to student's response—he or she simply goes on to something else.
− Negate		Teacher simply indicates that the student's response is incorrect (shakes head, says "No," "That's not right," "Hmmm," etc.).
−− Criticize		Teacher criticizes student, either in words ("You should know better than that," "That doesn't make any sense—you better pay close attention," etc.) or by expressing verbal negation in a frustrated, angry, or disgusted manner.
Gives Ans.	Teacher gives answer	Teacher provides the correct answer for the student.
Ask Other	Teacher asks another student	Teacher redirects the question, asking a different student to try to answer it.
Other Calls	Another student calls out answer	Another student calls out the correct answer, and the teacher acknowledges that it is correct.
Repeat	Repeats question	Teacher repeats the original question, either in its entirety or with a prompt ("Well?" "Do you know?" "What's the answer?").
Clue	Rephrase or clue	Teacher makes original question easier for student to answer by rephrasing it or by giving a clue.
New Ques.	New question	Teacher asks a new question (i.e., a question that calls for a different answer than the original question called for).

Figure 1.1a
Coding categories for question-answer-feedback sequences (Good & Brophy, 1987b)

NO.	Student Sex M.	F.	Student Response +	±	-	0	++	+	0	-	- -	Teacher Feedback Reaction Gives Ans.	Ask Other	Other Calls	Repeat	Clue	New Ques.
1		✓	✓					✓									
2	✓		✓					✓									
3	✓					✓										✓	
4	✓		✓				✓										
5	✓		✓				✓	✓									✓
6		✓			✓						✓						
7	✓		✓						✓								
8	✓		✓						✓								
9	✓		✓			✓					✓	✓					
10	✓																
11																	
12																	
13																	
14																	
15																	

Figure 1.1b
Coding response form (Good & Brophy, 1987b)

USE: Whenever the teacher praises an individual student
PURPOSE: To see what behaviors the teacher reinforces through praises, and to see how
    the teacher's praise is distributed among the students.

Behavior Categories	Student Number		Codes
1. Perserverence or effort; worked long or hard	14	1.	3
2. Progress (relative to the past) toward achievement	23	2.	34
3. Success (right answer, high score) achievement	6	3.	3
4. Good thinking, good suggestions, good guess, or nice try	18	4.	3
5. Imagination, creativity, originality	8	5.	1
6. Neatness, careful work	8	6.	1
7. Good or compliant behavior, follows rules, pays attention	8	7.	1
8. Thoughtfulness, courtesy, offering to share, prosocial behavior		8.	
9. Other (specify)		9.	
		10.	
		11.	
NOTES:		12.	
		13.	
All answers occurred during		14.	
social studies discussion		15.	
		16.	
Was particularly concerned		17.	
about #8, a low-achieving male.		18.	
		19.	
		20.	
		21.	
		22.	
		23.	
		24.	
		25.	

Figure 1.2
Coding form for measuring individual praise (Good & Brophy, 1987b)

>>> FIVE KEY BEHAVIORS CONTRIBUTING <<<
TO EFFECTIVE TEACHING

*What are some key
effective teaching
behaviors?*

Approximately 10 teacher behaviors show promising relationships
to desirable student performance, primarily as measured by classroom assessments and standardized tests. Five of these behaviors
have been consistently supported by research studies over the past
two decades (Brophy, 1989; Brophy & Good, 1986; Walberg, 1986;
Dunkin & Biddle, 1974; Rosenshine, 1971b). Another five have had
some support and appear logically related to effective teaching. The
first five we will call **key behaviors,** because they are considered
essential for effective teaching. The second five we will call **helping**

behaviors that can be used in combinations to implement the key behaviors. The five key behaviors are the following:

1. Lesson clarity — *present lesson clearly – at level of students*
2. Instructional variety — *variety of manipulatives/ideas for teaching subject.*
3. Teacher task orientation
4. Engagement in the learning process — *is teacher asking questions? Students participating?*
5. Student success rate

Lesson Clarity

This key behavior refers to how clear and interpretable a presentation is to the class. Assume for the moment that you are the teacher and ask yourself: Are your points understandable? Are you able to explain concepts clearly so your students are able to follow in a logical step-by-step order? Is your oral delivery to the class clear, audible, intelligible, and free of distracting mannerisms?

One result from research on teacher clarity is that teachers vary considerably on this behavior. Not all teachers are able to communicate clearly and directly to their students without wandering, speaking above students' levels of comprehension, or using speech patterns that impair the clarity of what is being presented. Some indications of a lack of clarity (Brown & Wragg, 1993; Wilen, 1991; Dillon, 1988a) follow:

Teachers need to speak in easy, clear sentences.

- The extent to which a teacher uses vague, ambiguous, or indefinite language ("might probably be," "tends to suggest," "could possibly happen").
- The extent to which a teacher uses overly complicated sentences ("There are many important reasons for the start of World War II but some are more important than others, so let's start with those that are thought to be important but really aren't").
- The extent to which a teacher gives directions that often result in student requests for clarification.

If you teach with a high degree of clarity, you will spend less time going over material. Your questions will be answered correctly the first time, allowing more time for instruction. Clarity is a complex behavior because it is related to many other so-called cognitive behaviors, such as your organization of the content, lesson familiarity, and delivery strategies (whether you use a discussion, recitation, question-and-answer, or small-group format). Nevertheless, research shows that both the *cognitive* clarity and *oral* clarity of

The more clearly you teach; less time you spend going over material.

Not only must you be clear but you must be able to know the material

presentations vary substantially among teachers. This in turn produces differences in student performance on cognitive tests of achievement (Marx & Walsh, 1988). Table 1.2 summarizes some of the indicators of lesson clarity and teaching strategies you will learn about in this text, especially in chapters 6 (direct instruction), 7 (indirect instruction), and 8 (questioning strategies).

Instructional Variety

This key behavior refers to the variability or flexibility of delivery during the presentation of a lesson. For example, it includes the planned mixing of different classroom behaviors, such as those measured by the classroom observation instruments shown earlier. Research indicates increased student achievement from the use of variety in instructional materials and techniques, the frequency and variety of reinforcements used, and the types of feedback given to students (Rohrkemper & Corno, 1988; Brophy & Good, 1986).

- ask many questions to clarify material

One of the most effective ways of creating variety during instruction is to ask questions. As you will learn in Chapter 8, many different types of questions can be asked, and when integrated into the pacing and sequencing of a lesson, they create meaningful variation (Palincsar & Brown, 1989; Gall, 1984). Therefore, the effective teacher needs to know the art of asking questions and how to discriminate among different question formats—fact questions, process questions, convergent questions, divergent questions. These question types will be introduced in Chapter 8 and expanded on in Chapter 9.

What kind of materials, equipment, displays & space is important to encourage student involvement.

Another aspect of variety in teaching is perhaps the most obvious: the use of learning materials, equipment, displays, and space in your classroom. The physical texture and visual variety of your classroom can actually encourage student involvement with lesson content. The display of reading materials, use of audio and visual devices, demonstration materials, and the organization of reference materials and learning resources can all contribute to instructional variety. This, in turn, influences student achievement on end-of-unit tests, performance assessments and student engagement in the learning process. For example, some studies found the amount of disruptive behavior to be less in classrooms that had more varied activities and materials (Emmer, Evertson, Clements, & Worsham, 1994). Other studies have shown variety to be related to student attention (Lysakowski & Walberg, 1981).

- using all kinds of devices: visual, audio, etc... helps the learning process

Some ways to incorporate variety into your teaching will be presented in Chapter 6 (direct instruction), Chapter 7 (indirect instruction), and Chapter 10 (cooperative learning and the collaborative

Being Clear (an effective teacher . . .)	Poor Clarity (an ineffective teacher . . .)	Examples of Teaching Strategies
1. Informs learners of the lesson objective (e.g., describes what behaviors will be tested or required on future assignments as a result of the lesson).	Fails to link lesson content to how and at what level of complexity the content will be used.	Prepare a behavioral objective for the lesson at the desired level of complexity (e.g., knowledge, comprehension, etc.). Indicate to the learners at the start of the lesson in what ways the behavior will be used in the future.
2. Provides learners with an advance organizer (e.g., places lesson in perspective of past and/or future lessons).	Starts presenting content without first introducing the subject with respect to some broader context.	Consult or prepare a unit plan to determine what task-relevant prior learning is required for this lesson and what task-relevant prior learning this lesson represents for future lessons. Begin the lesson by informing the learner that the content to be taught is part of this larger context.
3. Checks for task-relevant prior learning at beginning of the lesson (e.g., determines level of understanding of prerequisite facts or concepts and reteaches, if necessary).	Moves to new content without checking for the facts, concepts, or skills needed to acquire the new learning.	Ask questions of students at the beginning of a lesson or check assignments regularly to determine if task-relevant prior knowledge has been acquired.
4. Gives directives slowly and distinctly (e.g., repeats directives when needed or divides them into smaller pieces).	Presents too much clerical, managerial, or technical information at once, too quickly.	Organize procedures for lengthy assignments in step-by-step order and give as handout as well as orally.
5. Knows ability levels and teaches at or slightly above learners' current level of functioning (e.g., knows learners' attention spans).	Fails to know that instruction is under or over heads of students. Seems not to know when most learners have "tuned out".	Determine ability level from standardized tests, previous assignments, and interests and retarget instruction accordingly.
6. Uses examples, illustrations, and demonstrations to explain and clarify (e.g., uses visuals to help interpret and reinforce main points).	Restricts presentation to routine verbal reproduction of text or workbook.	Restate main points in at least one modality other than the one in which they were initially taught (e.g., visual vs. auditory).
7. Provides review or summary at end of each lesson.	Ends lesson abruptly without "repackaging" key points.	Use key abstractions, repetition, or symbols to help students efficiently store and later recall content.

Table 1.2
Indicators for clarity

process). Table 1.3 summarizes some of the indicators of instructional variety and teaching strategies that will be covered in these chapters.

Teacher Task Orientation

How much time does teacher devote to a Subject?

This key behavior refers to how much classroom time the teacher devotes to the task of teaching an academic subject. The more time dedicated to the task of teaching a specific topic, the greater the opportunity students have to learn. Some task-related questions a teacher must answer are: (1) how much time do I spend lecturing, asking questions, and encouraging students to inquire or think independently? (2) How much time do I spend organizing for teaching and getting my students ready to learn? And, (3) how much time do I spend assessing my learners' performance?

Teachers must ask themselves quest. that pertain to how students are learning, what's presented; is time used wisely?

These questions pertain to how much material gets presented, learned, and assessed, as opposed to how much time is delegated to procedural matters. All teachers need to prepare their students to learn and want them to enjoy learning. However, most researchers agree that student performance has been higher in classrooms with teachers who spent the majority of their time teaching subject-specific content as opposed to devoting large amounts of time to the process and materials that may be needed to acquire the content. It follows that classrooms in which teacher–student interactions focus more on intellectual content than on process issues (such as how to use materials or classroom rules and procedures) are more likely to have higher rates of achievement (Slavin, 1987; Rosenshine, 1983; Evertson & Emmer, 1982).

Also, teachers who are task oriented are highly conversant with topics that are likely to appear on performance assessments and end-of-year achievement tests. This is not to say that these teachers "teach to the test." Rather, their classroom instruction parallels the instructional goals and curriculum that guide the construction of assessments of student progress.

These topics are presented in chapters 4 and 5, which prepare you to write lesson and unit plans, and chapters 6 and 7, which show you how to execute them in your classroom. Table 1.4 summarizes some of the indicators of teacher task orientation and teaching strategies that will be covered in these chapters.

Engagement in the Learning Process

This key behavior refers to the amount of learning time devoted to an academic subject. This is one of the most recently researched teacher behaviors related to student performance. It is related to a

Using Variety (an effective teacher . . .)	Poor Variety (an ineffective teacher . . .)	Examples of Teaching Strategies
1. Uses attention-gaining devices (e.g., begins with a challenging question, visual, or example).	Begins lesson without full attention of most learners.	Begin lesson with an activity in a modality that is different from last lesson or activity (e.g., change from listening to seeing).
2. Shows enthusiasm and animation through variation in eye contact, voice, and gestures (e.g., changes pitch and volume, moves about during transitions to new activity).	Speaks in monotone, devoid of external signs of emotion; stays fixed in place entire period or rarely moves body.	Change position at regular intervals (e.g., every 10 minutes). Change speed or volume to indicate that a change in content or activity has occurred.
3. Varies mode of presentation, (e.g., lectures, asks questions, then provides for independent practice [daily]).	Lectures or assigns unmonitored seatwork for the entire period; rarely alters modality through which instructional stimuli are received (e.g., seeing, listening, doing)	Preestablish an order of daily activities that rotates cycles of seeing, listening, and doing.
4. Uses a mix of rewards and reinforcers (e.g., extra credit, verbal praise, independent study, etc. [weekly, monthly]).	Rarely praises or tends to use same words to convey praise every time.	Establish lists of rewards and expressions of verbal praise and choose among them randomly. Provide reasons for praise along with the expression of praise.
5. Incorporates student ideas or participation in some aspects of the instruction (e.g., uses indirect instruction or divergent questioning [weekly, monthly]).	Assumes the role of sole authority and provider of information; ignores student opinion and diversity.	Occasionally plan instruction in which student opinions are used to begin the lesson (e.g., "what would you do if . . . ").
6. Varies types of questions (e.g., divergent, convergent, [weekly] and probes (e.g., to clarify, to solicit, to redirect [daily]).	Always asks divergent, opinion questions (e.g., What do you think about . . . ?) without follow up; or overuses convergent, fact questions.	Match questions to the behavior and complexity of the lesson objective. Vary complexity of lesson objectives in accord with the unit plan.

Table 1.3
Indicators for variety

15

Being Task Oriented (an effective teacher . . .)	Poor Task Orientation (an ineffective teacher . . .)	Examples of Teaching Strategies
1. Develops unit and lesson plans that reflect the most relevant features of the curriculum guide or adopted text (e.g., each unit and lesson objective can be referenced back to curriculum guide or text).	Develops lessons almost exclusively from personal or student interests. Breadth and depth of lesson content fails to distinguish between primary and secondary content in the curriculum guide and text.	Key each lesson to a unit plan, the curriculum guide, and the text to test its relevance. Confer with other teachers concerning the most relevant portions of the text and curriculum guide.
2. Handles administrative and clerical interruptions (e.g., visitors, announcements, collection of money, dispensing of materials and supplies) by anticipating and deferring some tasks and deferring others to noninstructional time.	Attends to every administrative and clerical task in detail during the time normally devoted to instruction.	Establish a five-to-ten minute restriction on how much time per every hour of instruction you will devote to noninstructional tasks. Defer all other tasks to before or after the lesson.
3. Stops or prevents misbehavior with a minimum of class disruption (e.g., has preestablished academic and work rules to "protect" intrusions into instructional time).	Attends at length to specific misbehavior; singles out individual students for punishment and lectures on the offense during instructional time.	Establish rules for the most common misbehaviors and post them conspicuously. Identify only the offender and offense during instructional time, deferring consequence to later.
4. Selects the most appropriate instructional model for the objectives being taught (e.g., primarily uses direct instruction for knowledge and comprehension objectives and indirect instruction for inquiry and problem-solving objectives).	Uses inefficient instructional methods for achieving lesson objectives (e.g., frequently attempts to teach facts, rules, and action sequences through discussion or concepts, patterns, and abstractions through drill and practice).	Using your unit plan, curriculum guide, or adopted text, divide the content to be taught into (1) facts, rules, and action sequences, and (2) concepts, patterns, and abstractions. Generally, plan to use direct instruction for the former content and indirect instruction for the latter.
5. Builds to unit outcomes with clearly definable events (e.g., weekly and monthly review, feedback, and testing sessions)	Has no systematic milestones toward which to work (e.g., tests on Fridays, major review every fourth Monday) which keep the class on schedule and moving toward a clearly defined goal.	Establish a schedule in which major classroom activities begin and end with clearly visible events (e.g., minor and major tests, and review and feedback sessions).

Table 1.4
Indicators for teacher task orientation

teacher's task orientation and to content coverage. A teacher's task orientation should provide students the greatest possible opportunity to learn the material to be assessed.

For example, Table 1.5 shows the results achieved in second-grade reading when the teacher's task orientation—or time teaching an academic subject—was increased over a five-week period. Increasing the time devoted to this instructional objective from 4 minutes to 52 minutes a day, over an average of only 25 school days, yielded an increase of 27 percentile points (from 39 to 66) on a standardized achievement test. The researchers who recorded these data indicated that, although such large increases in instructional time might appear unusual, they actually were achieved by teachers in these elementary school classrooms.

The more time the students spent w/ a subject, increased chances of higher points.

Distinctively different from the amount of time you devote to teaching a topic is the time your students will be *actively engaged* in learning the material. This has been called the engagement rate or the *on-task* behavior of students.

Engagement rate is the percentage of time devoted to learning when the student is actually on task, engaged with the instructional materials and benefiting from the activities being presented. Even though a teacher may be task oriented and may provide maximum content coverage, the students may be disengaged. This means that they are not actively thinking about, working with, or using what is being presented (Savage, 1991; Marx & Walsh, 1988).

engagement rate

Students may become disengaged eventhough the material is covered at its max.

Table 1.5
Learning time and student achievement: Example from second-grade reading

Reading Score at First Testing (October)		Student Engaged Time in Reading with High Success Rate		Estimated Reading Score, Second Testing (December)	
Raw Score (out of 100)	Percentile	Total Time Over 5 Weeks (Minutes)	Average Daily Time (Minutes)	Raw Score (out of 100)	Percentile
36	50	100	4	37	39
36	50	573	23	43	50
36	50	1300	52	52	66

Note: An average of twenty-five school days occurred between the first and the second testing.

Source: From Charles W. Fisher et al., *Teaching and Learning in the Elementary School: A summary of the Beginning Teacher Evaluation Study.* Beginning Teacher Evaluation Study Report VII-I. (San Francisco, CA: Far West Laboratory for Research and Development, 1978)

The proper use of space and the display of learning materials in the classroom create a visual texture and variety that encourages students to become involved with lesson content.

Such disengagement can involve an emotional or mental detachment from the lesson that may or may not be obvious. When students jump out of their seats, talk, read a magazine, or leave for the restroom, they obviously are not engaged in instruction, however clear and thorough the teacher's presentation. Students also can be disengaged in far more subtle ways, such as looking attentive while their thoughts are many miles away. An unpleasant fact of life is that a quarter of a class may be "tuned out" at any one time. Correcting this type of disengagement may be much more difficult, requiring changes in the structure of the task itself and the cognitive demands placed on the learner (Bennett & Desforges, 1988; Doyle, 1983). Strategies for composing tasks and activities that elicit the active participation of your learners are presented in chapters 6, 7, 8, and 9.

Several research studies have contributed useful data for increasing learning time and, more important, student engagement. From these data, Crawford et al. (1978) identified behaviors having potential for increasing learning time, resulting in increased on-task behavior. Their work, recently updated by Emmer et al. (1994), has provided the following suggestions for teachers to promote student engagement:

Suggestions for teachers to promote student engagement—

1. Set rules that let pupils attend to their personal and procedural needs without obtaining your permission each time.
2. Move around the room to monitor pupils' seatwork and to communicate your awareness of student progress.

3. Ensure that independent assignments are interesting, worthwhile, and easy enough to be completed by each pupil without your direction.
4. Minimize time-consuming activities such as giving directions and organizing the class for instruction by writing the daily schedule on the board. This will ensure that pupils know where to go and what to do.
5. Make abundant use of resources and activities that are at, or slightly above, a student's current level of functioning.
6. Avoid "timing errors." Act to prevent misbehaviors from occurring or increasing in severity so they do not influence others in the class.

These teaching practices have been extended to small groups and independent seatwork by Anderson, Evertson, and Brophy (1982) and Anderson, Stevens, Prawat, and Nickerson (1988). These and other more specific ways of increasing the engagement rates of students will be explored in chapters 6, 7, 8, and 9. Table 1.6 summarizes some of the indicators of student engagement and teaching strategies that will be covered in these chapters.

Student Success Rate

This key behavior refers to the rate at which students understand and correctly complete exercises.

A crucial aspect of the research on task orientation and student engagement has been the level of difficulty of the material presented. In these studies, level of difficulty was measured by the rate at which students understood and correctly completed exercises. Three levels of difficulty are as follows:

- high success, in which the student understands the task and makes only occasional careless errors
- moderate success, in which the student has partial understanding but makes some substantive errors
- low success, in which the student does not understand the task at all

Findings indicate that a teacher's task orientation (instructional time) and student engagement are closely related to student success rate, as shown in Figure 1.3. Consistently, instruction that produces a moderate-to-high success rate results in increased performance, because more content is covered at the learner's current level of

[handwritten margin note: How well does student understand & completely correctly completes material?]

[handwritten margin note: When more content is covered at the learners level, there is a moderate–high success rate.]

Engaging Students Effectively in the Learning Process (an effective teacher . . .)	Engaging Students Ineffectively in the Learning Process (an ineffective teacher . . .)	Examples of Teaching Strategies
1. Elicits the desired behavior immediately after the instructional stimuli (e.g., provides exercise or workbook problems with which the desired behavior can be practiced).	Fails to ask learners to attempt the desired behavior.	Schedule practice exercises or questions to immediately follow each set of instructional stimuli.
2. Provides opportunities for feedback in a nonevaluative atmosphere (e.g., asks students to respond as a group or covertly the first time through).	Formally evaluates the initial practice (e.g., individually calls on students to give correct answer in ways that could be threatening or embarrassing).	Require covert responding or nonevaluative (e.g., group) feedback at the start of a guided practice session.
3. Uses individual and group activities (e.g., performance contracts, programmed texts, games and simulations, and learning centers as motivational aids) when needed.	Fails to match instructional methods to the learning needs of special students (e.g., less able or bilingual learners).	Have individualized instructional materials available (e.g., remedial exercises or texts) for those who may need them.
4. Uses meaningful verbal praise to get and keep students actively participating in the learning process.	Fails to provide rewards and reinforcers that are timely and meaningful to the student (e.g., never says why something is "good").	Maintain a warm and nurturing atmosphere by providing verbal praise and encouragement that is meaningful (e.g., explain why the answer was correct). Praise partially correct answers, with qualification.
5. Monitors seatwork and frequently checks progress during independent practice.	Does not monitor student progress during seatwork evenly (e.g., spends too much time with some students, failing to observe work of other students).	Limit contact with individual students during seatwork to about 30 seconds each, providing instructionally relevant answers. Circulate among entire class.

Table 1.6

Indicators for engaging students in the learning process

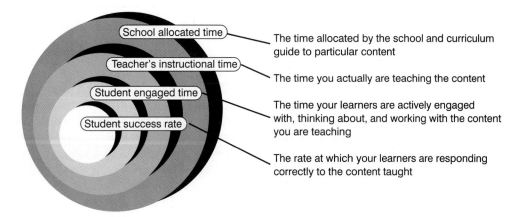

The time allocated by the school and curriculum guide to particular content

The time you actually are teaching the content

The time your learners are actively engaged with, thinking about, and working with the content you are teaching

The rate at which your learners are responding correctly to the content taught

Figure 1.3
Levels of time

understanding. This result was initially found for expository or didactic forms of instruction with which learners are taught basic academic skills most easily learned through practice and repetition (Rosenshine, 1983). But, more recent research has extended these findings to thinking skills instruction (Costa & Lowery, 1989) and project-based learning (Blumenfeld et al., 1991). Research has also shown that instuction that promotes low error rates (high success) can contribute to increased levels of student self-esteem and to positive attitudes toward the subject matter and the school (Slavin, 1991b).

The average student in a typical classroom spends about half of the time working on tasks that provide the opportunity for high success. But researchers have found that students who spend more than the average time in high-success activities have higher achievement, better retention, and more positive attitudes toward school (Wyne & Stuck, 1982; Brophy & Evertson, 1976). These findings have led to the suggestion that students spend about 60 to 70 percent of their time on tasks that allow almost complete understanding of the material being taught with only occasional errors (Rosenshine, 1983; Brophy & Evertson, 1976).

Moderate-to-high success rates will produce mastery of the lesson content. But they also can provide the foundation for your students to apply learned knowledge in some practical way, such as thinking critically and independently. This has been the unique contribution of strategies for self-directed learning and learning to learn, which will be studied in Chapter 9. These strategies encour-

[handwritten margin note: Moderate/High Success provides foundation for Stud. to apply learned Knowledge (such as critically + independent]

age learners to "construct" their own understandings and meanings from lesson content. They also encourage learners to reason, problem solve, and think critically about the content they are learning. By varying the complexity and variety of the tasks provided, such strategies provide opportunities for individual patterns of thinking to emerge through various forms of classroom discussion and dialogue (Duffy & Roehler, 1989; Rohrkemper & Corno, 1988).

Many teachers devote insufficient time to this stage of learning, which is particularly crucial for attaining the goals of problem solving and critical thinking. A key behavior for the effective teacher is organizing and planning instruction that yields moderate-to-high success rates, but then challenges the learner to go beyond the information given. You will discover ways to use moderate-to-high success rates to attain the goals of problem solving and critical thinking in chapters 7 and 9. Table 1.7 summarizes some of the indicators of student success and teaching strategies that will be covered in these chapters.

>>> SUMMARY OF KEY BEHAVIORS <<<

The five key behaviors—lesson clarity, instructional variety, teacher task orientation, student engagement, and success rate—are essential for effective teaching. Without the knowledge and skill to present lessons that are clear, that incorporate variety, that are task oriented, and that actually engage students in the learning process at moderate-to-high rates of success, a teacher cannot be effective in producing desirable patterns of student achievement and attitude. The following chapters present the tools and techniques you will need to use these five key behaviors effectively in your classroom.

Classroom researchers undoubtedly will discover other effective teaching behaviors, and attain a more thorough understanding of those already described. However, for the first time, research has provided a basis for better definitions of effective teaching and for training teachers. As classroom research continues, additions to and modifications of these five key behaviors undoubtedly will be discovered. But today, these five stand as a practical starting point for defining the effective teacher. They are the skeleton on which the remainder of this text will construct the heart, mind, and body of the effective teacher.

You learned earlier that there can be no simple answer to the question, "What is an effective teacher?" As suggested, many behaviors must be orchestrated into *patterns of behavior* for your teaching to be effective. You can see this both in the overlapping relationships among the five key behaviors and the many other behaviors that may

Moderate-to-High Rates of Success (an effective teacher . . .)	Poor Rates of Success (an ineffective teacher . . .)	Examples of Teaching Strategies
1. Establishes unit and lesson content that reflects prior learning (e.g., planning lesson sequences that consider task-relevant prior information).	Fails to sequence learning in advance to ensure that all task-relevant prior knowledge has been taught before moving to next lesson.	Create a top-down unit plan in which all the lesson outcomes at the bottom of the hierarchy needed to achieve unit outcomes at the top of the hierarchy are identified. Arrange lessons in an order most logical to achieving unit outcomes.
2. Administers correctives immediately after initial response (e.g., shows model of correct answer and how to attain it after first crude response is given).	Leaves students to practice and learn independently immediately after presenting instructional stimuli; waits until next day to show correct responses.	Provide for guided practice prior to independent practice and provide means of self-checking (e.g., handout with correct answers) at intervals of practice.
3. Divides instructional stimuli into small chunks (e.g., establishes bite-size lessons that can be easily digested by learners at their current level of functioning).	Packages instruction in chunks that are too large or small (e.g., teaches too complex of a lesson too early in an instructional sequence).	Plan interdisciplinary thematic units to emphasize relationships and connections that are easily remembered.
4. Plans transitions to new material in easy to grasp steps (e.g., changes instructional stimuli according to a preestablished thematic pattern so that each new lesson is seen as an extension of previous lessons).	Abruptly changes instructional topics and perspectives from one lesson to another without themes and interconnections.	Extend unit-plan hierarchy downward to more specific lessons that are tied together above with a single unit theme and outcome.
5. Varies the pace at which stimuli are presented and continually builds toward a climax or key event.	Maintains same pace for too long a time, leading to a monotonous and static level of intensity and expectation.	Use review, feedback, and testing sessions to form intervals of increasing and decreasing intensity and expectation.

Table 1.7
Indicators for student success

23

be needed to successfully carry out any one or combination of the key behaviors. The identification of only five behaviors makes teaching appear deceptively simple. However, as the following sections will reveal, your success in implementing these five key behaviors in the classroom will be assisted by many other "helping" behaviors.

>>> SOME HELPING BEHAVIORS RELATED <<< TO EFFECTIVE TEACHING

What are some behaviors that can help me perform the key teaching behaviors?

To fill out our picture of an effective teacher, more than five general keys to effective teaching are needed. You also need behaviors to help you implement the five key behaviors in your classroom. Let's consider some additional behaviors that can be thought of as catalytic, or helping, behaviors for performing the five key behaviors.

Research findings for helping behaviors, although promising, are not as strong and consistent as those that identified the five key behaviors. There is general agreement on the importance of these helping behaviors, but the research has not been so accommodating as to identify explicitly how these behaviors should be used. Nor has it linked these behaviors to student performance and progress as strongly as the key five. This is why helping behaviors need to be employed *in the context of other behaviors* to be effective, making them catalysts rather than agents unto themselves. These helping behaviors include the following:

1. Using student ideas and contributions
2. Structuring
3. Questioning
4. Probing
5. Teacher affect

Use of Student Ideas and Contributions

This behavior includes acknowledging, modifying, applying, comparing, and summarizing student responses to promote the goals of a lesson and to encourage student participation. Note how any one of these activities (suggested by Flanders, 1970) could be used in achieving one or more of the five key behaviors:

Acknowledging: using the student's idea by repeating the nouns and logical connectives expressed by him or her (to increase lesson clarity).

Modifying: using the student's idea by rephrasing it or conceptualizing it in your words or another student's words (to create instructional variety).

Applying: using the student's idea to teach an inference or take the next step in a logical analysis of a problem (to increase success rate).

Comparing: taking a student's idea and drawing a relationship between it and ideas expressed earlier by the student (to encourage engagement in the learning process).

Summarizing: using what was said by an individual student or a group of students as a recapitulation or review of concepts taught (to enhance task orientation).

More recently, the use of student ideas and contributions has been extended to reasoning, problem solving, and independent thinking. This has been achieved through **teacher-mediated dialogue** that helps learners restructure what is being learned using their own ideas, experiences, and thought patterns. Teacher-mediated dialogue asks the learner not just to respond to textual material, but to internalize its meaning by elaborating, extending, and commenting upon it using the learner's own unique thoughts. In this manner, learners are encouraged to elaborate and communicate the processes by which they are learning, thereby creating their own meanings and understandings of the content. We will present strategies for teacher-mediated dialogue in the chapters ahead, and especially in Chapter 9.

teacher helps student understand what's being learned by using the student's past experiences/ideas—

Use of student ideas and contributions also can increase a student's engagement in the learning process. Thus, it has become a frequently used catalyst for helping achieve that key behavior (Emmer et al., 1994). Consider this brief instructional dialogue that uses student ideas to promote engagement:

— ∙ — ∙ — ∙ — ∙ — ∙ — ∙ — ∙ — ∙ — ∙ — ∙ — ∙ — ∙ —

Teacher: Tom, what is the formula for the Pythagorean theorem?
  Tom: $c^2 = a^2 + b^2$.

— ∙ — ∙ — ∙ — ∙ — ∙ — ∙ — ∙ — ∙ — ∙ — ∙ — ∙ — ∙ —

At this point the teacher simply could have said "Good!" and gone on to the next question. Instead, this teacher continues:

— ∙ — ∙ — ∙ — ∙ — ∙ — ∙ — ∙ — ∙ — ∙ — ∙ — ∙ — ∙ —

Teacher: Let's show that on the board. Here is a triangle; now let's do exactly as Tom said. He said that squaring the altitude, which is *a*, and adding it to the square of the base, which is *b*, should give us the square of the hypotenuse, which is *c*. Carl, would you like to come up and show us how you would find the length of *c*, using the formula Tom just gave us?

Carl: Well, if *a* were equal to 3 and *b* equal to 4, the way I would solve this problem would be to add the squares of both of them together and then find the square root—that would be *c*.

Teacher: So, we square the 3, square the 4, add them together, and take the square root. This gives us 5, the length of the hypotenuse.

─ ─ ─ ─ ─ ─ ─ ─ ─ ─ ─ ─ ─ ─ ─ ─ ─ ─ ─

Which of the five ways of using student ideas are in this dialogue? First, by putting Tom's response graphically on the blackboard, this teacher *applied* Tom's answer by taking it to the next step, constructing a proof. Second, by repeating orally what Tom said, the teacher *acknowledged* to the entire class the value of Tom's contribution. And third, by having someone come up to prove the correctness of Tom's response, a *summary* of the concept was provided. All this was accomplished from Tom's simple (and only) utterance. "$c^2 = a^2 + b^2$."

Research reveals that student ideas and contributions, especially when used in the context of the naturally occurring dialogue of the classroom, are more strongly and consistently related to student engagement than simply approving a student's answer with "Good!" (Brophy, 1981). The standard phrases we use to acknowledge and reward students ("correct," "good," "right") are so overused that they may not convey the reward intended and often fail to contribute to the goals of your instruction.

Although the use of student ideas looks simple, it takes skill and planning. Even when your response is unplanned, you must be pre-

Student ideas and contributions elicited during the naturally occurring dialogue of the classroom add content to a lesson and reinforce previous learning. However, some expressions of the approval of student ideas and contributions, such as "correct," "good," or "right," have become so overused they may no longer convey the reward intended.

Handwritten margin note: A teacher can use a student's ideas to help strengthen the key behaviors

pared to seize opportunities to incorporate student ideas into the lesson. In later chapters you'll see how using student ideas can be a catalyst in other ways to performing each of the key teaching behaviors.

Structuring

Teacher comments made for the purpose of organizing what is to come, or summarizing what has gone before, is called *structuring*. Used prior to an instructional activity or question, structuring can serve as an organizer for students, aiding their understanding and retention of the material to be taught. Used at the conclusion of an instructional activity or question, structuring reinforces learned content and places it in proper relation to other content already taught. Both forms of structuring are related to student achievement and are effective catalysts for performing the five key behaviors (Doenau, 1987; Gage, 1976).

Typically, "before" and "after" structuring takes the following form:

Teacher: (at beginning of lesson) OK, now that we have studied how the pipefish change their color and movements to blend in with their surroundings, we will study how the pipefish gathers its food. Most important, we will learn how the pipefish grow and provide the means for other fish, like the kind we eat for food, to flourish deep below the ocean's surface.

Teacher: (at end of lesson) So, we have discovered that the pipefish protects itself by changing colors to blend in with plants on the ocean's floor and by swaying back and forth to fool its enemies. We might conclude from this that the pipefish evade rather than capture their natural enemies and feed close to the ocean's floor where they can't be noticed. Can you think of when this clever strategy might not work, making the pipefish prey to other fish deep below the ocean's surface? (adapted from Palincsar & Brown, 1989)

This sequence illustrates some of the many ways that you can use structuring. One way is to *signal* that a shift in direction or content is about to occur. A clear signal alerts students to the impending change. Without such a signal, students may confuse new content with old, missing the differences. Signals such as "Now that we have studied how the pipefish change their color and movements . . . we will learn . . . " help students switch gears and provide a perspective that makes new content more meaningful.

[handwritten marginal notes:] Teacher lists & organizes what students will need to do – Structuring

– This helps students retain their information best when the teacher summarizes the material.

When a teacher emphasises what's important, the student acknowledges & understands the activity best.

Teachers use verbal markers to help emphasis important points —

Another type of structuring uses *emphasis.* Can you find a point of emphasis in the previous dialogue? By using the phrase "most important," this teacher alerts students to the knowledge and understanding expected at the conclusion of this activity. This provides students with an organizer for what is to follow, called an *advance organizer.*

In this instance, the students are clued to consider the factors that extend beyond the color and movement of the pipefish to include how they grow and provide the means for other fish to flourish. This makes the teacher's final question more meaningful ("Can you think of when this clever strategy might not work, making the pipefish prey to other fish deep below the ocean's surface?"). The students have been clued that such a question might be raised and that generalizations beyond the concepts discussed will be expected. Phrases such as "Now this is important," "We will return to this point later," and "Remember this" are called *verbal markers.* They emphasize your most important points.

In addition to verbal markers and advance organizers, the effective teacher organizes a lesson into an activity structure. An *activity structure* is a set of related tasks that differ in cognitive complexity and that to some degree may be placed under the control of the learner. Activity structures (Marx & Walsh, 1988) can be built in many ways (e.g., cooperatively, competitively, independently) to vary the demands they make upon the learner and to give tempo and momentum to a lesson. For the effective teacher, they are an important means for engaging students in the learning process and moving them from simple recall of facts to the higher response levels that require reasoning, critical thinking, and problem-solving behavior (Bennett & Desforges, 1988; Doyle, 1983). These important means of structuring your learning activities will be covered in chapters 8 and 9.

Questioning

Questioning is another important helping behavior. Few other topics have been researched as much as the teacher's use of questions (Brown & Wragg, 1993; Dillon, 1988b; Gall, 1984). One of the most important outcomes of research on questioning has been the distinction between *content* questions and *process* questions, which we will look at next.

Content Questions.   Teachers pose content questions to have the student deal directly with the content taught. An example is when a teacher asks a question to see if students can recall and understand specific material. The correct answer is known well in advance by the teacher. It also has been conveyed directly in class, in the text, or both. Few, if any, interpretations or alternative meanings of the question are possible.

Researchers have used various terms to describe content questions, such as the following:

Direct: question requires no interpretation or alternative meanings.

Lower-order: question requires the recall only of readily available facts, as opposed to generalizations and inferences.

Convergent: different data sources lead to the same answer.

Closed: question has no possible alternative answers or interpretations.

Fact: question requires the recall only of discrete pieces of well-accepted knowledge.

Following are examples of content-oriented questions:

- What is the meaning of the word *ancient* in the story we just read?
- What was the mechanical breakthrough that gave the cotton gin superiority over all previous machines of its type?
- What is one of the chemical elements in the air we breathe?
- What is the function of a CPU in a microcomputer?
- What is the result of the number 47 divided by 6?

Some estimates show that up to 80 percent of the questions teachers ask refer directly to specific content and have readily discernable and unambiguous "right" answers (Gall, 1984). Perhaps even more important is the fact that approximately the same percentage of test items (and behavioral objectives) are written at the level of recall, knowledge, or fact (Kubiszyn & Borich, 1996). Therefore, test items, behavioral objectives, and most instruction seem to emphasize readily known facts as they are presented in curriculum guides, workbooks, and texts.

The art of questioning will become one of your most important skills as a teacher. The variety you convey to your students will be determined in large measure by your flexible use of questions. Questions are rarely ends in themselves but rather a means of engaging students in the learning process by getting them to act on, work through, or think about the material presented. Chapter 8 will have more to say about the many types of questions that can increase the variety of your lessons plans and the engagement of your learners.

Process Questions. From the discussion above you can see why not all questions should be content questions. There are different purposes for which questions can be asked, with the intent of encouraging different mental processes. To problem solve, to guide, to arouse (e.g., curiosity), to encourage (e.g., creativity), to analyze, to synthesize, and to judge also are goals of instruction that should be reflected in your questioning strategies. For these goals, content is not an end itself, but a means of achieving what are called "higher-order" goals.

Researchers have used various terms to describe process questions, such as the following:

Indirect: question has various possible interpretations and alternative meanings.

Higher-order: question requires more complex mental processes than simple recall of facts (e.g., making generalizations and inferences).

Divergent: different data sources will lead to different correct answers.

Open: a single correct answer is not expected or even possible.

Concept: question requires the processes of abstraction, generalization, and inference.

Following are examples of process-oriented questions:

- What are some of the ways you have used the word *ancient?*
- What were the effects of the invention of the cotton gin on attitudes in the North?
- From what we know about the many forms of pollution today, what would be one of the first things we have to do to clean up the air we breathe?
- How have recent advances in computer technology influenced the life of your family?
- Using examples of your own choosing, can you tell us some of the ways division and subtraction are similar?

Can you see the difference between this set of process questions and the list of content questions that preceded it? Notice that the process questions above encourage more thinking and problem solving by requiring the learner to use personal sources of knowledge to actively construct her or his own interpretations and meanings rather than acquiring understanding by giving back knowledge already organized in the form in which it was told. This view of teaching and learning represents a movement in education, called *constructivism.* **Constructivist teaching strategies** emphasize the learner's direct experience and the dialogue of the classroom as instructional tools while deemphasizing lecturing and "telling." Process questions and the use of probes, our next helping behavior, are important aids in constructivist thinking and action in the classroom. We will have more to say about the role of direct experience and the use of constructivist strategies in the classroom in many of the chapters ahead, and especially in chapters 7 and 8.

What are "constructivist strategies" of teaching?

Probing

Another helping behavior is probing. *Probing* refers to teacher statements that encourage students to elaborate upon an answer, either their own or another student's. Probing may take the form of a general question or can include other expressions that *elicit* clarification of an answer, *solicit* additional information about a response, or *redirect* a student's response in a more fruitful direction. Probing often is used to shift a discussion to some higher thought level.

Generally, student achievement is greatest when the eliciting, soliciting, and (if necessary) redirecting occur in cycles. This systematically leads the discussion to a higher level of complexity, as when interrelationships, generalizations, and problem solutions are being sought (Zahorik, 1987; Gage, 1976). In this manner, you may begin a lesson with a simple fact question; then, by eliciting clarification of student responses, soliciting new information, or redirecting an answer, you can move to a higher level of questioning.

A typical cycle might occur in the following manner:

Teacher: Bobby, what is a scientific experiment?

Bobby: Well, it's when you test something.

Teacher: But, what do you test?

Bobby: Mmm. Something you believe in and want to find out if it's really true.

Teacher: What do you mean by that?

Mary: He means you make a prediction.

Teacher: What's another word for "prediction"?

Tom: Hypothesis. You make a hypothesis, then go into the laboratory to see if it comes true.

Teacher: OK. So a scientist makes a prediction or hypothesis and follows up with an experiment to see if it can be made to come true. Then what?

Billy: That's the end!

Teacher: (No comment for 10 seconds; then . . .) Is the laboratory like the real world?

David: The scientist tries to make it like the real world, but it's much smaller, like the greenhouse pictured in our book.

Teacher: So what must the scientist do with the findings from the experiment, if they are to be useful? (No one answers, so the teacher continues . . .) If something important happens in my experiment, wouldn't I argue that what happened could also happen in the real world?

Bobby: You mean if it's true in a specific situation it will also be true in a more general situation?

Betty Jo: That's making a generalization.

Teacher: Good. So we see that a scientific investigation usually ends with a generalization. Let's summarize. What three things does a scientific investigation require?

Class: A prediction, an experiment, and a generalization.

Teacher: Good work, class.

— — — — — — — — — — — — — — — — — — — —

Can you find the teacher's soliciting, eliciting, and redirecting behaviors in this dialogue? In Chapter 8 you will fully explore dialogues such as this and learn how to produce them, but a few examples should make clear the concept of probing. Notice that all of the ingredients in this teacher's lesson were provided by the class. The concepts of hypothesis, experiment, and generalization were never defined for the class. The students defined these concepts for themselves with only an occasional "OK" or "Good" to let them know they were on track. The teacher's role was limited to eliciting clarification ("What do you mean by that?"), soliciting additional information ("What's another word for it?"), and redirection ("Is the laboratory like the real world?").

The purpose of this cycle of eliciting, soliciting, and redirection was to promote inquiry, or independent discovery of the content of the lesson. Generally, *retention* of material learned has been greater from inquiry teaching than from formal lecturing methods (Paul, 1990).

Teacher Affect

Anyone who has ever been in a classroom where the teacher's presentation was lifeless, static, and without vocal variety can appreciate the commonsense value of affective behavior. However, unlike the behaviors discussed previously, affect cannot be captured in transcripts of teaching behavior or by classroom interaction instruments. Consequently, narrowly focused research instruments often miss a teacher's affective behavior, which may be apparent from a more holistic view of the classroom.

What the instruments miss, the students see clearly. Students are good perceivers of the emotions underlying a teacher's actions, and they often respond accordingly. A teacher who is excited about the subject being taught and shows it by facial expression, voice inflection, gesture, and general movement is more likely to hold the attention of students than one who does not exhibit these behaviors. This is true whether or not teachers consciously perceive these behaviors in themselves.

Students take their cues from such behavioral signs and lower or heighten their engagement with the lesson accordingly. A presentation that is drab and static and that lacks praise, nonverbal approval, and a warm, nurturing, encouraging attitude is a sure formula for putting students to sleep mentally, if not physically. The very presence of this behavior on the part of the teacher is a message to the students that comparable behavior on their part is acceptable.

Enthusiasm is an important aspect of a teacher's affect. *Enthusiasm* is the teacher's vigor, power, involvement, excitement, and interest during a classroom presentation. We all know that enthusiasm is contagious, but how is it so? Enthusiasm is conveyed to students in many ways, the most common being vocal inflection, gesture, eye contact, and animation. A teacher's enthusiasm is related to student achievement (Bettencourt, Gillett, Gall, & Hull, 1983; Rosenshine, 1971a). It also is believed to be important in promoting student engagement in the learning process.

Obviously, no one can maintain a heightened state of enthusiasm for very long without becoming exhausted emotionally. Nor is this what is meant by enthusiasm. A proper level of enthusiasm is far more subtle, and perhaps that is why it has been so difficult to

When a teacher shows good attitude, the students are more motivated to learn.

Enthusiasm is important. It's vigor, power, excitement & interest in a classroom.

Enthusiasm is an important aspect of a teacher's affect. It is related to student achievement and is believed to be important in promoting student engagement in the learning process. Teachers convey enthusiasm to students in many ways, the most common being vocal inflections, gestures, eye contact, and animation.

research. A proper level of enthusiasm involves a delicate balance of vocal inflection, gesturing, eye contact, and movement. It employs each of these behaviors in only moderate ways. *In combination*, these behaviors send to students a unified signal of vigor, involvement, and interest. It is the use of these behaviors in moderation and at the right times that conveys the desired message.

Timing and the ability to incorporate these behaviors into a consistent pattern make possible an unspoken behavioral dialogue with students that is every bit as important as your spoken words. Letting students know that you are ready to help by your warm and encouraging attitude is essential if your enthusiasm is to be taken as an honest and sincere expression of your true feelings. We will return to this important topic in the chapters ahead.

>>> THE NEED FOR MULTIPLE DEFINITIONS <<<

Why are multiple definitions of "effective teaching" necessary?

You may have noticed this book's use of the plural when discussing *definitions* of effective teaching. There must be multiple definitions because effective teaching varies with the age of the student population (elementary, junior high, or secondary), the subject matter (reading vs. math), and even the background characteristics of the students (high vs. low socioeconomic status). These factors produce multiple definitions of effective teaching, each of which applies to a particular teaching context, thereby defining effective teaching more accurately.

Herein lies one of the major problems with earlier attempts to define effective teaching by describing ideal types or by describing a teacher's personality, attitude, experience, achievement, and aptitude. These attempts failed to consider (or even acknowledge) that *different* teaching contexts require *different* teaching behaviors. The complexity and difficulty of learning to teach arises from the complexity of the varied decision-making contexts in which teaching must occur. Thus, any single definition of effective teaching would be simplistic and inaccurate because of its insensitivity to the different learners, curricula, grade levels, and instructional materials with which teaching and learning must take place. It is the proper mix of key and helping behaviors in the context of your classroom that will come to define effective teaching for you. In the chapters ahead you will learn how to vary this mix accordingly, giving each key and helping behavior its proper emphasis within your grade, subject, learners, and curriculum.

Now let's turn to the importance of certain behaviors in several different teaching contexts.

>>> TEACHING EFFECTIVENESS <<< ACROSS SES AND CONTENT

In addition to the teaching behaviors that have elicited achievement across a wide variety of students and content, researchers have uncovered other behaviors of special importance to certain types of students and content. Two subareas of findings having the most consistent results are the teaching of lower- and higher-socioeconomic status (SES) students and the teaching of reading and mathematics.

Teaching Lower-SES and Higher-SES Students

The phrase *socioeconomic status* can mean many different things, but generally it is an approximate index of one's income and education level. For the classroom researcher, the SES of a student is determined directly by the income and education of his or her parents, or indirectly by the nature of the school the student attends.

How does effective teaching differ across socioeconomic level, culture, and ethnicity?

Some schools are in impoverished areas where the income and education level of the community are low, whereas other schools are located in more affluent communities. Many schools in impoverished areas qualify for special financial assistance from the federal government, based upon the median income of their students' parents. Researchers consider these "Chapter I" schools to be those where the majority of students come from lower-SES homes, are disadvantaged, and/or are "at risk" of dropping out of school. They are usually among the most culturally and ethnically diverse schools.

Because lower-SES and higher-SES students are facts of life that are likely to exist for some time, classroom researchers have determined what teacher behaviors promote the most achievement in these two types of students. Brophy and Evertson (1976), using a sample of elementary school classrooms, were among the first to provide suggestions for teaching these two types of students. Many of their suggestions have been confirmed by subsequent research in culturally diverse classrooms (Bowers & Flinders, 1991; Hill, 1989). A few of the most important teaching behaviors to emphasize for these two groups are summarized in Table 1.8.

Notice in the table that teacher affect seems to be particularly important in lower-SES classrooms. Also, notice that some of these teaching behaviors received little or no mention in our preceding discussions, because those discussions applied generally to students representing the full range of SES. Four of the behaviors shown for lower-SES classrooms (student responses, overteaching/overlearning, classroom interaction, and individualization) can be seen as spe-

Table 1.8
Important teaching behaviors for lower-SES and higher-SES students

	Findings for Lower-SES Pupils
Teacher Affect	Provide a warm and encouraging classroom climate by letting students know help is available.
Student Responses	Encourage an initial response, however crude, before moving to the next student.
Content Organization	Present material in small pieces, with opportunity to practice what has been learned after each piece. Show how the pieces fit together and are to be applied before each new segment of instruction begins.
Classroom Instruction	Emphasize knowledge and applications before teaching patterns and abstractions. Present most concrete learnings first. Monitor each student's progress at regular intervals. Use progress charts to help record learner improvement. Help students who need help immediately. Use peer and cross-age tutors, if necessary. Minimize disruptions by maintaining structure and flow between activities. Organize and plan transitions in advance.
Individualization	Supplement standard curriculum with specialized materials to meet the needs of individual students. Use media, learning resources, and the personal experiences of the students to promote interest and attention.
	Findings For Higher-SES Pupils
Correcting	Check right answers by requiring extended reasoning.
Thinking and Decisionmaking	Pose questions that require associations, generalizations, and inferences. Encourage students to use this same level of questioning. Supplement curriculum with challenging material, some of which is slightly above students' current level of attainment. Assign homework and/or extended projects that require independent judgment, discovery, and problem solving using original sources of information obtained outside the classroom.
Classroom Interaction	Encourage student-to-student and student-to-teacher interactions in which learners take responsibility for evaluating their own learning.
Verbal Activities	Actively engage students in verbal questions and answers that go beyond text and workbook content.

Based on Kennedy (1991), Bowers & Flinders (1991), and Bennett (1990).

cial ways of creating student engagement at high rates of success. This presents a particular challenge when teaching lower-SES and/or culturally diverse learners who may be inattentive, disinterested, or "at risk."

Also, frequently correcting wrong answers in the the absence of warmth or encouragement could be construed as a personal criticism by the lower-SES student, who already may have a poor self-concept. Therefore, feedback that could be construed as criticism may need to occur in the context of a more consistently warmer and encouraging environment than may be needed for the higher-SES learner. Also, activities such as discussion and problem solving may require more structure (and preparation) in the lower-SES classroom than in the higher-SES classroom.

Because much of the research on SES has been conducted in elementary classrooms, it is as yet uncertain to what extent these teaching behaviors apply to the secondary classroom. However, many of the learning characteristics of higher-SES and lower-SES students appear to be similar across these school contexts. Therefore, your success as a teacher in a predominantly lower-SES or higher-SES classroom may depend on your ability to vary the extent to which you emphasize the behaviors in Table 1.8. In subsequent chapters we will return to these and other characteristics of teaching and learning that apply to the culturally diverse classroom.

Teaching Reading and Mathematics

Another set of findings pertains to the different teaching behaviors that distinguish reading from mathematics instruction (Reynolds, 1989; Good & Grouws, 1979; Brophy & Evertson, 1976). Although not all teachers will teach either reading or mathematics, this set of findings may be generalized to some extent to other types of content that are similar in form and structure.

How does effective teaching differ across content areas?

For example, social studies, history, and language instruction all have high reading content and share some structural features with reading. General science, biology, physics, and chemistry are similar to the science of mathematics in that concepts, principles, and laws all play a prominent role. Also, visual forms and symbolic expressions are at least as important to understanding science subjects as is the written word. Therefore, some cautious generalizations may be made about the teaching behaviors important for reading and mathematics instruction and for subjects similar to each.

Some important findings are summarized in Table 1.9. Notice the two different approaches implied by the behaviors listed. For mathe-

Table 1.9

Important teaching behaviors for reading and mathematics instruction

Findings for Reading Instruction	
Instructional Activity	Spend sufficient time during reading instruction discussing, explaining, and questioning to stimulate cognitive processes and promote learner responding.
Interactive Technique	Use cues and questions that require every student to attempt a response during reading instruction.
Questions	Pose thought-provoking questions during reading instruction that require the student to predict, question, summarize, and clarify what has been read.

Findings For Mathematics Instruction	
Instructional Materials	Use application- and experience-oriented activities and media during mathematics instruction to foster task persistence.
Instructional Content	Maximize coverage of instructional applications during mathematics instruction through the use of activity sheets, handouts, and problem sets at graduated levels of difficulty.
Instructional Organization	Emphasize full-class or small-group instruction during mathematics instruction. Limit unguided or independent work, especially when it may interfere with on-task behavior and learner persistence.

Based on Reynolds (1989), Good & Grouws (1979), and Brophy & Evertson (1976).

matics instruction, a formal, direct approach appears to be most effective, especially when teaching the basics or fundamentals. This approach includes maintaining a high degree of structure through close adherence to texts, workbooks, and experience-oriented activities. It also maximizes instructional coverage by teaching to the full class as much as possible, minimizing unstructured independent work that could diminish engaged learning time. On the other hand, reading instruction allows a more interactive and indirect approach, using more classroom discussions and question-and-answer sessions.

These approaches, however, are not mutually exclusive. What the research shows is that, in general and over time, a more direct instructional approach during mathematics tends to result in greater student progress than would, say, the exclusive use of an inquiry approach. For reading, the reverse appears to be true: an exploratory, interactive approach that encourages the use of classroom discussion and student ideas tends to result in greater student progress over time.

These different approaches represent *degrees of emphasis*, and not exclusive strategies. Clearly, teaching mathematics will at times require an inquiry approach, just as reading sometimes requires a lecture or "telling" approach. More important than either of these approaches or the behaviors that represent them is the ability of the teacher to be flexible. The effective teacher senses when a change from one emphasis to another is necessary, regardless of the content being taught (Marx & Peterson, 1981).

>>> REVIEW OF SOME IMPORTANT TEACHER <<< EFFECTIVENESS INDICATORS

If this chapter were reduced to simple advice for you to improve your teaching, the result would be a return to a simplistic definition of an effective teacher. However, if you ask for some indicators of teaching effectiveness that have demonstrated importance in improving student achievement, the following list will help. These are some of the general indicators of effective teaching that are currently supported by the research literature. These indicators will be used in the chapters ahead to introduce specific instructional practices that will help you create these same behaviors in your own classroom.

What are some important indicators of teaching effectiveness?

The effective teacher:

- Takes personal responsibility for students' learning and has *positive expectations* for every learner.
- *Matches* the difficulty of the lesson with the ability level of the students and *varies* the difficulty when necessary to attain moderate-to-high success rates.
- Gives students the *opportunity to practice* newly learned concepts and to receive timely feedback on their performance.
- *Maximizes instructional time* to increase content coverage and to give students the greatest opportunity to learn.
- Provides direction and control of student learning through *questioning, structuring,* and *probing.*
- Uses a *variety of instructional materials and verbal and visual aids* to foster use of student ideas and engagement in the learning process.
- *Elicits responses* from students each time a question is asked before moving to the next student or question.
- Presents material in *small steps* with opportunities for practice.
- Encourages students to *reason out* and *elaborate on* the correct answer.
- Engages students in *verbal questions and answers.*
- Uses naturally occurring *classroom dialogue* to get students to *elaborate, extend,* and *comment on* the content being learned.

- Gradually *shifts some of the responsibility for learning to the students*—encouraging *independent thinking, problem solving,* and *decision making.*
- *Provides* learners with *mental strategies* for organizing and learning the content being taught.

At this point, you might think that an effective teacher simply is one who has mastered all of the key behaviors and helping behaviors. But, teaching involves more than a knowledge of how to perform individual behaviors. Much like an artist who blends color and texture into a painting to produce a coherent impression, so must the effective teacher blend individual behaviors to different degrees to promote student achievement. This requires orchestration and integration of the key and helping behaviors into meaningful patterns and rhythms that can achieve the goals of instruction within your classroom.

The truly effective teacher knows how to execute individual behaviors with a larger purpose in mind. This larger purpose requires placing behaviors side by side in ways that accumulate to create an effect greater than can be achieved by any single behavior or small set of them. This is why teaching involves a sense of timing, sequencing, and pacing that cannot be conveyed by any list of behaviors. It is the behaviors that connect these behaviors together, giving each its proper emphasis in the context of your classroom, that are so important to the effective teacher. And, it is the combination of curriculum, learning objectives, instructional materials, and learners that provides the decision-making context for the proper connection. Considerable attention will be devoted to this important decision-making context in the chapters ahead.

This chapter has presented some key and helping behaviors for becoming an effective teacher. These are not all of what the effective teacher is or does, but they are an important basis—perhaps the most valid basis—for beginning to understand the effective teacher. For us they will form the backbone and skeleton of an effective teacher. In the chapters ahead we will assemble the remainder of this complex person called the effective teacher.

As you have seen, the major teaching goals representing effective teaching are lesson clarity, instructional variety, task orientation, student engagement in the learning process, and student success. Some of the more specific means of achieving these goals have included the use of student ideas and contributions, structuring, questioning, probing, and teacher affect. The remaining chapters will represent teaching practices and decisions that can help you orchestrate these components into patterns that will create a lasting impression on your students. It is to this important task that we now turn.

Summing Up

This chapter introduced you to definitions of effective teaching and key behaviors that help achieve it. Its main points were as follows:

1. Early definitions of effective teaching focused primarily on a teacher's goodness as a person and only secondarily on his or her behavior in the classroom.

2. The psychological characteristics of a teacher—personality, attitude, experience, achievement, and aptitude—do not relate strongly to the teacher's behavior in the classroom.

3. Most modern definitions of effective teaching identify patterns of teacher–student interaction in the classroom that influence the cognitive and affective performance of students.

4. Classroom interaction analysis is a research methodology in which the verbal interaction patterns of teachers and students are systematically observed, recorded, and related to student performance.

5. Five key behaviors for effective teaching and some indicators pertaining to them are the following:

- Lesson clarity: logical, step-by-step order, clear and audible delivery free of distracting mannerisms.
- Instructional variety: variability in instructional materials, questioning, types of feedback, and teaching strategies.
- Task orientation: achievement (content) orientation as opposed to process orientation, maximum content coverage, and time devoted to instruction.
- Engagement: maintaining on-task behavior, limiting opportunities for distraction, and getting students to work on, think through, and inquire about the content.
- Success rate: 60–70 percent of time spent on tasks that afford moderate-to-high levels of success, especially during expository or didactic instruction.

6. Five helping behaviors for effective teaching and some indicators pertaining to them are the following:

- Use of student ideas and contributions: using student responses to foster the goals of the lesson, and getting students to elaborate on and extend learned content using their own ideas, experiences, and thought patterns.
- Structuring: providing advance organizers and mental strategies at the beginning of a lesson and creating activity structures with varied demands.
- Questioning: using both content (direct) and process (indirect) questions to convey facts and to encourage inquiry and problem solving.
- Probing: eliciting clarification, soliciting additional information, and redirecting when needed.
- Enthusiasm: exhibiting vigor, involvement, excitement, and interest during classroom presentations through vocal inflection, gesturing, eye contact, and animation.

7. The key behaviors appear to be consistently effective across all or most teaching contexts.

8. Other teaching behaviors, such as use of student ideas and contributions, structuring, and questioning, may be more important with some learners and objectives than with others.

9. Effective teaching involves the orchestration and integration of key and helping behaviors into meaningful patterns to achieve specified goals.

*1. In the following list, place the number *1* beside those indicators that most likely would appear in early definitions of effective teaching, based on the characteristics of a "good" person. Place the number *2* beside those indicators that most likely would appear in later definitions of effective teaching, based on the psychological characteristics of teachers. Place the number *3* beside those indicators most likely to appear in modern definitions of effective teaching, based on the interaction patterns of teachers and students.

____ is always on time for work
____ is intelligent
____ stays after class to help students
____ works well with those in authority
____ has plenty of experience at his or her grade level
____ varies higher-level with lower-level questions
____ likes his or her job
____ uses attention-getting devices to engage students in the learning task
____ is open to criticism
____ shows vitality when presenting
____ has worked with difficult students before
____ always allows students to experience moderate-to-high levels of success
____ matches the class content closely with the curriculum guide

2. In your opinion, which of the following helping behaviors on the right would be *most* helpful in implementing the key behaviors on the left? (The helping behaviors may be used more than once across key behaviors, and more than a single helping behavior may be used for a given key behavior.) Compare your results with those of another and discuss the reasons for any differences.

Lesson clarity ____	1. student ideas
Instructional variety ____	2. structuring
Task orientation ____	3. questioning
Engagement in the learning task ____	4. probing
Success rate ____	5. enthusiasm

*3. Using Table 1.8, identify one way in which you would try to achieve each of the following for *either* a lower-SES classroom or a higher-SES classroom: Individualization, teacher affect, thinking and decision making, classroom interaction.

4. Which two teaching effectiveness behaviors would you emphasize if you were teaching fifth-grade mathematics? Which two would you emphasize when teaching fifth-grade reading? Justify your choices from the summary research tables in this chapter.

5. Indicate your perceived strengths in exhibiting the five key and five catalytic behaviors, using the following technique. First, notice the number assigned to each of the key behaviors.

1 lesson clarity

2 instructional variety

3 teacher task orientation

4 engagement in the learning process

5 student success rate

Now, for each of the following rows of numbers listed, circle the number representing the key behavior in which you perceive yourself to have the greater strength.

1 versus 2	2 versus 4
1 versus 3	2 versus 5
1 versus 4	3 versus 4
1 versus 5	3 versus 5
2 versus 3	4 versus 5

Count up how many times you circled a 1, how many times you circled a 2, a 3, etc., and place the frequencies on the following lines.

1. _____
2. _____
3. _____
4. _____
5. _____

---

* Answers to asterisked questions (*) in this and the other chapters are in Appendix B.

Your perceived greatest strength is the key behavior having the highest frequency. Your perceived least strength is the key behavior with the lowest frequency. In subsequent chapters, underscore material related to your perceived least strength and note the suggested readings related to it.

6. Repeat the paired comparison technique in the same manner for the five helping behaviors.

1 use of student ideas

2 structuring

3 questioning

4 probing

5 enthusiasm

1 versus 2	2 versus 4
1 versus 3	2 versus 5
1 versus 4	3 versus 4
1 versus 5	3 versus 5
2 versus 3	4 versus 5

1. _____

2. _____

3. _____

4. _____

5. _____

7. Recall a particularly good teacher you had during your high-school years—and a particularly poor one. Try to form a mental image of each one. Now rate each of them on the five key behaviors in the following table. Use *1* to indicate strength in that behavior, *2* to indicate average performance, and *3* to indicate weakness in that behavior. Are the behavioral profiles of the two teachers different? How?

Behavior	Teacher X (good)	Teacher Y (poor)
Lesson clarity	____	____
Instructional variety	____	____
Task orientation	____	____
Engagement in the learning process	____	____
Success rate	____	____

8. Now do the same for the five helping behaviors, using the same two teachers. Is the pattern the same? What differences in ratings, if any, do you find across key and catalytic behaviors for the same teacher? How would you account for any differences that occurred?

Suggested Readings

Anderson, L. (1987). Opportunity to learn. In M. J. Dunkin (Ed.), *International encyclopedia of teaching and teacher education.* New York: Pergamon.

 A brief and authoritative introduction to the key behavior of engagement in the learning process.

Bolin, F. S. (1988). Helping student teachers think about teaching. *Journal of Teacher Education, 39*(2), pp. 48–54.

 The author describes how student teachers develop a concept of teaching and think about their role as teachers. Through a case study of one preservice teacher's journal entries and interviews with a university supervisor, the author describes stages of development and the role of self-awareness and reflection in becoming an effective teacher.

Borich, G. (1995). *Becoming a teacher: An inquiring dialogue for the beginning teacher.* Bristol, PA: Falmer Press.

 A set of 13 conversations between a young journalist, school principal, and teachers describing an effective school and effective teaching. Through conversational dialogue, the author identifies and illustrates practical ways schools and teachers become effective.

Cruickshank, D. (1990). *Research that informs teachers and teacher educators.* Bloomington, IN: Phi Delta Kappa.

This summary of research (1971–1989) identifies the most studied and talked-about characteristics of effective teachers and effective schools. The author provides a helpful summary table at the end that identifies 45 characteristics of effectiveness pertaining to principals, teachers, and the classroom. See also *Effective Schools: A Summary of Research.* Arlington, VA: Educational Research Service (1983).

Grossman, P. A., Wilson, S., & Shulman, L. S. (1989). Teachers of substance: Subject matter knowledge for teaching. In M. C. Reynold, *Knowledge base for beginning teachers.* New York: Pergamon.

This article explains that one of the first challenges facing beginning teachers is the transformation of their subject matter knowledge into a form that is relevant to students and specific to the task of teaching. The authors identify and illustrate several practical ways teachers can make this transformation.

Rosenshine, B., & Stevens, R. (1986). Teaching functions. In M. C. Wittrock (Ed.), *Handbook of research on training* (3rd ed., pp. 376–391). Englewood Cliffs, NJ: Merrill/Prentice Hall.

Summarizes some of the more generally applicable findings from recent research on teaching effectiveness, with particular emphasis on those teaching functions related to student achievement.

Webb. R. (Ed.) (1990). *Practitioner research in the primary school.* New York: Falmer.

This book provides models and actual examples of how teachers can become practitioner-researchers in their own classrooms and, in the process, acquire a capacity for directing their own professional development.

CHAPTER 2

Understanding Your Students

 This chapter will help you answer the following questions:

1. What is a reflective teacher?
2. How can I adapt my instruction to the needs and abilities of individual learners?
3. To what extent can I expect my learners performance to be determined by their intelligence?
4. What is the relative contribution of general and specific intelligence to learning?
5. Can the intelligence of my learners be raised by my instruction?
6. What is the relationship between the socioeconomic level of a learner and his or her readiness to learn?
7. How can I help my learners acquire friendships and a positive self-concept?
8. How does "learning style" differ across culture and ethnicity?
9. What are some of the ways I can use peer group membership to foster the goals of my instruction?
10. What are some ways I can promote family–school partnerships in my classroom?

This chapter will also help you learn the meaning of the following:

▶ adaptive teaching
family–school linking mechanisms
field dependence and field independence
general versus specific intelligence
learning structures
learning styles
reflective teacher
social competence
state and trait anxiety
student self-concept
systems-ecological perspective
task-relevant prior behaviors
vertical and horizontal relationships

C hapter 1 explained that teaching is not simply the transmission of knowledge from teacher to learner but rather
is the interaction of teacher with learner. For this reason,
effective teaching practices are always defined by who is
being taught and under what conditions (curriculum,
learning objectives, instructional materials, and learners). This idea appeared in Chapter 1: some teaching
behaviors are more effective with some types of learners
(higher-SES vs. lower-SES) and content (math vs. reading) than with others. This chapter discusses the decisions you must make about whom you will teach. In subsequent chapters, we will consider the decisions you
must make about what and how you will teach.

It was not so long ago that some teachers thought of
their students as blank slates onto which they were to
transfer knowledge, skills, and understanding. They perceived their task to be the skilled transmission of appropriate grade-level content as it appeared in texts, curriculum guides, workbooks, and the academic disciplines.
Students were viewed as empty vessels into which the
teacher poured the contents of the day's lesson.

You can see how contradictions arose from such a
simplistic definition of teaching and learning. For example, this definition could not explain why some "bright"
students get poor grades and some "dull" students get
good grades. Nor could it explain why some students
want to learn while others do not even want to come to
school; why some students do extra homework while others do none at all; or why some students have attitudes
conducive to learning while others talk harshly to their
peers about the value of schooling.

These are just some of the individual differences
existing in every classroom; they will influence the outcome of your teaching, regardless of how adept you may
be at transmitting content. Your transmission of knowledge onto the blank slate will be interrupted by more
than a few of these individual differences.

Adapting your teaching to individual differences will
require that you make many decisions about your learners that cannot be reduced to simple formulas or rules. It
will require that you become a **reflective teacher,** which
means that you take the time to ask tough questions
about the appropriateness and success of your teaching
efforts. Reflective teachers are thoughtful and self-critical

Many differences among students in every classroom.

What is a reflective teacher?

[Margin note: Need to adapt to students needs....]

about their teaching. That is, they take the time necessary to adapt their lessons to their learners' needs, prior histories, and experiences, and to analyze and critique their lessons afterward.

[Margin note: Reflective teachers are thoughtful, self critical about their teaching.]

To help adapt subject matter content to the world of their learners, reflective teachers use the direct experiences of their learners and their classroom interactions (questions, discussion, projects, cooperative activities) as instructional tools. With these and other instructional tools you will learn about in this text, they get their learners to use their own experiences to actively construct understandings that make sense to them, while deemphasizing lecturing and "telling." In other words, they bridge the gap between teaching and learning by actively engaging students in their lessons and encouraging them to gradually accept greater responsibility for their own learning. In the chapters ahead, we will have more to say about how you can become a reflective teacher who adapts subject matter to the individual differences of learners and who uses direct experiences and the dialogue of the classroom to actively engage students in the learning process.

[Margin note: Teachers get their students to use their own experiences to learn.]

But, for now, you should know that becoming an effective teacher includes not only learning to be knowledgeable about content and how to teach it, but also how to adjust both content and teaching practices to the individual differences that exist among learners. This chapter contains some important facts about the psychology of learners that will help you understand and appreciate their individual differences.

[Margin note: An effective teacher not only is knowledgeable but must know how to teach; adjust to ea. individual student/learners.]

>>> WHY PAY ATTENTION TO <<<
INDIVIDUAL DIFFERENCES?

Any observer in any classroom quickly notices that schoolchildren vary in their experiences, learning ability, achievement, personality, interests, creativity, and self-discipline. Of what consequence is such an obvious observation? After all, you must teach all the students assigned to you, regardless of their differences.

Two of the reasons for being aware of individual differences among learners in your classroom are as follows:

[Margin note: Kids learn at diff. levels.]

To help students best because of indiv differences using diff. instruct. methods -

1. By recognizing individual differences, you may be able to match or adapt your instructional method to the individual learning needs of your students. That is, you will be better able to help them use their own experiences and past learning histories to bring their own meanings and understandings to what you are teaching.

2. When counseling students and consulting with parents about the achievement and competencies of those who have difficulty learning or who are learning above expectations, you will be able to convey the reasons for the behavior you are describing. Understanding your students' behavior provides perspective for parents, counselors, and other teachers when they wonder why Jared is not learning, why Anita learns without studying, or why Angela does not even want to learn.

Understanding individual differences among learners will enable you to adapt instructional methods to their needs. For example, information about learner experiences, learning ability, prior achievement, personality, and interests may be used to select the most appropriate teaching style or method for a given instructional objective. Researchers are discovering many content areas and individual differences where the application of different instructional strategies to different types of learners has significantly improved their performance (Corno & Snow, 1986; Cronbach & Snow, 1977).

Student-centered discussions help students significantly.

In one instance, student-centered *discussions* were found to significantly improve the achievement of highly anxious students, while teacher-centered *lecture* classes significantly improved achievement among low-anxiety students (Dowaliby & Schumer, 1973). These results were explained by the more informal, nurturing climate accompanying the student-centered discussion, which allowed the highly anxious students to focus more intently on the content, resulting in greater learning. In contrast, the low-anxiety students achieved better under the more efficient direct-lecture approach in which a faster pace was achieved.

Students learn under diff. approaches to teaching

In another example involving the teaching of reading, the *linguistic* approach resulted in higher vocabulary achievement for students *high* in auditory ability, while the *whole-word* approach was more effective for students *low* in auditory ability (Stallings & Keepes, 1970). Achievement was maximized when the instructional method favored the learners' natural abilities. In this case, those who learned best by *seeing* benefited from the whole-word approach, while the auditory approach was better for those who learned best by *hearing*.

Adaptive Teaching

The general approach to achieving a common instructional goal with learners whose prior achievement, aptitude, or learning styles differ widely is called **adaptive teaching.** Adaptive teaching techniques apply different instructional strategies to different groups of learners so that the natural diversity prevailing in the classroom does not prevent any learner from reaching the common goal. Two approaches to adaptive teaching have been reported to be effective (Corno & Snow, 1986). They are the remediation approach and the compensatory approach.

The Remediation Approach. The *remediation* approach provides the learner with the prerequisite knowledge, skill, or behavior needed to benefit from the planned instruction. For example, in the first research example cited (discussion vs. lecture), you might first attempt to lower the anxiety of the high-anxious group, so that the lecture method could equally benefit all students. In the second example (linguistic vs. whole-word), you might attempt to raise the auditory (listening) skills of those who are deficient in them so that both groups could profit equally from the linguistic approach (which, due to limitations in time and materials, may be the only method available).

The remediation approach to adaptive teaching will be successful to the extent that the desired prerequisite information, skill, or behavior to overcome a deficiency can be taught within a reasonable period of time. However, this often is not possible or represents an inefficient use of classroom time, and the compensatory approach to adaptive teaching must be taken.

The Compensatory Approach. The *compensatory* approach chooses an instructional method to circumvent or compensate for deficiencies in information, skills, or ability known to exist among learners. With this approach to adaptive teaching, content presentation is altered to circumvent a fundamental weakness or deficiency. This is done by using alternate modalities (e.g., pictures vs. words) or by supplementing content with additional learning resources (games and simulations) and activities (group discussions, hands-on experiences). This may involve modifying the instructional technique to compensate for known deficiencies and to use known strengths. Techniques include the visual representation of content, using more flexible instructional presentations (films, pictures, illustrations), shifting to alternate instructional formats (self-paced texts, simula-

How can I adapt my instruction to the needs and abilities of individual learners?

tions, experience-oriented workbooks), or using authentic, performance-based assessment procedures that might require students to assemble a portfolio of their experiences, understandings, and products pertaining to a topic.

For example, students who are poor at reading comprehension and lack a technical math vocabulary might be taught a geometry unit supplemented with visual handouts. Portraying each theorem and axiom graphically emphasizes the visual modality. Other students having an adequate reading comprehension and vocabulary level might skip this more time-consuming approach and proceed by learning the same theorems and axioms from a highly verbalized text, thereby emphasizing the verbal modality.

Benefits of Adaptive Teaching.   Notice that adaptive teaching goes beyond the simpler process of ability grouping, in which students are divided into "slow" and "fast" learners and then presented approximately the same material at different rates. Some research suggests that differences in academic performance between high and low achievers may actually *increase* with the use of ability grouping, creating a loss of self-esteem and motivation for the low group (Slavin, 1991a; Kerchoff, 1986; Good & Stipek, 1983).

Adaptive teaching, on the other hand, works to achieve the common goal with all students, regardless of their individual differences. It does so either by remediation (building up the knowledge, skills, or abilities required to profit from the planned instruction) or by compensation (circumventing known weaknesses by avoiding instructional methods/materials that rely on abilities that may be less well developed). Therefore, adaptive teaching requires an understanding of your students' learning abilities and the alternative instructional methods that can maximize their strongest receptive modalities (e.g., visual vs. auditory).

The chapters ahead provide a menu of such strategies from which to choose. Some of the most promising instructional alternatives in adaptive teaching include the following:

High/low vividness of materials

Inductive/expository presentation

Rule-example/example-rule ordering

Inductive/deductive presentation

Teacher-centered/student-centered presentation

Structured/unstructured teaching methods

Lecture/student presentation

[Handwritten margin notes: "When students are grouped 'slow' 'fast' learners, this increases loss of self-esteem/motivation for 'low' ability group." "Important" "Remediation ① build knowledge" "Compensation ② develop on weakness"]

Group phonics/individualized phonics instruction

Presence/absence of advance organizers

Programmed/conventional instruction

Each of these teaching methods or presentation styles has been found more effective for some types of learners than for others (Rohrkemper & Corno, 1988; Cronbach & Snow, 1977). The research literature and curriculum texts in your teaching area offer many examples of specific content areas in which a particular instructional method—in association with a particular student characteristic—has enhanced student performance. However, common sense and classroom experience will suggest many other ways in which you can alter teaching to fit the individual needs of your students. By knowing your students and having a variety of instructional methods available, you can adjust your instruction to the learning needs of your students with one of these two methods of adaptive teaching.

>>> THE EFFECTS OF GENERAL <<< INTELLIGENCE ON LEARNING

One thing everyone remembers about elementary school is how some students seemed to learn so easily, while others had to work so hard. In high school there was an even greater range of "smartness." In a practical sense, we associate the terms *smart, bright, ability to solve problems, learn quickly,* and *figure things out* with intelligence. Both in the classroom and in life it is obvious that some have more "intelligence" than others. This observation often has been a source of anxiety, concern, and jealousy among learners. Perhaps because the topic of intelligence can so easily elicit emotions like these, it is the most talked about and least understood aspect of student behavior.

One of the greatest misunderstandings that some teachers, parents, and school administrators have about intelligence is that it is a single, unified dimension. Such a belief is often expressed by the use of word pairs such as *slow/fast, smart/dumb, bright/dull* when referring to different kinds of learners. These phrases indicate that a student is *either* fast *or* slow, *either* bright *or* dull, *either* smart *or* dumb, when in fact, each of us (regardless of our intelligence) is *all* of these at one time or another. On a particular task of a certain nature, you may appear to be "slow and dull," but given another

To what extent can I expect my learners' performance to be determined by their intelligence?

Intelligence – least understood behavior.

At one time or another we have all expressed fast/slow, bright/dull, smart/dumb at one time or another

task requiring different abilities, you may be "fast and bright." How do such vast differences occur within a single individual?

Everyone knows from personal experience in school, hobbies, sports, and interpersonal relationships that degree of intelligence depends on the *circumstances* and *conditions* under which the intelligence is exhibited. Observations such as these have led researchers to study and identify more than one kind of intelligence. This relatively new way of looking at intelligence has led to a better understanding of classic contradictions like why Carlos is good in vocabulary but not in mathematics, why Angela is generally good in social studies but specifically bad at reading maps, or why Tamara is good at analyzing the reasons behind historical events but poor at memorizing the names and dates that go along with them. Each of these seemingly contradictory behaviors can be explained by the special abilities required by each task. It is these specific abilities, in which we all differ, that are the most useful for understanding the learning behavior of your students.

There are some controversial issues about the use of general intelligence tests you should be aware of when discussing "intelligence" with parents, other teachers, and school administrators. These issues often strongly divide individuals into two camps, known as the environmentalist position and the hereditarian position.

The Environmentalist Position

The *environmentalist* position criticizes the use of general IQ tests in the schools in the belief that they are culturally biased. Environmentalists believe that differences in IQ scores among groups such as African Americans, Hispanics, and Anglos can be attributed largely to social class or environmental differences. They reason that some groups of students, particularly minorities, may come from impoverished home environments in which the verbal skills generally required to do well on intelligence tests are not practiced. Therefore, a significant part of minority-student scores on any IQ test represents the environment in which they grew up and not their true intelligence.

Environmentalists conclude (and some research supports) that the effect of home environment is at least as important as heredity in contributing to one's IQ (Bloom, 1981; Smilansky, 1979). This group believes that intelligence tests are biased in favor of the white middle class, who, it is believed, are able to provide their children with more intense patterns of verbal interaction, greater reinforcement for learning, more learning resources, and better physical health during the critical preschool years in which cognitive growth is fastest.

The Hereditarian Position

The *hereditarian* position concludes that heredity rather than environment is the major factor determining intelligence. Hereditarians base their beliefs on the research and writings of Arthur Jensen (1969). They believe that not all children have the same potential for developing the same mental abilities. They contend that efforts such as compensatory education programs to make up for environmental disadvantages in the early elementary grades through remediation can have only limited success because the origin of the difference is genetic and not environmental (Herrnstein & Murray, 1994).

← belief of hereditarian

Belief Intelligence is Hereditary

General versus Specific Intelligence

School grades

Common sense tells us there is some truth in both arguments. However, despite how parents, other teachers, and even your own students may feel, these positions are highly dependent on the notion of **general intelligence.** They become less relevant in the context of specific abilities. General intelligence tests only moderately predict school grades, whereas **specific intelligence** abilities tend to predict not only school grades but also more important real-life behaviors that school grades are supposed to represent. For example, tests of general intelligence do not predict success as a salesperson, factory worker, carpenter, computer programmer, or teacher, because they measure few of the abilities required for success in these occupations.

What is the relative contribution of general and specific intelligence to learning?

Specific intelligence predicts grades + real-life behaviors

If we think of school learning as a pie and IQ as a piece of it, we can ask the question: How large a piece of the classroom learning pie is taken up by IQ? Another way of asking this same question is: What percentage of school learning can be attributed to IQ and what percentage to other factors? Scarr (1981) indicates that many factors, in addition to IQ, will contribute to your learners' success: their motivation, support from parents, prior knowledge, health, use of learning strategies, emotional stability and the quality of your teaching to name only some. Scarr classifies these factors under the term **social competence.** What percentage of school learning can be assigned to IQ and what percentage to all the other factors, Scarr's social competence? The answer, illustrated in Figure 2.1, is that only about 25 percent can be attributed to IQ; about 75 percent must be assigned to "social competence." So, knowing your learners' *specific* strengths and weaknesses and altering your instructional goals and activities accordingly will contribute far more to your effective teaching than will categorizing your students' performances in ways that indicate only their *general* intelligence.

Teachers who know learners specific strengths weaknesses & altering instructional goals can be very effective.

Figure 2.1
Factors contributing to school
learning

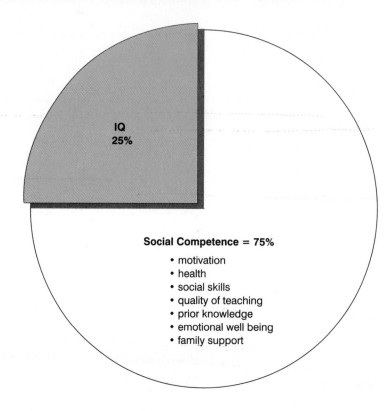

IQ
25%

Social Competence = 75%
- motivation
- health
- social skills
- quality of teaching
- prior knowledge
- emotional well being
- family support

>>> THE EFFECTS OF SPECIFIC <<<
ABILITIES ON LEARNING

Specific definitions of intelligence and the behaviors they represent commonly are called *aptitudes* or *factors.* As a teacher, you are unlikely to measure aptitudes in your classroom, but you need to know of their influence on the performance of your students. Your students may already have been aptitude-tested in a districtwide testing program, or you can ask the school counselor or psychologist to measure a specific aptitude to find the source of a specific learning problem. Your acquaintance with the division of general intelligence into specific aptitudes will help you see how a learner's abilities in specific areas can directly affect the degree of learning that takes place.

Thurstone's Specialized Abilities

Some of the many specialized abilities that have been reliably measured include *verbal comprehension, general reasoning, memory, use of numbers, psychomotor speed, spatial relations, and word fluency.* This list of abilities resulted from the work of L. L. Thurstone (1947). Instead of reinforcing the idea of a single IQ score, Thurstone's work led to the development of seven different IQs, each measured by a separate test. In this manner the concept of general intelligence was divided into component parts; it had the obvious advantage that a specific score for a given part could be related to certain types of learning requirements.

Some learning activities require a high degree of memory, such as memorizing long lists of words in preparation for a spelling bee or a vocabulary test. Likewise, spatial relations, use of numbers, and general reasoning ability are essential for high levels of performance in mathematics. Such differences in aptitude are far more useful than general intelligence in explaining to parents why Alexis can get excellent scores on math tests that emphasize number problems $(12 + 2 \times 6 =)$ but poor scores on math tests that emphasize word problems (If Bob rows 4 mph against a current flowing 2 mph, how long will it take him to row 16 miles?). Such apparent contradictions become more understandable in the light of specific aptitudes.

While Thurstone's dimensions were among the earliest, other components of general intelligence have been hypothesized. For example, Gardner and Hatch (1989) propose seven different "intelligences" based on skills found in a modern technological society. Their seven abilities, along with some representative individuals who would be expected to possess high levels of these abilities, are identified in Table 2.1. Gardner and his associates have developed instructional materials and modules to teach some of these abilities.

Their theory derives from the observation that many individuals who are successful in life do not score high in traditional indicators of ability, such as verbal or mathematical reasoning. Gardner and his associates suggest that these individuals, to be successful, used other abilities, such as those in Table 2.1, to minimize their weaknesses in some areas and compensate for weaknesses in others. Their theory may have particular relevance for teaching at-risk learners, some of whom may not learn from school in the traditional classroom setting using the traditional curriculum. These researchers reason that alternative forms of learning could "tap into" other dimensions of intelligence that in the traditional classroom may go unnoticed or underutilized.

Content area specialists have identified still other specific forms of intelligence nestled within those suggested by Thurstone and by Gardner and Hatch. For example, content specialists in reading have identified no fewer than nine verbal comprehension factors, which indicate the ability to do the following:

[Handwritten margin notes:]
Gard. M. Intel
table shows
Students have different levels of learning.
— stronger in some ex: math areas than others.
— Some Day intelligence isn't teachable but w/ instruction + Students can fine their strengths of their talents — may have one or more strengths
helpful?!
"true"

Table 2.1

Gardner's multiple intelligences

Dimension	Example
Linguistic intelligence: Sensitivity to the meaning and order of words and the varied uses of language	Poet, journalist
Logical-mathematical intelligence: The ability to handle long chains of reasoning and to recognize patterns and order in the world	Scientist, mathematician
Musical intelligence: Sensitivity to pitch, melody, and tone	Composer, violinist
Spatial intelligence: The ability to perceive the visual world accurately, and to recreate, transform, or modify aspects of the world based on one's perceptions	Sculptor, navigator
Bodily-kinesthetic intelligence: A fine-tuned ability to use the body and to handle objects	Dancer, athlete
Interpersonal intelligence: The ability to notice and make distinctions among others	Therapist, salesperson
Intrapersonal intelligence: Access to one's own "feeling life" *(inventor)*	Self-aware individual

SOURCE: Adapted from Gardner & Hatch, 1989

Know word meanings

See contextual meaning

See organization

Follow thought patterns

Find specifics

Express ideas

Draw inferences

Identify literary devices

Determine a writer's purpose

In other words, a learner's general performance in reading may be affected by any one or a combination of these specific abilities. This and similar lists point up an interesting and sometimes controversial aspect of intelligence: once aptitudes such as memory, use of numbers, reasoning, verbal comprehension, and so on are defined by their underlying factors, is it possible to *teach* these so-called components of intelligence?

Hereditarians say that intelligence is not teachable, but it seems logical that, with proper instruction, a learner could be taught to draw inferences, find specifics, and determine a writer's purpose. As general components of intelligence, such as those defined by Thurstone and by Gardner and Hatch become divided into smaller and more specific aptitudes, the general concept of intelligence has become "demystified." At least some elements of intelligence depend on achievement in certain areas that *can* be influenced by instruction. Therefore, another advantage of the multidimensional approach to intelligence is that some specific deficiencies once thought to be unalterable can be remedied by instruction.

Sternberg's Theory of Intelligence

One of the most recent conceptions of specialized abilities comes from Sternberg (1989). He believes that intelligence, as defined by its components, can be altered through instruction. Sternberg's work has been important in forming new definitions of intelligence that allow for intellectual traits, previously believed to be inherited and unalterable, to be improved through instruction. Further, Sternberg suggests not only that intelligence can be taught but also that the classroom is the logical place to teach it.

Let's look more closely at the theory from which this fascinating claim is made. Sternberg's theory of intelligence is called *triarchic* because it consists of three parts: the individual's internal world, how the individual acquires intelligence, and the individual's external world.

Can the intelligence of my learners be raised by my instruction?

[handwritten note: Sternberg belief that intelligence can be altered w/ instruction. — feels classroom is best place to teach ...]

1 The Individual's Internal World. The first part of Sternberg's theory relates to the individual's internal world that governs thinking. Three kinds of mental processes occur, instrumental in (1) planning what things to do, (2) how to learn to do them, and (3) how to actually perform them. The first of these processes is used in planning, monitoring, and evaluating the performance of a task. In essence, this is an "executive" component that tells all other components of our intelligence what to do, like the boss who gives directions but who does none of the work. Hence, this component's role is purely administrative.

A second component of this internal world of intelligence governs behavior in actual task performance. This component controls

[handwritten: Know ↗]

Some aspects of the age-old concept of intelligence, once thought to be unalterable, now may be taught in the classroom.

the various strategies used in solving problems. For example, one strategy is to guide you to the most relevant details of a problem and steer you away from the irrelevant. Thus, individuals can become more or less "intelligent" by learning which details need attention and which to ignore.

A third component of this internal world of intelligence governs what previously acquired knowledge we bring to a problem. It is here that Sternberg's theory differs most from other concepts of intelligence. In his view, the innate and less alterable characteristics of memory, manipulating symbols, or mental speed are not particularly important to intelligence. Instead, he sees the *previously acquired knowledge* that one brings to problem solving as more important to thinking intelligently.

Sternberg points out that one of the biggest differences between "experts" and "nonexperts" in the real world is not the mental processes they use in performing a task, but their previously acquired knowledge. The task in expanding intelligence or "expertness," then, is to understand how experts acquire needed information, when nonexperts seemingly fail to acquire it. This notion leads to the second part of Sternberg's triarchic theory.

2 How the Individual Acquires Intelligence. Sternberg proposes that intelligence is the ability to learn and to think using previously discovered patterns and relationships to solve new problems in unfamiliar contexts. By experiencing many novel tasks and conditions early in life, we discover the patterns and relationships that tell us how to solve new problems with which we may be totally unfamiliar. In other words, the greater our experience in facing unique and novel conditions, the more we grow and can adapt to the changing conditions around us.

Sternberg suggests that confronting novel tasks and situations and learning to deal with them is one of the most important instructional goals in learning intelligent behavior. His writings provide many practical exercises and examples of how to become facile at learning to deal with novel tasks and situations that provide the patterns and relationships with which to enhance our intelligence.

3   The Individual's External World.   The third part of Sternberg's theory relates intelligence to the external world of the individual. This is where an individual's intelligence shows most and can be altered quickest. This part of intelligence is governed by how well one learns to adapt to the environment (changes his or her way of doing things to fit the world), to select from the environment (avoid unfamiliar things and choose familiar and comfortable ones), and to shape the environment (change it to fit a personal way of doing things). Thus, "intelligent" people *learn* to adapt, select, and shape their environment better and faster than do "less intelligent" people. Therefore, perhaps the most important aspect of Sternberg's theory is that intelligence results as much from how people learn to *cope* with the world around them as it results from the internal mental processes with which they are born (e.g., memory, symbol manipulation, mental speed).

This notion of coping is expressed by 20 characteristics that Sternberg suggests often impede intelligent behavior and, therefore, are often found in the "unintelligent" or the "nonexpert":

Lack of motivation

Lack of impulse control

Lack of perseverance

Using the wrong abilities

Inability to translate thought into action

Lack of a product orientation

Inability to complete tasks and to follow through

Failure to initiate

Fear of failure

Handwritten margin notes:

"The greater the experience in facing unique novel conditions, the more we grow and adapt to changing conditions around us."

How well one adapts to the way we do things to fit the world.

Procrastination

Misattribution of blame

Excessive self-pity

Excessive dependency

Wallowing in personal difficulties

Distractibility and lack of concentration

Spreading oneself too thin

Inability to delay gratification

Inability or unwillingness to see the forest for the trees

Lack of balance between critical thinking and creative thinking

Too little or too much self-confidence

From these 20 impediments to intelligent thinking, you can see why Sternberg believes many aspects of intelligence can and should be taught and why the classroom may be a logical place to convey the attitudes and behaviors that can help learners avoid these impediments to intelligent behavior.

>>> THE EFFECTS OF PRIOR <<<
ACHIEVEMENT ON LEARNING

Closely related to Sternberg's notion of intelligence are the prior knowledge and skills of your learners—specifically, their task-relevant knowledge and skills. *Task relevant* means those facts, skills, and understandings that must be taught if subsequent learning is to occur. Mastery of these behaviors makes possible future learning. Thus, their identification is important not only in planning instruction but also in accounting for why learning does not occur in some situations and for some students.

These task-relevant facts, skills, and understandings come in various shapes and sizes. In each content area they are part of the logical progression of ideas with which a lesson is conveyed. For example, various orders of reasoning may be used—general-to-detailed, simple-to-complex, abstract-to-concrete, or conceptual-to-procedural. These logical progressions are **learning structures** that identify at each step those behaviors needed before new learning can take place (e.g., procedures must come before concepts, and simple facts must come before complex details).

Chapters 6, 7, and 8 present more about the many logical progressions with which teaching can be structured, but for now it is important to appreciate that many task-relevant prior learnings are embedded within these progressions. It is upon these that the final outcomes of a lesson or unit depend. This point is illustrated in Figure 2.2 for an instructional unit on government and Figure 2.3 for a unit on writing skills.

Notice that in Figure 2.2, the concepts of "presidential" and "parliamentary" would have to be learned before the concept of a "representative" democracy could be understood. And, the concepts of "monarchy," "oligarchy," and "democracy" would have to be learned prior to an understanding of "types of government." These task-relevant prior achievements provide a structure for learning that allows larger concepts, principles, and generalizations to be learned at the end of a lesson or unit. Regardless of the type of progression that may apply in a specific instance, notice that a breakdown in the flow of learning at almost any point will prevent learning from taking place at any subsequent point. Failure to attain concepts at higher levels in the instructional plan, therefore, may not indicate a lack of ability or specialized aptitude but a failure to adequately grasp **task-relevant prior behaviors.**

Chapter 5 indicates how to plan instructional units using different types of "learning structures." Chapters 7, 8, and 9 present some of the many classroom activities with which these learning structures can be taught.

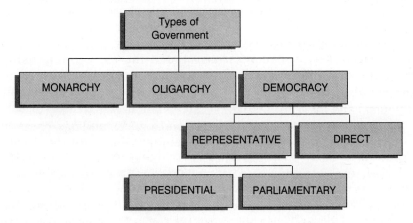

Figure 2.2
Organization of content indicating a logical progression for a unit on government

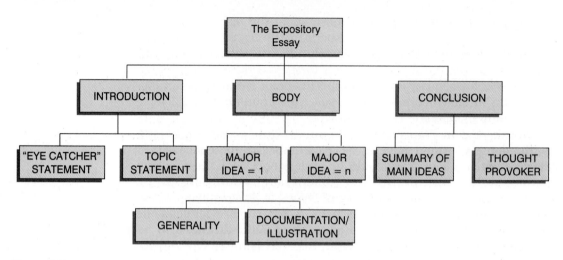

Figure 2.3
Organization of content indicating a logical progression for a unit on writing skills

>>> THE EFFECTS OF HOME AND <<< FAMILY ON LEARNING

What is the relationship between the socioeconomic level of a learner and his or her readiness to learn?

It is well known that a close relationship exists between social class and educational achievement. The effect of socioeconomic status (SES) on achievement has been so pronounced in some instances that it has lead to identifying different teaching behaviors for higher-SES and lower-SES students, as noted in Chapter 1. Traditionally, students from lower-class and lower middle-class families have not performed as well on standardized achievement tests as have students from middle-class and upper-class families.

In this regard, observers have noted the close relationship among social class, race/ethnicity, and school achievement (Mansnerus, 1992; Sleeter & Grant, 1991). Their studies generally conclude that most differences in educational achievement occurring by race and ethnicity can be accounted for by social class, *even after the lower socioeconomic status of minority groups is considered* (Gamoran, 1992; Levine & Havinghurst, 1984). In other words, if you know the socioeconomic status of a group of students, you can predict their achievement with reasonable accuracy. Information about their racial and ethnic group does little to improve the prediction. This indicates the powerful effect social class can have upon the behavior of your students. You will see in chapters 11 and 12 that this effect can extend to the affective and emotional makeup of your students as well as to their cognitive achievement.

General conclusion are that if you know a students SES, then you can predict their achievement w/ accuracy!

Why SES Is So Important in Learning

It is now appropriate to ask, "What is it about one's socioeconomic status that creates such large and important differences in the classroom?" and "What can I, a teacher, do to lessen these differences?" Obviously, if SES plays such an influential role in student achievement, it must stand for something more specific than income and the educational level of parents. Research shows that associated with income and educational level are a number of more meaningful characteristics in which the home and family lives of higher-SES and lower-SES families differ. It is these characteristics—which are indirect results of income and education—that are thought to influence the achievement of schoolchildren.

One important characteristic that seems to distinguish children of the lower class from those in the middle and upper socioeconomic class is that the latter are more likely to acquire knowledge of the world outside their home and neighborhood at an earlier age (Lambert, 1991; Delgado-Gaitan, 1991). Through greater access to books, magazines, social networks, cultural events, and other families that value these learning resources, middle-class and upper-class students develop their reading and speaking abilities more rapidly. This, in combination with parental teaching (which tends to use the formal or elaborated language that trains the child to think independently of the specific communication context), may give students in the middle and upper classes an advantage at the start of school.

This contrasts with children who come from lower-class homes where values and attitudes may emphasize obedience and conformity rather than independent thinking. Researchers who have studied lower-SES families report that they generally are more likely than middle-SES and higher-SES families to emphasize physical punishment rather than reasoning and to encourage rote learning (memorization, recall of facts, etc.) rather than independent, self-directed learning (Christenson, Rounds, & Franklin, 1992; Leler, 1983; Grave, Weinstein, & Walberg, 1983).

And why do these differences exist between lower-SES and higher-SES learners? Contributing to the problem of the low-SES learner is the fact that 70 percent of working-age mothers of disadvantaged students must work. This leaves at least four million latchkey children of school age home alone (Hodgkinson, 1988). In the last 30 years, the composition of the family has undergone a dramatic change. The traditional family unit is no longer the rule, but the exception. As recently as 1965, more than 60 percent of American families were traditional: a working father and a mother who kept the house and took care of the children. Only 10 percent of

[Handwritten margin notes:]

Characteristics SES

Middle/Upper SES class seem to acquire more knowledge at earlier age — magazines, books, networks etc — develop good reading/speaking abilities

Lower SES students — emphasis physical punishment.

today's families represent the traditional family of past generations. The Internal Revenue Service currently recognizes no fewer than 13 variations of the family. Today's family is more likely to be a dual-career family, a single parent family, a stepfamily, or a family that has moved an average of 14 times. All of these conditions affect the fabric of the family and the development of the schoolage learners within it.

By some estimates, the majority of children now being born will live in a household in which there is no adult 10 to 12 hours a day. Fewer involved parents, more distracting lifestyles, greater job and occupational stress, and the increased rate of divorce all have contributed to the growing number of disadvantaged and lower-SES learners. Levin (1986) has estimated that educationally disadvantaged youth comprise more than one-third of all schoolage children.

The Teacher's Role in Improving Lower-SES Achievement

The classroom is the logical place to begin the process of reducing some of the achievement differences that have been noted between lower-SES and middle/upper-SES students. Many formal interventions are trying to reduce the differences, from preschools to federally funded compensatory education programs. However, these interventions and programs are not likely to make a major impact on achievement differences among various groups of students who have highly divergent home and family lifestyles.

This leaves you, the classroom teacher, to deal with these differences as a daily fact of life. The general tendencies are clear: the home and family backgrounds of lower-SES and higher-SES students differentially prepare them for school. For the classroom teacher the task becomes one of planning instruction around these differences in ways that reduce them as much as possible.

There are several ways to make the achievement differences between social classes in your classroom more easily altered by your instructional methods. One of these is your willingness to incorporate a variety of learning aids, such as audiovisuals, learning centers, and exploratory materials, into your lessons, which encourage your learners to use their own experiences, past learnings, and preferred learning modalities (for example, visual vs. verbal) in which to construct and demonstrate what they have learned. Thus, lesson variety can be an important resource for those who may benefit from alternative ways of learning.

Another way in which to reduce achievement differences due to social class is to have high expectations for all your students, and to reward them for their accomplishments. Sufficiently high expectations and rewards for learning may not be present in the home environments of some of your learners. Your role in providing high expectations, support, and encouragement could be instrumental in making students aware that someone cares about them.

Finally, as an effective teacher you should seek opportunities for getting lower-SES students to talk about their experiences. This is particularly important for encouraging learners to construct and express understandings and meanings of their own in a form that is most comfortable to them. One of the most significant differences among students coming from different social classes is that lower-SES students have poorer self-concepts than higher-SES students. Getting students to talk about personal experiences and using these to help attain the instructional goals of your classroom has a double effect. It promotes student cooperation and interest in your subject while showing them that someone thinks they have something worthwhile to say. We will present strategies for accomplishing this in chapters 9 and 10.

Express understandings & meanings of their own form that's confortable to them.

>>> THE EFFECTS OF PERSONALITY ON LEARNING <<<

*✻ Personality ✻
integration of one's
- traits, motives,
  beliefs, & abilities
  emotional
  responses —
  Character &
  morals.*

Preceding sections discussed the potential influence on learning of students' general intelligence, specific aptitude, task-relevant prior achievement, and home life. In this section your students' personalities will be added to this equation.

When words such as *trustworthy, creative, independent, anxious, cheerful, authoritarian,* or *aggressive* are used to describe a student, they refer to an aspect of that student's personality. *Personality* is the integration of one's traits, motives, beliefs, and abilities, including emotional responses, character, and even morals. The notion of personality is indeed broad and, according to some authors, even subsumes intelligence and specialized abilities. It is not necessary to take so broad a view of personality here because not every part of what is considered to be personality is equally applicable to classroom learning. On the other hand, several aspects of personality are so important to learning that learning probably could not occur without them. These aspects of personality are called traits.

Traits are enduring aspects of a person's behavior that are consistent across a variety of settings. Traits are not specific to subject matter content, grade level, or instructional objective, as are aptitude and achievement. However, this does not mean that variations in content, grade level, and objectives are unimportant to personality. In fact, many things within an environment, such as a classroom, can trigger some personality traits and not others. Some parts of personalities lie dormant until stimulated to action by some

TRAITS —

particular perception of the world. This is the reason teachers often are dismayed to hear, for example, that an aggressive and verbally abusive child in fifth-period social studies is shy and cooperative in someone else's seventh-period mathematics. It also is the reason that some students and teachers may never quite see eye to eye. Fortunately, such personality conflicts are rare, but they can be devastating to classroom rapport if left to smolder beneath the surface.

Erikson's Crises of the School Years

How can I help my learners acquire friendships and a positive self-concept?

Some psychologists believe that different personality traits dominate at certain periods of our lives. For example, Erikson (1968), who developed a theory on how we form our personalities, hypothesized eight different stages of personality growth between infancy and old age that he called "crises." Three of these stages, shown in Figure 2.4, occur during the school years:

1. The crisis of accomplishment versus inferiority, which occurs sometime during the elementary school years.
2. The crisis of identity versus role confusion, which occurs sometime during the adolescent or high school years.
3. The crisis of intimacy versus isolation, which occurs in adolescence and early adulthood.

During the first crisis of accomplishment versus inferiority, the student seeks ways of producing products or accomplishments that are respected by others. In this manner the child creates a feeling of worth to dispel feelings of inferiority or inadequacy that result from competing in a world where adults appear confident and competent. At first such accomplishments may take the easiest course—being good at sports, being good in school, or being helpful at home. For the teacher this is a particularly challenging time, because student engagement at high rates of success is needed to keep some feelings of worth focused in the classroom. Seeing that every student has some successful experiences in the classroom can be an important vehicle for helping students through this crisis.

Erikson's second crisis during the school years is precipitated by the student's need to come to an understanding of self—to find his or her identity, the "real me." One's sex, race, ethnicity, religion, and physical attractiveness can play important roles in producing—or failing to produce—a consistent and acceptable self-image. This is a process of accepting oneself, as one truly is, apart from illusions, made-up images, and exaggerations.

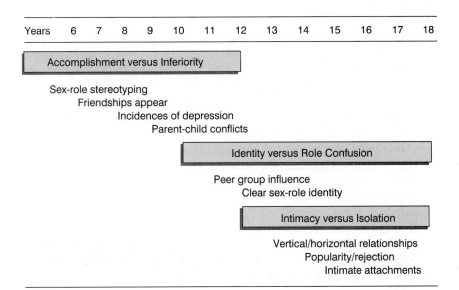

| Years | 6 | 7 | 8 | 9 | 10 | 11 | 12 | 13 | 14 | 15 | 16 | 17 | 18 |

Accomplishment versus Inferiority

Sex-role stereotyping
   Friendships appear
      Incidences of depression
         Parent-child conflicts

Identity versus Role Confusion

Peer group influence
Clear sex-role identity

Intimacy versus Isolation

Vertical/horizontal relationships
Popularity/rejection
Intimate attachments

Figure 2.4
Personal and social development during Erikson's three crises during the school years

Social psychologists believe that in the process of finding and accepting oneself during this crisis the individual must experience *recognition*, a sense of *control* over her or his environment, and *achievement*. Being a member of a group intensifies these needs. Social psychologists, such as Patricia and Richard Schmuck (Schmuck & Schmuck, 1988), urge teachers to recognize that groups give rise to needs for recognition, control, and achievement and to use this heightened motivation to achieve academic goals. And, they caution that classrooms that fail to satisfy these three basic needs may have large numbers of learners who feel rejected, listless, and powerless, creating motivational and conduct problems within the classroom.

A task orientation in which the teacher plans to actively involve learners in ways they can express themselves and their uniqueness (such as with discussions, demonstrations of learning, cooperative activities, and portfolios and exhibits) can help to reduce the emotional temperature of a classroom, which may have during these times the fictitious quality of a movie set more than a place for learning. The effective teacher not only understands and empathizes with the conflicting emotions of students at this stage, but also provides the structure and realism needed to help resolve the crisis.

Erikson's third crisis during the school years is that of giving up part of one's identity to develop close and intimate relationships

[Handwritten margin notes: "being a part of a group is impt. to non-adolescents..." / "Students need to feel these 3 basic needs." / "Teachers need to provide structure & realism to help resolve crisis"]

with others. For some, this stage may occur after the high school years, but for most its roots are in high school. Forming relationships, especially with the opposite sex, may be one of the most important and traumatic experiences of school. For some students it may represent the only reason for coming to school. It is not unusual for students during this crisis to form emotional relationships with their teachers as well, especially when relationships with their peers are thwarted due to differences in maturity, attractiveness, interests, or even physical size. There are no simple ways to deal with these emotions. Be aware of their occurrence, try to cushion their impact on the student, and try to channel the student's emotions productively.

Therefore, learning how to get along with teachers, parents, and classmates is one of the key developmental tasks learners must master to successfully resolve this crisis. Successful relationships with parents and teachers, referred to as **vertical relationships** (Hartup, 1989), meet a learner's needs for safety, security, and protection. Successful relationships with peers, referred to as **horizontal relationships,** are of equal developmental significance for learners. They meet learners' needs for belonging and allow them to acquire and practice important social skills. Providing opportunities for learners to develop healthy relationships when they enter school helps them develop skills important in getting along with others, helping others, and establishing intimacy. The failure to experience healthy horizontal relationships and learn friendship-building attitudes and skills can have undesirable consequences. This failure is often described by the terms *unpopularity* and *social rejection.*

Current research suggests that rejected children are more likely to be aggressive and disruptive in school (Hartup, 1989), experience intense feelings of loneliness (Cassidy & Asher, 1992), and suffer emotional disturbances in adolescence and adulthood (Dishion, Patterson, Stoolmiller, & Skinner, 1991). Nevertheless, researchers have shown that learners can be taught some of the social skills necessary to gain acceptance by peers. More importantly, by helping your learners construct their own well-functioning horizontal relationships, you may eliminate the need of having to teach how to acquire these relationships.

Personality differences due to *anxiety, learning style* and *self-concept* are important in all three of Erikson's crises of the school years. Researchers have confirmed the significant influence of anxiety, learning style, and self-concept on learning, their close relationship to one another, and differences among them across social classes. Let's see what the researchers have to say about them.

[Handwritten margin notes:]
Vertical Relationship — Successful relation w/ parents, teachers

Horizontal Relationship — relationship w/ peers.

Anxiety

Everyone finds anxiety uncomfortable, if only because of its debilitating effect on getting things done. Anxiety makes even the simplest tasks seem difficult. One feels threatened, fearful of the unknown, and generally tense. Among your acquaintances, and perhaps within yourself, you have observed at least two types of anxiety. They are called state anxiety and trait anxiety.

State Anxiety.   **State anxiety** (Spielberger, 1966) is an experience of fear or threat related to a particular environmental situation. A common example is the anxiety felt before taking a test. This represents a state or condition that is *momentary* and produced by some specific stimulus in the environment (a test, a report card, a speech before the class, a first date). Levels of state anxiety vary with different environmental stimuli. However, given the right stimulus, this anxiety can occur at any time.

There is a positive side to state anxiety: some is necessary for learning. Without fearing the negative consequences of a failing grade, Mary may not do the studying required for a passing grade. Without some fear of injury in a poorly executed lab experiment, Damian may not be cautious enough to avoid the danger. Without fear of doing poorly in front of his peers, Billy may not organize his speech well enough to avoid embarrassment. Grades, report cards, and assignments are some of the ways the effective teacher provides the level of state anxiety necessary to motivate students to respond successfully.

Trait Anxiety.   A second type of anxiety is a general disposition to feel threatened by a wide range of conditions perceived to be harmful. This type of anxiety has been labeled **trait anxiety,** indicating its stability over time. No single stimulus, such as a grade or assignment, can be identified as the source of the anxiety. It results instead from many ill-defined sources. Unlike state anxiety, which all students experience to some degree, this type of anxiety tends *not to fluctuate* within individuals. It exists in different amounts from person to person. In sum, this type of anxiety is a fairly stable characteristic of one's personality, with different individuals having different amounts of it.

High levels of trait anxiety seem to go with high motivation and the need to achieve. But, like state anxiety, extremely high levels can be immobilizing, especially when the need to achieve is guided more by a fear of failure (shame, ridicule by peers, punishment from parents) rather than by a wish to do well. When fear of failure is the primary motive among high-anxiety students, more assignments may be completed with more accuracy, but they will be completed in a mechanical, perfunctory way allowing for little more than the most obvious and expected learning outcomes.

Research shows that when motivation among high-anxiety students is guided more by a desire to do well (e.g., to produce a perfect product, create something new and different, gain the respect of others, tackle the impossible) rather than by fear of failure, more work is accomplished toward a given goal in less time and in ways that engage students in discovery types of learning experiences that result in higher achievement (Covington & Omelich, 1987).

This suggests that one of your tasks as an effective teacher is to control the learning conditions of high-anxiety students. In the case of high *trait* anxiety, conveying a feeling of warmth, encouragement, and support prior to the assignment can turn fears of failure into more productive motives involving a desire to do well. Structuring the assignment in ways that provide for a *range of acceptable responses* serves to focus the high-anxiety student on an attainable end product and away from general fears of being unable to achieve an acceptable level of performance. As we will learn in Chapter 15, performance assessment and student portfolios also are excellent ways of accomplishing this goal.

Learning Style

A second aspect of personality which will influence your learners' achievement is their learning style. **Learning style** refers to the classroom or environmental conditions under which someone prefers to learn. Learning style preferences fall in the following categories:

Physical environment: seating arrangements, lighting, temperature, noise level, etc.

Social environment: working alone vs. in small groups; cooperative vs. competitive instructional formats; with or without the presence of adults

Emotional environment: friendly, helpful vs. aloof, solitary; preference for a nurturant, people oriented vs. self-reliant, materials- or text-oriented learning environment

Instructional environment: lecture vs. discussion; preference for certain types of tests; direct, indirect, self-directed instructional formats; preference for activities involving visual, tactile, or kinesthetic sense modalities

Managerial environment: many vs. few rules; written down vs. unstated rules; clear vs. implied consequences; number of classroom routines; preferences for particular leadership styles

These learning style characteristics represent preferred ways individuals have for engaging in the learning process. Some learners are quick to respond when presented a problem to solve or question to answer. Others are more reflective despite being as informed and expert as the more impulsive group. Although there are a number of learning styles, the one most studied has been that identified with the characteristics of **field dependence** and **field independence.**

Field Dependence versus Field Independence. Much has been written about how some learners are more "global" than "analytic" in how they approach learning (Franklin, 1992). Some use the terms *holistic/visual* to describe "global" learners, and *verbal/analytic* to describe the opposite style or orientation (Tharp & Gallimore 1989). Still others (Hilliard, 1976) prefer the term *field sensitive* to refer to the holistic/visual learning style and the term *field insensitive* to refer to the verbal/analytic learning style. To what are these researchers referring?

Basically, these terms have come to refer to how people view the world. People who are field dependent see the world in terms of large, connected patterns. Looking at a volcano, for example, a field-dependent person would notice its overall shape, and the larger colors and topographical features that make it up. A field-independent person, on the other hand, would tend to notice the discrete parts of a scene. Thus, she might notice more the individual trees, the different rocks, the size of the caldera, where the caldera sits in relation to the rest of the structure, topographical features showing the extent of lava flow, and so on. To better understand what field dependence and field independence mean, and what these terms suggest about how different children learn, let's look at what some of the researchers say about them.

Franklin (1992), Tharp (1989), and Garger and Guild (1984) believe that field dependence and independence are stable traits of individuals that affect different aspects of their lives, especially their approach to learning. Table 2.2 summarizes some of the characteristics associated with both types of learners. These researchers agree that the different personality characteristics or traits of field-dependent and -independent learners suggest that at least some learners think about and process information differently during classroom learning activities. They suggest that each group would benefit from different instructional strategies, as suggested in Table 2.3.

Table 2.2
Field-dependent and field-independent learner characteristics

Field-dependent (Field-sensitive) Learners	Field-independent Learners
1. Perceives global aspects of concepts and materials.	1. Focuses on details of curriculum materials.
2. Personalizes curriculum—relates concepts to personal experience.	2. Focuses on facts and principles.
3. Seeks guidance and demonstrations from teacher.	3. Rarely seeks physical contact with teacher.
4. Seeks rewards that strengthen relationship with teacher.	4. Formal interactions with teacher are restricted to tasks at hand—seeks nonsocial rewards.
5. Prefers to work with others and is sensitive to their feelings and opinions.	5. Prefers to work alone.
6. Likes to cooperate.	6. Likes to compete.
7. Prefers organization provided by teacher.	7. Can organize information by him/herself.

How does "learning style" differ across culture and ethnicity?

Learning Style and Culture. There has been interest among educators in the relationship between learning style and culture. The work of several researchers has suggested that Native Americans, Hispanic Americans, and African Americans are more field-dependent than Anglo Americans and Asian Americans (Bennett, 1990; Cushner, McClelland, & Safford, 1992; Garcia, 1991; Tharp, 1989; Hilliard, 1992). They advocate that teachers who work with these groups of learners use more field-dependent teaching styles.

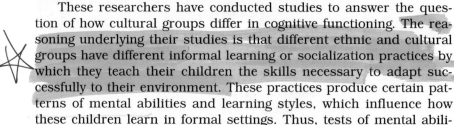

These researchers have conducted studies to answer the question of how cultural groups differ in cognitive functioning. The reasoning underlying their studies is that different ethnic and cultural groups have different informal learning or socialization practices by which they teach their children the skills necessary to adapt successfully to their environment. These practices produce certain patterns of mental abilities and learning styles, which influence how these children learn in formal settings. Thus, tests of mental abilities and tests of learning style should reveal different patterns of scores when comparing one cultural group to another.

What evidence have these studies found which suggests that minority groups have different learning styles than Anglo Americans? While the evidence is sometimes inconsistent, in general, there is some support that minority learners are more holistic/global/visual or field sensitive in their approach to learning than verbal/analytic or field independent. For example, Native Amer-

Table 2.3
Instructional strategies for field-dependent and field-independent learners

Field-dependent (Field-sensitive) Learners	Field-independent Learners
1. Display physical and verbal experiences of approval or warmth. Show referent power.	1. Be formal in interactions with learners; show expert power.
2. Motivate by use of social and tangible rewards.	2. Motivate by use of nonsocial rewards such as grades.
3. Use cooperative learning strategies.	3. Use more mastery learning and errorless teaching strategies.
4. Use corrective feedback often.	4. Use corrective feedback only when necessary.
5. Allow interaction during learning.	5. Emphasize independent projects.
6. Structure lessons, projects, homework, etc.	6. Allow learners to develop their own structure.
7. Assume role of lecturer, demonstrator, checker, reinforcer, grader, materials designer.	7. Assume role of consultant, listener, negotiator, facilitator.

icans consistently score higher on tests requiring spatial ability and manipulation skills (arranging puzzles, solving mazes, drawing figures) than on tests requiring primarily verbal abilities (detecting similarities and differences in concepts, analyzing proverbs for their underlying meaning, etc.) (Browne, 1984; Gallimore, Tharp, Sloat, Klein, & Troy, 1982; Cohen, 1985; Tharp, 1987).

Shade (1982), Cohen (1969), and Hilliard (1976) present evidence suggesting that African American learners have a learning style emphasizing field-sensitive abilities as well as a preference for person-oriented classroom activities (cooperative learning and activities that focus on people and what they do, rather than on things or objects). Other researchers (Ramirez & Castaneda, 1974; Knight & Kagan, 1977) conclude that Mexican Americans are more field sensitive as a group than Anglo Americans. They explain the superior relative performance of this group on measures of field sensitivity by pointing out that the childrearing practices of this group stress strong family ties and a respect and obedience to elders—experiences they conclude lead to a more field-sensitive learning style.

Cultural Differences in Learning Styles: Some Cautions.   Is there sufficient justification to advocate field-sensitive teaching styles in classrooms with significant numbers of minority learners? Should teachers make greater use of instructional practices that emphasize cooperative learning, person and movement/action-oriented activities, visual/holistic learning, and so on when teaching significant numbers of African, Hispanic, or Native American learners? Before implementing culturally responsive teaching without qualification, keep in mind the following cautions:

1. *Beware of perpetuating stereotypes.* Grant (1991) cautions that cultural information such as that described previously may be used to "perpetuate ideas from the cultural deficit hypothesis that encourages teachers to believe that these students have deficits and negative differences and, therefore, are not as capable of learning as white students" (p. 245). Others (Weisner, Gallimore, & Jordan, 1988) claim that cultural explanations of differential achievement of minority groups often result in global and stereotypical descriptions of how minority cultures behave that go beyond available evidence. Kendall (1983) argues that it is one thing to be aware of the potential effect of culture specific learning and learning styles on classroom achievement but another to expect a child of a particular group to behave and to learn in a particular way.

2. *Note within-group differences.* Almost all studies of the learning style preferences of different minority groups have shown that differences within the cultural groups studied were as great as the differences between the cultural groups (Tharp, 1989; Cushner et al., 1992; Henderson, 1980). In other words, Native Americans, Hispanic Americans, African Americans, and Anglo Americans vary considerably on tests of field dependence and independence. There will be Anglo Americans who are as field dependent in their pattern of scores as there will be Native Americans who are field independent. On the average, the groups may differ. But, around these averages are ranges of considerable magnitude. Thus, using a field-dependent teaching style, even in a monocultural classroom, may fail to match the preferred learning style of at least some learners.

3. *Culturally responsive teaching may be more difficult in multicultural classrooms.* Culturally responsive teaching appears to be most efficient and practical in monocultural classrooms. In classrooms that are multicultural, it may be difficult, maybe impossible, to match the different learning styles of 30 or more children who may represent several different cultures.

4. *Culturally responsive concerns may take the focus away from "expert practice."* Educators, such as Englemann and Carnine (1982) and Lindsley (1992), argue that before assuming that differences in achievement are due to characteristics within the learner (for example, learning style), fac-

tors external to the learner, such as ineffective teaching practices, should be ruled out. Also, the quality of instruction provided minority learners should be equivalent to that of Anglo Americans. Majority- and minority-group learners should experience similar schooling in terms of resources, quality of teachers, expectations, expert practice in instruction, testing, and motivation techniques before embracing specialized techniques specifically adapted to minorities. Although there is some evidence that African American and Native American children improve in reading and math with culturally responsive teaching techniques (Tharp, 1989; Franklin, 1992), studies fail to indicate that expert instruction using traditional instructional methods could not have achieved the same or similar results.

Self-Concept

A third aspect of personality that will influence your learners' achievement is self-concept. **Self-concept** represents the beliefs, feelings, and attitudes we have about ourselves. Our self-concept grows out of interactions with *significant others,* such as parents, teachers, and peers. Significant others act as mirrors for our behavior. That is, they reflect the images we create of ourselves, sometimes in modified and revised form. When the image that is returned looks good, is acceptable to others, and is consistent with what we want it to be, a positive self-concept is formed. When the reflected image does not look good, is unacceptable to others, and is inconsistent with our beliefs about ourselves, a less favorable self-concept is formed.

The formation of self-concept is perhaps one of the most fascinating aspects of personality. It has captured the attention of many psychologists and researchers who have studied the relationship of self-concept to student achievement. The research thus far is sketchy and focuses only on certain grades and subjects. However, some evidence indicates that a positive self-concept may be moderately related to achievement (Beane, 1991; Walberg, 1986; Hansford & Hattie, 1982). This research has been taken as an encouraging sign that a student's concept of self can affect the extent to which he or she *becomes actively engaged in the process of learning,* even if it is not always strongly related to scores on tests of academic performance.

Does a positive self-concept promote achievement? Or does achievement promote a positive self-concept? We don't know. However, the intuitive value of having a positive self-concept is so pervasive in our culture that the order of the relationship may not be all that important. An increase in self-concept is believed to have positive results on behavior, either directly on school achievement or indirectly on one's ability to relate to others, to cope with the problems of daily life, and ultimately to be successful in a career or occupation.

Such important outcomes are not measured by tests of academic achievement. However, good performance on school tests might improve one's self-concept. This, in turn, could influence the other important life outcomes. This is reason enough for engaging students in the learning process at moderate-to-high rates of success: to provide a mirror with a positive image. It also is one reason why high rates of success are so important to lower-SES students. It is these students who have been found to have the poorest self-concepts and whose home life may provide few opportunities for improving them.

The crucial question asked by every student in the process of forming a self-concept is "How am I being perceived?" In the school environment, this reflected self-image is derived most often from direct, personal interaction with you, the teacher. As a teacher it is your task to be sensitive to and understanding of the impact of the images you are reflecting to students by your words and deeds. You will not always want to reflect what your students believe about themselves. On the other hand, consider that any image you send back by interactions and performance evaluations may have implications far beyond the time when you deliver the message. The message you reflect may contribute to the ever-growing complement of data used by each of your students to form the self-concept they will "wear" for years to come.

Finally, it is not a question of *whether* you will influence the self-concept of your students, but *how*. Your performance as an effective teacher—as a significant other—is always guided by a belief in the inherent value of the unique talents and contributions of each individual student. The secret to improving students' self-concepts lies in the process of finding and reflecting back to students the value of their unique talents.

>>> THE EFFECTS OF THE PEER <<<
GROUP ON LEARNING

One of the most powerful but least noted influences on a student's behavior is the peer group. Often considered as the source of a "hidden curriculum," the peer group can influence and even teach students how to behave in class, study for tests, converse with teachers and school administrators, and can contribute to the success or fail-

Friendship patterns in the classroom often are created through peer groups that exhibit strong commitments of loyalty, protection, and mutual benefit. The importance of peer group characteristics lies with their power to create, promote, and reinforce behaviors that can be conducive or disruptive to the goals of the classroom.

ure of performance in school in many other ways. From the play group in the elementary school to the teenage clique in high school, a student learns from peers how to behave in ways that are acceptable and that will establish status in the eyes of others. Establishing such status reflects group approval, which promotes a good self-concept.

The power of the peer group in influencing individual student behavior stems from the fact that it is the *voluntary* submission of one's will to some larger cause. Teachers and parents must beg, plead, punish, reward, and cajole to exact appropriate behavior from their students, sons, and daughters. But peer groups need not engage in any of these behaviors to obtain a high level of conformity to often unstated and abstract principles of behavior. Trendy school fashions, new slang words, places to "hang out," acceptable social mates, and respected forms of out-of-school activities are communicated and learned to perfection without lesson plans, texts, or even direct verbalization. Instead, these and other behaviors are transmitted by "salient others" and received by those who anxiously wish to maintain membership in or gain acceptance to a particular peer group.

The power of the peer group to influence the behavior of others was underscored in a 1984 survey by John Goodlad of more than 17,000 junior high and senior high students in 1000 classrooms across the United States. In Goodlad's survey, each student was

A student can learn from peers and behave in ways that are acceptable to the eyes of others.

— it establishes status — approval

— promotes good self-concept.

Peer Groups

Friendship patterns create strong commitments of loyalty, protection, & mutual benefit.

— may cause rivalry against education.

Passive learner / troublemaker

not successful

asked "What is the *one* best thing about this school?" The most frequent response, "my friends," occurred more than twice as often as any other. Teachers were mentioned least often.

Friendship patterns often are created through peer groups and sometimes are adhered to with strong commitments of loyalty, protection, and mutual benefit. These commitments can create individual peer cultures or even gangs within a school. Such cultures can rival the academic commitments made in the classroom and frequently supersede them in importance. Studying for a test or completing homework frequently may be sacrificed for the benefit of the peer group. Peer groups can form on the basis of many different individual differences, such as intelligence, achievement, personality, home life, physical appearance, and personal and social interests. But they commonly result from complex combinations of these that are not always discernable to outsiders and sometimes not even to those within the peer group (Hartup, 1989; Schmuck & Schmuck, 1992).

The importance of peer group characteristics in the classroom lies in the extent to which they can create, promote, and reinforce behaviors that are disruptive to teaching objectives. More specifically, to what extent can the hidden rules, regulations, and rituals often required by a peer group affect a member's engagement with the learning process?

Some peer groups can promote an increased activity in the learning process. When intelligence, a high need to achieve, and acceptance of responsibility are the basis of a peer group, it well may promote a conformity among its members to achieve in accord with the highest academic standards. Membership in the National Honor Society, ambition to enroll in college, and a desire to pursue certain types of careers sometimes are the "glue" that holds such peer groups together.

However, combinations of individual differences also can combine to promote two types of problem learners (Lightfoot, 1983). One is the passive learner, in which minimum effort is the standard (nothing extra is volunteered). The other is the so-called "troublemaker" whose willingness to disrupt, intimidate, and provoke is reinforced and accorded special tribute by peer group members. The latter learner, in contrast with the passive learner who simply is not motivated or successful in school, actually fights against the conformity and routine demands of the classroom by waging a surreptitious war in which authority figures become targets.

You may have little influence in the formation of peer groups in your classroom. But, here are several approaches effective teachers have used to foster the goals of the classroom.

What are some of the ways I can use peer group membership to foster the goals of my instruction?

Drug use creates a psychological dependence or bonding with the drug that has been related to an erosion of the self-discipline required for learning as well as truancy, dropping out, and crime. More than half of all adolescent suicides are suspected to be drug related.

1. *Stress group work in which members are from different peer groups.* When forming work or cooperative groups be sure group members represent different backgrounds and interests, which can bring different skills and talents to an assignment. When different types of individuals are assigned to work cooperatively, group behavior tends to follow a middle ground, discouraging extreme or disruptive behavior.

2. *Conduct a group discussion of class norms, describing what class members should and should not do to be socially acceptable.* Tell group members what you expect of them and give some examples of what they might expect of others. Glasser (1990) suggests discussing with students ideas on how the class might be run, problems that may interfere with the group's performance, and needed rules and routines.

3. *Build group cohesiveness by promoting the attractiveness of each student to one another.* Provide opportunities for your students to know one another through one or more of the following: Constructing a bulletin board around the

theme of friendships, having students write a brief biography about themselves for all to read, publishing a class directory that includes names, hobbies, jobs, and career aspirations, have students bring something they have made or really care about (a toy, tool, model, etc.).

4. *Assign older or more mature students who are more likely to be respected as role models to interact with and help younger students in a peer tutoring situation.* Many schools have a formal peer tutoring program in which tutors may be chosen from higher grades, called *cross-age tutoring,* to help younger students who may be at risk, or discouraged learners. Research has shown that tutoring has been most successful when tutors have been trained and given explicit instruction on how to tutor.

>>> THE EFFECTS OF SOCIAL <<< CONTEXT ON LEARNING

Closely connected with the influence of the peer group on learning is the social context in which your learners live, play, and work. Among the most prominant sources of influence in this context will be your learners' family and its relationship to the school.

In 1990, the National Governors Conference for educational reform set forth a formidable agenda for educators. At this conference, the following goals were to be achieved by the first decade of the twenty-first century:

1. All children in America will start school ready to learn.
2. The high school graduation rate will increase to at least 90%.
3. American students will leave Grades 4, 8, and 12 having demonstrated competency over challenging subject matter in the sciences and humanities.
4. American students will be the best in the world in mathematics and science achievement.
5. Every adult American will be literate and will possess the knowledge and skills to compete in a global economy and exercise the rights and responsibilities of citizenship.
6. Every school in America will be free of drugs and violence and will offer a disciplined environment conducive to learning.

A theme throughout the commentaries on the governors' agenda was the realization that schools would have to develop genuine partnerships with parents to achieve these goals. A singular focus on just teachers, parents, or administrators as the agents of reform would not produce the hoped-for results. Rather, only the active participation of parents, community groups, and educators in partnership with one another would bring about the desired objectives (Lambert, 1991).

When parents and teachers become partners, not only can student achievement increase but also parents learn about you and your school. Research studies confirm that coordination and collaboration between home and school improves learner achievement, attitude toward school, classroom conduct, and parent and teacher morale (Cochran & Dean, 1991). Establishing genuine partnerships with the parents and guardians of your learners is as essential a teacher practice as those that involve building a cohesive classroom climate, establishing a well-managed work environment, developing goals and objectives, conducting effective instruction, and assessing student performance.

The practice of parent involvement requires that you develop and strengthen throughout the school year "linking mechanisms" for parent participation and collaboration. **Family–school linking mechanisms** are opportunities for school and family involvement and may involve parent-teacher conferences, home visits, participation of teachers in community events, newsletters, phone calls, personal notes, volunteering as classroom aides, and the use of home-based curriculum materials. These efforts require more than just a handout sent home to parents at the beginning of the school year, an obligatory presentation during back-to-school night, or an occasional note home. The opportunities to develop and nurture linking mechanisms will be the culmination of your efforts to build a successful classroom workplace. The challenge of the twenty-first century will be to establish such linking mechanisms in your classroom.

To assist in this process, Bronfenbrenner (1989, 1979) has urged us to view the family–school partnership from a **systems-ecological perspective.** Bronfenbrenner looks at the learner as a naturalist looks at nature—as an ecosystem. In the learner's ecosystem the major systems include the family, school, and, as we have seen in the previous section, the peer group.

One way to picture the learner's ecosystem is as a series of concentric circles, as shown in Figure 2.5. Each of these circles and their connections has a special term. The most central layer is called the *microsystem*. It includes all those settings where the child lives or spends significant portions of his or her time: the family, school, classroom, day care setting, playground, and job setting if the child is old enough. Bronfenbrenner refers to these settings as *subsystems.*

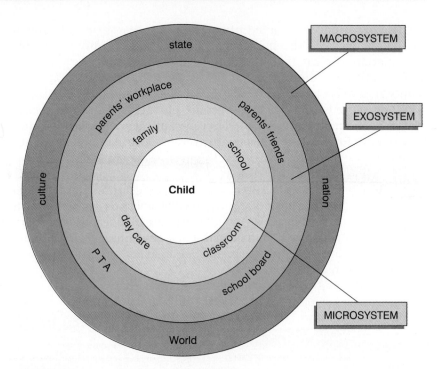

Figure 2.5
The child from a systems-ecological perspective

Each subsystem can be viewed within itself as a system. The school system is made up of subsystems that include teachers, administrators, support personnel, school board members, and learners. The family system includes a marital, parental, sibling, and often a grandparent subsystem. The peer system includes social friendships, academic friendships, and sports or hobby friendships.

The next layer of the system includes those subsystems the child does not directly experience, but which affect the child because of the influence they exert on the microsystem. This layer is called the *exosystem*. It may include the parents' workplace, their friends, the PTA, the school board, and so on.

Finally, both microsystems and exosystems exist in a larger setting called the *macrosystem*. This system refers to the larger culture or society in which the micro- and exosystems function. Figure 2.6 indicates some of the relationships among these systems.

A systems-ecological perspective urges us to view a learner's behavior, whether in school or at home, not as a product of that individual alone but as a product of the learner and the demands and forces operating within the systems of which the learner is a

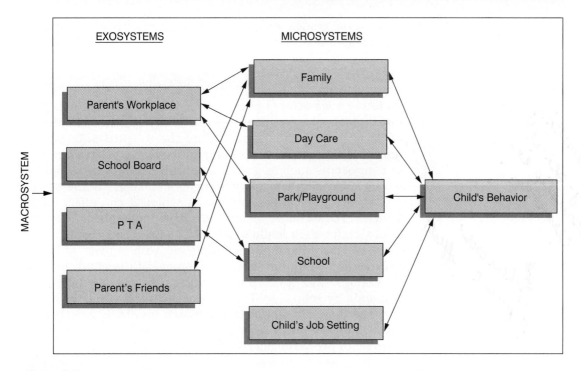

EXOSYSTEMS   MICROSYSTEMS

MACROSYSTEM

Parent's Workplace

School Board

P T A

Parent's Friends

Family

Day Care

Park/Playground

School

Child's Job Setting

Child's Behavior

Figure 2.6
The child's ecosystem

member. Family experiences and the culture of the family system, influence school behavior and performance which, in turn, affect the family system. School adjustment problems, which may be influenced by problems within the family may, in turn, exacerbate conditions within the family system itself. For example, the parent who never signs and returns a note home may not be an uninterested and uninvolved parent—as might be assumed. Dynamics within the family system (for example, other siblings who demand extensive care or adjustment to a new child) may explain the parent's apparent lack of involvement in his or her child's education.

Thus, when trying to understand the behavior of parents, teachers, and learners, the systems-ecological perspective recommends that we first ask ourselves, "What forces within the family–school environment impel the person to act this way?" When the goal is to promote the academic and social development of the learner, the systems-ecological perspective focuses our most immediate concern on the family–school partnership.

What are some ways I can promote family–school partnerships in my classroom?

[handwritten: Promoting family–school partnership in classroom]

[handwritten: Phone calls to parents – affects]

[handwritten: — Working families — Single parent. — divorced fa...]

Here are some guidelines for understanding and promoting family–school partnerships in your classroom.

1. *View the family from a systems-ecological perspective.* Avoid viewing the behavior of your learners or their mothers or fathers, as simply products of individual psychological forces. Instead, recognize that the family system is made up of several subsystems, including the *marital* subsystem, *parental* subsystem, the *sibling* subsystem, and *extrafamily* or exosystems such as grandparents and employers. Changes in one subsystem inevitably bring about changes in the other.

   When a child has problems in school it can affect other systems. For example, phone calls to parents during working hours about their child's school behavior can result in an employer reprimanding the employee, an argument at home between husband and wife, punishment of the child, teasing by siblings, and concern and criticism by in-laws. Likewise, demands by school staff that parents do something at home to make the child complete homework inevitably reverberate throughout the entire family system. These effects may be so great as to preclude any change in parental behavior.

   Thus, when you ask a parent to take greater responsibility for getting their child to bed earlier at night, or to supervise their child's homework more closely, or to take away privileges for school misbehavior, these demands may affect more than one parent. It very likely will affect a variety of family subsystems.

2. *Acknowledge changes in the American family.* Most families have two working parents. Research on teacher beliefs regarding families where both parents work shows that teachers believe that working parents are less involved with their children's education (Linney & Vernberg, 1983). However, a study conducted by Medrich, Roizen, Rubin, and Burkley (1982) concludes that working and nonworking mothers spend the same amount of time in child-related activities. Furthermore, their data show that children of working mothers are just as involved in extracurricular activities as are the children of nonworking mothers.

   Single-parent families make up about 25 percent of the families of children in school. Yet many teachers view this family pattern as an abnormality (Carlson, 1992). Joyce Epstein, a researcher at the Johns Hopkins Center for Research on Elementary and Middle Schools reports that teachers have lower expectations for the achievement of children from single-parent families despite the fact that no data support this (Epstein, 1987).

Some researchers suggest that the requirements in single-parent families for organization, schedules, routines, and division of responsibilities better prepare children to accept such structure in schools (Linney & Vernberg, 1983). Carlson (1992) concludes that it is family income and not single or dual parenting alone that affects child achievement in school.

3. *View parent participation from an "empowerment model" rather than a "deficit model."* Delgado-Gaitan (1991) proposes that we view parent participation as a process that involves giving parents both the power and the knowledge to deal with the school system. Typically, non–systems-ecological and "deficit model" explanations have been offered for reasons why culturally different parents have not become involved with schools. These perspectives sometimes have portrayed parents as passive, lazy, incompetent, or unskilled to help their children. They propose that parents are unable to become involved in their children's education because they work long hours away from the home, or are simply not interested. But, Delgado-Gaitan (1992) points out, when examined closely, research has shown that Hispanic families who speak a different language and have a different culture from that of the school do indeed care about their children and possess the capacity to advocate for them. This holds true for African Americans, Hispanic Americans, Native Americans, and other cultural and linguistic groups as well. The question is not can they become genuine partners with the school but how to empower them to do so.

involving parents in schools.

4. *Recognize the unique needs of mothers and fathers when planning opportunities to involve parents.* Turnbull and Turnbull (1986) urge teachers to promote nonsexist views of parenting and parent involvement. They stress that teachers recognize the importance of mothers *and* fathers when designing home–school linkages. Encourage visiting opportunities for both parents, and develop flexible schedules to accommodate the working schedules of both parents. Send information about the children and schooling to both parents. Seek to promote teaching skills in fathers as well as mothers. Finally, give consideration to the father's interests and needs when suggesting ways for parents to work with their children at home.

encourage parents to visit

5. *Appreciate that parents are just like you—they experience periodic emotional, family, and economic problems.* Many parents may have personal, family, work, health, or other

problems that remain hidden. Make a special effort to provide the benefit of the doubt, particularly when parents fail to respond in a timely manner to your requests. Carlson (1992) documents the overwhelming economic as well as divorce, custody, and career problems of single parents. Their failure to monitor their child's homework, or attendance, or tardiness to class may be due less to a lack of interest than to attempts to cope with day-to-day personal, social, and economic problems. When parents do not live up to your expectations, avoid trying to assign personal blame.

6. *Understand the variety of school–family linkages and respect family preferences for different degrees of school participation.* As you are planning for parent involvement early in the school year, consider and evaluate the full range of ways in which parents can participate. These activities can be placed on a continuum anchored on one end by activities that involve parents as receivers of information (parent-teacher conference, notes home, classroom newsletter) and on the other end by those that involve parents as active educational decision makers (school and classroom advisory councils, site-based management teams, tutoring).

Developing partnerships with the parents of your learners should be as much a focus of your planning for a new school year as your classroom rules, routines, instructional goals, and objectives. As the research suggests, your learners' achievement of academic goals, their adherence to rules and routines, and their attitudes and expectations about school can be enhanced by having parents as partners.

>>> SCHOOLS, NEIGHBORHOODS, SUBCULTURES, <<< AND THE LEARNING ENVIRONMENT

There is no question that your students' individual differences in intelligence, achievement, personality, home life, peer group, and social context can dramatically affect teaching methods and learning results. So, why place such diverse students in the same classroom? Would it not be more efficient to segregate students by intelligence and achievement level, personality type, degree of disadvantage due to home life, or even according to the most advantageous peer group? The result of such grouping might be quite astounding, if it were tried.

It is difficult to imagine life in such a segregated environment, for we live, work, and play in a world that is complex and diverse.

[handwritten margin note: We can't expect our students to be placed in same level classrooms etc... because our world we live in, work in isn't that way!]

However, our forefathers seriously considered this very question. Their answer is in the first 10 amendments to the U.S. Constitution, known as the Bill of Rights, and in the *Declaration of Independence,* which gives every citizen the unqualified right to "life, liberty, and the pursuit of happiness." This constitutional guarantee specifically precludes any attempt to advance a single group at the expense of any other group. It even precludes segregating groups when "separate but equal" treatment is accorded them, because even the labeling of groups as "different" implies inequality, regardless of the motives for forming them.

These are important constitutional implications for the American classroom. They promote an environment that not only tolerates differences among individuals but also is conducive to integrating diverse individuals. This constitutional implication has been called the "pluralistic ideal."

The Pluralistic Ideal

The pluralistic ideal has become a guide at national and state levels for making our most important societal decisions on housing, job opportunities, college and professional school admissions, transportation, elementary and secondary education, and the dispersal of public services. What is not always evident is that the pluralistic ideal also provides the rationale for the composition of our neighborhoods, schools, and classrooms. And it is not limited to cultural and minority issues; it extends to the integration and mixture of all types of individuals, including those marked by the individual differences discussed in this chapter.

It is important to note why the pluralistic ideal has become an insightful constitutional legacy. The pluralistic ideal has two advantages that our forefathers recognized. First is the realization that our country is and always will be a melting pot of enormous diversity. Second is the need for such diversity.

The Melting Pot.   America's diversity two centuries ago resulted from the varied nationalities and religious persuasions that contributed to our general culture. It later was enriched by different ethnic groups and most recently by increasingly diverse lifestyles, politics, and values.

With all this diversity, clearly a cultural core would be difficult as a common ground from which to govern all the people. The role of our pluralistic ideal was to acculturate and to socialize vastly different groups to a general core of values that could provide the framework of a government. The means of accomplishing this was the U.S. Constitution. It promotes the integration and mixing of all individuals in the land, regardless of how different they are. The Constitution makes illegal the segregation of individuals into any group that, by labeling or any other means, would limit their life, liberty, and the pursuit of happiness, or deny maximum individual development. The Constitution encourages and promotes the establishment of a core culture to which all individuals adhere, regardless of their personal values and cultural preference.

By having to work, live, and play with diverse individuals in our public lives we have established a common cultural heritage. This heritage has rules (e.g., paying taxes), loyalties (going to war), rituals (observing specified holidays), and laws (respecting the rights of others). We all have come to accept these, regardless of our differences.

The Need for Diversity.   A second insight reflected in the pluralistic ideal was the shared realization that, in a world complicated by such social and technological problems as pollution, disease, illiteracy, and congestion, we need divergent viewpoints, different abilities, and diverse values to address these problems. No single set of skills, attitudes, temperament, personality, or aptitude can provide all that is needed to solve our problems.

By allowing and encouraging this diversity in human potential, our country has possessed for the better part of its history the most enviable work force in the world. It has been responsible for impressive breakthroughs in medicine, electronics, energy, and aerospace, and highly creative approaches to problems in health, education, and the behavioral sciences. This has been accomplished as a result of, *not* in spite of, the cultural diversity and differences that flourish in our communities, schools, and classrooms. This flourishing diversity directly results from the pluralistic ideal.

Your Role in the Pluralistic Ideal.   To continue this success, you as an effective teacher must carry on the pluralistic ideal by respecting and accepting the diversity of human potential that lies within your classroom, and every classroom. Even more important, you must fully develop such potential if the pluralistic ideal is to serve us in the future as it has in the past. Your flexibility in teaching allows for adapting instruction to students' group-related learning styles, using different instructional approaches in teaching students of differing ethnic and racial backgrounds, and adapting instruction to the concerns and needs of the community. Above all, your teaching strategies must emphasize the importance of all students working cooperatively with their peers and with teachers. In the chapters ahead we will explore many ways of accomplishing these important goals.

We all can contribute... We & each have diff ideas of addressing certain problems.

We must accept diversity in our classrooms.

>>> A FINAL WORD <<<

This chapter discussed individual differences that affect learning and determine your success in teaching different types of learners. Individual differences are many and their apparent influence on the learning process is great. Your teaching will be successful to the extent that you (1) become acquainted with the individual differences operating in your classroom and (2) can adapt your teaching style to accommodate these differences.

You have seen in this chapter the considerable influence on learning exerted by your students' aptitudes, prior achievements, personalities, home lives, peer groups, and social contexts. Your students are far from being blank slates onto which you impart knowledge and understanding of your subject matter. On the contrary, your students, with all of their individual differences, are an active force in determining your success at transmitting your knowledge and understanding. In other words, not only your own behavior but also that of your students will affect how successfully you can execute the key teaching behaviors of lesson clarity, instructional variety, task orientation, engagement in the learning process, and student success.

Summing Up

This chapter introduced the diversity of students found in classrooms and how this diversity must be acknowledged in your teaching methods. Its main points were the following:

1. Early conceptions of teaching viewed students as empty vessels into which the teacher poured the content of the day's lesson. These conceptions failed to consider the effect of individual differences on learning.

2. A knowledge of the individual differences among learners is important (1) to adapt instructional methods to individual learning needs and (2) to understand and place in perspective the reasons behind the school performance of individual learners.

3. One misunderstanding that some teachers and parents have about intelligence, or IQ, is that it is a single, unified dimension.

4. Specific aptitudes or factors of intelligence are more predictive of success in school and specific occupations than is general intelligence.

5. Knowing your learners' specific strengths and weaknesses and altering instructional goals and methods accordingly will contribute to greater learning than will categorizing and teaching your students according to their general intelligence.

6. Task-relevant prior learning represents the facts, skills, and understandings that must be taught if subsequent learning is to occur. Mastery of task-relevant prior learning often is required for subsequent learning to take place.

7. Traditionally, students from lower-class and lower middle-class families have not performed as well on standardized achievement tests as students from middle-class and upper-class families. Most of the differences in educational achievement that occur by race and ethnicity can be accounted for by social class.

8. An important characteristic that distinguishes lower-class children from middle-class and upper-class children is that the latter more rapidly acquire knowledge of the world outside their homes and neighborhoods.

9. Lower-SES families are more likely than middle-SES and higher-SES families (1) to emphasize physical punishment rather than independent judgment and (2) to encourage rote learning (memorization, recall of facts, etc.) rather than independent, self-directed learning.

10. Some instructional strategies to meet the learning needs of lower-SES students include (1) use a variety of audiovisual and exploratory materials that require alternate modalities (e.g., sight vs. sound), (2) have high expectations and reward intellectual accomplishments, and (3) get students to talk about personal experiences to improve their self-concepts.

11. Erikson's (1968) three crises during the school years are: (1) accomplishment versus inferiority, occurring during the elementary school years; (2) identity versus confusion, occurring during the adolescent or high school years; and (3) intimacy versus isolation, occurring in early adulthood.

12. State anxiety is a temporary condition produced by some specific stimulus in the environment, such as a test.

13. Some state anxiety is necessary for learning; grades, report cards, and assignments generally provide proper levels of state anxiety to motivate students to engage in the learning process.

14. Extreme levels of state anxiety can be avoided by putting in perspective the value (importance) of a specific assignment compared to other assignments, and by clarifying its relative importance in the total context of assignments.

15. Trait anxiety is stable within individuals over time but varies among individuals. It is produced by a wide range of ill-defined conditions perceived by an individual to be harmful.

16. High levels of trait anxiety are associated with high motivation and a need to achieve, but extreme levels are associated with an intense fear of failure that dampens creativity and results in perfunctory, mechanical responses.

17. Extreme levels of trait anxiety sometimes can be avoided by making a range of alternative responses acceptable for a given assignment.

18. Learning style refers to the classroom or environmental conditions under which someone prefers to learn. One of the most frequently studied learning styles is field independence/dependence.

19. Research has shown that some learners tend to be field sensitive—or holistic/visual learners—while others tend to be less field sensitive—or verbal/analytic learners.

20. Before implementing instructional strategies to match students' learning styles, teachers should be cautious not to perpetuate stereotypes and ignore within-group differences.

21. Self-concept has only a modest relationship to school achievement but has a strong relationship to active engagement in the learning process and success in one's career or occupation. You can improve students' concept of self by finding and reflecting back to them the value of their unique talents.

22. Peer groups are an influential source of learner behavior both in and out of the classroom. Group work, group norms, group cohesiveness, and cross-age tutoring are means of using peer group influence to foster instructional goals of the classroom.

23. Closely connected with the influence of peer group on learning is the social context in which your learners live, play, and work. Among the most prominant sources of influence in this context will be your learners' family and their relationship to the school.

24. The pluralistic ideal describes the bringing together of diverse individuals so that (1) a common core of values can be established to provide the framework for a system of cooperation and government and (2) the unique and individual talents of individuals can be applied to solving the problems common to all.

*1. In what two ways might you use knowledge of the individual differences in your classroom to become a more effective teacher?

*2. Describe briefly the environmentalist and hereditarian positions concerning the use of general IQ tests in schools. Devise a counterargument you could use in responding to an argument from an extremist in each camp.

*3. Explain the role that "social competence" is believed to play in school learning. If behaviors solely related to SES could be eliminated, how might differences in the tested IQ among subgroups of learners change?

*4. Identify aptitudes or factors that are likely to be more predictive than general IQ of success in selected school subjects and occupations.

5. For each of the following, give an example of a school subject or content area in which you might expect a high score on an aptitude test to predict a high score on a test of subject-matter achievement.

Aptitude	School Subject or Content Area
verbal compre- hension	_____
general reasoning	_____
memory	_____
use of numbers	_____
psychomotor speed	_____
spatial relations	_____
word fluency	_____

6. Give an example of task-relevant prior knowledge that might be required before each of the following instructional objectives could be taught successfully.

  a. Adding two-digit numbers
  b. Reading latitude and longitude from a map
  c. Writing a four-sentence paragraph
  d. Seeing an amoeba under a microscope

  e. Correctly pronouncing a new two-syllable word
  f. Understanding how the executive branch of government works
  g. Playing ten minutes of basketball without committing a foul
  h. Responding correctly to a fire alarm
  i. Solving the equation
  $$c^2 = a^2 + b^2$$
  j. Punctuating two independent clauses

7. What might be some of the home-life characteristics of lower-SES students that make them consistently score lower than higher-SES students on standardized achievement tests? What are some teaching practices that might shrink differences in standardized achievement due to SES?

*8. Identify one approach that might be used to improve the poor self-concept of a lower-SES student.

*9. Which indicators best represent state anxiety and which best represent trait anxiety?

  a. Looks scared and exhausted before a test
  b. Becomes nervous whenever asked about where he lives
  c. Continuously combs hair and puts on makeup
  d. Has an incessant drive to get into college
  e. Skips school whenever an oral presentation is required
  f. Never fails to complete an extra credit assignment
  g. Always boasts and exaggerates about the number of girls he dates
  h. Copies others' homework often
  i. Wants to become the most respected athlete in the school
  j. Never brings home papers that have received a grade lower than "A"

10. Identify two types of learners who have different learning style preferences. What different types of products would they likely submit to you for their portfolio assessment as evidence of their learning?

*11. Identify two methods for dealing with a disruptive peer group in your classroom.

12. Using specific examples in the life of a child, explain what is meant by a systems-ecological perspective.

13. Explain in your own words what is meant by the *pluralistic ideal.* What are some signs in a typical school that show the commitment made by our country, its people, and its government toward this ideal?

_____

*Answers to asterisked questions (*) in this and the other chapters are in Appendix B.

Suggested Readings

Harter, S. (1990). Processes underlying adolescent self-concept formation. In R. Montemajor, G. R. Adams, & T. P. Gullota (Eds.). *From childhood to adolescence: A transitional period?* (pp. 205–239). Newbury Park, CA: Sage.

This chapter reviews how one acquires self-concept during the critical adolescent years and the many sources of influence within a school that can shape its development.

Hartup, W. (1989). Social relationships and their developmental significance. *American Psychologist, 44,* 120–126.

Description of the role of horizontal and vertical friendships and how they can influence the social-emotional development of the school child.

Hill, H. (1989). *Effective strategies for teaching minority students.* Bloomington, IN: National Educational Service.

A guide to successfully teaching minority youth and developing cultural sensitivity that promotes learning and achievement.

Gardner, H., & Hatch, T. (1989). Multiple intelligences go to school. *Educational Researcher, 18* (8), 4–10.

An introduction to how the concept of "multiple intelligences" can be used in the classroom.

Delgado-Gaitan, C. (1991). Involving parents in the schools: A process of empowerment. *American Educational Research Journal, 100* (1), 20–46.

A report of research involving several minority communities in which strategies were successful in getting parents involved in their neighborhood schools.

Schmuck, R., & Schmuck, P. (1992). *Group process in the classroom: 6th Edition.* Dubuque, IA: William C. Brown.

A thorough discussion of the role of norms and peer group influence in the classroom—and how teachers can use them to advantage.

Sinclair, K. (1987). Students' affective characteristics. In M. J. Dunkin (Ed.), *International encyclopedia of teaching and teacher education.* New York: Pergamon.

An interesting article on the complex social and emotional behaviors of school learners and their potential effects in the classroom.

CHAPTER 3

Instructional Goals and Plans

This chapter will help you answer the following questions:

1. What are the differences among an instructional aim, a goal, and an objective?
2. Where do instructional goals come from?
3. What are some important educational goals for the year 2000?
4. How can I plan for a "thinking curriculum" in my classroom?
5. What sources of information do I use as inputs to the planning process?
6. How do I determine the appropriate content and methods to use with my learners?
7. On what basis should I revise my instruction?
8. How can I plan to eliminate biases I might have in labeling, grouping, and interacting with my learners?
9. How can I move from a concern for my own well-being to a concern for my impact on learners?

This chapter will also help you learn the meaning of the following:

aims
biases in labeling and grouping
community priorities
content organization
goals
goals for the year 2000
learning needs
objectives
societal concerns
tacit knowledge
teacher concerns
teaching methods
the "thinking curriculum"

C hapters 1 and 2 introduced some behaviors expected of you as a teacher and some individual differences you can expect among your students. This chapter combines these two topics to show you how to organize your thinking about who, what, and how you will teach. First, let's consider the distinction among aims, goals, and objectives and their use in instructional planning.

>>> AIMS, GOALS, AND OBJECTIVES <<<

What are the differences among an instructional aim, a goal, and an objective?

The words *aims, goals,* and *objectives* often are used interchangeably without recognizing their different, albeit related, meanings. **Aims** are general expressions of our values that give us a sense of direction. They are broad enough to be acceptable to large numbers of individuals, such as "taxpayers," "parents," or "the American people." Examples of aims are the following:

Every citizen should be prepared to work in a technological world.

Every adult should be functionally literate.

Every American should be able to vote as an informed citizen in a democratic society.

Aims such as these are important in expressing *values* and communicating societal concerns with which many individuals can agree. However, aims are so broad and general that their implementation is difficult. To be useful, aims require greater specification in the form of goals and objectives.

Goals, like aims, provide a sense of direction, but are more specific. Goals tell your learners why you are teaching the lessons you have planned. Your ability to express important subject matter goals conveys to learners a sense of purpose from which they can make a commitment to learn. This is why goals are important—they energize and motivate students to become actively engaged in and committed to the learning process. As you read the goals below, see how well they answer the question "Why am I teaching this?"

Students should understand the use of the microcomputer at home and at work.

Students should be able to read and write well enough to become gainfully employed.

Students should know how to choose a candidate and vote in an
   election.

Notice that these goal statements, although written for the
teacher, are expressed from the learner's point of view. In other
words, goals identify what your *students* will learn from your
instruction. For example, the statement, "The teacher will show students examples of logical arguments," would fail as an educational
goal because it describes what *you will do,* not what *your students
will learn.* "Learners will acquire the ability to construct a convincing argument," qualifies as a goal statement because it identifies
what is expected of your students.

How do you choose goals for learners? What is the best way to
find proper goals given the diversity and complexity that exists
across subjects and grades? Several approaches to formulating educational goals have been developed to help you. One approach
comes from the work of Tyler (1974).

Tyler's Goal Development Approach

Tyler's approach to generating educational goals has had a major
influence on curriculum development over the past three decades.
Tyler believes that as society becomes more complex there are more
things for people to learn. But, the time to learn this ever-expanding
amount of knowledge and skills may actually decrease in a techno-
logically complex society. Consequently, educators must make
informed choices about which goals are worth teaching.

*Where do instruc-
tional goals come
from?*

Tyler identified five factors to consider when establishing priorities for what students should learn. First, goals must include

1. the subject matter we know enough about to teach (subject
   matter mastery),
2. **societal concerns,** which represent what is valued in both
   the society at large and the local community, and
3. student needs and interests and the abilities and knowledge
   they bring to school.

Secondly, these goals must be refined to match

4. your school's educational philosophy and your **community's
   priorities,** and
5. what instructional theory and research tells us can be taught.

Figure 3.1
Tyler's considerations in goal selection

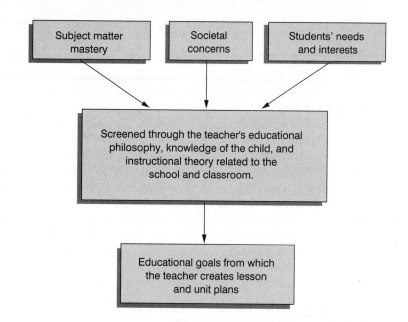

Tyler's approach to establishing educational goals is illustrated in Figure 3.1.

Goals will be important to you because they tell your learners, their parents, and the community *why* you are teaching the lessons you have planned, which, then, energize and motivate them to become actively engaged in and committed to the learning process. Educational goals

1. provide direction for your unit and lesson planning,
2. communicate the importance of your instruction to parents and to the community, and
3. energize your learners to higher levels of commitment and engagement in the learning process.

From Educational Goals to Classroom Accomplishments

Educational goals provide direction for planning, communicate the importance of what you are teaching, and increase your students commitment to learn. They also can provide a practical framework around which to organize and sequence your instruction.

But, while goals answer the question, "Why am I teaching this?," they are not a satisfactory response to what or how you will teach on any given day. Goals give you little direction as to what strategies to

Goals increase students commitment to learn--

use to achieve them or when or even if they are met. A satisfactory answer to these questions requires that you prepare lesson **objectives,** which convey to your learners the *specific behavior* to be attained, the *conditions* under which the behavior must be demonstrated, and the *proficiency level* at which the behavior is to be performed. We will visit the topic of lesson objectives in the next chapter, but, for now, let's look at the three previously stated goals, now converted to objectives:

- Students will, using their own choice of microcomputer, produce an edited two-page manuscript free of typographical errors in 15 minutes or less.
- Students will, at the end of the 12th grade, be able to write a 500-word essay with no more than two grammatical and punctuation errors and to read newspapers and magazines with no errors in comprehension.
- Students will, at the end of an eighth-grade unit on government, participate in a mock election by choosing a candidate from the prescribed list and giving three reasons for their choice.

Objectives like these often are included in curriculum guides and teacher's manuals that accompany textbooks and workbooks. But, they may not always be well written, or fit a particular class of students or the way you choose to structure your lessons. Therefore, you will find it necessary to reformulate objectives to fit the individual needs of students, the instructional priorities of your school district, and your organization of content.

Table 3.1 summarizes the distinctions among aims, goals, and objectives. Figure 3.2 illustrates the translation of aims into objectives as a funneling or narrowing of focus in which the general aims of society gradually are translated into specific objectives for instruction.

>>> SOCIETAL GOALS FOR EDUCATION <<<
FOR THE YEAR 2000

In the past decade there have been several important developments that have highlighted concerns about academic goals and how we measure them. Several presidential commissions have completed comprehensive studies of the state of education in American elementary and secondary schools (Goodlad, 1984; Sizer, 1985; Holmes Group, 1990). They concluded that instruction at all levels

Table 3.1

Aims, goals, and objectives

Category	Description	Examples
Aims	Broad statements of very general outcomes that 1. do not include specific levels of performance 2. do not identify specific areas of the curriculum 3. tend to change infrequently and in response to societal pressure	Become a good citizen Be competent in the basic skills areas Be creative Learn problem solving Appreciate art Develop high-level thinking skills
Goals	More narrowly defined statements of outcomes that 1. apply to specific curricula 2. may be formulated on an annual basis 3. are developed by program coordinators, principals, and other school administrators	Students receiving the new reading program should realize achievement gains on the Iowa Test of Basic Skills.
Objectives	Specific statements of learner behavior or outcomes that state the conditions under which the behavior is to be exhibited (e.g., given a list of 25 vocabulary words at the 8th-grade level) and the proficiency to be attained (e.g., the student will correctly provide synonyms for 20 out of the 25). These behaviors are expected to be attained at the end of a specified time of instruction.	By Friday, the students will be able to recite the names of the months in order. The student will be able to take apart and reassemble correctly a one-barrel carburetor with the tools provided within 45 minutes.

educ. commissions want to develop a more "thinking" curriculum

is predominantly focused on memorization, drill, and workbook exercises. These commissions called for a commitment to developing a "thinking curriculum," one that focuses on teaching learners how to think critically, reason, and problem solve in real-world contexts. Four teacher organizations—the National Council of Teachers of Mathematics, the National Council for the Social Studies, the National Council for Improving Science Education, and the National Council of Teachers of English—took up the challenge of these commissions by publishing new curriculum frameworks. These frameworks advocated that American schools adopt such a **thinking cur-**

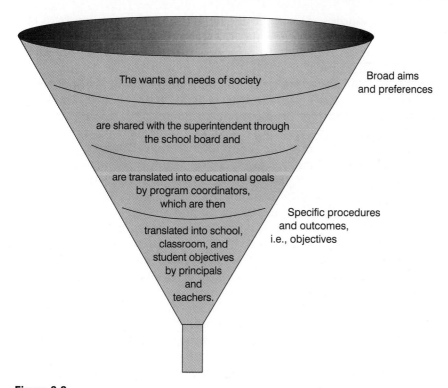

Figure 3.2
The funneling of societal aims into objectives

From *Educational Testing and Measurement: Classroom Application and Practice,* 4th Edition by Tom Kubiszyn and Gary Borich. Copyright © 1993 by HarperCollins College Publishers. Reprinted by permission.

riculum and a performance-based examination system that would adequately measure complex cognitive skills (Mitchell, 1992; Loucks-Horsley et al., 1990; Parker, 1991; Willoughby, 1990).

These commissions were stimulated in part by a disenchantment with the quality of public school education voiced by many segments of our society, including parents, taxpayers, legislators, business and military leaders, and some teacher groups. This disenchantment was not limited to matters of curriculum. It extended to the quality of teaching, leading in some cases to recommendations for teacher competency testing and new requirements for certification. Each of the commissions registered its own concerns, but together they expressed a consensus about what was wrong with American education and what to do about it.

For example, several reports agreed that our schools needed to strengthen curricula in math, science, English, foreign languages,

What are some important educational goals for the year 2000?

and social studies. Also, high technology was represented by a call for more computer science and computer literacy, both as separate courses and as adjuncts to other courses. The reports called for renewed effort in teaching higher-order thinking skills, including the teaching of concepts, problem solving, and creativity (as opposed to rote memorization and parroting of facts, lists, names, and dates divorced from a larger problem-solving context).

Not surprisingly, all the reports recommended increasing both grading standards and the number of required core courses (as opposed to elective courses), especially at the secondary level. This recommendation went hand in hand with the suggestion that colleges raise their admission requirements by requiring more course work in core subjects, especially math and foreign languages.

Most of the reports recommended increasing school hours and homework time. For example, one report suggested a minimum seven-hour school day (some schools have fewer than six hours) and a 200-day school year (many have a 180-day year). Presumably, students would spend more time actively engaged in the learning process if they took more courses and spent more time in school. Time spent on extracurricular and other noninstructional activities was to be reduced accordingly, as would administrative interruptions. These recommendations foreshadowed a tough new policy in which many school districts went on record as wanting to reverse the more flexible curriculum, grading standards, and school management style of a decade earlier.

By taking a broad view of our educational establishment, these reports recommended the following:

Students should be trained to live and function in a technological world.

Students should possess minimum competencies in reading, writing, and mathematics.

Students should possess high-order thinking, conceptual, and problem-solving skills.

Students should be required to enroll in all the core subjects each school year, to the extent of their abilities.

Students should be trained to work independently and to complete assignments without direct supervision.

Students should improve school attendance and stay in school longer each day and year.

Students should be given more tests that require problem-solving skills and higher grading standards.

The basis of these goals was the perception that our schools had lost sight of their role in teaching students *how to think*. Traditionally, this was accomplished through the core curriculum (English, math, science, foreign languages, and social studies). However, with fewer advanced offerings in these areas and with additional time being spent in remedial activities, the time devoted to teaching children how to think may have been seriously curtailed. These reports suggested that schools should reverse this trend by requiring students to study both the basic core and more advanced areas. Such instruction would require homework, higher testing and grading standards, and complex thinking skills and performance assessments of what was learned. Mastering thinking skills, such as problem solving, decision making, and learning to make value judgments, was considered important because they are required both in the world of work and to gain admittance to advanced education and training opportunities (Resnick & Resnick, 1991).

Although other goals can be derived from these reports, the preceding list illustrates how a broad national consensus can guide the formulation of goals and objectives and how they are to be assessed. In Chapter 5 we will show how you can translate the spirit of these goals into your own unit and lesson plans. In Chapter 15 we will show how these goals can be measured using performance and portfolio assessment.

How can I plan for a "thinking curriculum" in my classroom?

>>> INPUTS TO THE PLANNING PROCESS <<<

You are now ready to consider planning and its relationship to decisions you make in the classroom. *Planning* is the systematic process of deciding what and how your students should learn. Teachers make one such decision on the average of every two minutes while they are teaching, according to an estimate by Clark and Peterson (1986). However, these "in-flight" decisions are only part of the decision-making process. Teachers also make many other decisions involving priorities and judgments about the form and content of their instruction, such as how much lecturing, questioning, and discussing to do, how much material to cover in the allotted time, and how in-depth to make the instruction. In the previous section you saw the importance of *aims* and *goals* in the planning process. Now, let's consider three other inputs to the planning process: knowledge of the *learner*, knowledge of your *subject matter*, and knowledge of *teaching methods.*

An important recommendation for curriculum reform in the 1990s is that learners be better trained to work independently and to attain more high-level thinking, conceptual, and problem-solving skills.

Knowledge of the Learner

What sources of information do I use as inputs to the planning process?

Planning – being aware of the students level of learning

Chapter 2 showed the importance of understanding learner needs and individual differences in preparing to teach. In fact, a review of six research studies on planning found that teachers spent more of their planning time on learner characteristics (an average of 43%) than on any other area (Clark & Peterson, 1986). Recall the major influences on student learning: ability and achievement, personality (including anxiety, learning style, and self-concept), peers, and home and family. These are windows through which you "see" special **learning needs.** They also are the psychological characteristics that reflect how ready your students are to learn, telling you at what level to begin your instruction.

Planning with respect to learners includes consciously noting their characteristics in these areas and recording significant departures from what might be expected within the traditional curriculum. These departures can signal special learning needs that require you to select content, materials, objectives, and methods that match your students' characteristics. These inputs are instrumental in helping you organize, select, sequence, and allocate time to various topics of instruction.

Knowledge of Subject Matter

A second primary input to planning is knowledge of your academic discipline and grade level. As a student, you have spent much time and

Organizing the subj you teach [handwritten annotation]

effort becoming knowledgeable in the subjects you will teach. You also have learned a subtle yet important aspect of your discipline, perhaps without realizing it. You have observed and absorbed valuable information about how textbook authors, your instructors, and subject matter specialists *organize* concepts in your teaching area. This includes how parts relate to the whole, how content is prioritized, how transitions are made between topics, and which themes are major or minor.

Figure 3.3 illustrates three of the many ways of organizing content in lesson and unit planning. These and other **content organization** schemes are used by teachers, curriculum designers, and textbook authors to make learning easier, more orderly, and more

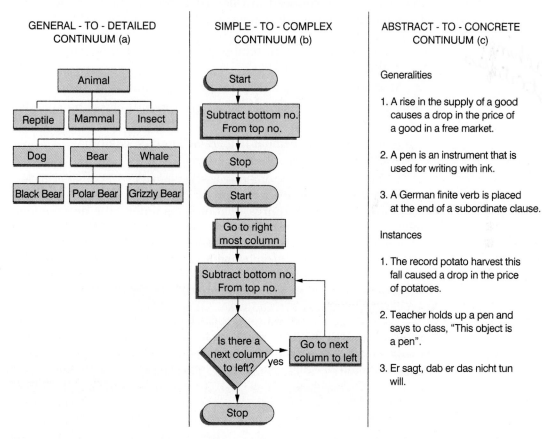

Figure 3.3

Some ways of organizing content

From *Instructional Design Theories and Models: An Overview of Their Current Status* (p. 345) by C. Reigeluth, 1983, Hillsdale, NJ: Lawrence Erlbaum Associates, Inc. Copyright © 1983 by Lawrence Erlbaum Associates, Inc. Reprinted by permission.

conducive to retention and later use (Clark & Yinger, 1979). These organizational schemes are provided by subject matter specialists in textbooks, instructional materials, and curriculum guides. Deriving your content organization from these sources will be instrumental in helping you select, sequence, and allocate time to instruction.

Knowledge of Teaching Methods

A third input to the planning process is your knowledge of **teaching methods.** With this knowledge comes an awareness of different teaching strategies with which you can implement the key and helping behaviors introduced in Chapter 1. Also included under teaching methods are your decisions about the following:

Appropriate pacing or tempo (e.g., the speed at which you introduce new material)

Mode of presentation (e.g., lecture vs. group discussion)

Class arrangement (e.g., small groups, full class, independent study)

Classroom management (e.g., raise hand, speak out)

Included in the planning process is your careful consideration of these dimensions and how to interweave them during content presentation. Teaching requires relationships among the decisions you make during the orchestration of both key and helping behaviors. Therefore, your decisions about pacing, mode of presentation, class arrangement, and classroom management should work together to form a coherent whole from which you present individual lesson objectives. This strategy must also be planned to add momentum, expectancy, and forward movement to your classroom.

Another aspect of your knowledge of teaching methods is your selection and use of teaching materials. Your decisions about textbooks and curriculum materials, workbooks, films, tests, and reference works are crucial to planning. Therefore, you will want to keep a record of the materials and media that may be useful in meeting instructional goals in your subject matter and grade level. As you gain experience in your content area or grade level through observation and student teaching, be sure to list texts, workbooks, and media, and, when possible, obtain copies of handouts, activity sheets, and assessment tools directed to your learners' ages and grade levels. This is an important part of the planning process.

Summary of Inputs to Planning

To recap, the four primary inputs to the planning process are the following:

1. Aims and goals, reflected by national and state policies and legislation, school district curriculum guides, and adopted textbooks and materials.
2. Learner characteristics and individual differences, reflected by student aptitude and achievement, personality traits (anxiety, learning style, and self-concept), peer influence, and home and family life.
3. Knowledge of academic discipline and grade-level curriculum, reflected by content organization (such as general-to-detailed, simple-to-complex, abstract-to-concrete), ordering of priorities (such as connections and transitions among and between parts), major and minor themes (such as most important/least important), and content-specific facts, rules, concepts, and principles.
4. Knowledge of teaching methods, reflected by key and helping behaviors (such as lesson clarity, instructional variety, task orientation, and student engagement in the learning process at moderate-to-high rates of success), pacing, mode of presentation, class arrangement, classroom management, and selection and use of textbooks, media, and materials.

Shulman (1992) identifies four sources from which you may obtain knowledge about aims and goals, learners, content, and teaching methods: (1) *practical experiences,* such as classroom observation, student teaching, and regular teaching, (2) reading *case studies* about what successful and unsuccessful teachers have done, (3) reading *theoretical articles* about important ideas, conceptual systems, and paradigms for thinking about teaching, and (4) reading *empirical studies* about what the research says about your subject and how to teach it. Each of these is a valuable source for extending and updating your knowledge of learners, content, and teaching methods, which we will visit in the chapters ahead.

>>> DECISION MAKING AND TACIT UNDERSTANDING <<<

As a beginning teacher, you probably regard your content and method knowledge as hard won during four long years of schooling.

Figure 3.4
Inputs to the planning process

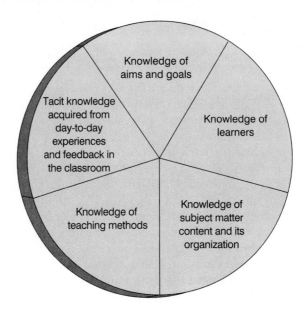

To be sure, it is—but you've only just begun. Your knowledge in content and methods will change with the *interaction* of "book learning" and classroom experience.

This change will result from what is called tacit, or personal knowledge (Elbaz, 1983; Polanyi, 1958). **Tacit knowledge** represents "what works" discovered over time and through experience. Through everyday experiences, such as observation, experience in schools, lesson planning, and student teaching, you will compile tacit knowledge that can guide your actions as effectively as knowledge from texts and formal instruction. This knowledge can add to the quality of your planning and decision making by bringing variety and flexibility to your lessons. Tacit knowledge can make your planning less rigid and over time add fresh insights to your teaching style, which can become stale and outdated through habit or routine.

Effective teachers reflect on their day-to-day experiences in the classroom and use them as yet another input to the planning process. Lesson plans that include your day-to-day experiences will give your teaching the variety, flexibility, and creativity it deserves. Thus, we add this fifth input to the planning process, shown in Figure 3.4.

>>> STEPS IN THE PLANNING PROCESS <<<

You have seen that planning includes gathering and recording information from five inputs. Recall that the five inputs are aims and goals, knowledge of learner characteristics, knowledge of subject matter, knowledge of teaching methods, and tacit knowledge acquired from your day-to-day classroom experience. Each is a step in the planning process for which decisions must be made. For example, consider the following planning-related questions:

1. Which aims and goals should I try to achieve?
2. To which learner needs should I direct my instruction?
3. What should I teach, and in what ways can I structure the content to produce maximum learning (for example, establish sequences, make transitions, highlight important points, interweave themes)?
4. How can I orchestrate various teaching methods to meet my objectives (for example, question and answer, discussion, review and practice)?
5. What instructional media and materials should I use to deliver the content and assess whether it has been learned?
6. On what basis should I revise my instruction?

For each question there are many alternatives. Selecting an instructional goal, organizing content for maximum learning and retention, selecting instructional methods and materials, and assessing your learners—all require planning skills that must reduce the alternatives to the most practical and effective ones. These planning skills include the ability to *generate alternatives,* to *recognize value assumptions* contained in the choice of alternatives, and to extend or *change previously chosen alternatives* when needed. Now, let's consider how these skills can be used for planning your lessons and units.

Generating Alternatives

Generating alternative courses of action is one of the first steps in good planning. For example, you must (1) choose among different instructional goals to select the learner characteristics to which your instruction will be tailored, (2) organize the content, and (3) select teaching methods and instructional materials. Each of these tasks requires choices. Some possibilities can be eliminated due to their impracticality for a specific set of learners, lack of resources, or the time required. Others will stand out as viable alternatives.

The first step in planning, then, is to describe alternative courses of action and determine what is practical considering the content, learning needs, time, and resources. Here are some example alternatives:

How do I determine the appropriate content and methods to use with my learners?

make choices about what methods to use w/ my learners

1. Possible instructional goals (from curriculum guide and text-book):
   ☐ Teach facts regarding . . .
   ☐ Teach appreciation of . . .
   ☐ Teach analytical thinking in . . .
   ☐ Teach how to make decisions about . . .
2. Possible learning needs (from previous testing, prior class-room assignments, and informal observation):
   ☐ Remediate deficiencies
   ☐ Improve problem solving
   ☐ Acquire new skills
3. Possible content organizations (from curriculum guide, text, subject matter references, and tacit knowledge):
   ☐ Simple-to-complex ordering
   ☐ Most-interesting-to-least-interesting ordering
   ☐ First-step-to-last-step ordering
   ☐ General-to-specific ordering
4. Possible methods (from knowledge of teaching methods):
   ☐ Independent, programmed learning
   ☐ Question and answer
   ☐ Small-group discussion
   ☐ Lecture and recitation

For this lesson, four different goals appear possible, three different learning needs have been identified, four organizational patterns seem applicable to the goals, and four instructional methods or combinations have been selected as possibilities.

Recognizing Value Assumptions

Now, you must match up goals, learning needs, organization, and methods. Match goals with learning needs, and then tie them to a specific organizational pattern and instructional arrangement to make the best "goal–learning need–organization–method" match. For example, a reasonable match might be the teaching of facts (goal) to remediate deficiencies (learning need) using simple-to-complex ordering (organization) in small groups (method). Another might be teaching skills (goal) to improve problem-solving performance on weekly quizzes (learning need) using general-to-specific ordering (organization) in a discussion format (method). Laying out the possibilities in accord with the four planning process inputs permits a practical matching of alternatives at the time of lesson planning. This lets you prioritize different goal–learning need–organization–method matches, so you can pursue other combinations in priority order over longer periods of time as resources permit.

One of the most important results of prioritizing your goal–learning need–organization–method matches is that you will recognize the *value assumptions* that such ordering implies. For example, if your highest priority is teaching analytical skills to improve problem solving using most-complex-to-least-complex organization in a lecture format, this implies that time and resources may not be available to teach the facts needed to remove existing deficiencies. When you recognize the values implied by your choices, and their conflict with other value sources such as those of the school and community, you may reconsider your selection and might divide your time and resources more evenly among various matches.

This part of the planning process is successful to the extent that it makes you *consider and reconsider* all practical and available instructional alternatives. Matching and prioritizing are planning activities that encourage you to actively consider the consequences of your decisions. Recognizing the values implied by a choice is an effective means of promoting thoughtful planning.

Revising Alternatives

You need not identify all instructional alternatives before you begin to teach. You also can choose alternatives based on feedback you receive during instruction. In other words, you can use the tacit knowledge acquired through day-to-day experience with your learners as an input to the planning process. Suppose that you selected a particular goal–learning need–organization–method match to achieve a certain outcome (e.g., improved basic skills, greater problem-solving ability, more critical thinking). If feedback from work samples, tests, and classroom performance indicates that you are not obtaining your intended result, you can shift to another content organization or teaching method to obtain a better match to improve the outcome.

Remember that feedback from the observation and assessment of learners is an important input to the planning process. Sensitivity to these data provides your best means of monitoring the consequences of your instructional decisions, and the most effective means of revising them. This part of the planning process is shown in Figure 3.5.

On what basis should I revise my instruction?

Keep trying diff. methods of instruction

— may be on feedback recieved during instruction

— day to day exper... etc..

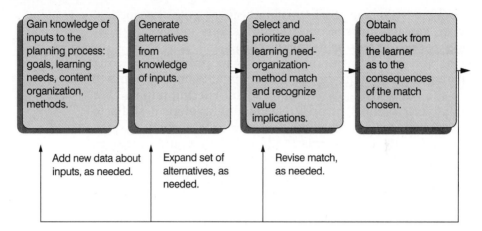

Figure 3.5
Stages of the planning process

>>> PLANNING TO ELIMINATE BIAS <<<

Planning to eliminate bias in classroom teaching can be one of the most significant aspects of becoming an effective teacher. Researchers recently have brought to our attention that, consciously or unconsciously, everyone has biases of one kind or another (Gage & Berliner, 1992). When applied in ways that affect only your own behavior and not that of others, we use the word *preference.* Preferences are the harmless results of values manifest in choosing clothing, cars, music, etc.

Biases, on the other hand, are not harmless; they can injure the personal growth and well-being of others. The fact that many biases are covert and unconscious makes them even more devastating and difficult to control, especially in a culturally diverse classroom. Your biases, if left unchecked, can significantly affect the growth and development of learners. As the previous section showed, one purpose of planning is to raise to a conscious level the thoughts, feelings, and understandings that you may have acquired tacitly or informally. You also can use this process to become aware of biases that influence how and what you teach. Let's look at some of the ways you might show bias.

Biases in Labeling and Grouping

A particularly alarming case of bias was uncovered by Rist (1970) when he studied a single class of ghetto students from kindergarten through second grade. Rist observed that from the time these students entered kindergarten, they were divided into three groups—"tigers," "cardinals," and "clowns"—each seated at a different table. Initial placement into these groups in kindergarten was made by the teacher according to SES, using information from registration forms and from interviews with mothers and social workers. The highest status children, called tigers, were seated closest to the teacher and quickly labeled "fast learners." The lowest status children, called clowns, were farthest removed from the teacher and quickly were led to believe they were "slow learners."

In reality, each of the three groups had a mixture of slow and fast learners; but the slow learners seated farthest from the teacher seldom got the opportunity to interact with her, while those closest to the teacher frequently received attention. Before long the abilities of each group were taken as fact rather than as creations of the teacher, so much so that it was increasingly difficult for the "clowns" to be considered other than slow by their teachers in the following grades.

At no time did the teacher seem to be aware that the arrangement was biased or that seating certain students consistently in the back of the room would reduce their contact with her. Thus, this teacher's bias became a self-fulfilling prophecy that extended even to subsequent grades and classes—all as a result of biased labeling during the early years of schooling.

Good and Brophy (1987b) describe the sequence of how biases lead to self-fulfillment in the following way:

- Based on what you read, hear, or see about your students, you naturally expect different achievement and social behavior from different students;
- these expectations affect your decisions while you are teaching—you call on certain students and not others; you wait longer for some students to give answers than others; you seat students in different parts of the room; you check the work of some students more frequently; you give easier or harder assignments;
- your students eventually learn what they are and are not expected to do, and behave accordingly; and, so,
- you observe the student behavior that confirms your original expectations, and the cycle repeats itself.

Many other examples of teacher biases have been catalogued. For example, Brophy and Good (1974) summarize how teachers sometimes respond unequally to high and low achievers by communicating low expectations and thereby accepting, and unintentionally encouraging, a low level of performance among some students. Brophy and Good identified the following areas in which some teachers responded differently toward low and high achievers:

- Wait less time for lows to answer.
- Give lows the answer after their slightest hesitation.
- Praise marginal or inaccurate answers of lows.
- Criticize lows more frequently for having the wrong answer.
- Praise lows less when the right answer is given.
- Do not give feedback to lows as to why an answer is incorrect.
- Pay attention to (e.g., smile at) and call on lows less.
- Seat lows farther from the teacher.
- Allow lows to "give up" more.

Generally, these findings confirm that teachers usually do not compensate for differences between high and low achievers in allowing more response opportunities and more teacher contact for the latter.

Biases in Interacting

Other types of bias can affect interactions with students. For example, Gage and Berliner (1992) identified several biased ways in which teachers interact with their students and then analyzed the extent to which experienced teachers actually exhibited these biases in their classrooms. Their biases included interacting with or calling on students disproportionately in these ways:

Seated in front half of class vs. seated in back half of class

Nicer-looking students vs. average-looking students

More-able students vs. less-able students

Nonminority group members vs. minority group members

Gage and Berliner calculated the number of student–teacher interactions that would be expected by chance for these classifications, and then from observation determined the actual number of interactions that occurred. Somewhat surprisingly, their results indicate that *every* teacher showed some bias in these categories. In other words, every teacher favored at least one student classification over another by naming, calling on, requiring information from, and otherwise interacting with those in some classification disproportionally to those not in that classification.

Such biases may be meaningless over a single class period but can have significant and long-lasting emotional impact on students if

Bias in interacting with students can routinely occur when potential sources of bias are not identified beforehand and steps are not taken to avoid them. For example, calling on some students more than others is an open message that some are less desirable and less worthy than others, regardless of how unintentional the bias may be.

continued throughout weeks, months, or the entire school year. The accumulated effect of systematic bias in a classroom is an open message to some students that they are less desirable and less worthy of attention than others, regardless of how unintentional the bias may be. If the message is received, and it surely will be, the result is change in motivation, self-concept, and even anxiety level of some students in ways that impede their development and learning.

Bias in the way a teacher interacts with students is undesirable in any form, but it is particularly distasteful when it pertains to students' ethnicity. As we saw in Chapter 2, our nation as well as our educational system is based on the pluralistic ideal and respect for individual differences of all types. This means that our classrooms become one of the most important showplaces of our democratic values. It is disturbing that researchers report frequent ethnic bias or cultural insensitivity during student–teacher interactions in classrooms of African Americans, Hispanic Americans, Asians, and Anglos.

In one study of interactions between teachers and Anglo American and Hispanic American students in 429 classrooms in the American Southwest, interaction frequently favored Anglos in teacher questioning, positive responses, use of student ideas, and praise and encouragement (Civil Rights Commission, 1973). More recent studies (Dillon, 1989; Tharp & Gallimore, 1989) point out that many actions of teachers diminish the classroom participation of minority students and/or build resentment because their actions are culturally incongruent. Reverse bias also has been observed between African Americans and Anglos in inner-city schools, where teacher–student interaction favors the African American majority. Regardless of the direction, biases can be brought to a conscious level and cultural sensitivity heightened through the planning process.

Certain actions of teachers diminish class participation of minority students.

How can I plan to eliminate biases I might have in labeling, grouping, and interacting with my learners?

Bowers and Flinders (1991) and Gage and Berliner (1992) make the following planning suggestions for eliminating bias and increasing cultural sensitivity in the classroom:

1. Plan to spread your interactions as evenly as possible across student categories by deciding in advance which students to call on. Because the many classifications of potential bias are cumbersome to deal with, choose one or two bias categories you know or suspect you are most vulnerable to.

2. If you plan on giving special assignments to only some of your students, choose the students randomly. Place all of your students' names in a jar and have one student draw the names of individuals needed for the special assignment. This protects you from inadvertently choosing the same students repeatedly and conveying the impression that you have "pets."

3. Try consciously to pair opposites in what you believe to be a potential area of bias for you—for example, pair minority with nonminority, more able with less able, easy to work with and difficult to work with, etc. In this manner, when you are interacting with one member of the pair you will be reminded to interact with the other. Occasionally change one member of the pair so that your pairing does not become obvious to the class.

4. When you discover a bias, plan a code to remind you of the bias and then embed it within your class notes, text, or lesson plan at appropriate intervals. For example, should you discover you systematically favor more able (MA) learners over less able (LA) learners, place the code "LA" on the margins of your exercise to remind you to choose a less able learner for the next response.

>>> A HIERARCHY OF PLANNING NEEDS <<<

At this point in your training, you probably see yourself in the role of teacher and you may have constructed some images or pictures of your first class. You may have promised yourself that you are going to be better than some of the teachers that taught you when you were in elementary or high school. And, you probably hope to be as good as some other teachers you have known. But, as you begin your first regular teaching assignment you will find that there is a difference between your student teaching experience and "the real world of teaching." First, the classrooms you have been in came with a made-to-order instructional and behavior management system. All you had to do was adjust to it. Soon, no such system will exist and you will have to create one of your own.

During student teaching, you will have some instructional materials and lessons to draw on as aids to help you plan and teach. This may not be the case when you start your first teaching assignment. You will have to make many decisions about what, for how long, and in what manner to teach a group of learners you know little about.

And, finally, your cooperating teacher will be an important advisor and confidante during your student teaching experience, someone you can go to for advice on how to teach particular learners or on how to cope with the psychological and physical demands of teaching. No such mentor may exist in your first regular teaching assignment.

This transition to the real world of teaching ushers in the first stage of teacher development, sometimes called the *survival stage* (Fuller, 1969; Burden, 1986; Ryan, 1992; Borich, 1993). The distinguishing feature of this first stage of teaching is that your **teaching concerns** and plans will focus on your own well-being more than on the teaching task or your learners. Bullough (1989) has described this stage as "the fight for one's professional life" (p. 16). During it, your concerns typically are focused on the following:

- Will my learners like me?
- Will they listen to what I say?
- What will parents and other teachers think of me?
- Will I do well when I'm being observed?

Typically, during this time behavior management concerns become a major focus of your planning efforts. For most teachers, survival—or *self*—concerns begin to diminish rapidly during the first months of teaching, but there is no precise time when they end. What signals their end is the transition to a new set of concerns and planning priorities. This new set of priorities focuses on how best to deliver instruction. Various labels have been used to describe this second stage, such as the mastery stage of teaching (Ryan, 1992), consolidation and exploration (Burden, 1986), and trial and error (Sacks & Harrington, 1982). Fuller (1969) described this stage as one marked by concerns about the teaching *task*.

At this stage you are beginning to feel confident that you can manage the day-to-day routines of the classroom and deal with a variety of behavior problems. You are at the point where you now can plan your lessons without an exclusive focus on managing your classroom. Your planning turns instead toward improving your teaching skills and achieving greater mastery over the content you are teaching.

Typically your concerns during this stage are with the following:

- Where can I find good instructional materials?
- Will I have enough time to cover the content?

- Where can I get ideas for a learning center?
- What's the best way to teach writing skills?

The third and highest level of teacher planning is characterized by concerns which have less to do with management and lesson delivery and more with the impact of your teaching on learners. This stage of planning is sometimes referred to as the *impact* stage. At this stage you will naturally view learners as individuals and will be concerned that each of your students fulfills her or his potential to learn. At this time, your principal concerns will be the following:

- How can I increase my learners' feelings of accomplishment?
- How do I meet my learners' social and emotional needs?
- What is the best way to challenge my unmotivated learners?
- What skills do they need to best prepare them for the next grade?

Fuller (1969) speculated that concerns for *self, task,* and *impact* are the natural stages that most teachers pass through, representing a developmental growth pattern extending over months and even years of a teacher's career. Although some teachers may pass through these stages more quickly than others and at different levels of intensity, Fuller suggested that almost all teachers can be expected to move from one to another, with the most effective and experienced teachers expressing student-centered (impact) concerns at a high level of commitment. The lack of adequate knowledge or emotional support during the critical preteaching and student teaching experience can result in a slower, more labored shift in focus from self to task to impact.

Fuller's "concerns theory" has several other interesting implications. A teacher might return to an earlier stage of concern—move from a concern for students back to a concern for task as a result of having to teach a new grade or subject, or move from a concern for task back to a concern for self as a result of having to teach different and unfamiliar students. The second time spent in a stage might be expected to be shorter than the first. Finally, the three stages of concern need not be exclusive of one another. A teacher could have concerns predominately in one area while still having concerns at lesser levels of intensity in the other stages. Fuller's three stages of teacher concerns are summarized in Figure 3.6.

How can I move from a concern for my own well-being to a concern for my impact on learners?

An important question for you as a prospective teacher is what type of knowledge and experiences are needed to pass successfully from an exclusive concern for self to a concern for the impact you are having on your students. The chapters ahead will convey the types of

Figure 3.6
Hierarchy of planning needs and
teacher concerns

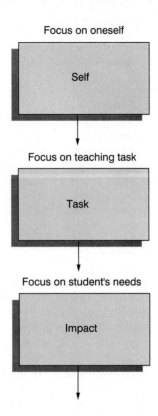

knowledge you will need to move quickly up the planning hierarchy
from self to task to impact. But, before learning about the tools and
techniques that will help you progress through the stages of teacher
concerns, you will want to determine your own levels of concern for
self, task, and impact at this point in your teaching career. Appendix
A contains the Teacher Concerns Checklist, a 45-item self-report
instrument and scoring instructions for assessing the stages of concern with which a teacher most strongly identifies. Using the Teacher
Concerns Checklist, rank your own level of concern and determine
which stage of concern you identify with most closely.

The Teacher Concerns Checklist has been administered to both
preservice and inservice teachers. From their responses it was possible to construct a hierarchy of planning needs based upon the
three stages of concern. This hierarchy suggests the concerns most
frequently expressed by teachers for each of the three stages and
provides suggestions for reducing high levels of concern for a
prospective teacher at each stage. This hierarchy appears in Table
3.2 within the three-step planning framework presented earlier.

Table 3.2

Planning aids for three stages of concerns using selected items from the Teacher Concerns Checklist (Appendix A)

Stage	Concern	Generating an Approach	Recognizing the Value Assumptions	Altering or Extending the Approach
Self	Whether the students really like me	Construct a simple attitude instrument to measure your student's attitudes toward your organization, clarity, and fairness at the end of a major unit. Then try altering your instructional procedures in the areas in which you were rated the lowest until some improvement can be noted. If possible, compare your results with those of another student teacher using the same instrument.	You may want to value your own intuition. Keep in mind that some students will be chronic complainers while others are forever silent. Your own instincts may be the best guide to whether your students like you.	At times the most honest and helpful responses as to how well you are doing are acquired informally rather than from evaluation instruments. Choose a few students of high, average, and low ability and find out how you are doing by asking them the things they thought were the easiest to learn and why, and the things that were the most difficult to learn and why.
	Feeling under pressure too much of the time	Organize your planning time so that a specified amount of time is allotted for planning and organizing each major instructional activity you have responsibility for. Allot more time to your hardest subjects, less to your easiest. Then stick to your schedule.	Feeling under pressure is normal and may even make you perform better by forcing you to "rise to the occasion" when special demands are being placed upon you.	Rotate from lecturing, to question and answer, to assigning seatwork on alternate days or periods thereby reducing the type and amount of planning you must do each day.
	Doing well when a supervisor is present	Ask your supervisor if your first observation can be in a more informal instructional activity, such as tutoring, working with small groups, or cooperatively teaching with the classroom teacher.	Most supervisors are aware of your anxiety during your first few observations and take this into account in evaluating your performance.	Practice performing three specific instructional activities that are among the most often used in your classroom (e.g., probing, asking a higher-level question, using media to illustrate a point). Then use them at the time you are being observed.

Stage	Concern	Generating an Approach	Recognizing the Value Assumptions	Altering or Extending the Approach
Self	Clarifying the limits of my authority and responsibility	Ask your supervisor what is expected at your school, and then ask another teacher. Consider all of what both say as the limits of your authority and responsibility.	Often times the limits of behavior can only be defined as a result of trial and error. Increasing in *small degrees* your authority and responsibility over your instructional decisions until a problem is noted is one way to define these limits in concrete ways.	Observe in other classrooms and especially in the classrooms of other student teachers in your department or grade to gain a sense as to how much authority and responsibility is expected.
	Feeling more adequate as a teacher	Recall past microteaching experiences, exercises, or simulations in which you were judged adequate by external standards. Use your performance during these experiences as a baseline for your performance now. Devote time in your classroom to fine tuning these already acquired skills.	Few teachers, even those who are experienced, rarely feel completely adequate, regardless of outward signs to the contrary. The intensity and complexity of the teaching task separates it from most other occupations and often makes perfection unattainable.	Identify those areas in which you have signs you are less adequate than desired. Seek specific references and materials that address those areas and observe other teachers for their behavior in these areas. Then practice what you have learned in small-group settings.
	Being accepted and respected by professional persons	To become a meaningful part of your school, not just another student teacher, accept responsibilities beyond those you are specifically assigned. With the permission and cooperation of the classroom teacher, try innovative ideas even when they require extra or difficult planning. Include the classroom teacher in the planning of these	Student teachers and beginning teachers are, in general, accepted and respected less as a result of their newness and transient nature in the school than are older, more experienced teachers. *Complete* acceptance and respect results from the acquaintance of others with you over time, which may not be sufficient	Let your skills and personality be known outside of your classroom by becoming familiar with the members of the various organizations represented at your school, working voluntarily with other teachers who sponsor clubs and activities in which you have an interest, and attending sports functions that are important to your

Table 3.2, *continued*

Stage	Concern	Generating an Approach	Recognizing the Value Assumptions	Altering or Extending the Approach
Self		ideas from the very start.	during your student teaching experience.	students. The first step of being accepted and respected is being involved.
Task	The nature and quality of instructional materials	Catalogue the materials available to you along with the advantages and disadvantages of each. Specifically, note those for which the disadvantages outweigh the advantages and show this to the classroom teacher for possible alternatives.	Inadequate materials do not always translate into inadequate learning, and sometimes may be a result of personal preferences, not inadequate or poor design. How materials are used and what they are supplemented with often can reduce inadequacies.	Pair weak or inadequate materials with other more adequate resources which might compensate, in part, for their poor coverage, accuracy, or difficulty level.
	Maintaining the appropriate degree of class control	Establish specific classroom rules in all important areas, e.g., speaking out, leaving seats, leaving room, talking, neatness, etc. prior to your first teaching day. Hand out and/or display these rules prominently in your classroom.	The amount of class control that is desirable will change according to your objectives and instructional activities. While you must always be in control, there is a degree of control which can be chosen for a specific objective, such as when students are to explore and discover in small groups versus listening to you lecture.	Anticipate and carefully structure in advance those activities that may cause discipline problems, such as discussion sessions, question and answer periods, problem solving exercises—especially those requiring more student talk.
	Being fair and impartial	Establish your grading standards *before* grading tests and evaluating papers, and stick to it. If changes in your standards seem called for,	Concern with being fair and impartial can lead to too low a grading standard and over-reactions to student complaints. Your own intuition as to	After important tests and papers, ask students if they believe the grade they received accurately represented their knowledge and effort.

Stage	Concern	Generating an Approach	Recognizing the Value Assumptions	Altering or Extending the Approach
Task		make them starting on the *next* test or paper, not on the present test or exam.	your fairness and impartiality may be the best guide.	Use this information and your own judgment to decide if your grading standards or procedures need changing.
	Work with too many students each day	For large classes, vary your instructional procedures each day, e.g., from lectures one day to discussion or question and answer the next. For small groups and tutorials combine similar groups or individuals into a single group and employ peer teaching when possible.	Working with fewer actual students each day, that is, having a reduced class load, may not make instruction easier, since small classes often require more attention to individual needs and can represent a student mix that can be as difficult to teach as a larger class.	Identify those in your class who are most in need of special attention. Then, attend to the special learning needs of these individuals, giving special attention to others as time permits and allowing those who are capable to work independently when possible.
	Insufficient time for class preparation	Reserve the first 10 minutes of each class for a review of previous concepts and the last 10 minutes for a summary of what was just covered. This should reduce the amount of new planning you will have to do each day, while providing needed instruction and review.	Rarely is there a teacher who has sufficient time for preparation. The fact that teachers generally do not have sufficient time to prepare during the school day should encourage you to plan efficiently but not feel guilty for an instructional arrangement that can not always provide time for adequate preparation.	Use a variety of teaching techniques that make students more responsible for their own learning, such as question-and-answer groups, small-group discussion, research assignments, and seatwork employing exercises and self-instructional workbooks.
	Adequately presenting all of the material	Rearrange content in workbooks and texts so that conceptually similar content is taught at the same	This is an often-expressed concern of teachers both experienced and inexperienced. Having the	Individualize content coverage to the extent possible by providing self-instructional materials and teaching

Table 3.2, *continued*

Stage	Concern	Generating an Approach	Recognizing the Value Assumptions	Altering or Extending the Approach
Task		time. Emphasizing concepts more than facts will give your students the tools to learn whatever content was not covered on their own at a later time.	concern itself does not necessarily mean, however, that sufficient material will not be adequately presented. Much of the work of teaching involves making compromises in the use of teaching time and content covered. The nature of the compromise is more important than the fact that a compromise must be made.	activities at your students' current level of functioning. Temporary groups can be formed to avoid unnecessary or unproductive content coverage that may be too easy or too hard for some students.
	The wide diversity of student ethnic and socioeconomic backgrounds	Determine the range of ability in your classroom from standardized achievement scores recorded on school records. Note from these data if placement changes to higher or lower classes would be in the best interest of the student. Where such changes conform with school policies, refer appropriate students to a school counselor.	Diversity of ethnic and socioeconomic backgrounds does not necessarily imply that teaching and learning will be more difficult. These are outward signs that may or may not indicate diverse learning needs. Your experience with and the achievement of specific students must determine exactly how diverse the instructional needs are in your classroom.	Use task-related grouping based upon prior achievement, motivation, and individual strengths to create homogeneous subgroups to which specific materials and objectives can be directed.
	Increasing students' feeling of accomplishment	Use a flexible system of reward and feedback that adjusts your standards and expectations to the students' current level of functioning. In this manner gain or growth from a	Reward and reinforcement to be meaningful must actually be earned. Simply bestowing undeserved or unearned praise on a student may actually lessen a student's feeling of	Each week choose a few students from your class to congratulate on having done well by writing them a note on which you identify the work or deed being praised. Singling different students out in this

Stage	Concern	Generating an Approach	Recognizing the Value Assumptions	Altering or Extending the Approach
		baseline of each student's own behavior can be used as a source of praise and accomplishment in addition to how the student performs against an objective class standard.	accomplishment by drawing attention to the fact that something was said that was known to be untrue.	manner over time can often increase the feeling of accomplishment of your entire class.
Impact	Diagnosing student learning problems	Assign ample exercises and seatwork activities during the first few days and weeks of school in order to obtain a reasonable sample of your students' performance with respect to grade-level expectations. Large discrepancies should be brought to the attention of the school counselor. Smaller discrepancies can be your individualized agenda for working with these students the remainder of the year.	Diagnosing the learning problems of individual students may be beyond the scope and even expertise of most teachers. Although learning problems at the class level must be dealt with through your lesson planning, diagnosing the special learning needs of individual students may not be practical in the average classroom and such needs when severe may best be dealt with by bringing them to the attention of the counselor, special educators, or school administrators.	Choose students with the most severe learning problems and arrange a learning center where the students can go to obtain special reference material, media exercises, and peer tutoring geared to their special problems. Their work at the center can also be used to further diagnose their learning problem.
	Challenging unmotivated students	At the beginning of the year, record each student's personal interests and unique experiences. Where possible, select materials and assignments for poorly motivated students that match	Some students may remain unmotivated regardless of what is done to accommodate their interests in the classroom. For these students the reasons for their lack of motivation may lie outside	Choose learning materials for unmotivated students that are visually oriented and concrete in nature. Allow them more flexibility to substitute these materials for regular school curricula.

Table 3.2, *continued*

Stage	Concern	Generating an Approach	Recognizing the Value Assumptions	Altering or Extending the Approach
Impact		their interests and experiences.	your classroom and out of your control.	
	Whether students apply what they learn	At the end of each major unit of instruction include a real-world problem-solving exercise whose solution calls for the practical application of some of the concepts you have taught.	Oftentimes being able to successfully apply what one "knows" requires extensive interactions with problems in the real world. While school must help prepare individuals for the real world, being able to actually apply school concepts with efficiency and proficiency must, in part, be the result of experience in other classrooms, with other teachers, and in the community and home.	Assign action research projects, experiments, demonstrations, and fieldwork to help relate classroom learning to the types of problem-solving contexts in which this learning will be most likely used.
	Slow progress of certain students	When slow progress persists, test to see if remediation is indicated and, if so, assign remedial work in place of regular school assignments until some progress is made.	Slow progress is a fact of life for some students, calling for patience and understanding from the teacher. Slow progress, if it persists, may require adjusting standards for a particular student.	Examine the alternative modes of instruction that may exist in your school, such as more basic coursework and materials, remedial programs, or federally-funded districtwide programs that provide special instruction or materials for less-able learners. Use these when learner needs match program objectives.
	Helping students to value learning	Relate learning to real-world accomplishments wherever possible, indicating the cause and effect relationship between	To value is to have a deep and unwavering belief in something. Such a belief comes from many different experiences over	Incorporate into your planning ways in which learning can be made fun, exciting, or unusual. Instructional games, simulations,

Stage	Concern	Generating an Approach	Recognizing the Value Assumptions	Altering or Extending the Approach
Impact		them. Use examples that support the fact that knowledge is "power" by indicating the knowledge of individuals that preceded and made possible modern-day inventions, discoveries, and personal successes.	years of someone's life. School is only one context in which the value of learning can and should be taught. Others are the home, workplace, and community.	and cooperative grouping can encourage students to value learning for its own sake if they are planned in ways that lead to discoveries within oneself and a greater understanding of self.
	Recognizing the social and emotional needs of students	Follow up unusual expressions of need or distress through observation and direct student contact to determine if a social or emotional need is being expressed that hinders the learning process.	Practically all students have social and emotional needs, only some of which will be debilitating to the learning process. Although social and emotional needs are important to recognize seldom can they be sufficiently met solely in the instructional context of the classroom.	A warm and nurturing attitude toward your students can reduce some of their most important emotional needs by providing a climate of acceptance, security, and understanding in which learning can occur unhampered by personal embarrassment and competition.

>>> A FINAL WORD <<<

This chapter has made a distinction between the process of planning and that of writing a lesson plan. A written lesson plan, which we will discuss in Chapter 5, would be sterile and ineffective if not preceded by a consideration of goals, learning needs, content, and teaching methods and revised from time to time by your tacit knowledge acquired from observation and experience. This chapter has described these inputs to the planning process and how they can be used in preparing to write lesson plans.

The next chapter presents one other useful tool on our way to developing lesson plans—*lesson objectives.* Objectives are an important link between the planning concepts discussed in this chapter and the preparation of lesson plans (Chapter 5). Recall that goals are useful inputs for guiding the planning process, but goals do not indicate how to carry out a course of action or what to measure to determine if the action chosen was effective in meeting learner needs. This is the unique role of objectives, which identify the specific behaviors to be learned, the conditions under which the behaviors are to be achieved, and the level of proficiency at which the behaviors are to be performed.

Summing Up

This chapter introduced aims and goals, recent educational reform, the planning process and its inputs, how to handle bias, and the three concerns of self, task, and students. The main points were as follows:

1. The words *aims, goals,* and *objectives* often are used interchangeably but have different meanings.

2. Aims are expressions of societal values that are broad enough to be acceptable to large numbers of individuals.

3. Goals bring aims down to earth by connecting them to some tangible aspect of the school curriculum.

4. Objectives are more specific than goals; they describe the specific behavior a learner is to attain, the conditions under which the behavior must be demonstrated, and the proficiency level at which the behavior is to be performed.

5. Aims are translated into goals and goals into objectives by a process of funneling or narrowing.

6. Student needs and interests can expand or enhance societal aims and establish a curriculum sensitive to particular learners.

7. With the publication of five specially commissioned reports, American education began a period of reform that called for the following:

- Strengthening of the curriculum in math, science, English, foreign language, and social studies.
- Renewed effort to teach higher-order thinking skills.
- Raising school grading standards.
- Raising college admission standards.
- More work in the core subjects, especially math and foreign language.

8. Planning is the process of deciding what and how teachers want their students to learn. The preparation of lesson plans, often confused with the planning process, is the *result* of this process.

9. The process of planning structures and prioritizes behavior so that only the most effective teaching behaviors are employed for attaining a given objective, providing maximum instruction in minimum time.

10. The following are the five primary inputs to the planning process:

- Aims and goals
- Learner characteristics and individual differences
- Knowledge of academic discipline and grade-level content
- Knowledge of teaching methods
- Tacit knowledge acquired from day-to-day experience in the classroom

11. Knowledge of aims and goals is reflected by national and state policies and legislation, school curriculum guides, and adopted texts.

12. Knowledge of learner characteristics and individual differences is reflected by student aptitude and achievement data; student anxiety, motivation, and self-concept levels; home life indicators; and peer-group influences.

13. Knowledge of academic discipline and grade-level content is reflected by a knowledge of content and its organization.

14. Knowledge of teaching methods is reflected by the key and helping behaviors for effective teaching, teaching strategies that encompass these behaviors, classroom management techniques, and use and selection of instructional media and materials.

15. Tacit knowledge is knowledge derived from feedback received from learners about the success of your instruction. Tacit knowledge is useful in the planning process for revising teaching practices and making the planning process less rigid.

16. To be effective, the planning process must generate and distinguish among alternative courses of action, recognize the values

implied by each course of action, and revise the alternative courses of action as needed.

17. Generating and distinguishing among alternative courses of action means identifying the different goals, learners, content organization, and teaching methods that may be relevant to the classroom.

18. Recognizing the values implied by each course of action means examining various goal–learning need–organization–method matches for their practicality and conflict with school and community priorities.

19. Revising the alternatives chosen means altering the goal–learning need–organization–method match based on feedback about its effectiveness in the classroom.

20. Almost every teacher shows some type of bias in interacting with students. Bias may be avoided by

- Consciously spreading interactions across categories of students toward whom you have identified bias
- Randomly selecting students for special assignments
- Covertly pairing students who are opposite in your category of bias and then interacting with both members of the pair
- Coding class notes to remind yourself to call on students toward whom you may be biased

21. Most teachers express concerns related to self (e.g., Do students like me?), related to the teaching task (Is my coverage of content adequate?), and related to their impact on students (Are the students learning?). The three concerns of self, task, and student appear to be natural stages through which most teachers pass (and occasionally revisit), representing a developmental pattern extending over months and even years of a teacher's career.

*1. Distinguish aims from goals by placing an *a* to the left of each aim and a *g* to the left of each goal.

a To be able to live in a technological world *vary PC–*

g To know how to add, subtract, multiply, and divide

a To appreciate the arts, both nationally and internationally

g To know the historical reasons for World War II

a To work together cooperatively

To know parliamentary procedure

a To be able to read a popular magazine

g To experience literature from around the world

To understand the rudiments of health and hygiene

g To know how to swing a tennis racket

2. Select one of the aims identified in the previous question, (1) translate it into a goal, and (2) translate that goal into an objective. Make sure your objective is responsive to the aim from which it was derived.

3. In your own words, indicate some of the differences you see among aims, goals, and objectives. How are they the same?

4. Give an example of a student need or interest that might be used to expand or enhance curriculum goals in communities having these characteristics:

a. The average standardized grade equivalent reading achievement in the fourth grade is 2.7.

b. The average IQ is 117.

c. The dropout rate in high school last year was 42%.

d. One out of 10 adults in the surrounding community is believed to have received treatment for substance abuse in the past year.

e. The teen suicide rate is among the highest in the state.

f. The school sits within a stone's throw of the world's top three computer manufacturers.

g. Many students who want to go to the state college cannot get in because their SAT math scores are too low.

*5. Name five recommendations for the reform of American education shared by most of the national policy reports.

*6. If you had to sum up in a single phrase the most general and agreed-upon problem with our schools as seen by the authors of policy reports, what would it be?

7. Identify five changes that you now see being implemented in our schools as a result of the national policy reports and of local and state efforts to reform school curricula. Which, if any, do you *not* agree with, and why?

8. In your own words, how would you convince another teacher (who disagrees with you) that lesson plans are the *result* of the planning process, and are not the process itself? What improvements in the other teacher's performance might result from seeing the planning process as different from plan making (preparing lesson plans)?

*9. What are the five inputs to the planning process? Where can you get information about each?

10. If tacit, or personal, knowledge is known only through experience and cannot be found in the pages of a textbook or in a college lecture, what are examples of tacitly acquired knowledge that you might have at the end of your first full day of teaching?

11. For a particular lesson at your grade level or in your content area, construct a list of alternative goals, learning needs, ways of organizing the content, and teaching methods. Choose one alternative from each category to create a goal–learning need–organization–method match that you feel should be of highest priority in your classroom or that you would most like to teach. Now construct another match of highest priority (which may use some of the same alternatives). Construct a third match, if possible.

12. Consider the two or three matches you constructed for the previous question. What educational values did you assume were important when choosing your highest priority match? What educational values did you assume were important when choosing your next-highest priority match?

*13. Gage and Berliner (1988) identify a number of ways in which your interactions with students can be biased. Name four and then add one of your own that is not mentioned by Gage and Berliner.

*14. Identify four procedures for reducing or eliminating the biases you may have when interacting with your students.

*15. Name Fuller's three stages of concern and give an original example of a concern *you* have in each of the three areas.

16. Complete the Teacher Concerns Checklist in Appendix A according to the instructions provided. After completing the checklist, calculate your average score within each of the three categories using the key provided to determine the relative intensity of your concerns in each of these three areas. How does your score in each of the three areas compare with the average of the class?

*17. Teachers A, B, C, and D have the following profile of scores on the Teacher Concerns Checklist.

	Self	*Task*	*Impact*
Teacher A	low	medium	high
Teacher B	high	medium	low
Teacher C	low	medium	high
Teacher D	high	low	high

One teacher has been teaching for 4 months, another has taught the same subject in the same school for 8 years, another has taught in the same school for 11 years but just recently has been assigned to teach a subject he never taught before, and the fourth teacher has taught in the same school for 6 years but recently was declared "surplus" and reassigned to the same subject in an inner city vocational school. Which teacher most likely would have which profile, according to Fuller's concerns theory?

18. Using ideas from Fuller's concerns theory, how might you rearrange the course you are now taking? How might you extend your ideas to the design of a new undergraduate teacher training curriculum?

---

* Answers to asterisked questions (*) in this and the other chapters are in Appendix B.

Suggested Readings

Borich, G. (1993). *Clearly outstanding: Making each day count in your classroom.* Boston: Allyn & Bacon.

A self-improvement guide for how to be effective during your first year of teaching. This book traces the career development of three teachers through the stages of self, task, and impact.

Kennedy, M. (Ed.). (1991). *Teaching academic subjects to diverse learners.* New York: Teachers College Press.

This book contains chapters by subject area specialists in the areas of science and mathematics. The various authors discuss effective teaching methods specific to these disciplines. They also address the challenges that classes of diverse learners present to teachers.

Livingston, C., & Borko, H. (1989). Expert-novice differences in teaching: A cognitive analysis and implications for teacher education. *Journal of Teacher Education, 40,* July-August, 36–42.

The authors describe an investigation of the thoughts and actions of a small number of expert and novice teachers. The article presents differences between teacher planning from two perspectives—planning as a cognitive skill and planning as improvisation.

McCutcheon, G. (1980). How do elementary school teachers plan? The nature of planning and influences on it. *Elementary School Journal, 81,* 4–23.

An informative guide for elementary teachers on how to plan and what forces influence the planning process.

Moore, K. (1989). *Classroom teaching skills.* New York: Random House.

The author describes the skills needed to select and properly select instructional goals and plan for their implementation in the classroom.

Pasch, M., Sparks-Langer, G., Gardner, T. G., Starko, A. J., & Moody, C. D. (1991).

Teaching as decision-making: Instructional practices for the classroom teacher. New York: Longman.

This text contains numerous practical exercises to help teachers with instructional planning. It emphasizes the day-to-day decisions teachers must make when choosing goals, objectives, and strategies for learners.

Shavelson, R. (1987). Planning. In M. J. Dunkin (Ed.). *International encyclopedia of teaching and teacher education.* New York: Pergamon.

An overview of teacher planning and its relationship to effective teaching.

CHAPTER 4

Instructional Objectives

This chapter will help you answer the following questions:

1. Why do I need behavioral objectives?
2. How will I know if a behavior is observable?
3. What are the steps in writing a behavioral objective?
4. Is there a type of objective that allows for flexibility in the range of acceptable responses?
5. What is an authentic behavior?
6. How is a performance test different from a paper and pencil test?
7. What types of cognitive behaviors will I want to teach in my classroom?
8. What types of affective behaviors will I want to teach in my classroom?
9. What types of psychomotor behaviors will I want to teach in my classroom?
10. How can I be sure that I teach behaviors at all levels of behavioral complexity?

This chapter will also help you learn the meaning of the following:

▶ affective behavior
authentic behavior
behavioral objective
cognitive behavior
expressive objective
learning activity
learning condition
learning outcome
performance tests
proficiency level
psychomotor behavior

I n Chapter 3 we noted the purpose of having aims and goals: They provide a direction for curriculum development, state and national mandates, and local school district policies. However, aims and goals have weaknesses. They are not necessarily tied to a specific curriculum, they do not suggest strategies for attaining a particular result, and they do not provide a means for knowing when that result has been achieved. In this chapter you will learn how the classroom teacher plays an active role in translating aims and goals into specific classroom strategies and outcomes.

>>> THE PURPOSE OF OBJECTIVES <<<

Why do I need behavioral objectives?

Objectives have two practical purposes. The first is to tie general aims and goals to specific classroom strategies that will achieve those aims and goals. The second is to express teaching strategies in a format that allows you to measure their effects on learners. A written statement that achieves these purposes is called a **behavioral objective**.

— tie gen. aims/goals to classroom
— express teaching strategies

What Does *Behavioral* Mean?

Observable change in

How will I know if a behavior is observable?

When the word *behavioral* precedes the word *objective*, the learning is being defined as a change in *observable* behavior. Therefore, the writing of behavioral objectives requires that the behavior being addressed be observable and measurable (with a test, attitude survey, checklist, etc). Covert or mentalistic activities occurring in the seclusion of your learners' minds are not observable and thus cannot be the focus of a behavioral objective. Unobserved activities, such as the creation of mental images or rehearsing a response subvocally, can precede learning, but they *cannot constitute evidence that learning has occurred*, because they cannot be directly observed.

3 components your behavioral obj.
① specific

If ever you are unsure whether something is a "behavior," put it to the "Hey, Dad, watch-me-test." For example, "Hey, Dad, watch me draw a parallelogram (or recite the multiplication tables)," would pass the test, since Dad can see or hear you do it through his own eyes or ears. But, try "Hey, Dad, watch me feel (or think or have a belief)." These expressions fail the test, since they do not describe behaviors that can be observed directly.

Further, the behavior of your learners must be observable over a period of time during which specifiable content, teaching strategies, and instructional media (e.g., films, homework exercises, texts) have been used. This effectively limits a behavioral objective to a time frame consistent with the logical divisions in school curricula, such as lessons, chapters, units, and grading periods. Feedback from behavioral objectives (e.g., tests, work samples, and student observation) provides data for monitoring the consequence of your instructional strategy and for revising the goal–learning need–organization–method match.

Where Did the Notion of Objectives Come From?

Historically, the idea of an educational objective can be traced to the early part of the century when Tyler (1934) first conceived of the need for goal-directed statements for teachers. He observed that teachers were concerned far more with the content of instruction (what to teach) than with what the student should be able to do with the content (i.e., whether it could be applied in some meaningful context).

Tyler also noticed implicitly what Fuller later conceptualized (1969) as the stages of concern through which teachers move, starting with concerns for self (Can I make it through the day?), to concerns for task (What will I teach next?), and finally to concerns for students (Are they learning what I teach?). Recall from Chapter 3 Fuller's observation that beginning teachers, particularly those in their first weeks and months of teaching, are preoccupied with concerns for self, sometimes to the exclusion of concerns for their impact on students. In research reported by Clark and Peterson (1986), the average teacher planning time devoted to goals and objectives in four separate studies ranged from only 2.7 percent to 13.9 percent. These short times indicate that in some classrooms relatively little of a teacher's time may be focused on student outcomes.

To help teachers shift from self-concerns to a concern for their impact on students, Tyler developed the idea of behavioral objectives. In this chapter you will see how behavioral objectives can help you better plan and prepare lessons and focus your attention on what and how well your students are learning. Aside from the role of objectives in directing instructional decisions during lesson planning, they may be the single best way of shifting from an exclusive concern for self or the teaching task to a concern for your impact on students. Objectives will therefore be an important tool for reaching your highest and most mature level of professional performance.

>>> AN OVERVIEW OF BEHAVIORAL OBJECTIVES <<<

The goal of this chapter is to show you how to prepare useful objectives as painlessly as possible. Simply put, writing behavioral objectives involves three steps:

[handwritten: Know]

- Identify a specific goal that has an observable outcome (a learning outcome).
- State the conditions under which learning can be expected to occur (e.g., with what materials, texts, and facilities and in what period of time).
- Specify the criterion level—the amount of behavior that can be expected from the instruction under the specified conditions.

Before considering the actual written form of behavioral objectives, let's look at these three steps in more detail.

Specifying the Learning Outcomes

What are the steps in writing a behavioral objective?

The first step in writing a behavioral objective is to identify an observable **learning outcome.** Recall that for an objective to be behavioral, it must be observable. It also must be measurable so you can determine whether the behavior is present, partially present, or absent. The key to identifying an observable outcome is your choice of words to describe it.

[handwritten: Choosing words Carefully.]

Word choice in writing behavioral objectives is important because the same word may have different meanings, depending on who is reading or hearing it. The endless puns heard in our culture are humorous illustrations of this: Does "well-rounded person" mean broadly educated or well fed? Another illustration is the way that foreign visitors sometimes use words literally without awareness of subtle connotations. Words can express a concept not only accurately or inaccurately, but also specifically or vaguely. It is vague usage that gives us the most trouble in writing behavioral objectives.

In a behavioral objective, learning outcomes must be expressed directly, concretely, and observably, unlike the way behaviors usually are described in the popular press, television, and even some textbooks. If you took these everyday sources as a guide for writing the behavioral expressions needed in the classroom, you would quickly find that they could not be easily observed, and probably could not be measured, either. For example, we often hear these expressions as desirable goals:

mentally healthy citizens

well-rounded individuals

self-actualized schoolchildren

informed adults

literate populace

But, what do *mentally healthy, well-rounded, self-actualized, informed,* and *literate* actually mean? If you asked a large number of individuals to define these terms, you would receive quite an assortment of responses. These diverse responses would have widely divergent implications for how to achieve each desired behavior and for observing its attainment. The reason, of course, is that the words are vague and open to many interpretations. Imagine the confusion such vagueness could cause in your classroom if your objective for the first grading period were simply to make the class *informed* about the content or to make them *high achievers.* Johnny's parents would have one interpretation of "informed," and Betty's parents would have quite another. One hopes they both don't show up on parent-teacher night! Also, you might mean one thing by *high achievers,* but your principal might mean another.

The point is that vague behavioral language quickly becomes a problem for those who are held accountable for bringing about the behavior in question. Those who use vague language in everyday conversation, unlike teachers, are seldom accountable for teaching individuals to perform the behaviors they describe. Needless to say, school boards, school administrators, parents, and taxpayers may and often do call to account those who use vague or general language to describe the outcomes for which they are responsible. You can avoid this problem by writing behavioral outcomes in precise language that makes observation and measurement specific and noncontroversial. You can do so by exchanging such popular but vague expressions as *mentally healthy, well-rounded, self-actualized, informed,* and *literate* with expressions that show specifically what the individual must do to show mental health, well-roundedness, self-actualization, and so on.

One way to make your outcomes specific and noncontroversial is to choose behavioral expressions from a list of action verbs that have widely accepted meanings. These action verbs also allow easy identification of the operations necessary for displaying the behavior. For example, instead of expecting students to be informed or literate in a subject, expect them to

differentiate between . . .

identify outcomes of . . .

solve a problem in . . .

compare and contrast . . .

These action verbs describe what being *informed* or *literate* means by stating specific, observable behaviors that the learner must perform. Although we have not yet indicated how well the learner must be able to perform these behaviors, we are now closer to the type of evidence that can be used to determine whether these objectives have been achieved.

Although a behavioral objective should include an action verb that specifies a learning outcome, not all action verbs are suitable for specifying learning outcomes. Some are better suited to specifying **learning activities.** Unfortunately, learning outcomes often are confused with learning activities. For example, which of the following examples represent learning *outcomes* and which represent learning *activities*?

1. The child will <u>identify</u> pictures of words that sound alike.
2. The child will <u>demonstrate</u> an appreciation of poetry.
3. The student will <u>subtract</u> one-digit numbers.
4. The student will <u>show</u> a knowledge of punctuation.
5. The student will <u>practice</u> the multiplication tables.
6. The student will <u>sing</u> the "Star-Spangled Banner."

In the first four objectives, the action words *identify, demonstrate, subtract,* and *show* all point to outcomes—end products of instructional units. However, the action word in the fifth example, *practice,* is only a learning activity; it is not an end in itself and only can work toward a learning outcome. The sixth objective is more ambiguous. Is *sing* an outcome or an activity? It is hard to say without more information. If the goal is to have a stage-frightened student sing in public, then it is a learning outcome. However, if singing is only practice for a later performance, it is a learning activity. Learning activities are important, but only in relation to the specific learning outcomes, or end products, they are attempting to achieve. Without a learning outcome clearly in mind, there would be no way to determine the value of a learning activity for promoting desirable student outcomes.

The following examples differentiate between verbs used for learning outcomes and verbs used for learning activities:

Learning Outcomes (Ends)	*Learning Activities (Means)*
identify	study
recall	watch
list	listen
write	read

Behavioral objectives must include the end product, because you will use this end product in choosing your instructional procedures and evaluating whether you have achieved the desired result.

Identifying the Conditions — *asking what are tools used for certain activities*

The second step in writing a behavioral objective is to identify the specific **conditions** under which learning will occur. If the observable learning outcome can be achieved only through use of particular materials, equipment, tools, or other resources, state these conditions in the objective. Here are some examples of objectives that state conditions:

- Using examples from short stories by John Steinbeck and Mark Twain, differentiate between naturalism and realism in American literature.
- Using the map of strategic resources handed out in class, identify the economic conditions in the South resulting from the Civil War.
- Using an electronic calculator, solve problems involving the addition of two-digit signed numbers.
- Using pictures of fourteenth-to-eighteenth-century Gothic and Baroque European cathedrals, compare and contrast the styles of architecture.

If the conditions are obvious, they need not be specified. For example, it is not necessary to specify, "Using a writing instrument and paper, write a short story." On the other hand, when conditions can focus learning in specific ways, eliminating some areas of study and including others, the statement of conditions can be critical to attaining the objective and you should include it. For example, imagine that a student will be tested on the behavior indicated in the first objective in the preceding list, but without the condition indicated. Differentiating naturalism from realism without reference to concrete examples in the writings of specific authors who represent these styles is likely to produce a more general, less structured response. If students are told the conditions, they can focus their studying on the precise behavior called for (for example, applying learned distinctions to specific examples, as opposed to, say, memorizing a list of definitions).

Note also that without a statement of conditions to focus your instruction, your students may assume conditions different than you intend. In the absence of concrete examples, some students might prepare by studying the philosophical differences between the two styles of writing; others might focus on being able to apply their knowledge to examples in the literature. And, because objectives form the basis for tests, your tests might be more fair to some students than others, depending on the assumptions they make in the absence of stated conditions.

Notice in the other examples above that learning can take on different meanings, depending on whether students study and practice with or without the use of a map, electronic calculator, or pictures of fourteenth-to-eighteenth century cathedrals. Teaching and learning become more structured and resources more organized when conditions are stated as part of your objectives. And, as we have seen, objectives that specify conditions of learning lead to tests that are fairer.

Conditional statements within a behavioral objective can be singular or multiple. It is possible, and sometimes necessary, to have two or even three conditional statements in an objective to focus the learning. Although too many conditions attached to an objective can narrow learning to irrelevant details, multiple conditions often are important adjuncts to improving the clarity of the behavior desired and the organization and preparation of instructional resources. Here are examples of multiple conditions, indicated by italics:

- Using a centigrade *thermometer,* measure the temperature of two liters of *water* at a depth of 25 centimeters.
- Using a *compass, ruler,* and *protractor,* draw three conic sections of different sizes and three triangles of different types.
- Using four grams of *sodium carbonate* and four grams of *sodium bicarbonate,* indicate their different reactions in H_2O.
- *Within 15 minutes* and using the *reference books* provided, find the formulae for wattage, voltage, amperage, and resistance.
- Using a *microcomputer* with word processing capability, correct the spelling and punctuation errors on a *two-page manuscript* in 20 minutes or less.

It is important not to add so many conditions that learning is reduced to trivial detail. It is also important to choose conditions that are realistic—that represent real-life circumstances your learners are likely to find in as well as out of the classroom. The idea behind stating conditions, especially multiple conditions, is not to complicate the behavior but rather to make it more natural and *close to the conditions under which the behavior will have to be performed in the real world* and in subsequent instruction. Always check the conditions specified to see if they are those under which the behavior is *most likely to be performed outside the classroom or in subsequent instruction.*

Stating Criterion Levels — *states level of performance to meet an obj.*

The third step in writing a behavioral objective is to state the level of performance required to meet the objective. Recall that one of the most important reasons for translating goals into objectives is to provide some way of determining whether the behavior implied by the goal has been attained. Part of this purpose is accomplished by being specific about the behavior desired (e.g., "differentiate between" instead of "inform," and "identify outcomes of" rather than "educate"). Another part is accomplished by stating the conditions under which learning is expected to occur. Specifying the outcome and conditions reveals the procedures necessary for the behavior to be observed.

However, one important element is missing. You also must specify *how much* of the behavior is required for you to consider the objective to be attained. This element of objective writing is the *criterion level.* It is the level or degree of performance desired or the **level of proficiency** that will satisfy you that the objective has been met.

Setting criterion levels is one of the most misunderstood aspects of objective writing. At the root of this misunderstanding is failure to recognize that criterion or proficiency levels are value judgments as to what performance level is required for adequately performing the behavior in some later setting. The mistaken assumption is often made that a single "correct" level of proficiency exists and that once established it must forever remain in its original form. At first, criterion levels should be taken as educated guesses. They should indicate the approximate degree of proficiency needed to adequately perform the behavior in the next grade, another instructional setting, or the world outside the classroom. They should be adjusted periodically upward or downward to conform with how well your students are able to perform the behavior. This means that you should observe in other contexts your students use of the skills and behaviors you teach.

Often, criterion levels are set to establish a benchmark for testing whether an objective has been met, without recognizing that this level may not be relevant to subsequent learning tasks or instructional settings. To avoid this, always consider criterion levels to be adjustable and dependent on your evaluation of how well students can adequately use the behavior *at subsequent times* and *in contexts beyond your classroom.*

Criterion levels come in many sizes and shapes. For example, they can be stated in the following ways:

Number of items correct on a test

Number of consecutive items correct (or consecutive errorless performances)

Essential features included (as in an essay question or paper)

Completion within a prescribed time limit (where speed of performance is important)

Completion with a certain degree of accuracy

Recall the objective, "Using short stories by John Steinbeck and Mark Twain, differentiate between naturalism and realism in American literature." Is a criterion stated? Remember, a criterion level establishes the degree of behavior required for the objective to be met, the minimum level of proficiency that must be exhibited. How would the teacher know if a student's written response to this objective has demonstrated a minimum level of differentiation? With only the information given, it would be difficult and arbitrary, because no criterion level is stated. Now, let's add a criterion to this objective:

- Using short stories by John Steinbeck and Mark Twain, differentiate between naturalism and realism by selecting four passages from each author that illustrate differences in these writing styles.

Is there a type of objective that allows for flexibility in the range of acceptable responses?

Now there is a basis for evaluating the objective. This particular criterion level requires considerable skill in applying learned information in different contexts and allows for flexibility in the range of responses that are acceptable. This type of objective is sometimes called an **expressive objective** (Eisner, 1969) because it allows for a variety of correct responses or for the student to express himself or herself in a variety of forms for which there is no single correct answer. The amount of expressiveness in a response allowed by an objective is always a matter of degree. In other words, objectives can have more—or less—rigid criterion levels.

Consider another example:

- Using an electronic calculator, the student will solve problems involving the addition of two-digit signed numbers.

no single correct answer

Is there a stated criterion level for this objective? No. There is no unambiguous basis for deciding whether Mary met the objective and Bobby did not. Now, add a criterion level:

- Using an electronic calculator, the student will correctly solve 8 out of 10 problems involving the addition of two-digit signed numbers.

This objective now precisely identifies the minimum proficiency that must be observed to conclude that the desired behavior has been attained. Unlike the first objective, little flexibility is allowed in the required response (except that more than 8 out of 10 could be solved correctly). Notice that far less expression is possible in answering a question about mathematics than about literature; the former is more highly structured and more rigid in terms of possible responses. Notice also that this more structured approach to an acceptable response fits well with the nature of this particular objective, while the less structured approach fits well with the previous objective (differentiating between naturalism and realism).

Both of these objectives illustrate that the expressiveness of an objective is established by how you set an acceptable criterion. Also, the level of expressiveness that fits best often is a function of the objective itself—how many correct answers are possible. Different types of criterion behaviors will be discussed shortly, but for now keep in mind that you must establish the degree of expressiveness allowed, and that a proficiency level is alterable at any time. These two considerations—level of proficiency and expressiveness—are under your control. Continually reevaluate them and adjust them as you gain experience with the level and quality of your students' responses.

Here are some of the earlier objectives with criterion levels added in brackets (or italicized where a criterion already was included):

- Using a centigrade thermometer, measure the temperature of two liters of water at a depth of 25 centimeters [to within one degree accuracy].
- Using a compass, ruler, and protractor, draw *three* conic sections of *different sizes* and *three* triangles of *different types.*
- Using four grams of sodium carbonate and four grams of sodium bicarbonate, indicate their different reactions with H_2O [by testing the alkalinity of the H_2O and reporting results in parts per million (PPM)].

One essential ingredient of a well-written objective is that it identifies the proficiency level that must be displayed for the desired behavior to be achieved. Objectives can have either more rigid or less rigid levels of proficiency, the latter allowing for more flexibility in the response of the student.

- Within 15 minutes and using the reference books provided, find [and write correctly] the formulae for wattage, voltage, amperage, and resistance.
- Using a microcomputer with word processing capability, correct the spelling and punctuation errors for a two-page manuscript in *20 minutes* [with 100% accuracy].

These examples illustrate well-written behavioral objectives.

You have seen how to specify learning outcomes, state conditions for learning, and establish criterion levels. These are the three most important ingredients of well-written behavioral objectives. But, there is one more point to know about preparing objectives: Keep them simple.

Keeping Objectives Simple

Teachers often make the mistake of being too sophisticated in measuring learning outcomes. As a result, they resort to indirect or unnecessarily complex methods of measurement. If you want to know whether Johnny can write his name, ask him to write his name—but not while blindfolded! Resist the temptation to be tricky. Consider these examples:

- The student will show his or her ability to recall characters of the book *Tom Sawyer* by painting a picture of each.
- Discriminate between a telephone and television by drawing an electrical diagram of each.
- Demonstrate that you understand how to use an encyclopedia index by listing the page on which a given subject can be found in the *Encyclopedia Britannica.*

In the first example, painting a picture surely would allow you to determine whether the students can recall the characters in *Tom Sawyer,* but is there an easier (and less time consuming) way to measure recall? How about asking the students simply to list the characters? If the objective is to determine recall, listing is sufficient. For the second example, how about presenting students with two illustrations, one of a telephone, the other of a television, and simply ask them to tell (verbally or in writing) which is which?

The third example is on target. The task required is a simple and efficient way of measuring whether someone can use an encyclopedia index.

In this chapter you will begin writing objectives on your own. Be sure to include these three components in every objective you write: (1) observable learning outcome, (2) conditions, and (3) criterion level. Once you have written a behavioral objective, always analyze it to make sure that you have included these three essential components. Return to the examples given if you need help.

>>> THE COGNITIVE, AFFECTIVE, AND <<< PSYCHOMOTOR DOMAINS

You might have noticed that some of the example objectives shown earlier in this chapter have illustrated very different types of behavior. For example, compare the behaviors called for in these objectives:

- Using short stories by John Steinbeck and Mark Twain, differentiate between naturalism and realism by selecting four passages from each author that illustrate differences in these writing styles.
- Using a centigrade thermometer, measure the temperature of two liters of water at a depth of 25 centimeters to within one degree accuracy.

Common sense tells us that the behaviors called for require different patterns of preparation and study to attain. In the former objective, study and practice would focus on analysis—identifying the key aspects of naturalism and realism and explaining relationships between them, noting their similarities and differences and the application of these ideas to actual examples of the writings of a naturalist and a realist. Contrast this complicated process with how one might study to acquire the behavior in the second objective. Here the study and practice might consist simply of learning to accurately perceive distances between the markings on a centigrade scale. Such practice might be limited to training one's eyes to count spaces between the gradations and then assigning the appropriate number to represent temperature in degrees centigrade.

Note also the difference in study and preparation time required to achieve these two different objectives: the second could be learned in minutes, but the other might take hours, days, or even weeks. These different objectives represent only two examples of the variety of behavioral outcomes possible in your classroom.

Objectives can require vastly different levels not only of cognitive complexity but of affective and psychomotor complexity as well. The following section introduces behaviors at different levels of complexity for which behavioral objectives can be prepared. For convenience, these are organized into **cognitive behaviors** (development of intellectual abilities and skills), **affective behaviors** (development of attitudes, beliefs, and values), and **psychomotor behaviors** (coordination of physical movements and bodily performances). Let's look at each of these behavioral domains.

The Cognitive Domain

Bloom, Englehart, Hill, Furst, and Krathwohl (1984) devised a method for categorizing objectives according to cognitive complexity. They delineate six levels of cognitive complexity, ranging from the knowledge level (least complex) to the evaluation level (most complex). As illustrated in Figure 4.1, they presume the levels to be hierarchical—higher-level objectives are assumed to include, and to be dependent on, lower-level cognitive skills. Thus, objectives at the evaluation level are presumed to require more complex mental operations—higher cognitive skills—than objectives at the knowledge level.

Also, notice that higher-level objectives are "more authentic" than lower level objectives. In Chapter 15 we will discuss how to measure your objectives authentically using performance assessments of learning, but, for now, let's consider what *authenticity* means.

What is an authentic behavior?

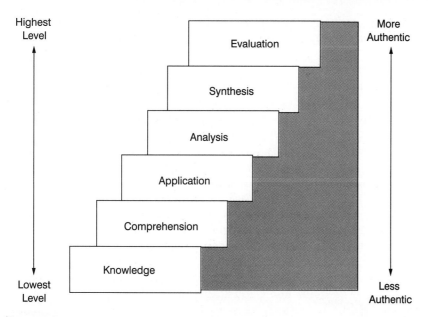

Figure 4.1
Taxonomy of educational objectives: Cognitive domain

So far in this chapter you have seen a variety of skills and behaviors that children learn in school. Some of these require learners to acquire information by memorizing, for example, vocabulary, multiplication tables, dates of historical events, or the names of important persons. Other skills and behaviors involve learning action sequences or procedures to follow when, for example, using drawing materials, performing mathematical computations, operating a calculator, or practicing handwriting. In addition, you saw some example objectives in which students had to acquire concepts, rules, and generalizations that allowed them to understand what they read, to analyze, and to write an essay.

Some of these skills are best assessed with paper and pencil tests, as we will see in Chapter 14. But, other skills—particularly those requiring independent judgment, critical thinking, and decision making—are best assessed with performance assessments. **Performance tests** measure a skill or behavior as it is used in the world outside your classroom.

Classroom assessment of learning, particularly beyond the early elementary grades, has been almost exclusively based on paper and pencil tests, which *indicate* rather than directly measure what children have learned (Gullickson & Ellwein, 1985). For example, you

How is a performance test different from a paper and pencil test?

may measure an understanding of the scientific method, not by having learners plan, conduct, and evaluate an experiment (a direct measure), but by asking them to list the steps in conducting an experiment, write about the difference between an hypothesis and a theory, or choose the correct definition of a control group from a list of choices (all indirect assessment). Or, you may measure children's understanding of money, not by observing them buy food, paying for it, and getting the correct change (direct assessment), but by asking them to recall how many pennies there are in a dollar, or writing down how much change they would get back from a 10-dollar bill if they paid $6.75 for a T-shirt (indirect assessment).

There are obvious advantages to indirect assessment of achievement and learning, not the least of which is efficiency. It would be very time consuming to directly measure all learning that goes on in a classroom. But, indirect assessment raises a problem: How do you know your test is telling you if your learners can *apply* the skills and behaviors you are teaching? Authentic tests ask learners to display their skills and behaviors in a way that they would be displayed outside the classroom—in the real world (making change from a real transaction, using the concept of an isosceles triangle to build a structure, conducting an experiment and reporting its results). Authentic tests measure directly the skills and behaviors teachers and learners really care about. In other words, they ask the learners to do what was modeled, coached, and practiced during instruction as it would be done outside the classroom. If learners saw you demonstrate how to focus a microscope, were coached to do this and practiced doing it, then an authentic assessment would ask them to focus a microscope and not label the parts of the microscope on a diagram. If, on the other hand, your learners only needed to know the parts of a microscope so that they could read a story about the invention of the microscope—not use one—asking them to label the parts could be an authentic assessment. However, as we study behaviors in the cognitive, affective, and psychomotor domains, it will become apparent that behaviors that represent higher cognitive skills (e.g., evaluation, synthesis, and analysis in the cognitive domain) are those behaviors most frequently needed in the real world—in occupations, advanced courses of study, and job training programs.

In chapters 14 and 15, we will present ways of measuring your objectives using a variety of methods of assessment. At this time, however, you should know that objectives requiring higher-level cognitive, affective, and psychomotor skills—those that most closely represent the "thinking curriculum" discussed in Chapter 3—are more **authentic behaviors** because they are more likely to represent the types of performances required of your learners in the world in which they must live, work, and play.

Now, let's look at how each behavior in the cognitive domain varies according to cognitive skill and authenticity. These behaviors are described below with examples of action verbs that represent them.

What types of cognitive behaviors will I want to teach in my classroom?

Knowledge.   Objectives at the knowledge level require your students to remember or recall information such as facts, terminology, problem-solving strategies, and rules. Some action verbs that describe learning outcomes at the knowledge level are:

define	list	recall
describe	match	recite
identify	name	select
label	outline	state

Here are example knowledge objectives that use these verbs:

- The student will recall the four major food groups, without error, by Friday.
- From memory, the student will match United States generals with their most famous battles, with 80 percent accuracy.

Comprehension.   Objectives at this level require some degree of understanding. Students are expected to be able to change the form of a communication; translate; restate what has been read; see connections or relationships among parts of a communication (interpretation); or draw conclusions or see consequences from information (inference). Some action verbs that describe learning outcomes at the comprehension level are:

convert	estimate	infer
defend	explain	paraphrase
discriminate	extend	predict
distinguish	generalize	summarize

Here are example comprehension objectives that use these verbs:

- By the end of the semester, the student will summarize the main events of a story in grammatically correct English.
- The student will discriminate between the *realists* and the *naturalists,* citing examples from the readings.

Application.   Objectives written at this level require the student to use previously acquired information in a setting other than the one in which it was learned. Application objectives differ from comprehension objectives in that application requires the presentation of a problem in a different and often applied context. Thus, the student can rely on neither the *content* nor the *context* in which the original learning occurred to solve the problem. Some action verbs that describe learning outcomes at the application level are:

change	modify	relate
compute	operate	solve
demonstrate	organize	transfer
develop	prepare	use

Here are example application objectives that use these or similar verbs:

- On Monday, the student will demonstrate for the class an application to real life of the law of conservation of energy.
- Given fractions not covered in class, the student will multiply them on paper with 85 percent accuracy.

Analysis. Objectives written at the analysis level require the student to identify logical errors (e.g., point out a contradiction or an erroneous inference) or to differentiate among facts, opinions, assumptions, hypotheses, and conclusions. At the analysis level students are expected to draw relationships among ideas and to compare and contrast. Some action verbs that describe learning outcomes at the analysis level are:

break down	distinguish	point out
deduce	illustrate	relate
diagram	infer	separate out
differentiate	outline	subdivide

Here are example analysis objectives that use these verbs:

- Given a presidential speech, the student will be able to point out the positions that attack an individual rather than that individual's program.
- Given absurd statements (e.g., A man had flu twice. The first time it killed him. The second time he got well quickly.), the student will be able to point out the contradiction.

Synthesis. Objectives written at the synthesis level require the student to produce something unique or original. At the synthesis level students are expected to solve some unfamiliar problem in a unique way or to combine parts to form a unique or novel solution. Some action verbs that describe learning outcomes at the synthesis level are:

categorize	create	formulate
compile	design	predict
compose	devise	produce

Here are example synthesis objectives that use these or similar verbs:

- Given a short story, the student will write a different but plausible ending.
- Given a problem to be solved, the student will design on paper a scientific experiment to address the problem.

Evaluation.   Objectives written at this level require the student to form judgments and make decisions about the value of methods, ideas, people, or products that have a specific purpose. Students are expected to state the bases for their judgments (e.g., the external criteria or principles they drew on to reach their conclusions). Some action verbs that describe learning outcomes at the evaluation level are:

appraise	criticize	justify
compare	defend	support
contrast	judge	validate

Here are example evaluation objectives that use these verbs:

- Given a previously unread paragraph, the student will judge its value according to the five criteria discussed in class.
- Given a description of a country's economic system, the student will defend it, basing arguments on principles of democracy.

The Affective Domain

Another method of categorizing objectives was devised by Krathwohl, Bloom, and Masia (1964). This taxonomy delineates five levels of affective behavior ranging from the receiving level (least complex and least authentic) to the characterization level (most complex and most authentic). As in the cognitive domain, these levels are presumed to be hierarchical—higher-level objectives are assumed to include and be dependent on lower-level affective skills (Figure 4.2). As one moves up the hierarchy, more involvement, commitment,

What types of affective behaviors will I want to teach in my classroom?

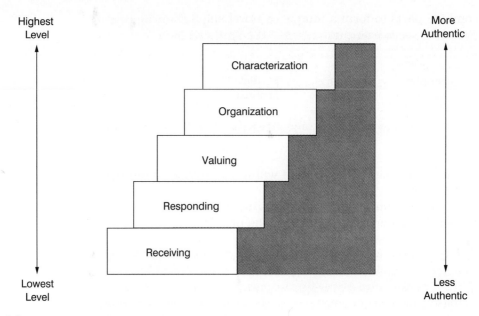

Figure 4.2
Taxonomy of educational objectives: Affective domain

and reliance on one's self occurs, as opposed to having one's feelings, attitudes, and values dictated by others.

For each level of the affective domain—receiving, responding, valuing, organization, and characterization—the following sections contain examples of action verbs indicating each level.

Receiving. Objectives at the receiving level require the student to be aware of, or to passively attend to, certain phenomena and stimuli. At this level students are expected simply to listen or be attentive. Some action verbs that describe outcomes at the receiving level are:

attend	discern	look
be aware	hear	notice
control	listen	share

Here are example receiving objectives that use these verbs:

- The student will be able to notice a change from small-group discussion to large-group lecture by following the lead of others in the class.
- The student will be able to listen to all of a Mozart concerto without leaving her or his seat.

Responding.   Objectives at the responding level require the student to comply with given expectations by attending or reacting to certain stimuli. Students are expected to obey, participate, or respond willingly when asked or directed to do something. Some action verbs that describe outcomes at the responding level are:

applaud	follow	play
comply	obey	practice
discuss	participate	volunteer

Here are example responding objectives that use these verbs:

- The student will follow the directions given in the book without argument when asked to do so.
- The student will practice a musical instrument when asked to do so.

Valuing.   Objectives at the valuing level require the student to display behavior consistent with a single belief or attitude in situations where he or she is neither forced nor asked to comply. Students are expected to demonstrate a preference or display a high degree of certainty and conviction. Some action verbs that describe outcomes at the valuing level are:

act	debate	help
argue	display	organize
convince	express	prefer

Here are example valuing objectives that use these verbs:

- The student will express an opinion about nuclear disarmament whenever national events raise the issue.
- The student will display an opinion about the elimination of pornography whenever discussing social issues.

Organization.   Objectives at the organization level require a commitment to a set of values. This level of the affective domain involves (1) forming a reason why one values certain things and not others, and (2) making appropriate choices between things that are and are not valued. Students are expected to organize their likes and preferences into a value system and then decide which ones will be dominant. Some action verbs that describe outcomes at the organization level are:

abstract	decide	select
balance	define	systematize
compare	formulate	theorize

Here are example organization objectives that use these verbs:

- The student will be able to compare alternatives to the death penalty and decide which ones are compatible with his or her beliefs.
- The student will be able to formulate the reasons why she or he supports civil rights legislation and will be able to identify legislation that does not support her or his beliefs.

Characterization. Objectives at the characterization level require that all behavior displayed by the student be consistent with his or her values. At this level the student not only has acquired the behaviors at all previous levels but also has integrated his or her values into a system representing a complete and pervasive philosophy that never allows expressions that are out of character with these values. Evaluations of this level of behavior involve the extent to which the student has developed a consistent philosophy of life (e.g., exhibits respect for the worth and dignity of human beings in all situations). Some action verbs that describe outcomes at this level are:

avoid	internalize	resist
display	manage	resolve
exhibit	require	revise

Some example objectives are:

- The student will exhibit a helping and caring attitude toward students with disabilities by assisting with their mobility both in and out of classrooms.
- The student will display a scientific attitude by stating and then testing hypotheses whenever the choice of alternatives is unclear.

The Psychomotor Domain

What types of psychomotor behaviors will I want to teach in my classroom?

A third method of categorizing objectives has been devised by Harrow (1972). This taxonomy delineates five levels of psychomotor behavior ranging from the imitation level (least complex and least authentic) to the naturalization level (most complex and most authentic). Figure 4.3 illustrates the hierarchical arrangement of the psychomotor domain. These behaviors place primary emphasis on neuromuscular skills involving various degrees of physical dexterity.

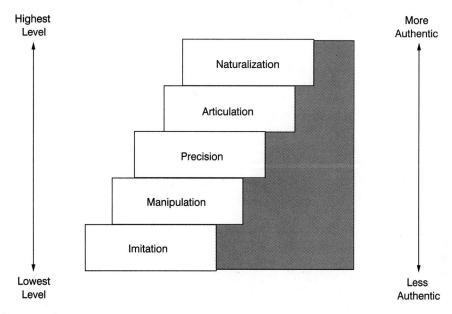

Figure 4.3
Taxonomy of educational objectives: Psychomotor domain

As behaviors in the taxonomy move from least to most complex and authentic, behavior changes from gross to fine motor skills.

Each of the levels—imitation, manipulation, precision, articulation, and naturalization—has different characteristics and is described in the following sections with examples of action verbs that represent each level.

Imitation.   Objectives at this level require that the student be exposed to an observable action and then overtly imitate it, such as when an instructor demonstrates the use of a microscope by placing a slide on the specimen tray. Performance at this level usually lacks neuro-muscular coordination (e.g., the slide may hit the side of the tray or be improperly aligned beneath the lens). Thus the behavior gener-ally is crude and imperfect. At this level students are expected to observe and be able to repeat (although imperfectly) the action being visually demonstrated. Some action verbs that describe outcomes at this level are:

align	grasp	repeat
balance	hold	rest (on)
follow	place	step (here)

Here are example imitation objectives that use these or similar verbs:

- After being shown a safe method for heating a beaker of water to boiling temperature, the student will be able to repeat the action.
- After being shown a freehand drawing of a parallelogram, the student will be able to reproduce the drawing.

Manipulation. Objectives at this level require the student to perform selected actions from written or verbal directions without the aid of a visual model or direct observation, as in the previous (imitation) level. Students are expected to complete the action from reading or listening to instructions, although the behavior still may be performed crudely and without neuromuscular coordination. Useful expressions to describe outcomes at the manipulation level are the same as at the imitation level, using the same action verbs, except they are performed from spoken or written instructions.

Here are example manipulation objectives:

- Based on the picture provided in the textbook, type a salutation to a prospective employer using the format shown.
- With the instructions on the handout in front of you, practice focusing your microscope until the outline of the specimen can be seen.

Precision. Objectives at this level require the student to perform an action independent of either a visual model or a written set of directions. Proficiency in reproducing the action at this level reaches a higher level of refinement. Accuracy, proportion, balance, and exactness in performance accompany the action. Students are expected to reproduce the action with control and to reduce errors to a minimum. Expressions that describe outcomes at this level include performing the behavior:

accurately	independently	with control
errorlessly	proficiently	with balance

Here are example precision objectives:

- The student will be able to accurately place the specimen on the microscope tray and use the high-power focus with proficiency as determined by the correct identification of three out of four easily recognizable objects.

- The student will be able to balance a light pen sufficiently to place it against the computer screen to identify misspelled words.

Articulation.   Objectives at this level require the student to display coordination of a series of related acts by establishing the appropriate sequence and performing the acts accurately, with control as well as with speed and timing. Expressions that describe outcomes at this level include performing the behaviors with:

confidence	integration	speed
coordination	proportion	stability
harmony	smoothness	timing

Here are example articulation objectives:

- Students will be able to write all the letters of the alphabet, displaying the appropriate proportion between upper case and lower case, in 10 minutes.
- Students will be able to accurately complete 10 simple arithmetic problems on a hand-held electronic calculator quickly and smoothly within 90 seconds.

Naturalization.   Objectives at this level require a high level of proficiency in the skill or performance being taught. At this level the behavior is performed with the least expenditure of energy and becomes routine, automatic, and spontaneous. Students are expected to repeat the behavior naturally and effortlessly time and again. Some expressions that describe this level of behavior are:

automatically	professionally	with ease
effortlessly	routinely	with perfection
naturally	spontaneously	with poise

Here are example naturalization objectives:

- At the end of the semester, students will be able to write routinely all the letters of the alphabet and all the numbers up to 100 each time requested.
- After the first grading period, students will be able to automatically draw correct isosceles, equilateral, and right triangles, without the aid of a template, for each homework assignment that requires this task.

Objectives that require a high level of proficiency in the psychomotor domain expect the learner to repeat the behavior naturally and effortlessly time and again.

>>> CREATING A CONTENT-BY-BEHAVIOR <<< BLUEPRINT WITH TEACHING OBJECTIVES

How can I be sure that I teach behaviors at all levels of behavioral complexity?

We have devoted a good deal of time to writing and analyzing objectives. It also is necessary to spend time on a technique that reminds you to write objectives at different levels. This technique is the *content-by-behavior blueprint.* Much like a blueprint used to guide the construction of a new building, the content-by-behavior blueprint guides your unit and lesson planning.

The blueprint for a building ensures that the builder will not overlook essential details. Similarly, the content-by-behavior blueprint ensures that you will not overlook details essential to good teaching. Specifically, it ensures that your lessons will address all the content areas covered in the curriculum guide and text, and all the behaviors that represent important learning needs.

Table 4.1 illustrates a content-by-behavior blueprint for an elementary school unit on reading. The intent of this blueprint is to be certain that behaviors related to all the levels of the cognitive domain would be taught over a unit of five short stories. The shaded portions of the blueprint indicate portions of the cognitive domain for which objectives would be written, tested, and given special

Table 4.1
Content-by-behavior blueprint for elementary school reading

	Behavior Categories											
CONTENT OUTLINE	A. Knowledge		B. Comprehension		C. Application		D. Analysis		E. Synthesis		F. Evaluation	
	Ability to list new words	Ability to use vocabulary	Ability to summarize meaning	Ability to translate into feelings	Ability to transfer meanings	Ability to organize main points	Ability to compare and contrast	Ability to see relationships	Ability to go beyond givens	Ability to compose new story line	Ability to express opinions	Ability to make judgments
	A.1	A.2	B.1	B.2	C.1	C.2	D.1	D.2	E.1	E.2	F.1	F.2
1. Story of the Knight (history)	■		■					■			■	
2. Animal Kingdom (nature)		■				■					■	
3. Wilderness Adventure (nature)									■			■
4. Christmas Surprise (fiction)					■					■		
5. Dark and Dungeon (science fiction)				■								

Shaded portions indicate behaviors to be tested.

Table 4.2
Content-by-behavior blueprint for secondary school mathematics

| CONTENT OUTLINE | A. Knowledge | | | B. Comprehension | | | | | C. Application | | | | D. Analysis | | | | |
	A.1 Ability to list specific facts	A.2 Ability to define terminology	A.3 Ability to state algorithms	B.1 Ability to summarize	B.2 Ability to distinguish principles, rules, and generalizations	B.3 Ability to infer mathematical structure	B.4 Ability to extend problem elements from one mode to another	B.5 Ability to defend a line of reasoning	C.1 Ability to solve routine problems	C.2 Ability to develop comparisons	C.3 Ability to operate on data	C.4 Ability to organize patterns, isomorphisms, and symmetries	D.1 Ability to separate out nonroutine problems	D.2 Ability to decide relationships	D.3 Ability to illustrate proofs	D.4 Ability to break down proofs	D.5 Ability to outline generalizations
Number systems																	
1.1 Whole numbers																	
1.2 Integers																	
1.3 Rational numbers																	
1.4 Real numbers																	
1.5 Complex numbers																	
1.6 Finite number systems																	
1.7 Matrices and determinants																	
1.8 Probability																	
1.9 Numeration systems																	
Algebra																	
2.1 Algebraic expressions																	

Behavior Categories

Behavior Categories

CONTENT OUTLINE	A. Knowledge			B. Comprehension					C. Application				D. Analysis				
	A.1 Ability to list specific facts	A.2 Ability to define terminology	A.3 Ability to state algorithms	B.1 Ability to summarize	B.2 Ability to distinguish principles, rules, and generalizations	B.3 Ability to infer mathematical structure	B.4 Ability to extend problem elements from one mode to another	B.5 Ability to defend a line of reasoning	C.1 Ability to solve routine problems	C.2 Ability to develop comparisons	C.3 Ability to operate on data	C.4 Ability to organize patterns, isomorphisms, and symmetries	D.1 Ability to separate out nonroutine problems	D.2 Ability to decide relationships	D.3 Ability to illustrate proofs	D.4 Ability to break down proofs	D.5 Ability to outline generalizations
2.2 Algebraic sentence																	
2.3 Relations and functions																	
Geometry																	
3.1 Measurement																	
3.2 Geometric phenomena																	
3.3 Formal reasoning																	
3.4 Coordinate systems and graphs																	

emphasis during each story. Table 4.2 illustrates a content-by-behavior blueprint for a much larger instructional sequence for secondary school mathematics. This blueprint illustrates a semester- or year-long state or school district curriculum in which different portions of the blueprint represent required essential skills for which a teacher should write classroom objectives. Both types of blueprint provide the teacher with a means of ensuring that each topic on the content outline is covered by one or more objectives at each level of the cognitive domain. Let's look now at how the components of the content-by-behavior blueprint are interrelated.

Content Outline Portion of Blueprint

The content outline listed down the side of the blueprint contains the topic areas to be taught; these are usually found in the curriculum guide and adopted text. It is for these topical areas that you will write objectives and test items. Generally, one objective within a behavior category is written for each topic area. Keep the number of topic areas to a manageable number within any single blueprint; otherwise, the number of objectives for unit plans, lesson plans, and tests will be too large.

Behavior Categories Portion of Blueprint

The categories listed across the top of the blueprint serve as a reminder or check on the behavioral complexity of your instruction. In the cells under each category, you can enter the number of test items needed to cover a particular area. Some units may contain objectives that do not go beyond the comprehension or application level. However, depending on the content outline, and your desire to foster a thinking curriculum, you will want to incorporate some behaviors at higher levels into your instruction and tests.

In summary, the information in the content-by-behavior blueprint indicates the following:

The content and behaviors for which objectives are to be written

Whether the instruction reflects a balanced picture of what is to be taught

Whether instruction will be planned for all topics and objectives specified in the curriculum and text

Seldom can a perfectly balanced blueprint that incorporates all levels of behavior for each content area be attained—nor is such a balance always desirable. However, the little extra time required to construct a blueprint can suggest levels of behavioral complexity that were not originally planned, but which you can and should incorporate into your unit and lesson plans. With a content-by-behavior blueprint you avoid not only spotty instruction but also the necessity of having to go back to teach concepts you discover are needed for subsequent instruction.

A content-by-behavior blueprint also is essential to good test construction, ensuring that your tests include a variety of items that tap different levels of behavioral complexity and authenticity. You will feel a special sense of satisfaction from using a framework that will help create fair and representative tests for the objectives you have taught. In Chapter 14 we will look at how to use the content-by-behavior blueprint for writing test items.

>>> SOME MISUNDERSTANDINGS <<< ABOUT BEHAVIORAL OBJECTIVES

Before beginning to write objectives, you should be aware of several misconceptions that have grown up around behaviors associated with the cognitive, affective, and psychomotor domains. These misconceptions are the understandable result of categorizing behaviors into many different levels, in the hopes of providing a practical tool that can be used across many different content areas. Following are some cautions to be mindful of when using behavioral objectives.

Are Some Behaviors More Desirable Than Others?

One misconception that often results from study of the cognitive, affective, and psychomotor domains is that the simple-to-complex ordering of behavior within each of these domains also represents an ordering from least to most *desirable*. Some believe that simple behaviors, like the recall of facts and dates, are less desirable than more complex behaviors requiring the cognitive operations of analysis, synthesis, and decision making. However, the behaviors within the cognitive, affective, and psychomotor domains do not imply desirability, because many lower-order behaviors (such as memorizing facts) must be learned before higher-order behaviors can even be attempted.

Some teachers pride themselves on preparing objectives almost exclusively at the highest levels of cognitive complexity; they do not recognize that objectives at a lower order of complexity always will be required for some students to stay actively engaged in the learning process with moderate-to-high rates of success. Without adequate instruction in the simpler behaviors, students will not be actively engaged when behaviors of greater complexity are taught. In this case, neither task-relevant prior knowledge nor skills necessary for acquiring more complex behaviors will have been taught. This may cause high error rates and predictably less active engagement in the learning process at the higher levels of behavioral complexity.

One of the most important uses of the taxonomies of behavior we have studied is to provide a menu of behaviors at different levels of complexity. As with any good diet, variety and proper proportion are the keys to good results.

What Is an Authentic Behavior?

Another misconception involves the meaning of the word *authentic.* The word *authentic* means relevant to the real world. If a learner would need to list the names of the presidents *in the real world*—on a job, at home, in a training program—that behavior could be measured authentically by asking the learner to repeat the names of the presidents, perhaps in the order in which they held office. Your measurement of this objective would be authentic because you are asking that the behavior be displayed in your classroom exactly as it would be performed outside. However, few occupations, courses, or programs of study will probably require your learners to recite the names of the presidents. Behaviors that have less relevance in the real world as they are taught in your classroom will be less authentic behaviors. Knowledge (in the cognitive domain), receiving (in the affective domain), and imitation (in the psychomotor domain) are seldom sufficient, in and of themselves, in the world outside the classroom. Although they often are necessary in acquiring more complex behaviors, they seldom take on importance by themselves. Behaviors representing higher cognitive skills often do take on importance outside the classroom exactly as they are taught. Evaluation (in the cognitive domain), characterization (in the affective domain), and naturalization (in the psychomotor domain) are examples of such behaviors. Deciding what candidate to vote for, assuming the responsibility of an informed citizen, and being able to complete a voting ballot legibly are all authentic behaviors because they are *necessary performances in daily life.* Therefore, higher cognitive skills often are more authentic than lower cognitive skills because they represent more integrated behaviors necessary for living, working, and performing in the world outside your classroom. This is one of the best reasons for teaching higher cognitive skills *in* your classroom.

Are Less Complex Behaviors Easier to Teach?

Another misconception is that behaviors of less complexity (e.g., recall of facts) are easier to teach than behaviors of greater complexity (e.g., problem solving). This is an appealing argument because intuition and common sense indicate that this should be so. After all, complexity—especially cognitive complexity—often has been associated with greater difficulty, greater amounts of study time, and more extensive instructional resources.

Although simpler behaviors may be easier to teach some of the time, it often is just the opposite. For example, consider the elaborate study card and mnemonic system that might be needed to recall the periodic table of chemical elements, as opposed to the simple visual demonstration of an experiment to promote problem-solving activity. In this case, the so-called less complex behavior requires greater time and instructional resources. Also, whether a behavior is easier or harder to teach always will depend on the ability level, motivation, discipline, and prior achievement of the students. It is quite possible that the teaching of dull but important facts to less able, poorly motivated students will be considerably more difficult than demonstrating the practical application of those facts to the same students.

These examples point out that errors of judgment can easily be made by automatically assuming that lower-order, less complex behaviors necessarily require little preparation, fewer instructional resources, and less teaching time than do higher-order, more complex behaviors. The ease with which a behavior can be taught is not synonymous with the level of the behavior in the taxonomy (i.e., lower or higher). These designations refer to the mental—or cognitive—operations *required of the student* and *not* the complexity of the activities *required of the teacher* to produce the behavior.

Are Cognitive, Affective, and Psychomotor Behaviors Mutually Exclusive?

Finally, categorizing behaviors into cognitive, affective, and psychomotor domains does not mean that behaviors listed in one domain are mutually exclusive of those listed in other domains. For example, it is not possible to think without having some feeling about what we are thinking, or to feel or have a response without some cognition. Also, much thinking involves physical movements and bodily performances that require psychomotor skills and abilities. For example, conducting a laboratory experiment requires not only thought but pouring from one test tube to another, safely igniting a Bunsen burner, adjusting a microscope correctly, and so on. Legible handwriting requires neuromuscular coordination, timing, and control.

It is convenient for an objective to contain behavior from only one of the three domains at a time. But keep in mind that one or more behaviors from the other domains also may be required for the behavior to occur—for example, a good attitude is required for the memorization of facts to occur. This is one of the best reasons for preparing objectives in all three domains: it is evidence of your awareness of the close and necessary relationship among cognitive, affective, and psychomotor behaviors.

To sum up, keep in mind the following cautions when using and writing behavioral objectives:

- Behaviors listed within the cognitive, affective, and psychomotor domains do not imply that some behaviors will be more or less desirable in your classroom than others.
- The word *authentic* means relevant to the real world. Higher cognitive skills often are more authentic than lower cognitive skills because they represent more integrated behaviors necessary for living, working, and performing outside your classroom.
- Less complex behaviors within the cognitive, affective, and psychomotor domains do not imply that less teacher preparation, fewer instructional resources, or less teaching time will be required than for more complex behaviors.
- Although objectives usually contain behaviors from only one of the three domains, one or more behaviors from the other domains may also be required for the behavior to occur.

>>> THE CULTURAL ROOTS OF OBJECTIVES <<<

Finally, you should be prepared to have the source of your objectives questioned by parents, community members, and students. The technical process of writing objectives sometimes can obscure the forest because of the trees; that is, prevent you from recognizing the obvious because you were working so hard to produce objectives in the correct technical form. Therefore, your responses about the source of objectives may include "from textbooks," "from curriculum guides," or "from department policies."

These answers are technically correct but miss the fundamental point, which is that objectives have roots much deeper than any single text, curriculum guide, or set of policies. These roots lie in the educational values we espouse as a nation. While parents, students, and other teachers may argue with the text used, the curriculum guide followed, or the department policies accepted, it is quite another thing to take exception to the values we share as a nation and that were created by many different interest groups over many years of thoughtful deliberation.

Texts, curricula, and policies are interpretations of these values shared at the broadest national level and translated into practice through goals and objectives. Texts, curriculum guides, and school district policies can no more create objectives than they can create values. Goals and their objectives are carefully created to reflect our values from sources such as curriculum reform committees, state and national legislative mandates, and national educational policies. This is why you must have a knowledge of these ultimate sources from which you have derived your objectives, or else you may continually be caught in the position of justifying a particular text, curriculum, or policy to parents, students, and peers— some of whom will always disagree with you. Reference to any one text, curriculum, or policy can never prove that your students should appreciate art or know how to solve an equation.

On the other hand, our *values,* as indicated by curriculum reform committees, state and national mandates, and national educational policies, can provide appropriate and adequate justification for intended learning outcomes. Attention to these values as reported by the press, professional papers and books, curriculum committees, and national teacher groups is as important to teaching as the objectives you write.

Summing Up

This chapter introduced instructional objectives. Its main points were as follows

1. Objectives have two purposes: (1) to tie general aims and goals to specific classroom strategies that will achieve those aims and goals, and (2) to express teaching strategies in a format that allows you to measure their effects upon your learners.

2. When the word *behavioral* precedes the word *objective,* the learning is being defined as a change in *observable* behavior that can be *measured* within a *specified period of time.*

3. The need for behavioral objectives stems from a natural preoccupation with concerns for self and task, sometimes to the exclusion of concerns for the impact on students.

4. Objectives that express the desired outcomes provide the means for evaluating the chosen goal–learning need–organization– method match.

5. Simply put, behavioral objectives do the following:

- Focus instruction on a specific goal whose outcomes can be observed.
- Identify the conditions under which learning can be expected to occur.
- Specify the level or amount of behavior that can be expected from the instruction under the conditions specified.

6. Action verbs help operationalize the learning outcome expected from an objective

and identify exactly what the learner must do to achieve the outcome.

7. The outcome specified in a behavioral objective should be expressed as an end (e.g., to identify, recall, list) and not as a means (e.g., to study, watch, listen).

8. If the observable learning outcome is to take place with particular materials, equipment, tools, or other resources, these conditions must be stated explicitly in the objective.

9. Conditional statements within a behavioral objective can be singular (one condition) or multiple (more than one condition).

10. Conditions should match those under which the behavior will be performed in the real world.

11. A proficiency level is the minimum degree of performance that will satisfy you that the objective has been met.

12. Proficiency levels represent value judgments, or educated guesses, as to what level of performance will be required for adequately performing the behavior in some later setting beyond your classroom.

13. The expressiveness of an objective refers to the amount of flexibility allowed in a response. Less expressive objectives may call for only a single right answer, whereas more expressive objectives allow for less structured and more flexible responses. The expressiveness allowed is always a matter of degree.

14. "Complexity" of a behavior in the cognitive, affective, or psychomotor domain pertains to the operations required of the student to produce the behavior, not to the complexity of the teaching activities required.

15. Behaviors in the cognitive domain, from least to most complex, are knowledge, comprehension, application, analysis, synthesis, and evaluation.

16. Behaviors in the affective domain, from least to most complex, are receiving, responding, valuing, organization, and characterization.

17. Behaviors in the psychomotor domain, from least to most complex, are imitation, manipulation, precision, articulation, and naturalization.

18. A content-by-behavior blueprint is a graphic device for ensuring that the lesson and tests adequately address and provide a balanced coverage of (1) all the content areas identified in the curriculum guide, and (2) all the important cognitive, affective, and psychomotor behaviors.

19. Behavioral objectives have their roots in the educational values we espouse as a nation. Texts, curricula, and department and school policies are interpretations of these values shared at the broadest national level and translated into practice through behavioral objectives.

20. Four important cautions in using the taxonomies of behavioral objectives are as follows:

- No behavior specified is necessarily more or less desirable than any other.
- Higher cognitive skills often are more authentic than lower cognitive skills.
- Less complex behaviors are not necessarily easier to teach, less time consuming, or dependent on fewer resources than are more complex behaviors.
- Behavior in one domain may require one or more behaviors in other domains to be achieved.

For Discussion and Practice

*1. Identify the two general purposes for preparing behavioral objectives. If you could choose only one of these purposes, which would be more important to you? Why?

*2. Explain what three things the word *behavioral* implies when it appears before the word *objectives*.

*3. Identify the three components of a well-written behavioral objective and give one example of each component.

*4. Historically, why did the concept of behavioral objectives emerge?

*5. Why are action verbs necessary in translating goals such as *mentally healthy* *citizens, well-rounded individuals,* and *self-actualized schoolchildren* into behavioral outcomes?

*6. Distinguish learning outcomes (ends) from learning activities (means) by placing an *O* or *A* beside the following expressions:

_____ working on a car radio
_____ adding signed numbers correctly
_____ practicing the violin
_____ playing basketball
_____ using a microscope
_____ identifying an amoeba
_____ naming the seven parts of speech
_____ punctuating an essay correctly

*7. Define a *condition* in a behavioral objective. Give three examples.

*8. How can the specification of conditions help students study and prepare for tests?

*9. In trying to decide upon what condition(s) to include in a behavioral objective, what single most important consideration should guide your selection?

*10. What is the definition of *criterion level* in a behavioral objective? Give three examples.

11. Provide examples of two behavioral objectives that differ in the degree of expressiveness they allow.

*12. Column A contains objectives. Column B contains levels of cognitive behavior. Match the levels in Column B with the most appropriate objective in Column A. Column B levels can be used more than once.

Column A	Column B
_____ 1. Given a two-page essay, the student can distinguish the assumptions basic to the author's position.	a. knowledge b. comprehension c. application d. analysis e. synthesis f. evaluation
_____ 2. The student will correctly spell the word *mountain.*	

_____ 3. The student will convert the following English passage into Spanish.

_____ 4. The student will compose new pieces of prose and poetry according to the classification system emphasized in lecture.

_____ 5. Given a sinking passenger ship with 19 of its 20 lifeboats destroyed, the captain will decide, based on his perceptions of their potential worth to society, who is to be placed on the last lifeboat.

13. Make up two objectives for each of the knowledge, comprehension, application, analysis, synthesis, and evaluation levels of the taxonomy of cognitive objectives. Select verbs for each level from the lists provided in the chapter. Try to make your objectives cover the same subject.

14. Exchange the objectives you have just written with a classmate. Have the classmate check each objective for (1) an observable behavior, (2) any special conditions under which the behavior must be displayed, and (3) a performance level considered sufficient to demonstrate mastery. Revise your objectives if necessary.

15. A parent calls to tell you that, after a long talk with her son, she disapproves of the objectives you have written for health education—particularly those referring to the anatomy of the human body—but which you have taken almost verbatim from the teachers' guide to the adopted textbook. Compose a response to this parent that shows your understanding of the roots of objectives and justifies your decision to teach these objectives.

---

* Answers to asterisked questions (*) in this and the other chapters are in Appendix B.

Suggested Readings

Cohen, S. (1987). Instructional alignment: Searching for the magic bullet. *Educational Researcher, 16* (8), 16–20.

This article explains what an effective objective is and the important process of matching learning activities with objectives called "instructional alignment."

Gronlund, N. (1995). *How to write and use instructional objectives* (5th ed.). Englewood Cliffs, NJ: Merrill/Prentice Hall.

This is a practical text written especially for teachers on how objectives can be used for effective teaching across different grades and content areas.

Gronlund, N., & Linn, R. (1995). *Measurement and evaluation in teaching.* Englewood Cliffs, NJ: Merrill/Prentice Hall.

This text contains several excellent chapters on the many possible types of objectives and how to put them to use in preparing classroom tests.

Kubiszyn, T., & Borich, G. (1996). *Educational testing and measurement: Classroom application and practice* (5th ed.). New York: HarperCollins.

This text includes chapters on instructional goals and objectives, measuring learning outcomes, and the content-by-behavior blueprint.

McClelland, D. (1985). How do elementary school teachers plan? The nature of planning and influences on it. In W. Doyle & T. Good (Eds.), *Focus on Teaching.* Chicago: University of Chicago Press.

An account of how teachers can use objectives along with texts, tests, and curriculum guides to focus their instruction.

Pophan, W. (1990). *Modern educational measurement.* Englewood Cliffs, NJ: Prentice Hall.

Contains several chapters that cogently state the case for the use of objectives in the schools and their application to testing. Widely read and often referenced.

Sardo-Brown, D. (1988). Teachers' planning. *The Elementary School Journal, 89,* 68–87.

A report on how a sample of elementary school teachers actually used objectives in planning their lessons and units.

CHAPTER 5

Unit and Lesson Planning

This chapter will help you answer the following questions:

1. How do I use a curriculum guide to plan a lesson?
2. How do I choose behavioral outcomes that match my learners?
3. How can I keep the "big picture"—or unit goal—in mind while preparing individual lessons?
4. How do I make a unit plan?
5. How do I make an interdisciplinary thematic unit plan?
6. How do I decide the level of behavioral complexity at which to begin a lesson?
7. How can my lessons provide for student diversity?
8. What are some new technologies I can use to deliver my lessons?
9. What is in a lesson plan?

This chapter will also help you learn the meaning of the following:

 disciplinary thematic units
hierarchy
interactive individualized practice activities
interdisciplinary thematic units
lesson plans
peer and cross-age tutoring
system perspective
task ability grouping
the "living curriculum"
tutorial and communication technologies
vertical and lateral planning

n Chapter 3 we noted that, before you can prepare a **lesson plan,** you must decide on instructional goals, learning needs, content, and methods. These prelesson planning decisions are crucial for developing effective lesson plans, because they give structure to lesson planning and tie it to important sources of societal and professional values. In this chapter, unit and lesson plans are presented as tools for tying these values to the classroom and the school curriculum. Before discussing how to prepare unit and lesson plans, however, let's review the inputs to the planning process that were covered in Chapter 3.

These inputs represent the first part of a three-stage process that includes (1) prelesson planning, (2) actual preparation of lesson plans, and (3) evaluation of lesson plans. In the prelesson planning stage covered in Chapter 3, you learned of an approach for organizing your instructional planning according to the inputs shown in Figure 5.1. In this chapter you will learn specific ways to use these inputs to build unit and lesson plans. In chapters 14 and 15 you will learn how to evaluate the success of your lessons with learners.

>>> UNIT AND LESSON PLANS <<<

The important process of unit and lesson planning begins with implementing the five planning inputs (Figure 5.1). This stage of the planning process takes a **system perspective,** meaning that your lessons will be part of a larger system of interrelated learning, called a unit.

The word *system* brings to mind phrases like *school system, mental health system,* and *legal system.* Schools, mental health services, and criminal justice agencies are supposed to work as systems. This means that their component parts, departments, and branches are to interrelate and build toward some unified concept: an educated adult, a mentally healthy individual, a rehabilitated offender. For example, in a school system, discrete facts, skills, and understandings learned by the completion of sixth grade not only are important in themselves but also are important for successful completion of seventh grade. This, in turn, is important for completion of eighth grade, and so on through the educational system until

Figure 5.1
Inputs to the planning process

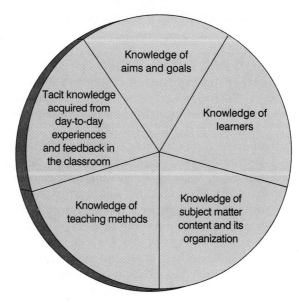

the high school graduate has many of the facts, skills, and understandings necessary for adult living.

Notice that these skills, facts, and understandings are not
acquired from twelfth-grade instruction alone but are *accumulated*
through the entire schooling process, which is a sequence of many
different learning activities. At no one point or time could it be said
that Johnny's education was complete (not even at grade twelve);
nor could Brenda's facts at grade seven, Bobby's skills at grade ten,
and Betty Jo's understandings at grade twelve be added together to
define an educated adult. This illustrates not only how dependent a
system outcome is upon the outcomes of all its component parts,
but also the importance of the relationship among its parts.

The strength of a system is that "the whole is greater than the
sum of its parts." But how can anything be more than the sum of its
parts? Can a unit of instruction comprised of individual lessons
ever add up to anything more than the sum of the individual
lessons? This sounds like getting something for nothing, a concept
that does not ring true. But, if the system of individual lessons
really does produce outcomes in learners that are greater than the
sum of the outcomes of the individual lessons, then there must be a
missing ingredient that we haven't mentioned.

That missing ingredient is *the relationship among the individual lessons.* This relationship must allow the outcome of one lesson
to build upon the outcomes of preceding lessons. Knowledge, skills,

and understanding evolve gradually through the joint contribution of many lessons arranged to build more and more complex outcomes. It is this invisible but all-important relationship among the parts of a system, or instructional unit, that allows the unit outcomes to be greater than the sum of the lesson outcomes.

This does not mean that anything labeled a system or an instructional unit necessarily will achieve outcomes greater than the sum of its parts. If the relationship among parts of the system or instructional unit is not painstakingly planned to ensure that earlier lessons become building blocks for later lessons, a true system will not exist. Instead, only a mixture of bits and pieces bound together by some common unit title may exist, like the accumulation of junk in an attic or in the glove compartment of a car. Nothing works in harmony with anything else to produce a coherent whole or a unified theme. One of the goals of this chapter is to provide concepts and tools to help your individual lessons add up to more than the sum of their individual outcomes.

Of considerable importance is the relationship of your district's curriculum guide to your unit and lesson plans. _Units generally extend over an instructional time period of one to four weeks._ They usually correspond to well-defined topics or themes in the curriculum guide. _Lessons,_ on the other hand, are considerably shorter, spanning a single class period or occasionally two or three periods. Because lessons are relatively short, they are harder to associate with a particular segment of a curriculum guide. This means that you can expect unit content to be fairly well structured and defined but lesson content to be much less detailed.

This is as it should be, because the arrangement of day-to-day content in the classroom must be flexible to meet individual student needs, your instructional preferences, and special priorities and initiatives in your school and district. So, although the overall picture at the unit level may be clear from the district's curriculum guide, at the lesson level you must apply considerable independent thought, organization, and judgment. Figure 5.2 indicates the flow of teaching content from the state level to the classroom, illustrating the stages through which a curriculum framework is translated into unit and lesson plans.

>>> MAKING PLANNING DECISIONS <<<

Unit planning begins with an understanding of the alternative goals, learning needs, content, and methods that are involved in writing lesson plans. These inputs to the learning process result from pre-

Figure 5.2
Flow of teaching content from the state level to the classroom level

State Curriculum Framework

- provides philosophy that guides curriculum implementation
- discusses progression of essential content taught from grade to grade; shows movement of student through increasingly complex material
- notes modifications of curriculum to special populations (e.g., at-risk, gifted, or bilingual learners, or learners with disabilities)

District Curriculum Guide

- provides content goals keyed to state framework
- enumerates appropriate teaching activities and assignment strategies
- gives outline for unit plans; lists and sequences topics
- reflects locally appropriate ways of achieving goals in content areas

Teacher's Unit and Lesson Plans

- describes how curriculum guide goals are implemented daily
- refers to topics to be covered, materials needed, activities to be used
- identifies evaluation strategies
- notes adaptions to special populations

Teacher's Grade Book

- records objectives mastered
- identifies need for reteaching and remediation
- provides progress indictators
- guides promotion/retention decisions

lesson planning, in which you consult sources of societal and professional values, and select as relevant certain goals, learning needs, content, and methods. This selection is made in part by the curriculum adopted by your school district, because both societal and professional values were instrumental in curriculum selection.

However, the entire job of determining goals, learning needs, and content has not been completed by this selection process. You must decide the relative degree of emphasis to place upon these goals, and determine toward what learning needs and what area of content the goals are directed. Let's look closer at several types of decisions you will make pertaining to goals, learners, content, and how your content is organized.

Goals

How do I use a curriculum guide to plan a lesson?

Curriculum guides at the grade, department, and school district level usually clearly specify what content must be covered in what period of time. But they may be far less clear about the specific behaviors that students are expected to acquire. For example, an excerpt from a curriculum guide for English language instruction might take this form:

I. Writing concepts and skills. The student shall be provided opportunities to learn:
   A. The composing process.
   B. Descriptive, narrative, and expository paragraphs.
   C. Multiple paragraph compositions.
   D. Persuasive discourse.
   E. Meanings and uses of colloquialism, slang, idiom, and jargon.

Or for a life-science curriculum:

I. Life science. The student shall be provided the opportunity to learn:
   A. Skills in acquiring data through the senses.
   B. Classification skills in ordering and sequencing data.
   C. Oral and written communication of data in appropriate form.
   D. Concepts and skills of measurement using relationships and standards.
   E. Drawing logical inferences, predicting outcomes, and forming generalized statements.

Notice in these excerpts the specificity at which the content is identified (e.g., the composing process; descriptive, narrative, and expository paragraphs; multiple paragraph composition). In contrast, note the lack of clarity concerning the *level of behavioral complexity* to which the instruction should be directed. This is typical of many curriculum guides. Recalling the taxonomy of behavior in the cognitive domain (Chapter 4), you might ask the following questions:

For which of these content areas will the simple *recall* of facts be sufficient?

For which areas will *comprehension* of those facts be required?

For which areas will *application* be expected of what the student comprehends?

For which areas will higher-level outcomes be desired, involving *analysis, synthesis,* and *decision-making* skills?

Decisions made about goals often involve (1) selecting the level of behavioral complexity for which teachers will prepare an instructional unit or lesson and (2) the level at which they will expect student outcomes and test for them. The flexibility afforded by most curriculum guides in selecting the behavioral level to which instruction can be directed often is both purposeful and advantageous for you. For the curriculum guide to be adapted to the realities of your classroom, a wide latitude of expected outcomes must be possible. These depend on the unique behavioral characteristics of your students, the time you can devote to a specific topic, and the overall behavioral outcomes desired at the unit level.

Learners

Curriculum guides allow you the flexibility of adapting your instruction to the individual learning needs of your students. Chapter 2 presented several categories of individual differences that will be characteristic of students in your classroom. These included differences in ability, prior achievement, anxiety, self-concept, learning style, and home and family life. These factors can reflect entire classrooms as well as individuals. Other categories of learners— at-risk, bilingual, and gifted learners, and learners with disabilities—add even greater diversity to the classroom. They may create the need for task-related subgroups that require instruction individ-

How do I choose behavioral outcomes that match my learners?

ually or time-limited ability groups, alternatives we will address in the chapters to come.

You will also want to remain flexible in choosing the behavioral complexity of your unit and lesson outcomes. For these decisions, the information you will need to adapt the complexity of your objectives to the needs of your learners will come from their in-class oral responses, practice exercises, performance assessments, homework, and tests. You will want to use these often to adjust the level of your instruction to your learners.

Content

Perhaps foremost in the mind of beginning teachers is the content to be taught. Your content decisions appear easy inasmuch as textbooks, workbooks, and curriculum guides were selected long before your first day in the classroom. Indeed, as you saw in the excerpts from the curriculum guide, content often is designated in great detail. Textbooks and workbooks carry this detail one step further by offering activities and exercises that further define and expand the content in the curriculum guide. From this perspective it appears that all of the content has been handed to you, if not on a silver platter, then surely in readily accessible and highly organized tests, workbooks, and curriculum materials.

Although every teacher might wish this were true, most quickly realize that as many decisions must be made about content—what to teach—as about behavioral goals and learning needs. You will quickly come to realize that adopted texts, workbooks, and even detailed curriculum guides identify the content to be taught but do not select, organize, and sequence that content *according to the needs of your learners.* For this task, you must select from among textbook and curriculum guide content and expand upon it to strengthen the relationship between your behavioral goals and learner needs.

Thus, the content you present cannot be decided until you have determined your learners' characteristics (e.g., level of achievement, motivation, cultural diversity, etc.) and selected the level of authenticity of your desired behavioral outcomes (e.g., knowledge, comprehension, application, etc.). Although textbook and curriculum guides indicate the content coverage to strive for, the effective teacher knows that this content must be *selected from* for some behavioral goals and learners and *added to* for other goals and learners to engage them in the learning process at the *most appropriate level of behavioral complexity.*

Organization

Chapter 3 provided examples of content organization that illustrated several ways in which to interrelate lesson and unit content to form a *learning structure* (e.g., simple-to-complex, abstract-to-concrete, general-to-detailed, etc.). Establishing lesson interrelationships is one of the most important planning decisions you will make. How your lessons interrelate can even determine if and how well your learners achieve higher levels of cognitive, affective, and psychomotor behavior at the unit level. This, in turn, will determine how well your unit and lesson plans reflect a thinking curriculum.

These higher levels of behavior (analysis, synthesis, evaluation; value, organization, characterization; precision, articulation, naturalization) can rarely if ever be achieved in a single lesson. Thus, lessons must be placed within a unit (system) in which individual lessons build on previously taught behaviors to achieve these higher-order behaviors. This is why your structuring of content is so important to unit planning: without it, behavioral outcomes at the unit's end probably would be no different than the outcomes achieved at the completion of each single lesson. Unlike junk in the attic or the glove compartment of your car, units must have a coherent, unified theme that rises above the cognitive, affective, and psychomotor complexity of any single lesson.

Thus far, we have spoken as though the way you choose to sequence instruction or to relate lessons to one another is a matter of personal preference. However, the way you organize lesson content should be decided with both your goals and learners in mind. For example, one reason for choosing a specific-to-general organization of instructional content might be to achieve outcomes at a higher level of behavioral complexity (application, analysis, and synthesis) with poorly motivated learners. Your reason might be that, since the more difficult content will come at the conclusion of the unit, the most specific or concrete lesson content should be presented first. Thus, learners can more easily acquire the needed basics and achieve a higher level of interest before moving deeper into the topic. Or, the reason for choosing a particular series of lessons (for example, on "acid rain," "new technologies," or "heroic deeds") might be to show how several disciplines that your students are studying can be brought together with a single theme for the purpose of solving a problem, thinking critically, and forming an independent judgment. In each case, the unit goal and needs of your learners will play an important role in selecting a particular organization. Thus, your decisions about unit structure will depend both on clearly stated goals and a knowledge of your learners.

As noted in Figure 5.1, choosing a teaching method is yet another important decision area in the planning process. Chapters 6–13 are devoted exclusively to helping you acquire these methods.

>>> VERTICAL AND LATERAL UNIT PLANNING <<<

In the following two sections, we will introduce unit plans and how to communicate them in a clear and orderly manner. Our first approach to unit planning will show you how to plan and to teach knowledge and understanding "vertically." **Vertical unit planning** is a method of developing units within a discipline in which the content to be taught is arranged hierarchically or in steps (e.g., from least to most complex, or from concrete to abstract) and presented in an order that ensures that all task-relevant prior knowledge required for subsequent lessons has been taught in previous lessons.

Following our discussion of vertical unit planning, we present a second means of communicating knowledge and understanding to your learners, called lateral planning. **Lateral unit planning** is often used for planning thematic units that integrate bodies of knowledge across disciplines in order to convey relationships, patterns, and abstractions that bind different aspects of our world together in some systematic way. Lateral unit plans move across the established boundaries of disciplines, subject matter, and content areas to elicit problem solving, critical thinking, cooperative activity, and independent thought and action that emphasizes that the whole is greater than the sum of its parts. As you will see, both vertical and lateral unit planning are valuable tools for acquiring the skills of an effective teacher.

>>> DISCIPLINARY (VERTICAL) <<<
THEMATIC UNIT PLANS

How can I keep the "big picture"—or unit goal—in mind while preparing individual lessons?

An old Chinese proverb states, "A picture is worth a thousand words." In this chapter we will apply this age-old idea to unit planning by showing how you can develop a unit plan by creating a visual blueprint of your thematic unit. In this section we will show you how to use a written and graphic format to express a unit plan within a discipline, subject matter, or content area. In the next section, we will show you how to use a similar format to express an interdisciplinary thematic unit that spans more than a single discipline, subject matter, or content area.

While a visual device cannot substitute for a written description or outline of what you plan to teach, it is an effective means of organizing your thinking—i.e., your planning. Scientists, administrators, engineers, and business executives long have known the value of visuals in the form of flow charts, organization charts, blueprints, technical diagrams, and even "doodles" to convey the essence of a concept, if not the details. From the beginning, teachers have used this basic method, too. Pictures not only communicate the results of planning but are useful during that process to select, organize, and revise a unit plan, and to see the "big picture"—or final outcome— you are working hard to achieve.

Although teaching parallels many other fields by using visual devices in planning, in many ways teaching is a unique profession. Unlike business, education's product does not roll off an assembly line, nor does education build its product with the mathematical laws and physical substances used by the scientist and engineer. Consequently, your visual blueprints differ from those of others, but at the same time must reflect the qualities that have made pictures so important to planning in these other professions. You already have been introduced to two of these qualities: the concept of **hierarchy,** which shows the relationship of parts to the whole (lessons to unit), and the concept of *task-relevant prior knowledge,* which shows the necessity for a certain order of events (lesson sequence). In vertical unit planning, both concepts are put to work in creating a visual picture of a unit; such a picture can both stimulate and organize your thoughts and communicate the results to others in an easy-to-follow graphic format.

There are two simple rules used in drawing a picture of a vertically planned unit. The first is to diagram how the unit goal is divided into specific lessons. The second is to show the sequence of these lessons and how their outcomes build on one another to achieve the unit goal. Let's look at these two rules.

Visualizing Specific Teaching Activities

Our first rule simply uses boxes to picture areas of content—or instructional goals—at various levels of generality. In other words, any goal at the unit level can be broken into its component parts at the lesson level. Those component parts represent everything that is important for attaining the goal. This idea is illustrated in Figure 5.3.

How do I make a unit plan?

Notice that Figure 5.3 has three levels. For now, focus on the top and bottom levels. The top shows the unit's general intent, which is derived from the curriculum guide and adopted textbook, which in turn are based upon societal, state, or locally stated goals. The bottom row shows unit content, expressed at a level specific enough to

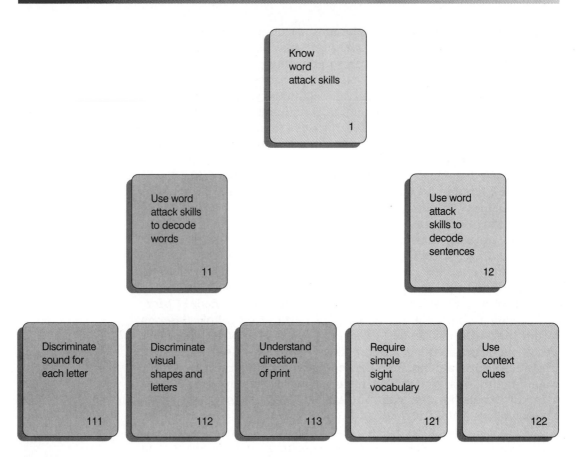

Figure 5.3
Example of a hierarchy of reading content at different levels of specificity

prepare individual lessons. Notice that, in the judgment of this unit planner, ending the plan at a more detailed level than boxes 111, 112, and 113 would result in content sized for less than one lesson; beginning the plan with content at a more general level than box 1 (top) would result in content sized too big for one unit.

This unit plan ends with bite-sized chunks that together exhaust the content specified at the higher levels. Just as in the story of Goldilocks and the three bears, the bottom of the unit plan hierarchy must end with the portion of content being served up as "not too big and not too small, but just right." How can you know whether you have achieved the right size and balance for a single lesson?

The second level of Figure 5.3 is a logical means of getting from the general unit goal to specific lesson content. It is an intermediate thinking process that produces the lower level of just-right-sized pieces. How many intermediate levels should you have? There is no magic number; this depends on how broadly the initial goal is stated and the number of steps needed to produce content in just the right amounts for individual lesson plans. Experience and judgment are the best guides, although logical divisions within the curriculum guide and text are helpful, too.

In some cases, the route from unit to lesson content can be very direct (two levels), while in other instances several levels may have to be worked through before arriving at lesson-sized chunks. If you have trouble getting sufficiently specific for lesson-sized content, you may need to revise the unit goal by dividing it into two or more subgoals and beginning a new hierarchy from each subgoal. This was done in Figure 5.3, where one subgoal is shaded (representing word-specific content), and the other is unshaded (representing sentence-specific content). Starting at such a high level of generality, the unit planner had to devise two units of instruction.

Notice that this is done in the same way that you create an outline, beginning with Roman numerals (I, II, III, etc.), their subdivisions (A, B, C, etc.), and perhaps further subdivisions. The initial statement of unit content (top box) often turns out to be more comprehensive than you expected, representing a cluster of units. This was the case in Figure 5.3; what initially was seen as an individual lesson (11) turned out to be a whole unit (111, 112, 113).

This process of building a content hierarchy will guide you in making the important distinction between unit and lesson content and will prevent many false starts in lesson planning.

Visualizing the Sequence of Activities

The second rule, equally simple, shows the sequence among lessons and how lesson outcomes build on one another to achieve a unit goal. This second rule, illustrated in Figure 5.4, shows the order of the individual lessons, when order is important. Notice that in Figure 5.4, we chose the first box (11) from the second level of the hierarchy in Figure 5.3 as our unit goal. The procedure is to indicate the intended unit outcome with an arrow extending from the right of this box, as shown in Figure 5.4. The outcome of all the lessons derived from it, taken together, should be the same as this unit outcome. This will always be true, whether or not the sequence of your lessons is important. In some instances this sequence may be arbitrary (Figure 5.5a), while for others a partial sequence may be appropriate (Figure 5.5b).

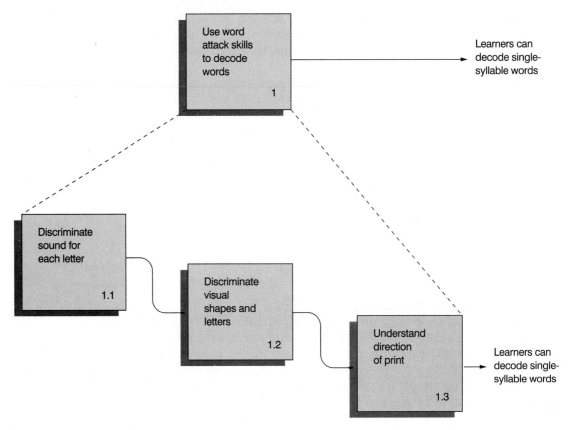

Figure 5.4
A unit plan showing a sequence among lessons

This second rule recognizes how previous lessons can *modify* or *constrain* the outcomes of subsequent lessons. It encourages you to use sequence, building on previously taught learning to provide increasingly more authentic and behaviorally complex outcomes at the unit level. This will be important if your unit plan is to promote a thinking curriculum. If lesson outcomes are unrelated, it is unlikely that your unit outcome will be at any higher a level of cognitive, affective, or psychomotor complexity than your individual lesson outcomes. As an effective teacher, you should plan the interrelationships among lessons in a way that encourages higher-order behaviors to emerge at the unit level.

You can see that picturing your unit plan visually has several advantages. Seeing a lesson in context with other lessons that share the same purpose focuses your attention on the importance of task-

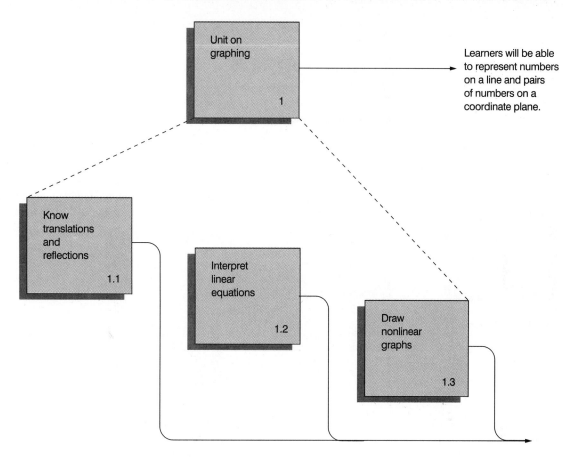

Figure 5.5a
A unit plan without lesson sequence (Lessons 1.1, 1.2, and 1.3 can occur in any order)

relevant prior knowledge to lesson success. Recall that if prerequisite knowledge and skills relevant to your lesson have been inadequately acquired (or not acquired at all), your lesson objective probably will not be attained by some or most of your learners. One purpose of seeing lessons within a unit plan is to determine whether all task-relevant prior knowledge required by each lesson has been provided. Because unit plans precede lesson plans, overlooked lessons and objectives prerequisite to later lessons can be added easily to the unit plan. You can draw your unit plans graphically, as shown in this chapter, using the word processing or graphics software on your personal computer.

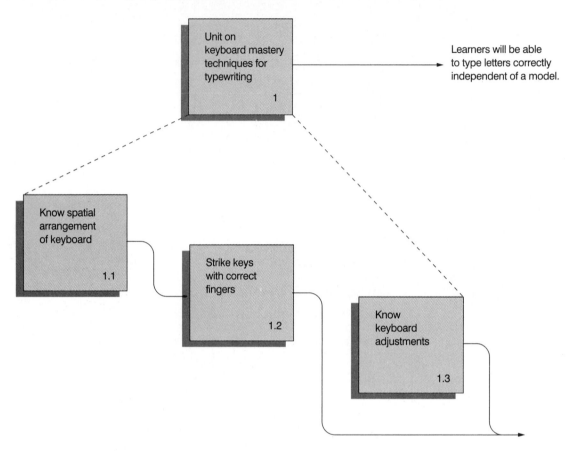

Figure 5.5b
A unit plan with partial lesson sequence (Lesson 1.1 must precede lesson 1.2)

The Written Unit Plan

Planning units graphically will be helpful in organizing, sequencing, and arriving at bite-sized pieces of content at the lesson level. But, you will also need a description that will communicate details of the unit to others (and to remind yourself) at a later time.

One format for a written version of a unit plan appears in Figure 5.6. This format divides a written plan into its (1) main purpose, (2) behavioral objectives, (3) content, (4) procedures and activities, (5) instructional aids and resources, and (6) evaluation methods. To this written plan attach your visual blueprint to indicate at a glance the organization, sequence, and sizing of the unit and to provide an introduction and overview of the written details. Together, they will give you a powerful tool for communicating your unit plans.

Grade: 10

Unit Topic: Pizza with Yeast Dough Crust

Course/Subject: Contemporary Home Economics

Approximate Time Required: One week

1. Main Purpose of the Unit: The purpose of this unit is to acquaint the students with the principles of making yeast dough by making pizza. The historical background, nutritional value, and variations of pizza will also be covered.
2. Behavioral Objectives
   The student will be able to:
   A. Describe the functions of each of the ingredients in yeast dough. (Cognitive-knowledge)
   B. Explain the steps in preparing yeast dough. (Cognitive-comprehension)
   C. Make a yeast dough for a pizza crust. (Cognitive-application and psychomotor-imitation)
   D. State briefly the history of pizza. (Cognitive-knowledge)
   E. Match the ingredients in pizza to the food groups they represent. (Cognitive-knowledge)
   F. Classify and give examples of different types of pizza. (Cognitive-analysis)
   G. Create and bake a pizza of their choice. (Cognitive-synthesis and psychomotor-precision)
3. Content Outline
   A. Essential ingredients in yeast dough
      (1) Flour
      (2) Yeast
      (3) Liquid
      (4) Sugar
      (5) Salt
   B. Non-essential ingredients
      (1) Fats
      (2) Eggs
      (3) Other, such as fruit and nuts
   C. Preparing yeast dough
      (1) Mixing
      (2) Kneading
      (3) Rising (fermenting)
      (4) Punching down
      (5) Shaping
      (6) Baking

   D. History of pizza
      (1) First pizza was from Naples.
      (2) Pizza is an Italian word meaning pie.
      (3) Originally eaten by the poor, pizza was also enjoyed by royalty.
      (4) Italian immigrants brought pizza to the United States in the late 1800s.
   E. Types of pizza
      (1) Neapolitan
      (2) Sicilian
      (3) Pizza Rustica
      (4) Pizza de Polenta
   F. Nutritional value of pizza
      (1) Nutritious meal or snack
      (2) Can contain all four food groups
      (3) One serving of cheese pizza contains:
         (a) Protein
         (b) Vitamins
         (c) Minerals
   G. Making a pizza
      (1) Prepare dough
      (2) Roll out dough
      (3) Transfer to pan
      (4) Spread sauce
      (5) Top as desired
      (6) Bake
4. Procedures and Activities
   A. Informal lecture
   B. Discussion
   C. Demonstration of mixing and kneading dough
   D. Filmstrip on pizza
   E. Education game (Pizzeria): Each time a student answers correctly a question about yeast dough or pizza, he gets a part of a paper pizza. The first to collect a complete pizza wins.
   F. Cooking lab
5. Instructional Aids or Resources
   A. Text: Guide to Modern Meals (Webster, McGraw-Hill, 1970)
   B. Filmstrip: Pizza, Pizza 10 minutes
   C. Pizza, Pizza booklets by Chef Boyardee
   D. Educational game (Pizzeria)
   E. Bake-it-easy Yeast Book by Fleischmann's Yeast
   F. Poster (showing different kinds of pizza from Pizza Hut)
6. Evaluation
   A. Unit test
   B. Lab performance

Figure 5.6
Example unit plan

From *Curriculum Planning: A Ten-Step Process* by W. Zenger and S. Zenger, 1982, Palo Alto, CA: R and E Research Associates. Copyright © 1982 by R and E Research Associates. Reprinted by permission.

Finally, notice that in Figure 5.6 both objectives and individual learners progress from the lower levels of cognitive and psychomotor behavioral complexity (comprehension, application, imitation) to the higher levels (analysis, synthesis, precision). This illustrates how early lessons in a unit can be used as building blocks to attain higher levels of authenticity at unit's end, helping to achieve a thinking curriculum.

>>> INTERDISCIPLINARY (LATERAL) <<< THEMATIC UNIT PLANS

How do I make an interdisciplinary thematic unit plan?

Results of recent research indicate that a curriculum unit in which the subjects are integrated and instructional techniques are used that involve students in interactive learning, problem solving, critical thinking, and independent thought and action can lead to high levels of thinking and meaningful learning (Aschbacher, 1991; Shavelson & Baxter, 1992; Richmond, & Striley, 1994).

An interdisciplinary thematic unit is a laterally planned unit of study in which topics and materials across content areas are integrated to provide a focus on a specific theme or subject. This approach to learning helps students visualize connections beyond the textbook. The principal aim of interdisciplinary instruction is to present learners with an opportunity to discover relationships and patterns that often go beyond a specific discipline and that bind together different aspects of our world in some systematic way. For example, interdisciplinary units often represent themes that can be related to several different disciplines or subject matter areas at the same time, such as to English or reading, science, social studies, and the expressive arts. Effective interdisciplinary units also often require learners to go beyond the instruction provided—to conduct research that requires the cooperation of other learners, the independent use of materials, and classroom dialogue in which learners are expected to reason critically, ask questions, make predictions and, with the aid of the teacher, evaluate the appropriateness of their own responses.

For example, Roberts and Kellough (1996) describe one teacher who planned an interdisciplinary unit for her middle school students by having them read a story about a young boy who travels through time and journeys to a fantasy planet. As the boy struggles to adapt to his new culture, he experiences the familiar themes of isolation, loneliness, domination, and imprisonment at the hands of those in charge of his new world. To relate this story to several different disciplines based on their reading, the teacher planned a unit in which the following relationships were drawn between and within disciplines:

- *Related to English.* The students discussed changes in the novel's setting, the development of the plot, and the author's use of the literary device of foreshadowing.
- *Related to expressive arts.* The students made a model of the planet and a floor plan of some of the buildings, and designed a robot that was described in the story. They also staged a dramatic reenactment of a scene in the novel.
- *Related to science.* Some students studied the flora and fauna on the planet and compared it to the plants and animals of their own state, while others attempted to identify the chemical composition of the environment on the planet and identify a probable location for it in our solar system.
- *Related to social studies.* The students engaged in a map study of the planet, developed a government for the fantasy planet, compared the segregation practiced in the story with segregation elsewhere, compared the freedoms of the inhabitants on the planet with the freedoms in our own Bill of Rights, and discussed issues of prejudice and class structure.
- *Related to additional research.* The students studied popular research on dreams and experiments about the sleep of humans, which played a predominant role in the story.

Notice how the relationships and patterns across subject areas in this unit did not just happen. This teacher developed her unit from a carefully constructed list of interrelated themes that she could select from and add to when determining the areas of the curriculum to be taught. To prepare her unit plan, this teacher developed a list of possible themes, like those shown in Table 5.1. These thematic concepts, topics, and categories were mapped onto existing subject matter in her and other teachers' classrooms and brought to life through the interdisciplinary thematic unit.

Table 5.1
Theme development for interdisciplinary units

Concepts	Topics	Categories
freedom	individual	autobiographies
cooperation	society	dreams
challenge	community	fantasies
conflict	relationships	tall tales
discovery	global concerns	experiences
culture	war	first-hand accounts
change	partnerships	
perseverance		

You should design interdisciplinary units to help you achieve the following objectives:

1. Emphasize that the process of learning is sometimes best pursued as an interconnected whole rather than as a series of specific subjects that always must be learned one after the other.
2. Encourage students to work cooperatively in partnerships and small groups that focus on the social values of learning.
3. Teach students to be independent problem solvers and thinkers.
4. Assist students to develop their own individual interests and learning styles.
5. Help students find out what they need to know and what they need to learn rather than always expecting the curriculum to teach it to them.

A key component of thematic units is the varied structure of the instructional strategies used. Give students a variety of activities, materials, and learning strategies within each of the content areas to facilitate comprehension and create a desire to read more about a topic. Have students work independently at times, but also collaborate in groups to read stories, investigate problems, and complete projects. In this way, students interact and learn from each other. Your role is that of a facilitator of learning.

The Spectrum of Integrated Curricula

Roberts and Kellough (1996) and Stevenson and Carr (1993) identify four ways you can implement integrated thematic teaching in your classroom, which represent different degrees of involvement:

Level 1. At this level, you would use a thematic approach to relate content and material from various disciplines during the same day. For example, the theme, "Natural Disasters Cause Social Effects," could originate from the topics of "weather" normally taught within a science or geography lesson and the topic of "community" taught within a social studies lesson. You would convey the theme of this interdisciplinary lesson to learners at the beginning of the unit in the form of a question, such as, "What necessary functions in a community are often disrupted after a natural disaster?" Encourage students to suggest adding other content and questions that represent other disciplines. For example, "What should be the role of the federal government in helping communities affected by a natural disaster?"

Level 2.   The next level of implementation requires you to consult with other teachers and agree on a common theme. Each teacher who decides to participate in the interdisciplinary unit teaches to that theme in their own classroom. In this manner students learn from a teacher in one classroom something that is related to what they are learning in another classroom. In the early elementary grades, a single teacher can perform this same function by referring back, say, during reading instruction, to a related concept in social studies, math, or science. Display on the bulletin board a list of themes developed beforehand based on interconnections among subject areas to remind both you and your learners to identify and discuss the connections. Encourage students to suggest additional content and questions related to the theme.

Level 3.   At the third level, you and your students work together to form a list of common themes across subject areas. For example, in the later elementary and high school grades, you might give an assignment to search the table of contents of your text and those of other teachers for the topic of a thematic unit you might teach within your classroom. If other teachers agree on the theme developed they, too, can be encouraged to mutually reinforce the connections identified in their classrooms, thereby providing momentum across disciplines for your thematic unit. This level of implementation is an effective way to initiate a team approach to your interdisciplinary teaching.

Level 4.   At the fourth level, your students develop on their own a list of common themes or problems across disciplines. Your charge to students is to arrive at one or more themes in which a traditional subject, discipline, or content area would be inadequate for addressing a theme or resolving a problem. In other words, you instruct your students to find current, contemporary dilemmas, moral issues, and problems that defy solution in the context of any one or small number of traditionally defined subject areas. Students may therefore be challenged to raise such thorny problems as, "How can we know when someone has really died?", requiring the simultaneous consideration of latest advances in the fields of medicine, religion, and philosophy, or, "How can we rid our planet of life-threatening pollution?", possibly requiring your class to consider knowledge from general science, physics, and chemistry and from social studies, government, and the law. At this level, your students are playing the role of independent and socially responsible thinkers and you are playing the role of resource, guiding their thoughts in increasingly productive avenues for elaborating relationships, patterns, and abstractions for adult living.

Visualizing Your Interdisciplinary Unit

Since interdisciplinary units emphasize lateral knowledge, their graphic portrayal is different than disciplinary units, which emphasize vertical knowledge. The graphic technique you use for expressing lateral knowledge must allow for content to be woven in and out of lessons as the opportunity arises. Hence, a more free form, or web type, visual format is required. This type of format shows how content is *nestled* within other content, how different subject areas *share* a common theme, how a single theme is *threaded* through different content areas, or how one field of study is *immersed* in another. Thus, all important themes and issues in an interdisciplinary plan are shown simultaneously in association with one another. The rules for creating these types of graphic outlines or webs are as follows:

- Identify the single most essential theme or idea.
- Place this theme or idea in the center of your web.
- Use arrows or lines going outward from the main idea to show relationships with other, subordinate issues, topics, or content, which can become the topics of individual lessons.
- Label the arrows and all key concepts with code words or phrases to describe the relationships you have expressed.

Figures 5.7 and 5.8 provide examples of thematic webs for expressing an interdisciplinary thematic unit.

The Written Unit Plan

The written format for an interdisciplinary unit plan is the same as that for a disciplinary unit. Recall that a written unit is divided into its (1) main purpose, (2) behavioral objectives, (3) content, (4) procedures and activities, (5) instructional aids and resources, and (6) evaluation methods. An example of a written interdisciplinary plan appears in Figure 5.9. To this written plan attach the visual outline or web of your theme and its interrelationships.

>>> MAKING LESSON PLANS <<<

Up to this point we have emphasized the importance of choosing unit outcomes at a higher level of behavioral complexity than lesson outcomes in order to achieve a thinking curriculum. If you plan lessons without a higher-level unit outcome in mind, your students' attention will fall exclusively on each individual lesson without noticing the

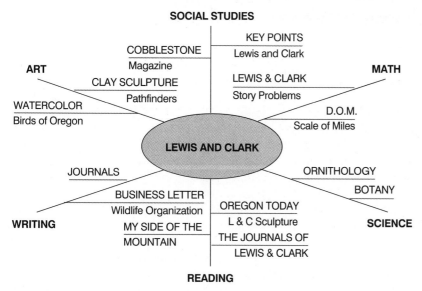

Figure 5.7
Visual representation of the interdisciplinary unit theme, "Adventures of Lewis and Clark"

From Kovalik, S. *The Classroom of the 21st Century,* 1994, Kent, WA: Books for Educators. Copyright ©
1994 by S. Kovalik. Reprinted with permission.

relationship among lessons. This relationship may appear deceptively unimportant until it becomes apparent that your lessons seem to pull students first in one direction (e.g., knowledge acquisition) and then abruptly in another (e.g., problem solving), without instruction to guide them in the transition. The result of such isolated lesson outcomes may well be confusion, anxiety, and distrust on the part of your students, regardless of how well you prepare each individual lesson and how effective they are in accomplishing their stated—but isolated—outcomes. Because outcomes at higher levels of behavioral complexity rarely can be attained within the time frame of a single lesson, they must be achieved in the context of unit plans.

Before actually writing a lesson plan, two preliminary considerations are necessary for your unit plan to flow smoothly: (1) determining where to start, and (2) providing for learner diversity. We discuss these in the following sections.

Determining Where to Start

Perhaps most perplexing to new teachers is deciding the level of behavioral complexity at which a lesson should begin. Do you always begin by teaching facts (instilling knowledge), or can you

How do I decide the level of behavioral complexity at which to begin a lesson?

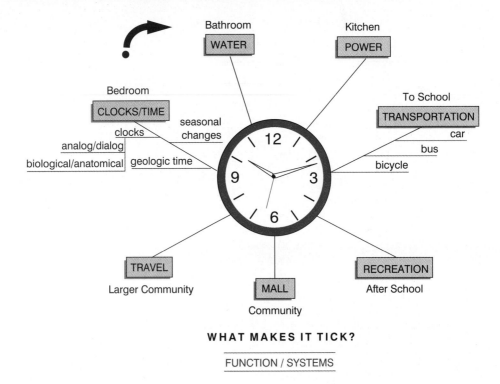

WHAT MAKES IT TICK?

FUNCTION / SYSTEMS

Figure 5.8
Visual representation of the interdisciplinary unit theme, "Dimensions of Time"
From Kovalik, S. *ITI: The Model,* 1994, Kent, WA: Books for Educators. Copyright © 1994 by S. Kovalik.
Reprinted with permission.

begin with activities at the application level, or even at the synthesis and decision-making levels? Both alternatives are possible, but each makes different assumptions about the behavioral characteristics of your students and the interrelationship among your lessons.

Beginning a lesson or a sequence of lessons at the knowledge level (e.g., to list, to recall, to recite, etc.) assumes that the topic you will be teaching is mostly new material. Such a lesson usually occurs at the beginning of a sequence that will progressively build this knowledge into more authentic behavior—perhaps ending at the application, synthesis, or evaluation level. When no task-relevant prior knowledge is required, the starting point for a lesson often is at the knowledge or comprehension level. When some task-relevant prior knowledge has been taught, lessons can begin at higher levels of behavioral complexity. Notice from the list of of objectives in Figure 5.6 that each lesson having an outcome at a higher level of behavioral complexity is preceded by a lesson at some lower level.

Grade: 5

Unit Topic: Gold Rush

Course/Subject: Interdisciplinary

Approximate Time Required: One Month

1. **Main Purpose of the Unit**

   The purpose of this unit is to acquaint the students with the excitement, the hardships and the challenges of the nineteenth century gold rush.

2. **Behavioral Objectives**

   The student will be able to:

   A. *History/Social Science*—Give reasons why people came to California in the 1840s.

   B. *History/Social Science*—Describe the three routes the pioneers took to California.

   C. *History/Social Science*—Compare life in the United States in the 1840s to life in the United States now.

   D. *History/Social Science*—List supplies brought by the pioneers on the trip West.

   E. *Language Arts*—Write a journal entry to describe some of the hardships associated with the trip West.

   F. *Science*—Research and write a report on how gold is mined.

   G. *Math*—Weigh gold nuggets (painted rocks) and calculate their monetary value.

   H. *Art*—Design a prairie quilt pattern using fabric scraps.

3. **Content Outline**

   A. Reasons people came to California in the 1840s
      1. Gold
      2. Job opportunities
      3. Weather
   B. Supplies for the trip
      1. Tools
      2. Personal supplies
      3. Food
      4. Household items

   C. Life on the trip West
      1. Weather conditions
      2. Roles of men, women, children
      3. Hazards of the trail
   D. Life in California after arrival
      1. Inflated prices
      2. Staking a claim
      3. Striking it rich
      4. A typical day in the life of a miner

4. **Procedures and Activities**

   A. Read aloud
   B. Small-group reading
   C. Independent reading
   D. Discussion
   F. Journal entries
   G. Measurement
   H. Cooking
   I. Singing

5. **Instructional Aids and Resources**

   A. Literature selections
      1. *Patty Reed's Doll*
      2. *By the Great Horn Spoon*
      3. *If You Traveled West in a Covered Wagon*
      4. *Children of the Wild West*
      5. *Joshua's Westward Journal*
      6. *The Way West, Journal of a Pioneer Woman*
      7. *The Little House Cookbook*
   B. Items indicative of the period (if obtainable)
      1. Cast iron skillet
      2. Bonnet or leather hat
      3. Old tools

6. **Assessment/Evaluation**

   Develop a rubric to grade these.

   A. Essay—Choose one route that the pioneers took to get to California and describe the journey.
   B. Gold Rush Game Board—Design a board game detailing the trip to California. The winner arrives in California and strikes it rich!

Figure 5.9

Example interdisciplinary thematic unit

(Written by Cynthia Kiel, teacher, Glendora, California)

The behavioral complexity with which each lesson starts depends on the behavioral outcome of the lessons that preceded it.

As we have seen, unit plans should attempt to teach a range of behaviors that end with a higher level of behavioral complexity than that which the unit began. Some units might begin at the application level and end at a higher level, if a previous unit has provided the task-relevant prior knowledge and understandings required. It also is possible to progress from one behavioral level to another within a single lesson. This may be increasingly difficult when lessons start at high levels of behavioral complexity, but it is possible and often desirable to move from knowledge to comprehension and on to application activities within a single lesson. This is illustrated in the flow of behaviors for the following third-grade social studies lesson.

Unit Title: Local, State, and National Geography
Lesson Title: Local Geography
Behaviors:

- Student will know geographical location of community relative to state and nation (knowledge).
- Student will be able to describe physical features of community (comprehension).
- Student will be able to locate community on map and globe (application).
- Student will be able to discuss how the community is similar to and different from other communities (analysis).

In this lesson a comprehensive span of behaviors is required in relatively brief time (a single lesson) by using objects already known to the students (their own community; map; globe) and by dovetailing one behavior into another so that each new activity is a continuation of the preceding one. When a transition across behavioral levels is planned within a single lesson, the necessary question before each new level of complexity is, "Have I provided all the required task-relevant prior knowledge?" Only when you can answer "Yes" will the lesson be directed at the students' current level of understanding, and only then can students attain the unit objective.

Providing for Learner Diversity with Alternative Methods and New Technologies

How can my lessons provide for student diversity?

A second consideration before writing a lesson plan is the extent to which the lesson provides for student diversity. Thus far, we have considered all the students within a class to be identical, sharing the same behavioral characteristics and task-relevant prior knowledge. Of course, diversity is the rule in any classroom, and in Chapter 2 we presented some of the varieties of students that you are likely to encounter.

Regardless of where you position the entry level of a lesson, some students will be above it and other students will be below it. Much of the work of unit and lesson planning is playing a game of averages in which you attempt to provide *most* of the instruction at the current level of functioning of *most* of the learners. Unless an entire course of study is individualized (sometimes the case with programmed and computer-assisted instruction curricula), most instruction must be directed at the "average" learner in your classroom.

However, there are instructional methods and **tutorial and communication technologies** that can supplement the game of averages. These methods and technologies share the following characteristics:

What are some new technologies I can use to deliver my lessons?

- Allowing rapid movement within and across content depending on the learners' success at any given time.
- Allowing students the flexibility to proceed at their own pace and level of difficulty.
- Providing students immediate feedback as to the accuracy of their responses.
- Gradually shifting the responsibility for learning from teacher to student.

Before you begin your lesson plan, decide on the extent to which methods and technologies for individualizing instruction are needed by the diversity of learning needs in your classroom. The following methods describe some of your options for individualizing instruction.

Task Ability Grouping.   Your class can be grouped for a specified period of time by the skills required to learn the material you are presenting. For example, more able readers can read ahead and work independently on advanced exercises while your lesson is directed to the average and less able reader. Lesson plans, objectives, activities, materials, and tests can be divided into two or more appropriate parts, when learners exhibit noticeable strengths and weaknesses that cannot be bridged in a single lesson. The intent is to group learners homogeneously by learning skills relevant to a specific task or lesson, after which regrouping is considered.

Learning Centers.   Students tend to learn better when solving real-life problems. As a result, many schools are working to reorganize curriculum to support real-world problem solving and application (Boyer, 1993). One way to promote real-world problem solving and help individual learners apply what they have learned is through the use of a learning center. Learning centers can individualize a lesson by providing resources for review and practice for those who may lack task-relevant prior knowledge or skills. When a learning center can contain media, supplemental resources, and/or exercises directly related to applying your lesson content, include it as an integral part of your lesson plan.

Review and Followup Materials.   Some of your lessons will need to stimulate the recall of task-relevant prior knowledge. An oral summary, together with a supplementary handout on which individual learners may look up the required information, can bring some students to the required level while not boring others. The key to this procedure is to carefully prepare a *summary and review sheet* covering the critically needed prerequisite knowledge for the day's lesson. This lets you limit your review to the essentials and to the least amount of time.

Instructional Games and Simulations.   Games and simulations can be used either cooperatively or independently by students who need an alternative or supplementary means of attaining your classroom objectives. Lessons may begin with whole-class instruction and, depending on interests and abilities, some students can be directed to instructional games and simulations to receive hands-on experiences that may remediate or enrich skills taught during full-class instruction. Textbook publishers are increasingly providing computer simulations and practiced-based instruction that teach and reteach basic skills relevant to your curriculum guide. Some of these curriculum supplements can be used by learners in cooperative groups.

Programmed Instruction.   Programmed instruction refers to written instructional materials that students work with by themselves at their own level and at their own pace. Programmed instruction materials typically break skills down into small subskills, such as might be identified in a learning hierarchy, through which students work in small steps. Questions and prompts along the way actively engage learners in formulating responses to which they are given immediate knowledge of whether they are correct, usually directly beneath or near the question or prompt. Programmed instruction has not been found to be more effective than more conventional methods, when it has been used as the sole source of new instruction (Bangert, Kulik, & Kulik, 1983; Slavin, 1984). However, when self-instructional materials have covered more familiar content and learners work in mixed ability learning teams in which teammates help each other (called "Team Assisted Individualization"), programmed materials have been effective in increasing achievement (Slavin, 1985).

Tutoring.   **Peer tutoring** is when one student teaches another at the same grade and age level. **Cross-age tutoring** is when one tutor is several years and grade levels above the learner receiving the instruction. Cross-age tutoring, generally, has been more effective than peer tutoring owing to the fact that older students are more likely to be familiar with the material and are more likely to be respected as role models (Devin-Sheehan, Feldman, & Allen, 1976). It has been recommended that cross-age tutors be separated by two or three grades. As with programmed instruction, tutoring has been most successful as an adjunct to regular instruction usually in the form of providing greater amounts of instructional practice than could be provided in a whole-class or group setting. Tutoring has been most successful when tutors have been trained and given explicit instruction on how to tutor.

Computer-assisted Instruction (CAI).   Computer-assisted instruction provides many of the same practice opportunities of programmed instruction and tutors, but with the aid of a computer. CAI programs are now available at many different grade levels and content areas to give students practice, assess understanding, and provide remediation, if needed. The advantage of CAI over written programmed materials and tutors is that the accuracy of student responses to practice activities can be quickly assessed and the sequence and difficulty of the activities changed to correspond with the learners' current level of functioning. In this manner practice can be "tailored" to each individual learner depending on how well he or she is responding at a certain level of difficulty. More time can be spent on a particular topic or skill or the "program" can return to an earlier sequence of instruction to review or reteach prerequisite learning. Computer-assisted instruction also has the capability of providing color pictures, charts, and diagrams, which can motivate learners and enhance the authencity of the practice experience. Most computer-assisted instruction is now presented to learners on personal computers in the classroom with software developed by publishers of the textbooks used at the various grades and content areas in which instruction is being given. As with other individual-ized learning methods, CAI has been found most effective when pro-viding practice opportunities for content already taught (Atkinson, 1984; Kulik & Kulik, 1984).

Interactive Videodiscs and CD-ROM. Interactive videodiscs—or laser discs—are similar to the compact discs used for recording music. CD-ROM (compact disc—read-only memory) discs are similar to videodiscs but are smaller and can store more information. Except for the smaller size and greater information storage capacity, inter-active videodiscs and CD-ROM share the same advantages over either written or computer-assisted programmed material. These new laser technologies can present to the learner *any combination* of text, diagrams, slides, maps, films, and animations on demand, thereby greatly increasing the flexibility of the recorded content over traditional programmed instruction. They can also hold different sound tracks, for example, one in English and another in Spanish. The learner can freeze frames indefinitely and locate any frame or sequence of frames on the disk almost instantaneously. And, unlike written texts or computer software (diskettes), they are sealed under a protective plastic surface through which light passes, making them nearly indestructible.

Because of these characteristics, interactive videodiscs and CD-ROM technology are particularly suited to simulating and modeling higher-order thinking skills and real-life experiences—such as labora-tory experiments, physical motion, and even noises and sounds, which can make learning "come alive." For this reason interactive videodisc and CD-ROM technology is quickly becoming the preferred medium for providing **interactive individualized practice activities.**

Fiber Optics/Telecommunications. This technology offers the most oppor-tunities to stimulate the senses through multimedia, making the learning environment more fluid and personalized. Often referred to as the "**living curriculum,**" the combination of laser technology and telecommunications has many of the same features of interactive videodisc technology with the added advantage that the subject mat-ter being studied no longer must reside on a videodisc inside a per-sonal computer. Students may acquire information nearly instanta-neously from communication "superhighways," which can give the individual learner rapid access to human and textual resources across schools, geographical locations, and the world.

With the aid of a computer, learners create their own "living cur-riculum" with which to practice and apply the content learned. By selecting information networks and pathways that increasingly bring

Learning centers containing media, supplemental resources, demonstration materials, and exercises can help individualize a lesson for those who may lack the prerequisite knowledge or skills required at the beginning of the lesson. The use of a learning center should be indicated in the lesson plan whenever applicable.

authentic detail and professional expertise to learners, responsibility for retaining and applying content passes gradually from the teacher to learners and to the world outside the classroom, encouraging cooperative ventures with other students, professionals, and resources. Once established, these information pathways provide students with many opportunities, among which are the following:

- Search beyond their local libraries; for example, browse through holdings on "early flight" in the Library of Congress, visually take a tour of a space station circling in space, or ask questions of a curator at the Air and Space Museum via electronic mail.
- Become more specialized and focused on current issues; for example, query a database being compiled by *The New York Times* on a fast-breaking story, scan a recent index of *Scientific American* for latest advances on gene splicing, or communicate via electronic mail with a researcher stationed in Antarctica.
- Cooperate with other learners at a distance; for example, team up with students in another school, state, or nation to share information of mutual interest on acid rain, deforestation, or the global economy.

- Work with cross-age mentors outside their own school; for example, to explore connections between academic work and job opportunities, or to see how principles and concepts are used at more advanced levels, such as in subsequent courses, in the workplace, or in different community contexts.

These methods and communication technologies are only some of the ways your lesson plans can provide for diverse learning needs among your students. We will return for a closer look at some of these in the chapters ahead.

>>> EVENTS OF INSTRUCTION <<<

What is in a lesson plan?

After you have determined where to start the lesson and how to provide for diverse learning needs, you are ready to start planning the lesson. At this time, you will specify the key events that occur during the lesson—and for which you are responsible. By placing the responsibility on you for providing these events, we distinguish between teaching and learning. *Learning* refers to the internal events that go on inside your learners' heads. *Teaching* is the sum of the instructional activities you provide to influence what goes on in your learners' heads.

The sequence of steps you follow in lesson planning assumes that the instructional events you plan will influence learning. It is not unusual for teaching to be unrelated to learning, as when teachers teach and students listen, but nothing "sinks in." The process of getting instructional events to sink in is one of planning instruction that fosters a close relationship between the external events of instruction and the internal events of learning, *actively engaging your learners in the learning process.*

You can achieve this tightly knit relationship between teaching and learning by considering seven instructional events suggested by Gagné and Briggs (1979).[1] These steps include the most relevant parts of other models of lesson preparation. For example, Hunter (1982) proposes a sequence of events, called the Mastery Learning Program, which is related to those of Gagné and Briggs (see Figure 5.10). Although not all of the events in either model are applicable to every lesson, they provide a basis—or menu—from which you can formulate many different lesson plans. Let's consider the types of instructional activity that each event entails and how you can relate them to the internal processes of learning.

---

[1] Although less useful for lesson planning, these steps also appear in a slightly revised form in Gagné and Briggs (1992).

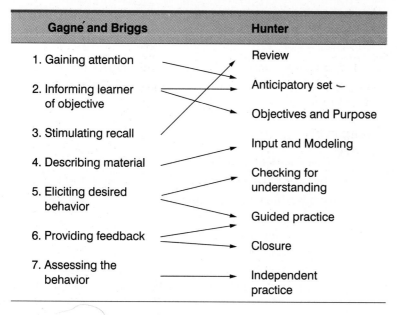

Gagné and Briggs	Hunter
1. Gaining attention	Review
2. Informing learner of objective	Anticipatory set
	Objectives and Purpose
3. Stimulating recall	Input and Modeling
4. Describing material	Checking for understanding
5. Eliciting desired behavior	Guided practice
6. Providing feedback	Closure
7. Assessing the behavior	Independent practice

Figure 5.10
Two related perspectives on events of instruction

1. Gaining Attention

Without your students' attention, little of your lesson will be heard, let alone actively engage your students in the learning process. Thus, each lesson plan begins with an instructional event to engage student interest, curiosity, and attention. In some classes this will mean raising their attention from almost complete disengagement to where their vision and hearing are receptive. In other classes this may mean raising their attention from an already receptive mode to a higher level of curiosity, interest, and attention. The intensity of your attention-gaining event will depend on the starting point of your learners. A fifth-period class that meets after lunch may require a more dramatic attention-getting event than will an eager first-period class. You will need to find the right event for gaining your students attention.

One of the most common attention-gaining devices is to arouse curiosity. Often this can be accomplished by asking questions:

Have you ever wondered how we got the word "horsepower"? Who would like to guess? (from a lesson on energy)

Can anyone think of a popular automobile with the name of a Greek god? (from an introductory lesson on mythology)

Have you ever wondered how some creatures can live both in the water and on land? (from a lesson on amphibious animals)

These questions, called *openers,* are designed not to have any single correct answer or even to accurately reflect the fine details of what is to follow. Instead they *amuse, stimulate, or even bewilder* students so that they become receptive to the content and questions that follow. Following are other thought-provoking openers:

Why do some scientists think that traveling to the planets will make the space traveler younger? (from a lesson in physics)

Why do we have the word i-t-s and another word i-t-apostrophe-s? (from a lesson in punctuation)

Why is the dollar worth more today in Mexico than in Switzerland? (from a lesson in economics)

Why do you think some eloquent lawyers become disliked by the juries they speak to? (from a lesson in public speaking)

Another useful technique for gaining students' attention is to present

- an apparent *contradiction:*
  Why do you think the Greek empire collapsed when it was at its strongest?
- or a seeming *inconsistency* in real life:
  Why do some lower forms of animal life live longer than human beings?
- or something that at first appears to be *illogical:*
  Why must something go backward every time something else goes forward?

For example, introducing a lesson in signed numbers by informing your learners that the multiplication of two negative numbers always results in a positive product may puzzle them, but it can arouse their curiosity about how two negatives could result in something positive. You could continue by explaining the mathematical rules behind this apparent contradiction.

Diagrams, pictures, illustrations, scale models, and films are other attention-getting aids. Use these devices to appeal to your learners' sense of vision while your oral presentation appeals to their sense of hearing. Graphics or visuals are particularly effective openers with students who are known to be more oriented and responsive to visual than auditory presentations. A visual opener can include samples of materials for the day's lesson so that students can touch them before the lesson begins. A visual opener also can show equipment you will use during the lesson (e.g., scales, meters).

2. Informing Learners of the Objective

Just because your learners have been turned on with some attention-getting device does not mean they will be tuned to the wavelength at which you present the lesson. Now you need to tell them the channel on which your lesson is being transmitted. The most effective way to focus your learners' receptivity is to inform them of the behavioral outcome they will be expected to attain by the end of the lesson. You can do this by telling them early in the lesson or unit how they will be examined or expected to show competence. For example, such expectations might be expressed in the following ways:

- Remember the four definitions of *power* that will be presented (science).
- Be able to express ownership orally in a sentence to the class (English).
- Identify correctly a mystery specimen of lower animal life using the microscope (life science).
- State your true feelings about the laws dealing with pornography (social studies).

Such statements allow learners to know when they have attained the expected level of behavior and to become selective in how to use and remember the lesson information. If your students know they will be expected to recall four definitions of power at the end of your lesson on energy, then they know to focus their search, retrieval, and retention processes *during the lesson* on the definitions or categories of power you present.

Informing learners of your objective helps them organize their thinking in advance of the lesson by providing mental "hooks" on which to hang the key points. This activates the learning process and focuses your learners on obtaining the required behavioral outcome.

The key to the success of this instructional event is to communicate your objective clearly. Therefore, choose your words with your learners' vocabulary and language level in mind, and record what you tell them as a reminder in this second part of your lesson plan. The best way to communicate your objective is to provide examples of tasks that you expect your students to be able to perform after the lesson. This effectively translates the action verb associated with a level of behavioral complexity into some ways this behavior might be measured on tests, in class discussions, and in question-and-answer sessions.

For example, you might write on the blackboard the following examples of expected behavior at the beginning of a unit on lower forms of animal life, and then checkmark the ones that most apply at the start of each day's lesson:

☒ Define an amoeba.

☒ Draw the cellular structure of an amoeba.

☐ Explain the reproduction cycle of an amoeba.

☐ Using a microscope, properly distinguish an amoeba from other single-celled animals.

Notice that these behavioral outcomes range from recounting a fact to making decisions and judgments in a real biological environment. Without knowing in advance at which of these levels they are expected to perform, your learners will have no way of selecting and focusing their attention on those parts of the instruction leading to the desired behavior. This is not to say that they should ignore other aspects of the presentation, but students can now see the other aspects as tools or means for gaining the highest level of behavior required, and not as ends in themselves.

3. Stimulating Recall of Prerequisite Learning

Before you can proceed with the new lesson content, one final preliminary instructional event is needed. Because learning cannot occur in a vacuum, the necessary task-relevant prior information must be retrieved and made ready for use. This calls for some method of reviewing, summarizing, restating, or otherwise stimulating the key concepts acquired in previous lessons. This information is instrumental for achieving the level of behavioral complexity intended in the present lesson.

For example, if your goal is to have learners use a microscope to properly distinguish an amoeba from other single-celled animals, it is clear that some previously acquired facts, concepts, and skills are relevant to this new task. Definitions of single-celled animals, unique characteristics of an amoeba that make it distinguishable from other one-celled animals, and skill in using the microscope are among the task-relevant prior knowledge that will influence their attainment of this outcome.

Before the actual presentation of new content begins, the necessary task-relevant prior information must be retrieved and made ready for use. This can be accomplished by reviewing, summarizing, and restating, stimulating into action the key concepts acquired in previous lessons.

Helping students retrieve earlier information requires condensing the key aspects into brief, easily understood form. Obviously, it is not practical to summarize all of it in a few minutes. You need to use thought-provoking and stimulating techniques to focus upon sizable amounts of prior learning, but without reviewing all the content that was previously covered or that is needed for the new learning. Questions can help your students recall the most significant and memorable parts of earlier lessons:

Do you remember why Johnny couldn't see the amoeba in the microscope? (it was on low magnification instead of high)

Do you remember Betty Jo's humorous attempt to relate the reproduction cycle of an amoeba to that of human beings? (she had equated cell division with waking up one morning to find a new baby in the family)

Do you remember the three-color picture Bobby drew of the cellular structure of an amoeba? (everyone had commented on how lifelike the picture was)

Such questions help students retrieve task-relevant prior learning—not by summarizing that learning, but by tapping into a single *mental image* that recalls that learning. Once the image has been retrieved, students can turn it on and off at will to search for details that may be nestled within it, achieving still greater recall. Describing how to stimulate the recall of prerequisite learning, then, is the third entry in your lesson plan.

4. Presenting the Stimulus Material

This will be the heart of your lesson plan. At first glance, this component may seem to require little explanation, but several important considerations for completing it often go unnoticed. These pertain to the authenticity, selectivity, and variety of your lesson presentation. Let's look closely at each of these.

Authenticity.   Recall our discussion of authenticity in Chapter 4. In order to teach a behavior that is authentic, your lesson must present content in a way in which it will be used by your learners on performance tests, in subsequent grades, and on the job. If your goal is to teach learners to use a microscope to identify single-celled animals, then teaching them to label the parts of a microscope would not be authentic. Although naming the parts may be a prerequisite skill and an important objective of an earlier lesson, it would not be sufficient to attaining the desired goal of this lesson. Similarly, if your students are to fully understand signed numbers, they should be given examples using both single-digit and multiple-digit numbers in various formats, just as they are found in subsequent grades, on the job, and in tasks required in real life. In other words, how you use a behavior in daily life must always be how you teach a behavior in order for it to be authentic.

You can make the behaviors you teach more authentic by changing the *irrelevant* aspects of what you are teaching as often as possible, and in as many different ways as possible, so that students learn which dimensions are irrelevant. This prevents learning an objective under only one condition but not under others that may be encountered in subsequent lessons, grades, and courses. Following are examples of changing the irrelevant aspects of a learning stimulus:

- In math, show both stacked format and line format:

$$-2 \text{ as well as } -2 + 5 =$$
$$\underline{+5}$$

- Introduce learners to examples of proper punctuation by using popular magazines and newspapers as well as the text and workbook (English or a foreign language).
- Show how the laws of electricity apply to lightning during a thunderstorm as well as to electrical circuitry in the laboratory (science).

- Relate rules of social behavior found among humans to those often found among animals (social studies).
- Compare the central processing unit in a microcomputer to the executive processes in the human brain (computer science).
- Show how the reasons for a particular war also can be applied to other conflicts hundreds of years earlier (history).

In each of these examples the lesson designer is changing the irrelevant dimensions of the objective by applying key lesson ideas in different contexts. As a result, learners are more likely (1) to focus upon correct mathematical operations and not the format of the problem, (2) to notice improper punctuation when it appears in a slick or popular publication, (3) to understand the universality of physical laws governing electricity, (4) to not think that social behavior is a uniquely human phenomenon, (5) to not confuse the wonders of data processing with the hardware and equipment that only sometimes are needed to perform it, and (6) to understand that some reasons for conflict, war, and hostility are general as well as specific.

Selectivity. A second consideration during this stage of lesson preparation is emphasizing the content most important to your lesson. Not everything in a chapter, workbook, film, lecture, or on the chalkboard will be of equal importance to the day's objective. Consequently, highlighting key aspects of the text and workbook at the *beginning* of the lesson will help students selectively review and retain the main points of your lesson. For example, focusing your learners' attention on the "six concepts on the bottom of page 50" or the "tables and figures at the end of Chapter 3" can help your learners place the day's lesson in the context of their curriculum and provide an anchor for future reference.

You will also want to highlight content *during* your lesson. Examples of such highlighting include verbally emphasizing the importance of certain events; telling students what to look for in a film (even stopping it to reinforce an idea, if need be); emphasizing key words on the chalkboard with underlining, circling, or color; and using verbal markers ("This is important"; "Notice the relevance of this"; "You'll need this information later"). These and other methods for selectively emphasizing key parts of your lesson will be taken up in later chapters, but remember to consider them at this stage of your lesson plan.

Variety. A key behavior of the effective teacher described in Chapter 1 was instructional variety. Gaining students' attention at the start of the lesson is one thing, but keeping their attention is quite another. Variety in the modalities of instruction (e.g., visual, oral, tactile) and instructional activity (large-group lecture, question and answer, small-group discussion) stimulates student thinking and interest. Shifting from visually dominated instruction to orally dominated instruction (or using both simultaneously) and breaking a lesson into several instructional activities (e.g., explanation followed by question and answer) is important.

Planning changes in modality and instructional activities presents the lesson in varied contexts, giving learners the opportunity to grasp material in several different ways, according to their individual learning styles. Such changes also give students the opportunity to see previously learned material used in different ways. This reinforces learned material better than simply restating it in the same mode and form. It also encourages learners to extend or expand material according to the new mode or procedure being used. For example, material learned in a lecture may be pushed to its limit in a question-and-answer period when the learner answers a question and finds out that previous understandings were partly incorrect due to the limited context in which they were learned. Quite apart from the well-known fact that instructional variety helps keep students attentive and actively engaged in the learning process, it also offers them a more memorable and conscious learning experience. Be sure to consider these and other methods of adding instructional variety to your lesson during this stage of your lesson plan.

5. Eliciting the Desired Behavior

After presentation of the stimulus material, provide your learners an opportunity to show whether they can perform the behaviors at the intended level of complexity. Learning cannot occur effectively in a passive environment—one that lacks activities to engage the learner in the learning process at moderate-to-high rates of success. Active engagement in the learning process at an appropriate level of difficulty must be a goal of every lesson, because without it little or no learning occurs.

Such engagement can be accomplished in many ways. It may even occur spontaneously as a result of getting your students' attention, informing them of the objectives, stimulating the recall of prerequisite learning, and presenting the stimulus material—but don't count on it! Active engagement, especially at an appropriate level of difficulty, is a slippery concept. If left to chance, it rarely occurs to the extent required for significant learning. While all of the instructional events presented thus far are required to actively engage your learners, they cannot guarantee engagement. Therefore, a fifth instructional event is needed; when added to a lesson plan it encourages and guides learners through a process that can be expected to produce the behavior intended.

This fifth event—eliciting the desired behavior—differs from the four preceding ones in that it seeks the individual's covert and personal engagement in the learning process. Each learner must be placed in a position of grappling in a trial-and-error fashion with summarizing, paraphrasing, applying, or solving a problem involving the lesson content. It is not important that the behavior be produced at this stage in a recognizable form, as long as the activity provided stimulates an *attempt to produce the intended behavior.* This activity encourages the learner to *organize a response* that meets the level of behavioral complexity stated when the student was informed of the objective.

The primary ways of staging this instructional event include workbooks, handouts, textbook study questions, verbal and written exercises, and questions that have students apply what was learned, if only in the privacy of their minds. The idea is to pose a classroom activity that encourages students to use the material in a nonevaluative atmosphere, as close in time as possible to presentation of new material. Sometimes such activities can be inserted throughout the lesson at the end of each new chunk of information, which also adds variety. In other instances, these activities occur near the end of presenting the new material.

Either way, the eliciting activity is brief, nonevaluative, and focused exclusively on posing a condition for which the learner must organize a response (such as a question, problem, or exercise). This response may be written, oral, or subvocal (students respond in their own minds). Eliciting activities can be as simple as your posing a question anywhere in a lesson, or as complex as a problem exercise completed in a workbook at lesson's end. The main attribute is that these activities be *nonevaluative,* to encourage a response unhampered by the anxiety and conservative response patterns that generally occur during testing. Rosenshine and Stevens (1986) suggest additional ways of eliciting the desired behavior:

- Preparing a large number of oral questions beforehand.
- Asking many brief questions on main points, on supplementary points, and on the process being taught.
- Calling on students whose hands are not raised in addition to those who volunteer.
- Asking students to summarize a rule or process in their own words.
- Having all students write their answers (on paper or the chalkboard) while you circulate.

- Having all students write their answers and check them with a neighbor (this is frequently used with older students).
- At the end of a lecture/discussion (especially with older students), writing the main points on the chalkboard and then having the class meet in groups to summarize the main points to each other.

6. Providing Feedback

The sixth instructional event is closely connected in time to the fifth event (eliciting the desired behavior). Eliciting the desired behavior promotes learning to the extent that learners come to understand the correctness of their responses. The response itself must be an individual attempt to recall, summarize, paraphrase, apply, or problem-solve, but the feedback that immediately follows can be directed to the entire class. For example, you can anonymously report to the class an individual's correct answer or hold up several students' answers for comparison.

However, as stated, an eliciting activity's main attribute is that it is *nonevaluative*. At this stage of the learning process, it is important to respond to a wrong answer encouragingly, to maintain the nonevaluative flavor of the eliciting activity. Responses such as, "That's a good try," "That's not quite what I'm looking for this time," or "Keep thinking," can switch the focus to more useful responses without penalizing students for responding.

Ways of confirming a correct response are to read aloud the correct answers from a workbook, or provide a handout with the correct answers, or provide a copy of the exercise with correct answers penciled in. You could use a transparency to pose the eliciting activity and then record volunteered answers. If students are working silently at their seats, you can walk about the room, using a simple nod and smile to indicate the correctness of an individual performance or to encourage the revision of a wrong response. This part of the lesson plan, then, should include the means by which feedback will be given learners about their responses. These and additional ways of providing feedback to individual students, small groups, and the entire class are summarized in Table 5.2.

7. Assessing the Behavior

You do not have to provide all your eliciting activities and feedback within a single instructional period. There are other ways to engage

Table 5.2
Some methods of providing feedback

Individual Students	Small Groups	Class
Nod while walking past	Sit with group and discuss answers	Place answers on a transparency
Point to correct answer in workbook or text	Have one group critique another group's answers	Provide answers on a handout
Show student the answer key	Give each group the answer key when finished	Read answers aloud
Place check alongside incorrect answers	Assign one group member the task of checking the answers of other group members	Place answers on the chalkboard
Have students grade each others' papers by using the text, or assign references as a guide		Have selected students read their answers aloud
		Have students grade each others' papers as you give answers

your students in the learning process, to organize a response, and to create a product. These include tests and homework problems that are returned the next day, or extended assignments that are returned days or weeks later (essays and research papers). However, tests, essays, term papers, and projects result from several individual lessons and therefore are considerably larger than the elicitation activities discussed thus far. These larger activities are particularly valuable for eliciting more complex behavior than could be expected at the end of any single lesson and for evaluating how well behaviors are performed.

This final instructional event specifies what activity you will use to evaluate the behavior. As we have seen, eliciting activities can be immediate or delayed (an oral question vs. a research paper), and evaluative or nonevaluative. The fifth event described an immediate and nonevaluative eliciting activity. But for this instructional event—assessing the behavior—you will describe a *delayed* eliciting activity that is primarily *evaluative.*

Evaluative eliciting activities such as tests, research papers, graded homework and classroom performances, and student portfolios can be disadvantageous at earlier stages of learning because they limit risk-taking—or exploratory—behavior and their feedback lacks immediacy. Both of these factors can be counterproductive to learning when the instructional goal is to get learners to respond for the first time. Consequently, do not use a delayed eliciting activity to the exclusion of immediate and nonevaluative eliciting activities early in the lesson.

The means for completing this event can include the following:

Tests and quizzes

Homework exercises

In-class workbook assignments

Performance evaluations

Lab assignments

Oral presentations

Extended essays

Research papers

Independent practice

Portfolios

>>> EXAMPLE LESSON PLANS <<<

We are now ready to place these seven instructional events into a brief but effective lesson plan. To be both practical and effective, lesson plans must be short and yet provide all the ingredients needed to deliver the lesson. Following are some example plans on various subjects and grade levels that show how easy lesson planning can be when the task is organized by these seven instructional events. Let's review each of them with some examples.

Unit Title: Reading: Word Attack Skills (vertically planned unit)
Lesson Title: Sound Discrimination, Letters of the Alphabet—Lesson 2.1

This indicates the general content of the lesson and its placement in a unit on word attack skills. The lesson identifier, 2.1, indicates that this lesson is the first one in Unit 2. It would appear on the graphic unit plan as indicated in Figure 5.11.

Next appears the elaboration of each of the seven instructional events for delivering this lesson to students.

1. Gaining attention	Play an audiotape of a voice articulating the sounds.

This instructional event gains student attention and focuses them on what is to be presented. Whatever device or procedure you use should not only gain their attention but also motivate their continued concentration well into the lesson. Keep in mind that students, especially young ones, have trouble picking up subtle transitions in classroom activities. Often their attention is steadfastly on what has immediately preceded the lesson, and they are reluctant to change focus unless something new, interesting, or exciting is on the horizon.

Visual or auditory stimuli often are effective as attention getters, because their ability to penetrate the senses exceeds that of more neutral stimuli like written words, verbal expressions, or pronounce-

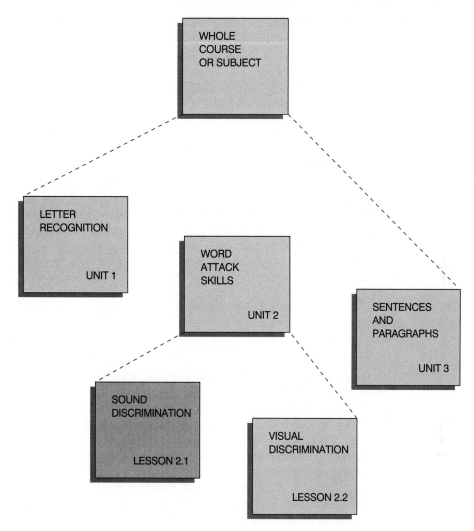

Figure 5.11
The relationship among lessons, units, and a course or domain

ments. Changing sensory modalities from listening to looking (or vice versa) often provides the incentive necessary to more selectively perceive and receive the message about to be communicated.

2. Informing the learner of the objective

When the tape is finished, indicate that at the end of the lesson students will be expected to repeat the vowel sounds out loud, independently of the tape.

This instructional event translates the behavioral objective for the lesson into a form that is meaningful to students. In this example, the transfer of information from one modality (listening) to another (speaking) is being sought, indicating that the objective for this lesson is written at the comprehension level of the cognitive domain. Your attention-getting device should be chosen to lead into the objective for the lesson. Simply clapping one's hands to gain attention, followed by the objective, would not be as effective as having the objective actually *contained within* the attention-getting procedure.

In this example, the audiotape was directly related to the lesson's content, allowing these two instructional events to work together to produce a unified theme, enhancing the learners' attention. Other simple but effective attention getters that easily can be made to reflect the lesson objective are a picture or chart, a question on the chalkboard, or a demonstration derived directly from lesson content.

3. Stimulating recall of prerequisite learning

Show how each vowel sound is produced by the correct positioning of the mouth and lips.

Identifying and successfully communicating task-relevant prior knowledge to students is critical to attaining the lesson objective. Unless you paraphrase, summarize, or otherwise review this information, at least some students will be unable to comprehend the information to be conveyed. Among the most frequent reasons that learners are unable to attain lesson outcomes is that they lack the needed skills and understandings of previously taught lessons necessary for subsequent learning to occur.

Prerequisite content must be recalled or stimulated into action for it to play a meaningful role in acquiring new learning. Most lessons require some previous facts, understandings, or skills, and these should be recalled and identified at this step of the lesson plan. You can achieve this by touching on the high points of this prior learning.

4. Presenting the stimulus material

Say each vowel sound and then have the class repeat it twice, pointing to a chart of the position of the mouth and lips during the articulation of each vowel sound. Do the most commonly used vowels first.

You may feel that this is the heart of the lesson. You are partly right, except that there are six other hearts, each of which could entail as much effort in planning and instructional time as this event does. Beginning teachers tend to pack their lessons almost entirely with new stimulus material. They devote far less effort to gaining attention, to informing the learner of the objective, to recalling prerequisite learning, and to other instructional events that must follow the presentation of new material.

Obviously the presentation of new material is indispensable, but it need not always encompass most (or even a large portion) of the lesson. The result of devoting a large portion of the lesson to new material, exclusive of the other instructional events, is that the lesson is likely to present content in pieces too big for learners to grasp. This often results in considerable reteaching during subsequent lessons and ultimately less content coverage at the end of a unit.

Although the presentation of new stimulus material is an important part of most lessons, it does not always have to comprise the majority of instructional time. Just as the first three instructional events must come before the presentation of new material for this material to be meaningful, the next three instructional events will make clear that this new stimulus material must itself be a stimulus for something more to come.

5. Eliciting the desired behavior	Have students silently practice forming correct mouth and lip positions for each vowel sound, following the pictures in their workbooks.

For this instructional event the learner is given guidance in how to perform the behavior and an opportunity to practice it—two activities that must go hand in hand if learning is to occur. Eliciting the desired behavior for the first time without providing an opportunity to practice it diminishes the effect of this instructional event. The stimulus material described in the previous event should be presented in a form that affords the learner the opportunity repeatedly to use the behavior in a nonthreatening, nonevaluative environment. Grading or performance evaluations, therefore, should not be part of the performance being elicited in this instructional event, where spontaneity, freedom to make mistakes, and an opportunity for immediate feedback are the goals.

6. Providing feedback	Randomly choose students to recite the vowel sounds; correct their errors to demonstrate to the class the desired sound.

Feedback should be given immediately after the eliciting activity. As short a time as possible between performance and feedback is one of the most essential elements of learning: the closer the correspondence between a performance and feedback, the more quickly learning will occur.

Your feedback can be part of the eliciting activity, or it can be a separate activity. In the previous example (the fifth instructional event), feedback was not provided and learners had no way of knowing the correctness of their behavior (mouth and lip movements). Pictures in the text guided their behavior, but because students could not see themselves performing the movements, they couldn't tell if they performed accurately. In this case, feedback would have to follow the eliciting activity, making this instructional event essential for learning. The previous eliciting activity, however, might have included feedback if, for example, students were asked to recite aloud the vowel sounds and the teacher determined the accuracy of their utterances. The correspondence of an eliciting activity and feedback is a matter of degree, but these two events should take place as closely in time as possible.

7. Assessing the behavior | This lesson objective is assessed as part of the unit test on word attack skills and from exercises completed in the workbook.

Few lesson objectives are assessed by individual lesson tests. Amounts of content larger than that contained in a single lesson usually are necessary to make tests efficient and practical. However, it is important to indicate which unit or subunit tests cover the lesson content and what means, other than formal tests (such as classroom performances, projects, and portfolios), you will use to grade the behaviors.

This entry on the lesson plan will remind you to include the lesson's content on subsequent tests or to find other means of checking learners' attainment of it. Some assessment method always should be designed into a lesson plan (tests, workbook exercises, homework, handouts, worksheets, oral responses, etc.). This information provides important feedback about students' readiness for new stimulus material and possible reasons for poor performance in later lessons for which the current material is prerequisite.

Unit Title: Gold Rush (laterally planned unit)
Lesson Title: Westward Journals
Subject Areas: History/Social Science, Language Arts, Art
Written by Cynthia Kiel

This indicates the general content of the lesson and the unit of which it is a part. This lesson appears on an interdisciplinary unit

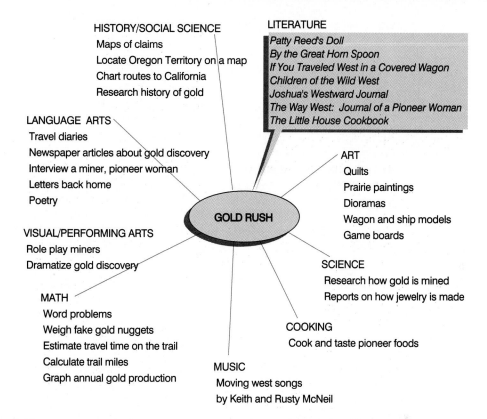

HISTORY/SOCIAL SCIENCE
Maps of claims
Locate Oregon Territory on a map
Chart routes to California
Research history of gold

LITERATURE
Patty Reed's Doll
By the Great Horn Spoon
If You Traveled West in a Covered Wagon
Children of the Wild West
Joshua's Westward Journal
The Way West: Journal of a Pioneer Woman
The Little House Cookbook

LANGUAGE ARTS
Travel diaries
Newspaper articles about gold discovery
Interview a miner, pioneer woman
Letters back home
Poetry

ART
Quilts
Prairie paintings
Dioramas
Wagon and ship models
Game boards

VISUAL/PERFORMING ARTS
Role play miners
Dramatize gold discovery

GOLD RUSH

SCIENCE
Research how gold is mined
Reports on how jewelry is made

MATH
Word problems
Weigh fake gold nuggets
Estimate travel time on the trail
Calculate trail miles
Graph annual gold production

COOKING
Cook and taste pioneer foods

MUSIC
Moving west songs
by Keith and Rusty McNeil

Figure 5.12

Visual representation of the interdisciplinary unit theme, "Gold Rush," which includes the lesson, "Westward Journals"

(Developed by Cynthia Kiel, teacher, Glandora, California)

plan as a lesson in reading or literature titled, "Westward Journals," as shown in Figure 5.12.

1. Gaining attention	Display items or pictures of items that pioneers may have brought with them on their trip West. These may include a diary, bonnet, old tools, *Bible*, and cast-iron skillet.
2. Informing the learner of the objective	Students will be expected to choose one of the routes to California and write a diary entry from the 1840s detailing a day on the trip. Students may be cre-

ative in their presentation of this product, choosing to design a diary, journal, or perhaps write their entry on a construction paper ship or wagon.

3. Stimulating recall of prerequisite learning	As a class, brainstorm on a large chart the main events learned about the trip West.
4. Presenting the stimulus material	Read excerpts from *The Way West, Journal of a Pioneer Woman* by Amelia Stewart Knight and *Joshua's Westward Journal* by Joan Anderson. Lead a discussion of how each author details and summarizes events on the journey.
5. Eliciting the desired behavior	Ask the students to pretend they are a child in a wagon train or aboard a ship on the trip West in the 1840s. Tell them to write a journal or diary about their experiences. Provide a variety of writing paper and construction paper and invite creativity in designing their journal.
6. Providing feedback	While the students are writing, periodically ask individuals to share an excerpt from their entries. Point out how the students are including items listed on the brainstorm chart made at the beginning of the lesson.
7. Assessing the behavior	Design a rubric to grade the journal entries. Criteria may include adherence to factual events in 1840, descriptive language, and creativity.

Table 5.3 presents the *approximate* amount of time during a 50-minute class period that you might devote to each instructional event. Some periods will differ considerably from these amounts of time, such as when the entire lesson is devoted to a review or when recall of prior learning and assessing behavior is not relevant to the day's lesson. Keep in mind that experience, familiarity with content, and common sense always are your best guides for the percentage of time to devote to each instructional event.

Table 5.3

Approximate distribution of instructional time across instructional events for a hypo-thetical 50-minute lesson

Instructional event	Ranges in minutes	Ranges in percentages of time
Gaining attention	1–5	2–10
Informing learners of the objective	1–3	2–6
Stimulating recall of prerequisite learning	5–10	10–20
Presenting the stimulus material	10–20	20–40
Eliciting the desired behavior	10–20	20–40
Providing feedback	5–10	10–20
Assessing behavior	0–10	0–20

From Table 5.3 it is apparent that when you emphasize one instructional event, another must be deemphasized; tradeoffs always are necessary. Although every teacher would like to have more (sometimes less) time than allotted for an instructional period, decisions must be made that fit a lesson into the available time. Table 5.3 indicates some of the ways this might be done when planning a typical lesson.

We conclude with additional lesson plans that illustrate the seven instructional events in other content areas and grade levels.

Unit Title: United States History (Early Beginning through Recon-struction)
Lesson Title: Causes of the Civil War—Lesson 2.3

1. Gaining attention

Show the following list of wars on a transparency:
French and Indian War 1754–1769
Revolutionary War 1775–1781
Civil War 1861–1865
World War I 1914–1918
World War II 1941–1945
Korean War 1950–1953
Vietnam War 1965–1975

2. Informing the learner of the objective

Learners will be expected to know the causes of the Civil War and to show that those causes also can apply to at least one of the other wars listed on the transparency.

3. Stimulating recall of prerequisite learning	Briefly review the causes of both the French and Indian War and the Revolutionary War as covered in Lessons 2.1 and 2.2.
4. Presenting the stimulus material	(a) Summarize major events leading to the Civil War: —rise of sectionalism —labor-intensive economy —lack of diversification (b) Identify significant individuals during the Civil War and their roles: —Lincoln —Lee —Davis —Grant (c) Describe four general causes of war and explain which are most relevant to the Civil War: —economic (to profit) —political (to control) —social (to influence) —military (to protect)
5. Eliciting the desired behavior	Ask the class to identify which of the four causes is most relevant to the major events leading up to the Civil War.
6. Providing feedback	Ask for student answers and indicate plausibility of the volunteered responses.
7. Assessing the behavior	Assign as homework a one-page essay assessing the relative importance of the four causes for one of the wars listed on the transparency.

Unit Title: Writing Concepts and Skills
Lesson Title: Descriptive, Narrative, and Expository Paragraphs—Lesson 1.3

1. Gaining attention	Read examples of short descriptive, narrative, and expository paragraphs from Sunday's newspaper.
2. Informing the learner of the objective	Students will be able to discriminate among descriptive, narrative, and expository paragraphs from a list of written examples in the popular press.

3. Stimulating recall of prerequisite learning	Review the meanings of the words *description, narration,* and *exposition* as they are used in everyday language.
4. Presenting the stimulus material	Using a headline from Sunday's newspaper, give examples of how this story could be reported by description, narration, and exposition.
5. Eliciting the desired behavior	Take another front-page story from Sunday's newspaper and ask students to write a paragraph relating the story in descriptive, narrative, or expository form, whichever they prefer.
6. Providing feedback	Call on individuals to read their paragraphs, checking each against the type of paragraph he or she intended to write.
7. Assessing the behavior	Provide multiple choice examples of each form of writing on the unit test. Have students revise their paragraphs as needed and turn in as homework the following day.

Unit Title: Consumer Mathematics
Lesson Title: Operations and Properties of Ratio, Proportion, and Percentage—Lesson 3.3

1. Gaining attention	Display so all can see: (a) can of diet soft drink (b) one-pound package of spaghetti (c) box of breakfast cereal
2. Informing the learner of the objective	Learners will be expected to know how to determine ratios, proportions, and percentages from the information on labels of popular food products.
3. Stimulating recall of prerequisite learning	Review the definitions of *ratio, proportion,* and *percentage* from the math workbook.
4. Presenting the stimulus material	Place the information from the soft-drink label on a transparency and ask students to identify the percentage of sodium.

5. Eliciting the desired behavior

Write on the board the list of ingredients given on the cereal box; ask students to determine (a) the percentage of daily allowance of protein, (b) the proportion of daily allowance of Vitamin A, and (c) the ratio of protein to carbohydrates.

6. Providing feedback

Using the information on the board, point to the correct answer for a and b and show how to find the appropriate numerator and denominator for c from the ingredients on the label.

7. Assessing the behavior

Provide on the weekly quiz five problems covering ratios (two problems), proportions (two problems), and percentages (one problem) using labels from other consumer products.

Unit Title: Manipulative Laboratory Skills
Lesson Title: Use of the Microscope—Lesson 1.1

1. Gaining attention

Show the first five minutes of a film about making a lens.

2. Informing the learner of the objective

Learners will be expected to be able to focus correctly a specimen of one-celled animal life, using both high and low magnification.

3. Stimulating recall of prerequisite learning

Review procedures for selecting a slide from the one-celled specimen collection and mounting it on the specimen tray of the microscope.

4. Presenting the stimulus material

Using a student in front of the class as a demonstrator, help position his or her posture and hands on the microscope. Gently bend body and hands until the correct posture results. Demonstrate the position of the eyes and show clockwise and counterclockwise rotation of low and then high magnification adjustment.

5. Eliciting the desired behavior

Have each student obtain a specimen slide, mount it on a microscope and focus on low magnification. Randomly check microscopes, correcting slide, positions, and focus as needed with student observing. Repeat for high magnification.

6. Providing feedback

Feedback has been provided in the context of the eliciting activity (step 5) to increase immediacy of the feedback. Also, refer students to the text for examples of focused and unfocused specimens.

7. Assessing the behavior

At the completion of the unit, students will be assessed during a practical lab exam requiring the correct mounting and identification of three unknown specimens using the microscope.

Summing Up

This chapter introduced you to unit and lesson planning. Its main points were as follows:

1. A unit of instruction may be thought of as a "system"; individual lessons within the unit are its component parts.

2. Four primary activities within the planning process are establishing instructional goals, identifying learner needs, and selecting and organizing content.

3. The two purposes of unit planning are (1) to convert generally stated activities and outcomes into specific objectives and lessons, and (2) to provide a picture of long-term goals.

4. The concept of *hierarchy* tells us the relationship of parts to the whole (in this case, lessons to units and the concept of *task-relevant prior knowledge* tells us what must come before what in a sequence of events (lesson sequence). Systems thinking draws our attention to the relationship among parts of varying sizes to see what lessons make up what units.

5. Units can be planned vertically, emphasizing hierarchy of lesson content and task-relevant prior knowledge (sequence), or laterally, emphasizing themes that integrate bodies of knowledge across disciplines to convey relationships and patterns that bind different aspects of our world together.

6. In vertical planning, boxes illustrate areas of content, or instructional goals, at various levels of generality. Lines and arrows indicate sequences among lessons and how outcomes of lessons build on one another to achieve a unit goal.

7. Three activities of vertical unit planning are as follows:

- Classifying unit outcomes at a higher level of behavioral complexity than lesson outcomes by using one or more taxonomies of behavior.
- Planning the instructional sequence so that the outcomes of previously taught lessons are instrumental in achieving the outcomes of subsequent lessons.

- Rearranging or adding lesson content where necessary to provide task-relevant prior knowledge where needed.

8. In lateral planning, a central theme is identified and lines or arrows connected to it to indicate subordinate ideas for lesson content.

9. Three activities of lateral planning are the following:

- Identifying an interdisciplinary theme.
- Integrating bodies of knowledge across disciplines.
- Identifying relationships and patterns that bind different aspects of our world together.

10. Before starting the preparation of a lesson plan, you must determine the behavioral complexity level of the lesson (e.g., knowledge, application, evaluation), and to what extent provisions for student diversity must accompany the lesson plan (e.g., ability grouping, peer tutoring, learning centers, specialized handouts, cooperative groups).

11. *Learning* refers to internal events in the heads of learners that result from external teaching events you provide. Hence, the words *teaching* and *learning* refer to two different but related sets of activities.

12. The following external events can be specified in a lesson plan:

- Gaining attention
- Informing the learner of the objective

- Stimulating recall of prerequisite learning
- Presenting the stimulus material
- Eliciting the desired behavior
- Providing feedback
- Assessing the behavior

13. Gaining attention involves gaining your students' interest in what you will present and getting them to switch to the appropriate modality for the coming lesson.

14. Informing learners of the objective involves informing them of the complexity of the behavior expected at the end of the lesson.

15. Stimulating recall of prerequisite learning is reviewing task-relevant prior information required by the lesson.

16. Presenting the stimulus material is delivering the desired content in a manner conducive to the modality in which it is to be received, using procedures that stimulate thought processing and maintain interest.

17. Eliciting the desired behavior gets learners to produce the intended behavior by organizing a response corresponding with the level of complexity of the stated objective.

18. Providing feedback tells the learner the accuracy of her or his elicited response in a nonthreatening, nonevaluative atmosphere.

19. Assessing the behavior evaluates the learner's performance with tests, homework, and extended assignments.

For Discussion and Practice

*1. Identify the five inputs to the planning process from which the preparation of lesson plans proceeds.

*2. How can a unit outcome be more than the sum of individual lesson outcomes?

*3. Explain in your own words how the concepts of *hierarchy* and *task-relevant prior knowledge* are used in unit planning.

*4. How are the concepts of *hierarchy* and *task-relevant prior learning* related?

*5. Name the levels of behavioral complexity in each of the three domains (cognitive, affective, and psychomotor) that generally would be most suitable for a unit outcome.

*6. How are the boxes further down on a vertical unit plan different than the boxes higher up?

7. Vertically plan a three-lesson unit within a discipline in which the sequence of lessons is critical to achieving the outcome. Then, laterally plan a three-lesson interdisciplinary unit in which lesson sequence is unimportant. Be sure lesson outcomes for each unit reflect the unit outcome.

*8. Explain how a graphic unit plan for a vertical unit is different than a graphic unit plan for a lateral unit. In your own words, why must there be a difference?

*9. Identify some ways of providing for student diversity in the context of a lesson plan.

*10. Explain what is meant by mastery learning and its relationship to task-relevant prior knowledge.

*11. Name the seven events of instruction that can be described in a lesson plan. Give a specific example of how you would implement each one in a lesson of your own choosing.

*12. Identify the instructional event(s) for which the key behavior of *instructional variety* would be most important.

*13. Identify the instructional event(s) for which the key behavior of *student success* would be most important.

*14. Identify the instructional event(s) for which the key behavior of *engagement in the learning process* would be most important.

*15. Indicate how the instructional events of (1) providing feedback and (2) assessing behavior differ according to the evaluative nature of the feedback provided and the immediacy with which the feedback is given.

16. Following the form of the examples provided in this chapter, prepare a lesson plan for a topic in your major or preferred teaching area and another in your minor teaching area. Include the approximate number of minutes you expect to devote to each event out of a 50-minute class period.

---

* Answers to asterisked questions (*) in this and the other chapters are in Appendix B.

Suggested Readings

Block, J. (1987) Mastery learning models. In M. J. Dunkin (Ed.), *International encyclopedia of teaching and teacher education.* New York: Pergamon.

   An excellent article on how to achieve mastery learning and what this important concept means for effective teaching.

Dunkin, M.J. (1987). Lesson formats. In M. J. Dunkin (Ed.), *International encyclopedia of teaching and teacher education.* New York: Pergamon.

   A sampling of the many varieties of and ways to prepare lesson plans.

Gagné, R., & Briggs, L. (1992). *Principles of instructional design.* New York: Holt, Rinehart & Winston.

   A thorough and authoritative text on the design of instruction. Although less useful for writing lesson plans, the authors describe nine events of instruction, not the seven presented in this chapter.

Kovalik, S. (1993). ITU: The model/Integrated Thematic Instruction. Oak Creek, AZ: Books for Educators.

   The author describes how to follow an easy to use model for preparing thematic units. This book is written specifically for the classroom teacher.

Pasch, M., Sparks-Langer, G., Gardner, T. G., Starko, A. J., & Moody, C. D. (1991). *Teaching as decision making: Instructional practices for the successful teacher.* New York: Longman.

   This text provides plenty of examples of unit and lesson plans for the beginning teacher—along with many practical tips on how to design a lesson.

Pratt, D. (1980). *Curriculum, design and development.* New York: Harcourt, Brace, Jovanovich.

    An introductory text on how to design classroom instruction using many of the concepts presented in this chapter.

Roberts, P., & Kellough, R. (1996). A guide for developing interdisciplinary thematic units. Englewood Cliffs, NJ: Merrill/Prentice Hall.

    This book provides an up-to-date reference for writing ITUs that offers step-by-step directions and plenty of examples to guide the way.

Saylor, G., Alexander, W., & Lewis, A. (1981). *Curriculum planning for better teaching and learning* (4th ed.). Chicago: Holt, Rinehart & Winston.

    A companion volume to the previous one that relates lesson planning to unit planning to produce an integrated sequence of instruction.

CHAPTER 6

Direct Instruction Strategies

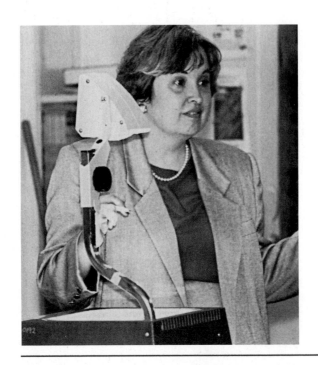

This chapter will help you answer the following questions:

1. What is the direct instruction model?
2. What student outcomes are best taught with direct instruction?
3. What teacher behaviors are required for direct instruction?
4. How can I use direct instruction to achieve mastery learning?
5. How can I efficiently check for prior learning at the start of a direct instruction lesson?
6. How do I organize lesson content to make it more effective for direct instruction?
7. How can I prompt learners to respond correctly during direct instruction?
8. How can I model for learners what I want them to learn?
9. How do I correct responses that are hesitant, responses that are careless, and responses that are incorrect due to lack of knowledge?
10. How can I encourage my learners to actively respond during direct instruction?
11. What is an effective practice activity?
12. What are some ways of promoting the goals of direct instruction in a culturally diverse classroom?

This chapter will also help you learn the meaning of the following:

daily review and checking
direct instruction model
direct instruction teaching functions
feedback and correctives
guided student practice
independent practice
lecture-recitation format
mastery learning
modeling
passive and active responding
presenting and structuring
verbal, gestural, and physical prompting
weekly and monthly review

T he previous chapter presented seven instructional events that form the skeletal structure of a lesson plan:

1. Gaining attention
2. Informing the learner of the objective
3. Stimulating recall of prerequisite learning
4. Presenting the stimulus material
5. Eliciting the desired behavior
6. Providing feedback
7. Assessing the behavior

To add flesh to this skeleton, this and subsequent chapters present different instructional strategies by which these seven events can be carried out with ease and perfection. This chapter presents strategies for direct teaching that include explanations, examples, review, practice, and feedback in the context of a lecture-recitation format. The next chapter presents strategies for indirect teaching that include guided questions, inductive and deductive logic, use of student ideas, and group discussion in an inquiry or problem-solving format. Subsequent chapters show how you can use the ideas in both chapters to teach your learners to direct, control, and regulate their own learning and to learn cooperatively with others.

Have you ever wondered why some teachers are more interesting than others? This is an ageless phenomenon, well known to anyone who has spent time in school. Students cannot wait to attend the classes of some teachers, but dread attending the classes of others. Interesting teachers often are described with phrases such as "is more intelligent," "has a better personality," and "is warmer and friendlier." Although these qualities may be present in teachers judged to be the most interesting, they are not the only reasons that a teacher can be interesting.

It may surprise you that one of the most important factors in how interesting teachers are to their students is their use of the key behavior instructional variety. In a study of experienced and inexperienced teachers (Emmer, Evertson, & Anderson, 1980), experienced teachers who showed flexibility and variety in their instructional strategies were found to be more interesting than inexperienced teachers who had no knowledge of alternative teaching strategies.

Knowledge of a variety of instructional strategies and the flexibility to change them both within and among lessons are two of the greatest assets a teacher can have (Emmer et al., 1994). Without variety and flexibility to capture the interest and attention of students, it is unlikely that any other key behavior, however well executed, will have an effect on them. This chapter provides a variety of teaching strategies you can use to compose lesson plans and to create and maintain an atmosphere of interest and variety in your classroom using a direct instruction format.

>>> CATEGORIES OF TEACHING AND LEARNING <<<

Just as the carpenter, electrician, and plumber must select the proper tool for a specific task, you must select the proper instructional strategy for a learning outcome. To help determine your choice of strategies, here are two broad classifications of learning outcomes:

Type 1: Facts, rules, and action sequences

Type 2: Concepts, patterns, and abstractions

Type 1 outcomes often represent behaviors at lower levels of complexity in the cognitive, affective, and psychomotor domains. As discussed in Chapter 4, these include the knowledge, comprehension, and application levels of the cognitive domain; the awareness, responding, and valuing levels of the affective domain; and the imitation, manipulation, and precision levels of the psychomotor domain.

Type 2 outcomes, on the other hand, frequently represent behaviors at the higher levels of complexity in these domains. They include objectives at the analysis, synthesis, and evaluation levels of the cognitive domain; the organization and characterization levels of the affective domain; and the articulation and naturalization levels of the psychomotor domain. Examples of Type 1 and Type 2 outcomes are shown in Tables 6.1 and 6.2.

These outcomes are two fairly broad distinctions and can overlap, but are useful guides in selecting an instructional strategy to maximize learning when the objectives include facts, rules, and action sequences or concepts, patterns, and abstractions. Some

Table 6.1

Example Type 1 outcomes: Facts, rules, and action sequences

Facts	Rules	Action Sequences
1. Recognize multiplication with two-digit numbers	Carrying with two-digit numbers	Multiplying to "1000"
2. Identify apostrophe "s"	Finding words with apostrophe "s"	Using apostrophe "s" in a sentence
3. Select multisyllable words from list	Pronouncing multisyllable words	Reading stories with multisyllable words
4. State chemical composition of water	Combining 2 parts hydrogen with 1 part oxygen	Writing the expression for water

important differences between instructional goals requiring these two types of learning are shown in Table 6.3.

Notice across the left and right columns of Table 6.3 that two types of learning are being required. In the left column, Type 1 tasks require combining facts and rules at the knowledge and comprehension level into a sequence of actions that could be learned by observation, rote repetition, and practice. Students can learn the "right answers" by memorizing and practicing behaviors that you model.

In the right column, a quite different learning type is called for. The "right answers" are not so closely connected to facts, rules, or action sequences that can be memorized and practiced in some limited context. Something more is needed to help the learner go

Table 6.2

Example Type 2 outcomes: Concepts, patterns, and abstractions

Concepts	Patterns	Abstractions
1. Positive and negative numbers	-3 (-4) 11 = 10 x (-6) =	Signed numbers
2. Possessive form	Policeman's daughter Mrs. Burns' paper	Ownership
3. Vowels (v) and consonants (c)	cv order cvc order	Vowel/consonant blends
4. Element, atomic weight, and valence	H_2O	Molecular structure

Table 6.3

Instructional objectives requiring Type 1 and Type 2 outcomes

Type 1: Objectives Requiring Facts, Rules, and Sequences	Type 2: Objectives Requiring Concepts, Patterns, and Abstractions
1. IF Objective is to *recognize* multiplication to "1000" THEN TEACH the multiplication tables, and then have student *find examples*	BUT IF Objective is to *understand* multiplication of signed numbers THEN TEACH the concept of negative and positive numbers and *show how they are multiplied*
2. IF Objective is to *identify* the apostrophe "s" THEN TEACH words using the apostrophe "s", and then have student *find words denoting possession*	BUT IF Objective is to *express* ownership THEN TEACH the concept of the possessive form, and then have student *practice writing paragraphs* showing forms of possession
3. IF Objective is to *select* multisyllable words THEN TEACH how to *find each of the words* on a list, and then have student write words	BUT IF Objective is to *pronounce* vowel/consonant blends THEN TEACH vowels and consonants, and then have student *read story aloud*
4. IF Objective is to *state* the chemical composition of water THEN TEACH the symbol for 2 parts hydrogen and 1 part oxygen, and then have student *write the chemical composition of water*	BUT IF Objective is to *determine* the molecular structure of chemical substances THEN TEACH the concept of element, atomic weight, and valence, and then have student *practice balancing the atomic weights of chemical substances*

beyond the facts, rules, or sequences to create, synthesize, and ultimately identify and recognize an answer that cannot be easily modeled or memorized. The missing link involves learning an abstraction called a *concept*.

For example, to learn the *concept* of a frog involves learning the essential characteristics that make an organism a frog, as distinguished from closely similar animals (e.g., a green chameleon). In other words, the learner needs to know not only the characteristics that all frogs have (e.g., green color, four legs, eats insects, amphibious) but also what characteristics distinguish frogs from other animals. If we classified frogs only on the characteristics of being green, having four legs, eating insects, and being amphibious, some turtles could be misidentified as frogs. Another category of knowledge must be learned that contains characteristics that separate frogs from similar animals (e.g., frogs have soft bodies, moist skin, strong hind limbs, and do not change color).

Figure 6.1 presents a diagram showing the information involved in learning the concept of *frog*. Notice that to properly classify a frog among other animals that may look like one, both *nonessential* and *essential* frog attributes need to be learned. The nonessential attributes can be learned only by studying nonexamples, thus allowing learners to eliminate characteristics that are not unique to frogs. Finally, as the learner gains more practice with both examples and nonexamples, the concept of a frog emerges as a tightly woven combination of characteristics. Now the learner is able to disregard superficial characteristics such as color and to focus on characteristics that are unique to frogs. Given pictures of various toads, chameleons, turtles, snakes, and so on, the student learns to identify correctly those that are frogs.

At this point the learner has discovered at least some of the essential attributes of a frog and has formed an initial concept. Notice how different this teaching/learning process is from simply having Johnny repeat some recently memorized facts about frogs: "Frogs are green, have four legs, eat insects, and can swim." This response does not tell you whether Johnny has the concept of a frog, or a pattern of which frogs are a part (e.g., amphibian), or even the most general and abstract frog characteristics (e.g., "water life"). Even if Johnny learns the considerably more complex task of how to care for frogs, he still has not learned the *concept* of a frog. He has grasped only how to arrange a constellation of facts into an action sequence.

The preceding demonstrates how the processes used to learn facts, rules, and action sequences are different from those used to learn concepts, patterns, and abstractions. And just as different

Concept: Frog
Pattern: Amphibians
Abstraction: Water life

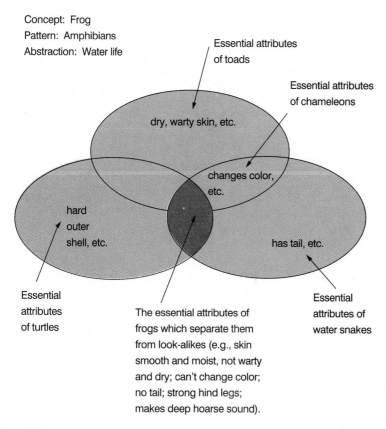

Figure 6.1
Learning the concept of *frog*

processes are involved in such learning, so are different instructional strategies needed to teach these outcomes. We most commonly teach facts, rules, and action sequences using strategies that emphasize *knowledge acquisition*. We most commonly teach concepts, patterns, and abstractions using strategies that emphasize *inquiry* or *problem solving*. These follow distinctions suggested by Anderson (1990), and Gagné, Yekovich, and Yekovich (1993), whose writings have highlighted the different instructional strategies required by these two types of learning.

Knowledge acquisition and inquiry are different types of learning outcomes, so each of them must be linked with the specific strategies most likely to produce them. This chapter presents a group of strategies for teaching knowledge acquisition involving facts, rules, and action sequences, called direct instruction. The next chapter presents strategies for teaching inquiry and problem solving involving concepts, patterns, and abstractions, called indirect instruction. In subsequent chapters, both types of learning are combined to show how, together, they can build additional teaching strategies that help learners solve problems, think critically, and work cooperatively.

>>> **INTRODUCTION TO DIRECT** <<<
INSTRUCTION STRATEGIES

What is the direct instruction model?

The teaching of facts, rules, and action sequences is most efficiently achieved through a process called the **direct instruction model.** Direct instruction, sometimes synonymous with expository or didactic teaching, is a *teacher-centered* strategy in which you are the major information provider. In the direct instruction model, your role is to pass facts, rules, or action sequences on to students in the most direct way possible. This usually takes the form of a lecture-recitation with explanations, examples, and opportunities for practice and feedback. The direct instruction **lecture-recitation format** is a multifaceted presentation requiring not only large amounts of verbal explanation but also teacher–student interactions involving questions and answers, review and practice, and the correction of student errors.

In the direct instruction model, the concept of a lecture in the elementary and secondary classroom differs considerably from the concept of a lecture that you might acquire from college experience. The typical one-hour college lecture rarely will be suitable for your classroom, because your learners' attention spans, interest levels, and motivation will not be the same as your own. Therefore, the "lecture" as presented here is neither a lengthy (and boring) monologue nor an open, free-wheeling discussion of problems that interest the student. Instead, it is a quickly paced, highly organized set of interchanges that you control, focusing exclusively on acquiring a limited set of predetermined facts, rules, or action sequences.

Rosenshine and Stevens (1986) have equated this type of instruction with that of an effective demonstration in which the following occurs:

1. You clearly present goals and main points by
   a. Stating goals or objectives of the presentation beforehand.
   b. Focusing on one thought (point, direction) at a time.
   c. Avoiding digressions.
   d. Avoiding ambiguous phrases and pronouns.
2. You present content sequentially by
   a. Presenting material in small steps.

   b. Organizing and presenting material so that one point is mastered before the next point is given.
   c. Giving explicit, step-by-step directions.
   d. Presenting an outline when the material is complex.
3. You are specific and concrete by
   a. Modeling the skill or process (when appropriate).
   b. Giving detailed and redundant explanations for difficult points.
   c. Providing students with concrete and varied examples.
4. You check for students' understanding by
   a. Being sure that students understand one point before proceeding to the next.
   b. Asking students questions to monitor their comprehension of what has been presented.
   c. Having students summarize the main points in their own words.
   d. Reteaching the parts that students have difficulty comprehending—either through further teaching, explanation, or by students tutoring each other.

The examples that appear later illustrate this type of lecture. For now, note the following action verbs that correspond to the objectives most suited for direct instruction:

What student outcomes are best taught with direct instruction?

Cognitive objectives	*Affective objectives*	*Psychomotor objectives*
to recall	to listen	to repeat
to describe	to attend	to follow
to list	to be aware	to place
to summarize	to comply	to perform accurately
to paraphrase	to follow	to perform independently
to distinguish	to obey	to perform proficiently
to use	to display	to perform with speed
to organize	to express	to perform with coordination
to demonstrate	to prefer	to perform with timing

These outcomes are learned through application of facts, rules, and action sequences that usually can be taught in a single lesson. You can most easily and directly test them with multiple-choice, listing, matching, and fill-in exercises. Test items would call for the listing of memorized names, dates, and other facts; summarizing or paraphrasing of learned facts, rules, or sequences; or connecting together and applying learned facts, rules, and sequences in a context slightly different than the one in which they were learned.

Both Rosenshine (1983) and Good (1979) have identified this type of learning as what results from direct instruction or "active teaching." This type of instruction most often is characterized by the following:

- Full-class instruction (as opposed to small-group instruction)
- Organization of learning around questions you pose
- Provision of detailed and redundant practice
- Presenting material so that one new fact, rule, or sequence is mastered before the next is presented
- Formal arrangement of the classroom to maximize recitation and practice

What teacher behaviors are required for direct instruction?

Table 6.4 presents some teacher behaviors most commonly associated with the direct instruction model. You can see that from these behaviors that a large share of teaching time is likely to be devoted to direct instruction, that is, to providing information directly to students interspersed with explanations, examples, practice, and feedback.

Whether explaining, pointing out relationships, giving examples, or correcting errors, there is much to say for using strategies that follow the direct instruction model. Research indicates that **direct instruction teaching functions** (see Table 6.4) and the teaching behaviors that comprise them (e.g., teacher reviews previous day's work, teacher provides feedback and corrections, teacher provides for student practice) are among the teaching functions that correlate highest with student achievement (Anderson et al., 1982).

>>> WHEN IS DIRECT INSTRUCTION APPROPRIATE? <<<

When direct instruction strategies are used for the proper purpose, with the appropriate content, and at the right time, they are important adjuncts to a teaching strategy menu. Most of these strategies are at their best when your purpose is to disseminate information not readily available from texts or workbooks in appropriately sized pieces. If such information were available, your students might well learn the material from these sources independently, with only introductory or structuring comments provided by you. However, when you must partition, subdivide, and translate textbook and workbook material into a more digestible form before it can be understood by your students, direct instruction is appropriate.

Another time for direct instruction strategies is when you wish to arouse or heighten student interest. Students often fail to complete textbook readings and exercises in the mistaken belief that the chapter is boring, is not worth their effort, or presents material

Table 6.4
Some direct instruction functions

1. Daily review, checking previous day's work, and reteaching (if necessary):
    Checking homework
    Reteaching areas where there were student errors
2. Presenting and structuring new content:
    Provide overview
    Proceed in small steps (if necessary), but at a rapid pace
    If necessary, give detailed or redundant instructions and explanations
    New skills are phased in while old skills are being measured
3. Guided student practice:
    High frequency of questions and overt student practice (from teacher and
        materials)
    Prompts are provided during initial learning (when appropriate)
    All students have a chance to respond and receive feedback
    Teacher *checks for understanding* by evaluating student responses
    Continue practice until student responses are firm
    Success rate of 80% or higher during initial learning
4. Feedback and correctives (and recycling of instruction, if necessary):
    Feedback to students, particularly when they are correct but hesitant
    Student errors provide feedback to the teacher that corrections and/or
        reteaching is necessary
    Corrections by simplifying question, giving clues, explaining or reviewing
        steps, or reteaching last steps
    When necessary, reteach using smaller steps
5. Independent practice so that student responses are firm and automatic:
    Seatwork
    Unitization and automaticity (practice to overlearning)
    Need for procedure to ensure student engagement during seatwork (i.e.,
        teacher or aide monitoring)
    95% correct or higher
6. Weekly and monthly reviews:
    Reteaching, if necessary

already learned. Your active participation in the presentation of content can change such misperceptions by mixing interesting supplemental or introductory information with the "dry" facts, by showing their application to future schoolwork or world events, and by illustrating with questions and answers that the material is neither "easy" nor previously mastered. Your direct involvement in presenting content provides the human element that may be necessary for learning to occur in many of your students.

How can I use direct instruction to achieve mastery learning?

Finally, direct instruction strategies are indispensable for achieving content mastery and overlearning of fundamental facts, rules, and action sequences that may be essential to subsequent learning (Anderson & Block, 1987). The degree of **mastery learning** that occurs is directly related to the time a student is actively engaged in the learning process. Therefore, efficient use of class time and active student practice are important ingredients of mastery learning.

The two goals of mastery learning—efficient use of class time and active student practice—are best achieved by an instructional sequence of review, presenting new content, practice, feedback, and reteaching, as shown in Figure 6.2. These repetitive cycles may compose nearly all of the time scheduled for a direct instruction lesson. Many examples in this chapter illustrate this type of instructional sequence. When the content to be taught represents task-relevant prior knowledge for subsequent learning, a direct instruction format is the best insurance that this knowledge is remembered and available for later use.

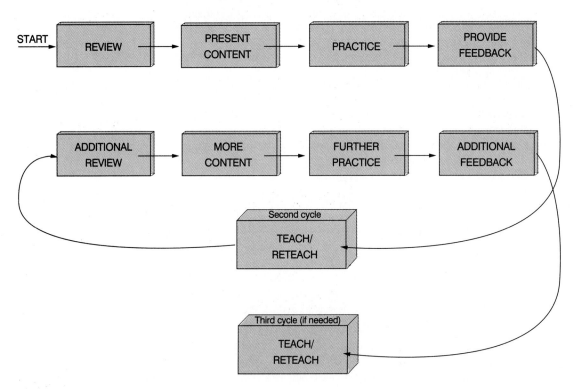

Figure 6.2
The direct instructional sequence for mastery learning

There also are times in which direct instruction strategies are inappropriate. When objectives other than learning facts, rules, and behavior sequences are desired, direct instruction strategies become clumsy, less efficient, and often far less effective than the inquiry or problem-solving strategies we will discuss in subsequent chapters. Teaching situations that need strategies other than direct instruction include (1) presenting complex material having objectives at the analysis, synthesis, and evaluation levels of the cognitive domain and (2) presenting content that must be learned gradually over a long period. Such material requires learner participation to heighten a commitment to the learning process and to create the intellectual framework necessary for learning concepts and recognizing patterns. You can attain this learner participation through carefully crafted classroom dialogue, which will be illustrated in chapters 7 and 8.

Finally, when students have already mastered the fundamentals and task-relevant prior knowledge required for more authentic outcomes at the problem-solving, critical thinking, and decision-making levels, direct instruction strategies can be inefficient and ineffective forms of instruction.

>>> AN EXAMPLE OF DIRECT INSTRUCTION <<<

To see what direct instruction looks like in the classroom, consider the following dialogue, in which the teacher begins a direct instruction sequence to teach the acquisition of facts, rules, and action sequences for forming and punctuating possessives. She begins by informing her students of the lesson's objective.

Teacher: Today we will learn how to avoid embarrassing errors such as this when forming and punctuating possessives (circles an incorrectly punctuated possessive in a newspaper headline). At the end of the period I will give each of you several additional examples of errors taken from my collection of mistakes found in other newspapers and magazines. I'll ask you to make the proper corrections and report your changes to the class. Who knows what a possessive is?

Bobby: It means you own something.

Teacher: Yes, a possessive is a way of indicating ownership. It comes from the word *possession,* which means "*something owned*" or "*something possessed.*"

Forming possessives and punctuating them correctly can be difficult, as this newspaper example shows (points to paper again). Today I will give you two simple rules that will help you form possessives correctly.

But first, to show ownership or possession, we must know who or what is doing the possessing. Mary, can you recall the parts of speech from last week's lesson? (Mary hesitates, then nods.) What part of speech is most likely to own or possess something?

Mary: Well, umm . . . I think . . . I think a noun can own something.

Teacher: Yes. A noun can own something. What is an example of a noun that owns something? Tommy.

Tommy: I don't know.

Teacher: Debbie.

Debbie: Not sure.

Teacher: Ricky.

Ricky: A student can own a pencil. The word *student* is a noun.

Teacher: Good. And who can remember our definition for a noun?

Jim: It's a person, place, or thing.

Teacher: Good. Our first rule is: Use the possessive form whenever an *of* phrase can be substituted for a noun (teacher points to this rule written on board). Let's look at some phrases on the board to see when to apply this rule. Johnny, what does the first one say?

Johnny: The daughter of the policeman.

Teacher: How else could we express the same idea of ownership?

Mary: We could say "the policeman's daughter."

Teacher: And, we could say "the policeman's daughter" because I can substitute a phrase starting with *of* and ending with policeman for the noun *policeman.* Notice how easily I could switch the placement of *policeman* and *daughter* by using the connective word *of.* Whenever this can be done you can form a possessive by adding an *apostrophe s* to the noun following *of.*

Now we have the phrase (writes on board) *policeman's daughter* (points to the apostrophe). Betty, what about our next example, *holiday of three days* (pointing to board)?

Betty: We could say "three days' holiday."

Teacher: Come up and write that on the board just the way it should be printed in the school paper. (Mary writes *three day's holiday.*)

Would anyone want to change anything?

Susan: I'm not sure but I think I would put the apostrophe after the *s* in days.

Teacher: You're right, which leads to our second rule: If the word for which we are denoting ownership already ends in an *s,* place the apostrophe after the *s,* not before it. This is an important rule to remember, because it accounts for many of the mistakes that are made in forming possessives. As I write this rule on the board, copy down these two rules for use later.

(Finishes writing second rule on board.) Now let's take a moment to convert each of the phrases on the overhead to the possessive form. Write down your answer to the first one. When I see all heads up again I will write the correct answer.

(All heads are up.) Good. Now watch how I change this first one to the possessive form; pay particular attention to where I place the apostrophe, then check your answer with mine. (Converts *delay of a month* to *month's delay*.) Any problems? (Pauses for any response.) OK, do the next one. (After all heads are up, teacher converts *home of Jenkins* to *Jenkins' home*.)

Any problems? (Johnny looks distressed.)

Teacher: Johnny, what did you write?

Johnny: *J-E-N-K-I-N apostrophe S.*

Teacher: What is the man's name, Johnny?

Johnny: Jenkins.

Teacher: Look at what you wrote for the second rule. What does it say?

Johnny: Add the apostrophe after the *s* when the word already ends in an *s.* Oh, I get it. His name already has the *s*, so it would be *s apostrophe.* That's the mistake you showed us in the headline, isn't it?

Teacher: Now you've got it. Let's continue. (Proceeds with the following in the same manner: *speech of the President* to *President's speech, the television set of Mr. Burns* to *Mr. Burns' television set, pastimes of boys* to *boys' pastimes.*)

Now open your workbooks to the exercise on page 87.

Starting with the first row, let's go around the room and hear your possessives for each of the sentences listed. Spell aloud the word indicating ownership, so we can tell if you've placed the apostrophe in the right place. Debbie . . . (looking at "wings of geese")

Debbie: geeses wings . . . spelled *W-I-N-G-S apostrophe.*

Teacher: That's not correct. What word is doing the possessing?

Debbie: The geese, so it must be *G-E-E-S-E apostrophe S.*

Teacher: Good. Next.

Now, let's look at our six direct instruction functions in Table 6.4 as they relate to the preceding dialogue.

>>> DAILY REVIEW AND CHECKING <<< THE PREVIOUS DAY'S WORK

This is the first ingredient in direct instruction (Table 6.4). **Daily review and checking** emphasizes the relationship between lessons so that students remember previous knowledge and see new knowledge as a logical extension of content already mastered. Notice that early in the example lesson the definition of a noun was brought into the presentation. This provided review of task-relevant prior knowledge needed for the day's lesson.

It also provided students with a sense of wholeness and continuity, assuring them that what was to follow was not isolated knowledge unrelated to past lessons. This is particularly important for securing the engagement of students who do not have appropriate levels of task-relevant prior knowledge or who may be overly anxious about having to master yet another piece of unfamiliar content.

Review and checking at the beginning of a lesson also is the most efficient and timely way of finding out if your students have mastered task-relevant prior knowledge sufficiently to begin a new lesson; if not, you may reteach the missing content, as shown in Figure 6.2.

How can I efficiently check for prior learning at the start of a direct instruction lesson?

You might think that beginning a lesson by checking previously learned task-relevant knowledge is a common practice. Yet, Good and Grouws (1979) found that only 50 percent of experienced teachers began a lesson in this fashion. This is unfortunate, because daily review and checking at the beginning of a lesson is easy to accomplish:

1. Have students correct each other's homework at the beginning of class.
2. Have students identify especially difficult homework problems in a question-and-answer format.
3. Sample the understanding of a few students who probably are good indicators of the range of knowledge possessed by the entire class.
4. Explicitly review the task-relevant information that is necessary for the day's lesson.

Dahllof and Lundgren (1970) proposed the use of a *steering group* of low achievers as a particularly effective way of determining the extent to which review and reteaching may be needed. An expanded notion of the steering group is a small number of low, average, and high performers who can be queried at the start of class on the task-relevant prior knowledge needed for the day's lesson. When high performers miss a large proportion of answers, this warns you that extensive reteaching for the entire class is necessary. When high performers answer questions correctly but average performers do not, some reteaching should be undertaken before the start of the lesson. And, finally, if most of the high and average performers answer the questions correctly but most of the low performers do not, then you need to use individualized materials, supplemental readings, summary and review sheets, or the tutorial arrangements and communication technologies described in Chapter 5. This ensures that large amounts of class time are not devoted to review and reteaching that may benefit only a small number of students.

Such strategies for daily review and checking, especially when used with a carefully selected steering group, are indispensable for

A major purpose of daily review and checking is to emphasize the relationship between lessons and to provide students with a sense of wholeness and continuity, assuring them that what is to follow is a logical extension of content already mastered.

warning you that previous instruction was over the heads of some or most of your students and, therefore, that additional review and reteaching is necessary.

>>> PRESENTING AND STRUCTURING <<<

Presenting new content is the second step in the direct instruction model (Table 6.4). One of the primary ingredients of the model is presenting material in small steps. Recall from Chapter 5 that lessons must be served up in small portions that are consistent with the previous knowledge, ability level, and interests of your students. Likewise, the content *within* the lessons must be partitioned and subdivided to organize it into small bits. No portion can be too large; if it is, you will lose your students' attention, which may lead to disruptive or distracting behaviors.

The key is to focus the material on one idea at a time and to present it so that one point is mastered before the next point is introduced. This is most easily accomplished by dividing a lesson into easily recognizable subparts, rules, or categories. It is no coincidence that the strategy of "divide and conquer" is as appropriate in the classroom as in military battles. Just like any great warrior, you can derive much benefit from it.

Remember that the subdivisions you use can be your own; they need not always follow those provided by the text, workbook, or curriculum guide. There is an important difference between content divisions used in books and content divisions needed in teaching: Content divisions in texts, workbooks, and curriculum guides generally are created for the purpose of communicating *content intended to be read,* not for the purpose of presenting *content that must be explained orally* to learners within the time frame of a specific lesson. Consequently, published divisions like chapter titles, subheadings, or Roman numerals in outlines sometimes are too broad to form bite-sized pieces that students can easily digest within a single lesson.

Unfortunately, many beginning teachers stick tenaciously to these formal headings without realizing either the volume of content that falls within them or the time it takes to orally explain, illustrate, and practice this content. The truth is that you are not discarding content by creating new organizational divisions; you only are breaking content into smaller steps suitable for presentation in a single period. You can create your own subdivisions consisting of rules ("here are some rules to follow"), steps ("we will do this, then that"), or practices ("here is the first of five things we will cover"). These subdivisions preorganize your instruction into bite-sized pieces and, most importantly, communicate this organization to your students.

How do I organize lesson content to make it more effective for direct instruction?

Chapter 3 introduced several methods of **structuring** content in ways that are meaningful to students (e.g., general to detailed, simple to complex, concrete to abstract). Following is an elaboration of four additional ways of organizing content that are particularly relevant to direct instruction. These are the part–whole, sequential, combinatorial, and comparative methods.

Part–Whole Relationships

A part–whole organizational format introduces the topic in its most general form ("What is a possessive?") and then divides the topic into easy-to-distinguish subdivisions ("Rule 1," "Rule 2"). This creates subdivisions that are easily digested and presents them in ways that always relate back to the whole. Students should always be aware of the part being covered at any particular time ("This is Rule 2") and its relationship to the whole ("This leads to our second rule for denoting ownership"). Use verbal markers to alert students that a transition is

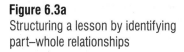

Figure 6.3a
Structuring a lesson by identifying
part–whole relationships

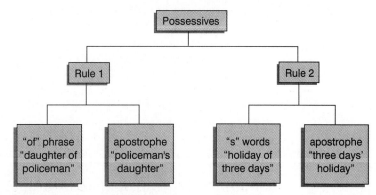

under way ("This is Rule 1," "Here is the first part," "This is the last example of this type; now let's move to the next type").

This type of organization creates bite-sized chunks; it helps students organize and see what is being taught and informs them of what portion they are on. Part–whole organization is illustrated in Figure 6.3a.

Sequential Relationships

Another way of structuring content is by sequential ordering; you teach the content according to the way in which the facts, rules, or sequences to be learned occur in the real world. Students may already have a feel for sequential ordering from practical experience.

In algebra, for example, equations are solved by first multiplying, then dividing, then adding, and finally subtracting. This order of operations must occur for a solution to be correct. A sequentially structured lesson, therefore, might introduce the manipulation of signed numbers in the order multiplication-division-addition-subtraction, which reinforces the way equations must actually be solved, making the skill and behavior you are teaching more authentic. In other words, all examples used in teaching signed-number multiplication would be completed before any examples about division would be introduced, thereby teaching the correct sequence as well as the intended content. Sequential ordering is illustrated in Figure 6.3b.

Combinatorial Relationships

A third way you can structure lesson content is to bring together in a single format various elements or dimensions that influence the use of

Figure 6.3b
Structuring a lesson by identifying sequential relationships

$$y = a - b + \frac{cd}{e}$$

1. First, let's determine cd when

   c = -1, d = 2

   c = 0, d = -4

   c = 2, d = -3

2. Next, let's determine $\frac{cd}{e}$ when

   cd = -2, e = -2

   cd = 0, e = 1

   cd = -6, e = 4

3. Now, let's determine $b + \frac{cd}{e}$ when

   $b = 1, \frac{cd}{e} = 1$

   $b = -2, \frac{cd}{e} = 0$

   $b = 2, \frac{cd}{e} = -1.5$

4. Finally, let's determine $a - b + \frac{cd}{e}$ when

   $a = 10, b + \frac{cd}{e} = 2$

   $a = 7, b + \frac{cd}{e} = -3$

   $a = 5, b + \frac{cd}{e} = .5$

facts, rules, and sequences. This allows an overall framework to direct the order of content by showing the logic of some combinations of facts, rules, and sequences and the illogic of other combinations.

For example, in teaching a direct instruction lesson in social studies, you might develop a scheme to reveal the relationship between marketable products and the various means of transporting them to market. You could draw an organizational chart (Figure 6.3c) to structure the content. You could show the chart to your students, and then teach all the relevant facts (e.g., relative weights of products), rules (the heavier the product, the more efficient the transportation system must be), and action sequences (first analyze the product's size and weight, then choose the best location). The shaded cells, then, identify the *combinations*, or dimensions of content, that are most relevant to the lesson objectives.

Comparative Relationships

In comparative structuring of content, you place different pieces of content side by side so that learners can compare and contrast them. Placing facts, rules, and sequences side by side across two or more categories lets students observe their similarities and differences. For example, you might want to compare and contrast governmental aspects of the United States and England. You could

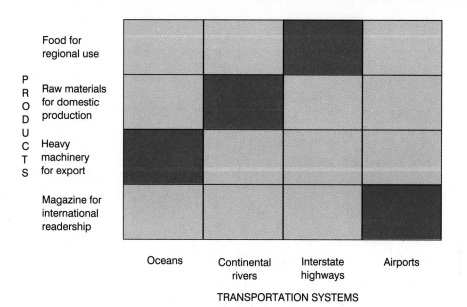

Figure 6.3c
Structuring a lesson by identifying combinatorial relationships

order the instruction according to the format shown in Figure 6.3d. Then you could teach the relevant facts (economic systems), politics (type of government), and source of laws (U.S. Constitution vs. legal codes) by moving first across the chart and then down. The chart structures content in advance, and students can easily see the structure and content to be covered.

Using the Methods

Whether you use one structuring method or a combination to organize a lesson, remember to divide the content into bite-sized pieces. To the extent that these structuring techniques divide larger units of content into smaller and more meaningful units, they will have served an important purpose.

Finally, note how the teacher in our classroom dialogue combined rules and examples in organizing and presenting the content. She always presented the rule first and then followed with one or more examples. Note also that after some examples illustrating the rule, she repeated it—either by having students write the rule after seeing it on the board, or by having a student repeat it to the class.

Points of Comparison	U.S.	England
Economics	capitalism	capitalism
Politics	representative democracy	parliamentary democracy
Source of laws	U.S. constitution	English legal codes
Representative body	Congress	parliament

Figure 6.3d
Structuring a lesson by identifying comparative relationships

Learning a rule in one sensory modality (e.g., seeing it on the board) and then recreating it in a different sensory modality (e.g., writing or speaking it) generally promotes greater learning and retention than seeing the rule only once or reproducing it in the same modality in which it was learned.

Giving a rule, then an example of the rule, followed by repetition of the rule is called the *rule-example-rule order.* It generally is more effective than simply giving the rule and then an example (rule-example order), or giving an example followed by the rule.

>>> GUIDED STUDENT PRACTICE <<<

This is the third step in the direct instruction model (Table 6.4). Recall from the structure of a lesson plan that presentation of stimulus material is followed by eliciting practice in the desired behavior. This section presents several ways of accomplishing this in the context of the direct instruction model. These elicitations are teacher guided, providing students with **guided practice** that you organize and direct.

Recall from Chapter 5 the important ingredients for eliciting a student response. One is to elicit the response in as nonevaluative an atmosphere as possible; this frees students to risk creating responses about which they may be unsure but from which they can begin to build a correct response. Any response, however crude or incorrect, can be the basis for learning if it is followed by proper feedback and correctives.

A second ingredient for eliciting a student response is the use of covert responses. This not only ensures a nonthreatening environment but also encourages student engagement in the learning task with the least expenditure of your time and effort. In the example, by having students privately write their responses before seeing the correct answers on the overhead, the teacher guided each student to formulate a response; it was not necessary to call on each of them. She guided the students into responding by encouraging, and later rewarding, their covert responses.

An equally important aspect of eliciting a desired response is to check for student understanding. When necessary, prompt to convert wrong answers to right ones. In the example, the teacher stopped after every item to see if there were problems, and prompted students to create correct answers when necessary. Prompting is an important part of eliciting the desired behavior, because it strengthens and builds the learners' confidence by encouraging them to use some aspects of the answer that have already been given in formulating the correct response (Gagné, et al. 1993). In the example, Johnny was encouraged to *rethink* his response, to *focus* consciously on the specific part of the problem causing the error, and to *remember* the rule that will prevent such errors in the future.

Prompting

During direct instruction the effective teacher often provides prompts, hints, and other types of supplementary instructional stimuli to help learners make the correct response. You can use three categories of prompts to shape the correct performance of your learners: verbal prompts, gestural prompts, and physical prompts.

How can I prompt learners to respond correctly during direct instruction?

Verbal Prompts. **Verbal prompts** can be cues, reminders, or instructions to learners that help them perform correctly the skill you are teaching. For example, saying to a first-grade learner as he is writing, "Leave a space between words," reminds him what you previously said about neat handwriting. Or saying, "First adjust the object lens," to a learner while she is looking at a microscope slide, prompts her as she is learning how to use a microscope. Verbal prompts help guide the learner to connect performances and prevent mistakes and frustration.

Gestural Prompts. **Gestural prompts** model or demonstrate for learners a particular skill you want them to perform. For example, if as the teacher above, you were to point to the fine adjustment knob on the microscope and make a turning gesture with your hand, you would be prompting, or reminding, the student to perform this step of the process. Gestural prompts are particularly helpful when you anticipate that the learner may make a mistake. You can use gestural prompts routinely to remind learners how to fold a piece of paper, how to grasp a pair of scissors, to raise their hand before asking a question, or to hold a pen properly when writing.

Physical Prompts.   Some learners may lack the fine muscle control to follow a demonstration and imitate the action being modeled. For example, you might verbally describe how to form the letter "A", and demonstrate this for the learner, and the learner may still be unable to write "A" correctly. In such a case, you might use your hand to guide the learner's hand as he writes. This is called a physical prompt. With a **physical prompt** you use *hand-over-hand* assistance to guide the learner to the correct performance. You can routinely use physical prompts to assist learners with handwriting, cutting out shapes, tying shoelaces, correctly holding a dissecting tool, or performing a complex dance routine.

Least-to-Most Intrusive Prompting.   It is generally recommended that you use the least intrusive prompt first when guiding a learner's performance. Verbal prompts are considered the least intrusive, while physical prompts are considered the most intrusive (Cooper, Heron, & Heward, 1987). Thus, it would be more appropriate, first, to say, "Don't forget the fine adjustment!" when guiding a learner in the use of a microscope than to take the learner's hand and physically assist her. The reasoning behind using a least-to-most intrusive order is that verbal prompts are easier to remove or fade than are physical prompts. Learners who are dependent on physical prompts to perform correctly will find it more difficult to demonstrate a skill independently of the teacher and to acquire authentic behavior.

Full-class Prompting.   You can also check for understanding and prompt for correct responses using the full class. The example dialogue showed one approach: all the students were asked to respond privately at the same time and then encouraged to ask for individual help ("Any problems?").

Another approach is to call on students whether or not their hands are raised, thereby seeking opportunities to prompt and correct wrong answers. One version of this is called *ordered turns,* in which you systematically go through the class and expect students to respond when their turn arrives. When groups are small, this approach is more effective in producing student achievement gains than randomly calling on students (Brophy & Evertson, 1976; Anderson et al., 1982). But, generally, this method is less efficient than selecting students to respond during full-class instruction (Anderson et al., 1982).

Yet another approach is to have students write out answers to be checked and perhaps corrected by a classmate. Finally, you can develop questions beforehand to test for the most common errors. Check student responses for accuracy and prompt when necessary. This approach has the advantage of assuming that not everyone understands or has the correct answer when no responses are received. It has been found to be particularly effective in increasing student achievement (Singer & Donlon, 1982; McKenzie, 1979).

Modeling

Modeling is a teaching activity that involves demonstrating to learners what you want them to do (in the form of action sequences), say (in the form of facts and concepts), or think (in the form of problem solving or learning to learn strategies).

How can I model for learners what I want them to learn?

When used correctly, modeling can assist learners to acquire a variety of intellectual and social skills more effortlessly and efficiently than with verbal, gestural, or physical prompts alone. Modeling is particularly effective for younger learners who may not be able to follow complex verbal explanations, visually dominant learners who may need to see how something is done before they can actually do it, and, as we will see in Chapter 9, for communicating mental strategies for problem solving to all ages of learners.

Bandura and his colleagues have studied how and why we learn from models (Bandura, 1977, 1986; Zimmerman, 1989). Their research on modeling is referred to as *social learning theory*, and attempts to explain how people learn from observing other people. From their work we know that children not only can learn attitudes, values, and standards of behavior from observing adults and peers, but may also learn physical and intellectual skills.

Some of this learning takes place by directly imitating what a model (for example, a teacher) is doing, while other learning takes place by inferring why the model is acting a certain way, or what type of person the model is. For example, learners acquire certain values about the importance of learning, caring for others, doing work neatly, or respect for other cultures by observing how their parents, friends, and teachers actually behave in the real world, and then inferring from their observations how they, too, should behave. Although teachers model all the time, we know that some forms of modeling are better than others. Zimmerman and Kleefeld (1977) found that teachers who were taught the practice of modeling were far more effective at helping young children to learn than teachers who were not.

Modeling is a direct teaching activity that allows students to imitate from demonstration or infer from observation the behavior to be learned. Four psychological processes need to occur for your learners to benefit from modeling:

1. Attention
2. Retention
3. Production
4. Motivation

Let's take a closer look at these to discover how students learn from what they see.

Attention. Demonstrations are only of value if learners are looking and/or listening to them. In other words, without attention there can be no imitation or observational learning. In the previous section we highlighted the importance of gaining a learner's attention. Modeling requires that you not only gain your learners' attention but that you retain it throughout the lesson. Bandura (1977) found that learners hold their attention better under the following conditions:

1. The model is someone who is respected as an expert in their field.
2. The model is demonstrating something that has functional value to the learner. Learners pay little attention to those things for which they see no immediate relevance.
3. The demonstration is simplified by subdividing it into component parts and presented in a clearly discernable step-by-step fashion.

Retention. Teachers model because they want their learners to be able to repeat their same actions when they are no longer present. For example, teachers typically model when they demonstrate how to add a column of numbers, sound out a word, or evaluate a short essay. But, the transfer of these actions will only occur if learners remember what they saw or heard. Demonstrations from which imitation is to occur must be planned with the goal of retention in mind.

Learners are more likely to remember the following types of demonstrations:

1. Those linked to previous skills or ideas that they have already learned. The more meaningful the demonstration, the more

likely it will be retained. ("Remember how yesterday we added one-digit numbers in a column? Well, today we will use the same procedure on numbers that have two or more digits.")

2. Those that include concise labels, vivid images, code words, or visual mnemonics (to be discussed in Chapter 9), which help learners hold new learning in memory. ("Look at how I hold my lips when I pronounce this next word.")

3. Those that are immediately rehearsed. This rehearsal can be overt, as when the teacher asks learners to say or do something immediately following the demonstration, or covert. Covert rehearsal occurs when the learner visualizes or mentally creates an image of what the teacher demonstrated. ("Now, everyone read the next passage to themselves, repeating silently the sequence of steps I just demonstrated.")

Production.   The third component of the modeling process occurs when learners actually do what the teacher demonstrated. In this stage of the process, the mental images or verbal codes learners retained in memory direct their actual performance of what the teacher demonstrated. Learners recall these images or codes by the practice situation the teacher creates and by the verbal cues given. Having been evoked, these images guide the actual performance of what was learned during the demonstration.

Learners are more likely to produce what they saw under the following conditions:

1. Production closely follows the retention phase. ("OK, now that you've practiced remembering the correct sequence of steps I demonstrated, let's use them to interpret the meaning of the following passage.")

2. The practice situation contains cues or stimuli that evoke the retained mental images or verbal codes. ("This next word requires you to position your lips exactly as you saw me do in the last example.")

3. The performance immediately follows mental rehearsal. ("Let's switch to several new examples that you haven't seen before.")

The production phase increases the likelihood that images of the demonstration learners have remembered will guide the production of newly acquired behavior. In addition, this phase allows the teacher to observe learners and give feedback on how well they have mastered the behavior. Giving learners information about the correctness of their actions—without expressing negativity or dissatisfaction—has been shown to increase the likelihood of a correct performance (Vasta, 1976).

Motivation.   The final stage of the process of learning through modeling occurs when learners experience desirable outcomes following their performance. Desirable outcomes usually take the form of some type of teacher praise, which motivates learners to want to imitate at some future time what they have seen. Learners are less likely to repeat the actions of a model if they have experienced punishing or unsatisfying consequences following their initial attempts to imitate the model.

On the other hand, learners are more likely to repeat the actions of a model both immediately and to transfer it to new situations over time when the following occur:

1. Praise and encouragement rather than criticism immediately follow performance. ("Your answer is partly correct; think some more about what we've just discussed," as opposed to, "Your answer is wrong. You're not listening again.")
2. The praise is directed at specific aspects of the performance. ("I like how you left enough space between your words," as opposed to, "That's neat.")
3. Directions rather than corrections follow incorrect performance. ("Remember, the first step is to generate a hypothesis," as opposed to, "You don't state the research design before you generate a hypothesis!")

>>> FEEDBACK AND CORRECTIVES <<<

How do I correct responses that are hesitant, responses that are careless, and responses that are incorrect due to lack of knowledge?

The next ingredient in the direct instruction model (Table 6.4) is provision of **feedback** and **correctives.** Simply put, you need strategies for handling right and wrong answers. Based upon several studies, Rosenshine (1983) identified four broad categories of student response: (1) correct, quick, and firm, (2) correct but hesitant, (3) incorrect due to carelessness, and (4) incorrect due to lack of knowledge. These are described in the following subsections, with some direct instruction strategies for handling them.

Correct, Quick, and Firm

The student response that teachers strive most to inspire is *correct, quick, and firm.* Such a response most frequently occurs during the latter stages of a lesson or unit, but it can occur almost anytime during a lesson or unit if you have divided the content into bite-sized portions. A moderate-to-high percentage of correct, quick, and firm responses is important if students are to become actively engaged in the learning process. Not every response from every student must be a correct one, but *for most learning that involves knowledge acquisition, make the steps between successive portions of your lesson small enough to produce approximately 60 to 80 percent correct answers in a practice and feedback session* (Bennett, Desforges, Cockburn, & Wilkinson, 1981; Brophy & Evertson, 1976).

This research suggests that your best response to a correct, quick, and firm student response is to ask another question of the same student. This increases the potential for feedback or, if time does not permit, to move on quickly to another question and student. Keep the lesson moving quickly, involving as many students as possible in the practice exercise, and covering as many stimulus problems as possible. Once 60 to 80 percent right answers are produced, you will have created a rhythm and momentum that heightens student attention and engagement and provides for a high level of task orientation. The brisk pace of right answers also will help minimize irrelevant student responses and classroom distractions.

Correct But Hesitant

The second student response is *correct but hesitant*. This type frequently occurs in a practice and feedback session at the beginning or middle of a lesson. Positive feedback to the student who supplies a correct but hesitant response is essential. The first feedback to provide in this instance is a positive, reinforcing statement, such as "good," or "that's correct," because the correct but hesitant response is more likely to be remembered when linked to a warm reply. This helps advance into the correct, quick, and firm category the student's next response to the same type of problem.

Affirmative replies, however, seldom effect significant change on a subsequent problem of the same type unless the reasons behind the hesitant response are addressed. Although discovering the precise reason for a hesitant response is desirable, it takes time. A quick restatement of the facts, rules, or steps needed to obtain the right answer often accomplishes the same end more efficiently. This restatement not only aids the student who is giving the correct but hesitant response, but also helps reduce subsequent wrong answers or hesitant responses among other students who hear the restatement.

Incorrect Because of Carelessness

The third student response is *incorrect because of carelessness*. As many as 20 percent of student responses fall into this category, depending on the time of day and the students' level of fatigue and inattentiveness. When this occurs, and you feel that they really know the correct response, you may be tempted to scold, admonish, or even verbally punish students for responding thoughtlessly (e.g., "I'm ashamed of you," "That's a dumb mistake," "I thought you were brighter than that"). However, resist this temptation, no matter how justified it seems. Nothing is more frustrating than to repress genuine emotions, but researchers and experienced teachers agree that you do more harm than good if you react emotionally to this type of problem.

Verbal punishment rarely teaches students to avoid careless mistakes. Further, experience shows that the rhythm and momentum built and maintained through a brisk and lively pace can easily be broken by such off-task attention to an individual student. Emotional reaction rarely has a positive effect, so the best procedure is to acknowledge that the answer is wrong and to move immediately to the next student for the correct response. By doing so, you will make a point to the careless student that he or she lost the opportunity for a correct response and the praise that goes with it.

Incorrect Because of Lack of Knowledge

Perhaps the most challenging response is *incorrect because of a lack of knowledge*. Such errors typically occur, sometimes in large numbers, during the initial stages of a lesson or unit. It is better to provide hints, probe, or change the question or stimulus to a simpler one that engages the student in finding the correct response than to simply give the student the correct response. After all, the goal is not to get the correct answer from the student, but to *engage the learner in the process by which the right answer can be found.*

In the example, the teacher tried to focus Johnny on the *s* he had missed at the end of the proper noun *Jenkins* and to restate the rule concerning formation of possessives in words ending in *s*. Likewise, the teacher probed Debbie after her wrong answer by asking, "What word is doing the possessing?" Each of these instances led to the right answer without actually telling the student what the right answer was. When your strategy channels a student's thoughts to produce the right answer without actually giving it, you provide a framework for producing a correct response in all subsequent similar problems.

Strategies for Incorrect Responses

The most common strategies for incorrect responses are the following:

1. Review key facts or rules needed for a correct solution.
2. Explain the steps used to reach a correct solution.
3. Prompt with clues or hints representing a partially correct answer.
4. Take a different but similar problem and guide the student to the correct answer.

Such strategies used with one student benefit all the rest by clarifying information that they may have been learned only partially. Because this type of corrective feedback is used with individual students, its effects on the entire class will be evidenced by an increasing percentage of correct responses. Reviewing, reexplaining, and prompting are effective until approximately 80 percent of the students respond correctly. After that point, make the correctives briefer, eventually guiding students who are making incorrect responses to helpful exercises in the text or to remedial exercises (Bennett & Desforges, 1988).

Finally, note that when using the direct instruction model for teaching facts, rules, and sequences, an incorrect answer must never go undetected or uncorrected. Respond to every wrong answer with one or more of the preceding strategies. Leaving an answer uncorrected due to inattentiveness or distraction signals students who do know the answer that paying attention and active responding are not to be taken seriously.

Lindsley (1992) and Hall, Delguardi, Greenwood, and Thurston, (1982) make a useful distinction between active and passive responding. **Active responding** includes orally responding to a question, writing out the correct answer, calculating an answer, or physically making a response (e.g., focusing a microscope), and so on. **Passive responding** includes listening to the teacher's answer, reading about the correct answer, or listening to classmates recite the right answer.

How can I encourage my learners to actively respond during direct instruction?

Greenwood, Delguardi, and Hall (1984) report that nearly half of a learner's day is involved in passsive responding. This is unfortunate because their research also demonstrates a strong relationship between learner achievement and active responding. These researchers urge you to plan your lessons so that learners spend *about 75 percent of their time engaged in active responding.*

A second finding of their research is that correct responses are more likely when you design your practice material (worksheets, seatwork, homework, etc.) to elicit correct responses 60 to 80 percent of the time. Many teachers purposefully design materials for learner practice to be overly challenging, i.e., with a strong likelihood that many learners will make mistakes. Researchers have demonstrated that learners acquire basic facts and skills faster when their opportunities for practice result in high rates of success (Lindsley, 1991).

In summary, when providing feedback and corrections:

- Give directions that focus on the response you want learners to make.
- Design instructional materials both for initial learning and practice so that learners can produce correct answers 60 to 80 percent of the time.
- Select activities to engage your learners in active responding about 75 percent of the time.

>>> INDEPENDENT PRACTICE <<<

The fifth ingredient in direct instruction is the opportunity for **independent practice** (Table 6.4). Once you have successfully elicited the behavior, provided feedback, and administered correctives, students need the opportunity to practice the behavior independently. Often this is the time when facts and rules come together to form action sequences. For example, learning to drive a car requires a knowledge of terminology (gear shift, ignition, accelerator) and rules (signaling, what to do at stoplights, parking on hills). But until the knowledge and rules are put together, meaningful learning cannot occur.

Independent practice provides the opportunity in a carefully controlled and organized environment to make a meaningful whole out of the bits and pieces. Facts and rules must come together under your guidance and example in ways that (1) force simultaneous consideration of all the individual units of a problem and (2) connect the units into a single harmonious sequence of action. Learning theorists call these two processes *unitization* and *automaticity* (La Berge & Samuels, 1974).

Notice the manner in which these two processes were required in the example lesson. The individual "units" were the definition of a possessive (a fact) and two statements about forming possessives (Rules 1 and 2). The lesson connected these units into a single harmonious sequence of action in two ways. First was the exercise with which the example ends, in which the teacher directed students to a workbook to provide independent practice opportunity. The workbook sentences should contain possessives similar to those found in

Table 6.5

Steps involved in translating the sentence, "In Mrs. Jones paper there was an article about a friend of Robert" into correct possessive form

---

Step 1   Is ownership indicated in this sentence?

Step 2   If yes, where?

       the paper belongs to Mrs. Jones

       the friend belongs to Robert

Step 3   Has an *of* phrase been substituted for a noun (Rule 1)?

       If yes, where?

       friend of Robert has been substituted for Robert's friend

Step 4   Does any word denoting ownership end in *s*? (Rule 2)

       If yes, where?

       Jones paper should be written *Jones' paper*

Step 5   Therefore, the correct possessive form of this sentence is "In Mrs. Jones' paper there was an article about Robert's friend."

---

any newspaper, magazine, or school essay. Second was the teacher's intention to provide examples of real mistakes occurring in newspapers and magazines for additional practice at the end of the lesson. Table 6.5 traces the steps a student might take in combining the facts and rules into an action sequence for one sentence in the workbook.

In the preceding direct instruction dialogue, we saw that the meaningful *application* of knowledge requires knowledge that is highly familiar to the learner and rich in examples and associations (e.g., month's delay, Jenkins' home) learned from detailed and redundant practice. In this sense, less complex levels of behavior almost always are required for more complex forms of learning to occur. It is important that facts and rules not be left dangling but be practiced with detailed and redundant examples that create more complex forms of learning, such as action sequences.

Examples of errors from newspapers and magazines provided students an opportunity to form action sequences from the facts and rules they learned. These real-life examples further increased the authenticity of their learning. In your own classroom, make opportunities for practice increasingly resemble applications in the real world until the examples you provide are indistinguishable from those outside the classroom. Using clippings from actual newspapers and magazines was this teacher's way of doing so.

The purpose of providing opportunities for all types of independent practice is to develop automatic responses in students, so they no longer need to recall each individual unit of content but can use all the units simultaneously. Thus, the goal of the example lesson was "to write a sentence using possessives correctly," and not "to recite Rule 1 and Rule 2." As we have seen, automaticity is reached through mastery of the units comprising a complete response and sufficient practice in composing these pieces into a complete action sequence. Your goal is to schedule sufficient opportunities for independent practice to allow individual responses to become "composed" and automatic (Samuels, 1981).

Regardless of the type of practice activity used, there are several guidelines for promoting effective practice that you should keep in mind:

What is an effective practice activity?

- *Students should understand the reason for practice.* Practice often turns into busywork, which can create boredom, frustration, and noncompliance. Learners should approach classroom practice with the same enthusiasm that an Olympic athlete pursues laps in the pool or on the track. This is more likely to occur if (1) you make known to learners the purpose of the practice ("We will need to be proficient at solving these problems in order to go on to our next activity"), and (2) practice occurs during as well as after new learning ("Let's stop right here, so you can try some of these problems yourselves").
- *Effective practice is delivered in a manner that is brief, nonevaluative, and supportive.* Practice involves more than simply saying, "OK. Take out your books, turn to page 78, and answer questions 1, 3, 7, and 9. You have 20 minutes." Rather, your introduction to a practice activity should accomplish three objectives: (1) inform the learners that they are going to practice something they are capable of succeeding at ("You've done part of this before, so this shouldn't be much different"); (2) dispel anxiety about doing the task through the use of nonevaluative and nonthreatening language ("You've got part of it right, Anita. Now, think some more and you'll have it"); and (3) let the learners know that you will be around to monitor their work and support their efforts ("I will be around to help, so let me know if you have a problem").
- *Practice should be designed to ensure success.* Practice makes perfect only when those practicing are doing so correctly. If your learners are making many math, punctuation, or problem-solving mistakes, practice is making imperfect. Design your practice to produce as few errors as possible. Worksheets, for example, should be developed to ensure that most learners complete correctly at least 60 to 80 percent of the problems.
- *Practice should be arranged to allow students to receive feedback.* As we learned earlier in our discussion of modeling,

feedback exerts a powerful effect on learning. Develop procedures and routines for rapid checking of work so that learners know as soon as possible how well they are performing. Using peers to correct one another's practice is an efficient way to give feedback. Also, having answer sheets handy so that learners can check their own work can be a simple and effective means of providing feedback.

- *Practice should have the qualities of progress, challenge, and variety.* Kounin (1970) found that the key to preventing learners from becoming bored was to design practice opportunities so that learners actually see that they are making progress. ("Don't forget to check your answers with the key on the board.") In addition, introduce practice in a challenging and enthusiastic manner. ("This will really test your understanding with some new and interesting kinds of problems.") Finally, practice exercises should include a variety of examples and situations.

You should perform the following activities to ensure that students become actively engaged in the practice you provide:

1. **Direct** the class through the first independent practice item. This gives the scheduled seatwork a definite beginning, and students who are unclear about the assignment can ask questions without distracting others. This also provides a mental model for attaining a correct answer, which students can use in subsequent problems.

2. **Schedule** seatwork as soon as possible after the eliciting and feedback exercises. This helps students understand that independent practice is relevant to the guided practice provided earlier. If opportunities for independent practice are not provided immediately but on a later day, there likely will be a high number of requests for information; this will lead you inefficiently to repeat key portions of the previous day's lesson. As with all forms of learning, *practice should follow the time of learning as soon as possible* for maximum recall and understanding.

3. **Circulate** around the classroom while students are engaged in independent practice, to provide feedback, ask questions, and give brief explanations (Emmer et al., 1994). Spend circulation time equally across most of your students—don't concentrate on a small number of them. Try to average 30 seconds or less per student (if you average 30 seconds per student, and have 30 students, that consumes 15 minutes of

class time). Minimize your scanning of written responses, prompting for alternative answers, or reminding students of facts and rules so as not to reduce your time available for monitoring the work of other students. Monitoring student responses during independent seatwork can be an important direct instruction function if you keep contacts short and focused on specific issues for which a brief explanation is adequate.

>>> WEEKLY AND MONTHLY REVIEWS <<<

The sixth and final direct instruction function involves conducting **weekly and monthly reviews** (Table 6.4). Periodic review ensures that you have taught all task-relevant information needed for future lessons and that you have identified areas that require the reteaching of key facts, rules, and sequences. Without periodic review you have no way of knowing whether direct instruction has been successful in teaching the required facts, rules, and sequences.

Periodic review has long been a part of almost every instructional strategy. In the context of direct instruction, however, periodic review and the recycling of instruction take on added importance because of the brisk pace at which direct instruction is conducted. You usually establish the proper pace by noting the approximate percentage of errors occurring during guided practice and feedback; 60 to 80 percent correct responses indicates a satisfactory pace.

Weekly and monthly reviews also help determine whether the pace is right or whether to adjust it before covering too much content (Cooper et al., 1987; Englemann, 1991). When student responses in weekly and monthly reviews are correct, quick, and firm about 95 percent of the time, the pace is adequate. Independent practice and homework should raise the percentage of correct responses from approximately 60 to 80 percent during guided practice and feedback to approximately 95 percent on weekly and monthly reviews. If results are below these levels—and especially if they are substantially below—your pace is too fast and some reteaching of facts, rules, and sequences may be necessary, especially if they are prerequisite to later learning.

Another obvious advantage of weekly and monthly reviews is that they strengthen correct but hesitant responses. Reviewing facts, rules, and sequences that are the basis of task-relevant prior understandings for later lessons will give some learners a second chance to grasp material that they missed or only partially learned the first time around. These reviews often are welcomed by students; it is a chance to go over material that they may have missed, that was difficult to learn the first time through, and that may be covered on unit tests.

During independent practice, the teacher circulates around the classroom scanning written responses, prompting for alternative answers, and reminding students of necessary facts or rules, being careful to keep interchanges short so that the work of as many students as possible can be checked.

Finally, a regular weekly review (not a review "every so often") is the key to performing this direct instruction function. The weekly review is intended to build momentum. Momentum results from gradually increasing the coverage and depth of the weekly reviews until it is time for a comprehensive monthly review (Posner, 1987). The objective is to create a review cycle that rises and falls in about a month. The low point of this cycle occurs at the start of a direct instruction unit, when only one week's material need be reviewed. The weekly reviews then become increasingly comprehensive until a major monthly review restates and checks for understanding of all the previous month's learning. Momentum is built by targeting greater and greater amounts of instruction for review. This is done in gradual stages so that students are not overwhelmed with unfamiliar review content and so they always know what will be covered in the next review.

Table 6.6 presents the lesson plan for direct instruction based on the dialogue about possessives presented in this chapter.

>>> OTHER FORMS OF DIRECT INSTRUCTION <<<

So far, direct instruction has been discussed as though it occurs only in a lecture-recitation format. This is perhaps the most popular format for direct instruction, but is by no means the only one. Other ways of executing the direct instruction model (either independent

Table 6.6
Lesson plan: Direct instruction

Unit Title: Punctuation
Lesson Title: Forming and punctuating possessives

1. Gaining attention	Display October school newspaper with punctuation error in headline. Point to error.
2. Informing the learner of the objective	At the end of the period students will be able to find mistakes in the newspapers (on file under "Punctuation") and make the necessary changes.
3. Stimulating recall of prerequisite learning	Review part of speech most likely to own or possess something by asking for the definition of a noun.
4. Presenting the stimulus material	Present two rules of possession: Rule 1. Use the possessive form whenever an *of* phrase can be substituted for a noun. Rule 2. For words ending in *s*, place the apostrophe after, not before, the *s*. Write rules on board.
5. Eliciting the desired behavior	Display the following examples on a transparency and ask students to convert them to the possessive form one at a time. On transparency: delay of a month home of Jenkins speech of the President the television set of Mr. Burns (See Smith, G. [1995]. *Understanding Grammar*. New York: City Press, pp. 101–103 for other examples.)
6. Providing feedback	Write the correct possessive form on the transparency as students finish each example. Wait for students to finish (all heads up) before providing the answer for the next example. Probe for complete understanding by asking for the rule.
7. Assessing the behavior	Use the exercise on page 87 of the workbook to assess student understanding and to provide additional practice. Use ordered recitation until about 90% correct responses are attained. Place 10 possessives on the unit test requiring the application of Rule 1 and Rule 2. Use examples in Smith (1995), pp. 101–103.

of the lecture-recitation format or in association with it include programmed instruction, computer-assisted instruction, peer and cross-age tutoring, various kinds of audiolingual and communication tools (such as recorded lessons for learning to read in the early grades), and the use of the computer as an information provider. These were discussed in Chapter 5.

Some of these approaches have been creatively programmed to include all, or almost all, of the six direct instruction functions (daily review, new content, guided practice, feedback and correctives, independent practice, and periodic review). There is little question that some of these alternatives to the lecture-recitation format have been successful with certain types of content and students (Atkinson, 1984; Kulik & Kulik, 1984). However, because they are much less under your control than is the lecture-recitation format you create, you should carefully consider their applicability to your specific instructional goals and students. Although programmed texts, computer-assisted instructional software, and various drill and practice media, such as described in Chapter 5, often are associated with the direct instruction model, their treatment of the intended content may be far from direct. Therefore, whenever using these formats and associated "courseware," be sure to preview both their method and content for close adherence to the six functions of the direct instruction model.

Finally, programmed texts, computer-assisted instruction software, specialized media, and information and communication technologies follow a direct instruction model most closely when they are programmed for basic academic skills. This is where the direct instruction format can be of most benefit in increasing student achievement (Lindsely, 1991, 1992). At the same time, it can relieve you of the sometimes arduous chore of providing individualized remedial instruction to a small number of students. Building a library of individualized courseware that covers the basic skills most frequently needed in your grade level and content area will be an important goal for your classroom.

>>> PROMOTING THE GOALS OF DIRECT INSTRUCTION <<< IN THE CULTURALLY DIVERSE CLASSROOM

We have seen that a task-oriented teacher maximizes content coverage and gives students the greatest opportunity to learn. Likewise, students who are involved in, acting on, and otherwise thinking about the material being presented have the greatest opportunity to learn. The key to bringing these two important dimensions of effective teaching together—task orientation and student engagement—rests with how you interact with your students to invoke a willingness to respond and apply what they have been learning. In classrooms where individual, cultural, and ethnic differences are prominent, student engagement in the learning process during direct instruction can be a major challenge to achieving performance outcomes.

What are some ways of promoting the goals of direct instruction in a culturally diverse classroom?

One facet of research dealing with cultural diversity and student engagement has focused on differences in fluency and oral expression among learners during lecture-recitation. For example, Kendon (1981) has studied how student fluency or quickness to respond can be influenced by nurturing and expressive qualities of the teacher. The implication of these findings is that student hesitancy in responding and becoming engaged in the learning process may, for some cultural groups, be more a function of the attitude and cultural style of the teacher than of student ability. Douglas (1975) has shown that student engagement is, in part, an expression of the interactive process between student and teacher. Specifically, her research has found that body posture, language, and eye contact form a pattern of *metacommunication* that is recognized by the learner—and acted upon according to the message being conveyed, intentionally or not. For example, a formal body posture and questions posed in an expressionless voice, without eye contact, may not invoke a commitment to respond. In other words, teachers must convey a sense of caring about the learner before engagement can take place. Engagement techniques alone (for example, presenting new content, guiding student practice, providing feedback and corrections) will not be sufficient to actively engage students in the learning process unless they are accompanied by the appropriate metacommunication expressing nurturance and caring. Bowers and Flinders (1991) suggest some of the ways teachers can promote student engagement by conveying a sense of nurturance and caring:

- Use appropriate examples to clarify concepts and model performance. "Let me give you an example that will help you see the relationship."
- Accept student's way of understanding new concepts. "That's an interesting answer. Would you like to tell us how you arrived at it?"
- Reduce feelings of competitiveness. "Today, those who wish can work with a partner on the practice exercise."
- Increase opportunities for social reinforcement. "If you like, you can ask someone sitting nearby how they worked the problem."

- Facilitate group achievement. "When you're finished with your work, you might join another group to help them solve the problem."
- Use and expect culturally appropriate eye contact with students. "Amanda, I'm going to sit down next to you and watch you work the first problem."
- Recognize longer pauses and slower tempo. "Take your time. I'll wait for you to think of an answer."
- Respond to unique or different questions during a response. "You're asking about something else. Let me give you that answer then we'll go back to the first question."
- Balance compliments and reinforcement equally. "Let's not forget, both Angel and Damen got the right answer but in different ways."

Although much still needs to be known about cultural diversity and student engagement during direct instruction, one thing is clear: Students of any culture are more likely to engage in the learning process in an atmosphere that (1) emphasizes the importance of unique learner responses, (2) reduces feelings of individual competitiveness, (3) teaches social reinforcement and peer interaction, and (4) conveys a sense of nurturance and caring.

[handwritten margin note: Students of any culture more likely to engage in learning]

>>> A FINAL WORD <<<

This chapter has emphasized some of the direct, or more didactic, functions of teaching. As you have seen, these functions are particularly useful for teaching facts, rules, and action sequences, which tend to correspond to objectives at lower levels of behavioral complexity. When used in the proper sequence and with the behavioral objectives for which they are best suited, direct teaching functions can make teaching easier, more efficient, and more effective.

The next chapter discusses another and equally valuable model of instruction, emphasizing still other teaching strategies. This model not only complements a menu of direct instructional strategies with other varieties of instruction, but also is an approach that enables you to move your teaching to higher levels of behavioral complexity. As noted in Chapter 5, behaviors at these higher levels should comprise a significant portion of the outcomes planned at the unit level. Because these behaviors are among those most frequently required outside of the classroom, techniques through which your students can acquire them are indispensable additions to your teaching strategy menu.

This chapter introduced you to direct instruction strategies. Its main points were as follows:

1. Two broad classifications of learning are facts, rules, and action sequences (Type 1) and concepts, patterns, and abstractions (Type 2).

2. Type 1 outcomes generally represent behaviors at the lower levels of complexity in the cognitive, affective, and psychomotor domains; Type 2 outcomes frequently represent behaviors at the higher levels of complexity in these domains.

3. Type 1 teaching activities require combining facts and rules at the knowledge and comprehension level into a sequence of actions that can be learned through observation, rote repetition, and practice. Type 1 outcomes have "right answers" that can be learned by memorization and practice.

4. Type 2 teaching activities go beyond facts, rules, and sequences to help the learner create, synthesize, identify, and recognize an answer that cannot be easily modeled or memorized. Type 2 outcomes may have many "right answers" that contain criterial attributes forming a concept or pattern.

5. The learning of facts, rules, and action sequences are most commonly taught with teaching strategies that emphasize knowledge acquisition; the learning of concepts, patterns, and abstractions are most commonly taught with teaching strategies that emphasize inquiry or problem solving.

6. The acquisition of facts, rules, and action sequences is most efficiently achieved through a process known as the *direct instruction model*. This model is primarily teacher centered; facts, rules, and action sequences are passed on to students in a lecture format involving large amounts of teacher talk, questions and answers, review and practice, and the immediate correction of student errors.

7. The direct instruction model is characterized by full-class (as opposed to small-group) instruction; by the organization of learning based on questions posed by you; by the provision of detailed and redundant practice; by the presentation of material so that one new fact, rule, or sequence is mastered before the next is presented; and by the formal arrangement of the classroom to maximize drill and practice.

8. Direct instruction is most appropriate when content in texts and workbooks does not appear in appropriately sized pieces, when your active involvement in the teaching process is necessary to arouse or heighten student interest, and when the content to be taught represents task-relevant prior knowledge for subsequent learning.

9. Techniques for daily review and checking include the following:

- Have students identify difficult homework problems in a question-and-answer format.
- Sample the understanding of a few students who are likely to represent the class.
- Explicitly review task-relevant prior learning required for the day's lesson.

10. Techniques for presenting and structuring new content include the following:

- Establish part–whole relationships.
- Identify sequential relationships.
- Find combinatorial relationships.
- Draw comparative relationships.

11. Techniques for guiding student practice include the following:

- Ask students to respond privately and then be singled out for help.
- Call upon students to respond whether or not their hands are raised.
- Prepare questions beforehand and randomly ask students to respond.

12. Providing appropriate feedback and correctives involves knowing how to respond to answers that are (1) correct, quick, and firm, (2) correct but hesitant, (3) incorrect but careless, and (4) incorrect due to lack of knowledge.

13. For a correct, quick, and firm response, acknowledge the correct response and either ask another question of the same student or quickly move on to another student.

14. For a correct but hesitant response, provide a reinforcing statement and quickly restate the facts, rules, or steps needed for the right answer.

15. For a correct but careless response, indicate that the response is incorrect and quickly move to the next student without further comment.

16. For an incorrect response that is not due to carelessness but to a lack of knowledge, engage the student in finding the correct response with hints, probes, or a related but simpler question.

17. For most learning involving knowledge acquisition, the steps between successive portions of your lesson should be made small enough to produce approximately 60–80 percent correct answers in a practice and feedback session.

18. Reviewing, reexplaining, and prompting is effective until approximately 80 percent of your students respond correctly, after which correctives should be made briefer or stu-

dents should be guided to individualized learning materials.

19. Design independent practice so that the learner puts together facts and rules to form action sequences that increasingly resemble applications in the real world. Make opportunities for independent practice as soon after the time of learning as possible.

20. Pace instruction so that student responses to questions posed in weekly and monthly reviews are correct, quick, and firm about 95 percent of the time.

21. Use independent practice and homework to raise the percentage of correct responses from approximately 60–80 percent during guided practice and feedback to approximately 95 percent on weekly and monthly reviews.

22. Student engagement in the culturally diverse classroom is promoted by accepting unique learner responses, reducing competitiveness, teaching, peer interaction, and conveying a sense of nurturance and caring.

For Discussion and Practice

*1. Identify the learning outcomes associated with Type 1 and Type 2 teaching strategies. To what levels of behavior in the cognitive domain does each type of learning apply?

*2. What type of learning outcomes are most commonly produced by instructional strategies that emphasize knowledge acquisition? What type of learning outcomes are most commonly produced by instructional strategies that emphasize inquiry or problem solving?

*3. Describe five instructional characteristics that define the direct instruction model.

*4. Give examples of action verbs that describe the type of outcomes expected by using the direct instructional model. Provide three examples each in the cognitive, affective, and psychomotor domains.

*5. Identify three areas of content in your teaching field in which the use of the direct

instruction model would be especially appropriate.

*6. Identify four techniques for reviewing and checking the previous day's work.

*7. Identify and provide one original example of each of the four techniques for structuring content and presenting it in bite-sized portions.

*8. Identify the order in which rules and examples of the rules should be given to promote the greatest amount of comprehension and retention of content. Provide a real-life example of such a sequence.

*9. Explain why providing guided student practice in a nonevaluative atmosphere is important for learning to occur.

*10. How is prompting used to provide guided student practice, and for what purpose is it used?

*11. Name four different types of student responses that vary in their correctness and describe how you would respond to each.

12. The following second-grade student responses were received by a teacher after asking the question, "What does 5 plus 3 equal?"

Mary: I think it's 8.
Tommy: 9.
Bob: 53.
Betty: 8.

Role play an appropriate teacher response to each of the answers.

13. The following tenth-grade student responses were received by a teacher who asked, "What was one of the underlying reasons for the Civil War?"

Tim: The South wanted the land owned by the North.
Robert: Religious persecution.
Ken: Well, let me think . . . it had something to do with slavery.
Tracy: The economic dependency of the South on slavery.

Role play an appropriate teacher response to each of these answers.

*14. Identify four different strategies for responding to an incorrect response and give a real-life example of each.

*15. What approximate percentage of correct answers should you work toward in a practice and feedback session? Identify how you would change your instructional approach if only 30 percent of your student responses were correct in a practice and feedback session.

*16. What is the primary purpose of independent practice? How should the exercises used for independent practice change as additional time for practice becomes available?

*17. Identify two recommendations for being more effective in monitoring student work while you circulate around the classroom during independent practice.

*18. Approximately what percentage of student responses during weekly and monthly review sessions should be correct, quick, and firm?

*19. Explain how a review cycle could be planned to rise and fall in one-month cycles.

20. What metacommunication techniques might you use in a culturally diverse classroom to promote engagement during instruction?

---

* Answers to asterisked questions (*) in this and the other chapters are in Appendix B.

Suggested Readings

Bennett, D. (1982). Should teachers be expected to learn and use direct instruction? *Association for Supervision and Curriculum Development Update, 24*(4), 5.

    A statement on some of the uses of direct instruction and when it is most likely to be effective.

Berliner, D. (1982). Should teachers be expected to learn and use direct instruction? *Association for Supervision and Curriculum Development Update, 24*(4), 5.

    A critical statement on when and where direct instruction is most applicable.

Brophy, J. (1982). Successful teaching strategies for the inner-city child. *Phi Delta Kappan, 63,* 527–530.

    A case for direct instruction employing research results confirming its positive effects on the achievement of inner-city students.

Gagné, R. M. (1992). *Principles of instructional design.* Orlando, FL: Harcourt, Brace Jovanovich.

    An excellent reference for preparing unit and lesson plans that include the direct instruction model.

Gagné, R. M. (1985). *Conditions of learning and theory of instruction: 4th edition.* New York: Holt.

This classic text sets out many of the learning principles from which the direct instruction model was derived.

Good, T., Grouws, D., & Ebmeier, H. (1983). *Active mathematics teaching.* New York: Longman.

An explanation of how best to apply direct instruction in mathematics.

Lindsley, O. R. (1992). Precision teaching: Discoveries and effects. *Journal of Applied Behavior Analysis, 24* (1), pp. 51–57.

The author describes a technique called "precision teaching," which contains many of the ingredients of the direct instruction model that have been found effective for teaching basic skills.

McKeachie, W. J. (1990). Learning, thinking, and Thorndike. *Educational Psychologist, 25,* 127–142.

Some of the most basic principles of learning and thinking are discussed from a direct instruction model.

Rosenshine, B. (1983). Teaching functions in instructional programs. *The Elementary School Journal, 83,* 335–351.

An oft-cited article that describes all of the functions of the direct instruction model as described in this chapter.

CHAPTER 7

Indirect Instruction Strategies

This chapter will help you answer the following questions:

1. What is the indirect instruction model?
2. What are constructivist strategies for teaching?
3. What are integrated bodies of knowledge?
4. How does direct instruction differ from indirect instruction?
5. What student outcomes are best taught with indirect instruction?
6. What teacher behaviors are required for indirect instruction?
7. What is an advance organizer?
8. How do I teach inductively and deductively?
9. How do I use examples and nonexamples to help learners discriminate and generalize?
10. How do I use questions to help students find their own meaning from what I teach?
11. How do I use student ideas and contributions to encourage students to think independently?
12. How do I get learners to evaluate their own performance?
13. How do I arrange group discussions that promote inquiry and problem solving?
14. What are some ways of promoting the goals of indirect instruction in a culturally diverse classroom?

This chapter will also help you learn the meaning of the following:

    constructivism
    criterial and noncriterial attributes
    generalization and discrimination
    group discussion
    hypothetico-deductive method
    indirect instruction model
    indirect teaching functions
    inductive and deductive reasoning
    integrated bodies of knowledge
    pair and team discussion
    social framing

What is the indirect instruction model?

Direct instruction =

Indirect instruction =
- result of discovery
- its problem
- ~~problem~~ process is inquiry

Chapter 6 introduced you to direct instruction for teaching facts, rules, and action sequences. Now we will consider strategies using the **indirect instruction model** for teaching concepts, patterns, and abstractions. These behaviors most often are associated with the words inquiry, problem solving, or discovery learning.

Inquiry, problem solving, and discovery learning each are different forms of the more general concept of indirect instruction. Indirect instruction is an approach to teaching and learning in which (1) the learning process is inquiry, (2) the result is discovery, and (3) the learning context is a problem.

These three ideas of inquiry, discovery, and problem solving are brought together in special ways in the indirect model of teaching and learning. This chapter presents instructional strategies you can use to compose your own indirect teaching approach. In subsequent chapters we expand on these concepts to present other indirect strategies, including self-directed and cooperative learning. Before we begin, let's look at two lessons, each designed to teach fractions differently.

It is the third six weeks of the fall semester and Tim Robbins is teaching a unit on fractions to his fourth-grade class.[1] During the first 12 weeks of the year, all fourth graders learned about numbers and number theory. They covered such topics as odd, even, positive, and negative numbers. The fourth graders are also familiar with such numerical concepts as multiples, factors, and the base 10 system for writing numbers.

On the day we observe Mr. Robbins, he is teaching a lesson about equivalent fractions as different ways of representing the same amount. During the four lessons prior to this one, his learners have studied about fractions as quantities and learned how fractions that look different (for example, ½, ¾) actually represent the same amount. The present lesson is intended to reinforce this idea.

Mr. Robbins begins the lesson with a quick review of the previous lesson. On the overhead projector he shows pictures of objects such as pies and loaves of bread divided to represent different fractions of the whole. In rapid-fire fashion his learners call out the fractions. He then projects a chart with undivided whole objects and

---

[1]Adapted from Borich, G., and Tombari, M. (1995), *Educational psychology: A contemporary approach.* New York: HarperCollins, pp. 182-184.

Figure 7.1
Mr. Robbins's chart for teaching fractions

$\frac{1}{4} \times \frac{25}{25}$	$\frac{25}{100}$	.25
$\frac{1}{2} \times \frac{}{50}$	$\frac{}{100}$	.
$\frac{1}{5} \times$	$\frac{}{100}$	.
$\frac{2}{5}$	$\frac{}{100}$	.
$\frac{3}{4}$	$\frac{}{100}$	.
$\frac{5}{4}$	$\frac{}{100}$	.
$\frac{3}{2}$	$\frac{}{100}$	.

has learners come up and divide them into halves, thirds, fourths, and so on while other learners do the same on worksheets. Each learner gets immediate feedback on his or her answers.

Next, he signals the class to clear their desks except for a pencil and draws their attention to a large, brightly colored chart hanging from the front blackboard. (The chart is shown in Figure 7.1.)

He passes out a similar dittoed chart to the students. Mr. Robbins explains that for each row the students are to complete the fraction with a denominator of 100 that equals the fraction in the row. Then, they are to fill in the third square with the decimal equivalent of that fraction.

Mr. Robbins first models how to do this. He demonstrates (pointing out that they have already learned this) how to make an equivalent fraction by multiplying the original fraction by a fraction that equals 1. He works several examples to be sure that his students have the concept and copy the examples onto their chart.

He then calls on several students to come to the front of the room and demonstrate several more examples for the class. Mr.

Robbins has the students state as they work, for the class to hear, how they are solving the problems. He checks that the rest of the class correctly fills in the chart at their desks.

Finally, he breaks the class into small groups and directs them to fill out the remainder of the chart. He provides each group with a key to immediately check their responses when finished. As the learners busily engage in their seatwork, Mr. Robbins moves from group to group, checking, giving feedback, correcting, or praising as needed.

Mr. Robbins has designed this lesson to show that fractions that look different can be equal in order to point out the relationship of decimals and fractions, and to use this as a foundation for teaching the relationships between dollars, decimals, and fractions in a subsequent lesson.

In the classroom next door to Mr. Robbins, Kay Greer also is teaching a unit on fractional equivalents. Let's look in on her lesson.[2]

As the lesson begins, Mrs. Greer asks Denisha to tell the class what she said yesterday about fractions. "A fraction like ½ isn't a number," she asserts, "because it isn't on the number line," Denisha points to the number line running along the top of the front blackboard. "See! There's no ½. Just 1, 2, 3, 4, . . . like that!"

"Well, class, let's think about what Denisha says. Let me give you a problem and we'll study it and, then, maybe come to some conclusion about if a fraction is a number." She turns on the overhead and projects the following for all to see:

> A boy has four loaves of bread that he bought at the local supermarket. He has eight friends and he wants each friend to get an equal part of the bread. How much bread should he give each of his friends?

Mrs. Greer draws the four loaves on the overhead and watches as the children, arranged in six groups of five children, copy the drawings into the notebook. She walks around the classroom occasionally prompting groups with the question, "How much bread is each one going to get?"

The children argue amongst themselves: "You can't do it!" "There isn't enough bread!" "How many slices are in each loaf?" After about 10 minutes Mrs. Greer asks, "Does anyone need more time to work on this? How many are ready to discuss?"

---

[2]Adapted from Ball, D. L. (1991). Teaching mathematics for understanding: What do teachers need to know about subject matter? In Kennedy, M. L. (Ed.), *Teaching academic subjects to diverse learners.* New York: Teachers College Press, pp. 67–69.

A few raise their hands. The rest are busy drawing and redrawing loaves of bread, sketching lines across them. Several minutes go by and Mrs. Greer says, "OK, would someone like to show their solution?"

Frank raises his hand, walks to the overhead and draws his solution. "I'm not sure it's right," he hedges. Frank draws four loaves of bread and divides each loaf into eight slices.

He looks up and announces to the class, "Each friend gets four slices!"

"That's wrong!" challenges Rosa. "Each friend gets two slices, see!" She walks to the overhead, draws four loaves of bread and divides each loaf into four slices. "Each friend gets two slices," she asserts, pointing to the equal portions.

"Why not just give each friend half a loaf?" asks Albert.

"Come up here and draw your solution," says Mrs. Greer. Albert walks up to the overhead and sketches his proposal to the class. "Can you write the number that each gets?" she asks. Albert writes the number "½" on the board.

"Well, Albert's and Rosa's slices are bigger than mine," protests Frank.

"Frank," asks Mrs. Greer, "why not write the number that shows how much of the bread your eight friends get? Albert's number is ½. How much is one slice as Albert sees it?" she asks the class.

"One-eighth," proposes Cal.

"Can you write that?" inquires Mrs. Greer. Cal comes up to the overhead and writes ⅛ next to Frank's drawing.

As children write different numbers for their solutions, Mrs. Greer asks, "Well, how can we have three different numbers for each of these solutions? We have one-half, two-fourths, four-eights," pointing to the different quantities and fractions on the overhead.

After several moments of silence several hands shoot up and one by one the children give explanations for the seeming discrepancy.

The lesson continues in this vein until five minutes before the bell. Mrs. Greer reviews what was concluded and sets the goal for the next lesson on fractions.

Now, let's compare the lessons of Mrs. Greer and Mr. Robbins. Both lessons had the same goal: to help learners understand the concepts of quantity and equivalence pertaining to fractions. But, they have designed two very different lessons to achieve this same end!

You may have noticed that the direct instruction approach has heavily influenced Mr. Robbins's lesson. He designed his lesson to elicit a minimum of mistakes. His activities elicit practice of correct responses followed by immediate feedback. For Mr. Robbins, learning involves correct responding, which is best accomplished by a teacher-directed or teacher-centered lesson.

Mrs. Greer, on the other hand, has a more indirect approach to learning. She is less focused on correct, rapid responses than on thought processes involving reflection, problem solving, analysis, and inquiry. Her lesson takes into consideration that her learners already have information and beliefs about fractions that may or may not be correct.

She wants to expose misconceptions and challenge learners to acquire new, more accurate perceptions through their own powers of reasoning. She carefully avoids providing answers. Her objective is to help learners understand fractions by influencing the cognitive processes by which they can elicit correct responses. Let's look at some of the cognitive processes around which she planned her lesson.

>>> THE COGNITIVE PROCESSES OF LEARNING <<<

Cognitive psychologists have identified three essential conditions for meaningful learning (Mayer, 1987): reception, availability, and activation. The *reception* and *availability* conditions are met when teachers focus their learners' attention on a problem and provide them with an anticipatory set or advance organizer. Teachers fulfill the *activation* condition by modeling the inquiry process and by skilled questioning techniques. As learners develop greater skill at inquiry and problem solving, the teacher gradually fades assistance and allows learners to assume more and more responsibility for their own learning.

What are constructivist strategies for teaching?

Supporting this approach to learning and instruction is a movement called **constructivism,** in which lessons are designed and sequenced to encourage learners to use their own experiences to actively construct meaning that makes sense to them, rather than acquiring understanding by having it presented in an already organized format.

Constructivists believe that knowledge results from the individual constructing "reality" from her or his own perspective. Learning occurs when the learner creates new rules and hypotheses to explain what is being observed. The need to create new rules and formulate hypotheses is stimulated by classroom dialogue, problem-solving exercises, and individual projects and assignments that create discrepancies—or an imbalance—between old knowledge and new observations. Direct experience (Piaget, 1977), project-based learning (Blumenfeld et al., 1991), and social interaction (Vygotsky, 1962) are used to restore the balance, while deemphasizing the role of lecturing and "telling." Recent subject matter advances in reading, writing, mathematics, and social studies have followed constructivist thinking and the indirect instructional strategies that support it.

Reading

For most of the twentieth century, reading curricula have taught the skills of decoding, blending, sequencing, finding main ideas, and so on outside the context of reading itself. These skills were usually practiced with contrived stories written in basal readers. Constructivist-influenced reading curricula now teach basic reading skills within a problem-focused context, such as through the reading of literature while engaged in a search for meaning. Learners often work in small groups, cooperatively reading to one another and asking and answering questions based on extended reading assignments. Skill- or fact-oriented worksheets are deemphasized.

Writing

Constructivist-oriented approaches to writing instruction provide a problem-solving context by focusing learners' attention on the importance of communication. They practice writing skills not in isolation but while working on writing activities that require learners to communicate ideas meaningfully. From their very earliest attempts at writing, learners realize that someone will read what they write. Thus, what they write must be understandable. Writing instruction, then, involves a process of developing initial drafts, revising, and polishing.

Mathematics

Authentic problems, such as the one presented in the dialogue with Mrs. Greer at the beginning of this chapter, are the focus of constructivist approaches to math instruction. In such approaches we see little time spent on the rote drill and practice of individual math skills. Rather, students are taught within a problem-solving or application context from the very beginning. The teacher attempts to have learners become actively involved in exploring, predicting, reasoning, and conjecturing.

Social Studies

Constructing meaning of own experience (handwritten margin note)

Constructivist approaches to social studies have the goal of helping learners acquire a rich network of understandings around a limited number of topics. Parker (1991) advocates that the K–12 social studies curriculum should focus on five essential learnings: the democratic process, cultural diversity, economic development, global perspectives, and participatory citizenship. The blending of these critical elements within a single curriculum requires a constructivist view of teaching and learning that promotes the following (Parker, 1991):

1. In-depth study—the sustained examination of a limited number of important topics
2. Higher-order challenge—the design of curriculum and instruction that requires students to gather and use information in nonroutine applications
3. Authentic assessment—pointing students' schoolwork toward standard-setting exhibitions of learning

These subject matter advances assume that students construct their own understanding of skills and knowledge rather than having it "told" or given to them by the teacher. Therefore, lesson plans are expected to have the following characteristics:

What are integrated bodies of knowledge?

1. Present instructional activities in the form of problems for students to solve.
2. Develop and refine students' answers to problems from the point of view of the student.
3. Acknowledge the social nature of learning by encouraging the interaction of teacher with students and students with one another.

As indicated, one goal of constructivist teaching is to present **integrated bodies of knowledge.** Integrated units and lessons stress the connections between ideas and the logical coherence of interrelated topics (Calfee, 1986; Rosenshine, 1986), as shown in Figure 7.2 for the social studies curriculum suggested by Parker (1991).

Figure 7.2
Five essential learnings spiral
upward through each grade to form
an integrated body of knowledge
(From Parker, W., 1991. *Renewing the
Social Studies Curriculum.* Alexandria, VA:
ASCD, p. 2.)

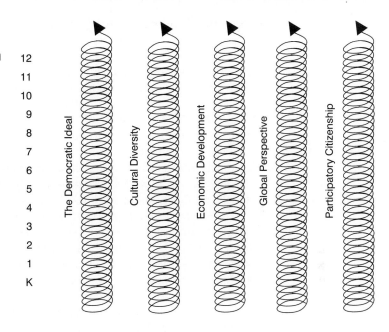

History - Geography - Civics

These interconnections between lessons and units were also apparent in the laterally planned units in Chapter 5. The role of the constructivist approach is to present authentic problems using the interaction and naturally occurring dialogue of the classroom to foster
integrated bodies of knowledge. Let's see how this is done using the
indirect model of instruction.

>>> COMPARING DIRECT AND <<<
INDIRECT INSTRUCTION

Recall from Chapter 6 the distinction between strategies for teaching
facts, rules, and action sequences and strategies for teaching concepts, patterns, and abstractions (Table 6.3 summarized this).
Because direct instruction strategies are best suited for the teaching
of facts, rules, and action sequences, it should be no surprise to
learn that indirect instruction strategies are best suited for teaching
concepts, patterns, and abstractions.
   When you present instructional stimuli to your learners in the
form of content, materials, objects, and events and ask them to go

*How does direct
instruction differ from
indirect instruction?*

beyond the information given to make conclusions and generalizations or find a pattern of relationships, you are using the indirect model of instruction. *Indirect* means that the learner acquires a behavior indirectly by transforming—or constructing—the stimulus material into a meaningful response or behavior that differs from both (1) the content used to present the learning and (2) any previous response given by the student. Because the learner can add to the content and rearrange it to be more meaningful, the elicited response or behavior can take many different forms. In contrast to direct instruction outcomes, there is rarely a single, best answer when using the indirect model of instruction. Instead, the learner is guided to an answer that goes beyond the problem or content presented.

Indirect instruction would be inefficient for teaching many facts, rules, or action sequences because the desired response is almost identical to the stimulus material and no new constructions or meanings are necessary. For example, rules for forming decimals and fractions are most efficiently taught by giving students the rules and practice applying them, as was illustrated in Mr. Robbins's lesson. In that example, knowledge acquisition and application were taught with a direct instruction strategy, because the stimulus material—Mr. Robbins' chart for teaching fractions—already contained the form of the correct answers, and the purpose of the lesson was to apply the rules, not to discover them or to invent new ones.

You might wonder why, if direct instruction is so effective in these instances, it is not used all the time. The answer is that not all desired outcomes call for responses that resemble the stimulus material. The direct instruction model requires from the learner very little construction of, or change in, the stimulus material. Direct instruction is limited to (1) learning units of the stimulus material so they can be remembered and (2) composing parts of the stimulus material into a whole, so a rapid and automatic response can occur. As noted in the previous chapter, these two cognitive processes are called *unitization* and *automaticity*.

Learning at the lower levels of the cognitive, affective, and psychomotor domains places heavy reliance on these two processes. Both can be placed efficiently into action by stimulus material that closely resembles the desired response (e.g., "Look at this word and then say it," "Watch me form a possessive and then you do the next one," "Read the instructions, then focus the microscope.") The desired response need not go much beyond what is provided. The task for the learner is simply to produce a response that mirrors the form and content of the stimulus. A great deal of instruction involves behavior that requires only unitization and automaticity. For this, the direct instruction model is most efficient and effective.

But not all learning is limited to the lower levels of behavioral complexity or requires only unitization and automaticity. In fact, if most lessons required only these two processes, students would not function successfully in subsequent grades or the world outside the classroom. This is because most jobs, responsibilities, and activities performed outside school require responses at higher levels of behavioral complexity and authenticity.

Real-world activities often involve analysis, synthesis, and decision-making behaviors in the cognitive domain, organization and characterization behaviors in the affective domain, and articulation and naturalization behaviors in the psychomotor domain. This complicates instruction, because these behaviors are not learned by memorizing the parts and reassembling them into a whole rapidly and automatically as are behaviors at lower levels of complexity. Instead, they must be constructed by the learner's own attempts to use personal experiences and past learnings to bring meaning to and make sense out of the stimulus material. While lower-level behaviors are required to attain more complex behaviors, much more is needed by both teacher and learners before higher-level behaviors can be learned. As you will see in this chapter, the teaching of higher-level behaviors requires a different set of instructional strategies.

>>> EXAMPLES OF CONCEPTS, <<<
PATTERNS, AND ABSTRACTIONS

Before describing the strategies that allow your learners to acquire higher-level behaviors, let's consider some examples of topics that require complex behavior to master:

Concept of a quadratic equation (algebra)

Process of acculturation (social studies)

Meaning of *contact sports* (physical education)

Workings of a democracy (government)

Playing of a concerto (music)

Demonstration of photosynthesis (biology)

Understanding of the law of conservation of energy (general science)

Learning these topics requires not just facts, rules, and action sequences, but much more: *concepts, processes, meanings,* and *understandings.* If you teach just the facts, rules, and action sequences

What student outcomes are best taught with indirect instruction?

about quadratic equations—"Here is the *definition*," "Here are the *rules* for solving them," or "Follow this *sequence* of steps"—your students may never learn the concept that binds together quadratic equations of different forms, or how to use these equations in a new or novel situation. Instead, your students must learn to add to, rearrange, and elaborate upon the stimulus material you present, using more complex cognitive processes. Let's consider how this is done.

Recall from Chapter 6 (Table 6.3) the distinction between Type 1 and Type 2 behaviors. Type 1 behaviors become Type 2 behaviors by using facts, rules, and sequences to form concepts. Notice what would be required, for example, if students tried to learn the concept of "frog" in the same way they acquired facts, rules, and action sequences about a frog.

First, they would have to commit to memory all possible instances of frogs (of which there may be hundreds). Trying to retain hundreds of frog images *in the same form they were presented* would quickly overburden their memories. Second, even after committing many types of frogs to memory, learners could confuse frogs with similar animals. This is because the memorization process does not include the characteristics that exclude other animals from being frogs (e.g., a hard shell, dry skin, color changes, tail).

The process of generalization and discrimination, if planned for in the presentation of your lesson, can help students overcome both of these problems. **Generalization** helps them respond in a similar manner to stimuli that differ, thereby increasing the range of instances to which particular facts, rules, and sequences apply (e.g., to all types of frogs). In addition, **discrimination** selectively restricts this range by eliminating things that appear to match the student's concept (e.g., a chameleon) but that differ from it in critical dimensions (e.g., has a tail).

Generalization and discrimination help students classify visually different stimuli into the same category, based on *criterial attributes*. Criterial attributes (discussed later in this chapter) act as magnets, drawing together all instances of the same type without requiring the learner to memorize (or even see) all possible instances. As a concept (frog) becomes combined with other concepts to form larger patterns (amphibians), patterns of increasing complexity are produced. Figure 7.3 shows a hierarchy of concepts, patterns, and abstractions typically found in a science curriculum.

It is apparent that both your role as teacher and your organization of stimulus material need to be different for the learning of concepts, patterns, and abstractions. For outcomes at higher levels of behavioral complexity, the stimulus material cannot contain all possible instances of the concept being learned. However, it must pro-

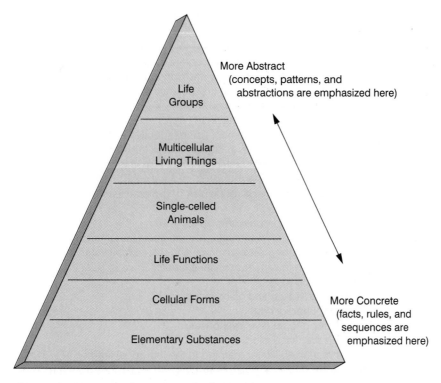

Figure 7.3
A hierarchy of abstraction representing possible units of instruction in a science curriculum

vide the appropriate associations or generalizations necessary to distinguish the most important dimensions—the criterial attributes—of the concept being learned. In this sense, there is less similarity between the stimulus material and the learner's written or oral response in the teaching of concepts, patterns, and abstractions than there is in the teaching of facts, rules, and action sequences.

The indirect instruction model uses instructional strategies that encourage the cognitive processes required to form concepts and to combine concepts into larger patterns and abstractions. Table 7.1 shows some of the **indirect teaching functions** performed by a teacher using this model.

You can see from Table 7.1 that indirect instruction is more complex than direct instruction in both teacher and student behavior. Classroom activities are less teacher centered. This brings student ideas and experiences into the lesson and lets students begin evaluating their own responses. Because the behaviors are more

What teacher behaviors are required for indirect instruction?

Table 7.1
Some indirect instruction functions

1. Provides a means of organizing content in advance
   Provides advance organizers and conceptual frameworks, which serve as "pegs" on which to hang key points that guide and channel thinking to the most productive areas
   Allows for concept expansion to higher levels of abstraction
2. Provides conceptual movement using inductive and deductive methods
   Focuses generalization to higher levels of abstraction by
   Inductive methods (selected events used to establish concepts or patterns)
   Deductive methods (principles or generalizations applied to specific instances)
3. Uses examples and nonexamples to
   Define critical attributes and promote accurate generalizations
   Gradually expand set of examples to reflect real world
   Enrich concept with noncritical attributes
4. Uses questions to
   Guide the search and discovery process
   Raise contradictions
   Probe for deeper level responses
   Extend the discussion
   Pass responsibility for learning to the individual learner
5. Encourages students to use examples and references from their own experience, to seek clarification, and to draw parallels and associations that aid understanding and retention
   Relates ideas to past learning and to students' own sphere of interests, concerns, and problems
6. Allows students to evaluate the appropriateness of their own responses and then provides guidance as necessary
   Provides cues, questions, or hints as needed to call attention to inappropriate responses
7. Uses discussion to encourage critical thinking and help students to
   Examine alternatives, judge solutions, make predictions, and discover generalizations
   Orient, provide new content, review and summarize, alter flow of information, and combine areas to promote the most productive discussion

complex, so too are your teaching strategies. To build toward outcomes that may require either advance organization or inductive and/or deductive reasoning, extended forms of reasoning and questioning are required. A variety of examples and group discussions are used to accomplish this.

The indirect instruction functions in Table 7.1 and the teaching behaviors that comprise them are among the teaching functions having the highest correlation with positive student attitudes (Fielding, Kameenui, & Gerstein, 1983). These also are the teaching functions thought to be most useful in providing behaviors that students will use in their adult lives (Mitchell, 1992; Palincsar & Brown, 1989).

>>> AN EXAMPLE OF INDIRECT INSTRUCTION <<<

Now let's examine a dialogue of indirect instruction and compare it to the dialogue of direct instruction in Chapter 6. The objective this time is Type 2 outcomes, not Type 1 outcomes. This dialogue reflects some facts, rules, and sequences that were taught previously, but the ultimate goal is the formation of concepts, patterns, and abstractions. This is a glimpse into a government class where a lesson on different economic systems is in progress. The teacher gets the students' attention by asking if anyone knows what system of government in the world is undergoing the most change. Marty raises his hand.

Teacher: Marty.

Marty: I think it's communism, because they've torn down the Berlin wall.

Teacher: That's right. And because this change will probably affect all our lives in the years ahead, it may be a good idea to know what communism is and why those who live under it want to change it. To get us started, let me ask if anyone knows where the phrase "government of the people, by the people, for the people" comes from. (Rena raises her hand.) Rena?

Rena: From Lincoln's Gettysburg Address . . . I think near the end.

Teacher: That's right. Most nations have similar statements that express the basic principles on which their laws, customs, and economics are based. Today, we will study three systems by which nations can guide, control, and operate their economies. The three systems we will study are *capitalism, socialism,* and *communism.* They often are confused with the political systems that tend to be associated with them. A political system not only influences the economic system of a country but also guides individual behavior in many other areas, such as what is taught in schools, what the relationship is between church and state, how people get chosen for or elected to political office, what jobs people can have, and what newspapers can print.

For example, in the United States we have an economic system that is based on the principles of capitalism—or private ownership of capital—but a political system that is based on the principle of democracy—or rule by the people. These two sets of principles are not the same, and in the next few days you will see how they sometimes work in harmony and sometimes create contradictions that require changes in an economic system, like those occurring today in Eastern Europe.

Today we will cover only systems dealing with the ownership of goods and services in different countries—that is, just the economic systems. Later I will ask you to distinguish these from political systems. Who would like to start by telling us what the word *capitalism* means?

Robert: It means making money.

Teacher: What else, Robert?

Robert: Owning land . . . I think.

Teacher: Not only land, but . . .

Robert: Owning anything.

Teacher: The word *capital* means tangible goods or possessions. Is a house tangible?

Betty: Yes.

Teacher: Is a friendship tangible?

Betty: Yes.

Teacher: What about that, Mark?

Mark: I don't think so.

Teacher: Why?

Mark: You can't touch it.

Teacher: Right. You can touch a person who is a friend but not the friendship. Besides, you can't own or possess a person. . . . So, what would be a good definition of *tangible goods*?

Betty: Something you own and can touch or see.

Teacher: Not bad. Let me list some things on the board and you tell me whether they could be called capital. (Writes the list)

>car
>stocks and bonds
>religion
>information
>clothes
>vacation

OK. Who would like to say which of these are *capital?* (Ricky raises his hand.)

Ricky: Car and clothes are the only two I see.

Barbara: I'd add stocks and bonds. They say you own a piece of something, although maybe not the whole thing.

Teacher: Could you see or touch it?

Barbara: Yes, if you went to see the place or thing you owned a part of.

Teacher: Good. What about a vacation? Did that give anyone trouble?

Mickey: Well, you can own it . . . I mean you pay for it, and you can see yourself having a good time. (The class laughs.)

Teacher: That may be true, so let's add one last condition to our definition of capital. You must be able to own it, see or touch it, and it must be *durable*—or last for a reasonable period of time. So now, how would you define *capitalism?*

Sue: An economic system that allows you to have capital—or to own tangible goods that last for a reasonable period of time. And, I suppose, sell the goods, if you wanted.

Teacher: Very good. Many different countries across the world have this form of economic system. Just to see if you've got the idea, who can name three countries, besides our own, that allow the ownership of tangible goods?

Joe: Japan, Germany, and Canada.

Teacher: Good. In all these countries capital, in the form of tangible goods, can be owned by individuals.

Now that we know a little about capitalism, let's look at another system by which a nation can manage its economy. Ralph, what does the word *socialism* mean to you?

Ralph: Well, it probably comes from the word *social.*

Teacher: And what does the word *social* mean?

Ralph: People coming together, like at a party—or maybe a meeting.

Teacher: And why do people usually come together at a party or a meeting?

Ralph: To have fun. (laughter)

Teacher: And what about at a meeting?

Ralph: To conduct some business or make some decisions, maybe.

Teacher: Yes, they come together for some common purpose and benefits. For example, they make decisions about the things they need to live and prosper. Does that sound like a basis for a kind of economic system? (no response from class) Suppose that a large number of individuals came together to decide what they needed to live and prosper? What types of things do you think they would consider?

Billy: You mean like a car or a home of your own?

Teacher: Yes, but let's say that the need for a car or a home of your own among individuals of the group is so very different that this group could never agree on the importance of these for everyone. What types of things could a group of people, say the size of a nation, agree on that would be absolutely essential for everyone's existence?

Ronnie: Food.

Teacher: Good. What else?

Billy: A hospital.

Teacher: Very good.

Sue: Highways.

Teacher: OK. Any others?

Ricky: If they couldn't agree on the importance of cars for everyone, then they would have to agree on some other form of transportation, like buses, trains, or planes.

Teacher: Yes, they would, wouldn't they? These examples show one of the purposes of a *socialist* economic system—that is, to control and make available to everyone as many things as possible that (a) everyone values equally and (b) everyone needs for everyday existence.

Sue: You mean free, without paying?

Teacher: Yes, or paying very little. In that way both rich and poor can use these services about equally.

Sue: But who pays?

Teacher: Good question. Who pays for the services provided under a socialist system?

Mark: The government.

Teacher: And who is the government?

Mark: Oh, I get it. The people pay taxes, just like us, and the government uses the taxes to provide the essential services.

Sue: So, how is that different from America?

Teacher: Good question. Who can answer that one?

Robert: It's the same.

Mark: No, it's not. Our government doesn't own hospitals, farms, trains, and that kind of stuff.

Teacher: Who owns Amtrak?

Robert: I think our government does.

Teacher: It also, believe it or not, owns some hospitals; and at least some local governments, like ours, own their own bus lines. (The class looks bewildered.) So, if you looked at our country's economic system and compared it to that of a socialist country, you might not see such a big difference. But there *is* a difference. What might that difference be?

Ralph, you began this discussion.

Ralph: I think it's a matter of degree. Almost all of the major things like hospitals and transportation systems that everyone needs are owned and run by the government under a socialist system, but only a few of these things are owned by the government in a capitalist system. On the other hand, there are things like highways, rivers, forests, and so on that are owned by the government under both systems.

Teacher: And how would the amount of taxes you pay differ in these two systems?

Ralph: You'd pay more taxes under a socialist economy than under a capitalist economy, but some services would be free—or almost—in a socialist system. In a capitalist country like ours, we'd pay more for these services but we'd also have more money to spend for them after taxes.

Teacher: That was a nice way of putting it. Now, what about our third economic system? What's a word similar to communism?

Billy: Oh . . . *community?*

Teacher: Yes. And who has ownership under communism?

Robert: The community.

Teacher: . . . which is represented by?

Robert: The government.

Teacher: Yes. Just a moment ago we discovered that much of the difference between capitalism and socialism, as economic systems, was a matter of degree. If this were also true of the difference between

	socialism and communism, how might you describe ownership under the communist economic system?
Sue:	More is owned by the community—I mean by the government.
Teacher:	Ronnie, you mentioned food before. Do you think food—or the farms on which the food is grown—is owned by the government under communism?
Ronnie:	I guess so. But, aren't they becoming more like us?
Teacher:	Yes, and that must mean . . . (nodding to Ronnie)
Ronnie:	. . . that it's harder or less efficient to grow food under the communist system.
Teacher:	So, you've given us one of the contradictions that may be making some countries that have a communist economic system to become more like us. Now, let's take some other examples. Billy, you mentioned hospitals; Sue, you mentioned highways; and Ricky, you mentioned planes. Who owns these in a communist economic system?
Class:	The government.
Teacher:	OK. Now let's create a chart that shows some examples of things likely to be owned by the governments under all three of our economic systems, so that we can see them side by side and compare them. (Teacher writes chart on board)

Capitalism	*Socialism*	*Communism*
highways	highways	highways
rivers	rivers	rivers
forests	forests	forests
	hospitals	hospitals
	planes	planes
	buses	buses
	trains	trains
		food supply
		housing
		industries

	Now, what kinds of things *don't* we find up here?
Richard:	Personal things, like clothes, watches, and television sets.
Teacher:	Good. Ownership of these items cannot be used to distinguish economic systems. What can distinguish economic systems, however, is the *degree* to which the goods and services that affect large numbers of individuals are owned by the government: The most is owned by the government under communism, and the least is owned by the government under capitalism. As we have seen in the past few years the balance of goods and services owned by governments under communism is changing—with the responsibility for greater numbers of goods and services being turned over to individuals just like in our own economic system. Now, how do you think the amount of taxes paid by individuals living under these three systems would differ?

Class: Communism would have the highest, then socialism, then capitalism.

Teacher: Good. And this is another point we will follow up. Tomorrow we will discuss other causes for some of the changes that have occurred in communism. Then we'll compare each of these three economic systems with the political systems that represent them. For tomorrow, look up in the encyclopedia the words *democracy* and *totalitarianism* and bring with you a one-page description of the major differences between these two political systems. Be prepared to know the differences between economic and political systems. Then, choose two countries that you think represent these different political systems, and we will discuss and study them further.

The previous dialogue illustrates one variation of the indirect model of instruction. Notice that this lesson used the naturally occurring dialogue of the classroom to encourage learners to bring their own experiences and past learnings to the topic, rather than to acquire an understanding by having it presented to them in an already organized form. This lesson required learners to build an understanding of the topic collectively under the guidance of the teacher using one another's predictions, hypotheses, and experiences. Table 7.1 summarized some of the teaching functions used in indirect instruction. Remembering these functions, let's consider the extent to which this example lesson contains key aspects of indirect instruction.

>>> ADVANCE ORGANIZERS <<<

What is an advance organizer?

Comparing the dialogues for direct and indirect instruction, what differences do you notice? Obviously they differ in length and complexity. This is not by chance, because teaching more complex behaviors takes more time and planning. The extensive planning needed for higher-order learning is one of the most overlooked aspects of indirect instruction. With more expansive and complex content, the lesson must be introduced with a framework or structure that organizes the content into meaningful parts *even before the content is presented.* This is the first element of planning for indirect instruction—organizing the content in advance (Table 7.1).

One way of providing this framework is to use advance organizers (Luiten, Ames, & Aerson, 1980; Ausubel, 1968). An advance organizer gives learners a *conceptual preview* of what is to come and helps prepare them to store, label, and package the content for retention and later use. In a sense, an advance organizer is a treelike structure with main limbs that act as pegs, or place holders, for the branches that are yet to come. Without these limbs on which to hang content, important distinctions can easily become blurred or lost.

For example, the lesson dialogue began with an introduction about coverage of the day's lesson. To set the stage, the teacher introduced two abstractions (economic systems and political systems), each comprised of a complex network of concepts (taxes, ownership, goods, services, etc.). At the beginning of the lesson, he alerted students to the reason for drawing such an early distinction between a political and an economic system ("*capitalism, socialism, and communism* . . . often are confused with the political systems"; "Today we will cover only . . . *economic* systems. Later I will ask you to distinguish these from political systems.")

Note that the overall ideas for which students are responsible on homework assignments and in the following day's lesson require them to distinguish between these systems. The important role of advance organization was to channel or focus student thinking for today's lesson onto the economic system branch of the overall organizer, while putting in place another branch on which additional content (political systems) will soon be placed. Figure 7.4 represents a graphic representation of an advance organizer which this teacher might have used to open the lesson.

Advance organizers, especially at the higher levels of behavioral complexity, are rarely single words or phrases that enlighten students when merely uttered. Instead, they are concepts woven into the lesson fabric to provide an overview of the day's work *and all topics to which it will subsequently relate.* Advance organizers can be presented orally or as charts and diagrams, as seen in Figure 7.4. Following are example advance organizing activities provided at the beginning of a lesson:

- Showing a chart that illustrates the skeletal evolution of humans prior to explaining the skeletal relationships among forms of animal life (biology).
- Drawing examples of right, equilateral, and isosceles triangles before introducing the concept of a right triangle (plane geometry).
- Discussing origins of the Civil War before describing its major battles (American history).
- Describing what is meant by a *figure of speech* before introducing the concepts of *metaphor* and *simile* (English).
- Listening to examples of both vowels and consonants before teaching the vowel sounds (reading).
- Showing and explaining the origins of the periodic table of elements before introducing any of the individual elements (chemistry).

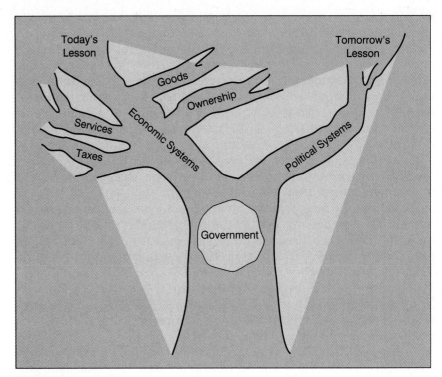

Figure 7.4
An advance organizer for a unit on government.

Notice that each of these examples presents a general concept into which fits the specific concept that is the subject of the day's lesson. This is not accomplished by reviewing earlier content, which often is confused with the idea of an advance organizer. Instead it is done by creating a conceptual structure—skeletal evolution, various triangular shapes, Civil War origins, figures of speech, the alphabet, an organized system of chemical elements—into which you can place not only the content to be taught but also the content for related lessons.

Therefore, these advance organizers set the groundwork for focusing the lesson topic. They prevent every lesson from being seen as something entirely new. Finally, they integrate related concepts into larger and larger patterns and abstractions that later become more authentic unit outcomes (evolution of man, triangular shapes, determinants of civil war, figures of speech). An advance organizer identifies the highest level of behavior resulting from a lesson sequence and to which the outcome of the present day's lesson will contribute. In the example, this higher-level outcome was to distinguish between economic and political systems, a distinction organized in advance by the teacher's introductory remarks.

Chapter 6 offered several suggestions for structuring content in ways particularly suited to direct instruction. You may recall that these were the part–whole, sequential, combinatorial, and comparative methods. This chapter adds several methods that are particularly suited for structuring content for indirect instruction. These methods are problem-centered, decision-making, and network approaches to organizing lesson content—and to composing advance organizers.

Problem Centered

A problem-centered approach identifies and provides students in advance with all the steps required to solve a particular problem. This approach begins by observing a specific event and concludes with how or why it occurred. For example, you might begin a general science lesson by demonstrating that liquid cannot be removed through a straw from a tightly sealed bottle. The question, "Why does this happen?" establishes the problem. You then might give your students a problem-solving sequence like the one shown in Figure 7.5a. Such a chart and its sequence of events become the advance organizer for the lesson. Each of its steps provides an organizational branch for a particular part of the lesson.

Decision Making

This same problem can also be organized hierarchically by showing the internal branching, or steps, that you must follow to arrive at a conclusion. While the problem-centered approach establishes the steps to be followed, the decision-making approach focuses on *alternative paths* that might be followed—or decisions that must be made—in exploring and discovering new information about a topic.

Figure 7.5b shows how this can be applied to the science question posed in the preceding paragraph. Although the students don't know at what level of the hierarchy the experiment will end, they could be shown the entire list of possible alternatives. This form of advance organizer is a particularly effective attention getter when you are asking students to contribute branches to the hierarchy and allowing them to trace the results of their inquiry as each decision point is reached (as indicated by the solid lines).

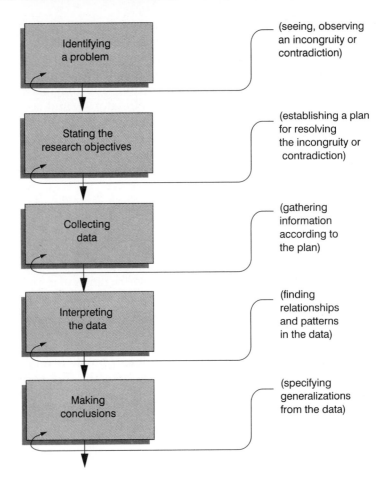

Figure 7.5a
Structuring a lesson using a problem-centered approach

Networking

Networking is a third type of organization often helpful for organizing and communicating the structure of a lesson in advance. Networking illustrates relationships among the data, materials, objects, and events that students must consider to solve a problem. When different aspects of a problem are to be considered in relation to each other, as in Figure 7.5c, a picture of the network of relationships becomes the advance organizer. The triangular network in Figure 7.5c is particularly important to the goals of the example sci-

Why doesn't the liquid flow through the straw?

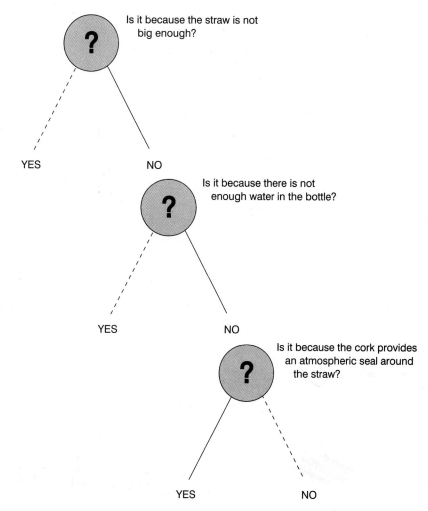

Figure 7.5b
Structuring a lesson using a decision-making approach

ence lesson, because it is the *relationship among several events* that may provide the best solution to this problem.

Each of these structuring methods—problem centered, decision making, networking—is a useful advance organizer when you communicate it to students in advance and when you tie key steps, decisions, or relationships back to the advance organizer as they occur

Figure 7.5c
Structuring a lesson using a network approach

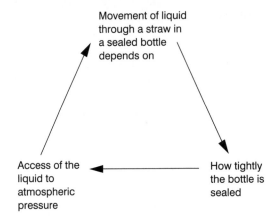

in the lesson. To the extent these structuring devices can provide the branches on which subsequent content can be placed, they serve a useful purpose as advance organizers. As we will see in Chapter 9, they also can become mental strategies by which students can learn similar subsequent content, independently of the teacher.

>>> CONCEPTUAL MOVEMENT— <<< INDUCTIVE AND DEDUCTIVE

This is the second element of planning for indirect instruction (Table 7.1). The words *inductive* and *deductive* refer to the way in which ideas flow. The following sections compare these methods.

Inductive Reasoning

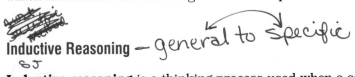

Inductive reasoning is a thinking process used when a set of data is presented and students are asked to draw a conclusion, make a generalization, or develop a pattern of relationships from the data. It is a process in which students observe specific facts and then generalize them to other circumstances. Common sense tells us that much of our everyday thinking proceeds in this manner. For example:

1. We notice that rain-slick roads are causing accidents on the way to school, so we reduce speed at all subsequent intersections.

2. We get an unsatisfactory grade on a chemistry exam, so we study six extra hours a week for the rest of the semester in all our subjects.

3. We see a close friend suffer from the effects of drug abuse, so we volunteer to disseminate information about substance abuse to all our acquaintances.

4. We get a math teacher who is cold and unfriendly, so we decide never to enroll in a math course again.

What these instances have in common is that they started with a specific observation of a limited set of data and ended with a generalization in a much broader context. Between the beginning and end of each sequence was an interpretation of observed events and the projection of this interpretation to all similar circumstances. Simply put, when we think inductively we believe that what happens in one place (e.g., at this intersection), can happen wherever or whenever circumstances are similar (at all other rain-slick intersections).

Deductive Reasoning — ~~specific to general~~ — ~~most closely to~~
G→S

Deductive reasoning, on the other hand, proceeds from principles or generalizations to their application in specific instances. Deductive thinking includes testing generalizations to see if they hold in specific cases. Typically, a laboratory experiment in the sciences (chemistry, physics, biology, psychology, mathematics, geology) follows the deductive method. In these fields the experimenter often begins with a theory or hypothesis about what should happen and then tests it with an experiment to see if it accurately predicts. If it does, the generalization with which the experiment began is true, at least under the conditions of the experiment. The following steps are frequently used in deductive thinking:

1. Stating a theory or generalization to be tested.
2. Forming a hypothesis in the form of a prediction.
3. Observing or collecting data to test the hypothesis.
4. Analyzing and interpreting the data to determine if the prediction is true, at least some of the time.
5. Concluding whether the generalization held true in the specific context in which it was tested.

Deductive methods are familiar in everyday life. For example, consider the four examples of inductive thinking listed previously to see how much change is required for them to become examples of deductive thinking. Here are the examples again—this time illustrating deduction:

1. We believe that rain-slick roads are the prime contributor to traffic accidents at intersections. We make observations one rainy morning on the way to school and find that, indeed, more accidents have occurred at intersections than usual— our prediction that wet roads cause accidents at intersections is confirmed.
2. We believe that studying six extra hours a week will *not* substantially raise our grades. We study six extra hours and find that our grades have gone up—our prediction that extra studying will not influence our grades is *not* confirmed.
3. We believe that drug abuse can be detrimental to one's physical and emotional well being. We observe and find physical and emotional effects of drug abuse in everyone that has admitted to using them—our prediction that drug abuse and physical and emotional impairment are related has been confirmed.
4. We believe that we could never like a subject if it is taught by a cold and unfriendly teacher, regardless of how good we are in it. We think back and remember that we had just such a teacher in high school, who taught math. We observe that we have always done everything possible to avoid a math course— our prediction that we could never like a subject taught by a cold and unfriendly teacher has been shown to be accurate.

These examples have in common the fact that they begin with a general statement of belief—a theory or hypothesis—and end with some conclusion based on an observation that tested the truth of the initial statement. Of course, we could be wrong, even though in some instances the prediction *appeared* to be true (e.g., you might have no problem liking sports despite the fact that you once had a cold and unfriendly gym teacher). As you might expect, deductive logic has been most closely associated with the scientific method. In the social, behavioral, and physical sciences, it is known as the **hypothetico-deductive method** (Kaplan, 1964) to emphasize the close connection between forming hypotheses and making predictions deduced from general beliefs and theories.

Applying Induction and Deduction

How do I teach inductively and deductively?

Both induction and deduction are important methods for teaching concepts, patterns, and abstractions. One application for such

Many forms of investigation and laboratory experiments follow the deductive method in which the student begins with a prediction about what should happen in a specific instance and then conducts an investigation to see if the prediction comes true.

teaching is to move into progressively deeper levels of subject complexity, using inductive and deductive methods and occasionally changing from one to the other:

> Greater levels of complexity are achieved using the *inductive* process when specific examples or events introduced earlier are later linked to other examples or events to create concepts and generalizations.

> Greater levels of complexity are achieved using the *deductive* process when generalizations and patterns introduced earlier in the lesson are later applied to specific instances, testing the adequacy of the generalizations.

In the earlier example of the government lesson about economic systems, consider how these two processes were employed. Using induction, the teacher built a definition of *tangible goods* beginning with a specific example: "Is a house tangible?" Notice how the examples increased not only in number, but also in abstraction (e.g., stocks and bonds). Also, he provided both examples and nonexamples to round out the definition of tangible goods in a capitalist system and to fine tune the concept. In other words, tangible goods could exist at different levels of abstraction, but some abstractions (e.g., friendships, vacation) could not qualify as tangible goods. This teacher skillfully used the inductive process, beginning with specific examples (making money and owning land) and increasingly broadening the examples to form a generalization (tangible goods that last for a reasonable length of time).

Also notice that a brief venture into deduction ended the teacher's introduction to capitalism. By asking students to name three countries that fit the concept of capitalism, he made them find specific instances that fit the general concept. He asked whether the general notion of ownership of tangible goods could be applied to the real world, and it could, of course, thereby testing the credibility of the more general statement.

Note that, although the concept of capitalism was understood by most students at the end of the first part of the lesson as "an economic system that allows the ownership of tangible goods that last," it was a rather crude interpretation that would fail many subsequent tests. For example, citizens of most socialist and communist countries own tangible goods that last a reasonable period of time (e.g., a wrist watch, a tie, a set of dinnerware). Recall that this crude version of the concept of capitalism emerged even after providing carefully planned examples and nonexamples. This means that the teacher's job was far from over at the end of the first part of the lesson. Further *conceptual movement* must be made to fine tune this concept, producing more accurate discriminations to be applied to the concept of capitalism.

This is precisely what occurs in subsequent portions of the lesson, in which the teacher can be seen moving students from the ownership of tangible goods as their working definition of an economic system to a definition that had the following five different elements:

1. The *degree* to which
2. goods and services
3. that all value
4. and see as essential for daily living
5. are owned by a government.

The teacher, using questions and examples, redefined the initial concept until it expanded to include a greater number of attributes, thereby making it more accurate. The teaching of concepts, patterns, and abstractions with the indirect instructional model is patterned around the inductive and deductive movement of concepts wherein you process initially crude and overly restrictive concepts into more expansive and accurate abstractions. Table 7.2 illustrates the different steps involved in inductive versus deductive teaching.

Table 7.2

A comparison of steps in inductive versus deductive teaching

Scientific Method

Teaching Inductively →	Teaching Deductively
1. Teacher presents specific data from which a generalization is to be drawn.	1. Teacher introduces the generalization to be learned.
2. Each student is allowed uninterrupted time to observe or study the data that illustrates the generalization.	2. Teacher reviews the task-relevant prior facts, rules, and action sequences needed to form the generalization.
3. Students are shown additional examples and then nonexamples containing the generalization.	3. Students raise a question, pose an hypothesis, or make a prediction thought to be contained in the generalization.
4. Student attention is guided first to the critical (relevant) aspects of the data containing the generalization and then to its noncritical (irrelevant) aspects.	4. Data, events, materials, or objects are gathered and observed to test the prediction.
5. A generalization is made that can distinguish the examples from nonexamples.	5. Results of the test are analyzed and a conclusion is made as to whether the prediction is supported by the data, events, materials, or objects that were observed.
	6. The starting generalization is refined or revised in accordance with the observations.

From Walter C. Parker, *Renewing the Social Studies Curriculum,* 1991, Alexandria, VA: Association for Supervision and Curriculum Development. Copyright © by ASCD. Used with permission.

>>> USING EXAMPLES AND NONEXAMPLES <<<

Both inductive and deductive methods help in concept teaching. Recalling our previous examples, one generalization was made after seeing several accidents: "accidents tend to occur at intersections on rainy days." Is there a concept, pattern, or abstraction here? Are there also facts, rules, and sequences?

There is no question that facts had to be known to form this generalization—facts about cars, streets, rain, and intersections. Rules also had to be present, such as "don't accelerate quickly on wet pavement," "slow down at intersections," and "a red light means stop." And, of course, sequences of actions had to be understood, such as "watch for intersections–look for signs–slow down–brake gently."

However, the intended generalization cannot be derived from these facts, rules, and sequences alone. Why? Because they are not sufficiently separated from specific examples to be applied appropriately in all circumstances. For example, you may learn the rule "stop at red lights" to perfection, but until you have seen examples of when to modify the rule (e.g., when an emergency vehicle with flashing lights is behind you), you do not have the complete concept of a red light—only the rule.

To learn concepts, your learners will need to go beyond the acquisition of facts, rules and sequences to be able to distinguish examples from nonexamples. Observing examples and nonexamples—when six extra hours of study pays off and when it does not, when disseminating drug abuse literature is likely to help and when it is not, when a cold and unfriendly teacher is likely to adversely affect your performance in a subject and when not—allows you to grasp *concepts*. *Examples* represent the concept being taught by including all of the attributes essential for recognizing it as a member of some larger class. *Nonexamples* fail to represent the concept being taught by purposely not including one or more of the attributes essential for recognizing it as a member of some larger class. Therefore, the third element for the teaching of concepts, patterns, and abstractions is the use of both examples and nonexamples that define the **criterial and noncriterial attributes** of a concept that are needed for producing accurate generalizations (Table 7.1).

As another example, consider the concept that private ownership of goods and services under socialism is more limited than under capitalism. How did this teacher develop this concept, moving from a definition of capitalism to a discussion of socialism? Recall that initially the concept was poorly understood by Billy, who concluded that "a car" and "a home of your own" were the types of capital that could become the basis for a socialist economic system. His response was reasonable, because both could be defined as tangible goods according to the discussion on capitalism.

However, this teacher would be in trouble and the outcome of the lesson would be in jeopardy if further concept expansion did not occur. The abstraction of an economic system at this point in the lesson was limited to one in which nearly all tangible goods could be privately owned. The teacher's job was to expand this initial version of the abstraction to include economic systems in which both goods and services are owned and to show that ownership extends to the government as well as to individuals.

Also, the teacher somehow had to make clear that ownership in the context of different economic systems is always a matter of degree. That is, the system determines not only *what* is owned by a government but *how much*, and therefore is unavailable for private ownership. Accordingly, the teacher arranged the next set of interchanges to bring out these specific points. Recall this exchange:

––·––·––·––·––·––·––·––·––·––·––·––·––·––

Teacher: . . . What types of things could a group of people, say the size of a nation, agree on that would be absolutely essential for everyone's existence?

Ronnie: Food.

Teacher: Good. What else?

Billy: A hospital.

Teacher: Very good.

Sue: Highways.

Teacher: OK. Any others?

Ricky: If they couldn't agree on the importance of cars for everyone, then they would have to agree on some other form of transportation, like buses, trains, or planes.

Teacher: Yes, they would, wouldn't they? These examples show one of the purposes of a socialist economic system—that is, to control and make available to everyone as many things as possible that (a) everyone values equally, and (b) everyone needs for everyday existence.

The teacher redirected the discussion by having students think about things that "a group of people, say the size of a nation, could agree on that would be absolutely essential for everyone's existence"—thereby encouraging them to broaden their earlier definitions. The question generated examples for discriminating between capitalism and socialism; some were useful (ownership of hospitals) and some were not (ownership of highways). Because some hospitals are owned by capitalist governments, these examples could be confusing; but Ralph makes the clarifying statement:

Ralph: I think it's a matter of degree. Almost all of the major things like hospitals and transportation systems that everyone needs are owned and run by the government under a socialist system, but only a few of these things are owned by the government in a capitalist system. On the other hand, there are things like highways, rivers, forests, and so on that are owned by the government under both systems.

The nonexample of *highways* clarifies the concept that neither socialism nor capitalism are mutually exclusive, all-or-none propositions. Some tangible things (highways and forests) are owned by both capitalist and socialist governments. Notice how this effective teacher used examples and nonexamples to expand the learners' concept of an economic system and to provide clear discrimination between capitalism and socialism.

How do I use examples and nonexamples to help learners discriminate and generalize?

These are not easy distinctions from a student's point of view. The teacher helped the students understand the concepts by using specific strategies:

1. Providing more than a single example.
2. Using examples that vary in ways that are important to the concept being defined (e.g., house is tangible, stocks and bonds are abstract, but both are instances of "tangible goods").
3. Including nonexamples of the concept that nonetheless possess important dimensions of the concept (e.g., a vacation can be bought or "owned" but is not an example of a "tangible good").
4. Explaining why nonexamples are nonexamples, even though they may share some of the same characteristics as examples (e.g., a vacation is not durable).

>>> THE USE OF QUESTIONS TO GUIDE <<< SEARCH AND DISCOVERY

Guiding the search-and-discovery process with questions is the fourth indirect instruction function (Table 7.1).

How do I use questions to help students find their own meaning from what I teach?

One difference you may have noticed between the direct and indirect instruction dialogues is *the way* in which the teachers asked questions. In the direct dialogue, the questions were specific and to the point, aimed at eliciting a single right answer. But in the indirect dialogue, questions steered the students to seek and discover the answer with minimum assistance from the teacher. In direct instruction, answering questions is how students show what they know (exhibit their level of understanding) so that you may provide clues, hints, and probes. In indirect instruction, your questions guide students into discovering new dimensions of a problem or ways of resolving a dilemma. This important distinction between questioning strategies will be demonstrated repeatedly in the following chapters.

For now, notice that the indirect instruction dialogue included several questions that guided the search-and-discovery process. For example, several major twists and turns in the dialogue begin and end with questions for which there are no single right answers:

"Who would like to start by telling us what the word *capitalism* means?"

"What does the word *socialism* mean to you?"

"What's a word similar to *communism?*"

These questions did not ask for specific definitions of capitalism, socialism, or communism; few students would know these accurately at the start of the lesson. Rather, they were asked in such a way that students could search for and find an answer that would be at least partially correct. By inserting a phrase such as " . . . means to you" or " . . . similar to," this teacher encouraged a response from almost every student who has ever heard these words and, thus, began students on the road to constructing their own meanings for these concepts.

Therefore, the purpose of this teacher's questions was not to quiz or even to teach, but to focus students' attention and to promote the widest possible discussion of the topic from the students' point of view. In this manner the class begins with everyone being able to participate, regardless of their task-relevant prior knowledge. By accepting almost any answer at the beginning, this teacher can use student responses to formulate subsequent questions and begin the process of shaping more accurate responses.

The point of using questioning strategies in indirect instruction, then, is not to arrive at the correct answer in the quickest and most efficient manner. The point is to stimulate a process that not only forms successively more correct answers, but also forms those answers using a personal search-and-discovery process chosen by the learner and guided by the teacher. For example, the teacher followed up Robert's response that capitalism means "making money" with the phrase, " . . . what else?", and followed Robert's next response ("owning land") with a leading response (" . . . not only land but . . "), encouraging Robert to broaden his answer.

By beginning with a broad question such as, "What does the word *capitalism* mean to you?", this teacher could have been confronted just as easily with the task of narrowing, not broadening, Robert's first response. In the next interchange this problem actually occurs, because Robert replies that capitalism means "owning anything." Now the job is to narrow or limit his response, which is accomplished by presenting the first criterial attribute of the concept of capitalism, tangible goods.

You can see that a single guided question in the context of indirect instruction is seldom useful in itself. Questions must dovetail into other questions that continually refocus the response (e.g., broaden, then narrow, then broaden slightly again) and keep the search going. The process is much like focusing a camera, because rarely is the camera initially set at the right focus for the subject. Similarly, we could not expect Robert's first response to perfectly represent the concept of capitalism. Just as one begins focusing the camera in the appropriate direction, often passing the point at which the subject is in focus, so also the teacher's followup probe led Robert to overshoot the mark and respond with too broad a response (e.g., owning anything). The teacher acknowledged the error and slightly narrowed Robert's response by noting that "The word *capitalism* means tangible goods or possessions."

Questions also can be used in the search-and-discovery process to do the following:

Present contradictions to be resolved—

"Who owns Amtrak?"

"But there is a difference. What might that difference be?"

Probe for deeper, more thorough responses—

"What does the word *social* mean?"

"Why do people usually come together at a party or a meeting?"

Extend the discussion to new areas—

"What things could a group of people, say the size of a nation, agree are absolutely essential for everyone's existence?"

"What types of things don't we find written here on the board?"

Pass responsibility back to the class—

"Good question. Who knows the answer to who pays for services provided under a socialist system?"

"Good question. Who can answer that one?"

Questions like these guide students to increasingly better responses through a search-and-discovery process. This process is one of the most useful for forming concepts and abstractions and for recognizing patterns. The back-and-forth focusing of student responses often is required to attain the appropriate level of generalization.

 **>>> USE OF STUDENT IDEAS <<<**

The Changing View

Until recently the use of student ideas was considered the center-piece of indirect instruction. Using student ideas meant incorporating student experiences, points of view, feelings, and problems into the lesson by making the student the primary point of reference. A completely student-oriented lesson might be initiated by asking students what problems they were having with the content; these problems would become the focus of the lesson. This approach was intended to heighten student interest, to organize subject content around student problems, to tailor feedback to individual students, and to encourage positive attitudes and feelings toward the subject. However, when a lesson attempts to accomplish only these objectives, it risks failing to achieve the most important objective of all: teaching students to reason, solve problems, and to think critically.

This is not to say that heightening student interest, focusing on student problems, providing individual feedback, and increasing positive attitudes are not important goals for the effective teacher. But these goals can and should be achieved *in the context of classroom dialogue that encourages students to think independently and assume responsibility for their own learning.*

This is where early attempts to use student ideas often went astray. The goals of incorporating student ideas, problems, feelings, and attitudes into the lesson in an open discussion format often became the end itself, rather than the means by which learning could be accomplished. Unfortunately, many forms of problem solving, inquiry, and discovery learning were thought to be synonymous with open, freewheeling discussions that began and ended with student-determined ideas and content. Also, some advocates believed such goals and approaches could be executed solely as processes, not requiring any of the formal structure or content of the traditional classroom. At least some of the curriculum reforms suggested by the national committees and reports reviewed in Chapter 3 were a response to just such misguided notions.

Where does this book stand on the matter? The position of this text, like that of recent research, is that while heightening student interest, selecting content based on student problems, providing individual feedback, and increasing affect are desirable goals, they can be achieved only in a carefully crafted teacher–student dialogue that promotes higher-order thinking. As we have seen earlier in the problem-centered, decision-making, and network approaches and in our example dialogue, even highly abstract content should be structured. Therefore, even in the indirect instruction model, which is designed to contribute to student-centered goals, these goals are only the means for achieving the essential outcomes of concepts, patterns, and abstractions. Thus, using student ideas is our fifth indirect instruction function (Table 7.1).

Productively Using Student-Centered Ideas

Used to guide their own thinking

So, how can student-centered ideas be used productively in the context of indirect instruction? In this context, you can use student ideas in the following ways:

- Encourage students to use *examples* and *references* from their own experience, from which they can construct their own meanings from text.
- Share mental strategies by which the students can learn more easily and efficiently.

How do I use student ideas and contributions to encourage students to think independently?

- Ask students to seek clarification of and to draw *parallels* to and *associations* from things they already know.
- Encourage understanding and retention of ideas by relating them to the students' own sphere of *interests, concerns,* and *problems.*

For examples of these uses of student ideas, recall again the dialogue about economic systems. By asking students to name three other countries that follow a capitalistic economic system, or to name the things a nation could agree on that are absolutely essential for everyone's existence, the teacher elicited examples and references from the learners' experience.

Perhaps more important than the questions themselves was the way in which the teacher incorporated student responses into the lesson. In one instance, the response even partially directed lesson content. This followed a general question, "What things could a group of people . . . agree on that would be absolutely essential for everyone's existence?" Almost any equally general response could be used, as when students contributed the concepts of food, hospitals, and highways, all of which were within the overall framework of the lesson established by the teacher. This allowed students to contribute almost any response without letting the choice itself alter the lesson agenda.

Also, by asking what the word *capitalism* "means to you," this teacher was asking students to express themselves by using parallels and associations they already understood—perhaps by having a job, or by recalling a conversation about occupations, or by remembering television images of life in Eastern Europe. Parallels and associations such as these are likely to be vastly different among students. This is desirable, both for heightening student interest and involvement and for exposing the students to a variety of responses, many of which may be appropriate instances of the concept to be learned.

A third way to incorporate student ideas into your lesson is to allow students to respond using their own interests, concerns, and problems. An instance of this occurred when the teacher asked students to name two countries having different political systems. Presumably these countries would be referred to in the future, perhaps in individual reports or research papers, perhaps in library reading or in a class discussion; in all of these cases, the individuality of each student's choice could be examined. Student interests—and especially individual choices affecting future assignments—can be important motivators for ensuring active student involvement in subsequent assignments that may be lengthy and time consuming.

Finally, notice that even within the context of these examples the instruction remained *content centered.* It allowed students to participate in determining the *form* in which learning occurred, but not the *substance* of what was learned. This substance usually is determined by the curriculum guide and textbook. Our example dialogue, therefore, contrasts with what is called *student-centered learning,* which allows both the form and substance to be selected by the student. This is sometimes associated with *unguided discovery learning,* wherein the goal is to maintain high levels of student interest, accomplished largely by selecting content based on student problems or interests and by providing individually tailored feedback.

Sometimes unguided discovery learning is desired in the context of independently conducted experiments, projects, portfolios, research papers, and demonstrations, where the topic may be selected by the student. However, even when unguided discovery learning is desired, the content still must fit within the confines of the curriculum. Therefore, whether your approach is the guided use of student ideas (as in this example) or unguided (as in research assignments), some preorganization and guidance always will be necessary prior to your soliciting and using student ideas. In the next two chapters, we will have more to say about using student ideas within the naturally occurring dialogue of the classroom.

>>> STUDENT SELF-EVALUATION <<<

The sixth ingredient of indirect instruction (Table 7.1) is to engage students in evaluating their own responses and thereby take responsibility for their own learning. Because there are many right answers when teaching concepts, patterns, and abstractions, it is virtually impossible for you to judge them all. In direct instruction, nearly all instances of the learned facts, rules, or action sequences likely to be encountered can be learned during guided and independent practice. But, because specifying all possible instances of a concept is neither possible nor efficient, you must use indirect instruction to have students look critically at their own responses.

How do I get learners to evaluate their own performance?

You can encourage self-evaluation by gradually giving control of the evaluation function to students and by letting them provide reasons for their answers so that you and other students can suggest needed changes. Recall that early in the dialogue, the teacher let the students know that some of the responsibility for determining appropriate answers would fall on them. After writing a list on the board, he said, "OK. Who would like to say which of these are *capi-*

tal?" The message is received when Ricky responds and Barbara modifies Ricky's response:

— · — · — · — · — · — · — · — · — · — · — · — · —

    Ricky: Car and clothes are the only two I see.
  Barbara: I'd add stocks and bonds. They say you own a piece of something, although maybe not the whole thing.

— · — · — · — · — · — · — · — · — · — · — · — · —

Even after Barbara's efforts to correct Ricky's response, the teacher still does not supply an answer, but instead keeps the evaluation of the previous responses going by responding with, "Could you see or touch it?"

The goal here was to create a student dialogue focused on the appropriateness of previous answers. The success of this self-evaluation strategy is most readily seen in the sequence of dialogue that occurs between students and teacher. This strategy promotes a student-to-student-back-to-teacher interchange, as opposed to the more familiar teacher-to-student-back-to-teacher interchange. The teacher's role is to maintain the momentum by offering hints or focusing statements that students can use to evaluate their previous responses.

An example of a student-to-student-to-teacher interchange took place when Sue, hearing that people in socialist countries pay taxes, asks, "So how is that different from America?"

— · — · — · — · — · — · — · — · — · — · — · — · —

  Teacher: Good question. Who can answer that one?
   Robert: It's the same.
    Mark: No, it's not. Our government doesn't own hospitals, farms, trains, and that kind of stuff.
  Teacher: Who owns Amtrak?

— · — · — · — · — · — · — · — · — · — · — · — · —

The answer obviously needs some evaluation, so the teacher simply keeps the ball rolling with, "Good question. Who can answer that one?" Robert responds with an incomplete answer and Mark quickly informs the class not only that the answer is wrong, but also why he thinks it is wrong. At that point the teacher retakes control and raises another question, suggesting that even Mark's response is not completely accurate.

In the process of these student-to-student-to-teacher exchanges, students learn the reasons for their answers in slow, measured steps. By allowing partially correct answers to become the bases for more accurate ones, this teacher is showing the class how to modify incorrect and partially correct answers into better ones. Especially for the learning of concepts, patterns, and abstractions that involve more than a single criterial attribute, these layers of refinement, gradually built up by student interchange, help the students develop a level of generalization.

Of course, there is no reason why such interchanges must be limited in size. Three, four, or even five successive exchanges among students before control returns to the teacher can work fine in circumstances that need less guidance and structuring. Classes of students who are more able or who have considerable knowledge of the content can sustain protracted exchanges without going so far astray that you need to restructure.

>>> USE OF GROUP DISCUSSION <<<

When student-to-student-to-teacher exchanges grow into long interactions among large numbers of students, a **group discussion** has begun. In these discussions, you may intervene only occasionally to review and summarize main points, or you may schedule periodic interaction to evaluate the group's progress and to redirect if necessary.

Group discussions can be useful for encouraging critical thinking, for engaging average and less able learners in the learning process, and for promoting the "reasoning together" that is necessary in a democratic society (Krabbe & Polivka, 1990; Dillon, 1988a). Because group discussion helps students think critically—examine alternatives, judge solutions, make predictions, and discover generalizations—it is yet another approach to teaching concepts, patterns, and abstractions. It is the seventh and last indirect instruction function in Table 7.1.

When your objective is to teach well-established concepts, patterns, or abstractions that already are structured in the text or workbook, a lecture-recitation may be more efficient and effective than a discussion. This might be the case with topics requiring little personal opinion and judgment, in which agreement about the topic may be so high as to preclude the controversy needed to promote discussion.

But sometimes you may prefer a group discussion to a lecture-recitation. When concepts, patterns, and abstractions have a less formal structure and are treated minimally in the text or workbook, then the lack of consensus can make a discussion rewarding. Examples of such topics are: Would photosynthesis be useful in space? How much aggression do you think it takes to start a war? In what ways can the legislative branch of government be influenced by the executive branch? Topics that are not formally structured by the text and for which a high degree of consensus does not yet exist make good candidates for discussion sessions for building, expanding, and refining concepts, patterns, and abstractions.

During the discussion, you are the moderator. Your tasks include the following:

How do I arrange group discussions that promote inquiry and problem solving?

1. Orienting the students to the objective of the discussion:
   "Today we will discuss when a nation should decide to go to war. Specifically, we will discuss the meaning of the concept of aggression as it has occurred in history. In the context of wars between nations, your job at the end of the discussion will be to arrive at a generalization that could help a president decide if sufficient aggression has occurred to warrant going to war."

2. Providing new or more accurate information where needed:
   "It is not correct to assume that World War II started with the bombing of Pearl Harbor. Many events occurred earlier on the European continent that some nations considered to be aggression."

3. Reviewing, summarizing, or putting together opinions and facts into a meaningful relationship:
   "Bobby, Mary, and Billy, you seem to be arguing that the forcible entry of one nation into the territory of another nation constitutes aggression, while the rest of the class seems to be saying that undermining the economy of another nation also can constitute aggression."

4. Adjusting the flow of information and ideas to be most productive to the goals of the lesson:
   "Mark, you seem to have extended our definition of aggression to include criticizing the government of another nation through political means, such as shortwave media broadcasts, speeches at the U.N., and so forth. But that fits better the idea of a cold war, and we are trying to study some of the instances of aggression that might have started World War II."

5. Combining ideas and promoting compromise to arrive at an appropriate consensus:
   "We seem to have two definitions of aggression—one dealing with the forcible entry of one nation into the territory of another, and another that has to do with undermining a nation's economy. Could we combine these two ideas by saying that anything that threatens either a nation's people or its prosperity, or both, could be considered aggression?"

Small-group discussions often require the teacher to become a moderator, visiting each group periodically to answer questions, review and summarize, redirect group work, provide new or more accurate information, and achieve consensus.

Group discussion can take several different forms. *Large-group discussions* in which all members of the class participate are the most familiar. Large groups can be difficult to handle, because discipline and management problems occur easily when numerous learners are interacting in student exchanges that you interrupt only occasionally. The moderating functions just listed allow you to control and redirect the discussion as necessary without overly restricting the flow of ideas. During a large group discussion, you should frequently perform one or more of these moderating functions. The frequency will vary with the topic and students, but the greater the consensus, the fewer the students, and the higher their ability to grasp the concepts and abstractions to be learned, *the more you can relinquish authority to the group* (Oser, 1986).

Small-group discussions of five to ten students also are useful for teaching concepts, patterns, and abstractions. When multiple topics must be discussed within the same lesson and time does not permit full class discussion of the topics in sequential order, try using two, three, or four small groups simultaneously. You have three tasks here: to form groups whose members can work together, to distribute students with diverse learning needs across groups, and to move along the groups as moderator. Stopping the groups periodically, either to inform the entire class of important insights discovered by a group or to apply moderating functions across groups, will help keep the groups close together and maintain your control and authority.

Another group format for indirect instruction is to have students work in pairs or teams. This can be effective when the discussion entails writing (e.g., a summary report), looking up information (in the text, encyclopedia, etc.), or preparing materials (chart, diagram, graph, etc.) (Slavin, 1990b; Johnson & Johnson, 1987). In the **pair** or **team discussion** arrangement, your role as moderator increases in proportion to the number of pairs or teams, so only brief interchanges with each may be possible.

The pair or team approach works best when the task is highly structured, when some consensus about the topic already exists, and when the orienting instructions fully define each member's role (e.g., student A searches for the information, student B writes a summary description of what is found, and both students read the summary for final agreement). Pairs or teams frequently become highly task oriented, so pairing or teaming tends to be most productive when discussion objectives go beyond just an oral report and include a product to be delivered to the class.

Table 7.3 presents the lesson plan for this indirect instruction lesson, following the written format provided in Chapter 5.

>>> COMPARISON OF DIRECT <<< AND INDIRECT INSTRUCTION

The direct and indirect instruction models were presented in separate chapters because each includes distinctive teaching strategies. As you have seen, the models have two different purposes:

The direct model is best suited to the teaching of facts, rules, and action sequences, and provides six teaching functions for doing so—daily review and checking, presenting and structuring new content, guided student practice, feedback and correctives, independent practice, and weekly and monthly reviews.

The indirect model is best suited for the teaching of concepts, patterns, and abstractions, and provides seven teaching functions for doing so—advance organization of content, inductive and deductive conceptual movement, use of examples and nonexamples, use of questions to guide search and discovery, use of student ideas, student self-evaluation, and group discussion.

Table 7.3
Lesson plan: Indirect instruction

Unit Plan: Economic Systems Lesson Plan: Comparisons and contrasts among capitalist, socialist, and communist economies	
1. Gaining attention	Ask if anyone knows where the phrase "government of the people, by the people, for the people" comes from, to establish the idea that the principles and rules by which a country is governed also influence its economic system.
2. Informing the learner of the objective	This session: To relate economic systems to the ownership of goods and services in different countries Next session: To be able to distinguish economic systems from political systems and to show why the communist economic system is changing.
3. Stimulating recall of prerequisite learning	Ask for a definition of capitalism and then refine with questioning and probing of the definition given. Continue probing until a definition is arrived at that defines capitalism as "an economic system that allows the ownership of tangible goods that last for a reasonable period of time." Check understanding by asking for three countries (other than ours) that have capitalist economies.
4. Presenting the stimulus material	A. Ask what the word *socialism* means. Refine definition by questioning and probing until a definition is arrived at that defines socialism as "an economic system that allows the government to control and make available to everyone as many things as possible that (a) everyone values equally, and (b) are seen as essential for everyday existence." Have students compare capitalism and socialism by degree of ownership of public services and degree of taxes paid under each system. B. Ask what the word *communism* means and establish its relationship to the idea of *community*. Refine definition, using the concept of degree of ownership by questioning and probing until still more examples of things owned and controlled by the government under communism are arrived at by the students.

Neither model should be used to the exclusion of the other. And, many times the two models can be effectively interwoven in a single lesson, as when a small number of facts, rules, or action sequences must be acquired prior to introducing a concept, pattern, or abstraction.

Table 7.3, *continued*

Unit Plan: Economic Systems
Lesson Plan: Comparisons and contrasts among capitalist, socialist, and communist economies

5. Eliciting the desired behavior	A. Use questions to encourage the identification of public services most commonly owned under socialism, for example, hospitals, trains, and communication systems. Some types of farms and industries will also be accepted when their relation to the public good is understood.
	B. Use questions to encourage the identification of those public services most commonly owned under communism, for example, food supply, housing, and industries. Emphasis will be placed on those services and goods that are different from those identified under socialism.
	C. Use questions to identify the amount and types of things owned by the government across the three systems, to establish the concept that differences among the systems are a matter of degree of ownership and degree of taxation.
6. Providing feedback	Questions will be posed in a manner that encourages the student to evaluate his or her own response and those of other students. Probes will be given until student responses approximate an acceptable answer. Placed side by side on the board will be those goods and services the students have identified as likely to be owned by the government in all three systems and those likely to be owned uniquely by any one or combination of systems. A distinction may be made between these and the personal items that may have been mentioned, such as clothes or household goods, but which cannot be used to distinguish economic systems.
7. Evaluating the behavior	After completion of a research paper describing three countries of the students' own choosing each of which represents a different economic system, students will be graded on their comprehension of the concepts of (a) degree of ownership, and (b) degree of taxation as discussed by L. Rutherford, (1995) *Economics in a Modern World*, Columbus, OH: Intex.

Let us now place the direct and indirect models of instruction side by side for comparison. Table 7.4 presents teaching events you can employ using both models.

Under direct instruction, the objective is rapid attainment of facts, rules, and action sequences. Content is divided into small,

Table 7.4

Some example events under the direct and indirect models of instruction

Direct Instruction	Indirect Instruction
Objective: To teach facts, rules, and action sequences	Objective: To teach concepts, patterns, and abstractions
Teacher begins the lesson with a review of the previous day's work.	Teacher begins the lesson with advance organizers that provide an overall picture and that allow for concept expansion.
Teacher presents new content in small steps with explanations and examples.	Teacher focuses student responses using induction and/or deduction to refine and focus generalizations.
Teacher provides an opportunity for guided practice on a small number of sample problems. Prompts and models when necessary to attain 60–80% accuracy.	Teacher presents examples and nonexamples of the generalization identifying critical and noncritical attributes.
Teacher provides feedback and corrections according to whether the answer was correct, quick, and firm; correct, but hesitant; careless; or incorrect.	Teacher draws additional examples from students' own experiences, interests, and problems.
Teacher provides an opportunity for independent practice with seatwork. Strives for automatic responses that are 95% correct or higher.	Teacher uses questions to guide discovery and articulation of the generalization.
Teacher provides weekly and monthly (cumulative) reviews and reteaches unlearned content.	Teacher involves students in evaluating their own responses.
	Teacher promotes and moderates discussion to firm up and extend generalizations when necessary.

easily learned steps through a lecture format involving brief explanations, examples, practice, and feedback. Both guided and independent practice, under tight control of the teacher, help ensure that students are actively engaged in the learning process at high rates of success. Everything that is not learned is revealed in weekly and monthly reviews and retaught as needed.

Under indirect instruction, the objective is to engage students in inquiry to eventually develop concepts in the form of patterns or abstractions. Here the teacher prepares for the complexity of the lesson by providing an overall framework into which the day's lesson is placed, allowing room for expansion of concepts. Initially crude and inaccurate responses are gradually refined through inductive and deductive movement, focusing the generalization to the desired degree. To do this, both examples and nonexamples (some drawn from the students' interests and experiences) are used to separate criterial from noncriterial attributes. Throughout, the teacher uses questions that guide students to discover the generalization and to evaluate their own responses. When the concepts are relatively unstructured and have moderate-to-low degrees of consensus, discussion groups may replace a more teacher-controlled format; in this case, the teacher becomes a moderator.

>>> PROMOTING THE GOALS OF INDIRECT <<< INSTRUCTION IN THE CULTURALLY DIVERSE CLASSROOM

What are some ways of promoting the goals of indirect instruction in a culturally diverse classroom?

One of the most recent developments in the area of cultural diversity and indirect instruction involves the concept of social framing. **Social framing** refers to the context in which a message, such as a lesson, is received and understood. Tannen (1986) defines a frame as a taken-for-granted context that delimits the sources from which meaning can be derived. When a teacher announces, "Today's lesson will expect you to know the differences between *capitalism, socialism,* and *communism,*" the teacher has implicitly set a frame for the lesson that conveys to learners what they are expected to learn. Recent research has examined how best to frame a lesson so that learners can derive understanding from the content presented, or how to alter the frame of a lesson so that it will be more understandable to cultural or ethnic groups that may be accustomed to an alternate frame. For example, Michaels and Collins (1984) report an example of an Anglo teacher who framed a story with linear, topic-centered patterns (for example, "Today I will read you a series of events that happened in the lives of three characters"), while her African-American students framed the task according to topic-associating patterns (for example, "She's going to tell us the kinds of things that can happen to people"). While one group primarily looked for a sequential list of events that unfolded from the beginning to end of the story, the other group made notes about the events and the memories they evoked. Thus, frames that are ambiguous or less appropriate to one group than another can alter how and what content is learned.

Bowers and Flinders (1991) make a case for understanding the context in which different cultures expect information to be transmitted that is particularly relevant during indirect instruction. They recommend that the teacher (1) present content from the frame most dominant to the classroom, (2) make explicit what the frame—

context—is through which learners must see the content (for example, as facts to be learned, skills to be performed, or concepts to think about), and/or (3) negotiate, when necessary, the frame with students at the start of the lesson.

Bowers and Flinders (1991) suggest three ways of establishing a frame at the start of a lesson that encourage students to respond in like manner. These approaches involve self-disclosure, humor, and dialogue:

- *Self-disclosure* involves being open about your feelings and emotions that lead up to the lesson. "I've been struggling to make this topic meaningful and here's what I've come up with." This will encourage similar statements of self-disclosure from students which can be used to frame the lesson.
- *Humor* at the start of a lesson establishes a flexible, spontaneous, expressive mood from which frames can become established. "Here's a funny thing that happened to me about what we're going to study today" will encourage students to share other personal episodes that can be used to provide a context for the lesson.
- *Dialogue* involves the back-and-forth discussion of lesson content involving random and simultaneous responding. Here every student can expect to be heard and lesson content is expressed idiosyncratically in the words of the learners. The responses of students, then, are used to further structure and elaborate lesson content.

Each of these framing techniques is believed to enhance student engagement during indirect instruction across cultural and ethnic groups, some of whom can be expected to be less responsive to the traditional frames of prepackaged lesson plans and textbooks.

>>> A FINAL WORD <<<

This chapter and the preceding one presented a variety of teaching strategies. When used with the appropriate content and purpose, these strategies can significantly improve your teaching effectiveness. Although both the direct and indirect models of instruction are significant contributions to teaching and learning, neither should exclusively dominate your instructional style. It would be unfortunate if you exemplified only the direct model or the indirect model, because the original purpose of introducing these models was to *increase the variety* of instructional strategies at your disposal.

These models and their strategies provide a variety of instructional tools that you can mix in many combinations to match your particular objectives and students. Just as different entrées have prominent and equal places on a menu, so too do the direct and indirect models have prominent and equal places in your classroom.

The underlying point of these two chapters, then, is that you should alternately employ the direct and indirect models to create tantalizing combinations of "educational flavors" for your students. Your own objectives are the best guide to what combination from the menu you will serve on any given day. In the chapters ahead we will extend this basic menu to provide still greater variety in the teaching methods at your command.

Summing Up

This chapter introduced you to indirect instruction strategies. Its main points were as follows:

1. Indirect instruction is an approach to teaching and learning in which the process of learning is *inquiry,* the result is *discovery,* and the learning context is a *problem.*

2. In indirect instruction, the learner acquires information by transforming stimulus material into a response that is different (1) from the stimulus used to present the learning and (2) from any previous response emitted by the student.

3. During indirect instruction, concepts, patterns, and abstractions are acquired through the processes of generalization and discrimination, which require the learner to rearrange and elaborate on the stimulus material.

4. The generalization process helps the learner respond in a similar manner to different stimuli, thereby increasing the range of instances to which particular facts, rules, and sequences apply.

5. The process of discrimination selectively restricts the acceptable range of instances by eliminating things that may look like the concept but that differ from it on critical dimensions.

6. The processes of generalization and discrimination together help students classify different-appearing stimuli into the same categories on the basis of criterial attributes. Criterial attributes act as magnets, drawing together all instances of a concept without the learner having to see or memorize all instances of it.

7. The indirect instruction model provides instructional strategies that encourage the processes of generalization and discrimination for the purpose of forming concepts, patterns, and abstractions.

8. The following are the instructional functions of the indirect model:

- Use of advance organizers
- Conceptual movement—inductive and deductive
- Use of examples and nonexamples
- Use of questions to guide search and discovery
- Use of student ideas
- Student self-evaluation
- Use of group discussion

9. An advance organizer gives learners a conceptual preview of what is to come and helps them store, label, and package content for retention and later use.

10. Three approaches to composing advance organizers are the problem-centered approach, the decision-making (hierarchical) approach, and the networking approach.

11. Induction starts with a specific observation of a limited set of data and ends with a generalization about a much broader context.

12. Deduction proceeds from principles or generalizations to their application in specific contexts. The testing of a generalization to see if it holds in specific instances is sometimes referred to as the *hypothetico-deductive* method.

13. Providing examples and nonexamples helps define the criterial and noncriterial attributes needed for making accurate generalizations.

14. Using examples and nonexamples correctly includes the following steps:

- Providing more than a single example
- Using examples that vary in ways that are irrelevant to the concept being defined
- Using nonexamples that also include relevant dimensions of the concept
- Explaining why nonexamples have some of the same characteristics as examples

15. In indirect instruction, the role of questions is to guide students into discovering new dimensions of a problem or new ways of resolving a dilemma.

16. Some uses of questions during indirect instruction include the following:

- Refocusing
- Presenting contradictions to be resolved
- Probing for deeper, more thorough responses
- Extending the discussion to new areas
- Passing responsibility to the class

17. Student ideas can be used to heighten student interest, to organize subject content around student problems, to tailor feedback to fit individual students, and to encourage positive attitudes toward the subject. Because these goals should not become ends unto themselves, you must plan and structure the use of student ideas to promote reasoning, problem solving, and critical thinking.

18. Student-centered learning, sometimes called unguided discovery learning, allows the student to select both the form and substance of the learning experience. This is appropriate in the context of independently conducted experiments, research projects, science fair projects, and demonstrations. However, pre-organization and guidance always are necessary to ensure that the use of student ideas fits within the prescribed curriculum.

19. Self-evaluation of student responses occurs during indirect instruction when students are given the opportunity to reason their answers so that you and other students can suggest needed changes. Self-evaluation is most easily conducted in the context of student-to-student-to-teacher exchanges, wherein you encourage students to comment on and consider the accuracy of their own and each others' responses.

20. A group discussion involves student exchanges with successive interactions among large numbers of students. During these exchanges, you may intervene only occasionally to review and summarize, or you may schedule periodic interaction to evaluate each group's progress and to redirect when necessary.

21. The best topics for discussion include those that are not formally structured by texts and workbooks and for which a high degree of consensus among your students does not yet exist.

22. Your monitoring functions during discussion include the following:

- Orienting students to the objective of the discussion
- Providing new or more accurate information that may be needed
- Reviewing, summarizing, and relating opinions and facts
- Redirecting the flow of information and ideas back to the objective of the discussion.

23. The greater the group consensus, the fewer the students in the group, and the higher their ability to grasp concepts and abstractions, then the more you can relinquish authority to the group.

24. Direct and indirect instruction generally are used together and you should not adopt one model to the exclusion of the other. Each contains a set of functions that can compose an efficient and effective method for the teaching of facts, rules, and sequences or concepts, patterns, and abstractions.

For Discussion and Practice

*1. What three learning concepts are brought together in the indirect model of instruction?

*2. What types of behavioral outcomes are the direct and indirect instructional models most effective in achieving?

*3. Where does the word *indirect* come from in the *indirect instruction model*?

*4. Why can direct instruction not be used all the time?

*5. Explain in your own words what is meant by the words *unitization* and *automaticity*. Give an example of a learning task in which only these two processes are required.

*6. Explain in your own words the meanings of *generalization* and *discrimination*. Given an example of a learning task in which both these processes are required.

*7. Identify which of the following learning tasks involve only facts, rules, or action sequences (Type 1) and which, in addition, involve concepts, patterns, and abstractions (Type 2).

(1) Naming the presidents
(2) Selecting the best speech
(3) Shifting the gearshift in a car
(4) Writing an essay
(5) Describing the main theme in George Orwell's *1984*
(6) Hitting a tennis ball
(7) Winning a tennis match
(8) Inventing a new soft drink
(9) Reciting the vowel sounds
(10) Becoming an effective teacher

*8. Describe two problems that would result if a concept or abstraction had to be learned using only the cognitive processes of unitization and automaticity by which facts, rules, and sequences are acquired.

9. Prepare a two-minute introduction to a lesson of your own choosing that provides your students with an advance organizer.

10. Provide one example each of an advance organizer using the problem-centered, decision-making, and networking approaches.

*11. In your own words, define *inductive* and *deductive* reasoning. Give an example of each, using content from your preferred teaching area.

*12. Identify the five steps to deductive reasoning commonly applied in the laboratory.

13. For each of the following, show with specific examples how the concept might be taught both inductively and deductively. Pay particular attention to whether your instruction should begin or end with a generalization.

Democracy

Freedom

Education

Effective teaching

Parenting

*14. For the concept of *effective teaching*, give five criterial attributes and five noncriterial attributes.

*15. Identify four ways in which examples and nonexamples should be used in the teaching of concepts.

*16. Distinguish the different purposes for asking questions in the direct and indirect models of instruction.

*17. Besides refocusing, what other types of questions can be used in the search-and-discovery process? Choose a lesson topic and provide an example of each of these.

*18. What type of learning might be represented by discussions that begin and end with student-determined ideas and content? How is this different from the use of student ideas in the context of the indirect instruction model?

*19. What are three ways student ideas might be incorporated into an indirect instruction lesson?

*20. Why is student self-evaluation more important in the indirect model of instruction than in the direct model of instruction?

*21. What are five monitoring responsibilities of the teacher during group discussion?

*22. For which of the following teaching objectives might you use the direct model of instruction, and for which might you use the indirect model? Teaching your class to do the following:

(1) Sing
(2) Use a microscope properly
(3) Appreciate Milton's *Paradise Lost*
(4) Become aware of the pollutants around us
(5) Solve an equation with two unknowns
(6) Read at grade level
(7) Type at the rate of 25 words per minute
(8) Write an original short story
(9) Build a winning science fair project
(10) Distinguish war from aggression

Are there any for which you might use both models?

23. Provide an example of social framing using a topic with which you are familiar.

---

* Answers to asterisked questions (*) in this and the other chapters are in Appendix B.

Suggested Readings

Brooks, J. (1990). Teachers and students: Constructivists forging connections. *Educational Leadership, 47*(5), 68–71.

This article explains how constructivist teaching and learning can be used to promote integrated bodies of knowledge.

Dillon, J. (1987). *Questioning and discussion: A multidisciplinary study.* Norwood, NJ: Ablex.

Presentation of the research and logic that underlies the discussion method.

Giaconia, R. (1987). Open versus formal methods. In M. J. Dunkin (Ed.), *International encyclopedia of teaching and teacher education.* New York: Pergamon.

An introduction to some of the most important differences between the direct and indirect models.

Joyce, B., & Weils, M. (1992). *Models of teaching.* Englewood Cliffs, NJ: Prentice-Hall.

A review of many of our most popular styles of teaching—a good complement to the two models described in this chapter.

Michaels, S., & Collins, J. (1984). Oral discourse styles: Classroom interaction and the acquisition of literacy. In D. Tannen (Ed.), *Coherence in spoken and written discourse.* Norwood, NJ: Ablex.

An introduction to the many styles of discourse that can be used during indirect instruction

Slavin, R. (1987). Small group methods. In M. J. Dunkin (Ed.), *International encyclopedia of teaching and teacher education.* New York: Pergamon.

An overview of some ideas on how to use small groups to promote a cooperative classroom environment.

Tannen, D. (1986) *That's not what I meant!* New York: Morrow.

Discusses the concept of "framing" and how it can determine the meaning of your message.

Watson, B., & Konicek, R. (1990). Teaching for conceptual change: Confronting children's experience. *Phi Delta Kappan, 71,* pp. 680–685.

An introduction to constructivist thought and logic with some interesting examples from the classroom.

Withall, J. (1987). Teacher-centered and learner-centered teaching. In M. J. Dunkin (Ed.), *International encyclopedia of teaching and teacher education.* New York: Pergamon.

An introduction to the direct and indirect models of instruction from the point of view of the teacher and learner.

CHAPTER 8

Questioning Strategies

? This chapter will help you answer the following questions:

1. What is an effective question?
2. How are different types of questions classified?
3. What percent of time should I devote to higher-level and to lower-level questions?
4. How can I match questions with the abilities of my learners?
5. What is a question-asking sequence?
6. How do I ask questions at different levels of cognitive complexity?
7. What types of student outcomes should be taught with convergent questions and which with divergent questions?
8. How can I redirect or restructure a discussion with the use of probes?
9. How long should I wait to respond after a question?
10. How do I ask questions that promote thinking and problem solving?
11. Should I vary questions according to the ethnicity or culture of the learner?

In this chapter you will also learn the meaning of the following:

convergent and divergent questions
culture-specific questioning
effective questions
eliciting
probes
question sequence
reacting
redirecting
sociolinguistics
soliciting
structuring
Wait-time 1
Wait-time 2

n the classroom dialogues of previous chapters, you saw
the important role of questions in the effective teacher's
menu. This is no coincidence, for most exchanges between
teachers and students involve questions in some form.
This chapter explores the definition of a question, the varied ways questions can be asked, and the types of questions that you should ask more frequently than others.

Also discussed is the closely related topic of probes.
Like questions, probes are effective catalysts for performing the five key behaviors of (1) lesson clarity, (2) instructional variety, (3) task orientation, (4) engagement in the
learning process, and (5) student success. Subsequent
chapters extend these questioning techniques, showing
how you can use them to form other types of teaching
strategies.

>>> WHAT IS A QUESTION? <<<

In the context of a lively and fast-paced exchange in a classroom,
questions are not always obvious. As observed by Brown and Wragg
(1993), students routinely report difficulty in distinguishing some
types of questions in the context of a classroom dialogue—and even
whether a question has been asked. For example, imagine hearing
these two questions:

Raise your hand if you know the answer.

Aren't you going to *answer the question?*

The first is expressed in command form (italics), yet it contains
an implicit question. The second sounds like a question, yet contains an implicit command. Will your students perceive both of
these statements as questions? Will they both evoke the same
response?

Voice inflection is another source of confusion; it can indicate a
question even when sentence syntax does not. For example, imagine
hearing the following two sentences spoken with the emphasis
shown:

You *said* the President can have two terms in office?

The President can have *two* terms in office?

The proper voice inflection can turn almost any sentence into a question, whether you intend it or not. In addition, a real question can be perceived as a rhetorical question because of inflection and word choice:

We all have done our homework today, *haven't we?*

Whether this is intended as a question or not, it is certain that all who failed to complete their homework will assume the question to be rhetorical.

Effective questions are ones for which students actively compose a response and thereby become engaged in the learning process. The previous examples show that effective questions depend on more than just words. Their effectiveness also depends on *voice inflection, word emphasis, word choice,* and the *context* in which the question is raised. Questions can be raised in many ways and each way can determine whether the question is perceived by your students, and how.

What is an effective question?

In this chapter any oral statement or gesture intended to evoke a student response is considered to be a question. And if it evokes a response that actively engages a student in the learning process, it is an *effective question.* With this distinction in mind, let us now explore many ways of asking questions that actively engage students in the learning process.

What Consumes 80% of Class Time?

In almost any classroom at any time you can observe a sequence of events in which the teacher structures the content to be discussed, solicits a student response, and then reacts to the response. These activities performed in sequence are the most common behaviors in any classroom. They were first described by Bellack, Kliebard, Hyman, and Smith (1966) as the following chain of events:

1. The teacher provides structure, briefly formulating the topic or issue to be discussed.
2. The teacher solicits a response or asks a question of one or more students.
3. The student responds or answers the question.
4. The teacher reacts to the student's answer.

The teacher behaviors in this chain of events compose the activities of **structuring, soliciting,** and **reacting.** The previous two chapters discussed strategies you can use for structuring the content. This chapter focuses upon the soliciting and reacting elements in this chain of events.

At the heart of this chain is soliciting, or question-asking behavior. Questions are the tool for bridging the gap between your presentation of content and the student's understanding of it. Many bridging strategies were presented in the previous chapters: advance organizers, guided practice, feedback and correctives, inductive and deductive logic, self-evaluation, discussion, and so on. These strategies included all possible ingredients of both direct and indirect instruction, ingredients whose function is to promote and stimulate thinking.

Just as these ingredients actively engage learners in the learning process, so can questions perform this same function and add still more variety to a teaching menu. The purpose of using questions must not be lost among the many *forms* and *varieties* of questions presented in this chapter. Like all the ingredients of direct and indirect instruction, questions are tools to encourage students to think about and act upon the material you have structured.

Classrooms and content can become boring if a teacher fails to have students do something with the content *as quickly as possible after presenting it.* This is why the effective teacher intersperses questions throughout a lesson and wraps them around small bits of content, to actively engage the student and evoke a response (sometimes *any* response). Consequently, the cycle of structuring, soliciting, and reacting is the most frequently occurring chain of events in any classroom.

The centerpiece of this chain—soliciting or questioning—is so prevalent that as many as 100 questions per class hour may be asked in the typical elementary and secondary classroom (Brown & Edmondson, 1984). Further, 80 percent of all school time is devoted to questions and answers (Gall, 1984). This enormous concentration on a single strategy attests both to its convenience and to its perceived effectiveness. But, as noted, not all questions are *effective* questions. That is, not all questions actively engage students in the learning process.

Are We Asking the Right Questions?

Some research data indeed show that not all questions actively engage students in the learning process. Early studies estimated that 70 to 80 percent of all questions require the simple recall of facts, while only 20 to 30 percent require the higher-level thought

processes of clarifying, expanding, generalizing, and making inferences (Haynes, 1935; Corey, 1940). Evidently little has changed
since these early studies. Recent work in the United States and England indicates that, of every five questions asked, three require data
recall, one is managerial, and only one requires higher-level thought
processes (Brown & Wragg, 1993; Dillon, 1988b).

This lopsided proportion of recall questions to thought questions is alarming. Behaviors most frequently required in adult life,
at work, and in advanced training—those at the higher levels of cognitive complexity involving analysis, synthesis, and evaluation—
seem to be the least-emphasized behaviors in the classroom. As we
have seen, there are good reasons for asking questions at the knowledge, comprehension, and application level. But there is little explanation for why such questions form so great a percentage, to the
exclusion of higher-level thought questions. Higher-level thought
questions not only develop the behaviors most frequently required
outside the classroom but also are believed to more actively engage
your students in the classroom.

>>> WHAT ARE THE PURPOSES OF QUESTIONS? <<<

It would be easy to classify all questions as either lower-order
(requiring the recall of information) or higher-order (requiring clarification, expansion, generalization, and inference). But such a broad
distinction would ignore the many specific purposes for which questions are used:

- To arouse interest and curiosity
- To focus attention on an issue
- To stimulate learners to ask questions
- To diagnose specific learning difficulties
- To encourage reflection and self-evaluation
- To promote thought and the understanding of ideas
- To review content already learned
- To help recall specific information
- To reinforce recently learned material
- To manage or remind students of a procedure
- To teach via student answers
- To probe deeper after an answer is given

Even this substantial list does not cover all the reasons why
questions are asked. Nevertheless, most reasons for asking questions can be classified into the following general categories:

How are different types of questions classified?

1. Interest-getting and attention-getting:
   "If you could go to the moon, what would be the first thing you would notice?"

2. Diagnosing and checking:
   "Does anyone know the meaning of the Latin word *via?*"

3. Recall of specific facts or information:
   "Who can name each of the main characters in *The Adventures of Huckleberry Finn?*"

4. Managerial:
   "Did you ask my permission?"

5. Encourage higher-level thought processes:
   "Putting together all that we learned, what household products exhibit characteristics associated with the element sodium?"

6. Structure and redirect learning:
   "Now that we've covered the narrative form, who can tell me what an expository sentence is?"

7. Allow expression of affect:
   "What did you like about *Of Mice and Men?*"

Most of the questions in these categories have the purpose of shaping or setting up the learner's response. In this sense, a well-formulated question serves as an advance organizer, providing the framework for the response that is to follow.

>>> WHAT ARE CONVERGENT AND <<< DIVERGENT QUESTIONS?

Questions can be narrow or broad, encouraging either a specific, limited response or a general, expansive one. A question that limits an answer to a single or small number of responses is called a **convergent** (or *direct* or *closed*) **question.** For such questions, the learner has previously read or heard the answer, and so has only to recall certain facts.

Convergent questions set up the learner to respond in a limited, restrictive manner: "Does anyone know the meaning of the Latin word *via?*" "Who can name the main characters in *The Adventures of Huckleberry Finn?*" The answers to these questions are easily judged right or wrong. Many convergent, or closed, questions are used in direct instruction. As mentioned, up to 80 percent of all questions may be of this type.

Another type of question encourages a general or open response. This is the **divergent,** or *indirect,* **question.** It has no single best answer, but it can have wrong answers. This is perhaps the most misunderstood aspect of a divergent question. Not just any answer will be correct, even in the case of divergent questions raised for the purpose of allowing students to express their feelings. If Johnny is asked what he liked about *Of Mice and Men* and says "Nothing," or "The happy ending," then either Johnny has not read the book or he needs help in better understanding the events that took place. A passive or accepting response on your part to answers like these is inappropriate, regardless of your intent to allow an open response.

Convergent and divergent questions, therefore, both have right and wrong answers. Divergent questions may have many right answers and therefore a much broader range of acceptable responses. But if you receive a wrong or meaningless response, or no response at all, you should guide the student to an appropriate response and have the student try again. You may need to hint, encourage, or probe further—"Now, why would you say death and tragedy make a happy ending?"

You can expect far more diverse responses from divergent questions than from convergent questions—which may explain why only 20 percent of all questions are divergent. It always will be easier to determine the right or wrong answer to a convergent question than it will be to sift through the range of acceptable responses to a divergent question. Even so, it is your responsibility to identify inappropriate responses, to follow them up, and to bring them back into the acceptable range. Thus, you often will need to follow up divergent questions with more detail, new information, or encouragement. In this sense, divergent questions become a rich source of lively, spontaneous followup material that can make your teaching fresh and interesting.

Note that the same question can be convergent under one set of circumstances and divergent under another. Suppose you ask a student to *decide* or *evaluate,* according to a set of criteria, which household products exhibit characteristics of the element sodium. If the student only recalls products from a previously memorized list, then the question is convergent. But if the student has never seen such a list, and must analyze the physical properties of products for the first time, then the question is divergent.

Convergent questions also can inadvertently turn into divergent questions. When the answer to a question thought to involve simple recall ("Does anyone know the meaning of the Latin word *via?*") has never been seen before, and the student arrives at the right answer through generalization and inductive reasoning (e.g., by thinking about the meaning of the English word *viaduct* or the phrase "via route 35"), then the question is divergent.

To complicate matters further, a convergent question in one context may be a divergent question in another, and vice versa. The question "What do you think of disarmament?" may require the use of evaluation skills by eighth graders but only the recall of facts by twelfth graders who have just finished memorizing the details of the Strategic Arms Limitation Treaty. Also, both of the questions "What do you think about disarmament?" and "What do you think about the Dallas Cowboys?" may require some analysis, synthesis, or decision making, but for most of your students disarmament will require a higher level of thought than will the Dallas Cowboys. As has been shown, effective questions depend on more than just words—they depend on the *context* of the discussion in which the question is raised, *voice inflection, word emphasis,* and *word choice.*

What Research Exists on Convergent vs. Divergent Questions?

Classroom researchers have studied the effects on student achievement of convergent and divergent questions (Dillon, 1988b; Gall, 1984). Remember that far more convergent questions are raised in classrooms than divergent questions; the ratio is about 4:1. Most rationales for using higher-level, divergent-type questions include promotion of thinking, formation of concepts and abstractions, encouragement of analysis-synthesis-evaluation, and so on. But interestingly, research has not clearly substantiated that the use of higher-level questions is related to gains in student achievement—at least not as measured by tests of *standardized* achievement.

Although some studies report modest improvements in achievement scores with the use of divergent questioning strategies, others have not. Some studies even report larger achievement gains with convergent questioning than with divergent questioning strategies. Although these studies found a large imbalance in favor of convergent questions, four important factors must be considered when looking at their results:

1. Tests of achievement—and particularly tests of *standardized* achievement—employ multiple-choice items that generally test for behaviors at lower levels of cognitive complexity. Therefore, the achievement measures in these studies may have been unable to detect increases in behaviors at the higher levels of cognitive complexity, increases that might have resulted from the use of divergent questions.

2. The diversity of responses normally expected from divergent questions, and the added time needed to build on and follow up on responses, may prohibit large amounts of class time from being devoted to higher-order questioning. Because less instructional time often is devoted to divergent questioning than to convergent questioning, some study results may simply reflect the imbalance in instructional time, not their relative effectiveness.

3. The content best suited for teaching more complex behaviors may constitute only a small amount of the content in existing texts, workbooks, and curriculum guides. Although this is changing as a result of constructivist views on teaching and learning, much of the typical curricula in math, science, English, and even the social sciences emphasize facts and understandings at the knowledge and comprehension level. This may be because such achievements are the most easily measured and because needed improvements can be identified from standardized tests. Until larger portions of curricula are *written to encourage or require higher-level thought processes,* the time teachers actually devote to these behaviors may not increase.

4. Thinking and problem-solving behaviors most closely associated with divergent questions may take much longer to become noticeable in the behavior of learners than less complex behaviors. Less complex behaviors (learning to form possessives, memorizing Latin roots, knowing multiplication tables) are quickly elicited with convergent questioning strategies and are readily detected with fill-in, matching, or multiple-choice exams at the end of a lesson or unit. But more complex and authentic behaviors (learning to distinguish economic systems from political systems, learning to analyze household products for their chemical components, recognizing forms of quadratic equations) may take a unit, a grading period, or even longer to build to a measurable outcome. This time span is beyond that of most, if not all, of the studies that have compared the effects of convergent and divergent strategies on school achievement.

What percent of time should I devote to higher-level and to lower-level questions?

Thus, the seeming imbalance in the use and effectiveness of divergent and convergent questioning strategies may have little to do with the strategies themselves. Because factual recall always will be required for higher-order thought processes, numerous convergent questions always will be a necessary precondition for achieving higher-level behaviors. Also, because more instructional time is needed for higher-order questioning to be used effectively, the consistent use of moderate amounts of divergent questions may be more effective than intense but brief episodes of divergent questioning. The most appropriate *convergent:divergent* question ratio may be about 70:30 in classrooms where lesson content emphasizes lower levels of behavioral complexity, to about 60:40 in classrooms where lesson content emphasizes higher levels.

It is important to note that many of the same studies that fail to link higher-order questioning with increases in school achievement indicate that higher-order questioning tends to encourage students to use higher thought processes in composing a response. Research (Dillon, 1988b) suggests that teachers who ask questions requiring analysis, synthesis, and evaluation elicit these behaviors from students more frequently than teachers who use fewer higher-level questions.

Therefore, these higher-level thought processes seem desirable, regardless of whether their effects show up on immediate tests of achievement. The effects of higher-level questioning on the thinking process in itself may justify applying higher-level questions consistently at moderate rates over extended periods.

>>> WHO ARE THE TARGETS OF QUESTIONS? <<<

How can I match questions with the abilities of my learners?

Research by Brown and Wragg (1993) and Brown and Edmondson (1984) suggests that questions at various levels of cognitive complexity can be directed to individuals, to groups, or to the entire class. Figure 8.1 shows some of the combinations possible. In heterogeneously grouped classes, questions at different levels of cognitive complexity can be targeted to individuals, groups, and the full class, depending on the content being taught. Occasionally posing questions over the heads of some learners and under the heads of others will keep all students alert and engaged in the learning process.

In more homogeneously grouped classes questions can be spread across individuals, groups, and the full class but crafted to fit the cognitive complexity most appropriate for the learners being taught. For example, a general question can be composed requiring less or more cognitive complexity and prerequisite knowledge, as illustrated in the following examples:

Less Complex	More Complex
"Tell me, Johnny, if you sat down to breakfast, what things at the breakfast table would most likely contain the element sodium?"	"Mary, what are some forms of the element sodium in our universe?"

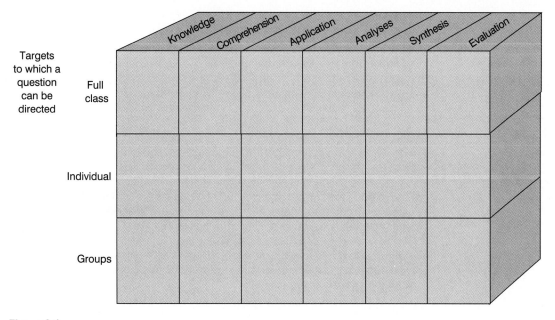

Figure 8.1
Possible targets and groups for framing questions

"After the death of Lenny in *Of Mice and Men,* what happens to the other main character?"

"What would be an example of an anticlimax in *Of Mice and Men?*"

"After thinking about the words *photo* and *synthesis,* who wants to guess what *photosynthesis* means?"

"Who can tell me how photosynthesis supports plant life?"

"Ted, if we have the equation $10 = 2/x$' do we find x by multiplying or dividing?"

"Rich, can you solve this problem for x? $10 = 2/x$'"

Notice that these examples vary not only in cognitive complexity but also in how they are framed, or phrased. More advance organizers, hints, and clues will be more appropriate for some types of learners than for others (Michaels & Collins, 1984).

One way of framing questions for heterogeneous classes is to design them so different responses at various levels of complexity will be correct. You can accept less complex responses as being just as correct as more complex answers, if they match the level of the question being asked. Although a response from some learners may not be

Table 8.1
Characteristics of more and less complex questions

More Complex Questions	Less Complex Questions
Require the student to generalize the content to new problems	Require the student to recall task-relevant prior knowledge
Stymie, mystify, and challenge in ways that do not have predetermined answers	Use specific and concrete examples, settings, and objects with which students are familiar
Are delivered in the context of an investigation or problem that is broader than the question itself	Use a step-by-step approach, where each question is narrower than the preceding one
Ask students to go deeper, clarify, and provide additional justification or reasons for the answers they provide	Rephrase or reiterate the answers to previous questions
Use more abstract concepts by asking students to see how their answers may apply across settings or objects	Suggest one or two probable answers that lead students in the right direction
Are part of a sequence of questions that builds to higher and more complex concepts, patterns, and abstractions	Are placed in the context of a game (e.g., 20 questions) with points and rewards

as complete, you can evaluate the response in terms of the behavioral complexity required by the question and the student's ability to respond to it. Therefore, the elaboration given and depth of understanding required may be less for one type of learner than for another.

In Chapter 13 we will have more to say about instructional strategies for heterogeneous classrooms. For now, keep in mind that although most of your questions will be aimed at the average learner in your class—or targeted to a mixture of abilities—you should specifically direct questions of varying complexity to the full class, smaller groups, and individuals. Table 8.1 suggests specific questioning strategies.

>>> WHAT SEQUENCES OF QUESTIONS ARE USED? <<<

What is a question-asking sequence?

Questions also can vary according to the sequence in which they are used. Recall that the most basic **question sequence** involves structuring, soliciting, and reacting. However, many variations are possible. Studies by Brown and Edmondson (1984), Wilen (1991), and Smith and Meux (1970) note that one of the most popular sequences employs divergent questions that lead to convergent questions. They report that many teachers begin the structuring-soliciting-reacting process by starting with an open question that leads to further structuring, and then to subsequent questions that involve recall or simple deduction.

This general-to-specific approach can take several twists and turns. For example, in the following dialogue, the teacher begins by encouraging speculative responses and then narrows to a question requiring simple deduction:

Teacher: What do astronauts wear on the moon?

Students: Spacesuits.

Teacher: So what element in our atmosphere must *not* be in the atmosphere on the moon?

It is the same approach when a teacher poses a problem, asks several simple recall questions, and then reformulates the question to narrow the problem still further:

Teacher: If the Alaskan Eskimos originally came from Siberia on the Asian continent, how do you suppose they got to Alaska?

Students: (No response)

Teacher: We studied the Bering Strait, which separates North America from Asia. How wide is the water between these two continents at their closest point?

Student: About 60 miles. The Little and Big Diomede Islands are in between.

Teacher: If this expanse of water were completely frozen, which some scientists believe it was years ago, how might Asians have come to the North American continent?

This type of funneling, adding conditions of increasing specificity to a question, was frequently employed by teachers in many studies reviewed by Redfield and Rousseau (1981). There is, however, no evidence that one sequencing strategy is any more effective in promoting student achievement than any other. The specific sequence chosen should depend on the behavioral objectives, the instructional content being taught, and the ability level of the students.

Other types of questioning sequences that can be implemented in a cycle of structuring, soliciting, and reacting, suggested by Hunk-

Table 8.2
Some sequences of questions

Type	Description
Extending ————	A string of questions of the same type and on the same topic
Extending and lifting	Initial questions request examples and instances of the same type, followed by a leap to a different type of question; a common sequence is likely to be recall, simple deduction and descriptions leading to reasons, hypothesis
Funneling	Begins with open question and proceeds to narrow down to simple deductions and recall or to reasons and problem solving
Sowing and reaping	Problem posed, open questions asked, followed by more specific questions and restatement of initial problem
Step-by-step up	A sequence of questions moving systematically from recall to problem solving, evaluation or open ended
Step-by-step down	Begins with evaluation questions and moves systematically through problem solving towards direct recall
Nose-dive	Begins with evaluation and problem solving and then moves straight to simple recall

From "Asking Questions" by G. Brown and R. Edmondson (pp. 97–119) in *Classroom Teaching Skills,* ed. E. Wragg. Copyright © 1984 by Nichols Publishing Company. Adapted by permission of Nichols Publishing Company.

ins (1989) and Brown and Edmondson (1984), are illustrated in Table 8.2. With the appropriate objectives, content, and students, all offer useful additions to your teaching menu.

>>> WHAT LEVELS OF QUESTIONS ARE USED? <<<

As we have seen, as an effective teacher you must be able to formulate divergent and convergent questions, to target questions to specific types of learners, and to arrange questions in meaningful sequences. You also must be able to formulate questions at different levels of cognitive complexity.

One of the best-known systems for classifying questions according to cognitive complexity is the taxonomy of objectives in the cognitive domain that was presented in Chapter 4. This system has the advantage of going beyond the simple recall-versus-thought dichotomy frequently used in the research cited previously. Not all recall questions should deal with the lowest and most mundane forms of learning (e.g., recall of names, dates, facts), and not all thought questions should deal with the highest and most superlative forms of learning (e.g., discovery, insight, judgment). A continuum of question complexity that fills the space between these ends of the scale is a useful addition to the art of asking questions.

Recall that the cognitive-domain taxonomy contains six levels of behavioral complexity:

Knowledge
Comprehension
Application
Analysis
Synthesis
Evaluation

Table 8.3 identifies the types of student behaviors associated with each level. Look at each level to get a feel for the question-asking strategies that go along with it.

Knowledge

Recall from Chapter 4 that knowledge objectives require the student to recall, describe, define, or recognize facts that already have been committed to memory. Some action verbs you can use to formulate questions at the knowledge level are:

How do I ask questions at different levels of cognitive complexity?

define   list
describe   name
identify   recite

Sample questions are:

What is the definition of capitalism?
How many digits are needed to make the number 12?
Can you recite the first rule for forming possessives?
What is the definition of a *straight line*?

Table 8.3

A question classification scheme

Level of Behavioral Complexity	Expected Student Behavior	Instructional Processes	Key Words
Knowledge (remembering)	Student is able to remember or recall information and recognize facts, terminology, and rules.	repetition memorization	define describe identify
Comprehension (understanding)	Student is able to change the form of a communication by translating and rephrasing what has been read or spoken.	explanation illustration	summarize paraphrase rephrase
Application (transferring)	Student is able to apply the information learned to a context different than the one in which it was learned.	practice transfer	apply use employ
Analysis (relating)	Student is able to break a problem down into its component parts and to draw relationships among the parts.	induction deduction	relate distinguish differentiate
Synthesis (creating)	Student is able to combine parts to form a unique or novel solution to a problem.	divergence generalization	formulate compose produce
Evaluation (judging)	Student is able to make decisions about the value or worth of methods, ideas, people, or products according to expressed criteria.	discrimination inference	appraise decide justify

Knowledge questions require recalling previously memorized facts. They do not require that the student understand what was memorized or be able to use the facts in a problem-solving context, for which higher-level questions will be needed.

Notice that each of these questions can be answered correctly simply by recalling previously memorized facts. They do not require understanding of what was memorized or the ability to use the learned facts in a problem-solving context. Robert could parrot the definition of *capitalism* (as given in our dialogue in Chapter 7) without having the slightest notion of the differences between capitalism and other economic systems—or even that he is living in a capitalist system.

It is not unusual for meticulously memorized facts to be forgotten within days or weeks. You probably can cite a personal experience of doing well on fact-type quizzes during the semester, only to do poorly on the end-of-semester exam. In such cases, either your time spent memorizing the facts was wasted because it did not stick, or the instructor failed to relate those facts to the higher-level and more authentic behaviors tested at the end of the course. (Your author vividly recalls his fifth-grade teacher, who spent nearly every social studies lesson having the class memorize dates of major historical events and administering brief oral quizzes about them. Indelibly etched into your author's memory are hundreds of dates—but not one was ever comprehended, applied, analyzed, synthesized, or evaluated!)

When facts are linked to other forms of knowledge, such as those in subsequent lessons and units, they become steppingstones for gradually increasing the behavioral complexity of teaching outcomes. To avoid the overuse or disconnected use of questions at the knowledge level, ask yourself: Do the facts required by my questions represent task-relevant prior knowledge for subsequent learning?

If your answer is "No," you might consider assigning text, workbook, or supplemental material that contains the facts, instead of incorporating them into your question-asking behavior. If your answer is "Yes," then determine in what ways the facts will be used in subsequent lessons, and raise questions that eventually will help form more complex behaviors.

Your students may *not* need the ability to recite the names of the presidents, the Declaration of Independence, or the elements in the periodic table, because these facts may not be task-relevant prior knowledge for more complex behavioral outcomes. On the other hand, it is likely that your learners *will* need to recite the multiplication tables, the parts of speech, and the rules for adding, subtracting, multiplying, and dividing signed numbers, for these will be used countless times in completing exercises and solving problems at more complex behavioral levels. Always take time to ask yourself: Are the facts that I am about to teach task-relevant prior knowledge for subsequent lessons? By doing so, you will avoid knowledge questions that may be trivial or irrelevant.

Comprehension

Comprehension questions require some level of understanding of facts the student has committed to memory. Responses to these questions should show that the learner can explain, summarize, or elaborate upon the facts that have been learned. Some action verbs you can use in formulating questions at the comprehension level are:

convert	paraphrase
explain	rephrase
extend	summarize

Sample questions are:

Can you, in your own words, explain the concept of capitalism?

How many units are there in the number 12?

In converting a possessive back to the nonpossessive form, what must be rephrased so that the first rule applies?

What steps are required to draw a straight line?

In responding to each of these questions, the student acts upon previously learned material by changing it from the form in which it was first learned. For example, the teacher asks not for the definition of capitalism, but "in your own words, explain the concept of capitalism." This requires translation or conversion of the original definition (the teacher's) into another (the student's).

There is an important step in moving from knowledge-level questions to comprehension-level questions. Knowledge-level questions require no cognitive processing—thinking—at the time of response, but comprehension-level questions do. In the former case, the learner actually may think about the material only once, at the time it was originally learned. In the latter case the learner must actively think about the content twice: once when the facts are memorized and again when they must be composed into a response in a different form. Although fact questions must logically precede comprehension questions, comprehension questions are superior to knowledge questions for arousing the cognitive processes of the learner and thereby encouraging long-term retention, understanding, and eventual use of the learned material in authentic contexts.

Application

Application questions extend facts and understanding to the next level of behavioral complexity. They go beyond memorization and translation of facts, requiring the student to use the previously acquired facts and understandings. Application questions require the student to apply facts to a problem, context, or environment that is different from the one in which the information was learned. Thus, the student can rely on neither the original context nor the original content to solve the problem.

Some action verbs you can use in formulating questions at the application level are:

apply	operate
demonstrate	solve
employ	use

Sample questions are:

What countries from among those listed do you believe have a capitalist economic system?

Can you show me 12 pencils?

Consider the first rule for forming possessives; who can apply it to the errors in the following newspaper article?

Can you draw for me a straight line between these two points?

These questions ask the learner to use previously learned facts and understandings to solve a problem. Your job in application questions is to present your learners with a context or problem different from that in which they learned the material. Application questions not only encourage the student to act upon learned material, thereby increasing engagement in the learning process, but also encourage the transfer of newly learned material to a new and different environment.

Application questions require two related cognitive processes: (1) the simultaneous recall and consideration of all the individual units (facts) pertaining to the question, and (2) the composing of units into a single harmonious sequence wherein the response becomes rapid and automatic. Recall that these two cognitive processes were introduced in chapters 6 and 7 as unitization and automaticity. They are required for all Type 1 behaviors—that is, for acquiring facts, rules, and action sequences. It is through these two processes that action sequences are created from the application of previously learned facts and rules.

Application questions ask students to compose (put together) previously learned responses under conditions approximating some real-world problem, with the goal of making the correct response rapid and automatic. You can see that action sequences require two precedents: learned facts and understandings acquired via knowledge and comprehension questions *and* the use of previously learned facts and rules in new contexts. The number and quality of your application questions will determine how rapid and automatic your learners' action sequences become.

The number of application questions you ask may be less important than your *consistency* in asking them. Many beginning teachers inappropriately believe that application questions should be reserved for the end of a unit—or even worse, for the end of a grading period. But, as you have seen, they are essential any time a rapid, automatic response involving facts or rules is desired, or when an action sequence is the lesson goal.

The quality of your application questions will be determined largely by how much you change the problem, context, or environment in which the facts or rules were learned. If your change is too small, transfer of learning to an expanded context will not occur, and your "parrots" will recite facts and rules from the earlier context. On the other hand, if your change is too great, the new context may require a response beyond the grasp of most of your learners. The key is to raise application questions that require the transfer of learning to new problems or contexts only after all task-relevant facts and rules have been taught. The easiest way to accomplish this is to change the context only a bit at first, and then gradually shift to more unfamiliar contexts.

Analysis

Questions at the analysis level require the student to break a problem into its component parts and to draw relationships among the parts. Some purposes of questions at the analysis level are to identify logical errors; to differentiate among facts, opinions, and assumptions; to derive conclusions; and to find inferences or generalizations—in short, to discover the reasons behind the information given.

Some action verbs you can use in formulating questions at the analysis level are:

break down	point out
differentiate	relate
distinguish	support

Sample questions are:

What factors distinguish capitalism from socialism?

Which of the boxes do not contain 12 things?

In what ways can you differentiate Rule 1 possessive errors from Rule 2 possessive errors in the following essay?

Which of the following pictures represents a straight line?

Analysis questions tend to promote Type 2 behaviors in the form of concepts, patterns, and abstractions. They generally are the most elementary form of the inquiry or problem-solving process, which is most closely associated with the functions of indirect instruction. In this respect, analysis questions are a movement away from the teaching of facts, rules, and action sequences and toward the more complex behavioral outcomes of concepts, patterns, and abstractions. You may consider analysis questions to be the start of the inquiry or problem-solving process, and the beginning of a change from direct to indirect instructional strategies.

Although not all Type 1 and Type 2 behaviors can be neatly divided between application and analysis, several important changes occur in the example questions at this level. Observe that the majority of the questions lack the single best answer so common in the teaching of facts, rules, and action sequences. Consequently, you will encounter and evaluate a much broader range of responses at the analysis level.

You may not anticipate all the varied responses you will receive (some in fact may be surprising). If you cannot prepare for all possible responses (which is very likely at the higher levels of behavioral complexity), then you should prepare yourself psychologically for the diverse responses that analysis questions generate. Preparing yourself psychologically may mean simply shifting your classroom to a less rigid, more deliberate, and slower-paced climate to give yourself some time to evaluate responses on the spot. It also may help to admit to yourself that some of the responses you hear may never have been heard before.

Synthesis

Questions at the synthesis level ask the student to produce something unique or original—to design a solution, compose a response, or predict an outcome to a problem for which the student has never before seen, read, or heard a response. This behavior level often is associated with *creativity,* which may be broader than what is intended here. The creativity sought at the synthesis level is not freewheeling ideas from out of the blue but *directed* creativity in which not all responses are equally acceptable. The facts, rules, action sequences, and any analysis questions that have gone before will define the limits and directions of the synthesis requested. Thus, the relationship of your synthesis questions to the Type 1 behaviors needed by students and the Type 2 behaviors you wish to create should be clear to your students.

Some action verbs you can use in formulating questions at the synthesis level are:

compare	formulate
create	predict
devise	produce

Sample questions are:

What would an economic system be like that combines the main features of capitalism and socialism?

What new numbers can you make by adding by 12s?

How could you write a paragraph showing possession without using any possessives?

How would you make a straight line without using a ruler?

This illustrates that even more diversity can be expected with synthesis questions than with analysis questions. This is due to the divergent nature of the questions used to teach Type 2 behaviors. Such openness is apparent at the analysis level, but it is even more pronounced at the synthesis level. Therefore, your preparation for diversity is critical to how your synthesis questions are received by your students.

A question asking for ways to identify undiscovered elements other than by using the periodic table opens up many possible responses. Some may not be acceptable ("consult an astrologer") but others will be ("analyze minerals from the moon and other planets"). Accept all reasonable answers, even though your own solutions may be limited to one or two efficient, practical, accurate solutions. Recognize that your question is sufficiently open that an acceptable answer need not be contingent on efficiency, practicality, or accuracy. Efficiency, practicality, and accuracy might be built from student responses, but you cannot initially expect it of them.

Another characteristic of higher-level questions is the multiple responses they are likely to generate. Multiple response questions are ones that actively encourage diverse responses and that are used to build increasingly more appropriate answers. Table 8.2 showed different types of questioning sequences, several of which are capable of molding student responses to be either more expansive or more restrictive than the original. You can use diverse responses to synthesis questions to draw out and direct creativity without restricting or narrowing the question itself, as the following dialogue illustrates:

■ ▪ ■ ▪ ■ ▪ ■ ▪ ■ ▪ ■ ▪ ■ ▪ ■ ▪ ■ ▪ ■ ▪ ■ ▪ ■

Teacher: In what ways other than from the periodic table might we predict the undiscovered elements?

Bobby: We could go to the moon and see if there are some elements there we don't have.

Betty: We could dig down to the center of the earth and see if we find any of the missing elements.

Ricky: We could study debris from meteorites—if we can find any.

Teacher: Those are all good answers. But what if those excursions to the moon, to the center of the earth, or to find meteorites were too costly and time consuming? How might we use the elements we already have here on earth to find some new ones?

Betty: Oh! Maybe we could try experimenting with the elements we do have to see if we can make new ones out of them.

——— · — · — — · — — · — — · — — · — — · — · — — · —

This simple exchange illustrates a funneling strategy: broad, expansive answers are accepted and then are followed up with a narrower question on the next round. In this manner, the diverse multiple responses that typically result from synthesis and other higher-level questions can be used to direct creative responses into gradually more structured avenues of inquiry, thereby contributing to critical thinking.

Evaluation

Questions at this highest level of behavioral complexity require the student to form judgments and make decisions using stated criteria. These criteria may be subjective (when a personal set of values is used in making a decision) or objective (when scientific evidence or procedures are used in evaluating something). In both cases, however, it is important that the criteria to be expressed be clearly understood—although not necessarily valued—by others.

Some action verbs you can use in formulating questions at the evaluation level are:

appraise	defend
assess	judge
decide	justify

Sample questions are:

Using evidence of your own choosing, do capitalist or socialist countries have a higher standard of living?

Which of the following numbers contain multiples of 12?

Using Rules 1 and 2 for forming possessives and assigning one point for each correct usage, what grade would you give the following student essay?

Given the following lines, which are curved and which are straight?

Evaluation questions have the distinct quality of confronting the learner with problems much as they appear in the real world. In this sense, evaluation questions link the classroom to the world outside.

Because decisions and judgments are prime ingredients of adult life, it is essential that classroom experiences start learners toward the world in which they will live, regardless of their age or maturity.

Unfortunately, evaluation questions often are reserved for the end of a unit, or even for the end of a larger block of instruction. Even more misguided is the notion that evaluation questions are more suited to junior high and high school than to elementary grades. Both misconceptions have reduced the impact of evaluation questions on learners and no doubt have contributed to the lower percentage of higher-order questions observed in classrooms. If learners are to cope with real-world problems, they must learn to do so starting at the earliest grades and throughout their schooling. Therefore, your ability to ask evaluation questions that can bring the world to your learners at their own level of knowledge and experience is one of the most valued abilities that you, the effective teacher, can have.

This ability, however, does not come easily. To be sure, all characteristics of the previously discussed higher-order questions— diversity of responses, opportunities for open-ended or divergent questioning, and multiple responses—are present in evaluation questions. But criteria must be applied to these in deciding the appropriateness of a solution. Notice in the preceding examples that the criteria (or their source) are identified: "using evidence of your own choosing," "if accuracy was your sole criterion," "using Rules 1 and 2," "given the graphs." The more specific your criteria, and the better your learners know them, the more actively engaged they will become in answering the question.

It is important to note that evaluation questions can be either convergent or divergent. When you ask "Is the equation $2 + 2 = 4$ correct?" you are asking an evaluation question for which only a single, narrow, correct response is possible. Here, the student's engagement in the learning process may be limited to simply conjuring up a memorized portion of the addition table. This evaluation question has far fewer implications for training learners to judge, to make decisions, and to think critically than one that asks, "What kinds of goods and services would be owned by a government under a socialist economic system that would not be owned by a government under a capitalist economic system?"

The first question is convergent, focusing on a single, best answer ("Yes, $2 + 2 = 4$ is correct."). The second question is divergent. It allows a range of responses, the acceptability of which could only be judged by applying a set of subjective or objective criteria. The criteria to apply in determining the appropriateness of the first question allow no room for judgment; the criteria to apply in the second question allow a great deal of judgment. Your fundamental criteria for evaluation questions are decisions and judgments as they are made in the real world.

>>> SUMMARY OF QUESTION TYPES <<<

What types of student outcomes should be taught with convergent questions and which with divergent questions?

You now know the levels of questions that can be asked of learners and some factors to consider in selecting the appropriate question type. To summarize:

* Type 1 behaviors (those calling for the acquisition of facts, rules, and action sequences) generally are most efficiently taught with convergent questions that have a single best answer (or a small number of easily definable answers). Type 1 behaviors are most effectively learned with a direct instruction model that focuses convergent questions at the knowledge, comprehension, and application levels of behavioral complexity.
* Type 2 behaviors (those calling for the acquisition of concepts, patterns, and abstractions) generally are most efficiently taught with divergent questions, for which many different answers may be appropriate. Type 2 behaviors are most effectively learned with an indirect instruction model that poses divergent questions at the analysis, synthesis, and evaluation levels of behavioral complexity.

Now that you are acquainted with these broad distinctions among types of questions, we turn to several specific techniques that can help you deliver these questions to your students with ease and perfection.

>>> HOW ARE PROBES USED? <<<

Recall from Chapter 1 the five catalytic or helping behaviors (use of student ideas and contributions, structuring, questioning, probing, teacher affect) that assist performance of the five key behaviors (lesson clarity, instructional variety, task orientation, engagement in the learning process, student success). In this section, we will look at one of the helping behaviors—probing—in the context of a questioning strategy.

A **probe** is a question that immediately follows a student's response to a question for the following purposes:

* Eliciting clarification of the student's response
* Soliciting new information to extend or build upon the student's response

- Redirecting or restructuring the student's response in a more productive direction

Use probes that *elicit clarification* to have students rephrase or reword a response so you can determine its appropriateness or correctness. **Eliciting** probes, such as "Could you say that in another way?" or "How would that answer apply in the case of _____?" induce learners to show more of what they know, thereby exposing exactly what they understand. The brief and vague responses often given in the context of a fast-paced and lively classroom discussion can mask partially correct answers or answers that are correct but for the wrong reason. When you are unsure how much understanding underlies a correct response, slow the pace with a probe for clarification.

Use probes that *solicit new information* following a response that is at least partially correct or that indicates an acceptable level of understanding. This time you are using the probe to push the learner's response to a more complex level (e.g., "Now that you've decided the laboratory is the best environment for discovering new elements, what kind of experiments would you conduct in this laboratory?" or "Now that you've taken the square root of that number, how could you use the same idea to take its cube root?").

This type of probe builds higher and higher plateaus of understanding by using the previous response as a steppingstone to greater expectations and more complete responses. This involves treating incomplete responses as part of the next higher-level response—not as wrong answers. The key to probing for new information is to make your followup question only a small extension of

Probes follow questions and are used to clarify a student's response, solicit new information, or redirect a response in a more productive direction.

your previous question; otherwise, the leap will be too great and the learner will be stymied by what appears to be an entirely new question. This type of probe, therefore, requires much the same process for finding the right answer as does the previously correct question, only this time applied to a different and more complex problem.

Use probes to *redirect the flow* of ideas instead of using awkward and often punishing responses such as "You're on the wrong track," "That's not relevant," or "You're not getting the idea." Probes for **redirecting** responses into a more productive area can accomplish the needed shift less abruptly and more positively, to avoid discouraging students from venturing another response. A probe that accomplishes this purpose moves the discussion sideways, setting a new condition for a subsequent response that does not negate a previous response.

For example, recall that, in our dialogue on socialism in Chapter 7, the teacher asked for "the kinds of things individuals would likely need to live and prosper." Ricky responded, "You mean like a car or a home of your own." But, because all individuals in a socialist economy might not agree on the value of these for everyone, the teacher had to redirect the discussion to objects more consistent with a socialist economy, without negating the value of the earlier response. He did this by stepping sideways and imposing two new conditions to get the discussion back on track: "What types of things could a *group of people,* say the size of a nation, agree on that would be *absolutely essential* for everyone's existence?" This probe successfully leaves behind objects such as cars and homes without negatively valuing Ricky's response.

How can I redirect or restructure a discussion with the use of probes?

Probing to redirect or restructure a discussion can be a smooth and effortless way of getting learners back on track. Notice in the following example how the teacher blends the use of all three types of probes in the context of a single discussion:

▬ ▬ ▬ ▬ ▬ ▬ ▬ ▬ ▬ ▬ ▬ ▬ ▬ ▬ ▬ ▬

Teacher: What do we call the grid system by which we can identify the location of any place on the globe? (To begin the questioning)

Bobby: Latitude and longitude.

Teacher: Good. What does longitude mean? (To solicit new information)

Bobby: It's the grid lines on the globe that . . . go up and down.

Teacher: What do you mean by *up and down?* (To elicit clarification)

Bobby: They extend north and south at equal intervals.

Teacher: OK. Now tell me, where do they begin? (To solicit new information)

Bobby: Well, I think they begin wherever it's midnight and end where it's almost midnight again.

Teacher: Let's think about that for a minute. Wouldn't that mean the point of origin would always be changing according to where it happened to be midnight? (To redirect)

Bobby:	Yes, so the grids must start at some fixed point.
Teacher:	Anybody know where they begin? (To solicit new information)
Sue:	Our book says the first one marked *0* starts at a place called Greenwich, England.
Teacher:	How can a grid that runs continuously north and south around the globe *start* anyplace, Sue? (To elicit clarification)
Sue:	I meant to say that it *runs through* Greenwich, England.
Teacher:	Good. Now let's return to Bobby's point about time. If we have a fixed line of longitude, marked *0*, how might we use it to establish time? (To solicit new information)
Bobby:	Now I remember. Midnight at the *0* longitude—or in Greenwich, England—is called *0* hours. Starting from there, there are time-lines drawn around the world, so that when it's midnight at the first timeline, it will be one o'clock back at Greenwich, England; and when it's midnight at the next timeline, it will be two o'clock back at Greenwich, England, and so on.
Teacher:	What does that mean? (To elicit clarification)
Bobby:	Each line equals one hour—so . . . so there must be 24 of them!
Teacher:	It should be no surprise to learn that time determined in reference to the *0* grid of longitude is called Greenwich Mean Time.

>>> HOW SHOULD YOU USE WAIT TIME? <<<

An important consideration during questioning and probing is how long to wait before initiating another question. Sometimes your "wait time" can be as effective in contributing to the desired response as the question or probe itself, especially when you give students time to thoughtfully compose their answers. Wait times that are either too short or too long can be detrimental, and when too long they also waste valuable instructional time. Obviously, wait time will be longer when students are weighing alternative responses (which often occurs during indirect instruction) than it will when their responses must be correct, quick, and firm (which often occurs during direct instruction).

Rowe (1986, 1987) distinguishes two different wait times. **Wait-time 1** refers to the amount of time a teacher gives a learner to respond to a question. Classrooms with short Wait-time 1s do not give learners much time to think before answering the question. In these classrooms, the teacher is repeating the question, or calling on another learner to answer the same question after only a two- or three-second period of silence.

Wait-time 2 refers to the interval of time after a learner's response until the teacher speaks. Teachers with long Wait-time 2s wait several seconds before asking a followup question, correcting the answer, or otherwise commenting on what the learner said. Classrooms with short Wait-time 2s are characterized by frequent interruptions of learners before they finish answering.

Rowe (1986) has found increasing either wait time has the following effects on learner responses:

- Learners give longer answers to questions.
- Learners volunteer more responses.
- There are fewer unanswered questions.
- Learners are more certain of their answers.
- Learners are more willing to give speculative answers.
- The frequency of learner questions increases.

How long should I wait to respond after a question?

Generally, you should wait *at least three seconds* before asking another question, or repeating the previous question, or calling on another student. During indirect instruction, where divergent questions may require thinking through and weighing alternatives, up to *15 seconds* of wait time may be appropriate.

These research findings provide impressive testimony to the important role that wait time can have on your learners' responses. If only a single piece of advice were given to beginning teachers concerning wait time, it would be: *slow down and pause longer between questions and answers than what at first feels comfortable.*

How do I ask questions that promote thinking and problem solving?

Finally, remember that questions are a principal means of engaging students in the learning process by getting them to think through and problem solve with the material you are presenting. Following are suggestions for using questions to promote your learners' thinking and problem solving:

- *Plan in advance the type of questions you will ask.* Although talk-show hosts make it appear as if their questions are spontaneous and unrehearsed, this seldom is the case. In reality, ad-libbing and spontaneity can lead to as much dead time on the air as they can in your classroom. The type of questions you select, their level of difficulty, and the sequence in which you ask them should be based on your lesson objectives.
- *Deliver questions in a style that is concise, clear, and to the point.* Effective oral questions are like effective writing—every word should be needed. Pose questions in the same natural conversational language you would use with any close friend.
- *Allow time for students to think—Wait-time 1.* Research on question asking points to the fact that many teachers do not allow learners sufficient time to answer a question before calling on someone else or moving to the next question. Gage and

Berliner (1992) and Rowe (1974) report that, on the average, teachers wait only about 1 second for learners to respond. These researchers recommend that you increase wait time to 3 to 4 seconds for lower-level questions and as much as 15 seconds for higher-level questions.

- *Keep the students in suspense.* First, deliver the question, then mention the student's name. Similarly, randomly select the students you want to answer your questions. You want your learners to anticipate that they can be called on at any time. This both increases accountability and maintains attention and alertness (Kounin, 1970).

- *Give students sufficient time to complete their response before redirecting the question or probing—Wait-time 2.* Wait-time 2 is the time you wait following a student answer before probing for deeper understanding or redirecting the question when the answer is incomplete or wrong. Teachers who are making a deliberate effort to maintain lesson momentum will often interrupt before a learner is finished responding. Some cultural and ethnic groups have a different Wait-time 2 than others. Tharp and Gallimore (1989) relate that in certain cultures a long Wait-time 2 makes the teacher appear disinterested in the lesson, while in other cultures this is a sign of respect for the speaker.

- *Provide immediate feedback to the learner.* Correct answers should be acknowledged and followed by either encouragement, elaborations on the response, further probing, or moving on to another question. The important point is to communicate to the learner that you heard and evaluated the answer. Often learners (unbeknown to the teacher) perceive that their answers have been ignored. Incorrect, incomplete, or inadequate answers should be followed by probes, or redirection of the question to another student. Research suggests that learners of different achievement levels and social class benefit from different redirecting and probing techniques.

>>> ARE QUESTIONING TECHNIQUES <<< CULTURE SPECIFIC?

Sociolinguistics is the study of how cultural groups differ in the courtesies and conventions of language rather than in the grammatical structure of what is said. Sociolinguistics examines the **culture-specific questioning** rules governing social conversation: with whom to speak, in what manner, when to pause, when to ask and answer questions, how to interrupt a speaker. Sociolinguists study,

Should I vary questions according to the ethnicity or culture of the learner?

for example, aspects of communication as revealed by the average length of utterances, time between utterances, speech rhythms, and rules for when, how, and about what people converse with each other. Among these aspects of communication, the most frequently studied are *wait time, rhythm,* and *participation structure.*

Wait time

Tharp (1989) reports that different cultures often have different wait times. Navaho children, for example, are raised in a culture with longer Wait-time 2s than Anglo children. Some studies show that Navaho children speak in longer sentences and volunteer more answers when taught by teachers with longer Wait-time 2s. Tharp reports that in Hawaiian culture interruptions are a sign of interest in the speaker and in what she is saying. Conversely, long Wait-time 2s suggest to Hawaiian learners that the speaker is uninterested or bored with the conversation. Other studies of Hispanic and African American learners appear as well to suggest that optimal wait times are culture and even context specific (Hill, 1989). Although specific prescriptions cannot be made from this research, it does suggest that the way a question is posed and the wait time between questions and answers must be determined within the cultural context and learning history of those being taught.

Rhythm

Conversational rhythm pertains to the tempo, inflections, and speed of conversations between two speakers as they converse. Young (1970) and Piestrup (1973) have observed that African American children and their mothers converse with one another using rapid rhythms and a "contest" style of interaction. Mothers encourage their children to be assertive. Directions for household chores and the children's responses to these directions take on an almost debate-like tone with the mother directing or calling and the children responding. Franklin (1992) suggests that this style of interaction creates a high-energy, fast-paced home environment that contrasts with the low-energy, slow-paced environment of the typical classroom.

Franklin speculates that this contrast between the pace of conversation at home and in school may be one reason why some African American children are referred for behavior problems in the classroom. Similarly, Anderson (1992) states that many Anglo teachers overreact to the conversational style of African American adolescents, which may explain the disproportionate referral of these children to programs for learners with behavior disorders. Anderson recommends that teachers allow African American learners to use in the classroom the conversational style they bring from home. This would include speaking more rhythmically, with greater variation in tonation, and engaging in more fast-paced verbal interplay.

Participation Structure

The typical classroom conversation occurs in a one-to-one, question-answer type participation structure or format. A teacher looks directly at a child, asks him or her a question, and waits for an answer before making a followup response. Tharp and Gallimore (1989) observe that such a participation structure results in very little participation by Hawaiian or Navaho children.

At home and in their communities, the typical participation structure when adults are present involves a relatively small group of children together with an encouraging, participating, but nondirective adult in an informal setting. When the classroom participation structures are based upon those found in the culture both Hawaiian and Navaho children, who rarely participated in classroom discussions or question-answer formats, become surprisingly "verbal" (Watson-Grego & Boggs, 1977).

Sociolinguists point out that children are more comfortable in classrooms where the sociolinguistic patterns (wait times, rhythms, participation structures, etc.) are compatible with those of their home and community. Bartz and Levine (1978) and Lein (1975) point out that often schools view African American or Hispanic migrant children as "nonverbal." Yet, when observed in familiar home or neighborhood environments they use vibrant, expressive, and creative language patterns. Their point is that the sociolinguistic patterns of the typical American classroom make certain minority group learners uncomfortable. This, in turn, causes them to participate less in class, in ways Anglo American teachers view as deficient or inappropriate, and achieve less.

>>> WHAT ARE COMMON PROBLEMS <<<
IN USING QUESTIONS?

Based on classroom observations of the question-asking behavior of beginning teachers, here are some of the most frequently observed problems to watch for, and suggested remedies.

Do You Use Complex, Ambiguous, or "Double" Questions?

One of the commonest question-asking problems of beginning teachers is the use of the complex, ambiguous, or "double" question. This is a question that is so long and complicated that students easily lose track of the main idea by the time it is completed. Sometimes, a teacher will unknowingly pack two (or even more) questions within its complicated structure.

Because such questions are delivered orally and are not written, students have no way of rereading the question to gain its full intent. It is unfortunate that these questions sometimes are so complicated that even the teacher cannot repeat the question precisely when requested, thus providing different versions of the same question. Consider the following three examples of needlessly complex questions and their simpler but equally effective revisions.

Example 1.

> *Complex Form:* "We all know what the three branches of government are, but where did they come from, how were they devised, and in what manner do they relate?"

This question is actually three questions in one, and requires too long a response if each point in the question were responded to individually. Besides, the first two questions may be redundant—or are they?—while the third is sufficiently vague to bewilder most students. Finally, what if some students do not know or cannot recall the three branches of government? For those students, everything that follows is irrelevant, opening the door to boredom and off-task behavior.

> *Simpler Form:* Recall that there are three branches of government: the executive, judicial, and legislative. What governmental functions are assigned to each by the Constitution?

Example 2.

> *Complex Form:* How do single-celled animals propagate themselves and divide up to create similar animal life that looks like themselves?

If you were to ask this question, you can be sure that some of your students would ask you to repeat the question, in which case you might not remember your own complex wording. This question fails to get to the point quickly and appears to ask the same thing three times: how do single-celled animals propagate . . . divide up

. . . create similar animal life? This redundancy could easily be mistaken for three separate questions by students struggling to understand single-celled reproduction at an elementary level. State your questions only one way and rephrase later, if need be, when students know that it is the same question being rephrased.

> *Simpler Form:* By what process do single-celled animals reproduce?

Example 3.
> *Complex Form:* What do you think about the Civil War, or the Vietnam War, or war in general?

Depending on what part of this question a student wants to hear, you may get noticeably different answers. The intention was to raise a question that would provide enough options to get almost any student involved in composing a response; but, unless you intend only to start a controversy, the range of responses will probably be so broad that moving to the next substantive point may be impossible. This question may leave students arguing feverishly for the entire period without being able to focus on the real purpose for raising the question in the first place (e.g., as an introduction to the Civil War, or to unpopular wars, or to the concept of war). This question is too broad, too open, and too divergent to be of practical value for framing a day's lesson.

> *Simpler Form:* What are the factors that you believe would justify a war among groups within the same nation?

Here are basic rules for avoiding complex, ambiguous, or "double" questions:

1. Focus each question on only one idea.
2. State the main idea only once.
3. Use concrete language.
4. State the question in as few words as possible.

Do You Accept Only the Answers You Expect?

Another common mistake of beginning teachers is to rely almost exclusively on the answer they expect. Recall the discussion in Chapter 3 regarding the bias that teachers sometimes have about whom they call on and interact with in classroom exchanges. Biases can extend to favorite answers as well as to favorite students. When teaching new content, which frequently is the case during your first year, you naturally strive to become more secure and confident by limiting answers to those with which you are most familiar. Your first reaction will be to discourage responses at the edge of what you consider to be the appropriate range. This range is directly related to the openness of your questions. Open questions encourage diversity, and it is this diversity that often catches the beginning teacher off guard and forces an expansive question into a limited one. Note in the following dialogue how this teacher's posture is changed by the nature of the response:

Teacher: OK, today we will study the European settlers who came to America, and why they came here. Why did they come to America?
Student 1: To farm.
Teacher: No, not to farm.
Student 2: To build houses and churches.
Teacher: No, that's not right either.

If this exchange were to continue for very long it no doubt would turn off many students, if only because they know that these responses cannot be entirely wrong even if they are not what the teacher wants. What does the teacher want? Probably, the desired answer is that the early Americans came because of religious persecution in their European communities. The last student's response, "to build houses and churches," was a perfect opportunity for a probe that simply asked "Why churches?" Unfortunately, this teacher missed that opportunity in favor of waiting for the exact response, because this teacher was unable or unwilling to *build on existing responses*. This teacher may have a long wait, in which case valuable instructional time will be lost by calling on student after student in the hope that the only acceptable answer will eventually emerge.

Answers that are just what you are looking for are always desirable, but remember that partially correct answers and even unusual and unexpected ones can become effective additions to the discussion through the use of probes. The solution to this problem is to use probes and build gradually toward your targeted responses.

Why Are You Asking This Question?

Perhaps the most serious error of all in question asking is not being certain of why you are asking a question. Remember, questions are tools that support the teaching and learning processes. Your first decision in using questions is to determine whether your lesson is teaching facts, rules, and action sequences or concepts, patterns, and abstractions. If the former is your goal, convergent questions at the knowledge, comprehension, or application levels probably are the ones to ask. If the latter is your goal, then divergent questions at the analysis, synthesis, or evaluation levels usually are the questions to ask. This decision strategy is summarized in Figure 8.2.

If you have not determined where you are on Figure 8.2, you are likely to ask the wrong type of question, and your questions will lack logical sequence. They may jump from convergent to divergent and move back and forth from simple recall of facts to the acquisition of concepts and patterns. Your students will find your questions disconcerting, because your ideas will not be linked by any common thread (at least, not by one that they can follow) and you will be seen as vague or lacking the ability to connect content in meaningful ways. Therefore, it is important that you decide in advance where your questioning strategy is going and then move toward this goal by choosing appropriate questions and levels of behavioral complexity.

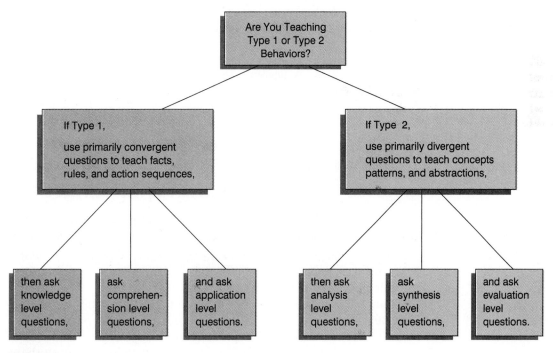

Figure 8.2
A decision tree for deciding on the types of questions to ask

Finally, it is important to note that just because your goal may be Type 1 or Type 2 behaviors, this does not mean that you cannot vary your questioning strategy across the levels shown on Figure 8.2. Questions should vary within types of learning (e.g., from knowledge to application or from analysis to synthesis) and across types of learning (e.g., from application to analysis). It is important to keep in mind your ultimate goal for the lesson and to choose the best combination of questions to reach that goal.

Do You Answer the Question Yourself?

Another common problem with beginning teachers is posing a question, and then answering it yourself. Sometimes a student begins a response but is cut off, only to hear the remainder of the response supplied by the teacher:

Teacher: So, who was the president who freed the slaves?
Student: Abraham—
Teacher: Lincoln! Yes, that's right.

Sometimes the reverse occurs: a student begins a response that the teacher knows is wrong and then is cut off by the teacher, who gives the correct response:

Teacher: So, who was the president who freed the slaves?
Student: George—
Teacher: No, no! It was Abraham Lincoln.

Needless to say, both outcomes demoralize the student, who either is deprived of the chance to completely give a right answer or is shown to have a response so incorrect that it is not even worth hearing in its entirety. Neither of these outcomes may be intended, but this is how your students will see it.

Your job is to use student responses to build to other more complex outcomes. Probes to elicit new information, to go beyond an already-correct answer, or to provide hints and clues after a wrong answer are particularly useful, because they extend to your students the right to give a full and deliberate response, right or wrong.

Teachers who frequently interrupt student responses because of a desire for perfect answers, a dominant personality, or talkativeness, may ultimately produce frustrated learners who never learn to give full and thoughtful responses or to participate voluntarily.

Do You Use Questions as Punishment?

Our final problem, and perhaps the most difficult, is the use—or rather, abuse—of questions to punish or to put a student on the defensive. Being asked a question can be a punishment as well as a reward. For example, questions can be used as punishment in the following ways:

1. A student who forgot to do the homework is deliberately asked a question from that homework.
2. A student who never volunteers is always asked a question.
3. A student gives a wrong response and then is asked an even harder question.
4. A student who disrupts the class is asked a question for which the answer cannot possibly be known.
5. A student who gives a careless response is asked four questions in a row.

Nearly every teacher has, at one time or another, used questions in one or more of these ways. Interestingly, some teachers do not always see these uses as punishment. Regardless of intent, however, such questions *are* punishment in that they (1) are unlikely to engage the student actively in meaningful learning, and (2) leave the student with a poorer self-image, less confidence, and more anxiety (perhaps anger) than was present before the question. These are behaviors that can only impede the learning process and which, therefore, have no place in your repertoire of questioning strategies. Each of the student-centered problems reflected in the preceding examples could have been handled more effectively, perhaps by doing the following:

1. Making a list of students who don't do homework.
2. Giving example questions beforehand to students who never volunteer.
3. Giving another try and providing hints and clues to students who give wrong responses until partially correct answers are received.

4. Giving disciplinary sanctions or reprimands to students who disrupt class.

5. Passing quickly to another student after receiving a careless answer.

Ample means are available for dealing with misbehavior and such means are far more effective than using questions. Questions are *academic tools* that should be prized and protected for their chosen purpose. To misuse them or to use them for any other purpose may affect how your questions will be perceived by your students (Did I get the hard question because she thinks I'm smart or because I'm being punished?). Such conflicts can drain students of the energy and concentration needed to answer your questions and may forever cast doubts on your motives.

The other side of questions is that they can be implicit rewards when used correctly. The opportunity to shine, to know and display the correct answer in front of others, and to be tested and get an approving grade are rewarding experiences for any learner. Consequently, every learner, regardless of ability level or knowledge of a correct response, should periodically experience these emotions.

Don't ignore students who have difficulty responding and don't accept wrong answers. Instead, occasionally try a broader criterion than correct/incorrect to help all students share in the emotional and intellectual rewards of answering questions. For example, try rewarding the most novel, most futuristic, most practical, and most thought-provoking answers along with the most accurate response. This will let every learner share in the challenge and excitement of questions.

>>> A FINAL WORD <<<

This chapter presented many aspects of the art of questioning. However, the most important lesson in this chapter is that questioning is a tool for actively engaging your learners in the learning process. All your teaching efforts will meet an untimely end unless you can get your learners to act upon, think about, or work on the content you present in ways that evoke the cognitive processes required by Type 1 and Type 2 learning. Guided practice, review, feedback and correctives, independent study, advance organizers, discussion, and so on are some approaches for setting in motion the cognitive processes necessary for meaningful learning to occur. Questions are another tool to add to your teaching menu. Because of their almost endless variety they may well be the most flexible tool on your menu.

This chapter introduced you to questioning strategies. Its main points were as follows:

1. An effective question is one for which students actively compose a response and thereby become engaged in the learning process.

2. An effective question depends on voice inflection, word emphasis, word choice, and the context in which it is raised.

3. The three most commonly observed teacher behaviors in the classroom are structuring, soliciting, and reacting.

4. Soliciting—or question-asking behavior—encourages students to act upon and think about the structured material as quickly as possible after it has been presented.

5. It has been estimated that 70 to 80 percent of all questions require the simple recall of facts, but only 20 to 30 percent require clarifying, expanding, generalizing, and the making of inferences. In other words, as few as one out of every five questions may require higher-level thought processes, even though behaviors at the higher levels of cognitive complexity are among those most frequently required in adult life, at work, and in advanced training.

6. Common purposes for asking questions include the following:

- Getting interest and attention
- Diagnosing and checking
- Recalling specific facts or information
- Managerial
- Encouraging higher-level thought processes
- Structuring and redirecting learning
- Allowing expression of affect

7. A question that limits possible responses to one or a small number is called a *convergent, direct,* or *closed* question. This type of question teaches the learner to respond in a limited, restrictive manner.

8. A question that has many right answers or a broad range of acceptable responses is called a *divergent* question. Divergent questions, however, can have wrong answers.

9. The same question can be convergent under one set of circumstances and divergent under another, as when so-called creative answers to a divergent question have been memorized from a list.

10. Research has not established that the use of higher-order questions is related to improved performance on standardized achievement tests. However, higher-order questions have been found to elicit analysis, synthesis, and evaluation skills, which are among the skills most sought in adult life.

11. Questions can be specifically worded for cognitive complexity as well as directed to individuals, groups, or the entire class.

12. Questions may be used in the context of many different sequences, such as funneling, where increasingly specific conditions are added to an original question, narrowing it to one requiring simple deduction.

13. In addition to being divergent, convergent, and targeted to specific types of learners, questions can be formulated at different levels of cognitive complexity that comprise the knowledge, comprehension, application, analysis, synthesis, and evaluation levels of the cognitive domain.

14. Knowledge questions ask the learner to recall, describe, define, or recognize facts that already have been committed to memory.

15. Comprehension questions ask the learner to explain, summarize, or elaborate on previously learned facts.

16. Application questions ask the learner to go beyond the memorization of facts and their translation and to use previously acquired facts and understandings in a new and different environment.

17. Analysis questions ask the learner to break a problem into its component parts and to draw relationships among the parts.

18. Synthesis questions ask the learner to design or produce a unique or unusual response to an unfamiliar problem.

19. Evaluation questions ask the learner to form judgments and make decisions, using stated criteria for determining the adequacy of the response.

20. A *probe* is a question that immediately follows a student's response to a question; its purpose is to elicit clarification, to solicit new information, or to redirect or restructure a student's response.

21. The key to probing for new information is to make the followup question only a small extension of the previous question.

22. The time you wait before initiating another question or turning to another student may be as important in actively engaging the learner in the learning process as the question itself. A wait time of at least three seconds should be observed before asking another question, repeating the previous question, or calling on another student.

23. Longer wait times have been associated with longer responses, greater numbers of voluntary responses, greater behavioral complexity of the response, greater frequency of student questions, and increased confidence in responding.

24. Avoid problems commonly observed in the question-asking behavior of beginning teachers:

- Do not raise overly complex or ambiguous questions that may require several different answers.

- Be prepared to expect correct but unusual answers, especially when raising divergent questions.

- Always establish beforehand why you are asking a particular question. Know the complexity of behavior you may expect as a result of the question.

- Never supply the correct answer to your own questions without first probing. Never prevent a student from completing a response to a question, even if incorrect. Use partially correct or wrong answers as a platform for eliciting clarification, soliciting new information, or redirecting.

- Never use questions as a form of embarrassment or punishment. Such misuse of questions rarely changes misbehavior, and questions are academic tools that should be prized and protected for their chosen purpose. To misuse them or to use them for any other purpose may affect how your questions will be perceived by your students.

For Discussion and Practice

*1. What is the definition of an *effective question* as used in this chapter?

*2. Identify the chain of events that forms the most frequently observed cycle of teacher–student interaction.

*3. Approximately what percentage of all school time may be devoted to questions and answers?

*4. Approximately what percentage of questions asked require simple recall of facts, and approximately what percentage require clarifying, expanding, generalizing, and the making of inferences?

*5. Identify seven specific purposes for asking questions and give an example of each.

*6. In your own words, what is a convergent question and what is a divergent ques-

tion? How do they differ with respect to right answers? How are they the same with respect to wrong answers?

7. Using the same question content, give an example of both a convergent and a divergent question.

*8. Under what circumstances might a divergent question such as "What propulsion systems might airplanes use in the year 2050?" actually function as a convergent question?

*9. Explain under what circumstances a convergent question such as, "What is 2 multiplied by 4?" might actually function as a divergent question.

*10. How does the asking of higher-order questions affect (1) a learner's standardized achievement score, and (2) a learner's use of analysis, synthesis, and evaluation skills in thinking through a problem?

11. Using the same topic, compose a question that is more cognitively complex and another that is less cognitively complex. How do these two questions differ in cues, hints, and advance organizers?

12. Write a brief dialogue, using realistic teacher and student responses, that illustrates a sequence of related questions that funnels student responses.

13. Using Table 8.2 as a guide, compose a sequence of related questions that extend and lift student responses.

14. Using the same content area as above, prepare one question that elicits the appropriate level of behavioral complexity at each level of the cognitive domain—knowledge, comprehension, application, analysis, synthesis, and evaluation.

15. In the context of a brief classroom dialogue, provide one example each of questions that (1) elicit clarification, (2) solicit new information, and (3) redirect or restructure a student's response.

*16. What is meant by the phrase *wait time?* Generally speaking, should beginning teachers work to increase or decrease their wait time?

*17. Identify and give an example of the five most troublesome question-asking problems for the beginning teacher.

18. What is "sociolinguistic" and why is it important in a culturally diverse classroom?

---

* Answers to asterisked questions (*) in this and the other chapters are in Appendix B.

Suggested Readings

Brown, G., & Wragg, E. (1993). *Questioning.* London: Routledge.

An update of research and practice on questioning with many examples of questioning strategies for the classroom.

Dillon, J. T. (1988). *Questioning and teaching: A manual of practice.* New York: Teachers College Press.

A valuable text for the beginning teacher, with many exercises and problems for practicing the fine art of questioning.

Doneau, S. (1987). Soliciting. In M. J. Dunkin (Ed.), *International encyclopedia of teaching and teacher education.* New York: Pergamon.

An overview of the many ways teachers can solicit responses from their students during a lesson.

Hunkins, F. P. (1989). *Teaching thinking through effective questioning.* Boston: Christopher-Gordon.

An excellent reference for learning how to raise questions at higher levels of cognitive complexity.

Redfield, D., & Rousseau, E. (1981). A meta-analysis of experimental research of teacher questioning behavior. *Review of Educational Research, 51,* 237–245.

A comprehensive review of research summarizing the most consistent findings on teacher questioning behavior.

Tobin, K. (1980). The effect of an extended teacher wait-time on science achievement. *Journal of Research in Science Teaching, 17,* 469–475.

An interesting report of research that shows the influence that wait time can have on your students' behavior.

Wilen, W. (1991). *Questioning skills for teachers (3rd ed.).* Washington, DC: NEA.

A revised edition of a practical and classic text on questioning with many specific examples for the elementary and secondary classroom.

CHAPTER 9

Self-Directed Learning

This chapter will help you answer the following questions:

1. What teaching behaviors are required for self-directed learning?
2. How can I effectively demonstrate the mental procedures I want my learners to use?
3. How can I use student errors to enhance learning?
4. How can my learners explore content through classroom dialogue?
5. How do I get learners to accept responsibility for their own learning?
6. Can my learners' inner speech help them to learn?
7. What is the difference between teaching for oral and verbal regurgitation and teaching for problem solving and decision making?
8. What are the steps in teaching self-directed inquiry to individual learners?
9. What are some cognitive learning strategies that can help my learners retain, order, and comprehend new information?
10. How can I engage my learners in problem-based learning?
11. How can I promote the goals of self-directed learning in a culturally diverse classroom?

This chapter will also help you learn the meaning of the following:

    activity structure
anticipatory teaching
cognitive learning strategies
declarative knowledge
functional errors
inner speech
mental modeling
metacognition
problem-based learning
procedural knowledge
reciprocal teaching
teacher-mediated learning
zone of maximum response opportunity

n this chapter on self-directed learning we will study an important method for engaging your students in the learning process. Recall that in Chapter 7 we studied indirect instruction, in which concepts, patterns, and abstractions are learned through the processes of generalization and discrimination. We used the word indirect to indicate that the learner acquires a behavior indirectly by transforming content (facts, rules, and action sequences) into a response that differs both from the original content presented and from any previous responses made by the learner. In chapters 7 and 8 we associated these two characteristics with the goals of constructivism, wherein instruction is designed and sequenced to encourage learners to construct meaning from their own perspective. Recall that constructivist teaching and learning emphasizes direct experience, problem solving, and social interaction while deemphasizing the role of lecturing and "telling."

This chapter carries this approach one step further. Here we show you how to teach learners to go beyond the content given—to think critically, reason, and problem-solve—using a self-directed approach to learning. You will see how to use self-directed strategies to actively engage your students in the learning process and to help them acquire the reasoning, critical thinking, and problem-solving skills required in today's complex society.

>>> SELF-DIRECTED LEARNING <<<

Much of today's classroom learning is focused on activities by which the learner acquires facts, rules, and action sequences. The majority of lessons require outcomes only at the lower levels of behavioral complexity—knowledge, comprehension, and application. This may explain why some national studies of the state of education in the United States (National Governors Association, in Lambert 1991; National Commission on Excellence in Education, 1983) found many students unable to think independently of the teacher or to go beyond the content in their texts and workbooks. These reports suggest that the manner in which most schooling occurs may not be teaching students to become aware of their own learning and to derive their own patterns of thought and meaning from the content presented.

Self-directed learning is an approach to teaching *and* learning that actively engages students in the learning process to acquire outcomes at the higher levels of behavioral complexity. Self-directed learning helps students construct their own understanding and meaning from textual content, and helps them to reason, problem-solve, and think critically about the content.

Self-directed learning requires you to perform several unique teaching functions:

What teaching behaviors are required for self-directed learning?

1. Provide information about when and how to use mental strategies for learning.
2. Explicitly illustrate how to use these strategies to think through solutions to real-world problems.
3. Encourage your learners to become actively involved in the subject matter by going beyond the information given, to restructure it in their own way of thinking and prior understanding.
4. Gradually shift the responsibility for learning to your students through practice exercises, question-and-answer dialogues, and/or discussions that engage them in increasingly complex thought patterns.

Consider the following excerpt, which illustrates how some of these teaching functions might be accomplished in a typical lesson:

— · — · — · — · — · — · — · — · — · — · — · — · — · —

Teacher: (A poem is written on the board; teacher reads it to class)

> Man is but a mortal fool
> When it's hot, he wants it cool
> When it's cool, he wants it hot
> He's always wanting what is not.

Today, I want to illustrate some ways to understand a poem like the one I've just read. This may seem like a simple poem, but its author put a lot of care and meaning into each one of its words. Now, let me give you an approach to studying poems like these and gaining from them the meaning intended by their authors. First, let's identify the key words in this poem. Bobby, what do you think are some of the most important ones?

Bobby: Well, I'd say the word "man" because it's the first.

Teacher: Any others? (still looking at Bobby)

Bobby: Not that I can see.

Teacher: Anita?

Anita: The words "hot" and "cool" have to be important, because they appear twice and they rhyme with the last words of the first and last lines.

Teacher: Any other key words? Rick?

Rick: Well, I think a "mortal fool" is supposed to be telling us something, but I don't know what.

Teacher: Good. So, now we've identified some words we think are especially important for understanding this poem. Why don't we look up in the dictionary the meanings of any of these words we don't know or are unsure of. That will be our second step. Ted, look up the word "mortal" for us, while we begin work on our third step. The third step is to paraphrase what you think this author is saying. Susan, can you paraphrase what he is saying?

Susan: I think he's saying we're always changing our minds and that's why we look so stupid sometimes.

Teacher: We are all human, so we certainly change our minds a lot, don't we? Rhonda looks like she wants to say something. Rhonda?

Rhonda: Well, I'd say it's not that we're stupid that we change our minds, but that it's just part of who we are—we can't help wanting what we can't have.

Teacher: So, you've added a little something to Susan's interpretation. What do you think, Susan? Do you agree?

Susan: Yeah, we're not stupid; we're just mortals.

Teacher: Chris, do you want to add anything?

Chris: I'd say that we're not stupid at all. That to really enjoy something, we must have experienced its opposite—otherwise we wouldn't know how good it is.

Teacher: Now, that brings us to our fourth and last step. Let's try to relate what Chris just said to our own experience. Anyone ready? Bobby?

Bobby: I agree with Chris, because I remember thinking how much I welcomed winter because of how hot it was last summer.

Teacher: (Marcia is waving her hand) Marcia, what do you have to say about this?

Marcia: But, now that it's winter, I can't wait for the cold weather to end, so I can go swimming again. (class nods in agreement)

Teacher: It looks as though Chris was right. We sometimes have to see both sides of something—hot/cold, good/bad, light/dark—to fully appreciate it. Now, Ted, what did you find for "mortal" in the dictionary?

Ted: It says "having caused or being about to cause death," "subject to death," and "marked by vulnerability."

Teacher: Which of those do you think best fits the use of "mortal fool" in our poem?

Ted: Well, hmm . . . the last one, because it kind of goes with what we have been saying about how we choose one thing and then another . . . like when we get too cold, dream of summer, and then when summer comes, think it's too hot.

Teacher: I agree; it fits with what we all have experienced in our lives—and that means we are on the right track to the interpretation the author intended. Now, let's go one step further. Putting all of our ideas together, what is this poet saying? (nodding to Alex)

Alex: Well, I'd say life's a kind of circle. We keep going around and around—back to where we've come, and then trying to escape to where we've been—maybe that's one kind of vulnerability—like it said in the dictionary.

Teacher: That's good thinking, Alex. Bobby, because we began with you, I'll let you have the final word.

Bobby: I think Alex got it, because now I understand why the author thinks we're all fools—we're like a dog going in circles chasing our tails, always wanting what we don't have. That explains the first and the last line, doesn't it? Because we are human, we are vulnerable to always " . . . wanting what is not." Yes, so we're "mortal fools." I get it.

Teacher: Very good. Now, let's think for a moment about the four steps we just went through to understand this poem. I will repeat them slowly while you write them down. They will become your guide for reading the rest of the poems we study.

━ ・ ━ ・ ━ ・ ━ ・ ━ ・ ━ ・ ━ ・ ━ ・ ━ ・ ━ ・ ━ ・ ━

Notice how this teacher contributed something to each of the four components of self-directed learning (how to use mental strategies for learning, how to think through solutions to real-world problems, actively involving learners in the subject, and shifting responsibility for learning to the student).

First, she provided the learners with a mental strategy for learning—in this case a framework of four easy-to-follow steps for interpreting poetry. These steps were sufficiently familiar and practical enough to be followed by almost any student, regardless of ability or experience. Notice that they were not just divisions of the task, but steps that ultimately *force learners to go beyond the content presented* to find their own meaning and understanding, based on personal experience and individual thinking. In other words, there were no wrong answers with this strategy—only answers that could be improved to raise the learner onto the next rung of the learning ladder.

Second, the strategy provided wasn't just routinely given to the learners by listing its steps on the board; the steps were *illustrated in the context of a real problem.* The application was real world and typical of other examples to which they would be asked to apply the strategy.

Third, the learners were invited to become *participants in the learning,* not just passive listeners waiting to be told what to do. By using a question-and-answer dialogue to provide a structure for the learners' opinions and experiences, students became an active part of the process by which new knowledge was being generated. They were, in a sense, their own teachers without knowing it. This was made possible through the format of an unscripted discussion, which removed any fear of producing a wrong response that might have prevented some learners from participating.

And fourth, note that as the lesson evolved, more and more of the most important conclusions were provided by the students, not the teacher. The highest level of interpretation with which the lesson ended came almost entirely from the summarizing remarks of students. By the end of the lesson the teacher's role was more that of a monitor and codiscussant than of an information provider—that role having been assumed by the students themselves as they actively applied each of the steps given earlier in the lesson.

Now let's look more closely at some of the invisible mental strategies that actually can be used by learners to acquire meaning and understanding from text.

>>> METACOGNITION <<<

One invisible strategy for self-directed learning is metacognition. **Metacognition** refers to mental processes that assist learners to reflect on their thinking by internalizing, understanding, and recalling the content to be learned. They include thinking skills such as self-interrogation, self-checking, self-monitoring, and analyzing, as well as memory aids (called *mnemonics*) for classifying and recalling content.

Metacognitive strategies are most easily conveyed to learners through a process called **mental modeling** (Duffy, Roehler, & Herrmann, 1988). This involves using instructional techniques whereby learners increasingly accept responsibility for their own learning by implementing and monitoring a previously modeled way of thinking. Mental modeling involves three important stages (Duffy & Roehler, 1989):

1. Showing students the reasoning involved.
2. Making students conscious of the reasoning involved.
3. Focusing students on applying the reasoning.

These steps usually are carried out through verbal statements that walk learners through the process of attaining a correct solution. They begin with *verbal markers* such as the following:

> "Now, I will show you how to solve this problem by talking out loud as I go through it, identifying exactly what is going on in my mind."

"Think about each decision I make, where I stop to think and what alternatives I choose—as though you are making the same decisions in your own mind."

Notice that the teacher is not giving the learner the mechanics of getting a right answer—do step A, then B, then C—but, more importantly, is providing an actual "live" demonstration of the mental procedures that may lie behind the routine completion of a problem.

Research on what makes a good demonstration (Gage & Berliner, 1992; Good & Brophy, 1987a) indicates that skilled demonstrators of mental procedures do the following:

How can I effectively demonstrate the mental procedures I want my learners to use?

- *Focus the learners' attention.* They begin their demonstration only when the attention of their learners is focused on them. Then, they direct students' attention to the thinking or reasoning skill they want them to learn.
- *Stress the value of the demonstration.* They briefly and concisely point out why their learners should observe what they are about to demonstrate. They relate the thinking skill to the content to be learned.
- *Talk in conversational language while demonstrating.* They back up to cover unfamiliar concepts and repeat actions when needed, use analogies to bridge content gaps, and use examples to reinforce learning. They then probe for understanding.
- *Make the steps simple and obvious.* They break complex actions into simple steps that can be followed one at a time. They point out what to do next and then describe the action as it is being performed by thinking out loud while acting.
- *Help learners remember the demonstration.* They go slow ("Stop me if I'm going too fast"), exaggerate certain actions ("Now I'll ask myself a question"), highlight distinctive features ("Notice where I pause"), and give simple memory aids to help learners retain what they've seen and heard.

These mental procedures help students to internalize, recall, and then generalize problem solutions to different content at a later time. You do not just convey information according to the preceding steps, but actually demonstrate the decision-making process as it occurs within your own thoughts. By contrast, the mechanical memorization of steps rarely helps learners to solve similar problems in other contexts or allows content to be recalled when the present topic has lost its immediate importance (no exam in sight or homework due).

You then monitor the process as it occurs in the learner, provide feedback, and adjust the complexity and flow rate of content as needed. This leads to a second important concept for self-directed learning called mediation.

>>> TEACHER MEDIATION <<<

On-the-spot adjustments to content flow and complexity that you make to accommodate idiosyncratic learning needs are called teacher mediation. Your role during **teacher-mediated learning** is to adjust the instructional dialogue to help students restructure their learning and move them closer to the intended outcome. In other words, the interactive dialogue you provide helps learners construct their *own* meanings from the content. This aids retention and the generalization of the reasoning process to other contexts.

The knowledge or skills that learners are to acquire are not given to them in the form of end products. Instead, you provide the cognitive stimulation at just the proper times for them to acquire the end products through their own reasoning. The need for adjustment of flow and content seldom can be anticipated. It requires mediation—your on-the-spot judgment of what new information would bring a learner's response to the next level of refinement of which the learner is capable at that moment. This next level reflects the content difficulty and behavioral complexity from which the student can most benefit at that moment.

The Zone of Maximum Response Opportunity

This level of content difficulty and behavioral complexity is the learner's **zone of maximum response opportunity.**[1] It is the zone of behavior that, if stimulated by you, will bring a learner's response to the next level of refinement. Thus, your response directed at the zone of maximum response opportunity must be at or near the learner's current level of understanding, but also designed to lift the learner's following response to the next higher level. Your directed response need not elicit the correct answer, because the learner at that precise moment may be incapable of benefiting from it. It should, however, encourage the learner to refine an initially crude response.

---

[1] The zone of maximum response opportunity is called the "zone of proximal development" by Vygotsky (Kozulin, 1990).

Here are two classroom dialogues in which the first teacher hits the "zone of maximum response opportunity," but the second misses it:

Teacher: When you see a proportion, such as ⅘ (writes it on board), think of the number on top as "what is" and the number on the bottom as "what could be." Think about a box of cereal that you make your breakfast from. If I wrote the proportion of cereal in the box as ¾ (writes it on board), I would say to myself, the full box is equal to the number 4—that's the "could be" part. But this morning, after I fixed my breakfast, what's left is only the number 3, which is the "what is" part. That's how I can tell the box is still pretty full, because the number for "what is" is close to the number for "what could be."

Now, Johnny, explain to me what it means when it says on a label that the proportion of vitamin C for one 4-ounce glass of orange juice is ½ the minimum daily requirement.

Johnny: I'm not sure.

Teacher: Okay, what words can we use to describe the number on top?

Johnny: You said it's "what is."

Teacher: What does that mean?

Johnny: I guess it's how much vitamin C is really in the glass.

Teacher: And, now for the bottom.

Johnny: You said the bottom is "what could be." Does that mean that it's all you need?

Teacher: Yes, it does—good. Now, think of another example—one of your own—in which something was less than it could have been.

Johnny: Well, I finished Ms. Enro's social studies test before the end of the period.

Teacher: And how long was the period?

Johnny: Umm, about 40 minutes, I guess.

Teacher: Using our words, what would you call that part of the problem?

Johnny: "What could be." OK, I get it. Then, the time I actually took is what really happened? Yeah, I finished the test in about 20 minutes.

Teacher: So, how would you express that proportion in numbers?

Johnny: It would be 20, for "what is," over 40, for "what could be." The top is half of the bottom, so I guess one glass of orange juice gives you half the vitamin C you need in a day.

Teacher: Okay. Let's retrace the steps you just followed for another problem. . . .

Now let's imagine that Johnny relives this episode in another classroom. After the same introductory remarks, Johnny is asked the identical question:

Teacher: Now, Johnny, explain to me what it means when it says on a label that the proportion of vitamin C for one 4-ounce glass of orange juice is ½ the minimum daily requirement.

Johnny: I'm not sure.

Teacher: Look, if the number 1 is on the top and the number 2 is on the bottom, it must mean the top is less than the bottom. Right?

Johnny: Right.

Teacher: So, if the top number represents what is and the bottom number what could be, "what is" is one half less than "what could be." And, that can only mean the glass contains half of the minimum daily requirement of vitamin C. Got it?

Johnny: Yep.

Well, maybe he does and maybe he doesn't. Notice in the first example that, by retracing the mental steps for Johnny to recall, the teacher hit Johnny's "zone of maximum response opportunity" because his prior understanding and response were taken into account in moving the dialogue forward, closer to the intended goal of the lesson. It provided a peg with which Johnny lifted himself onto the next rung of the learning ladder.

The second teacher simply provided the right answer. This gave Johnny no opportunity to construct *his own* response by using the mental steps provided and thereby derive a process to use for independently arriving at other right answers in similar circumstances. The first teacher focused upon developing for the learner a process of reasoning—a "line of thinking"—that would give the content its own individual meaning and yet be consistent with the intended goal of the lesson.

Through classroom dialogues such as these, you can encourage your learners to construct their own meanings and interpretations, for example, to substitute their own unique constructions for "what is" and "what could be," and to share them with others through discussion and classroom dialogue. Such diversity among self-directed learners activates their unique learning histories, specialized abilities, and personal experiences, thus engaging them in the learning process.

Hitting the Zone of Maximum Response Opportunity

The "zone of maximum response opportunity" is particularly important in self-directed learning, because you can rarely provide the most appropriate response to each learner at all times. This is the key difference between individualized learning (e.g., programmed

Diversity among self-directed learners can be activated by teacher interaction and the "gentle interplay" that taps the learner's zone of maximum response opportunity and provides appropriate steppingstones to higher levels of learning.

instruction) and self-directed learning. In individualized learning, the content writer anticipates the most probable errors and provides remedial or alternative learning routes (called *branching*) for all learners, regardless of their zones of maximum response opportunity. Because the instruction assumes that relatively homogeneous groups of "individual" learners will work through the content, the same types of errors must be anticipated for all learners. In some cases the remedial steps or alternative branching provided may fall within a learner's zone of development, but in some cases it may not.

Because self-directed learning almost always occurs during a student response–teacher reaction sequence, it affords the opportunity to more accurately aim your spoken or written reaction at the learner's zone of maximum response opportunity. However, there can be a variety of teacher reactions that fall within the learner's zone of maximum response opportunity with equal effect. After all, your target is not a point but a zone that in some instances may be as broad as the outfield in a major league ballpark.

In this broad field, a hit is a hit, whether it falls in left field, center field, or right field, as long as it is within the appointed zone.

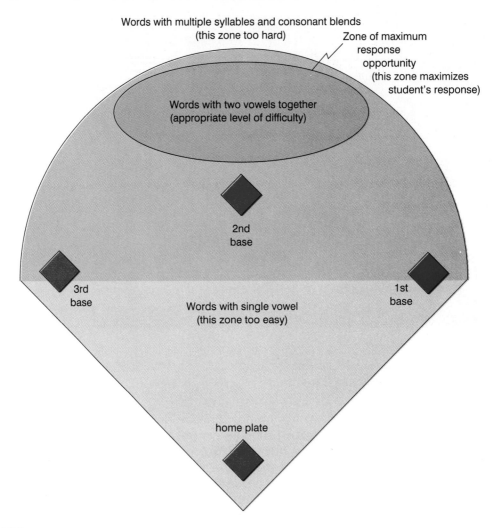

Figure 9.1
The zone of maximum response opportunity for a reading lesson

This is an important point, because aiming your reaction to a student response too sharply—to a fixed point like lower center field—may so restrict your response that it will exclude the learning history, specialized abilities, and personal experiences of the learner. And, it may not consider your own content knowledge, specialized abilities, and instructional style. Figure 9.1 illustrates the zone of maximum response opportunity for a lesson in reading.

Thus, the concept of a zone affords both you and your students some latitude within which to construct and to create meanings and understandings that consider the unique needs of both. In this manner, self-directed learning promotes a "gentle interplay" between the minds of learner and teacher, pulling and pushing each other in a student response–teacher reaction sequence designed to help the learner climb to the next rung of the learning ladder.

>>> FUNCTIONAL FAILURE (STUDENT ERRORS) <<<

Another concept important to self-directed learning is *functional failure.* Student errors play an important role in the "gentle interplay" between learner and teacher. If your reaction promotes an inaccurate and meaningless response, the interplay may not be so gentle, at least not in the learner's mind. But, if your reaction creates (or even intentionally promotes) a student response that is inaccurate *but* meaningful, interplay returns to a gentler state.

The latter condition describes a class of student errors called **functional errors.** Whether these errors are unexpected or are "planted" by you, they enhance the learner's understanding of content. Functional errors provide a logical steppingstone for climbing onto the next rung of the ladder, which may eliminate an erroneous thought process from ever occurring again in the learner's mind. For example, such an error may be necessary so the student will not arrive at the right answer for the wrong reason, thereby compounding the mistake in other contexts.

How can I use student errors to enhance learning?

Consider the following dialogue in which a student error becomes a functional steppingstone to the next level of understanding:

Teacher: As you recall from yesterday, we were studying the reasons behind the Civil War. Does anyone recall under what president of the United States the Civil War began?

Alexis: Our book says Jefferson Davis.

Teacher: Well, it so happens Jefferson Davis was a president at the time. But, that's not the right answer. Now, how do you think Jefferson Davis could be *a* president, but not *the* president of the United States at the time of the Civil War?

Alexis: Well, maybe at the start of the war there were two presidents, Jefferson Davis and someone else.

Teacher: As a matter of fact, there were two presidents, but only one could be President of the United States.

Alexis: Well, if he wasn't President of the United States he must have been president of the other side.
Teacher: But, do you recall the name of the government that represented the "other side?"
Alexis: Yeah, now I remember. It was the Confederacy. It was Lincoln who was the President of the North—which must have been called the United States—and Jefferson Davis, who must have been the President of the South, called the Confederacy. I guess I got confused with all the different names.

Even though the student response was incorrect, this teacher's reaction fell within the zone of maximum response opportunity, because from it directly followed a more correct response. Notice also how the teacher encouraged the learner to supply the answer, using her previous mistake as an aid to obtaining the correct answer. This strategy actually led to information that went beyond the question itself—to putting Jefferson Davis in geographic perspective and in correctly naming the governments representing both North and South.

But, what if this teacher had made a less thoughtful reaction, encouraging not only another inaccurate response but, worse, a blind alley not useful for refining or extending the student's initial response? What might such a reaction look like?

Teacher: Does anyone recall under what President of the United States the Civil War began?
Alexis: Our book says Jefferson Davis.
Teacher: I said President of the United States, not President of the Confederate States of America. See the difference?
Alexis: I guess so.
Teacher: Well, OK. Then, let's go on to Mark.

The interplay here becomes considerably less gentle, as the specter of failure is left hanging over the learner and the teacher has no easy way out of this awkward ending.

Self-directed learning requires considerable **anticipatory teaching.** This means you respond to the learner at the learner's current level of understanding, to promote a student response, correct *or* incorrect, that is functional for moving to the next rung of understanding on the way to the intended goal of the lesson. This is why scripted approaches to instruction (like programmed instruction), although useful in certain contexts, cannot replace the gentle interplay between student response and teacher reaction, supported by the classroom dialogue and group discussion methods of self-directed learning.

>>> RECIPROCAL TEACHING <<<

One way you can apply self-directed learning in your classroom is with a strategy called **reciprocal teaching** (Palincsar, 1987). Reciprocal teaching provides opportunities to explore the content to be learned via classroom dialogue. At the center of reciprocal teaching are group discussions in which you and your students take turns as leader in discussing the text.

Slavin (1990a) observed that most classroom discussions amount to little more than recitation of facts by students with the aid of question-and-answer sequences in which all or most of the answers are known. This leaves little opportunity for students to construct their own meaning and content interpretation so they can attain higher levels of understanding. In practice, many classroom discussions promote little meaningful dialogue that actually helps students struggle with the adequacy of their ideas and opinions on their way to arriving at acceptable solutions. More often, these discussions are driven by text content, with rapid-fire questions that stay close to the facts as presented in the text.

How can my learners explore content through classroom dialogue?

Reciprocal teaching is a strategy to make such a typical discussion into a more productive and self-directed learning experience. It accomplishes this through four activities—predicting, questioning, summarizing, and clarifying. These unfold into the following sequence, described by Palincsar and Brown (1989):

- *Predicting*—discussion begins by generating predictions about the content to be learned from the text, based on:
    - (a) its title or subheading in the text,
    - (b) the group's prior knowledge or information pertaining to the topic, and
    - (c) experience with similar kinds of information.

    Following the group's predictions about what they expect to learn from the text, the group reads and/or listens to a portion of it.
- *Questioning*—one individual is chosen to lead a discussion of each portion of the text that is read. Afterward, the discussion leader asks questions about the information. Students respond to the questions and raise additional questions.
- *Summarizing*—the discussion leader then summarizes the text and other students are invited to comment or elaborate on the summary.

- *Clarifying*—if points in the text were unclear (e.g., concepts or vocabulary), they are discussed until clarity is achieved. In this case, more predictions may be made and portions of the text reread for greater clarity.

The following dialogue (based on Palincsar & Brown, 1989) illustrates the four activities of predicting, questioning, summarizing, and clarifying that comprise reciprocal teaching:

Teacher: (reading from text) "The pipefish change their color and movements to blend with their surroundings. For example, pipefish that live among green plants change their color to a shade of green to match the plants."

Claire: (leading the discussion) One question that I had about this paragraph is: What is special about the way the pipefish looks?

Teacher: (clarifying) Do you mean the way that it is green?

Andy: (elaborating) It's not just that it's green, it's that it's the same color as the plants around it, all around it.

Claire: (continuing) Yes, that's it. My summary of this part tells how the pipefish looks and that it looks like what is around it. My prediction is that this is about its enemies and how it protects itself and who the enemies are.

Monty: (adding to the summary) They also talked about how the pipefish moves . . .

Keith: (rejoining) It sways back and forth . . .

Andy: (adding) . . . along with the other plants.

Teacher: (questioning) What do we call it when something looks like and acts like something else? The way we saw the insect called a "walking stick" yesterday? We clarified this word when we talked about the walking stick.

Angel: Mimic.

Teacher: That's right. We said we would say that the pipefish mimics the . . .

Students: (together) . . . plants.

Teacher: OK! Let's see if Claire's predictions come true. (class turns to the text)

Notice in this discussion how the teacher supports student participation in the dialogue. The teacher's aim is to engage as many students as possible in the learning process by providing reactions to student responses that are in their zones of maximum response opportunity. This is accomplished by elaborating on student responses and allowing ample opportunity for students to participate in the dialogue, from their perspective. This gives the teacher ample data upon which to form a reaction that is within their zone of maximum response opportunity.

As the discussion continues, more responsibility for reading and developing the dialogue is given over to the students until, over time, the teacher becomes more of an advisor—or coach—who refines responses instead of providing them. At that point, more and more of the discussion represents the internalization of the text by the students, who now express it through their unique learning histories, specialized abilities, and experiences.

The ultimate goal of reciprocal teaching is to sufficiently engage students in the learning process so that they become conscious of their reasoning process. This occurs through their own and other students' modeling, and the teacher's modeling of that process, and is refined in the context of classroom dialogues. This requires your continuous attention to the ongoing dialogue and to the meanings students are deriving from the text so you can continually adjust the instructional content to meet your learners' current level of understanding.

As students gradually accept the shift in responsibility from teacher to student, you reduce the amount of explaining, explicitness of cues, and prompting that may have marked the earlier part of the lesson. Figure 9.2 indicates some classroom activities that can guide the gradual shift of responsibility from teacher to learner during self-directed learning.

How do I get learners to accept responsibility for their own learning?

Palincsar and Brown (1989) summarize the teacher's role during reciprocal teaching:

- The teacher and students share responsibility for acquiring the strategies employed in reciprocal teaching.
- The teacher initially assumes major responsibility for teaching these strategies ("thinks aloud" how to make a prediction, how to ask a question, how to summarize, how to clarify), but gradually transfers responsibility to the students for demonstrating use of the strategies.
- All students are expected to participate in the discussion and are given the opportunity to lead it. The teacher encourages participation by supporting students through prompting, providing additional information, or raising/lowering the demand on students so that responses meaningful to learners will be achieved.
- Throughout each self-directed lesson, the teacher consciously monitors how successfully comprehension is occurring and adjusts the content as needed to the zone of maximum response opportunity.

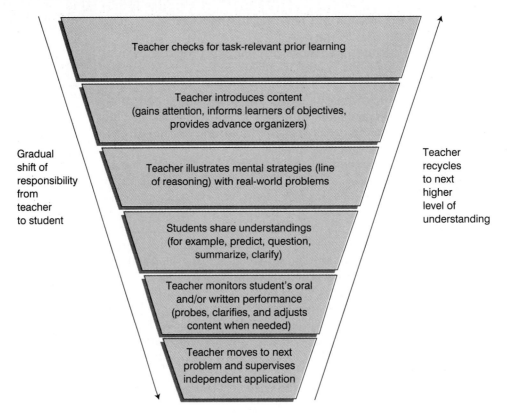

Gradual shift of responsibility from teacher to student

Teacher recycles to next higher level of understanding

Figure 9.2
Shifting responsibility from teacher to learners

>>> SOCIAL DIALOGUE <<<

As we have seen in the preceding dialogues, classroom conversation between teacher and students is central to self-directed learning. Verbal interactions within a classroom are vastly different from those occurring outside of it. In many classrooms, verbalizations are adult dominated, leaving students with little alternative but to respond to teacher requests for facts and information. These traditional teaching settings may offer few opportunities for students to elaborate or comment on the topic at hand.

However, self-directed learning strategies use classroom dialogue differently. Instead of verbalizations intended to confirm the teacher's authority, classroom dialogue is purposefully guided to gradually shift responsibility to the learner. The teacher "scaffolds," building the dialogue layer by layer, each time increasing the challenge to the learner to think independently of earlier constructions provided by the teacher.

Scaffolding must be done carefully to keep the challenge within the learner's zone of maximum response opportunity. This requires the following:

Your close monitoring of the learner's response

Your awareness of the learner's current functioning level (for example, familiarity with the task)

Your awareness of the understanding level the learner can attain at the moment (based on, for example, past learning performance)

Attention to these details lets you scaffold the cognitive demands placed on the learner. You do so to increasingly shift the learner from responding to textual material to internalizing its meaning by elaborating, extending, and commenting upon it.

As we have seen, the strategy of reciprocal teaching uses group discussion and rotating discussion leaders to achieve this goal. It does so not just by getting students to talk, as do many traditional discussions, but by getting them to expose and elaborate the *processes* by which they are learning the content. The clear articulation and rehearsal of these mental strategies (1) guides the learner in subsequent performances and (2) helps you adjust the flow and level of prompts, cues, and questions to hit inside the zone of maximum response opportunity.

>>> THE ROLE OF INNER SPEECH <<<

As we have seen, an important aspect of classroom dialogue in self-directed learning is the increasing responsibility it places on the learner for creating original verbalizations in the form of comments, elaborations, and extensions. These verbalizations, if properly scaffolded, are believed to create an "inner speech" within the learner (Vygotsky, 1962). This **inner speech** ultimately leads to private internal dialogue that takes the place of the teacher's prompts and questions and self-guides the learner through similar problems.

Can my learners' inner speech help them to learn?

As the responsibility for unique and original productions beyond the text gradually shifts to the learner, the learner increasingly acquires the ability to speak internally, modeling the same line of reasoning and mimicking the same types of questions, prompts, and cues used by the teacher at an earlier stage. In other words, the

Outward verbalizations by the learner, if properly scaffolded, can be turned into inner speech that eventually replaces the teacher's prompts and self-guides the learner through similar problems.

verbal interactions that were increasingly asked of the learner become internalized in a form of private speech used by the learner in the absence of direct teacher involvement.

It is at this point that the teacher's role turns to one of monitoring, prompting and cuing only when necessary to keep students on track. Ultimately, it is hoped that by internalizing the scaffold verbalizations of the teacher and recalling them at will in private dialogue, students become their own teachers, mimicking the logic and reasoning process modeled by the teacher. As we shall see in the following chapter (Cooperative Learning and the Collaborative Process), such self-direction can be stimulated by many different techniques in addition to reciprocal teaching, including many forms of cooperative and group learning.

The role of inner speech in guiding the behavior of both children and adults is central to self-directed learning strategies. The topic has long been a research interest and considerable evidence documents its usefulness in learning (Berk, 1993; Wiertsch, 1980; Bruner, 1978).

Although we adults seldom realize it, we often use inner speech to guide our actions. Most notably, when taking examinations, learners young and old verbally think through previously learned steps to obtain correct answers. During exams we talk to ourselves just as we talked ourselves through the same steps the night before, or were asked by our teacher to verbalize them before the class. These verbalizations gradually turn inward, from class discussions or recitations to private discussions with ourselves.

They become inner guideposts for thinking through and reasoning solutions to problems, using a process first modeled by a teacher and then gradually shifted to us through scaffolded verbalizations that "fade out" some portions of the model, requiring us to "pick them up" internally and to apply them on our own. This occurs most notably when the teacher no longer accepts regurgitations of the factual material in the text but begins to require their internalization through elaborations, comments, and extensions in our own unique constructions.

>>> SAMPLE DIALOGUES OF <<<
SELF-DIRECTED LEARNING

Let's look at three classroom dialogues that exhibit characteristics of self-directed inquiry. In different teaching contexts, these dialogues illustrate the following:

- How a teacher models the process by which meaning and understanding can be derived from textual material.
- How questions, prompts, and cues can be used to scaffold responses, gradually shifting the responsibility for learning to the student.
- How the teacher thereafter can monitor student responses for continued understanding.

First, let's look at a fourth-grade classroom in which Ms. Koker is teaching reading. We'll observe how she models the process by which meaning and understanding can be derived from text. Our discussion begins with Ms. Koker reading an excerpt from a short story to the class from the daily reader:

Ms. Koker: "Some of the coldest climate on earth occurs in the northern parts of Alaska. In this land, a small but hardy group of Native Americans lives and prospers in small villages where hunting and fishing is a way of life. This small group of villagers . . . "

Debbie: (interrupting) Ms. Koker, I don't know what the word "hardy" means.

Ms. Koker: What do you think it means, Debbie? (asking her to make a prediction)

Debbie:	Well, something that's hard—like, maybe, ice.
Ms. Koker:	Let's see if you are right. Let's think of some other words that might mean almost the same thing as "hard." (introducing the idea of synonyms)
Tim:	Something that's hard is strong.
Mickey:	Yeah, and it also lasts a long time.
Ann:	If you're strong, you can't be hurt.
Ms. Koker:	OK, now let's see if any of these ideas fit with the sentence, "In this land a small but hardy group of Native Americans lives and prospers in small villages where hunting and fishing is a way of life." What do you think, Tim? (encouraging the idea of fitting synonyms into the text to clarify meaning)
Tim:	Well, if we took the word "hardy" out and put in the word "strong," I think it would mean the same thing.
Ms. Koker:	What do you think, Barbara?
Barbara:	It makes sense, because when you're strong you can't be hurt—say by all the cold up north—and then you live a long time. (summarizing)
Mickey:	But, how do we know they live a long time, just because they're strong? (asking for clarification)
Ms. Koker:	That's a good point; we really don't know that yet, so what do you think? (calling for a prediction again)
Tina:	I think they won't live as long as us because of all the cold weather.
Ms. Koker:	So, how do you think they stay warm? Let's read on to see.

Notice that Ms. Koker was modeling a strategy for deriving meaning from text. To accomplish this, she introduced the idea of synonyms—by asking Debbie what she thought the word *hardy* meant and then by asking her students to insert the synonym into the text to check its appropriateness. Thus, she was conveying a model—a mental strategy—that can be used time and again by the students themselves, unaided by the teacher, whenever a word is unknown to them.

Next, let's observe Mr. Willis' junior high science class to see how he uses questions, prompts, and cues to encourage self-direction. In the following discussion, Mr. Willis is teaching a fundamental law of physics by providing questions and reactions that are scaffolded to his learners' zones of maximum response opportunity:

Mr. Willis:	Here you see a balloon, a punching bag, and a tire pump. Watch carefully as I let the air out of the balloon (lets air out), punch the bag (punches it), and press down on the pump handle (pushes handle). What did you notice about all three actions? Bobby?

Bobby: You got tired. (class laughs)

Mr. Willis: You're right, especially when I did the punching and pumping. (Then, reaching to Bobby's current level of understanding:) Yes, you saw a reaction in me; I got tired. What other action did you see?

Bobby: The balloon flitted across the room.

Mr. Willis: And, what else?

Bobby: The punching bag moved forward—and, well the pump handle went down and then a little up.

Mr. Willis: You saw several reactions, didn't you. What were they?

Bobby: Something happened to the object you were playing with and . . . well . . . I guess something else was going on too.

Mr. Willis: Anita, what did you see in all three cases?

Anita: Movement in two directions, I think.

Mr. Willis: What were the movements?

Anita: Well, for the balloon, it went forward, but also it pushed the air backward . . . over your face. And, for the punching bag, it went forward . . . umph (mimics the sound) . . . and stopped. I don't know what other movement there was.

Mr. Willis: (pushing to the next higher level of understanding now:) Think about what happened both after *and* before I punched the bag. To help you, write on the top of a piece of paper the words "before" and "after." Now, write down what you saw in each of these three instances—the balloon, the punching bag and the pump. Let's all take a minute to do this.

Anita: (after about a minute) Now I remember. The punching bag came back to hit your hand again. That was the second movement.

Mr. Willis: (checking for understanding among the others) And, what about the tire pump? Michael, you have your hand up.

Michael: When you pushed the pump handle down to inflate the tire, it came back up a little.

Mr. Willis: Yes, in each case there were two identifiable movements—which we will call an *action* and a *reaction*. Now, let's check to see if this is true for some other movements by identifying on your paper the action and reactions associated with the following. I'll say them slowly so you have time to write:

> The space shuttle taking off from Cape
>   Canaveral
> An automobile moving down the street
> A gunshot
> A football being kicked over a goalpost

Notice how Mr. Willis used questions targeted to his students' current level of understanding. This allowed them to respond in some meaningful way, which gave him the opportunity to build upon an earlier incomplete response to reach the next higher level of understanding. For example, Bobby's first crude response, aided by the prompt "What other action did you see?" was used to introduce the concept of action followed by a reaction. Each time the questioning turned to a new student, Mr. Willis' question, prompt, or cue was targeted higher, but still within the learners' zone of maximum response opportunity.

Also, the idea of thinking through a solution on paper—called *think sheets*—kept students actively engaged in working through their responses. At the same time, it provided a strategy from which they might more easily derive actions and reactions for the new problems presented at the end of the dialogue. Mr. Willis' use of questions, prompts, and cues at various levels of difficulty kept this class moving through the lesson with increasingly more sophisticated responses.

What is the difference between teaching for oral and verbal regurgitation and teaching for problem solving and decision making?

Now, let's look in on a third classroom. Mrs. LeFluir is teaching Spanish to a high school class not just by altering the level of questioning, as did Mr. Willis, but by altering the tasks from which learners experience the application of content first hand. Without realizing it, Mrs. LeFluir's class is experiencing the difference between **declarative knowledge**—knowledge intended for oral or verbal regurgitation—and **procedural knowledge**—knowledge intended to be used in some problem-solving or decision-making task:

Mrs. LeFluir: Today, we will study the gender of nouns. In Spanish all nouns are either masculine or feminine. Nouns ending in *o* are generally masculine, and those ending in *a* are generally feminine. Tisha, can you identify the following nouns as either masculine or feminine? (writes on board)

> libro
> pluma
> cuaderno
> gramática

Tisha: (correctly identifies each)
Mrs. LeFluir: Now, let's see how you identified each of the words and what each word means.
Tisha: Well, I followed the rule that if it ends in an *o* it will be masculine but if it ends in an *a*, it will be feminine. I think the words are book, pen, notebook, and grammar.
Mrs. LeFluir: Good. Now for the next step, you've all used indefinite articles *a* and *an* many times in your speaking and writing. In Spanish the word *un* is used for *a* or *an* before a masculine noun, and *una* is used for *a* or *an* before a feminine noun. In Spanish the article is repeated before each noun. Now, using the vocabulary

words on the board, let's place the correct form of the indefinite article in front of each word. (shifting the task demand:) Why don't you take the first one, Ted?

Ted: It would be *un libro*.

Mrs. LeFluir: Mary.

Mary: *Una pluma.*

Mrs. LeFluir: Bob and Mike, take the next two.

Bob: *Un cuaderno.*

Mike: *Una gramática.*

Mrs. LeFluir: OK. Now, we are ready to put our knowledge to work. I will give you a sentence in English and you translate it into Spanish, being sure to include the correct form of the indefinite article. (shifting the task demand again:) For this you will need to remember your vocabulary from last week. If you need to, look up the words you forgot. Mark, let's start with you. Come up to the board and write: Do you want a book?

Mark: (writes on board) *Desea usted un libro?*

Mrs. LeFluir: Good. And how did you decide to use *un* instead of *una?*

Mark: The noun ended in *o.*

Mrs. LeFluir: (Continues with three other examples)

> Do you need grammar?
> Do you want to study a language?
> Do you need a notebook?
> (After the students respond, she shifts the task demand again by moving to the following activity:) Now, read each sentence on the transparency and write down the correct form of the indefinite article that goes before the noun. (shows transparency)
>
> Yo necesito _____ gramática.
> Nosotros estudiamos _____ lengua.
> Necesita Tomás _____ libro?
> Es _____ pluma?

(After the students respond, she moves to a final activity and yet another task demand:) Now for the following sentences, I will speak in English, and I want you to repeat the same sentence entirely in Spanish. Be sure, once again, to include the correct form of the indefinite article....

Notice in this episode the different activities required of the students and how they differ in cognitive complexity. Mrs. LeFluir gradually changed the demands being placed upon her learners by shifting the tasks to which they were to respond. Her lesson began by asking only for the simple regurgitation of rules (declarative knowledge), but ended by engaging students in oral delivery of the kind that might be required in ultimately having a conversation in Spanish (procedural knowledge). She gradually shifted her tasks from declarative to procedural *in small enough degrees* to assure that all her students, or at least most of them, could follow.

This process also conveyed a language-learning model that will be helpful in subsequent contexts by providing a learning strategy that flows from memorization of rules and vocabulary, through completion and fill-in, to oral delivery. Notice that this sequence was completed even for this elementary lesson. This tells the learners that oral and written delivery, and not the regurgitation of rules, is the end goal to which all previous learning must contribute and toward which they must strive in their own individual learning and practice.

What are the steps in teaching self-directed inquiry to individual learners?

The systematic varying of task demands within a unit comprises an **activity structure.** Activity structures are most effective for self-directed learning when they vary the demands or problems being placed on the learner in ways that gradually require the learner to assume responsibility for learning the content at a higher level of understanding.

You can use the following steps in teaching self-directed inquiry to individual learners:

- Provide a new learning task and observe how the student approaches it (for example, reading a short selection in a history text that will be the basis for an essay exam).
- Ask the student to explain how she or he approaches the task of learning the textual information—for example, in preparation for the exam. (This helps the student analyze her or his own cognitive approach.)
- Describe and model a more effective procedure for organizing and accomplishing the task. For example, explain and demonstrate how to use the study questions at the end of the selection to help focus reading; highlight the main ideas in each paragraph of the selection with a fluorescent marker; write outline notes of key points on a separate sheet or on note cards as a study guide for later review. This gives the student new strategies for cognitively organizing the learning task.
- Provide the student with another, similar learning task for practicing the new cognitive strategies. Observe as the student proceeds with the task, giving reminders and corrective feedback.
- Model self-questioning behavior as you demonstrate analysis of a similar problem. For example, "What are the key questions you will need to answer?" or "What is the main idea in

this paragraph?" Write such questions on a small card for the student to use as a reminder.

- Provide another opportunity for the student to practice the skills using self-direction, decreasing your role as monitor.
- Check the result of the learning task by questioning for comprehension and asking the student to recall the specific learning strategies used.

>>> OTHER COGNITIVE STRATEGIES <<<

When you use a mental strategy to help you learn on your own, you have learned what psychologists call a **cognitive learning strategy.** Cognitive learning strategies are general methods of thinking that improve learning across a variety of subject areas. They accomplish this by helping the learner to retain incoming information (called *reception*), recall task-relevant prior knowledge (called *availability*), and build logical connections among incoming knowledge (called *activation*). These strategies include mnemonics (memory aids), elaboration/organization (for example, notetaking), comprehension-monitoring strategies, and problem-solving strategies (Goetz, Alexander, & Ash, 1992). Let's take a look at each of these.

What are some cognitive learning strategies that can help my learners retain, order, and comprehend new information?

Mnemonics

Cognitive psychologists such as Bruner (1966) and Ausubel (1968) advocate that teachers organize their lessons around a limited set of powerful ideas, called *key understandings* and *principles* (Brophy, 1992). Nevertheless, they recognize that all learners will have to learn facts as well in order to grasp the major ideas. These may be number facts, dates, names, rules, classifications, and so on. Bradsted and Stumpf (1982) describe several strategies that can aid the mental organization and retention of such facts.

Jingles or Trigger Sentences.   Jingles or trigger sentences can cue sequential letters, patterns, or special historical dates. For example, most music students learn some variation of the sentence, "Every Good Boy Does Fine," to recall the musical notes EGBDF on the lines of a music treble staff. "Spring forward, fall backward" helps one remember which way to adjust clocks at the spring and autumn time changes. And, many school children learn that, "In fourteen hundred and ninety-two, Columbus sailed the ocean blue." Such devices also can be used for recalling the steps of a mental strategy.

Narrative Chaining.   Narrative chaining is the process of weaving a list of key words you wish to remember into a brief story. For example, if you need to memorize the life cycle of a butterfly in sequence, including the key stages of egg, larva, pupa, and adult, you could invent a narrative such as the following:

> This morning I cooked an *egg* for breakfast, but I heated it so long that it looked like molten *lava* from a volcano. A *pupil* from a nearby school stopped by, and when he saw my egg-turned-*lava*, he yelled, "I'm just a *pupil!* You're the *adult!* Couldn't you cook an egg better than that?"

In this case, *lava* and *pupil* sound enough like *larva* and *pupa* to trigger memory of the correct words in the life cycle sequence.

Number Rhyme or Peg Word.   A number-rhyme or peg-word mnemonic system uses words that rhyme with a sequence of numbers as a basis for developing imaginative mental pictures that assist in memorizing a set of other, less related words.

Using the life cycle of the butterfly as an example again, you might employ the number-rhyme system this way:

one-sun	Imagine a big, fried *egg* hanging in the sky overhead in place of a brightly shining sun.
two-stew	Imagine a bubbling stew erupting from a gigantic volcano under the fried egg, drying to form molten *lava.*
three-sea	Imagine a tiny, screaming *pupil* afloat on a swirling, angry sea where the hot lava sizzles as it meets the seawater.
four-door	Imagine a golden door in the side of the volcano that is opened by a gentle, helpful *adult* who reaches out to pull the pupil from the sea near the lava that was heated by the egg-like sun.

Chunking.   Chunking or grouping bits of information into sets of five to seven discrete pieces also can assist in memorization. If this is combined by chunking the data into logical categories, the information is then doubly processed in a mental framework for improved recall. A common example is memorizing a grocery list by splitting it into logical categories (dairy products, vegetables, beverages, etc.) of several items each. Teaching students to employ such mental organizers gives them creative alternatives by which to manipulate ideas and information and retain mental strategies for learning, thus internally reinforcing their own learning.

Elaboration/Organization (Notetaking)

Elaboration involves teaching learners how to build internal connections between new knowledge and existing knowledge. Organization entails showing your learners how to order and systematize new information so that they can remember it and use it efficiently (Mayer, 1987). The most practical way to help your learners elaborate and organize new knowledge is to teach them how to take notes (Goetz et al., 1992).

Notetaking can improve information processing in several ways. It enhances reception by prompting learners to attend better to what they are hearing or seeing. Furthermore, notetaking assists activation by helping learners make internal connections among information and building a network of external connections with information in memory. You can give your learners several suggestions to help them take notes:

- Read the text before the lesson. This provides advance organizers for the new information.
- Watch for signals that indicate important information (gestures, key words, cues to the organization of the information).
- Write down the big ideas, not isolated facts. Try to be selective and not write down everything.
- When needed, use a more free-form outline format, called *webbing,* using pictures, arrows, and code letters. See Figure 9.3 for an example of webbing.
- Write down examples and questions as you listen.
- Leave blanks or some other prompt to indicate what you missed.
- Review your notes as soon as possible.

Comprehension Monitoring

Comprehension monitoring is a strategy wherein students learn to evaluate their own understanding by frequently checking their own progress during the course of a lesson. Brown (1980) used a strategy based on the reciprocal teaching method described earlier for helping poor as well as good readers understand. Teachers modeled for learners the following three skills:

1. Surveying the text and *making predications* about what it says.
2. *Asking questions* about the main idea of the text as it is being read.

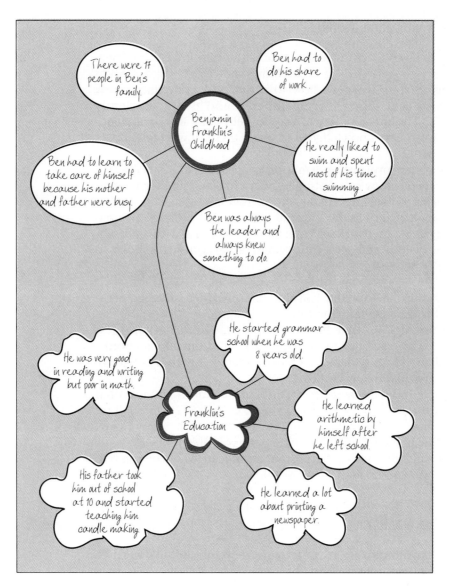

Figure 9.3
Webbing

From Dansereau, D. F. (1988). "Cooperative Learning Strategies." In C. F. Weinstein, E. T. Goetz, and P. A. Alexander (Eds.). *Learning and Study Strategies: Issues in Assessment, Instruction and Evaluation,* pp. 103–120. San Diego: Academic Press. Reprinted by permission.

3. Becoming aware of unclear passages by *monitoring one's own understanding*, asking: "Do I understand what I just read?"

Learners who used this strategy increased their reading comprehension from 50 to 80 percent after only four weeks of instruction. Comprehension monitoring strategies have in common the following skills:

- Setting goals: "What do I have to do?" "Why am I doing this?"
- Focusing attention: "What am I supposed to read?" "What activity must I complete?"
- Self-reinforcement: "Great, I understand this. Keep up the good work." "This strategy really works."
- Coping with problems: "I don't really understand this. I should go back and read it again." "That's a simple mistake. I can fix that."

Problem Solving

Cognitive learning strategists recommend that the school curriculum in most subject areas be organized around real-life problems that learners work on for days or weeks. According to some, we now have curricula isolated by disciplines (algebra, biology, geography, etc.) that identify lists of topics, facts, and skills to be covered by the end of a semester. Such curricula typically place learners in a relatively passive role and encourage rote or nonmeaningful learning.

As an alternative to this approach, growing numbers of educators advocate a type of learning called **problem-based learning** (Blumenfeld et al., 1991). Problem-based learning organizes the curriculum around loosely structured problems (Goetz et al., 1992) that learners solve by using knowledge and skills from several disciplines. Recall that we introduced this general approach to unit planning in Chapter 5 under the topic of interdisciplinary thematic units.

In order to benefit from problem-based learning, however, learners must know how to problem-solve. Since problem solving is a cognitive learning strategy in which few learners receive systematic instruction, teachers increasingly will be called upon to teach this skill to their learners.

There are many systems for solving problems that you may teach to learners (Mayer, 1987). These methods are generalizable to all curriculum areas and to a variety of problems, be they well-defined problems (such as the word problems typically seen in math curricula), or ill-defined problems with no one answer, many solution paths, and for which the nature of the problem shifts as learners work on them.

How can I engage my learners in problem-based learning?

One such problem-solving system is called IDEAL (Bransford & Steen, 1984). IDEAL involves five stages of problem solving:

1. *I*dentify the problem. Learners must first know what the problem or problems are before they can solve them. During this stage of problem solving learners ask themselves if they understand what the problem is and if they have stated it clearly.
2. *D*efine terms. During this stage the learner checks that he or she understands what each word in the problem statement means.
3. *E*xplore strategies. At this point in the IDEAL process, learners compile relevant information and try out strategies to solve the problem. This can involve options such as drawing diagrams, working backwards to solve a math or reading comprehension problem, or breaking complex problems into manageable units.
4. *A*ct on the strategy. Once learners have explored a variety of strategy options, they now use one.
5. *L*ook at the effects. During this final stage, learners ask themselves whether they have come up with an acceptable solution.

Teachers who incorporate cognitive strategies into their lessons have two broad goals: (1) enhancing learner acquisition of knowledge (declarative, procedural, metacognitive), and (2) enhancing cognitive processes (reception, availability, activation). They accomplish these goals when they design instruction that helps learners when they are studying and participating in lessons. They further increase the likelihood of achieving these two cognitive goals when they teach cognitive learning strategies (mnemonics, elaboration/organization, comprehension monitoring, and problem solving) to their students.

>>> PROMOTING THE GOALS OF SELF-DIRECTED <<< LEARNING IN THE CULTURALLY DIVERSE CLASSROOM

The work of Palincsar and Brown (1989) and Bowers and Flinders (1991) have underscored two important dimensions of the teacher's role in modifying classroom dialogue to foster the goals of self-directed learning in a culturally diverse classroom. One of these is that of teacher mediation—on-the-spot adjustments made by the teacher to extend or refocus a student response to move the learner to the next rung of the learning ladder. The second dimension is mental modeling—the active demonstration of strategies by which students can better learn and retain the content taught.

As we have seen in this chapter, teacher-mediated learning comprises adjustments in the level of content and pacing during a lesson for which the learner is an active participant. In teacher-mediated learning, more learners are encouraged to participate in the question-answer dialogue of the classroom, since the content and pacing is continually being adjusted to each participant's current level of understanding. Typically, researchers have found that student success rate (frequency of correct responses) increases during teacher-mediated dialogues compared with a traditional lesson in which the teacher conveys content exclusively through explaining and lecturing (Floden, 1991).

The explanation for these findings derives from the research on meaningful verbal learning (Ausubel, 1968) in which learners, given the opportunity to construct their own interpretations and meanings from content, were able to retain content longer and more easily generalize it to new contexts. The role of the teacher in these learning contexts was to take the acquired interpretations, experiences, and meanings expressed by learners to the next level of refinement through the use of followup questions, probes, and the responses of other learners. Thus, the teacher's response to a correct answer, a correct but hesitant answer, an incorrect or partially correct answer, or a careless answer could be chosen on the basis of the specific needs of the learner.

These results have been applied to the culturally diverse classroom through various forms of social interaction that encourage students to construct their own meanings and interpretations, and revise and extend them under the guidance of the teacher. As we have seen, among the techniques for promoting the concept of teacher mediation are reciprocal teaching (Palincsar & Brown, 1989) and problem-based learning (Blumenfeld et al., 1991). Both of these strategies involve the teacher eliciting student responses at the student's current level of understanding based on personal experiences with, assumptions about, and predictions from the content to be taught.

With these and similar self-directed approaches to learning, you will be able to support the participation of all your learners in the dialogue of the classroom. Your aim should be to engage as many students as possible in the learning process by providing reactions to student responses that are in their zones of maximum response opportunity. This can be accomplished by (1) adjusting the flow and complexity of content to meet individual learner needs, (2) offering

How can I promote the goals of self-directed learning in a culturally diverse classroom?

ample opportunity for all students to participate in the dialogue *from their perspective,* and (3) providing cognitive strategies with which they can better learn and remember the content taught. You can achieve these goals by asking yourself the following questions:

- Has my instruction been focused within my learners' zones of maximum response opportunity? Are learners bored because they have already mastered these skills or frustrated because the skills are beyond what they can be expected to learn?
- Has my instruction been too solitary? Have I met my learners' social learning needs by allowing for sufficient conversation, public reasoning, shared problem solving, and cooperative projects that reproduce the culture in which they spend the most time?
- Have I been expecting learners to acquire knowledge that is incompatible with their cultures? Do I use instructional methods that are culturally unfamiliar, irrelevant, or contradictory?

Summing Up

This chapter introduced you to strategies for self-directed learning. Its main points were as follows:

1. Self-directed learning is an approach to teaching and learning that actively engages students in the learning process for the purpose of acquiring outcomes at higher levels of cognitive complexity.

2. Self-directed learning involves the following sequence of activities:

- Providing information about when and how to use mental strategies for learning.
- Illustrating how the strategies are to be used in the context of real problems.
- Providing students the opportunity to restructure content in terms of their own ways of thinking and prior understandings.
- Gradually shifting the responsibility for learning to students through activities (exercises, dialogues, discussions) that engage them in increasingly complex patterns of thought.

3. *Metacognition* is a strategy for self-directed learning that assists learners in internalizing, understanding, and recalling the content to be learned.

4. Metacognitive strategies include self-interrogation, self-checking, self-monitoring, and techniques for classifying and recalling content, called *mnemonics.*

5. Metacognitive strategies are taught through mental modeling in which learners are "walked through" the process of attaining a correct solution. Mental modeling includes the following:

- Illustrating for students the reasoning involved.
- Making them conscious of it.
- Focusing learners on the application of the reasoning illustrated.

6. *Teacher mediation* is the teacher's on-the-spot adjustment of content flow rate and complexity to accommodate the individual learning needs of the student.

7. The role of teacher mediation is to adjust the instructional dialogue as needed to help the learner restructure what is being learned according to his or her unique abilities, learning history, and personal experiences.

8. A *zone of maximum response opportunity* represents the level of content difficulty and behavioral complexity from which the learner can most benefit at the moment a response is given.

9. The zone of maximum response opportunity is reached through a classroom dialogue in which the teacher provides reactions to student responses that activate the unique learning histories, specialized abilities, and personal experiences of the learner from which individual meanings and interpretations of the content can be acquired.

10. Functional errors are incorrect or partially correct answers made by the learner that can enhance the meaning and understanding of content and provide a logical steppingstone for climbing onto the next rung of the learning ladder.

11. Reciprocal teaching provides opportunities to explore the content to be learned via group discussion.

12. Reciprocal teaching involves a type of classroom dialogue in which students are expected to make predictions, ask questions, summarize, and clarify when learning from text.

13. Reciprocal teaching involves a sequence of activities, which include the following:

- An initial class discussion that generates predictions about the content to be learned from text.
- Reading and/or listening to a portion of the text.
- Choosing a discussion leader who asks questions about the text of other students, who then respond with questions of their own.
- A summarization of the text by the discussion leader on which other students are invited to comment or elaborate.

- A clarification of any unresolved questions and a rereading of portions of text for greater clarity, if needed.

14. The teacher's role during reciprocal teaching is to gradually shift the responsibility for learning to the students by reducing the amount of explaining, explicitness of cues, and prompting that may have marked earlier portions of the lesson.

15. During reciprocal teaching the teacher's role is to do the following:

- Jointly share the responsibility for learning with the students.
- Initially assume responsibility for modeling how to make a prediction, how to ask a question, how to summarize, and how to clarify, but then transfer responsibility to students for demonstrating use of these strategies.
- Encourage all students to participate in the classroom dialogue by prompting, providing additional information, and/or altering the response demand on students.
- Monitor student comprehension and adjust the rate and complexity of information as needed.

16. In self-directed learning, the teacher "scaffolds"—builds the dialogue within a discussion step by step—each time increasing the challenge to the learner to think independently of earlier constructions. Scaffolding must occur to the appropriate degree for each learner response to keep the challenge within the learner's zone of maximum response opportunity.

17. During self-directed learning, inner (private) speech helps the learner elaborate and extend the content in ways unique to the individual. As responsibility for learning beyond the text gradually shifts to the learner, the learner's inner-speech ability increases, modeling the same reasoning and using similar questions, prompts, and cues used by the teacher at an earlier stage.

18. The following are steps for teaching self-directed inquiry to individual learners:

- Provide a new learning task and observe how the student approaches it.
- Ask the student to explain how he or she would learn the content (e.g., preparing for an exam).
- Describe and model a more effective procedure for organizing and learning the content (e.g., using study questions, notes, or highlighting key features in the text).
- Provide another, similar task on which the student can practice the strategies provided.
- Model self-questioning behavior during the task to ensure the learner follows the strategies correctly (e.g., "Did I underline the key words?").
- Provide other opportunities for the student to practice, decreasing your role as a monitor.
- Check the result by questioning for comprehension and use of the strategies taught.

19. Other cognitive strategies can be helpful for organizing and remembering new material during self-directed learning:

- Mnemonics
- Elaboration/organization (notetaking)
- Comprehension monitoring
- Problem solving

20. Problem-based learning organizes curriculum around loosely structured or ill-defined problems that learners solve by using knowledge and skills from several disciplines.

21. Classroom dialogue can be modified to foster the goals of self-directed learning in a culturally diverse classroom in the following ways:

- Adjust the flow and complexity of content.
- Offer ample opportunity for all to participate.
- Teach cognitive strategies.

For Discussion and Practice

*1. Identify two purposes for engaging your students in self-directed learning.

*2. Identify four unique teaching functions associated with self-directed learning.

*3. What is *metacognition?* What do metacognitive strategies hope to accomplish?

*4. Identify the three stages of mental modeling.

5. Provide an example of a verbal marker in your content area that would alert learners that you are about to begin mental modeling.

*6. What specific outcomes can mental modeling help students acquire?

*7. What is the role of the teacher during "mediation"?

*8. Define *zone of maximum response opportunity* and give an example in the context of a classroom dialogue.

9. Give an example of a student response–teacher reaction that illustrates the concept of "functional failure."

*10. What is the purpose of reciprocal teaching?

*11. What is the sequence of activities comprising reciprocal teaching?

*12. What is the purpose of a classroom dialogue during self-directed learning?

*13. What is the role of inner (private) speech in self-directed learning?

14. Create a brief excerpt from a classroom dialogue to show what a scaffolded dialogue would be like in your teaching area.

*15. What is declarative knowledge as opposed to procedural knowledge? Give an example of each.

16. Provide an example of an activity structure in your own subject area or grade level that varies task demand.

*17. Describe the steps you would take to teach self-directed learning to an individual learner.

*18. Identify and give examples of each of four cognitive strategies for organizing and remembering new material.

---

* Answers to asterisked questions (*) in this and the other chapters are in Appendix B.

Suggested Readings

Borich, G., & Tombari, M. (1995). *Educational psychology: A contemporary approach.* New York: HarperCollins.

A review of the research that provides the foundation for self-directed learning and cognitive learning strategies (Chapter 5).

Duffy, G., & Roehler, L. (1989). The tension between information-giving and mediation: Perspectives on instructional explanation and teacher change. In J. Brophy (Ed.), *Advances in Research on Teaching*, Vol. 1, 1–33. Greenwich, CT: JAI Press.

A review of research by the authors and others in which metacognitive strategies were effective in promoting learner comprehension.

Duffy, G., Roehler, L., & Herrmann, B. (1988). Modeling mental processes helps poor readers become strategic readers. *The Reading Teacher, 41*(8), 762–767.

A practical application of metacognitive strategies in an elementary classroom.

Palincsar, A. (1986). The role of dialogue in providing scaffolded instruction. *Educational Psychologist, 21*, 73–98.

Some practical examples of the concept of "scaffolding," in which learners are moved toward increasingly complex patterns of thinking through classroom dialogue.

Palincsar, A., & Brown, A. (1989). Classroom dialogues to promote self-regulated comprehension. In J. Brophy (Ed.), *Advances in Research on Teaching*, Vol. 1, 35–71. Greenwich, CT: JAI Press.

The authors demonstrate how modeling and social dialogue in the classroom can contribute to student self-inquiry skills through reciprocal teaching.

Pressley, M., Borkowski, J., & Schneider, W. (1987). Good strategy users coordinate metacognition, strategy use, and knowledge. In R. Vasta & G. Whitehurst (Eds.), *Annals of Child Development* (Vol. 4, pp. 89–130). Greenwich, CT: JAI Press.

How metacognitive techniques can be combined with other effective teaching methods to increase independent thinking and problem solving.

Roehler, L., & Duffy, G. (1987). Why are some teachers better explainers than others? *Journal of Education for Teaching, 12*(3), 273–284.

Presents some techniques for achieving lesson clarity in which learners are encouraged to take responsibility for their own learning.

Rohrkemper, M., & Corno, L. (1988). Success and failure on classroom tasks: Adaptive learning and classroom teaching. *The Elementary School Journal, 88*(3), 298–312.

The authors discuss techniques by which learners can adapt classroom tasks to their individual learning styles to control their own learning.

Vygotsky, L. (1986). In A. Kozulin (Ed.), *Thought and language.* Cambridge, MA: Harvard University Press.

Introductions to the role of inner speech in learning and the concept of a zone of maximum response opportunity, by the author of these ideas.

CHAPTER 10

Cooperative Learning and the Collaborative Process

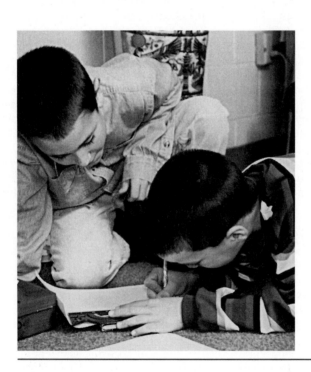

This chapter will help you answer the following questions:

1. What student outcomes can I expect from cooperative learning?
2. What must I do to plan a cooperative learning activity?
3. How do I structure a cooperative task?
4. How large should a cooperative group be?
5. How can I reduce the uninvolvement of learners during a cooperative learning task?
6. How much of a cooperative lesson should be devoted to individual group work?
7. What roles can I assign to group members?
8. What responsibilities do cooperative group members have toward one another?
9. What are some of the ways I can reward good group performance?
10. What are some collaborative skills I can teach my learners?
11. How can I evaluate the results of a cooperative learning activity?
12. How can I promote the goals of cooperative learning in the culturally diverse classroom?

This chapter will also help you learn the meaning of:

active and passive uninvolvement
cooperative attitudes and values
cooperative student roles
cooperative task structure
debriefing
integrated identity
prosocial behavior
role expectations
student-to-student interaction
task specialization
team-oriented cooperative learning

I n Chapter 9 you saw how self-directed learning could promote higher forms of thinking with the aid of metacognitive strategies. In this chapter, you will see how these same outcomes can be extended and reinforced through various forms of peer collaboration. You will learn how self-directed and cooperative learning share the complementary objectives of engaging students in the learning process and promoting higher thought processes and more authentic behaviors required in the world of work, family, and community.

>>> OUTCOMES OF COOPERATION <<<

What student outcomes can I expect from cooperative learning?

What good are critical thinking, reasoning, and problem-solving skills if your learners cannot apply them in interaction with others? Cooperative learning activities instill in learners important behaviors that prepare them to reason and perform in an adult world. Let's consider some of these behaviors.

Attitudes and Values

Adult learners form their attitudes and values from social interaction. Although we learn much about the world from books, magazines, newspapers, and audiovisual media, most of our attitudes and values are formed by discussing what we know or think with others. In this manner we exchange our information and knowledge with that of others who have acquired their knowledge in different ways. This exchange shapes our views and perspectives. It turns cold, lifeless facts into feelings, and then to attitudes and values that guide our behavior over longer periods of time.

These attitudes and values very often are left untaught in our schools. Many classrooms rely solely on formally acquired knowledge, with learners competing for grades and reinforcement. Yet, it is our attitudes and values that are one of the most important outcomes of schooling, because they alone provide the framework for guiding our actions outside the classroom, where there may be no formal sources of knowledge to fall back on. Cooperative learning is important in helping learners acquire from the curriculum the basic **cooperative attitudes and values** they need to think independently inside and outside of your classroom.

Prosocial Behavior

Models of acceptable behavior that contribute to the common good of family, friends, and community may not always be available in the home today. This is due in part to the dramatic increase in working couples, demanding occupations, and single-parent households. The "quality time" at home between adults and children is shrinking as our society becomes more technocratic, impersonal, and complex. For many, family burdens are heavy—driving long distances to and from work, finding appropriate and affordable afterschool child care, grocery shopping and housekeeping forced into the evenings and weekends. This complexity often places stress upon family members that can make intimate and meaningful contact among family members difficult or even impossible.

It is during close and meaningful encounters among family members that models of **prosocial behavior** are communicated. Children learn right from wrong implicitly through their actions and the actions of others that come to the attention of adult family members. These adults are quick to point out the effects of these actions on family, friends, and the community.

With the decreasing presence of adults in the homes of many schoolage learners, the classroom becomes an important vehicle for bolstering home and community values, or providing a substitute for them when none exist. Cooperative learning brings learners together in adultlike settings which, when carefully planned and executed, can provide appropriate models of social behavior.

Alternative Perspectives and Viewpoints

It is no secret that we form our attitudes and values by confronting viewpoints contrary to our own. Our likes and dislikes, the things we aspire to and avoid, come from our exposure to alternatives we could not have thought of on our own, given the limitations of our immediate context and experience. These alternatives—some of which we adopt, some we borrow from, and some we reject—are the raw material from which we form our own attitudes and values.

Confronted with these alternatives, we are forced into an objectivity necessary for thinking critically, reasoning, and problem solving. In other words, we become less self-centered. Depending on the merits of what we see and hear, we grow more open to exchanging our feelings and beliefs with those of others. It is this active exchange of viewpoints and the tension it sometimes creates within us that is the catalyst for our growth. Cooperative learning provides the context or "meeting ground" where many different viewpoints can be orchestrated, from which we form more articulate attitudes and values of our own.

Integrated Identity

One of the most noticeable outcomes of social interaction is its effect on how we develop our personalities and learn who we are. Social interaction over long periods forces us to "see ourselves"—our attitudes, values, and abilities—in many different circumstances. The main result is that inconsistencies and contradictions in who we are—or think we are—cannot be hidden, as might be the case in a single interaction or small number of social interactions.

If we say and think one way in one situation, and say and think another way in another situation, we cannot help but notice our own inconsistency and wonder why it exists. We attempt to resolve such contradictions, to clarify what we really believe and to believe what we really say. Our personality (at least what we show to others) becomes more coherent and integrated and is perceived by others as a more forceful and confident projection of our thoughts and feelings. Over time, repeated social interactions reduce the contradictions until our views become singular and consistent and we achieve an **integrated identity.**

Cooperative learning can be the start of stripping away the irrelevant, overly dramatic, and superficial appendages that mask our deepest thoughts and feelings. Thus we begin to gain an integrated sense of self—not coincidentally, one that we increasingly grow proud of.

Higher Thought Processes

If all of the preceding benefits of cooperative learning were not enough, the fact that it has been linked to increases in the use of higher thought processes in learners is another reason for its use (Slavin et al., 1985; Slavin, 1990b; Johnson & Johnson, 1991). As noted, cooperative learning actively engages the student in the learning process and seeks to improve the critical thinking, reasoning, and problem-solving skills of the learner. Critical thinking, reasoning, and problem solving cannot occur outside a context of attitudes and values, prosocial behavior, alternative perspectives and viewpoints, and an integrated identity. Cooperative learning provides the ingredients for higher thought processes to occur and sets them to work on realistic and adultlike tasks.

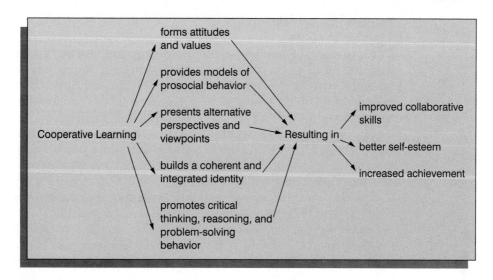

Figure 10.1
Model of cooperative learning

These higher thought processes—required for analyzing, synthesizing, and decision making—are believed to be stimulated more by interaction with others (peers and adults) than by books and lectures, which typically are not interactive. Books and lectures may be useful for teaching knowledge, comprehension, and application, but they seldom are sufficient to bring about the private, inner speech required for thinking critically, reasoning, and problem solving. These behaviors require interaction with others as well as oneself to "unleash" the motivation required for thinking and performing in complex ways.

The model of cooperative learning we have been discussing thus far is illustrated in Figure 10.1.

>>> COMPONENTS OF A COOPERATIVE <<<
LEARNING ACTIVITY

In the rest of this chapter you will see how to organize your classroom for cooperative learning. In planning a cooperative learning activity, you need to decide the type of interactions you will have with your students, the type of interactions your students will have with one another, the task and materials you select, and the role expectations and responsibilities you will assign. These four aspects are discussed in the following sections.

What must I do to plan a cooperative learning activity?

Teacher–Student Interaction

One purpose of teacher–student interaction during cooperative learning is to promote independent thinking. Much like student response–teacher reaction sequences during self-directed inquiry, exchanges between you and your learners in the cooperative classroom focus on getting learners to think for themselves, independently of the text. To accomplish this goal, you model, intervene, and collaborate with learners in much the same way as in the self-directed classroom. This should come as no surprise, as the goals of cooperative and self-directed inquiry are complementary. This also is why you may develop self-directed inquiry skills in your students first as an effective catalyst to cooperative learning.

However, the way you establish teacher–student interaction during cooperative learning is different from self-directed learning. In self-directed inquiry, the interaction usually is one on one, with verbal messages directed to individuals one at a time and adjusted to their zones of maximum response opportunity. On the other hand, cooperative learning occurs in groups that share a common purpose and task, so you must broaden interactions to fit the zone of maximum response opportunity that is common to most group members. And, instead of bringing individuals to a greater understanding and awareness of their own thinking, your goal now is to help the *group* become more self-reflective and aware of their own performance.

"Think about that some more," "Why not check with the reference at the learning center," and "Be sure you've followed the guidelines I've given you," are frequent expressions you will address to a group of four or five learners assigned a specific task. Your role is to intervene at critical junctures and then to retreat, allowing the group to grapple with the new perspective or information given. In this manner, you monitor and collaborate with the group during brief but focused interventions, keeping them on course and following a productive line of reasoning. Thus, teacher–student interactions take on an air of well-timed and brief intrusions into the group's thinking to periodically stimulate and stir a flurry of new ideas.

Student–Student Interaction

Interaction among students in cooperative learning groups is intense and prolonged. Unlike self-directed inquiry, in which the learner eventually takes responsibility for his or her own learning, students in cooperative learning groups gradually take responsibility for *each other's* learning. The effect may well be the same as in self-directed learning. Again, this is why cooperative and self-directed learning may be used as complementary learning strategies, with one reinforcing the skills acquired in the other.

During cooperative learning, the feedback, reinforcement, and support come from student peers in the group, as opposed to coming from you. **Student-to-student interaction** constitutes the majority of time and activity during cooperative learning, unlike the modest amount of direct student-to-student interaction that occurs in the self-directed classroom. Groups of four or five, working together in the physical closeness promoted by a common task, encourage collaboration, support, and feedback from the closest, most immediate source—one's peers. An essential ingredient of cooperative learning is each learner's desire to facilitate the task performance of fellow group members.

Task Specialization and Materials

Another component of cooperative learning is the task to be learned and the materials that comprise a cooperative learning activity structure. Cooperative learning tasks are preplanned activities; they are timed, completed in stages, and placed within the context of the work of others (for example, the tasks of other groups). This promotes the sharing of ideas and/or materials and the coordination of efforts among individuals. The choice of task and supporting materials is important to promote meaningful student–student interaction.

Cooperative learning typically uses **task specialization,** or "division of labor," to break a larger task into smaller subparts on which separate groups (sometimes individuals) work. Eventually these efforts come together to create the whole, and thus each member of the class has contributed. Therefore, each group may be asked to specialize, focusing its efforts on a smaller yet meaningful part of some larger end product for which the entire class receives credit. Groups may even compete against one another with the idea of producing a better "part" or more quality "product" than other groups. However, the purpose is not the competition that produces the final product, but the *cooperation* within and between groups that the competition creates.

Cooperative task structures have the goal of dividing and specializing the efforts of small groups of individuals across a larger task whose outcome depends on the sharing, cooperation, and collaboration of individuals within groups.

Role Expectations and Responsibilities

Proper assignment of roles is important to the success of cooperative learning activities. In addition to groups being assigned specialized tasks, individuals often are assigned specialized roles to perform within their groups. Some roles that can be assigned to facilitate a group's work and to promote communication and sharing among its members are group leader, researcher, recorder, and summarizer.

The success of a cooperative learning activity depends on your communication of **role expectations** and responsibilities and modeling them where necessary. This is another reason why cooperative learning has little resemblance to loosely formed discussion groups—not only must you divide labor among learners and specialized tasks, but you also must designate roles that foster the orderly completion of a task.

If someone's duties are unclear, or a group's assignment is ambiguous, cooperative learning quickly degenerates into undisciplined discussion, in which there may be numerous "uninvolved and passive participants." Uninvolved and passive participants are individuals who successfully "escape" sharing anything of themselves, choosing to rest within the confines of their own selfish behavior. This defeats the purpose of cooperative learning, for if a group produces an outstanding report but only a few students contributed to it, the group as a whole will have learned no more than if each member had completed the assignment alone. Worst of all, the critical thinking, reasoning, and problem solving that are so much a part of the shared effort of a cooperative learning activity will not have occurred.

>>> ESTABLISHING A COOPERATIVE TASK <<< STRUCTURE IN YOUR CLASSROOM

How do I structure a cooperative task?

Now let us put to work in your classroom the four components of cooperative learning—teacher–student interaction, student–student interaction, task specialization and materials, and role expectations and responsibilities. Establishing a **task structure** for a cooperative learning activity involves five specific steps:

1. Specifying the goal of the activity.
2. Structuring the task.
3. Teaching and evaluating the collaborative process.
4. Monitoring group performance.
5. Debriefing.

1—Specifying the Goal

The goal of a cooperative learning activity specifies the product and/or behaviors that are expected at the end of the activity. The outcome can take different forms:

- Written group reports
- Higher individual achievement on an end-of-activity test
- Oral performance, articulating the group consensus
- Enumeration of critical issues
- Critique of an assigned reading
- List of bibliographic references

To assure the desired outcome, your job is to identify the outcome, check for understanding, and set a cooperative tone. Each of these steps is described in the following subsections.

Identify the Outcome.   The form of the final product or performance must be clearly articulated from the beginning. For each of the outcomes just listed, you would illustrate the style, format, and length of the product that will constitute acceptable group work. For a written report, you might write on the board the acceptable length and format and display a sample report to guide group efforts. Or, if the goal is to increase test performance, you would identify the amount of improvement expected for each group as a standard to guide their performance. For oral performances, you would identify the nature of their content, thoroughness of research, and completeness. In each case, you must give your students signs of acceptable progress or milestones to be achieved and, where possible, examples of a successfully completed final product.

Following clear specification of the goal, you must place it in the context of past and future learning. Organize the content so that students will attach meaning and significance to it and see it in terms of their own experience. Typically, statements like "Remember when we had trouble with . . . " or "Next week we will need these skills to . . . " sufficiently highlight the importance of the impending activity. They also separate it from a casual exercise that has no consequences for either good or poor performance.

Check for Understanding.   Next, check for understanding of the goal and your directions for achieving it. Using a few average and high performers as a "steering group," ask for an oral regurgitation of your goal and directions. The entire class can benefit from hearing them again and you can correct them if needed. Because groups typically expend so much effort during a cooperative learning activity, misinterpretation of the goal and your directions for attaining it can severely affect classroom morale.

In self-directed learning, one individual can be led astray by poorly understood directives. But in cooperative learning, entire groups, not just occasional individuals, can wander off the path, leaving a significant portion of your classroom working toward the wrong goal. Having one member of each group restate the goal and your directions for attaining it is time well spent.

Set a Cooperative Tone. Your final task in introducing the goal of your cooperative learning activity is to set a tone of cooperation.

Students customarily begin cooperative learning activities as they have begun thousands of school activities before—as individuals competing against individuals. This competitive style has been ingrained in us from earliest childhood. It culminates in school with tests and grades that are placed on a "normal" or bell-shaped curve, which assures that for every test or graded performance there will be some winners and some losers. It may be difficult for some of your learners to get the competitive spirit out of their blood, because it has become so much a part of their schooling.

While competition has its place even within cooperative learning (for example, competing against other groups or one's own previous performance), effective group work depends on collaboration among its members, not competition. Therefore, your job at the start of a cooperative learning activity is to set the tone: "two heads are better than one." Other phrases such as "united we stand, divided we fall," or "work together or fail together," can remind groups of the cooperative nature of the enterprise. You could ask each group to choose or create a group motto (for example, "all for one and one for all") that provides a distinctive identity as well as reminding them that collaboration, not competition, is the goal.

As you will see shortly, your role also must be one of cooperation, and this too must be communicated at the outset. "I am here to help . . . to answer your questions . . . to be your assistant . . . your consultant . . . your information provider. . . . " These reassuring comments can lift your classroom from the realm of competition and into the world of cooperation.

2—Structuring the Task

As we saw earlier, the structure of the task is what separates just any group activity (like a discussion) from a cooperative learning activity.

Division of labor, often overlooked when structuring tasks, is critical to the success of group learning. Allowing students to analyze the task and identify divisions of labor can foster metacognitive growth and higher-order thinking.

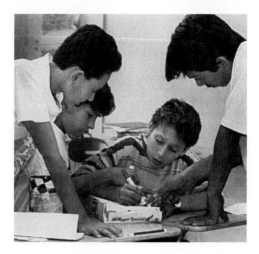

Group discussions have tasks, but they often are so generally defined (discuss the facts, raise issues, form a consensus) that they rarely allow for the division of labor, role responsibilities, collaborative efforts, and end products that so effectively promote critical thinking, reasoning, and problem solving in a cooperative learning activity.

In structuring a cooperative learning task, you must decide several factors in advance:

- How large will the groups be?
- How will group members be selected?
- How much time will be devoted to group work?
- What roles, if any, will be assigned to group members?
- What incentives/rewards will be provided for individual and group work?

Let's look at alternatives for each of these factors and how you can choose among them.

Group Size.   How many in the group? Group size is one of your most important decisions. Although influenced by the size of your class, the number of individual learners assigned to groups has far-reaching consequences for the following:

How large should a cooperative group be?

The range of abilities within a group

The time required for a group to reach consensus

The efficient sharing of materials within a group

The time needed to complete the end product

Each of these four factors will be altered by the number of members assigned to groups. This is why, when subtasks are comparable, group sizes should be made approximately equal.

The most efficient group size for attaining a goal in the least time is 4 or 5 members (Slavin, 1990b). Thus, in a class of 25 students, five or six groups can be formed. Smaller groups make monitoring of group performance more difficult, because the number of times you can interact with each group is reduced accordingly. On the other hand, groups of 7 or 8 generally argue more, reach consensus later, have more difficulty sharing limited materials (for example, a reference that must be shared), and take longer to complete the final product.

Thus, the rule of thumb is to compose groups of 4 or 5 members for single-period activities and slightly larger groups (of 5 or 6) when the activity stretches over more than a class period, requiring greater task complexity and role specialization. Keep in mind, however, that large groups—like large group discussions—often have more nonparticipants who more easily hide behind the work of others or find ways to maintain their anonymity in the context of a busy group.

Group Composition.   Whom will you select for each group? Unless the task specifically calls for specialized abilities, you will form most groups heterogeneously, with a representative sample of all the learners in a class. Therefore, you will assign to groups a mix of higher/lower ability, more verbal/less verbal, and more task-oriented/less task-oriented learners. This diversity usually contributes to the collaborative process by creating a natural flow of information from those who have it to those who need it. Surprisingly, it also promotes the transmission of alternative perspectives and viewpoints that often reverses the flow of information in unexpected and desirable directions.

Groups within a classroom generally should reflect the composition of the community outside it. This composition confronts learners with differences as well as similarities to provide the motivation for dialogue, the need for sharing, and the natural division of interests and abilities needed to get the job done.

It also is important that groups not only represent a diversity of talents, interests, and abilities but that typically nonengaged students be represented across groups. Social scientists long have observed that the pressure from peers working together often "pulls in" even recalcitrant and passive learners, sweeping them up in the excitement of some larger goal. This is especially true if they are deprived of the support of other passive or inactive participants.

Johnson and Johnson (1991) provide additional suggestions for forming groups:

1. Ask students to list three peers with whom they would like to work. Identify isolated students who are not chosen by any other classmates. Then, build a group of skillful and supportive students around each isolated learner.
2. Randomly assign students by having them count off; place the 1s together, the 2s together, and so forth. If groups of 5 are desired in a class of 30, have students count off by 6s.
3. To build constructive relationships between majority and minority students, between children with and without disabilities, and between male and female, use heterogeneous groups with students from each category.
4. Share with students the process of choosing group members. First, you select a member for a group, then that member selects another, and so on, alternating between your choice and students' choices until the group is complete.

One approach to drawing nonengaged learners into the cooperative activity is to structure the task so that success depends on the active involvement of all group members. Structuring the task reduces the problems of active and passive uninvolvement. **Active uninvolvement** is when a group member talks about everything but the assigned goal of the group. **Passive uninvolvement** is when a student doesn't care and becomes a silent member of the group. Here are ways you can structure a cooperative task to increase the likelihood that all group members will be actively involved:

How can I reduce the uninvolvement of learners during a cooperative learning task?

- Request a product that requires a clearly defined division of labor to generate (e.g., looking up new words, writing a topic sentence, preparing a chart, finding examples, etc). Then assign specific individuals to each activity at the start of the session.
- Within groups, form pairs that are responsible for looking over and actually correcting each other's work/contribution.
- Chart the group's progress on individually assigned tasks and encourage poor or slow performers to work harder to improve the group's overall progress. (A wall chart may be all that is needed.)
- Purposefully limit the resources given to a group, so that individual members must remain in personal contact to share materials and complete their assigned tasks (e.g., one dictionary or hand calculator to share).

● Make one stage of the required product contingent on a previous stage that is the responsibility of another person. This way, pressure will be applied or help provided by group members to those not performing adequately, so that they can complete their contribution.

Time on Task. How much time should you allot for group work? This obviously depends on task complexity (for example, single class period or multiple periods), but you must make some more refined estimates as well. You need to determine the time to devote to group work and the time to devote to all groups coming together to share their contributions. This latter time may be used for group reports, a whole-class discussion, debriefing to relate the work experiences of each group to the end product, or some combination.

Group work can easily get out of hand in the excitement, controversy, and natural dialogue that can come from passionate discussions. This requires you to place limits on each stage of the cooperative learning activity, so that one does not eclipse time from another and leave the task disjointed and incomplete in your learners' minds.

How much of a cooperative lesson should be devoted to individual group work?

Most time naturally will be devoted to the work of individual groups, where the major portion of the end product is being completed. This normally will consume 60 to 80 percent of the time devoted to the cooperative learning activity. The remaining time must be divided among individual group presentations and/or whole-class discussion that places the group work into the perspective of a single end product.

If you plan both group reports and a whole-class discussion for the same day, be aware that the whole-class discussion probably will get squeezed into a fraction of the time required to make it meaningful. To avoid this, schedule group discussions or debriefings for the following class day, so that class members have ample time to reflect upon their group reports and to pull together their own thoughts about the collaborative process, which may or may not have occurred as intended. Fifteen or twenty minutes at the beginning of class the next day usually provides students the proper distance to meaningfully reflect on their experiences the day before.

Role Assignment. What roles should you assign to group members? As you saw, division of labor within and across groups is an important dimension of cooperative learning that is not shared by most group discussion methods. It is this task specialization, and the division of labor it often requires, that promotes the responsibility and idea sharing that marks an effective cooperative learning activity. The acceptance of individual responsibility and idea sharing in a cooperative learning experience is encouraged by role assignments within groups and sometimes task specialization across groups. These roles and responsibilities are used to complement group work and to interconnect the groups.

Some of the more popular **cooperative student role** functions that can be assigned within or across groups are suggested by Johnson and Johnson (1991):

What roles can I assign to group members?

1. *Summarizer*—paraphrases and plays back to the group major conclusions to see if the group agrees and to prepare for (rehearse) the group's contribution before the whole class.
2. *Checker*—checks controversial or debatable statements and conclusions for authenticity against text, workbook, or references. Assures that the group will not be using unsubstantiated facts, or be challenged by more accurate representations of other groups.
3. *Researcher*—reads reference documents and acquires background information when more data are needed (for example, may conduct an interview or seek a resource from the library). The researcher differs from a checker in that the researcher provides critical information for the group to complete its task, while the checker certifies the accuracy of the work in progress and/or after it has been completed.
4. *Runner*—acquires anything needed to complete the task—materials, equipment, reference works. Far from a subservient role, this requires creativity, shrewdness, and even cunning to find the necessary resources, which may also be diligently sought by other groups.
5. *Recorder*—commits to writing the major product of the group. The recorder may require individuals to write their own conclusions, in which case the recorder collates, synthesizes, and renders in coherent form the abbreviated work of individual group members.
6. *Supporter*—chosen for his or her upbeat, positive outlook, the supporter praises members when their individual assignments are completed and consoles them in times of discouragement (for example, if proper references can't be found). Keeps the group moving forward by recording major milestones achieved on a chart for all the class to see, identifying progress made, and encouraging efforts of individuals, particularly those who may have difficulty participating or completing their tasks.

7. *Observer/Troubleshooter*—takes notes and records information about the group process that may be useful during whole-class discussion or debriefing. Reports to a class leader or to you when problems appear insurmountable for a group or for individual members.

Typically, any one of the preceding role functions also could serve as a group leader. However, because each of these roles entails some form of leadership, the formal designation of "leader" may not be necessary. This has the desirable effect of making all role functions more equal and eliminating an authority-based structure that can lead to arguments and disunity among members who may see themselves as more or less powerful than others.

What responsibilities do cooperative group members have toward one another?

In addition to these specific role functions assigned to individual group members, there are other responsibilities for all group members to perform. You may wish to provide students with the following reminders by writing them on the board or in a handout prior to a cooperative learning activity:

- Ask other group members to explain their points clearly whenever you don't understand.
- Be sure to check your answers and those of others in your group against references or the text.
- Encourage members of your group to go farther, to expand on their points to surpass previous accomplishments and expectations.
- Let everyone finish what they have to say without interrupting, whether you agree or disagree.
- Don't be bullied into changing your mind, if you really don't want to.
- Criticize ideas, not individuals.

What are some of the ways I can reward good group performance?

Providing Reinforcement and Rewards.   Besides deciding on group composition, size, time, and the individual responsibilities of group members, you need to establish a system of reinforcement and reward to keep your learners on task and working toward the goal. The following are among the reinforcement strategies that have been used effectively with cooperative learning activities:

- Grades—individual and group
- Bonus points
- Social responsibilities

Figure 10.2
Sample scales for evaluating individual and group effort in a collaborative activity

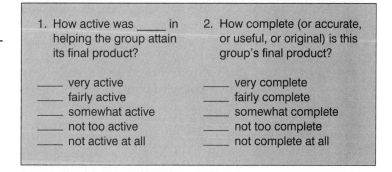

1. How active was _____ in helping the group attain its final product?

   _____ very active
   _____ fairly active
   _____ somewhat active
   _____ not too active
   _____ not active at all

2. How complete (or accurate, or useful, or original) is this group's final product?

   _____ very complete
   _____ fairly complete
   _____ somewhat complete
   _____ not too complete
   _____ not complete at all

- Tokens or privileges
- Group contingencies

Grades—the familiar type used in competitive learning—can be used to reinforce and reward the behavior of individuals and groups during cooperative learning. However, use of individual grades in the context of cooperative learning should stress the importance of individual effort in achieving *the group goal*. For this reason, cooperative learning grades usually incorporate both individual performance (quality and/or extensiveness of work toward accomplishing the group goal) and the thoroughness, relevance, and accuracy of the group product. Each individual's grade can be in two separate parts or can be a composite grade that combines his or her own plus the group's effort.

For example, individuals can rate each other on a five-point scale measuring the active involvement of each teammate in the group process, the average of which could be a score for individual effort. Also, you can rate the group's end product (or groups could rate one another and the average taken) on a five-point scale, providing two scores. Sample scales for measuring group and individual effort are illustrated in Figure 10.2. Scores from these scales could be recorded independently of one another (e.g., individual effort = 4, group product = 5) or as a ratio (e.g., 4/5 = .80). If the ratio method is chosen, each individual in the group would be given the same group score, either determined by you or by averaging each group's evaluation of one another. Ratios smaller than 1.0 indicate that the group product exceeded this individual's contribution. Scores greater than 1.0 indicate that the individual's contribution exceeded the group product.

Other types of grades also may be used as rewards:

1. Averaging of individual scores to determine the group grade.
2. Assigning all group members the average of the highest (or lowest) half of the members' scores.

3. Averaging an individual's score with the group score (for example, averaging an individual score of 4 with a group score of 5: 4 + 5 = 9, ÷ 2 = 4.5).
4. Adding points to the group score for each active participant within the group (or subtracting points from the group score for each nonparticipant), to be determined by the teacher.

Another reinforcement technique you can use in partnership with grades is bonus points, earned on the basis of how many group members reach a preestablished level of performance by the end of their group's activity. You might devise a group quiz (or take it from the text or workbook) and then assign an expected score for each individual member, which could vary according to ability or task. Those obtaining or exceeding their expected score would earn their group a bonus point.

Another popular form of reinforcement during cooperative learning includes rewarding individual efforts with desirable social responsibilities, such as granting the high performer the first pick of group role next time (observer, supporter, checker, etc.). Also, you can employ tokens or privileges to motivate individuals and group members. The highest-performing group might receive independent study time, time out, trips to the learning center, or use of special materials and/or resources. High-performing individuals within groups could be accorded these same privileges for exemplary performance.

Finally, group contingencies frequently have been used to motivate and reinforce members during cooperative learning. Johnson and Johnson (1991) describe three ways of rewarding the group based on the performance of its individuals:

1. Average-performance contingency, in which all members are graded or reinforced based on the average performance of all group members.
2. High-performance group contingency, in which the highest quarter of the group is the basis for grades, reinforcements, or privileges.
3. Low-performance group contingency, in which the lowest quarter of the group is the basis for individual grades or other forms of reinforcement.

3—Teaching and Evaluating the Collaborative Process

What are some collaborative skills I can teach my learners?

Another responsibility you have during cooperative learning is teaching the collaborative process. Most learners lack the collaborative skills needed to benefit from many cooperative learning activities. Therefore, you need to identify collaborative behaviors, place them in proper sequence, and demonstrate them. Just as self-directed learning strategies must be modeled, so must collaborative behaviors.

At the heart of collaborative skills is the ability to exchange thoughts and feelings with others at the same conceptual level. Students need to feel comfortable in communicating their ideas, beliefs, and opinions to others in a timely and efficient manner. Johnson and Johnson (1991) suggest some important "sending" skills and some of the ways you can encourage them:

1. *Teach how to communicate one's own ideas and feelings.* Encourage use of *I* and *my* to let students know it is *their* ideas and feelings that make the collaborative process work. Let students know that their personal experiences—events observed, problems encountered, people met—are valued information they can use to justify their own ideas and feelings.

2. *Make messages complete and specific.* Indicate that, along with the message being sent, there should be a frame of reference, perspective, or experience that led to the content of the message. For example, "I got this idea while traveling through a Pueblo Indian reservation in southern Colorado during our vacation last summer." Or, "I heard the President speak and his main point reminded me of . . . " or, "I read this newspaper article and it led me to believe some things about. . . . "

3. *Make verbal and nonverbal messages congruent.* Establish a serious tone in which hidden meanings or snide remarks are not acceptable. Indicate that voice and body language always are to reinforce the message being conveyed and that communicating serious information comically or overdramatizing will confuse both the message and the listener.

4. *Convey an atmosphere of respect and support.* Indicate that all students can contribute information, ideas, feelings, personal experiences, and reactions without fear of ridicule. Make clear that unsupportive behaviors ("You're crazy if you . . . ") are not allowed. Make clear that cooperation rests upon sharing both emotional and physical resources, receiving help, dividing responsibility, and in looking out for one another's well being.

5. *Demonstrate how to assess whether the message was properly received.* Instruct your learners in how to ask for interpretive feedback from listeners. Ask them to use phrases such as "What do you think about what I said?"

"Does what I said make sense?" "Can you see what I'm trying to say?" The more listeners are asked to paraphrase the message, the more the sender is sure the message has been received as intended.

6. *Teach how to paraphrase another's point of view.* Most learners will want to agree or disagree with the speaker without checking to see if they have the full intent of the message. Make it known that before one can be either critical or supportive of another's viewpoint, it must be paraphrased to the satisfaction of the sender. Teach the following rules of paraphrasing:

a. Restate the message in your own words—not those of the speaker.

b. Introduce your paraphrased remarks with phrases such as "It seems to me you're saying . . . "; "If I understand you, you believe that . . . "; "From what I heard you say, your position is. . . . "

c. During the paraphrasing, avoid any indication of approval or disapproval. For example, let it be known that responses such as "I disagree with you" or "I think you're right" should not be part of the paraphrased response, for its sole purpose is to determine whether the message has been accurately received.

7. *Demonstrate how to negotiate meanings and understandings.* Often one's understanding of a message must be corrected or fine tuned, because the message was ambiguous, incomplete, or misinterpreted. This means that paraphrases often must be recycled to a greater level of understanding, sometimes for the benefit of both sender and receiver. This requires tactful phrases from the sender such as "What I mean to say is . . . "; "What I forgot to add was . . . "; or "To clarify further. . . . " It also requires tactful phrases from the receiver, such as "What I don't understand is . . . "; "Can you say it some other way . . . ?" This approach is indispensable for refining the message and assuring more accurate interpretation. Sender and receiver each must provide a graceful means for the other to correct misperceptions of what was said or heard, without emotional injury to either.

8. *Teach participation and leadership.* Communicate the importance of the following:

Mutual benefit—what benefits the group will benefit the individual

Common fate—each individual wins or loses on the basis of the overall performance of group members

A teacher's role as monitor during group work includes identifying when additional resources may be needed by a group, redirecting group work in more productive directions, and providing emotional support to encourage commitment to the task.

Shared identity—everyone is a member of a group, emotionally as well as physically

Joint celebration—receiving satisfaction in the progress of individual group members

Mutual responsibility—being concerned for underperforming group members

4—Monitoring Group Performance

To establish a cooperative learning structure you must observe and intervene as needed to assist your learners in acquiring their group's goal. Your most frequent monitoring functions will be telling students where to find needed information, repeating how to complete the task, exhibiting the form of the product to be produced (in whole or part), and/or modeling for a group the process to be used in achieving the group goal. Your role is critical in keeping each group on track. Thus, your constant vigilance of group performance is necessary to discover problems and trouble spots before they hamper group progress.

One goal of your monitoring activity should be to *identify when a group needs assistance.* One common need will be to repeat or remind the group of its goal. Groups easily become disengaged or sidetracked, or will invent new and perhaps more interesting goals for themselves. Typically, you will move from group to group at least once at the beginning of a cooperative activity, repeating the task and the goal just to be certain each group understands it. You may have to return to a troubled group a second or even third time to repeat the goal. Some groups will require more vigilance than others.

A second goal of your monitoring activity should be to *redirect groups* that have discussed themselves into a blind alley. The heat of discussion and debate frequently distracts groups from productive thought, raising issues that may be only marginally relevant to accomplishing the group goal. Worse yet, group discussion can raise issues for which a consensus cannot be reached in reasonable time or for which resources or advanced knowledge are required that cannot be provided. When this happens, it is time for you to redirect the group's work and set them back on course.

Key to your monitoring is your ability to recognize when a group is at a difficult juncture. A group might pursue an avenue of fruitless discussion and waste valuable time, when a different avenue could set their course productively toward an attainable goal. Your close vigilance and direction of group work can make the difference between aimless talk and productive discussion.

A third monitoring activity you will perform during cooperative learning is to *provide emotional support and encouragement* to overwhelmed and frustrated group members. Not all group members will gladly accept their individual assignments, nor will all groups accept their designated goal. Your encouragement and support can instill the confidence some will need to complete a task they may be unsure of and that may not be of their own choosing. In between your periodic restatement and redirection of group goals, you may need to visit selected individuals or groups to bestow confidence, support, and technical advice on how to get the job done. Your expression of confidence in individuals often is all that is needed to nudge an inactive group participant into actively pursuing the group's goals.

5—Debriefing

Your feedback to the groups on how well they are collaborating is important to their progress in acquiring collaborative skills. You can accomplish **debriefing** and evaluation at the end of the collaborative activity:

1. Openly talk about how the groups functioned—ask students for their opinions. What were the real issues that enhanced

or impeded each group (a) in producing the product and (b) in completing the process?

2. Solicit suggestions for improving the process and avoiding problems so that higher levels of collaboration can be reached.

3. Get viewpoints of predesignated observers. You might assign one or two individuals to record instances of particularly effective and ineffective group collaboration and to report to the full class at the time of the debriefing.

Group members also can rate each other's collaborative skills during debriefing. Individual group members could receive their ratings privately while group averages could be discussed during the debriefing session to pinpoint strengths and deficiencies. Figure 10.3 is a scale for rating collaborative skills of group members. It can be used (1) by group members to rate each other, (2) by a group member (e.g., an observer) assigned the task of rating group members, or (3) by you, the teacher.

Use the scale as a checklist. On it, note the presence or absence of each skill for each group member by placing a checkmark in the appropriate box. Use *NA* (not applicable) for skills that do not apply for a given role or task. If you wish, instead of listing the names of group members, assign each member a number to keep the ratings anonymous. The whole group then could be assigned one point for each check placed on the scale and the "winning" group given a reward or special recognition.

Here is a summary of some obstacles to debriefing and how you can structure your cooperative learning activity to promote evaluation and feedback (based on Dishon & O'Leary, 1984):

How can I evaluate the results of a cooperative learning activity?

1. *There is not enough time for debriefing.* For many reasons (announcements, assemblies, ensuing lessons), teachers often believe they do not have the time to evaluate and gather feedback about the cooperative activity. Try the following:
   a. Do quick debriefing by asking the class to tell how well their groups functioned. You can do this by asking a question, such as "Did each group have enough time?" Then, have students indicate agreement or disagreement by answering *yes*—hand in air, *don't know*—arms folded, or *no*—hands down. Two or three questions can be asked and responded to in a minute or so.
   b. Do debriefing during the cooperative activity or have the class complete a questionnaire or checklist at home pertaining to how well their group functioned.

Collaborative Skills	Names of Group Members				
Provides knowledge and information to help group's progress					
Is open and candid to whole group with personal feelings					
Provides individual assistance and support to group members who need it					
Evaluates contributions of others in a nonjudgmental, constructive manner					
Shares physical resources—books, handouts, written information—for group to use					
Accurately paraphrases or summarizes what other group members have said					
Gives recognition to other group members when key contributions are made					
Accepts and appreciates cultural, ethnic, and individual differences					

Figure 10.3
Collaborative rating scale

2. *Debriefing stays vague.* When students conclude, "We did OK," "We did a good job," or "Everyone was involved" several times, you know that the feedback is not specific enough. Try the following:
   a. Give the group specific written questions to be answered about their group's functioning.
   b. Identify key events or incidents that occurred during the collaborative process for which students must indicate their comfort or satisfaction.
   c. Use student observers so that specific events indicating effective and ineffective group functioning are recorded.

3. *Students stay uninvolved in debriefing.* Occasionally there are groups whose members consistently stay uninvolved in the debriefing process. Try the following:
   a. Ask for a written report from the group, reporting the strengths and weaknesses of their group's functioning.
   b. Use questionnaires that require completion by everyone.
   c. Assign a student the job of debriefer for the group.
   d. Have each member sign a statement summarizing how their group functioned.
   e. Give bonus points for good debriefing reports.

4. *Written debriefing reports are incomplete.* Some groups may hand in incomplete debriefing reports. Try the following:
   a. Have group members read and sign each other's debriefing reports to show that each has been checked for accuracy and completeness.
   b. Give bonus points for completeness.

5. *Students use poor collaborative skills during debriefing.* When group members do not listen carefully to each other, when they are afraid to contribute to the debriefing process, or when the discussion becomes divisive, try the following:
   a. Assign specific roles for the debriefing.
   b. Have one group observe the debriefing of another group and discuss the results.

>>> TEAM-ORIENTED COOPERATIVE <<<
LEARNING ACTIVITIES

Recent research indicates that teams of heterogeneous learners can increase the collaborative skills, self-esteem, and achievement of individual learners (Slavin, 1993). Four **team-oriented cooperative learning** techniques have been particularly successful in bringing about these outcomes: Student Teams–Achievement Division

(STAD), Teams-Games-Tournaments (TGT), Jigsaw II, and Team-assisted Individualization (TAI). A brief summary of these follows, based on the work of Slavin (1993).

Student Teams–Achievement Division (STAD)

In STAD, students are assigned to four-or-five-member learning teams. Each team is made as heterogeneous as possible to represent the composition of the entire class (boys/girls, less able/more able, etc.)

Begin the cooperative learning activity by presenting new material via lecture or discussion and providing worksheets of problem sets, vocabulary words, questions, and such from which students can review the main points of the lecture or discussion. When your lecture, explanation, or introduction is complete, team members study your worksheets, quizzing each other. They work in pairs or in small groups in which team members discuss the worksheet content, clarifying difficult or confusing points among themselves and raising questions of you, when necessary.

Before team members begin, give one member of each group or pair the answers to all the questions or problems on the worksheet and assign this member the task of checking the written or oral responses of others. Allow team members sufficient time for everyone to complete the problems or questions on the worksheet (make the worksheet concise to encourage this).

After the teams have had sufficient time to practice with the worksheet and answer key, give individuals a written quiz over the material in which team members may not help one another. Score the quizzes immediately and form individual scores into team scores (for example, by averaging all, top half, or bottom half). Determine the contribution of individual students by how much each student's quiz score exceeds her or his past quiz average—or a preset score based on each student's learning history. This way, while the entire group receives a score based on each individual member's performance, individual learners also receive an improvement score based on the extent to which their individual score exceeds past performance or a preestablished standard that recognizes their learning history.

During STAD, you act as a resource person and monitor group study activities to intervene when necessary to suggest better study techniques ("Why not choose partners now and quiz each other on the questions you've been discussing?").

Research shows that, during Student Teams–Achievement Divisions, learners gain a sense of camaraderie and helpfulness toward fellow team members, pursue self-directed learning and rehearsal strategies modeled by the teacher, and become self-motivated through having some control over their own learning.

Teams-Games-Tournaments (TGT)

A cooperative learning activity closely related to STAD is the use of Teams-Games-Tournaments. TGT uses the same general format as STAD (four-to-five-member groups studying worksheets). However, instead of individually administered quizzes at the end of a study period, students play academic games to show their mastery of the topic studied.

Have students play games (e.g., 20 Questions) as weekly tournaments in which teams that are matched by ability based on previous performance compete against one another until one emerges the winner. Make the teams as heterogeneous and as evenly matched as possible so that none has a preponderance of high or low achievers. This assures that the competition is always seen as fair by the learners and that all learners have an opportunity to contribute to a winning team. Because games and tournaments naturally interest class members, let the teams take on competitive names, such as The Warriors against The Miracle Workers, The Scholars against The Pragmatists, and so on, to enhance the excitement. Often change teams (monthly) to create different heterogeneous groupings from which new cooperative relationships can emerge.

As in STAD, you can assign team points based on the number of questions answered correctly, and accumulated over a period of about four tournaments (weeks). Then, before exchanging team members, announce the winner for that month, along with the number of points accumulated by each member of the winning team (for example, number of total questions answered correctly in the past four tournaments). Keep both team and individual member statistics to see if a team and individual members can exceed the scores accumulated during any preceding month. Have an official scorekeeper keep a history of team and individual scores and record them on a handout or wall chart.

Again, you can see that TGT uses much the same format as STAD, except that academic games are substituted for individually administered quizzes, adding more intensity and competition to increase interest, participation, and excitement.

Jigsaw II

In the cooperative learning activity called Jigsaw II, you assign students to four-to-six member teams to work on an academic task that is broken into several subtasks, depending on the number of groups. You assign students to teams and then assign a unique responsibility to each team member. For example, assign each student within each team a section of the text to read. Then, give each team member a special task with which to approach the reading. Assign one team member to write down and look up the meanings of any new vocabulary words. Assign another to summarize or outline the main points in the text. Assign another the job of identifying major and minor characters, and so on.

When all team members have their specific assignments, "break out" from their original group all team members having the same assignment (e.g., finding and defining new vocabulary words) to meet as "expert groups" to discuss their assignment and to share their conclusions and results. Once in an "expert group," members may assist each other by comparing notes (e.g., definitions) and identifying points overlooked by other group members. When all the expert groups have had the opportunity to share, discuss, and modify their conclusions, return them to their respective "home groups." Each member then takes turns teaching their teammates about their respective responsibility.

Jigsaw II heightens interest among group members because the only way other team members can learn about the topics to which they were not assigned is to listen to the teammate who received that assignment. After each "expert" makes his or her presentation to the team, attempting to teach the group what they learned from their expert group, give individual quizzes to assess how much they have learned. As in STAD, you can assign both an overall group score as well as individual improvement score based on past performance. These scores become the basis for team and individual rewards for the highest scorers.

Team-Assisted Individualization (TAI)

One of the newest cooperative learning activities is Team-Assisted Individualization, which combines some of the characteristics of individualized and cooperative learning. Although originally designed for elementary and middle school mathematics classes, TAI can be used with any subject matter and grade level for which some individualized learning materials are available (for example, programmed or self-paced texts). In TAI, you start each student working through the individualized materials at a point designated by a placement test or previous learning history. Thus, students may work at different levels depending on the heterogeneity of abilities in the classroom.

Give each student a specified amount of content to work through (e.g., pages, problem sets, questions and answers) at his or her own pace. Also, assign each learner to a team selected to represent all ability levels and, therefore, individuals who enter the individualized materials at different levels of complexity. Heterogeneity within the teams is important, because you then ask each team member to have their work checked by another teammate. "Checkers" are expected to have completed portions of the materials that are more advanced than others. Have as many group members as possible assume the role of checker. When necessary, give the checkers answer sheets.

Have student monitors give quizzes over each unit and score and record the results on a master score card. Base team scores on the average number of units completed each week by team members and their scores on the unit quizzes. Reward those teams that complete a preset number of units with a minimum average quiz score (e.g., with certificates, time outs, learning center privileges). Assign one student monitor—rotate this assignment frequently—to each team to manage the routine checking, distribution of the individualized materials, and administering and recording the quizzes.

Because TAI uses individualized materials, it is especially useful for teaching heterogeneous classes that afford you few opportunities for whole-class instruction and little time to instruct numerous small groups who may have diverse learning needs.

Overviewing Team-Oriented Cooperative Learning Activities

Similarities and differences among the four cooperative learning methods are summarized in Table 10.1.

Many different forms of cooperative learning have been successfully used in classrooms of all grade levels and subject matter. Some of the most successful cooperative learning activities, however, have come from the ingenuity and creativity of individual teachers who, with little formal preparation, devise a group activity to promote social interaction when cooperative outcomes are encouraged by the nature of the content being taught. Although many versions of cooperative learning can be devised from the preceding four, as an effective teacher you should seize the opportunity to create a cooperative learning experience whenever content goals lend themselves to pro-

Table 10.1

Similarities and differences among four cooperative learning activities

Student Teams–Achievement Divisions (STAD)	Team-Games Tournament (TGT)	Jigsaw (II)	Team-Assisted Individualization (TAI)
1. Teacher presents content in lecture or discussion	1. Teacher presents content in lecture or discussion	1. Students read section of text and are assigned unique topic	1. Students are given diagnostic test/exercise by student monitor to determine placement in materials
2. Teams work through problems/questions on worksheets	2. Teams work through problems/questions on worksheets	2. Students within teams with same topic meet in "expert groups"	2. Students work through assigned unit at their own pace
3. Teacher gives quiz over material studied	3. Teams play academic games against each other for points	3. Students return to "home" group to share knowledge of their topic with teammates	3. Teammate checks text against answers and student monitor gives quiz
4. Teacher determines team average and individual improvement scores	4. Teacher tallies team points over four-week period to determine best team and best individual scorers	4. Students take quiz over each topic discussed	4. Team quizzes are averaged and number of units completed are counted by monitor to create team scores
		5. Individual quizzes are used to create team scores and individual improvement scores	

moting collaborative skills. This, in turn, can increase your learners' self-esteem, critical thinking, and problem-solving abilities.

>>> PROMOTING THE GOALS OF COOPERATIVE <<< LEARNING IN THE CULTURALLY DIVERSE CLASSROOM

One of the first things you will notice during cooperative learning activities is the variety of learning styles among your students. The variety you will observe in your students' independence, persistence, and flexibility during cooperative learning will be influenced, to some extent, by the predominant cultures and ethnicities in your school and classroom.

For example, Bennett (1990) points out how interactions among students and between students and teacher are influenced by learning styles that are modified by their culture. Cushner, McClelland, and Safford (1992) indicate how being a member of a subculture, minority, or ethnic group can enhance the nature of interpersonal relationships within a classroom by increasing its cohesiveness, informality, interpersonal harmony, and cooperativeness. Also, Bowers and Flinders (1991) provide examples of how the noise level, use of classroom space, turn taking, and negotiation can vary among social classes and ethnicities to create different but equally productive learning climates when properly managed and matched to cultural expectations.

In Chapter 2 we saw that learners could be distinguished on the basis of the cognitive processes they used to learn and whether they were presented a task *in a way that allowed them the opportunity to use their preferred learning style.* Two of the learning styles that have been frequently studied are field independence and field dependence. Recall from Chapter 2 (Table 2.1) that field-independent and field-dependent learners may be characterized in the following ways:

Field-independent Learner	Field-dependent Learner
Focuses on global issues	Focuses on details
Seeks out guidance	Enjoys independence
Prefers to work with others	Prefers to work alone
Prefers organization to be provided by teacher	Prefers to organize by himself or herself
Likes to cooperate	Likes to compete

The implications of field independence and field dependence for cooperative learning have been related to students' need for structure. Hunt (1979) identified characteristics of students who need more or less structure to maximize their opportunity to learn. Some of his characteristics, which have implications for how to plan a cooperative learning activity, follow:

Those needing more structure:

- Have shorter attention spans, like to move through material rapidly.
- Are reluctant to try something new and don't like to appear wrong.
- Tend not to ask many questions.
- May need reassurance before starting a task.
- Want to know facts before concepts.
- Usually give only brief answers.

Those needing less structure:

- Like to discuss and argue.
- Want to solve problems with a minimum of teacher assistance.
- Dislike details or step-by-step formats.
- Are comfortable with abstractions and generalities.
- Emphasize emotions and are open about themselves.
- Tend to make many interpretations and inferences.

How can I promote the goals of cooperative learning in the culturally diverse classroom?

Hunt goes on to suggest specific ways teachers can orient their cooperative activities to promote particular learning styles. Examples follow.

For students who require more structure:

1. Have definite and consistent rules.
2. Provide specific, step-by-step guides and instructions.
3. Make goals and deadlines short and definite.
4. Change pace often.
5. Assess problems frequently.
6. Move gradually from group work to discussion.

For students who require less structure:

1. Provide topics to choose from.
2. Make assignments longer, with self-imposed deadlines.
3. Encourage the use of resources outside the classroom.
4. Devote more time to group assignments with teacher serving as a resource.

5. Use and encourage interest in the opinions and values of others.

6. Provide opportunity for extended followup projects and assignments.

Although little is known about how these aspects of a teacher's task orientation relate to specific groups of learners during cooperative learning, Hilliard (1976) and Hill (1989) suggest that some cultural and ethnic groups tend to benefit more and adapt better to a task orientation that is less structured and more field dependent. These and other authors provide alternatives to the notion that the most effective task orientation for the teacher is always to stand in front of the classroom, lecturing or explaining to students seated in neatly arranged rows, who are assumed to have little or no expectations about or experiences with the content being taught. Recent findings suggest that not only may some task orientations, such as cooperative learning, be more appropriate for some groups but some of today's objectives (especially interdisciplinary objectives and objectives pertaining to integrated bodies of knowledge) may *require* cooperative and collaborative activities to achieve their goals.

Summing Up

This chapter introduced you to strategies for cooperative learning. Its main points were as follows:

1. Critical thinking, reasoning and problem-solving skills are of little use if they cannot be applied in cooperative interaction with others.

2. Self-directed and cooperative learning share the complementary objectives of engaging students in the learning process and promoting higher (more complex) patterns of behavior.

3. Cooperative learning activities can instill the following in your learners:

- Attitudes and values that guide the learner's behavior outside of the classroom
- Acceptable forms of social behavior that may not be modeled in the home

- Alternative perspectives and viewpoints with which to think objectively
- An integrated identity that can reduce contradictory thoughts and actions
- Higher thought processes

4. Planning for cooperative learning requires decisions pertaining to the following:

- Teacher–student interaction
- Student–student interaction
- Task specialization and materials
- Role expectations and responsibilities

5. The primary goal of teacher–student interaction during cooperative learning is to promote independent thinking.

6. The primary goal of student–student interaction during cooperative learning is to encourage the active participation and interdependence of all members of the class.

7. The primary goal of task specialization and learning materials during cooperative learning is to create an activity structure whose end product depends on the sharing, cooperation, and collaboration of individuals within groups.

8. The primary goal of assigning roles and responsibilities during cooperative learning is to facilitate the work of the group and to promote communication and sharing among its members.

9. Establishing a cooperative task structure involves five steps:

(1) Specifying the goal of the activity
(2) Structuring the task
(3) Teaching the collaborative process
(4) Monitoring group performance
(5) Debriefing

10. The goal of a cooperative activity may take different forms, such as the following:

- Written group reports
- Higher individual achievement
- An oral performance
- An enumeration or listing
- A critique
- Bibliographic research

11. You have four responsibilities in specifying the goal of a cooperative activity:

- Illustrate the style, format, and length of the end product.
- Place the goal in the context of past and future learning.
- Check for understanding of the goal and directions given for achieving it.
- Set a tone of cooperation, as opposed to competition.

12. Structuring the cooperative learning task involves the following decisions:

- How large the groups will be.
- How group members will be selected.
- How much time will be devoted to group work.
- What roles group members will be assigned.

- What incentives will be provided for individual and group work.

13. Generally, the most efficient size for a group to reach the desired goal in the least amount of time is four or five members.

14. Unless a group task specifically calls for specialized abilities, groups should be formed heterogeneously—or with a representative sample of all learners in the class.

15. Methods for selecting group members include the following:

(1) Asking students to list peers with whom they would like to work.
(2) Randomly assigning students to groups.
(3) Choosing matched opposites: minority/majority, male/female, with/without disabilities, etc.
(4) Sharing with students the process of choosing group members (for example, teacher selects first; then person selected chooses another; and so on).

16. An actively uninvolved group member is one who talks about everything but the assigned goal of the group; a passively uninvolved group member is one who doesn't care about the work of the group and becomes silent.

17. Methods for discouraging active and passive uninvolvement include the following:

- Requesting a product requiring division of labor.
- Forming pairs that oversee each other's work.
- Charting group progress on individually assigned tasks.
- Purposefully limiting group resources to promote sharing and personal contact.
- Requiring a product that is contingent on previous stages that are the work of others.

18. Group work should entail 60–80 percent of the time devoted to a cooperative activity, the remainder being devoted to whole-class discussion and debriefing.

19. Division of labor within a group can be accomplished with role assignments. The following are some of the most popular:

- Summarizer
- Checker
- Researcher
- Runner
- Recorder
- Supporter
- Observer/troubleshooter

20. The following are among the types of reinforcement strategies that can be used with cooperative learning activities:

- Individual and group grades
- Bonus points
- Social responsibilities
- Tokens or privileges
- Group contingencies

21. Teaching the collaborative process involves showing your learners how to do the following:

- Communicate their own ideas and feelings.
- Make messages complete and specific.
- Make verbal and nonverbal messages congruent.
- Convey respect and support.

- Assess if the message was properly received.
- Paraphrase another's point of view.
- Negotiate meanings and understandings.
- Actively participate in a group and assume leadership.

22. During the monitoring of group performance, the teacher's role is to see that each group remains on track, to redirect group efforts when needed, and to provide emotional support and encouragement.

23. During debriefing, there are several ways to gather feedback in a whole-class discussion about the collaborative process:

- Openly talk about how the groups functioned during the cooperative activity.
- Solicit suggestions for how the process could be improved.
- Obtain the viewpoints of predesignated observers.

24. Desirable outcomes have been documented for four popular team-oriented cooperative learning activities:

- Student Teams–Achievement Divisions (STAD)
- Teams-Games-Tournaments (TGT)
- Jigsaw II
- Team-assisted Individualization (TAI)

For Discussion and Practice

*1. What two complementary objectives do self-directed and cooperative learning share?

*2. Identify five specific outcomes that cooperative learning activities can instill in learners.

*3. What three general outcomes can result from these more specific outcomes?

*4. Identify the four most important components of a cooperative learning activity and one critical decision pertaining to each.

*5. What five specific steps are required for establishing a cooperative learning activity?

*6. List the forms of end products that a cooperative learning activity can take.

*7. Approximately how large should a cooperative learning group be to reach a specified goal in the least amount of time?

*8. Identify four methods for selecting group members.

*9. Identify three methods for minimizing passive and active uninvolvement in a cooperative learning activity.

*10. Name seven popular role functions that can be assigned to group members and briefly describe their responsibilities.

*11. Identify five types of reinforcement and reward that could be given to group members for appropriate performance. Create one specific example of each.

*12. Describe a procedure for combining individual and group work into a single score.

*13. Name the eight "sending" skills identified by Johnson and Johnson (1991) and give one specific example of how you would teach each.

*14. What three forms of intervention might you have to provide when monitoring group performance?

*15. Debriefing entails what three activities?

*16. Identify the five obstacles to debriefing identified by Dishon and O'Leary (1984) and one approach to dealing with each.

17. Describe four team-oriented cooperative learning activities with respect to the structure of the activity to be performed, the work of the teams, your role as teacher, and procedures for team scoring and recognition.

---

* Answers to asterisked questions (*) in this and the other chapters are in Appendix B.

Suggested Readings

Johnson, D. (1986). *Reaching out: Interpersonal effectiveness and self-actualization* (2nd ed.). Englewood Cliffs, NJ: Prentice-Hall.

   Presents some of the reasons why cooperative learning is so important, based on practical research and experience.

Johnson, D., & Johnson, R. (1991). *Learning together and alone* (3rd ed.). Englewood Cliffs, NJ: Prentice-Hall.

   One of the most popular and complete texts on cooperative learning, written especially for the beginning teacher.

Johnson, D., Johnson, R., Holubec, E., & Roy, P. (1984). *Circles of learning: Cooperation in the classroom.* Alexandria, VA: Association for Supervision and Curriculum Development.

   More practical activities for cooperative learning that can be implemented in any subject and at any grade level.

Slavin, R. (1990). *Cooperative learning: Theory, research and practice.* Englewood Cliffs: NJ: Prentice-Hall.

   A thorough review of the uses and benefits of cooperative learning—with important ideas for implementing cooperative learning in your classroom.

Slavin, R. (1991). Are cooperative learning and untracking harmful to the gifted? *Educational Leadership, 48,* 68–71.

   An important discussion of how cooperative learning can be of benefit in the heterogeneously grouped classroom.

Slavin, R. (1993). *Student team learning: An overview and practical guide.* Washington, DC: National Education Association.

   A concise and practical description of how to implement four cooperative learning activities in the classroom.

Slavin R., Sharan, S., Kagan, S., Hertz-Lazarowitz, R., Webb, C., & Schmuck, R. (1985). *Learning to cooperate, cooperating to learn.* New York: Plenum.

   A book of 16 individually authored chapters on many of the most important dimensions of cooperative learning, including cooperative learning activities in mathematics and science and multi-ethnic classrooms.

CHAPTER 11

Classroom Management

This chapter will help you answer the following questions:

1. What do I need to manage my classroom effectively?
2. How do I guide my learners through the natural stages of group development?
3. What can I do during the first weeks of school to get my learners to trust one another and feel as members of a group?
4. What can I teach my learners to help them discuss and resolve group conflicts on their own?
5. How do I get my class to develop group norms?
6. How can I create a social environment to match my instructional goals?
7. What types of classroom rules will I need?
8. How do I write an effective classroom rule?
9. How can I ensure orderly transitions between lesson activities?
10. How can I convey assignments positively and motivate learners to complete them?
11. How can I bring closure to a lesson?
12. How might I use the social organization of my classroom to bridge cultural gaps?

This chapter will also help you learn the meaning of the following:

centering behavior
crystallization of norms
culturally sensitive classroom management
diffusion of norms
distancing behavior
first-day planning
organizational environment
rules and procedures
social environment
social power
stages of group development

For most teachers, confronting some sort of behavior problem is a daily occurrence. These problems may include simple infractions of school or classroom rules, or they may involve more serious events, including disrespect, cheating, obscene words and gestures, and the open display of hostility. In this chapter and the next we will explore important issues pertaining to classroom management. In this chapter we present a framework for anticipating classroom behavior problems through an understanding and promotion of the processes by which cohesive and responsible groups are formed. In Chapter 12 we present strategies for resolving classroom behavior problems using your knowledge of group process and anticipatory management.

It is important that the management of your classroom begin with developing trusting relationships with your students. Without mutual feelings of trust and respect, you will be unable to assume the role of an instructional leader in your classroom. In this chapter we will discuss the many ways trusting relationships and a cohesive classroom can prevent and resolve many behavior problems before they occur. We will discuss how you can accomplish the following:

1. Design an orderly workplace that promotes your academic goals.
2. Develop rules for the workplace that create group norms that students respect and follow.
3. Adapt in the face of unproductive rules, routines, and procedures.
4. Maintain a workplace that fosters feelings of belonging and group solidarity.
5. Know how to seek help from other school professionals and from parents.

What do I need to manage my classroom effectively?

>>> EARNING TRUST AND BECOMING A <<< LEADER—THE "OLD-FASHIONED WAY"

What kind of group leader do you want to be? How do you want to be perceived by your students? How will you establish your leadership so as to help learners feel comfortable with you and one another? How will you make converts of some learners and compatriots of others?

According to social psychologists (French & Raven, 1959; Raven, 1974), to establish yourself as an effective leader you will have to gain your students' trust and respect the "old-fashioned way"—you'll have to earn it. But how? French and Raven provide a way of looking at how you earn respect by asking the question, "How do you achieve social power?" They identify five types of **social power** or leadership a teacher can strive for: *expert* power, *referent* power, *legitimate* power, *reward* power, and *coercive* power.

Expert Power

Certain individuals become leaders because others perceive them as experts. Successful teachers have *expert power*. Their students see them as competent to explain or do certain things and as knowledgeable about particular topics. Such influence is earned, rather than conferred by virtue of having a particular title. Teachers with expert power explain things well, show enthusiasm and excitement about what they teach, and appear confident and self-assured before their classes.

New teachers often find it difficult to establish leadership through expert power. Even though they are knowledgeable and competent in their field, uncertainty and inexperience in front of a group may make them appear less so. Students are attuned to body language suggesting lack of confidence and indecision and may test the competence and challenge the authority of a teacher who appears not to be in command of his or her subject.

Referent Power

Students often accept as leaders teachers whom they like and respect. They view such teachers as trustworthy, fair, and concerned about them (Goodlad, 1984). The term *referent power* is used to describe leadership earned in this way. Ask any group of junior high or high school students about why they like particular teachers and invariably the teachers they like are described as "fair," "caring" and "someone you can talk to." Without referent power, even teachers with expert power may have their authority challenged or ignored.

One often hears teachers say that they would rather be respected than liked, as if these two consequences were mutually exclusive. Research by Soar and Soar (1983) suggests that teachers can be both respected and liked: teachers who were both respected and liked were associated with greater student satisfaction and higher achievement. Glasser (1986) emphasizes that students' needs for belonging in a classroom will more likely be met by a teacher who is perceived as both warm and competent.

Legitimate Power

Some roles carry with them influence and authority by their very nature. Police officers, presidents, and judges exert social power and leadership by their very titles. Influence in such cases may be conferred by the role itself rather than being dependent on the nature of the person assuming the role. Savage (1991) refers to this type of power as *legitimate power* and, unlike expert and referent power, it may not be earned. Teachers possess a certain degree of legitimate power. Our society expects students to give teachers their attention, respect them, and follow their requests. Most families also stress the importance of "listening to the teacher." Every new teacher begins her or his first day of class with legitimate power.

Legitimate power, therefore, gives the new teacher some "breathing room" during the first few weeks of school. Most students will initially obey and accept the authority of a new teacher by virtue of her or his position of authority. However, building classroom leadership solely through legitimate power, bestowed by others, may be like building a house on a foundation of sand. The first challenge to authority may quickly erode any initial influence legitimate power may have provided. Teachers, therefore, should use their legitimate power to establish referent and expert power.

Reward Power

Individuals in positions of authority are able to exercise *reward power* in relation to the people whom they lead. These rewards can take the form of privileges, approval, or more tangible compensation, such as money. To the extent that students desire the rewards conferred by teachers, teachers can exert a degree of leadership and authority. There is, however, a relative paucity of rewards available to teachers and a great number of rewards available to students without the aid of a teacher. Students who don't care much about good grades or teacher approval are difficult to lead solely by exerting reward power, since students can attain outside of school much of what is reinforcing to them. In such cases some teachers resort to using tangible reinforcers such as access to desired activities, objects, and even food. In the next chapter, we will examine some of the ways you can use reinforcement in your classroom. In this chapter, you will learn that reward power can be an effective tool in the classroom but cannot substitute for referent and expert power.

Coercive Power

Through state and local government, teachers are allowed to act *in loco parentis*, i.e., in place of the parent. Consequently, within limits schools can punish students who defy the authority or leadership of the teacher by such techniques as suspension or expulsion, denial of privileges or removal from the classroom. Teachers who rely on such techniques to maintain social power in their classroom are said to be using *coercive power*. The use of coercive power may stop misbehavior for a time, but this will sometimes be at the cost of developing trust and meeting student needs. Overreliance on coercive power has the danger of increasing attitudes that may lead to the formation of subgroups antagonistic to classroom objectives, group cooperation, and achievement.

While each of these sources of power, when properly used, is a legitimate tool for managing the classroom, teachers, especially new teachers, should work to quickly achieve expert and referent power. You can achieve expert power by keeping up to date with developments in your teaching field, completing inservice and graduate programs, attending seminars and workshops, and by completing career ladder and mentoring activities provided by your school district. From your very first day in the classroom you can exhibit referent power by giving your students a sense of belonging and acceptance.

>>> STAGES OF GROUP DEVELOPMENT <<<

Social psychologists, such as Schmuck and Schmuck (1988), Johnson and Johnson (1987), and Schutz (1958), believe that the sources of social power you acquire are important for guiding your learners through the process of group development. They believe that every successful group passes through a series of **stages of development** during which it has certain tasks to accomplish and concerns to resolve. The way the group accomplishes these tasks and resolves these concerns determines the extent to which you can effectively and efficiently manage the group and accomplish the goals of your classroom. Mauer (1985) describes these stages:

How do I guide my learners through the natural stages of group development?

Stage 1: **Forming**—resolving concerns about acceptance and responsibilities

Stage 2: **Storming**—resolving concerns about shared influence

Stage 3: **Norming**—resolving concerns about how work gets done

Stage 4: **Performing**—resolving concerns about freedom, control, and self-regulation

Stage 1: Forming

When learners come together at the start of the school year, they usually are concerned about two issues: (1) finding their place in the social structure, and (2) finding out what they are expected to do. Schutz (1958) identifies this first issue as concerns about "inclusion" or group membership.

During the first several days of class, learners (and teachers) naturally ask, "How will I fit in?" "Who will accept or reject me?" "What do I have to do to be respected?" At this time, a phenomenon called *testing* takes place (Froyen, 1993). Learners engage in specific actions to see what kind of reaction they get from teachers and peers. This is the learner's way of finding out how the teacher and peers feel toward him or her. At this stage of group formation, learners are curious about one another. They want to know where other class members live, who their friends are, what they like to do, and where they like to go. As students learn more about one another, they begin to see how and with whom they fit in.

Putnam and Burke (1992) urge teachers to engage in activities during the first few weeks of school to help learners trust one another and feel as members of a group, activities that accomplish the following:

What can I do during the first weeks of school to get my learners to trust one another and feel as members of a group?

1. Help teachers and students learn about one another and to develop trust.
2. Foster appreciation for other students' abilities.
3. Inform learners about work expectations, rules, routines, and what life in the classroom will be like.
4. Promote learners' view of themselves having a voice in the running of the classroom.
5. Assess what learners know and can do.

Social psychologists caution teachers that there is a tendency during the first stage of classroom group development to concentrate almost exclusively on concerns about work and rules to the

Table 11.1

Important questions about group development

Stage 1: Forming	Stage 2: Storming	Stage 3: Norming	Stage 4: Performing
1. Are there activities for everyone to get to know about one another?	1. Are conflicts openly recognized and discussed?	1. Is there a process for resolving conflict?	1. Can this group evaluate its own effectiveness?
2. Has everyone had a chance to be heard?	2. Can the group assess its own functioning?	2. Can the group set goals?	2. Can the group and individuals solve their own problems?
3. Do learners interact with a variety of classmates?	3. Are new and different ideas listened to and evaluated?	3. Can learners express what is expected of them?	3. Does the group have opportunities to work independently and express themselves through a medium of their own choosing?
4. Do learners and teachers listen to one another?	4. Are the skills of all members being used?	4. Is there mutual respect between teacher and learners?	4. Can individuals evaluate themselves and set goals for personal improvement?
5. Have concerns and/or fears regarding academic and behavioral expectations been addressed?	5. Do all learners have an opportunity to share leadership and responsibility?	5. What happens to learners who fail to respect norms?	5. Is the group prepared to disband?

exclusion of concerns about inclusion. They warn that learners who have unresolved fears about acceptance by their teacher and where they fit in the peer group will find it difficult to concentrate on academic work without first developing trust and feeling as valued members of a group (Schmuck & Schmuck, 1992).

Table 11.1 lists questions you can ask to promote group development during the forming stage.

Stage 2: Storming

The goal of the forming stage of group development is to help learners feel secure and perceive themselves as members of a classroom group. Healthy group life at this stage occurs if learners have accepted the teacher as their leader, made some initial commitment to follow rules and procedures, and agree to respect other members of the class.

During the storming stage of group development, they begin to test the limits of these commitments (Froyen, 1993). This limit testing may take the form of amiable challenges to academic expectations (homework, classwork, tests, etc.) and rules in order to establish under what conditions they do and do not apply. Learners may question seating arrangements, homework responsibilities, seatwork routines, and so on. They may want further explanations for rules that they initially agreed to follow.

Social psychologists refer to these amiable challenges to teacher authority and leadership as examples of **distancing behavior**. They occur in any group where a leader initially establishes authority by virtue of his or her position rather than through competence or credibility. This distancing behavior represents reservations learners have at this stage of group development about the commitments they made during the forming stage to class expectations and group participation.

A second type of amiable limit testing, which often accompanies distancing behavior, is called **centering**. Centering occurs when learners question how they will personally benefit from being a group member. Their behavior can be described with the question, "What's in it for me?" The questions they ask and assertions they make reflect a preoccupation with fairness. They are quick to notice favoritism toward individual members of the group.

These distancing and centering conflicts arising between teachers and learners and among learners are a natural part of group development. Social psychologists caution teachers about feeling threatened or overreacting at this stage. The storming stage is best perceived as a desirable reflection on past commitments, which must occur on the journey to developing a healthy group life. During these types of conflicts, you will need to monitor compliance with rules and procedures, but be willing to reconsider those that may not be working.

Glasser (1986) and Putnam and Burke (1992) urge teachers to have class discussions centering around group conflict resolution. They recommend that teachers instruct their learners on how to problem-solve using the following guide:

What can I teach my learners to help them discuss and resolve group conflicts on their own?

1. *Problem agreement.* The teacher gets all members of the class to agree that there is a problem and that they will work together to solve it.

2. *State the conflict.* The teacher states concisely what the conflict is and assures all learners that they will have the opportunity to state their perspective.
3. *Identify and select responses.* Teachers and learners brainstorm and record solutions to the problem. They assess the short- and long-term consequences of the solutions and discard those that have negative consequences.
4. *Create a solution.* The class discusses and records a solution that all basically agree will resolve the conflict.
5. *Design and implement a plan.* The class discusses and works out the details of when, where, and how to resolve the conflict.
6. *Assess the success of the plan.* The class identifies information they can gather to determine the success of the plan. Checkpoints are identified to evaluate how the class is doing. When the conflict is resolved, the whole class discusses the value of the problem-solving process.

Table 11.1 lists questions you can ask to promote group development during the storming stage.

Stage 3: Norming

The security learners develop at the forming stage provides them with a safe foundation to challenge teacher authority during the storming stage. Skilled leadership during the storming stage assures learners that they will be listened to, treated fairly, and allowed to share power and influence. This assurance leads them during the norming stage to accept both academic expectations, procedures, and rules for the group and the roles and functions of the various group members.

Norms are shared expectations among group members regarding how they should think, feel, and behave. Social psychologists view norms as the principal regulators of group behavior (Zimbardo, 1992). They may take the form of either written or unwritten rules that all or most of the group voluntarily agree to follow. A classroom group has norms when learners, for the most part, agree on what is and is not socially acceptable classroom behavior.

Norms play an important role in governing behavior in the classroom. But, they do so differently than rules and procedures. Norms are more personally meaningful than rules, as seen in the following examples:

It's OK to be seen talking to the teacher.
Learners in this class should help one another.

We're all responsible for our own learning.

We shouldn't gloat when one of our classmates gives the wrong answer.

We need to respect the privacy of others.

The most important thing for this class is learning.

Social psychologists believe that positive norms serve several important functions in the classroom (Putnam & Burke, 1992; Schmuck & Schmuck, 1992; Froyen, 1993).

- Norms orient group members to what social interactions are and are not appropriate, and then regulate these interactions. When norms are present, learners can anticipate the ways others will behave in the classroom and also how they are expected to behave.
- Norms create group identification and group cohesiveness (Zimbardo, 1992). Social psychologists believe that the process of group formation begins when its members agree to adhere to the norms of the group. This process begins during the forming stage of group development and ends during the norming stage.
- Norms promote academic achievement and positive relationships among class members. Academic and social goals are more likely to be achieved in classrooms with consistent norms. For example, peer group norms represent one of the most important influences on school performance (Schmuck & Schmuck, 1992).

Group norms, whether in support of a teacher's goals or opposed to them, begin to develop on the first day of school during the forming stage of group development. Zimbardo (1992) identifies two basic processes by which norms develop: **diffusion** and **crystallization**. Diffusion takes place as learners first enter a group or class. They bring with them expectations acquired from experiences in other classes, from other group memberships, and experiences growing up. As learners talk and mingle with each other during breaks and recess, they communicate with one another. Their various expectations for academic and social behavior are diffused and spread throughout the entire class. Eventually, as learners engage in a variety of activities together, their expectations begin to converge and crystallize into a shared perspective of classroom life.

How do I get my class to develop group norms?

You should do all you can to influence the development of norms that support your classroom goals. It is important that you know how to positively influence the development of class norms and to identify and alter existing ones. Here are some suggestions for developing, identifying, and altering group norms:

- Explain to the class the concept of a *group norm*. Draw up a list of norms with the class and, over time, add and delete norms that either help or impede the work of the group.
- Conduct discussions of class norms and encourage learners to talk among themselves about them. Glasser (1986) suggests discussing with students ideas on how the class might be run, problems that may interfere with the group's performance, and needed rules and routines.
- Appoint or elect a class council to make recommendations for improving class climate and productivity. Have the group assess whether the norms are working.
- Provide a model of the respect, consistency, and responsibility for learning that you want your learners to exhibit.

Healthy group development at the norming stage is characterized by group behavior primarily focused on academic achievement. Assuming group development has proceeded successfully up to this point, group members now are concerned with both their own learning and that of the group. Learners feel secure and trust one another, accept their role as followers and the teacher's role as group leader, and are ready to get down to the business of the classroom. The norms that develop at this stage assure the group members that they know how to pursue and achieve their academic goals. Many teachers see the norming stage as the most satisfying and productive phase of group development.

Stage 4: Performing

By the time the group has reached the fourth developmental stage, learners feel at ease with one another, know the rules and their roles, accept group norms, and are familiar with the routine of the classroom. The principal concern for the group at this stage is establishing its independence.

Just as the storming stage of development was characterized by a testing of limits, the performing stage is characterized by learners wanting to show that they can do some things independently of the teacher. Social psychologists urge teachers to encourage the desire for independence at this stage by focusing less on classroom control and more on teaching the group how to set priorities, budget its time, self-evaluate, self-regulate, and self-discipline. Putnam and

Burke (1992) recommend that during this stage, in comparison to the others, teachers devote more time modeling to students how to reflect on what they have learned and to evaluate their own performance. These activities are important for exhibiting the performance behaviors that often occur concurrently with this stage.

The performing stage ends when the school year or semester ends. Thus, this stage represents a time of transition. Assuming all four stages of development have been successfully completed, learners will have developed relationships with one another and with their teacher through which they may manage themselves with the guidance and direction of the teacher. For this transition to successfully occur, however, you will need to establish a classroom climate in which group development can flourish through all four stages.

>>> ESTABLISHING AN EFFECTIVE <<< CLASSROOM CLIMATE

Classroom climate is the atmosphere or mood in which interactions between you and your students take place. Your classroom climate is created by the manner and degree to which you exercise authority, show warmth and support, encourage competitiveness or cooperation, and allow for independent judgment and choice. Although seldom recognized, the climate of your classroom is your choice, just as are your instructional methods.

Unfortunately, in many classrooms the climate is determined haphazardly. It is allowed to develop randomly, depending on what is occurring at the moment. This is not the case in a well-managed classroom. This section introduces two related aspects of an effective classroom climate: the **social environment**, meaning the interaction patterns you promote in the classroom, and the **organizational environment**, meaning your physical or visual arrangement of the classroom. Both are your choice, and you can alter them to create just the right climate for the proper objective.

The Social Environment

The social environment of your classroom can vary from *authoritarian*, in which you are the primary provider of information, opinions, and instruction, to *laizzez faire*, in which your students become the primary providers of information, opinions, and instruction. Between these extremes lies the middle ground in which you and your students *share responsibilities*: students are given freedom of

One aspect of an effective learning climate is the physical or visual arrangement of the classroom. This arrangement is a matter of choice that can be altered to create just the right climate for your learning objectives.

choice and judgment under your direction. Many variations are possible, and the variation you choose will have pronounced effects on the objectives you can and cannot achieve in your classroom.

For example, a group discussion might be a colossal failure in a rigid authoritarian climate, because the climate clues students that their opinions are less important than yours, that teacher talk and not student talk should take up most of the instructional time, and that the freedom to express oneself spontaneously is your right but not theirs. In a more open atmosphere this same attempt at discussion might well be a smashing success, because all the ingredients of a good discussion—freedom to express one's opinion, high degree of student talk, and spontaneity—have been provided by the classroom climate.

The social atmosphere you create, whether authoritarian, laissez faire, or somewhere between, is determined by how you see yourself: Are you a commander-in-chief who carefully controls and hones student behavior by organizing and providing all the learning stimuli? Or, are you a translator or summarizer of the ideas provided by students? Or, are you an equal partner with students in creating ideas and problem solutions? Consider the effects of each climate and how you can create it.

The effective teacher not only uses a variety of teaching strategies but also creates a variety of classroom climates. However, your ability to create a certain climate is less important than your ability to *change* the climate when the objectives and situation demand. Although early research in social psychology tried to identify the type of climate most conducive to individual behavior (Lippitt & Gold, 1959), the results suggest that different climates have both their advantages and disadvantages, depending on the intended goal.

Because goals change from lesson to lesson and week to week, so too must your classroom climate that supports the goals. When the goals change but your classroom climate does not, the stage is set for off-task, disruptive, and even antagonistic behavior among your students.

How can I create a social environment to match my instructional goals?

Competitive, Cooperative, or Individualistic.   We have already examined several ways you can vary your authority, and that of your students, in accordance with your objectives. These variations correspond not only with how much you relinquish your authority and therefore your control of the learning process, but also how competitive, cooperative, or individualistic you wish the interactions among members of your class to be. These three conditions are illustrated in Table 11.2.

You can see in the table that, as you shift classroom climate from competitive to cooperative to individualistic, you relinquish control over the learning process until, in the individualistic mode, students have almost sole responsibility for judging their own work. Note also that an individualistic mode all but eliminates student expressions of opinion, student talk, and spontaneity of responses, all of which are encouraged and promoted in a cooperative climate.

Each of the three climates has characteristic activities: the competitive mode features drill and practice in which students respond to your questions; the cooperative mode has group discussions in which both you and your students pose questions and answers; and the individualistic mode uses detailed seatwork assignments in which students practice independently. Your control and authority and the behaviors you can expect from your students will differ among these social climates, as indicated in Table 11.2.

Applying the Three Climates.   In addition to encouraging the proper climate for a given instructional activity (e.g., drill and practice, group discussion, or seatwork), you must decide to which segments of the class each climate applies. Figure 11.1 suggests that each climate can be applied to the full class, to groups, and to individuals with equal effectiveness. For example, it is not necessary that all group discussions be conducted in a cooperative climate.

You can form subgroups to compete against each other in a gamelike atmosphere (see Cell 21 in the figure), or individuals can work in a cooperative arrangement by exchanging papers and correcting each other's errors (Cell 32). Likewise, your entire class can

Table 11.2
Three types of classroom climate

Social climate	Definition	Example activity	Authority vested in students	Authority vested in teacher
Competitive	Students compete for right answers among themselves or with a standard established by the teacher. The teacher is the sole judge of the appropriateness of a response.	Drill and practice	None	To organize the instruction, present the stimulus material, and evaluate correctness of responses
Cooperative	Students engage in dialogue that is monitored by the teacher. The teacher systematically intervenes in the discussion to sharpen ideas and move the discussion to a higher level.	Small and large group discussion	To present opinions, to provide ideas, and to speak and discuss freely and spontaneously	To stimulate the discussion, arbitrate differences, organize and summarize student contributions
Individualistic	Students complete assignments monitored by the teacher. Students are encouraged to complete the assignment with the answers they think are best. Emphasis is on getting through and testing one's self.	Independent seatwork	To complete the assignment with the best possible responses	To assign the work and see that orderly progress is made toward its completion

	Competitive	Cooperative	Individualistic
Full Class	Students compete with other students by having the correct answer when it's their turn. <div align="right">11</div>	Students are allowed to call out hints or clues when a student is having difficulty finding the right answer. <div align="right">12</div>	The entire class recites answers in unison. <div align="right">13</div>
Groups	Subgroups compete against each other as opposing teams. <div align="right">21</div>	Subgroups work on different but related aspects of a topic combining their results into a final report to the class. <div align="right">22</div>	Each subgroup completes its own assigned topic which is independent of the topics assigned the other subgroups. No shared report is given to the class. <div align="right">23</div>
Individual	Individuals compete with each other by having to respond to the same question. The quickest most accurate response "wins." <div align="right">31</div>	Pairs of individuals cooperate by exchanging papers, sharing responses, or correcting each other's errors. <div align="right">32</div>	Individuals complete seat work on their own without direct teacher involvement. <div align="right">33</div>

Figure 11.1
Targets for three types of classroom climates

perform seatwork in lockstep fashion as though the class were a single individual (Cell 13), and subgroups can be asked to work as independent teams (Cell 23), and individuals can be teamed in pairs to compete with each other (Cell 31).

Although some cells in Figure 11.1 may be more popular than others, various arrangements of students and climates are possible, depending on your instructional goals. Your job is to ensure that the degree of authority you impose matches your instructional goal (e.g., the expression of student opinion you allow, the amount of time you devote to student talk, and the spontaneity with which you want your students to respond).

The Organizational Environment

In addition to arranging the social climate of your classroom, you also must arrange the physical climate. It goes without saying that a classroom should be attractive, well lighted, comfortable, and colorful. But, aside from a colorful bulletin board and neatness, you may have very little influence over the external features of your classroom (e.g., paint, lighting, windows, and even such things as the availability of bookshelves and a file cabinet). Attempts to improve these external conditions always are worth a try, but do not be surprised if your repeated requests are in vain. It is not unusual for teachers to bring their own essential items, such as a clock, bookcase, file cabinet, rug, or pedestal stool to the classroom at the beginning of the year and take them home again for the summer.

What may be more important than these items, however, is the way the internal features of your classroom (desks, chairs, tables) are arranged. Students quickly get used to and accept the external features of a classroom, good or bad. But the internal arrangement of the classroom will affect your students every day of the school year.

The most flexible furniture arrangement places your desk at the front of the room and aligns the student desks in rows. Although it may seem strange to associate this traditional format with flexibility, it is most flexible because you can use it to create competitive, cooperative, or individualistic environments, although not always with equal effectiveness. This fact, plus the difficulty of rearranging classroom furniture every time a change in social climate is desired, makes the traditional classroom arrangement almost as popular today as it was 50 years ago.

There are times, however, when you should change the arrangement to encourage a more cooperative, interactive, and group-sharing climate. Such a classroom arrangement has many variations that depend on the external features of the classroom and available furniture, but one such model is shown in Figure 11.2.

The important feature to note in this arrangement is the deliberate attempt to get people together. The barriers to interpersonal sharing and communication that sometimes result from the rigid alignment of desks are avoided in this setting by the more informal, but still systematic, furniture arrangement. As the internal features of the classroom turn from traditional to this less formal arrangement, so too will the social climate of the classroom change. Because this arrangement suggests that interpersonal communication and sharing is permitted, increased interpersonal communication and sharing will undoubtedly occur, whether you desire it or not.

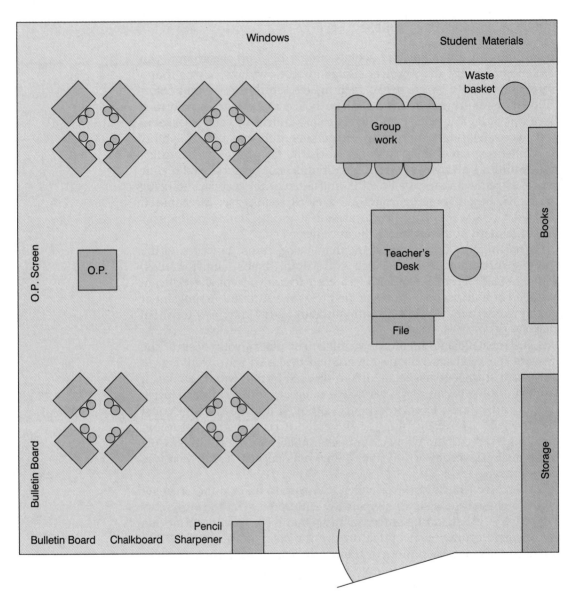

Figure 11.2
A classroom arrangement conducive to group work

From such an arrangement, expect more expression of student opinion, increased student talk, and greater spontaneity in student responses. This emphasizes the important notion that *the social climate created by your words and deeds always should match the organizational climate created by the physical arrangement of your classroom*. It also explains why the traditional or formal classroom actually is quite flexible and has remained so popular. A cooperative climate (e.g., for conducting a group discussion) always can occur in a formal classroom, but a competitive climate (e.g., for drill and practice) becomes exceedingly difficult in a less formal arrangement. This is not a reason to abandon the appeal of a less rigid classroom arrangement, but only to use it with a firm grasp of the student behavior it is likely to promote.

Of course, it always is refreshing to change the internal arrangement of a classroom from time to time for the sake of variety. This can be an effective psychological boost for both teacher and students in the midst of a long and arduous school year. Keep in mind, however, that time and effort allow for only so much back-and-forth switching. You might compromise by maintaining the basic nature of the formal classroom but, space permitting, setting aside one or two less formal areas (e.g., a learning center or group discussion table) for times when instructional goals call for interpersonal communication and sharing.

>>> ESTABLISHING RULES AND PROCEDURES <<<

Establishing **rules and procedures** to reduce the occurrence of classroom discipline problems will be one of your most important classroom management activities (Emmer et al., 1994). These rules and procedures, which you should formulate prior to the first school day, are your commitment to applying the ounce of prevention to avoid having to provide a pound of cure.

What types of classroom rules will I need?

Different types of rules and procedures are needed for effectively managing a classroom; these fall into four basic categories:

Rules related to academic work.

Rules related to classroom conduct.

Rules that must be communicated your first teaching day.

Rules that can be communicated later, at an appropriate opportunity.

The top half of Figure 11.3 identifies rules commonly needed the very first day of class, either because students will ask about

	Rules related to classroom conduct	Rules related to academic work
Rules that need to be communicated first day	1. where to sit 2. how seats are assigned 3. what to do before the bell rings 4. responding, speaking out 5. leaving at the bell 6. drinks, food, and gum 7. washroom and drinking privileges	8. materials required for class 9. homework completion 10. makeup work 11. incomplete work 12. missed quizzes and examinations 13. determining grades 14. violation of rules
Rules that can be communicated later	15. tardiness/absences 16. coming up to desk 17. when a visitor comes to the door 18. leaving the classroom 19. consequences of rule violation	20. notebook completion 21. obtaining help 22. notetaking 23. sharing work with others 24. use of learning center and/or reference works 25. communication during group work 26. neatness 27. lab safety

Figure 11.3
Classroom rules related to conduct and work

them or because incidents are likely to arise requiring their use. Notice that these rules are divided into seven conduct rules and seven work rules. For the elementary grades, it is best that you present them orally, *and* provide a handout, *and* post them for later reference by the students. In the lower grades, learners can forget oral messages quickly—or choose to ignore them if there is no physical representation of the rule as a constant reminder. In the later elementary grades and junior high, your recital of the rules while students copy them into their notebooks may be sufficient. For high school students, simply hearing the rules may be sufficient, as long as they are posted for later reference.

Not all "first day" rules are equally important, and other rules may have to be added as special circumstances require. But rules about responding and speaking out, making up work, determining grades, and violation of due dates are among the most important. It is in these areas that confusion often occurs on the very first day.

For example, following are some of the issues you must consider in these four rule areas:

Rule Area	Issues
Responding, speaking out	☐ Must hands be raised? ☐ Are other forms of acknowledgement acceptable (e.g., head nod)? ☐ What will happen if a student speaks when others are speaking? ☐ What will you do about shouting or using a loud voice?
Makeup work	☐ Will makeup work be allowed? ☐ Will there be penalties for not completing it? ☐ Will it be graded? ☐ Whose responsibility is it to know the work is missing?
Determining grades	☐ What percentage will quizzes and tests contribute to the total grade? ☐ What percentage will class participation count? ☐ When will notification be given of failing performance? ☐ How much will homework count?
Violation of due dates	☐ What happens when repeated violations occur? ☐ Where can a student learn the due dates if absent? ☐ What penalties are there for copying another person's assignment? ☐ Will makeup work be required when a due date is missed?

A few moments of thought before these issues are raised in class can avoid embarrassing pauses and an uncertain response when a student asks a question. You may want to identify alternative issues for the remaining rule areas in Figure 11.3 and to extend those just listed to your own grade level.

The bottom half of Figure 11.3 identifies areas for which rules can be communicated as the situation arises. Some are specific to a particular situation (e.g., safety during a lab experiment, notebook completion, obtaining help) and are best presented in the context to which they apply. They will be more meaningful and more easily remembered *when there is a circumstance or incident that applies to the rule and thus aids in its retention.* Many other rules in these areas, however, are likely to be needed in the first few days or weeks of school (e.g., tardiness/absences, leaving at the bell, notetaking). Even though you may not communicate these rules on the first day of school, they usually are required so soon afterward that you must compose a procedure for them prior to your first class day.

Some of the most troublesome behaviors in this category include students getting out of their seats, communicating during group work, completing in-class assignments early, and violating rules. Issues to be considered for these behaviors include the following:

Behavior	Issues
Getting out of seat	☐ When is out-of-seat movement permissible?
	☐ When can a student come to the teacher's desk?
	☐ When can reference books or learning centers be visited?
	☐ What if a student visits another?
Communicating during group work	☐ Can a student leave an assigned seat?
	☐ How loudly should a student speak?
	☐ Who determines who can talk next?
	☐ Will there be a group leader?
Early completion of in-class assignments	☐ Can work for other classes or subjects be done?
	☐ Can a newspaper or magazine be read?
	☐ Can the next exercise or assignment be worked on?
	☐ Can students rest their heads on their desks?
Rule violation	☐ Will names be written on the board?
	☐ Will extra work penalties be assigned?
	☐ Will you have after-class detention?
	☐ When will a disciplinary referral be made?

How do I write an effective classroom rule?

Here are several general suggestions for creating classroom rules:

• Make your rules consistent with the classroom climate you wish to promote. As a beginning teacher, now is the time to recognize your values and preferences for managing your classroom. Articulate your personal philosophy of classroom management and have your class rules reflect it. For example, do you want your classroom climate to emphasize independent judgment, spontaneity, and risk taking, or do you want it to emphasize teacher-initiated exchanges, formal classroom rules, and teacher-solicited responses?

- Don't establish rules that you can't enforce. A rule that says "No talking," or "No getting out of your seat," may be difficult to enforce when your personal philosophy continually encourages spontaneity, problem solving, and group work. Unfairness and inconsistency may result in applying rules you do not fully believe in.

- Specify only necessary rules. There are four reasons to have rules and each should reflect at least one of these purposes:

    Enhance work engagement and minimize disruption

    Promote safety and security

    Prevent disturbance to others or other classroom activities

    Promote acceptable standards of courtesy and interpersonal relations

- State your rules at a general enough level to include a range of specific behaviors. The rule, "Respect other people's property and person," covers a variety of problems, such as stealing, borrowing without permission, throwing objects, etc. Similarly, the rule, "Follow teacher requests immediately," allows you to put an end to a variety of off-task, disruptive behaviors that no list of rules could anticipate or comprehensively cover. However, be careful not to state a rule so generally that the specific problems to which it pertains remain unclear to your learners. For example, a rule stating simply, "Show respect," or "Obey the teacher," may be sufficiently vague to be ignored by most of your learners and unenforceable by you. If you follow this suggestion and the one above, you should have about four to six classroom rules.

It is a secure feeling to know that you have created procedures for dealing with the many possible problem areas. However, unless you clearly communicate your rules and apply them consistently, all your work in making them will be meaningless. Consistency is a key reason why some rules are effective while others are not. Rules that are not enforced or that are not applied evenly and consistently over time result in a loss of prestige and respect for the person who has created the rules and has the responsibility for carrying them out.

Following are the most frequently occurring reasons why a particular rule is not applied consistently (Emmer et al., 1994):

1. The rule is not workable or appropriate. It does not fit a particular context or is not reasonable, given the nature of the individuals to whom it applies.

2. The teacher fails to monitor students closely and consequently some individuals violating the rule are caught while others are not.
3. The teacher does not feel strongly enough about the rule to be persistent about its enforcement and thus makes many exceptions to the rule.

When you realize that any of the preceding conditions apply, think about changing the rule. One cannot state flatly that rules are made to be broken, but it is true that even good rules should be altered, changed, or even abandoned when circumstances change. If you allow a rule to be repeatedly ignored or broken, it will have the worst possible effect on your ability to manage your classroom effectively. On the other hand, rigidly clinging to a rule that obviously is not working or is not needed will have an equally detrimental effect.

Keep in mind that minor deviations in a rule may not be worth your effort to respond when (1) it would provide an untimely interruption to your lesson or (2) it is only momentary and not likely to recur. However, when problems in applying a rule persist over time, either increase your vigilance or adjust the rule to allow more flexibility in your response (e.g., coming up to the desk without permission for help may be acceptable, but coming up just to talk is not).

>>> PROBLEM AREAS IN <<<
CLASSROOM MANAGEMENT

A primary purpose of effective classroom management is to keep learners actively engaged in the learning process. Active engagement means getting learners to work with and act upon the material presented, as evidenced by carefully attending to the material, progressing through seatwork at a steady pace, participating in class discussions, and being attentive when called upon. This section describes four events that are particularly crucial for keeping students actively engaged in the learning process: *monitoring students, making transitions, giving assignments*, and *bringing closure to lessons*. Following are some effective classroom management practices in each of these areas.

Monitoring Students

Monitoring is the process of observing, mentally recording, and, when necessary, redirecting or correcting students' behaviors. Monitoring occurs when you look for active, alert eyes during discussion sessions, faces down and directed at the book or assignment during seatwork, raised hands during a question-and-answer period, and, in general, signs that indicate that learners are participating in what is going on. These signs of engagement (or their absence) indicate when you need to change the pace of your delivery, the difficulty of the material, or even the activity itself.

Kounin (1970) used the word *withitness* to refer to a teacher's ability to keep track of many different signs of engagement at the same time. Kounin observed that one of the most important distinctions between effective and ineffective classroom managers is the degree to which they exhibit withitness. Effective classroom managers who exhibited withitness were aware of what was happening in all parts of the classroom and were able to see different things happening in different parts of the room at the same time. Furthermore, these effective classroom managers were able to *communicate this awareness to their students.*

Few of us are blessed with eyes in the backs of our heads—or are capable of detecting multiple behaviors even when they occur in front of our heads. But there are several simple ways to increase your withitness and the extent of your students' active engagement in the learning process.

One way is to increase your physical presence through eye contact. If your eye contact is limited to only a portion of the classroom, you effectively lose withitness for the rest of the classroom. It is surprising to note that a great many beginning teachers consistently do the following:

Talk only to the middle-front rows.

Talk with their backs to the class when writing on the chalkboard.

Talk while looking toward the windows or ceiling.

Talk while not being able to see all students due to other students blocking their view.

In each of these instances, you see only a portion of the classroom, and *the students know only a portion of the classroom is seen.* Your eye contact that covers all portions of the classroom is one of the most important ingredients in conveying a sense of withitness.

A second ingredient for improving withitness is learning to monitor more than one activity at a time. Here, the key not only is to change your eye contact to different parts of the room, but also to change your focus of attention. For example, progress on assigned seatwork might be the focus of your observations when scanning students in the front of the class, but potential behavior problems might be your focus when scanning students in the back of the class.

You should switch back and forth from conduct-related observations to work-related observations at the same time you change eye contact. However, a great impediment to such switching is a tendency to focus exclusively on one student who is having either conduct- or work-related problems. Once other students realize you are preoccupied with one of their peers, problems with other students in other parts of the classroom may be inevitable.

Making Transitions

Another problem area is transitions. It is difficult to keep students' attention during a transition from one instructional activity to another. Switching from lecture to seatwork, from discussion to lecture, or from seatwork to discussion is a time for some students to misbehave. Moving the entire class from one activity to another in a timely and orderly manner can be a major undertaking. Problems in making these transitions often occur for two reasons: (1) learners are not ready to perform the next activity (or may not even know what it is), and (2) learners have unclear expectations about appropriate behavior during the transition.

When students are uncertain or unaware of what is coming next, they naturally become anxious about their ability to perform and make the transition. This is the time that transitions can get noisy, with some students feeling more comfortable clinging to the previous activity than changing to the next. The beginning of the school year is a time of noisy transitions as students fumble to find the proper materials (or guess which ones are needed) and to find out what is expected of them next. They will not rush headlong into a new activity, for fear they will not like it or will be unable to do well.

How can I ensure orderly transitions between lesson activities?

In this sense, transitions are as much psychological barriers as they are actual divisions between activities. Students must adjust their psychology for the next activity, just as they must adjust their books and papers. You can help in their adjustment by telling them the daily routine you expect of them. This routine becomes second nature after a few weeks, but it deserves special attention during the first days of school. This is the time for you to describe these daily activities and the order in which they will occur (e.g., 10 minutes of lecture, 15 minutes of questions and answers, 15 minutes of seatwork, and 10 minutes of checking and correcting).

Here are some suggestions for addressing the problems that occur during transitions:

Problems	Solutions
Students talk loudly at the beginning of transitions.	It is difficult to *allow* a small amount of talking and *obtain* a small amount. So, establish a no-talking rule during transitions.
Students socialize during the transition, delaying the start of the next activity.	Allow no more time than is necessary between activities (e.g., to close books, gather up materials, select new materials).
Students complete assignments before the scheduled time for an activity to end.	Make assignments according to the time to be filled, not the exercises to be completed. Always assign more than enough exercises to fill the allotted time.
Students continue to work on the preceding activity after a change.	Give five-minute and two-minute warnings before the end of any activity and use verbal markers such as "Shortly we will end this work," and "Let's finish this up so that we can begin. . . . " Create definite beginning and end points to each activity, such as "OK, that's the end of this activity; now we will start . . . " or "Put your papers away and turn to. . . . "
Some students lag behind others in completing the previous activity.	Don't wait for stragglers. Begin new activities on time. When a natural break occurs, visit privately with students still working on previous tasks to tell them that they must stop and change. Be sure to note the reason they have not finished (e.g., material too hard, lack of motivation, off-task behavior).
You delay the beginning of the activity to find something (file cabinet keys, materials, roster, references, etc.).	Be prepared—pure and simple! Always have the materials you need in front of you at the start of the activity.

Giving Assignments

Another crucial time for effective classroom management is when you are giving or explaining assignments. This can be a particularly trou-

One approach to moving the entire class from one activity to another in a timely and orderly manner is to communicate clearly the actual divisions in time between activities.

blesome time because it often means assigning work that at least some students will not be eager to complete. Grunts and groans are common student expressions of distaste for homework or other assignments that must be completed outside of the regular school day. At times like these, outbursts of misbehavior are most likely to occur.

Evertson and Emmer (1982) found that one difference between effective and ineffective classroom managers was the manner in which they gave assignments, particularly homework. Giving assignments appeared almost effortless for the effective managers, while for the ineffective managers the normal classroom routine sometimes abruptly halted, noise level went up, and much commotion ensued. The difference was attributed to several simple procedures that were commonplace among experienced teachers but not among inexperienced teachers.

One procedure was to attach assignments directly to the end of an in-class activity. By doing so, the teacher avoided an awkward pause and even the need for a transition, because the assignment was seen as a logical extension of what already was taking place. The practice of giving the assignment immediately after the activity to which it most closely relates, as opposed to giving it at the end of class or the day, may be much like getting an injection while the physician is engaging you in a friendly conversation and looking at you with a smile: if the conversation is engaging enough, you might not feel the pain.

By contrast, imagine how you might feel being given an assignment under these conditions.

Teacher A: I guess I'll have to assign some homework now, so do problems 1 through 10 on page 61.

Teacher B: For homework do the problems under Exercise A and Exercise B—and be sure all of them are finished by tomorrow.

Teacher C: We're out of time, so you'll have to finish these problems on your own.

In each of these assignments there is a subtle implication that the homework may not really be needed or that it is being given mechanically or as some sort of punishment. Why this homework is being assigned may be a complete mystery to most students, because none of the teachers mentioned either the in-class activities to which the homework presumably relates or the benefits that may accrue from the assignment. These explanations are important if you expect anything other than a mechanical or grudging response. Students expect and appreciate knowing why an assignment is made before they are expected to do it.

Now consider these assignments again, this time with some explanations added:

Teacher A: Today we have talked a lot about the origins of the Civil War and some of the economic unrest that preceded it. But some other types of unrest also were responsible for the Civil War. These will be important for understanding the real causes behind this war. Problems 1 through 10 on page 61 will help you understand some of these other causes.

Teacher B: We have all had a chance now to try our skill at forming possessives. As most of you have found out, it's a little harder than it looks. So let's try Exercises A and B for tonight, which should give you just the right amount of practice in forming possessives.

Teacher C: Well, it looks like time has run out before we could complete all the problems. The next set of problems we will study requires a lot of what we have learned here today. Let's complete the rest of these for tonight to see if you've got the concept. This should make the next lesson go a lot smoother.

———————————————————————————————————————

How can I convey assignments positively and motivate learners to complete them?

Keep in mind that effective classroom managers give assignments that immediately follow the lesson or activities to which they relate, that explain which in-class lessons the assignment relates to, and that avoid any *unnecessary* negative connotations (e.g., "finish them all," "be sure they are correct," "complete it on time"), which may make your assignment sound more like a punishment than an instructional activity.

It is also important that you convey assignments in a manner that motivates your students to complete them. Table 11.3 summarizes five different ways in which you can convey assignments positively and motivate your learners to continue engaging in the activity at a high level of involvement. These motivators involve the effective teaching practices of (1) using praise and encouragement, (2) providing explanations for why an assignment is being given, (3) offering to help students during the assignment, (4) accepting divergent, creative, or unusual responses, and (5) emphasizing the positive consequences of completing the assignment.

Finally, it always is a good idea to display prior assignments somewhere in your classroom so that students who have missed an assignment can conveniently look it up without requiring your time to remember or find an old assignment. A simple two-foot square sheet of art board, divided into days of the month and covered with plastic to write on, can be a convenient and reusable way of communicating past assignments on a monthly basis.

Bringing Closure

Another time for effective classroom management is when you are bringing a lesson to its end. This is a time when students sense the impending end of the period and begin in advance of your close to disengage themselves from the lesson. It is a time when noise levels increase and students begin to fidget with books, papers, and personal belongings in anticipation of the next class or activity. Typically, beginning teachers pay little attention to closure, and may end lessons abruptly:

Oops there's the bell!

We're about out of time, so we'll have to stop.

That looks like all we can do today.

Table 11.3
Some motivators and their appropriate uses

Motivator	Use phrases such as . . .	Avoid phrases such as . . .
Using praise and encouragement	You've got it.	That's a dumb answer.
	Good work.	You're being lazy again.
	Good try.	I can see you never study.
	That was quick.	You can never pay attention, can you?
Providing explanations	The reason this is so important is . . .	Today you will have to learn this, or else . . .
	We are doing this assignment because . . .	Complete this exercise; otherwise, there'll be trouble.
	This will be difficult, but it fits in with . . .	This is a long assignment, but you'll just have to do it.
	Experience has shown that without these facts the next unit will be very difficult.	We must cover this material, so let's get going.
Offering to help	Should you need help, I'll be here.	You should be able to do this on your own.
	Ask if you need help.	If you have to ask for help, you must not have studied.
	I'll be walking around; catch me if you have a problem.	Please don't ask a dumb question.
	Don't be afraid to ask a question if you're having trouble.	Raise your hand only if you're stuck on a difficult problem.

We'll have to finish tomorrow.

Our time is about gone; let's wrap things up.

Although phrases such as these do end the lesson, they do little else, especially when time remains for students to turn off task, anxiously waiting for the bell to ring or the activity to change. Recall

Table 11.3, *continued*

Motivator	Use phrases such as . . .	Avoid phrases such as . . .
Accepting diversity	That's not the answer I expected, but I can see your point.	That's not the kind of answer we can accept around here.
	That's not how I see it, but I can understand how others might see it differently.	I've never heard that expression before—so let's not start something new.
	This is not something I'm familiar with. Where did you get that idea?	Please use ideas that fit in with what I say in class.
	That is not a word I've heard before. Tell us what it means.	Don't ever use foreign words in this class.
Emphasizing reinforcement and reward	All homework completed means five extra points.	Five points off for missing homework.
	If you get a *C* or better on all the tests, I'll drop the lowest grade.	If you have less than a *C* average on all your tests, you'll have to take an extra test.
	Those who complete all the exercises on time can go to the learning center.	If you don't complete the exercise on time, there can be no use of the learning center.
	If you have a *C* average, you get to choose any topic for your term paper.	If you don't have a *C* average, you must choose your term paper topic from a restricted list of difficult topics.

from Chapter 5 that the attention-getting event can serve the double purpose of gaining students' attention and providing an advance organizer to mentally prepare students for the ensuing lesson. Closing comments also should serve a double purpose—not only ending the lesson but also keeping students actively engaged in the lesson until its very end by reviewing, summarizing, or highlighting its most important points. If good attention-getting devices help organize a lesson in advance, then good closing comments should keep students engaged in the lesson by having them acting on, thinking about, and working with the presented content.

Closure, therefore, is more than simply calling attention to the end of a lesson. It means keeping the momentum of a lesson going by reorganizing what has gone before into a unified body of knowledge that can help students remember the lesson and place it into perspective. Following are ways you can keep your learners actively engaged at the end of your lessons and help them retain what you have taught.

How can I bring closure to a lesson?

Combining or Consolidating Key Points.   One way of accomplishing closure is by combining or consolidating key points into a single overall conclusion. Consider the following:

Teacher: Today we have studied the economic systems of capitalism, socialism, and communism. We have found each of these to be similar in that some of the same goods and services are owned by the government. We have, however, found them different with respect to the *degree* to which various goods and services are owned by the government; the least number of goods and services are owned by a government under capitalism and the most goods and services are owned by a government under communism.

This teacher is drawing together and highlighting the single most important conclusion from the day's lesson. The teacher is doing so by expressing the highest-level generalization or conclusion from the lesson without reference to any of the details that were necessary to arrive at it. This teacher consolidated many different bits and pieces by going to the broadest, most sweeping conclusion that could be made, capturing the essence of all that went before.

Summarizing or Reviewing Key Content.   Another procedure for bringing closure to a lesson is by summarizing or reviewing key content. Here the teacher reviews the most important content to be sure everyone understands it. Obviously, not all of the content can be repeated in this manner, so some selecting is in order, as illustrated by the following:

Teacher: Before we end, let's look at our two rules once again. Rule 1: Use the possessive form whenever an *of* phrase can be substituted for a noun. Rule 2: If the word for which we are denoting ownership already ends in an *s*, place the apostrophe after, *not* before, the *s*. Remember, both these rules use the apostrophe.

—•—•—•—•—•—•—•—•—•—•—•—•—•—•—•—

Now the teacher is consolidating by summarizing, or touching on each of the key features of the lesson. The teacher's review is rapid and to the point, providing students with an opportunity to fill in any gaps about the main features of the lesson.

Providing a Structure. Still another method for closing consists of providing learners with a structure by which key facts and ideas can be remembered without an actual review of them. With this procedure, facts and ideas are reorganized into a framework for easy recall, as indicated in this example:

—•—•—•—•—•—•—•—•—•—•—•—•—•—•—•—

Teacher: Today we studied the formulation and punctuation of possessives. Recall that we used two rules—one for forming possessives wherever an *of* phrase can be substituted for a noun and another for forming possessives for words ending in *s*. From now on, let's call these rules the *of rule* and the *s rule*, keeping in mind that both rules use the apostrophe.

—•—•—•—•—•—•—•—•—•—•—•—•—•—•—•—

By giving students a framework for remembering the rules (the *of rule* and *s rule*), the teacher organizes the content and indicates how it should be stored and remembered. The key to this procedure is giving a code or symbol system whereby students can more easily store lesson content and recall it for later use.

Notice that in each of the previous dialogues, closure was accomplished by looking back at the lesson and reinforcing its key components. In the first instance this was accomplished by restating the highest-level generalization that could be made; in the second by summarizing the content at the level at which it was taught; and in the third by helping students to remember the important categories of information by providing codes or symbols. Each of these closings has the potential of keeping your learners engaged when the main part of your lesson has ended. Remember, closure means more than just calling attention to the end of a lesson. Endings to good lessons are like endings to good stories: they keep you engaged and in suspense and leave you with a sense that you have understood the story and can remember it long afterwards.

>>> LEARNER DIVERSITY AND <<< CLASSROOM MANAGEMENT

A number of authors have studied the effects of various styles of classroom management and their effects on learners. For example, Hall (1977) found a connection between spatial distance and classroom order. The greater the spatial distance between teacher and student, the more some students became passive listeners and engaged in off-task behavior. As the teacher moved closer to students, communication tended to become more interactive, with more students following the wishes of the teacher. Hall observed that standing closer to individual students can promote compliance to classroom rules, since students will be drawn into nonverbal forms of communication, such as eye contact and changes in voice and body movement, that send a message of involvement.

Similarly, Scollon (1985) found the use of space can communicate a sense of social power, which can promote involvement *or* uninvolvement. For example, Bowers and Flinders (1991) report a case of a teacher who moved from student to student checking work while on a swivel chair with casters. In this manner the teacher was able to elicit more spontaneous and relaxed student responses, resulting in greater student involvement and compliance with classroom rules. This was especially so among students who, by virtue of their language, culture, or ethnicity, did not wish to be spotlighted in the traditional teacher-dominated manner.

Other research has studied the compatibility of various classroom management techniques with the culture and ethnicity of the learner. Tharp and Gallimore (1989), Dillon (1989), and Bowers and Flinders (1991) present convincing arguments that different cultures react differently to nonverbal and verbal classroom management techniques that use space and distance (called *proximity control*), eye-contact, warnings, and classroom arrangement (e.g., cooperative vs. competitive). Furthermore, they cite numerous examples of how teachers of different cultures interpret disruptive behaviors of children differently.

For example, facial expressions during a reprimand have been found to communicate different messages concerning the importance of the reprimand (Smith, 1984). Research by Dillon (1989) has pointed out that many actions of teachers may diminish participation among minority students and/or build resentment because their actions are culturally incongruent. One of Dillon's suggestions is that teachers examine their own value and belief systems to become more aware how different they may be from their students

How might I use the social organization of my classroom to bridge cultural gaps?

Name _____   Class _____

1. What was the most interesting or exciting thing that you did this past summer?
   _____
   _____

2. What job would you like to have when you finish school?
   _____

3. What hobbies or interests do you like to spend time on after school?
   _____

4a. How difficult do you find
    school work?
    _____ very difficult
    _____ fairly difficult
    _____ a little difficult
    _____ not difficult

4b. How much do you enjoy
    coming to school?
    _____ very much
    _____ some
    _____ a little
    _____ not at all

5. Name something you look forward to about this coming school year.
   _____

6. What worries you the most about this coming school year?
   _____

7a. What subjects do you like
    the most?
    _____
    _____
    _____
    _____

7b. What subjects do you like
    the least?
    _____
    _____
    _____
    _____

Figure 11.4
Some questions for determining the interests of students at the beginning of the year

and use the social organization of the classroom to bridge cultural gaps:

- Establish an open, risk-free classroom climate where students can experience mutual trust and confidence.
- Plan and structure lessons that meet the interests and needs of students (see Figure 11.4).
- Implement lessons that allow all students to be active learners through activities and responsibilities that are congruent with the learners' cultures.

These are important considerations in understanding the culture and ethnicity of your classroom and establishing a **culturally sensitive classroom management** system.

>>> PLANNING YOUR FIRST DAY <<<

If your first class day is like that of most teachers, it will include some or all of these activities:

- Keeping order before the bell
- Introducing yourself
- Taking care of administrative business
- Presenting rules and expectations
- Introducing your subject
- Closing

Because your responses in these areas may set the tone in your classroom for the remainder of the year, let's consider your **first-day planning** in more detail to see how you can prepare an effective routine.

Before the Bell

As the sole person responsible for your classroom, your responsibility extends not just to when your classes are in session but to whenever school is in session. Consequently, you must be prepared to deal with students before your classes begin in the morning, between classes, and after your last class has ended—or anytime you are in your classroom. Your first class day is particularly critical in this regard, because your students' before-class peek at you will set in motion responses, feelings, and concerns that may affect them long after the bell has rung. Following are a few suggestions that can make these responses, feelings, and concerns positive ones.

To provide a sense of control and withitness, stand near the door as students enter your classroom. In this way you will come in direct contact with each student and be visible to them as they take their seats. Your presence at the doorway, where students must come in close contact with you, will encourage an orderly entrance (and exit) from the classroom. Remember, your class starts when the first student walks through your classroom door.

Another suggestion is to have approximately four to six rules, divided between conduct and work, clearly visible on the chalkboard, bulletin board, overhead, or in the form of a handout already placed on each student's desk. You may want to prepare rules for the areas shown in the upper half of Figure 11.3 that you feel will be most critical to your classes during the first few days of school. You can formally introduce these rules later, but they should be clearly visible as students enter your class the first day.

This communicates a sense of structure and organization which most students look for and expect, even on their very first day of school. It also occupies the attention of early arrivals, who otherwise may be inclined to talk loudly, move about the classroom, or talk with you, interfering with your ability to monitor students who are making the transition from hallway to classroom.

It is not unusual (considering the tension and anxiety associated with anyone's first day on the job) for you to be forgetful or to get sidetracked onto one activity (e.g., introducing yourself), leaving no time for other important business. Experience suggests that you may forget important business (e.g., reminding students of your classroom rules) or fall into a less logical order of activities if you do not use a reminder to keep yourself on track.

Therefore, it is important that you prepare a brief outline of your opening day's routine. This outline should list all the activities you plan to perform that day (or class period), in the order in which you will perform them. You can make a "cue card" for yourself—a simple 4" × 6" index card can be used to remind yourself:

1. Greet students and introduce yourself (5 min.)
2. Take roll (5 min.)
3. Fill out forms (10 min.)
4. Assign books (15 min.)
5. Present rules (10 min.)
   a. Conduct rules
   b. Work rules
6. Introduce course content (0–10 min.)
7. Remind students to bring needed materials (2 min.)
8. Close (3 min.)

In the elementary grades, this schedule easily can be amended to include an introduction to the entire day.

Let us look briefly at several of these activities for your first day.

Introducing Yourself

Introduce yourself by giving your name, the subject or class you are teaching, your special areas of expertise, and so on. However, after this formal introduction, you need to break the ice by showing a part of your personality at the same time that you maintain your role as a teacher. Frankly, this is not always easy. Some beginning teachers ramble too much about themselves, trying to convince students they are "regular people." Others maintain a cold and stern aura to keep students disciplined and at a distance. Both approaches are extreme and often create more problems than they solve. In the first instance students may get too friendly too soon, forgetting the discipline and order that school requires; and in the second instance students may stay frightened of you for weeks or even months.

Your personality will, and should, unfold in small degrees during the first few weeks of school. There is no need to rush it. However, a small glimpse of the kind of person you are outside of the classroom often is a nice touch for students, who would like to see you as a friend as well as a teacher. A short comment about your interests, hobbies, or special experiences—even family or home life—often is appreciated by students, who at the end of this first day will be struggling to remember just who you are.

Administrative Business

Your first opportunity to meet your students up close will be while taking the roll. This is when you may want to turn the tables and have your students not only identify themselves but indicate some of their own interests, hobbies, or special experiences. Such introductions tend to be lengthier in the elementary grades than in junior high and high school, where time is more limited.

Also, in the higher grades, interests, hobbies, or special experiences can be more efficiently determined with a brief interest inventory of the type shown in Figure 11.4. The advantage of using this approach is that time can be set aside in the future for looking through the student responses to help in planning future projects and lessons that coincide with your learners' special interests.

Your other administrative duties at this time can be considerable, and in some cases can consume most of the remainder of the class period at the upper grades and a full hour or more in the lower grades. Filling out forms requested by the school and school district, checking course schedules, guiding lost students to their correct rooms, and accepting new students during the middle of the class will make this first class day seem long and disorderly.

Rules and Expectations

Regardless of how much time administrative tasks require during your first day, plan to devote some time to discussing your classroom rules and your overall expectations about both conduct and work. This is the time to remove student uncertainties and let them know what to expect. There is no better way to begin this process than by referring to the conduct and work rules that either have been posted for all to see or that you have handed out.

In addition to your rules, however, there will be related concerns to address. For example, for younger students you will want to reiterate certain important school rules (e.g., what to do in the event of sickness, consequences of repeated tardiness or absence, procedures for going to the cafeteria) in addition to your own classroom rules.

You also will want to set the tone for the rigor and fairness with which you will grade and for the level of effort you expect. These comments should tell your students that you will "be fair but tough," "expect a lot but will reward hard work," "give difficult tests but teach what is needed to get a good grade," and "expect a lot of work but that the work will be interesting." Each of these phrases communicates not only your high standards, but also your understanding and fairness. This delicate balance is the most important impression with which you can leave your students on their first day.

Introducing Your Subject

Although time may not permit you to present much content on the first day, we offer several tips for presenting content during your first lessons.

First, begin your instruction to the whole class. This is a time when not all of your students will be eager to participate in group work or seatwork or be relaxed enough to meaningfully contribute to inquiry or problem-solving type assignments. Effective indirect and self-directed instruction formats depend on the trust and confidence that students acquire from their experience with you over time. They will be acquiring this trust and confidence during your first days and weeks in the classroom. Therefore, during your first week or so in the classroom, direct your lessons to the whole class.

Second, during your initial days in the classroom choose content activities that you believe everyone can successfully complete. This will go a long way toward building trust and confidence and promoting enthusiasm for the work that lies ahead. Avoid especially difficult tasks that may prohibit high rates of success; otherwise, some of your students may acquire a fear of failure that can suppress their true abilities well into the school year. At this time you will not yet know the difficulty level most appropriate for your learners, so use this time to gradually try out the types of tasks and activities you eventually will ask your learners to perform, beginning with those from which you expect the most student success.

Following are some examples of first-day activities that can give the flavor of a content area in which most students could demonstrate a high level of understanding and which could be used to begin to convey facts, rules, and action sequences:

- Conducting a brief experiment and explaining its consequences in real life (science).
- Reading a lively excerpt from a short story and providing an interpretation (language arts).
- Demonstrating a concrete procedure and having students practice it, such as using a calculator, equipment, charts, or tables (math and the sciences).
- Describing a typical current event and explaining how it can affect their lives (social studies).
- Teaching a few words of conversation and having students try them out (foreign language).

Closure

Your final first-day activity will be to close on a positive, optimistic note. Have a definite procedure for closing in mind (e.g., a preview of things to come, instructions to follow for tomorrow's class, a reminder of things to bring to class). Begin closing a full three minutes before the bell is to ring. End with a note of encouragement that *all* of your students can do well in your grade or class.

This chapter introduced you to motivation and classroom management. Its main points were as follows:

1. Five types of social power or leadership which a teacher can strive for are expert power, referent power, legitimate power, reward power, and coercive power.

2. Four stages in which a successful group passes through are forming, storming norming, and performing.

3. *Distancing* is a type of amiable limit testing in which group members challenge academic expectations and rules in order to establish under what conditions they do or do not apply.

4. *Centering* is a second type of amiable limit testing in which learners question how they will personally benefit from being a group member.

5. Two basic processes by which norms develop are *diffusion* and *crystallization*. The former occurs when different academic and social expectations held by different members are spread throughout the group. The latter occurs when expectations converge and crystallize into a shared perspective.

6. Classroom climate refers to the atmosphere or mood in which interactions between you and your students take place. A classroom climate can be created by the social environment, which is related to the patterns of interaction you wish to promote in your classroom, and by the organizational environment, which is related to the physical or visual arrangement of the classroom.

7. The social climate of the classroom can extend from authoritarian (in which you are the primary provider of information, opinions, and instruction) to laissez faire (in which your students become the primary providers of information, opinions, and instruction).

8. Your role in establishing authority in the classroom and the social climate can vary. You can adopt different roles, including the following:

- Commander-in-chief, who carefully controls and hones student behavior by organizing and providing all the stimuli needed for learning to occur

- Translator or summarizer of ideas provided by students
- Equal partner with students in creating ideas and problem solutions

9. The social climate of your classroom also can vary depending on how competitive, cooperative, or individualistic you wish the interactions among class members to be. Differences among these include extent of opportunities for students to express opinion, time devoted to student talk, and spontaneity with which your students are allowed to respond.

10. Organizational climate pertains to the physical or visual arrangement of the classroom and is determined by the positioning of desks, chairs, tables, and other internal features of a classroom.

11. The degree of competition, cooperation, and individuality in your classroom are a result of the social and organizational climate you create.

12. Rules can be divided into those that relate to one or more of four distinct areas:

- academic work
- classroom conduct
- information you must communicate your first teaching day
- information you can communicate later

13. Rules can be communicated orally, on the board, on a transparency, or in a handout. Rules for the early elementary grades should be presented orally, provided as a handout, and posted for reference. Rules for the elementary grades and junior high school may be recited and copied by students. Rules for high school may be given orally and then posted.

14. The following suggestions will help you develop classroom rules:

- Make rules consistent with your climate.
- Don't make rules that can't be enforced.
- Specify only necessary rules.
- State rules generally enough to include different but related behaviors.

15. Your inability to enforce a rule over a reasonable period of time is the best sign that you need to change the rule.

16. Monitoring students, making transitions, giving assignments, and bringing closure are four particularly troublesome areas of classroom management.

17. *Withitness* is a form of monitoring in which you are able to keep track of many different signs of student engagement at the same time.

18. You can convey assignments positively and motivate learners in the following ways:

- Using praise and encouragement
- Providing explanations
- Offering to help
- Accepting diversity
- Emphasizing reward, not punishment

19. Problems during transitions most frequently occur when learners are not ready to perform the next activity and do not know what behavior is appropriate during the transition.

20. Homework assignments should be given immediately following the lesson or activities to which they relate and without negative connotations.

21. Closing statements should gradually bring a lesson to an end by combining or consolidating key points into a single overall conclusion, by summarizing or reviewing key content, or by providing a symbol system whereby contents of the lesson can be easily stored and later recalled.

22. You may use the following methods to bridge cultural gaps in the classroom:

- Establish an open, risk-free climate.
- Plan lessons that meet student interests and needs.
- Allow for activities and responsibilities congruent with learners' cultures.

For Discussion and Practice

*1. Describe in your own words the two types of social power beginning teachers should most quickly achieve. How would you achieve each?

*2. Imagine a group of learners similar to the classroom in which you will teach. Using specific examples of student behavior, identify the four stages of group development you will have to bring them through in order for them to function as a cohesive group.

3. Using realistic episodes of group behavior, illustrate the group behaviors of distancing and centering.

*4. What is meant by the diffusion and crystallization of norms? In what order can you expect these two basic processes of norm development to occur?

*5. What are three roles that communicate different levels of authority that you can assume in your classroom? How will expression of student opinions, proportion of student talk to teacher talk, and spontaneity of

response change as a function of each of these three roles?

*6. Provide example classroom activities that would result in (1) a competitive, (2) a cooperative, and (3) an individualistic classroom climate.

7. Draw three diagrams of the internal features of a classroom, each illustrating how to promote one of the three classroom climates in question 6.

8. Identify four academic rules and four conduct rules (that must be communicated your first day of class) that you believe are among the most important. Write out a rule for each of these eight areas, exactly as it might be shown to your students on a handout or transparency on the first day of class.

*9. Identify two rules whose retention might be aided if they were communicated in the context of a circumstance or incident with which to associate the rule.

*10. State three effective suggestions for developing classroom rules. Identify four rules that, in your opinion, follow these suggestions.

*11. Identify a practical criterion for deciding when a rule should be revised or eliminated.

12. Explain in your own words what *withitness* means. Give an example from your own experience of when you displayed withitness, and when you did not but should have. What were the consequences of each event?

*13. What four teaching practices can help avoid misbehavior during a transition?

*14. What are two ways out-of-class assignments can be made more meaningful and acceptable to your students?

*15. Identify three ways of bringing your lesson to an end that can help students to organize your lesson in retrospect.

16. Identify the characteristics you might reveal about yourself when introducing yourself on the first day of class.

*17. If you were teaching in a culturally diverse classroom, in what ways would you try to bridge the different cultures to form a productive and cohesive classroom?

---

* Answers to asterisked questions (*) in this and the other chapters are in Appendix B.

Suggested Readings

Borich, G. (1993). *Clearly outstanding: Making each day count in your classroom.* Boston: Allyn & Bacon.

Through the eyes and ears of three teachers, Angela, Kurt, and Sheila, this book shows how teachers can establish a positive relationship with their class and as a result improve the effectiveness of their teaching. It also illustrates how the beginning teacher grows professionally and personally from the challenges presented by teaching groups of learners.

Bowers, C. A., & Flinders, D. J. (1990). *Responsive teaching: An ecological approach to patterns of language, culture, and thought.* New York: Teachers College Press.

An original and thoughtful analysis of how cultural patterns of thought and language effect a teacher's classroom management decisions.

Charles, C. M. (1992). *Building classroom discipline: From models to practice* (3rd ed.). New York: Longman.

A comprehensive survey of the major theoretical approaches to classroom discipline, it presents helpful suggestions for developing your own personalized system of classroom management.

Cohen, E. G. (1986). *Designing groupwork: Strategies for the heterogeneous classroom.* New York: Teachers College Press.

A practical guide for teachers on how to prepare and conduct group classroom work.

Emmer, E., Evertson, C., Clements, B., & Worsham, M. (1994). *Classroom management for secondary teachers* (2nd ed.). Englewood Cliffs, NJ: Prentice-Hall.

Presents detailed, step-by-step activities and principles for planning and organizing junior and senior high school classrooms. The recommendations are derived from observations of the best practices of effective teachers.

Glasser, W. (1990). *The quality school: Managing students without coercion.* New York: Harper.

Glasser takes his theories of student needs and student motivation and demonstrates how they can be applied to restructuring American classrooms.

Jones, V. F., & Jones, L. S. (1990). *Comprehensive classroom management* (3rd ed.). Boston: Allyn & Bacon.

Presents a detailed comprehensive discussion of the classroom management tradition. It offers many practical suggestions to both elementary and secondary school teachers on how to promote positive behavior.

Schmuck, R. A. & Schmuck, P. A. (1992). *Group processes in the classroom* (6th ed.). Dubuque, IA: William C. Brown.

Applies theories and research in social psychology to the understanding of classroom group processes. Contains numerous practical activities to promote group cohesiveness.

Classroom Order and Discipline

This chapter will help you answer the following questions:

1. What is an effective classroom management plan?
2. How can I correct the misbehavior of learners in a way that does not blame, scold, or humiliate?
3. How can I build a friendly workplace based on the principles of cooperation?
4. How can I modify student behavior using positive and negative reinforcement?
5. What behaviors do effective classroom managers possess?
6. How can I stop minor misbehaviors without disrupting the flow of a lesson?
7. What types of consequences for misbehavior are fair and just?
8. How can I condition my students to use natural reinforcers to motivate their behavior?
9. Which is more effective in changing the behavior of learners: rewards or punishment?
10. When should I use warnings to prevent minor problems from intensifying?
11. How do I plan a parent-teacher conference?
12. What is culturally responsive classroom management?

This chapter will also help you learn the meaning of the following:

behavioral antecedents
behavior modification
culturally responsive teaching
Ginott's congruent communication
Glasser's cooperative learning
low-profile classroom control
natural reinforcers
operant conditioning
positive and negative reinforcement
reactive and preventive systems of classroom management
surface behaviors

Anyone who reads the newspaper, listens to candidates running for public office, attends school board meetings, or overhears conversations in the teachers' lounge quickly realizes that classroom order and discipline are among education's most frequently discussed topics. Inability to control a class is one of the most commonly cited reasons for dismissing or failing to reemploy a teacher, and beginning teachers consistently rate classroom discipline among their most urgent concerns (Rogan, Borich, & Taylor, 1992).

Problems in maintaining classroom order and discipline, however, can be exaggerated. Candidates for public office and some community members may speak from time to time as though discipline in the schools is nonexistent or minimal, while newspapers readily report incidents that do occur. The facts are that major disciplinary problems (for example, vandalism, violent fighting, physical abuse toward teachers) rarely occur in most schools. Unfortunately, these are the incidents that attract the most attention, and often are reported to the exclusion of the many positive events that also occur. This chapter will address some major discipline problems, but the primary focus will be on the many less dramatic problems that, without an effective classroom management plan, can divert your attention from the instructional process.

Although minor in nature, research shows that some teachers spend nearly 50 percent of their time dealing with misbehavior that can be described as "amiable goofing off" (Jones, 1987). Thus, although you may worry about how to handle rare incidents of fighting, open defiance, property destruction, or swearing and cursing, the reality is that you will spend most of your management time coping with students who pass notes, whisper, stare out the window, ignore your requests, squirm in their seats, sleep, do work unrelated to your class, or do no work at all.

In Chapter 11, you learned how to form cohesive groups that regulate their own behavior and to manage your classroom in ways that anticipate problems before they occur. This chapter focuses on developing systematic procedures for stopping or altering misbehavior that is about to occur or has already occurred. As noted in the previous chapter, anticipating discipline problems and planning to avoid them is preferable to dealing with dis-

cipline problems once they have occurred. Nevertheless, not all misbehaviors can be anticipated and not all classroom management techniques for avoiding them work every time. This chapter is devoted to techniques for dealing with these types of misbehaviors.

>>> SYSTEMS OF CLASSROOM MANAGEMENT <<<

Approaches to dealing with classroom management can be grouped into three traditions. One tradition emphasizes the critical role of communication and problem solving between teacher and students. This approach is called the *humanist tradition* of classroom management (Ginott, 1972; Glasser, 1986, 1990). The second tradition comes from the field of *applied behavior analysis*. This approach to classroom management emphasizes behavior modification techniques and reinforcement theory applied to the classroom (Canter, 1989; Jones, 1987; Alberto & Troutman, 1986). The third approach is the most recent, emphasizing the teaching skills involved in organizing and managing instructional activities and in presenting content, and is called the *classroom management tradition* (Emmer et al., 1994; Good & Brophy, 1990; Doyle, 1986; Kounin, 1970). This approach, more so than the humanistic and applied behavior analysis traditions, underscores the critical role of prevention in managing classroom behavior. In this chapter we will briefly summarize the main features of these traditions, point out how they are used in the classroom, and show how the best features of each can be combined into a single approach. To begin, let's identify six criteria of an effective classroom management plan:

What is an effective classroom management plan?

1. *Establish positive relationships among all classroom participants.* A positive, supportive classroom environment that meets students needs for building trusting relations is a necessary foundation for managing an orderly classroom. In the previous chapter we saw some of the ways in which you could build trusting relations.
2. *Prevent attention-seeking and work-avoidance behavior.* Time devoted to managing the classroom should be directed to engaging students in the learning process and preventing behaviors that interfere with it. Engagement and prevention include both arrangement of physical space and the teaching of rules for working in this space. In the previous chapter we

saw the importance of classroom climate and provided some guidelines and examples for teaching classroom rules.

3. *Quickly and unobtrusively redirect misbehavior once it occurs.* Most classroom problems take the form of minor off-task and attention-seeking behaviors. Techniques for coping with these events should not cause more disruption than the behavior itself.

4. *Stop persistent and chronic misbehavior with strategies that are simple enough to be used consistently.* Management systems that require responses to every act of positive or negative behavior may not be sufficiently practical to be implemented consistently in today's busy classrooms.

5. *Teach self-control.* Students should be allowed the opportunity to exercise internal control before external control is imposed. When external controls are imposed, they should be implemented with plans for fading them out.

6. *Respect cultural differences.* Verbal and nonverbal techniques for redirecting disruptive behavior do not mean the same thing to all cultural groups. Likewise, systematic strategies involving rewards and consequences can violate important cultural norms.

Now, let's learn something about each of our three approaches to classroom management. As you read about them, see how each meets these criteria.

>>> THE HUMANIST TRADITION IN <<<
CLASSROOM MANAGEMENT

The principles underlying the humanist tradition come from the practice of clinical and counseling psychology. It is called *humanist* because its primary focus is the inner thoughts, feelings, psychological needs, and emotions of the individual learner. Humanist approaches emphasize the importance of allowing the student time to develop control over his or her behavior rather than insisting on immediate behavioral change or compliance. They hope to achieve these ends through interventions stressing the use of communication skills, an understanding of student motives, private conferences, individual and group problem solving, and the exercise of referent and expert power.

Ginott's (1972) cooperation through congruent communication (also called the communication skills approach) and Glasser's (1990) cooperation through individual and group problem solving (also called cooperative learning and reality therapy) are examples of the humanist tradition. While each emphasizes a different area of skill the effective classroom manager should possess, they essentially represent two sides of the same coin.

Ginott's Congruent Communication

The cardinal principle underlying Ginott's (1972) **congruent communication** skills approach is that learners are capable of controlling their own behavior if only teachers would allow them to do so. Teachers foster this self-control by allowing learners to choose how they wish to change their own behavior and how the class will be run. In addition, they help their students to deal with their inner thoughts and feelings through the use of effective communication skills.

Communication skills is the primary vehicle for influencing learners' self-esteem, which, in turn, is the primary force underlying acceptable behavior. Therefore, this tradition tries first and foremost to influence student behavior by enhancing student self-esteem. According to the proponents of this approach, congruent communication is the vehicle for promoting self-esteem.

Teachers have many opportunities during the school day to engage their students in congruent communication, usually during private conferences with students who misbehave. However, such communication also can go on during problem solving with the whole class. At such times, teachers communicate congruently when they do the following:

How can I correct the misbehavior of learners in a way that does not blame, scold, or humiliate?

1. *Express "sane" messages.* Sane messages communicate to students that their behavior is unacceptable but do so in a manner that does not blame, scold, preach, accuse, demand, threaten, or humiliate. Sane messages describe what should be done rather than scold what was done. "Rosalyn, we are all supposed to be in our seats before the bell rings," in contrast to, "Rosalyn you're always gossiping at the doorway and coming late to class."

2. *Accept rather than deny feelings.* Teachers should accept the feelings of students about their individual circumstances rather than argue about them. If a student complains, "I have no friends," the teacher should accept the student's feeling of isolation and identify with the student, such as by saying, "So, you're feeling that you don't belong to any group," rather than try to convince the student that he or she has misperceived the social situation.

3. *Avoid the use of labels.* When talking to students about what they do well or poorly, teachers should avoid terms such as *lazy, sloppy,* and *bad attitude,* as well as *dedicated, intelligent,* or *perfectionist.* Instead, teachers should describe, in purely behavioral terms, what they like or don't like about students. "You have a lot of erasures and white-outs on your homework," versus, "Your homework is sloppy." "You form your letters correctly," versus, "You are a good writer."

4. *Use praise with caution.* Ginott believes that many teachers use praise excessively and manipulatively to control student behavior rather than to acknowledge exceptional performance. They use praise judgmentally ("Horace, you are a good student"), confuse correctness with goodness (referring to a student who completes work with a minimum of mistakes as a "good child"), praise students performing minimally acceptable behavior as a way of influencing other students ("I like the way Joan is sitting in her seat"), and praise so often that the statements lose all significance and aren't even heard by the students. Ginott urges teachers to use praise only to acknowledge exceptional performance and in terms that separate the deed from the doer, for example, "That essay showed a great deal of original thought and research."

5. *Elicit cooperation.* Once a teacher and student have identified behavioral concerns, Ginott encourages teachers to offer them alternatives to solving the problem rather than using coercive power to tell them what to do. "Cooperate, don't legislate," is a convenient maxim to remember this point.

6. *Communicate anger.* Teachers are people, too. They get frustrated and angry just as anyone else. Ginott believes that teachers should express their feelings through the use of "I messages" instead of "you messages." The former focuses on your feelings about the behavior or situation that angered you ("You talked when the guest speaker was lecturing and *I feel* very unhappy and embarrassed by that"). The latter puts the focus on the students and typically accuse and blame ("You were rude to the guest speaker"). "I messages" should be used when you own the problem, that is, when you are the one who is angry or upset.

If you were to resolve a classroom management problem using the humanist tradition, you might have an open discussion with your students to draw their attention to the problem. Then, you would invite their cooperation in developing mutually agreed rules and consequences. Finally, as problems arise, you would have indi-

According to Glasser, one response to disruptive behavior is discussing the problem with the student. During that time you stress the importance of right choices and accept no excuses for wrong ones.

vidual conferences with your students during which time you would use the preceding steps 1 through 6 to engage them in congruent communication.

Glasser's Cooperative Learning

Glasser (1990) points out that effective classroom managers create a learning environment where students want to be, develop mutually agreed standards of behavior that must be followed to remain in this environment, and conduct problem-solving conferences with those who violate the standards. Glasser advocates **cooperative learning** as a way to make the classroom a place learners want to be. Glasser believes classrooms emphasizing cooperative learning motivate all children to engage in learning activities. He believes whole-group instruction, in which students compete with one another for limited rewards, inevitably causes 50 percent of the students to be bored, frustrated, inattentive, or disruptive.

For Glasser, dealing with disruptive students is straightforward, given a classroom where students experience belonging, power, and freedom—in other words, a classroom the learner would regret leaving. Faced with a student who persists in violating classroom rules the group believes are essential, Glasser states that the teacher should hold a brief, private conference with the student during which the rules are recalled, the disruptive behavior described, the need for following such rules asserted, and the consequence for not obeying them made clear, for example, removal from the room until the learner chooses to follow the rules. Glasser cautions teachers not to accept excuses from students for why they can't control their own behavior. He disagrees with teachers who use socioeconomic or sociocultural conditions as scapegoats or excuses for learners not making the "right" choices. For Glasser, there can be no excuse for disrupting an environment designed to meet learners' needs. Furthermore, when faced with removal from such an environment, Glasser believes students will choose, and will not need to be forced, to behave.

Glasser would have a clear directive for you as you begin to manage your classroom: Begin building a more friendly workplace based on principles of cooperative learning. He would have specific recommendations:

How can I build a friendly workplace based on the principles of cooperation?

- Develop with your students rules for the workplace.
- Get support from school administrators for having an area to which disruptive students can be removed.
- Have private conferences with disruptive students during which you stress the importance of right choices and accept no excuses for wrong ones.
- Follow through when students must be removed but always allow them the opportunity to return when they choose to follow class rules.

>>> THE APPLIED BEHAVIOR ANALYSIS <<< TRADITION IN CLASSROOM MANAGEMENT

This tradition is closely linked with Skinner's (1953) theory of learning called *behaviorism*, or *operant conditioning*. The techniques underlying the practice of behavior modification derive from this theory. Applications of behavior modification to changing socially important behaviors in the fields of education, business, and the social sciences has been called *applied behavior analysis* (Baer, Wolf, & Risley, 1968). To introduce both the strengths and weaknesses of this tradition, we first review the components of behavior modification that have resulted from this approach.

Behavior Modification

Behavior modification, as its name implies, focuses on changing or modifying behavior. Behavior is something a person does that is seen, heard, counted, or captured, say, in a snapshot or a home video.

Figure 12.1 summarizes some of the most important concepts of behavior modification. As Figure 12.1 indicates, when you want to teach a new behavior or make an existing behavior occur more frequently (for example, spell more words correctly), you must follow the behavior with some type of reinforcement. Reinforcement can be both positive and negative. **Positive reinforcement** occurs when a desired stimuli or reward you provide after a behavior increases its frequency of occurrence. **Negative reinforcement** occurs when the frequency of a behavior is increased by ending or terminating some painful, uncomfortable, or aversive state. In other words, the actions you take to turn off an annoying sound (shut the radio off), or relieve a headache (aspirin), or end a frustrating experience (walk away) will likely be repeated again (learned) the next time you experience a similar source of annoyance, discomfort, or frustration.

Negative reinforcement refers to escape or avoidance learning to strengthen the behavior, not simply to the application of discomfort or punishment. Thorndike (1913), for example, used negative rein-

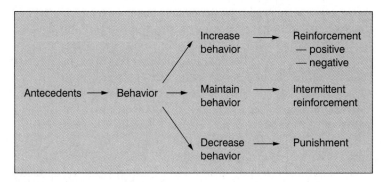

Figure 12.1
The process of behavior modification

forcement to teach cats how to escape a puzzle box. In order to get out of the box, the cat had to pull a cord hanging from the top of the box. As soon as the cat succeeded, the door opened and it escaped. The next time the cat was placed in the same box, the cat pulled the cord because it had learned how to escape to avoid the uncomfortable condition.

The reason negative reinforcement is important in the classroom is that learners often experience events they want to avoid: boring or difficult work, a scolding, requests to do something they don't want to do, or to stop doing something they want to continue. For example, when a shy student learns that when she doesn't look at the teacher the teacher stops calling on her, not-looking-at-the-teacher behavior becomes negatively reinforced. Or, when a learner makes distracting sounds during a lecture to get the teacher to send him out of the room, the teacher negatively reinforces the making-of-annoying-sounds behavior. Or, when some learners don't pay attention to get the teacher to stop the lesson, their not-paying-attention behavior becomes negatively reinforced. In other words, the teacher has taught these learners to pursue certain behaviors to escape or avoid an unpleasant condition.

As these examples illustrate, a teacher may inadvertently fall into the trap of "negative reinforcement" that learners unconsciously set. In fact, some psychologists believe that more inappropriate behavior is learned through negative than positive reinforcement, that is by learning what it takes to avoid or escape something undesirable than by being rewarded for doing something appropriate (positive reinforcement) (Iwata, 1987).

When you are satisfied with a particular behavior and how frequently it occurs, *intermittent reinforcement* can be applied to maintain the behavior at its present level. For example, consider a student who at the start of the school year was consistently late and unprepared for class, but now is beginning to arrive on time. You can maintain this behavior by reinforcing the student on a random or intermittent schedule, for example, every second day, every fourth day, or on randomly selected days, etc. This procedure is called intermittent reinforcement. Intermittent reinforcement is why you keep putting tokens into a slot machine long after your last "win" or keep fishing in the same spot long after your last nibble.

Behavioral antecedents are events (or stimuli), present when you perform a behavior, that elicit or set off the behavior. Antecedents can be *sounds* (for example, a noisy room influences students to become more noisy, an insult from a peer influences you to give an insult back, or the tone of voice in a teacher's demand influences a child to argue back), *sights* (the teacher raises finger to lips to indicate silence, or flips the light switch on and off), *people* (the principal walks in and everyone gets quiet), *materials* (math worksheets elicit a groan), or *places* (the auditorium elicits different behaviors than the principal's office). Behaviorists believe that much of our behavior has come under the control of antecedents (called *antecedent control*), because of the repeated pairing of reinforcers or punishers following the behavior with environmental stimuli (sounds, sights, people, and materials).

Applications of these principles to schools have produced a variety of systems or procedures for changing a student's behavior. Some of these procedures involve ignoring disruptive behavior and immediately reinforcing positive behavior. The assumption underlying these procedures is that disruptive students may have learned misguided ways of satisfying their needs for recognition. These disruptive behaviors will become less frequent when they learn that they will only gain recognition and rewards (receive positive reinforcement) when they behave well.

Other systems are built on the assumption that children learn desired behavior most efficiently when inappropriate behavior is immediately punished and appropriate behavior is immediately rewarded. The authors of these systems believe that more rapid improvement in how a child behaves will be made by using both timely punishment and timely reward than the use of either punishment or reinforcement alone. These systems routinely involve such punishment procedures as "time out," where the student is immediately removed to an area where they can experience no reinforcement of any kind following a disruptive act; "response cost" where a privilege or reinforcer that the student has in their possession is removed contingent on disruptive behavior (also called *fines*); or "overcorrection," where students not only make amends for what they did wrong, but also go beyond it by contributing something positive. For example, a student who defaces a desk is required not only to clean the desk he wrote on, but every other desk in the room as well. Or, a student who insults another student apologizes to that student *and* to the whole class.

There are literally hundreds of techniques available for applying procedures of reinforcement and punishment. But, how does one determine whether to use reinforcement or punishment or both? Applied behavior analysis has approached this problem by determining the most effective set of procedures for a given situation and behavior in two ways: the cookbook method and the functional analysis method.

Cookbook Method

The cookbook method is best described by Sparzo and Poteet (1989) and Canter (1976, 1989). According to this approach, the procedure you select (reinforcement or punishment) depends simply on what you want to happen to the behavior you wish to change. If you want to *increase* a behavior, you apply reinforcement. If you want to *decrease* the behavior, you apply punishment. Proponents of this approach usually provide teachers with lists of techniques that research has shown to decrease aggression, disruption, or inappropriate attention seeking for various ages and grades. Canter's *Assertive Discipline* (1989) recommends specific reinforcement and punishment techniques to use in modifying disruptive class behavior.

Functional Analysis Method

The functional analysis method holds that first you must determine the specific antecedents of a behavior and the consequences that motivate it before selecting an appropriate way in which to change the behavior. Proponents of this approach reason that it is the function of the behavior (that is, the motivation underlying it) that should dictate the choice of a behavior change, not simply the goal to reduce or increase it.

For example, one of the cookbook method recommendations for dealing with a child who disrupts class by speaking out of turn or getting out of her or his seat to bother other children is to place the child in a time-out area. This intervention may stop the behavior *if* the motivation behind it is to get attention from the teacher or other students. On the other hand, *if* the motivation behind the behavior were to get out of doing boring work, time out could lead to an increase in disruption through the ineffective use of negative reinforcement.

Thus, the functional analysis method would dictate that not only must the teacher assess the motivation behind the behavior in question before intervening (for example, to get attention, to escape demands, to get the teacher to let me do something better than boring seatwork), but the teacher should also determine what is reinforcing or punishing for each individual learner. Functional analysts argue that there is no reason to assume that any event will be reinforcing or punishing for any given person. Children from different cultures and different socioeconomic backgrounds who have had different experiences both inside and outside of school may not be motivated by the same reinforcers or punishers. Cookbook approaches, generally, recommend certain reinforcers or punishers to be applied to all children universally without consideration of individual likes and dislikes that may have been conditioned by culture, previous history, interests, and abilities. This can present an ethical dilemma to teachers who may decide to use the cookbook approach, since it makes little attempt to match reinforcers or punishment to the characteristics of individual learners, culture, or ethnicity (Donnelan & LaVigna, 1990).

Although specific approaches may vary, if you were to invite an applied behavior analyst to help you with a behavior problem, he or she would likely suggest the following steps for improving a learner's behavior:

How can I modify student behavior using positive and negative reinforcement?

- Identify both the inappropriate behavior you wish to change *and* the appropriate behavior you want to take its place.
- Identify the antecedents to both the inappropriate and appropriate behavior (e.g., influential peer) and make necessary changes in the classroom environment (e.g., change seating arrangement) to prevent the former from occurring and to increase the likelihood of the latter.
- Identify the student's goal or purpose behind the inappropriate behavior (e.g., attention seeking) and discontinue actions on your part (or those of peers) that satisfy this purpose.
- Establish procedures for reinforcing the appropriate behavior that you want to replace the inappropriate behavior.
- Use punishment only as a last resort.

>>> THE CLASSROOM MANAGEMENT TRADITION <<<

Throughout much of the latter half of this century, classroom discipline was focused on the question of how best to respond to student misbehavior. The humanist and the applied behavior analysis approach to classroom management shared the spotlight about equally during this period. As we have seen from the previous sections, both of these traditions are primarily **reactive** rather than **preventive systems of classroom management**. That is, they tend to emphasize solutions to misbehavior after rather than before it occurs. The 1970s and 1980s, however, provided another approach to classroom management which framed the question of classroom order and discipline, not in terms of reaction, but in terms of prevention. This approach was based on classroom research that examined what effective teachers do to prevent misconduct and what less effective teachers do to create it.

Some of this research involved observation and analysis of both experienced and inexperienced teachers while they taught. The major conclusion of this research was that more effective and less effective classroom managers can be distinguished more by what they do to *prevent* misbehavior than how they respond to misbehavior. In this section we will explain how the researchers came to this conclusion and the characteristics of effective classroom managers they found. But, first, let's look at one study of classroom management and how it was conducted.

Emmer, Evertson, and Anderson (1980) recruited 27 third-grade teachers in eight elementary schools into a year-long observation study. Using the average rate of student engagement and student off-task behavior obtained after the first three weeks of school, the teachers were classified into two groups, one consisting of the more effective managers and the other consisting of the less effective managers. Those teachers who were categorized as more effective classroom managers had significantly higher student engagement rates (more students actively engaged in the goals of the lesson) and significantly lower student off-task behavior (fewer reprimands and warnings) throughout the school year. Then, observation data pertaining to the classroom management procedures of these teachers during the first three weeks of school were used to compare the two groups.

During the first three weeks of school, observers gathered several types of information on each of the teachers, including room arrangement, classroom rules, consequences of misbehavior, response to inappropriate behavior, consistency of teacher responses, monitoring, and reward systems. In addition, observers counted the number of students who were on task or off task at 15-minute intervals to determine the extent to which students were attending to the teacher.

The more effective managers established themselves as instructional leaders early in the school year. They worked on rules and procedures until they were learned. Instructional content was important for these teachers, but they also stressed group cohesiveness and socialization, achieving a common set of classroom norms. By the end of the first three weeks, these classes were ready for the rest of the year.

In contrast to the more effective managers, the less effective managers did not have procedures well worked out in advance. This was most evident among the first-year teachers being observed. For example, the researchers described one new teacher who had no procedures for using the bathroom, pencil sharpener, or water fountain, and as a result the children seemed to come and go, complicating the teacher's instructional tasks.

The poorer managers, like the better managers, had rules, but there was a difference in the way the rules were presented and followed up. In some cases, the rules were vague: "Be in the right place at the right time." In other cases, they were introduced casually without discussion, leaving it unclear to most children when and where a rule applied.

The poorer managers were also ineffective monitors of their classes. This was caused, in part, by the lack of efficient routines for pupil activities. In other cases this was the result of teachers removing themselves from the active surveillance of the whole class to work at length with a single child. A major result of the combination of vague and untaught rules and poor procedures for monitoring and establishing routines was that students were frequently left without sufficient guidance to direct their own activities.

One further characteristic of the less effective managers was that the consequences of good behavior and inappropriate behavior were either not in evidence in those classrooms or were not delivered in a timely manner. For example, sometimes teachers issued general criticisms that failed to identify a specific offender or a particular event. Some of these teachers would frequently threaten or warn children but not follow through, even after several warnings. This tended to allow children to push the teacher to the limits, causing more problems. Others issued vague disciplinary messages ("You're being too noisy") that were not adequately focused to capture the attention of any one child or subgroup of children to whom they were intended. It was easy to see how deficiencies in the areas of rules, establishment of routines, monitoring, and praise and reward structure negatively affected the overall management and organization of the classroom. Most of the time these deficiencies became "windows of opportunity" that prompted a wider range of pupil misconduct, off-task behavior, and disengagement from the goals of the classroom. After only a few weeks had elapsed in the less effective managers' classrooms, there was a tendency for undesirable patterns of behavior and low teacher credibility to become established that persisted throughout the school year.

From this and related studies of classroom management (Evertson et al., 1994; Evertson & Emmer, 1982), we learn that effective classroom managers possess three broad classes of effective teaching behaviors:

What behaviors do effective classroom managers possess?

- They devote extensive time prior to and during the first few weeks of school to planning and organizing their classroom to minimize disruption and enhance work engagement.
- They approach the teaching of rules and routines as methodically as they approach teaching their subject area. They provide their students with clear instructions about acceptable

behavior and monitor student compliance with these instructions carefully during the first few weeks of school.

• They inform students about the consequences for breaking rules and enforce these consequences consistently.

As you can see, the classroom management tradition is essentially a preventive approach. It has a lot to say about how to ensure behavior problems do not occur. But, it offers few immediate solutions after the problem has occurred, since it emphasizes planning in anticipation of problems, not their resolution afterwards. You will need a comprehensive plan incorporating elements of all three traditions to make your classroom a positive environment for learning.

>>> AN INTEGRATED APPROACH TO <<< CLASSROOM MANAGEMENT

All three approaches to classroom management have their advantages and limitations. While each has made a significant contribution to our understanding of an effective classroom manager, there is no need to select one tradition over another. In fact, the research conducted by Emmer et al. (1980), Evertson and Emmer (1982), and Doyle (1986) has shown that effective classroom managers are able to blend together the best parts of different approaches. Let's look at some of the ways effective teachers have been able to accomplish this.

Low-Profile Classroom Control

Rinne (1984) has used the expression **low-profile classroom control** to refer to coping strategies used by effective teachers to stop misbehavior without disrupting the flow of a lesson. These techniques are effective for "surface behaviors" (Levin & Nolan, 1991), which represent the majority of disruptive classroom actions. Examples of surface behaviors are laughing, talking out of turn, passing notes, daydreaming, not following directions, combing hair, doodling, humming, tapping, and so on. They are labelled **surface behaviors** because they are the normal, developmental behaviors that children find themselves doing when confined to a small space with large numbers of other children. They do not indicate some underlying emotional disorder or personality problem. However, they can disrupt the flow of a lesson and the work engagement of others if left unchecked.

Figure 12.2 depicts the components of low-profile classroom control. Low-profile control for dealing with surface misbehavior is

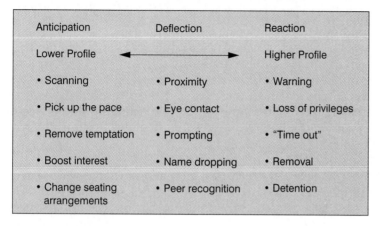

Anticipation	Deflection	Reaction
Lower Profile ⟵——————⟶		Higher Profile
• Scanning	• Proximity	• Warning
• Pick up the pace	• Eye contact	• Loss of privileges
• Remove temptation	• Prompting	• "Time out"
• Boost interest	• Name dropping	• Removal
• Change seating arrangements	• Peer recognition	• Detention

Figure 12.2
Characteristics of low-profile control

actually a set of techniques that requires *anticipation* by the teacher to prevent problems *before they occur*; *deflection* to redirect disruptive behavior that is *about to occur*; and *reaction* to unobtrusively stop disruptions immediately *after they occur*. Let's look at each of these.

Anticipation. Alert teachers have their antennae up to sense changes in student motivation, attentiveness, arousal level, or excitability, as these changes are or are about to happen. They are aware that at certain times of the year (before and after holidays), or week (just before a major social event), or day (right after an assembly or physical education class) the readiness of the class for doing work will be different from what usually can be expected. Skilled classroom managers are alert not only to changes in the groups' motivational or attention level but also to changes in specific individuals, which may be noticed as soon as they enter class.

At these times *anticipation* involves scanning back and forth with active eyes to quickly "size up" the seriousness of a potential problem and head it off before it emerges or becomes a bigger problem. For example, you may decide to pick up the pace of the class to counter some perceived lethargy in the class after a three-day weekend, or remove magazines or other objects that may distract attention from the individual or group before a long holiday. Some teachers maintain a reserve of activities likely to boost the interest of their students during times when it is difficult to stay focused on normal day-to-day activities. Others boost interest by forcing themselves to be more positive or eager in the face of waning student enthusiasm, for example, by raising and lowering the pitch of their voice and moving to different parts of the room more frequently. At other times it may be necessary to quickly change seating arrangements to minimize antagonisms when arguments between students occur. Anticipation involves not only knowing what to look for but also where and when to look for it. It also involves having a technique ready, no matter how small, for changing the environment quickly and without notice to your students to prevent the problem from occurring or escalating.

Deflection. As noted, good classroom managers sense when disruption is about to occur. They are attuned to verbal and nonverbal cues that in the past have preceded disruptive behavior. The applied behavior analysts would call these behavioral cues *antecedents* or *precursors*. They take the form of a glance, an abruptly closed textbook, sitting and doing nothing, squirming, asking to be excused, ignoring a request, a sigh of frustration, or a facial expression of annoyance or anger. Although not disruptive by themselves, these behaviors may signal that more disruptive behavior is about to follow.

Some teachers can detect the significance of these antecedents and deflect them by simply moving nearer to the student who may be about to misbehave, thus preventing a more disruptive episode from occurring. Other teachers may make eye contact with the learner combined with certain facial expressions, for example, raising of eyebrows or slight tilt of the head, to communicate a warning. Both these techniques effectively use nonverbal signals to deflect a potential problem. But verbal signals are also effective. Verbal deflection techniques include *prompting*, where the teacher reminds the class of the rule or says, "We are all supposed to be doing math, now"; *name dropping*, when the target student's name is inserted into the teacher's explanation or lecture, as in, "Now if Angela were living in Boston at the time of the Boston Tea Party, she might have . . . "; and *peer recognition*, in which the teacher notices a peer engaged in appropriate behavior and acknowledges this to the class. As potential for the problem to escalate increases, the effective manager shifts from nonverbal to verbal techniques to keep pace with the seriousness of the misbehavior that is about to occur.

Reaction. Anticipation and deflection can efficiently and unobtrusively prevent actions from disrupting the flow of a lesson. They allow students the opportunity to correct *themselves*, thus fostering the development of self-control. However, the classroom is a busy place and you will have many demands on your attention, which may make a behavior difficult to anticipate or to deflect.

When disruptive behavior occurs that you cannot anticipate or unobtrusively redirect, your primary goal should be to end the disruptive episode as quickly as possible. Effective classroom managers, therefore, must at times react to a behavior by providing a warning or an incentive to promote positive self-control. Your reaction requires first that you have included among your class rules a rule that corresponds with the behavior in question and the consequences for violating the rule. Glasser (1990) points out that an effective consequence for breaking a rule is temporary removal from the classroom—provided that your classroom is a place where that student wants to be—or loss of privileges, school detention, loss of recess, or other activity that the learner would miss.

When disruptive behavior occurs, your anticipation-deflection-reaction would be similar to the following:

How can I stop minor misbehaviors without disrupting the flow of a lesson?

1. As soon as a student disrupts, acknowledge a nearby classmate who is performing the expected behavior, "Carrie, I appreciate how hard you are working on the spelling words." Then, wait 15 seconds for the disruptive student to change his or her behavior.
2. If the disruption continues say, "Carlos, this is a warning. Complete the spelling assignment and leave Carrie alone." Wait 15 seconds.
3. If the student doesn't follow the request after this warning, say, "Carlos, you were given a warning. You must now leave the room for 5 minutes (*or* you must stay inside during lunch or cannot go to the resource center today). I'll talk to you about this during my free period."

Dealing with Persistent Disruptive Behavior

The low-profile techniques of anticipation, deflection, and reaction when used skillfully should promote lesson flow. Occasionally, when these techniques do not work for a particular student or group of students, it may be a signal that the needs of the student (for example, for trusting relationships, as discussed in Chapter 11) are not being met. When disruptive behavior persists and you have assured yourself that you have taken low-profile steps to deal with it, you may need to increase the intensity of your involvement in responding to the problem.

Table 12.1 lists some common discipline problems and typical teacher responses. The effective classroom manager prepares procedures in advance for these. In some cases, schoolwide rules and

Table 12.1

Some common discipline problems and typical teacher responses

Problems	Typical Teacher Responses
Talking out	Mary, if you have something to say; raise your hand.
Acting out	Bobby, if you don't stop clowning around, you'll be punished.
Talking back	Joan, you know I dislike your talking back to me.
Getting out of seat	Mary, that's the last time I'm going to stand for you leaving your seat to visit.
Note passing	Let me have that.
Noncompliant	I told you three times to open your workbook.
Ignoring rules	You know that makeup assignments must be due the same week they are assigned.
Obscene words or gestures	If I see that again, you'll go straight to the office.
Fighting	Tom and Joe, stop it immediately or you're both in big trouble.
Cheating	Mark, I can see you have another piece of paper under your test.
Stealing	Karl, where did you get this stapler?
Vandalism	Who wrote their initials on this desk?
Substance abuse	Tom, do I smell alcohol on your breath?

policies adequately address a problem (e.g., tardiness, cutting class, plagiarism). But in other cases, your classroom will be center stage for both the problem and its resolution.

How you handle these problems is as important as the problem itself. You must decide on how you will use your authority to bring about a resolution. At least three alternatives are available to you: (1) you alone decide the consequence for the misbehavior; (2) you and the student participate in choosing the consequence; or (3) you choose the consequence from among alternatives provided by the student.

You Alone Decide Punishment. You may decide that you are the ultimate authority. You will be the only judge of what occurred, you alone will decide the punishment, and you are the only one available or qualified to determine if the conditions of punishment are met. When a misbehaving student is unable to take responsibility for her or his own actions or to admit to the misbehavior, this approach is the most practical and effective. It may not, however, be the best approach to every situation.

You and Student Participate in Choosing Punishment.   In some situations it may be desirable for you and the student to discuss and agree on the consequence. One approach is for *you to provide* some alternative consequences from which the *student must choose*, thereby giving the student some choice in deciding his or her own fate. These consequences could be determined on the basis of group norms established by the entire class earlier in the year. Providing students with an opportunity to participate in the punishment phase of the misbehavior sometimes can reduce both their hostility toward you for disciplining them and the likelihood that the infraction will occur again.

You Choose Punishment from Student Alternatives.   A third alternative is to allow the students to participate in choosing their own consequence by *having them provide alternatives from which you choose.* This can work well with students mature enough to judge the severity of the wrongdoing and to suggest consequences accordingly, but may be inappropriate for students who cannot take responsibility for their own actions and who may not even be willing to own up to having misbehaved. Contrary to what you might expect, experience reveals that when students pose alternatives for their own punishment, the punishments they suggest often are harsher than those assigned by teachers.

Responses to Misbehavior

There are many responses at your disposal for dealing with misbehavior. You may choose to ignore an infraction if it is momentary and not likely to recur (e.g., when students jump out of and back into their seats to stretch their legs after a long assignment). At the other extreme, you may call an administrator to help resolve the problem. Between these extremes are many alternatives; listed here in order of increasing severity:

- Looking at the student sternly
- Walking toward the student
- Calling on the student to provide the next response
- Asking the student to stop
- Discussing the problem with the student
- Assigning the student to another seat

- Assigning punishment, such as a writing assignment
- Assigning the student to detention
- Writing a note to the student's parents
- Calling the student's parents

These alternatives vary in severity from simply giving the student a look of dissatisfaction to involving parents in resolving the problem. More important than the variety these alternatives offer, however, is your ability to *match the correct response to the type of misbehavior that has occurred.* One of the most difficult problems you will encounter in effectively maintaining classroom discipline will be deciding on a response that is neither too mild nor too severe.

What types of consequences for misbehavior are fair and just?

Although all rule violations consistently must receive some response, the severity of the consequence can and should vary according to the nature of the violation and the frequency with which such a violation has occurred in the past. If you respond too mildly to a student who has violated a major rule many times before, nothing is likely to change. If you respond too severely to a student who commits a minor violation for the first time, you will be unfair. Flexibility is important in the resolution of different discipline problems and must take into account *both the context in which the violation occurs and the type of misbehavior that has occurred.*

Here is some general advice for dealing with mild, moderate, and severe misbehavior:

- Mild misbehaviors like talking out, acting out, getting out of seat, disrupting others, and similar misbehaviors deserve a mild response, *at first.* But if they occur repeatedly, a moderate response may be appropriate. In unusual cases, such as continual talking that disrupts the class, a severe response may be warranted.
- Moderate misbehaviors like cutting class, abusive conduct toward others, fighting, and use of profanity deserve a moderate response, *at first.* But if these behaviors become frequent, a severe response may be warranted.
- Severe misbehaviors like cheating, plagiarism, stealing, and vandalism deserve a severe response. But don't try to handle major incidents of vandalism, theft, incorrigible conduct, and substance abuse in your classroom. Immediately bring these to the attention of school administrators.

Table 12.2 presents responses you can make to mild, moderate, and severe misbehavior.

Table 12.2

Examples of mild, moderate, and severe misbehaviors and some alternative responses

Misbehaviors	Alternative Responses
Mild misbehaviors	**Mild responses**
Minor defacing of school property or property of others	Warning
Acting out (horseplaying or scuffling)	Feedback to student
Talking back	Time out
Talking without raising hand	Change of seat assignment
Getting out of seat	Withdrawal of privileges
Disrupting others	Afterschool detention
Sleeping in class	Telephone/note to parents
Tardiness	
Throwing objects	
Exhibiting inappropriate familiarity (kissing, hugging)	
Gambling	
Eating in class	
Moderate misbehaviors	**Moderate responses**
Unauthorized leaving of class	Detention
Abusive conduct toward others	Behavior contract
Noncompliant	Withdrawal of privileges
Smoking or using tobacco in class	Telephone/note to parents
Cutting class	Parent conference
Cheating, plagiarizing, or lying	In-school suspension
Using profanity, vulgar language, or obscene gestures	Restitution of damages
Fighting	Alternative school service (e.g., clean up, tutoring)
Severe misbehaviors	**Severe responses**
Defacing or damaging school property or property of others	Detention
Theft, possession, or sale of another's property	Telephone/note to parents
Truancy	Parent conference
Being under the influence of alcohol or narcotics	In-school suspension
Selling, giving, or delivering to another person alcohol, narcotics, or weapons	Removal from school or alternative school placement
Teacher assault or verbal abuse	
Incorrigible conduct, noncompliance	

Reinforcement Theory Applied in the Classroom

Clearly, there are multiple ways to use your authority in managing discipline problems (you alone decide the consequence; you have students share in the responsibility; you choose the consequence from alternatives provided by the student) and multiple levels of response severity (from a stern glance to calling parents). But still more options exist. In this section you will learn how learners respond to reward and to punishment, why they respond to them differently, and how you can use them effectively in your classroom.

Reinforcement theory states that behavior can be controlled by the consequences that immediately follow it. The word *controlled* means that the consequences of a particular behavior can change the likelihood that the behavior will recur. Consider the following:

Event	Consequence	Future Event
You start going to the library to study.	Your test grades go up.	You begin going to the library more often.
You go to a new restaurant.	You get lousy service.	You never go there again.
You give your boyfriend or girlfriend a word of encouragement before a big test.	He or she gives you a kiss and a hug.	You give a word of encouragement before every big test.

When the consequence following a behavior changes the probability of that behavior's occurrence (test grades go up; you don't go there again; you get more kisses and hugs), reinforcement has occurred.

In your classroom, many events and their consequences will demonstrate the effects of reinforcement—whether you intend it or not. You may be surprised to learn that you are unintentionally increasing the frequency of some misbehaviors in your classroom through reinforcement. How can this happen? Consider another sequence of behaviors that, unknown to you, may occur in your classroom:

Event	Consequence	Future Event
Johnny cheats on a test.	He gets a good grade.	Johnny plans to cheat again.
Mary passes a note to her boyfriend.	Her boyfriend is able to pass a note back.	Mary buys a special pad of perfumed paper for writing more notes in class.

| Bobby skips school. | He earns five dollars helping a friend work on a car. | Bobby plans to skip again the next time his friend needs help. |

In each instance an undesirable behavior was reinforced (with a good grade; a returned note; five dollars). In each case the probability of recurrence increased because the consequence was desirable. In these examples, there is nothing you could have done, because your vigilance cannot be perfect—you didn't know about the cheating, note, or that school was missed for the wrong reason. But here are some ways you may unwittingly reinforce undesirable behaviors, which you *can* do something about:

- A student complains incessantly that her essay was graded too harshly. To quiet her, you add a point to her score. Reinforced, she complains after every essay for the rest of the year.
- Parents complain to you about their child's poor class participation grade. You start calling on the student more often, probing and personally eliciting responses. Reinforced, the student believes she no longer needs to volunteer or raise her hand.
- A student talks back every time you call on him, so you stop calling on him. Reinforced, he does the same in his other classes, to be left alone.

In each of these cases, the link connecting the behavior, the consequence, and the students' perception of the consequence might not be immediately apparent to you. Nevertheless, reinforcement of an undesirable behavior occurred.

The problem in each instance was that you chose to remove the misbehavior in a way that rewarded the student, thereby actually reinforcing the misbehavior. Notice that in each case you considered the consequence of your actions *only from your own point of view* (e.g., quieting an annoying student, preventing a parent from calling back, avoiding an ill-mannered student), without realizing that your actions *reinforced* the very behavior you wished to discourage.

Now that you see how reinforcement theory works, here are some guidelines for making it work not against you, but for you.

Rewards and Reinforcement.   Many types of rewards and reinforcement are available to increase the probability of a desirable response. A reward or reinforcement can be *external*, delivered by some other person, or *internal*, provided by the learner himself or herself.

Rewards consistent with the goals of your classroom and matched to student interests keep learners engaged in the learning process and responding at high rates of success.

Here are some familiar external rewards commonly found in the classroom:

- Verbal or written praise
- Smile, a head nod
- Special privileges (e.g., visit to the learning center, library, etc.)
- Time out of regular work to pursue a special project (e.g., lab experiment)
- Permission to choose a topic or assignment
- Getting to work in a group
- Extra points toward grade
- "Smiley face" stickers on assignments
- Note to parents on top of a test or paper
- Posting a good exam or homework for others to see
- Special recognitions and certificates (e.g., "most improved," "good conduct award," "neatest," "hardest worker," etc.)

Not all of these external rewards may be equally reinforcing, however. Some learners may disdain verbal praise; others will have no desire to visit the library or learning center. Some students like to be called on; others may be too shy and dislike the added attention. A reinforcement for one student may be completely irrelevant to another.

Educators have sometimes been criticized for creating a generation of learners who are hooked on artificial or extrinsic rewards in order to learn and behave in classrooms (de Charms, 1976). This has led to an increased interest in the use of internal rewards, also called **natural reinforcers**. An internal (natural) reward or reinforcer is one that is naturally present in the setting where the behavior occurs.

The most effective kind of natural reinforcer is one that results from the very performance of the behavior we want the learner to perform, and which motivates the learner to want to perform the behavior again. For example, the natural reinforcer for hitting the correct keys on a piano is the pleasurable sound that the behavior brings. Similarly, the natural reinforcer for writing correct letters is the satisfaction the first-grader experiences on seeing the letters forming on the page. Children who enjoy solving puzzles are receiving natural reinforcement for doing so. Likewise, learners who write poetry, play the guitar, study about history, read novels, compete in gymnastics, and so on are receiving natural reinforcement. What these examples have in common is that learners are engaging in the behaviors again and again without the need for external praise or other reinforcers delivered by another person.

Some learners are naturally reinforced by learning to write, read, color, answer questions, play sports, solve equations, answer textbook questions, and write essays. But, some are not. Many learners may require external reinforcers to begin to engage in certain classroom activities they do not find naturally reinforcing. For such children, external reinforcers have an important role to play: they (1) allow you to shape and improve the behaviors you desire through the use of positive reinforcement and (2) enable you to transfer their control over the learner's behavior to natural reinforcers. This transfer from external to internal control is called **operant conditioning** (Horcones, 1992). Over the past decade, researchers have developed strategies for transferring the control of extrinsic reinforcers to that of natural reinforcers:

Step 1. Select the target behavior.

This could be forming letters correctly, solving multiplication problems, drawing geometric figures, bisecting angles, writing compositions, or whatever is appropriate.

Step 2. Identify the natural consequences of the selected behavior.

For example, writing on a piece of paper produces many natural consequences: a scratching sound, the formation of letters, the filling up of a page, the gradual wearing away of a pencil point. Writing an essay has similar natural consequences but, in addition, produces sentences that express thoughts, ideas, images, and so on.

How can I condition my students to use natural reinforcers to motivate their behavior?

Step 3. Choose intrinsic consequences.

From your list of natural consequences, select those likely to be reinforcing to the person and relevant to the purpose of the activity. For example, the formation of the letters is a more appropriate consequence to focus on than the scratching sound on the paper or the filling up of the page.

Step 4. Identify those consequences the learner may more easily notice.

The more conspicuous the consequence to the learner, the easier it will be to condition this as a natural reinforcer. For example, the shape of a printed word is a conspicuous consequence of correct handwriting, and may serve as a natural reinforcer. Likewise, writing a complete thought, coming up with an answer that matches that in the back of the textbook, or the feeling you get when something is finished can all serve as natural reinforcers.

Step 5. Design your lessons in such a way that you make conspicuous the occurrence of natural consequences.

Rather than focusing only on the right answer to a problem, point out and describe for the learner the sequence involved. In general, focus on how something was done, not just on the end result. Some learners may not notice or direct their attention to the natural consequences of their work. By setting up instructional conditions to do this, you allow for natural reinforcers to acquire power over behavior.

Step 6. Select appropriate backup reinforcers.

To transfer the power an extrinsic reinforcer has over behavior to a natural consequence, you must select extrinsic or backup reinforcers. These reinforcers should have educational value, be available in your classroom and, ideally, involve you in the reinforcing activity (Horcones, 1991).

Step 7. Condition the natural reinforcer.

Have your learners engage in the behavior. As soon as possible, give informational feedback, pointing out the natural consequences that you hope will become natural reinforcers. Immediately, give the backup reinforcers. Gradually, remove these reinforcers from the learning setting but continue to point out and illustrate the natural consequences of what the learner did. Gradually, point out the natural consequences less and less. Deliver and intermittently pair the backup reinforcers with the natural reinforcers.

Which is more effective in changing the behavior of learners: rewards or punishment?

Punishment. Punishment is used to decrease the probability or likelihood that a behavior will occur. For example, you can try to keep

Johnny in his seat either (1) by giving him an extra assignment every time he is out of his seat, or (2) by giving him a trip to the reading center for every 30 minutes he stays in his seat. In the first instance you are giving Johnny a *punishment* to encourage him to do what's expected, and in the second you are giving him a *reward* to achieve this same end. Punishment creates an avoidance response to an undesirable behavior. On the other hand, a reward encourages a desirable behavior to recur by dispensing something pleasant or rewarding immediately after the desirable behavior.

But rewards and punishments generally are not equally effective in promoting a desired behavior. Given two choices to keep Johnny in his seat—the punishment of extra homework, or reward of something interesting to work on—the reward usually will be more successful. Here are several reasons:

Punishment does not guarantee that the desired response will occur. The extra homework may indeed keep Johnny in his seat the next time he thinks of moving about, but it by no means ensures that he will pursue the truly desired behavior, which is to perform some meaningful instructional activity while he is there. Instead, he can daydream, write notes to friends, or even pull Mary's hair. All succeed in keeping him from being punished again for getting out of his seat. Punishment in the absence of rewards can create other undesired behaviors.

The effects of punishment usually are specific to a particular context and behavior. This means that extra homework is not likely to keep Johnny in his seat when a substitute teacher arrives, because it was not *that* teacher who assigned the punishment. Also, *that* punishment is not likely to deter Johnny from pulling Mary's hair, because the punishment was associated only with keeping him in his seat. Punishment rarely keeps one from misbehaving beyond the specific context and behavior to which it was most closely associated.

The effects of punishment can have undesirable side effects. If extra homework is truly an aversive for Johnny—if it is a highly undesirable and painful consequence in his eyes—he may decide never to risk leaving his seat again, even to ask for your assistance or to use the rest room. Johnny may decide to take no chances about leaving his seat, and not even to trust his own judgment about when an exception to the rule may be appropriate.

Punishment sometimes elicits hostile and aggressive responses. Although any single punishment is unlikely to provoke an emotional response, students receive punishment in various forms all day long, both at school and at home. If your punishment is the "straw that breaks the camel's back," do not be surprised to observe an emotional outburst that is inconsistent with the amount of punishment rendered. This is not sufficient reason to avoid assigning punishment when it is needed, but it is reason to use it sparingly and in association with rewards.

The punishment can become associated with the punisher. If you use punishment consistently as a tool for increasing the likelihood that a desirable behavior will occur, you may lose the cooperation you must have for managing your classroom effectively. With this cooperation gone, you will find that the vital link for making management techniques work is gone. *Plan not to solve every discipline problem by using punishment*; otherwise, the punishment could become more strongly associated with you than the desired behavior you wish to encourage.

Punishment that is rendered to stop an undesired *behavior, but which is not immediately associated with the* desired *behavior, seldom has a lasting effect.* If the desired behavior is not clear to your students at the time punishment is administered, the punishment will be seen only as an attempt to hurt and not as an attempt to encourage the desired behavior.

When should I use warnings to prevent minor problems from intensifying?

Warnings. Warnings can prevent minor problems from intensifying to where punishment is the only recourse. For the misbehaviors listed as "mild" in Table 12.2, it is not unusual to provide several warnings before dispensing some kind of consequence. However, after two or three warnings you should assign some type of consequence, because waiting longer reinforces the student's belief that you are not serious about the misbehavior. This undermines the integrity of the rule being violated and your credibility, as well.

Some "moderate" misbehaviors also may receive warnings. In the case of "severe" behaviors, however, warnings are generally insufficient. For these behaviors, the consequences of recurrence may be too damaging to others and to your classroom. Therefore, warnings are untimely and you must take action immediately, while at the same time giving a clear indication of the expected behavior.

Corporal Punishment. Absent from the common forms of punishment listed in Table 12.2 is any form of corporal punishment, such as paddling a student. Such punishment, although permissible in

some school districts when administered by a specifically designated school authority, has not proven particularly effective in deter-
ing misbehavior.

A reason is that the heightened emotion and anxiety on the part
of the student (and the administrator) at the time of the punishment
often prevents rational discussion of the appropriate behavior that
the punishment is supposed to encourage. In addition, corporal
punishment easily can provoke aggression and cause hostility in
both students and parents. This can outweigh any immediate benefit that might accrue from the punishment.

Generally, you should not have physical contact with a student,
because such contacts are easily misunderstood. This applies
whether the contact is to administer punishment or, in the case of
older students, is a reward (patting a student for doing a good job)
or assistance (placing your arm around a student in times of high
anxiety). Although your own judgment, the situation, and age of the
student will be your best guides, the only clear exception is a situation where your assistance is needed immediately. Examples of such
situations are breaking up a fight to prevent physical injury, curtail-
ing the movement of a student who is hurting another, or restraining
a student from self-injury. At such times, you should call an administrator as quickly as possible.

>>> THE PARENT-TEACHER CONFERENCE <<<

When a major infraction of a school or classroom rule has occurred,
more effective than any form of corporal punishment is the parent-
teacher conference. This is your opportunity to inform one or both
parents of the severity of the misbehavior and for eliciting their
active help in preventing it. As we saw in Chapter 2, without the
support of the student's family in providing the appropriate rewards
and punishment at home, there is little chance that interventions at
school will have a lasting effect in deterring the misbehavior (Rotter,
Robinson, & Fey, 1987).

Being "grounded" for the week, having to be in at a certain time,
completing extra study time in the quiet of one's bedroom, or performing extra chores around the house *always will have more
impact than any aversive that can be administered during the
school day*, as long as these family aversives are administered with
a complete understanding of the desired behavior (Rich, 1987).

Notifying parents that a conference is desired usually is the
responsibility of the principal or a counselor. However, because the
request for a conference is the result of a specific problem in your

classroom, you will be involved in preparing any formal notification telling the parents why a conference is being requested. This notification should consist of a letter sent through the mail containing the following:

1. Purpose of the conference, including a statement of the joint goal of supporting the student's success in school
2. Statement pointing out the integral role of the parent in the discipline management process (this may include a citation from any state or school policy regarding such matters)
3. Date, time, and location of conference
4. A contact person (and phone number)
5. A response form for parents' reply, preferably with a self-addressed stamped envelope

How do I plan a parent-teacher conference?

If the request for a conference is made to the student's parents by phone, these same points can be orally presented; it is important that the date, time, location, and contact person for the conference are recorded by the parent at the time of the call.

During the conference you should do the following:

- Try to gain the parents' acknowledgment of the problem and their participation in the discipline management process.
- Present a plan of action for addressing the problem at home and at school.
- Identify followup activities (e.g., note home each week indicating progress, immediate phone call if problem should recur, a review of the situation at the next parent-teacher night).
- Document what took place at the conference, including the agreements and disagreements.

Conducting the Parent Conference

In addition to these general guidelines, during the parent conference you will be expected to talk plainly, listen, and use "I messages" (Swap, 1987).

Plain Talk.

> When my son, Bruce, entered the first grade, his report card said, "He verbalizes during class and periodically engages in excursions up and down the aisles." In the sixth grade, his teacher said, "What can we do with a child who does not relate to social interaction?" (I ran home and got out my dictionary.) At the start of his senior year, Bruce's advisor said, "This year will hopefully open up options for

your son so he can realize his potential and aim for tangible goals."
On my way out, I asked the secretary, "Do you speak English?" (She
nodded.) "What was she telling me?" "Bruce is goofing off," the secretary said flatly. I don't know if education is helping Bruce or not,
but it's certainly improving my vocabulary! (Bombeck, 1984, p. 17)

Practice speaking plainly. Here are just some of the terms educators use naturally, but which mean little to most parents: *norms,
fine-motor skills, behavioral objectives, learning set, negative
reinforcement, developmental needs, homogeneous or heterogeneous grouping, cognitive skills, discovery learning, percentiles,
linguistic approach, knowledge acquisition, prosocial behavior,
standardized test, higher-order thinking, basic skills, portfolios,
prerequisite skills.*
New teachers—particularly when they first meet parents or
address them at group meetings—rely on familiar jargon, which may
be incomprehensible to parents. Jargon, however familiar to you,
will diminish rather than increase your credibility with parents.

Listen.   Listening is your most important communication skill. Parents, particularly when they are upset, want to be heard. One of the
most frequent complaints leveled by parents against teachers is that
they don't listen (Gordon, 1974). The Appalachian Educational Laboratory (Shalaway, 1989) offers the following list of hints for you to
become a good listener:

- Maintain eye contact.
- Face the speaker and lean forward slightly.
- Nod or give other noninterrupting acknowledgements.
- When the speaker pauses, allow him or her to continue with-
  out interrupting.
- Ignore distractions.
- Wait to add your comments until the speaker is finished.
- Ask for clarification when necessary.
- Check your understanding by summarizing the essential
  aspects of what the speaker tried to say or the feeling he or
  she tried to convey.

Gordon (1974) refers to this last skill as *active listening*. It is
particularly valuable during reactive parent conferences or conferences requested by parents who are upset over something they perceive that you said or did. Such conferences can be emotionally
charged. Teachers typically take a defensive or aggressive posture
when confronted by an angry parent. Rather than listen to what the
parents have to say—regardless of how inaccurate it may seem—the

teacher follows the parents' statement with a denial, or a defensive statement, or a refusal to talk further.

Gordon believes that active listening, in which the listener provides feedback to the speaker on the message heard and the emotion conveyed, opens doors to further communication by letting the speaker know that she or he was being understood and respected. Active listening is an essential communication skill to be used with the parents of learners and the learners themselves. But it is a difficult skill to learn. It requires the ability to concentrate on what someone is saying even when you strongly object to what is being said. Like any skill, it must be practiced before it can be used naturally and automatically.

Use "I Messages" to Express Your Feelings. We have discussed Ginott's model of congruent communication (Ginott, 1972) in reference to learners. The use of sane messages is just as important when speaking with their parents. Particularly when you are upset about the actions of a learner or the words and actions of a parent, it is important that you clearly communicate your feelings. However, the way to do this is not by criticizing or blaming (with a "you message") but rather by describing (1) what you find offensive ("When you . . . " or "When your . . . "), (2) the feeling or emotion you experience when the offensive condition occurs (" . . . I feel . . . "), and (3) a statement of the reason for the feeling ("because . . . "). For example, "When Amanda talks back to me her behavior is disruptive to the entire class, and that makes me angry because I have to take time away from all the other students in the class to deal with her." This message focuses on your reaction to the problem rather than on what the child said or did. It opens up avenues to further communication rather than sets up barriers, which might be the case if you said, "What gives Amanda the right to talk back to me in my own classroom?"

Evaluating the Parent Conference

Following the conference, summarize for yourself what was said and agreed on and make a list of any actions to be taken by you or the parent. Make followup calls, send notes, and follow through on whatever you committed yourself to. Finally, take a moment to reflect on how well you communicated with the parents and achieved your goals and what you might change or do differently next time you have a parent conference. This moment of reflection will be one of the most important aids to sharpening your parent conferencing skills.

The Group Conference

Bringing parents together in one group can save you the time of having to repeat the same information about your goals, objectives, teaching methods, and evaluation activities to interested parents. Group conferences also give parents the opportunity to meet one another and develop friendships.

Some elementary school teachers conduct group conferences by allowing parents to follow their children throughout a regular school day. When the learners are at art, music, or physical education, the teacher talks to all the parents. Teachers who have tried this technique report that it makes the individual conference more meaningful and interesting to the parent (Shalaway, 1989).

Other forms of group conferences that have been found to contribute to learner achievement and improvement in classroom behavior are monthly parents' night, neighborhood meetings with school staff, early morning breakfasts, and monthly Dad's or Mom's nights, in which parents get together at the school for room decoration parties or to play basketball, volleyball, or a nonathletic game. When feasible, have translators when non–English speaking parents are present.

>>> THE INFLUENCE OF HOME AND FAMILY <<<
ON CLASSROOM BEHAVIOR PROBLEMS

Finally, it is important to note that some of the discipline problems you will face in your classroom have their origin at home. Living in a fast-paced, upwardly mobile society has created family stresses and strains that our grandparents could not have imagined. Their lives while growing up were not necessarily any easier than yours or your students', but they were most assuredly different, particularly in the intensity and rapidity with which children today experience developmental stages and life cycle changes.

For example, by some estimates, boys and girls are maturing earlier than they did 50 years ago. This means that they come under the influence of the intense emotions of sex, aggression, love, affiliation, jealousy, and competitiveness far earlier than our own parents probably did. Teachers of the seventh and eighth grades no longer are surprised by the depth of understanding and ability of young students to emulate the media's attractively packaged images of adult behavior and lifestyles, especially as they relate to sex, clothes, relationships, and dominance.

Although not often recognized, these generational differences sometimes are even more difficult for parents to accept than for you, the teacher. This often leads to major conflicts at home that surface in your classroom as seemingly minor but persistent misbehaviors. You can have little influence over home conflicts, except to understand that they originate in the home and not in your classroom.

There will be times when no amount of reward or punishment will work, because the source of the problem is within the home and may be far more serious than you suppose—including marital discord, verbal or physical abuse, competition among brothers and sisters, financial distress, and divorce. You need to realize that one or more of these family disturbances easily could be occurring in the families of some of your students.

These are not trivial burdens for students, especially when combined with the social and academic demands of school, the uncertainties of a future job or education, and the tension that school-age children always feel between youth and adulthood. If a problem persists and your rewards and punishments are to no avail, you must consider the possibility that such a family problem may be occurring. Although there is no easy way to know what is happening in the lives of your students at home, many students welcome the opportunity to reveal the nature of these problems, *when they are asked*. For some it will be just the opportunity they have sought to shed some of the emotional burden these events are creating in their lives.

It is not your role to resolve such problems, but knowing the reason they are occurring may explain why your rewards and punishments may not be working. Knowing the reason also can help you decide whether to refer the problem to other professionals who are in a position to help (such as a social worker, counselor, school psychologist).

>>> CULTURALLY RESPONSIVE <<<
CLASSROOM MANAGEMENT

What is culturally responsive classroom management?

One of the most interesting and encouraging advances in the understanding of classroom management is the emerging field of **culturally responsive teaching** and behavior management. As we saw in previous chapters, the writings and research of Tharp and Gallimore (1989), Dillon (1989), and Bowers and Flinders (1991) present convincing arguments that different cultures react differently to nonverbal and verbal behavior management techniques, including proximity control, eye contact, warnings, and classroom arrangement. Furthermore, they cite numerous examples of how teachers from one culture interpret disruptive behaviors of children differently than those of another culture. Therefore, it is important to be aware that many of the behavioral management techniques presented in this and the previous chapter may be culturally sensitive, and that the effective classroom manager matches not only the technique he or she uses with the situation but also with the cultural history of the learner.

If the research supporting "culturally responsive teaching" has yet to provide explicit prescriptions for teaching culturally different learners, what does it tell us about better understanding students in multicultural classrooms?

The traditional method of conducting classroom research is to study large groups of teachers, classify their teaching methods, give learners achievement tests, and try to find relationships between achievement test scores and particular teaching practices. Dillon (1989), however, used a different approach. She studied one teacher, Mr. Appleby, and his class for a year using a research method called *microethnography*. Her study, published in the *American Educational Research Journal*, provided valuable insights into what a teacher can do to create a classroom where culturally different learners experience academic and personal success.

Dillon's conclusion was that Appleby's effectiveness as a classroom teacher was due to his ability to assume the role of "translator and intercultural broker" between the middle-class culture of the school and the lower-class African American culture of his students. As a cultural broker and translator, Appleby was thoroughly knowledgeable about the backgrounds of his learners and, as a result, was able to bridge the differences between school and community/home cultures.

With this cultural knowledge, Appleby created a classroom with three significant attributes:

1. He created a social organization where teacher and learners knew one another, trusted one another, and felt free to express their opinions and feelings. In other words, Appleby created a climate characterized by the type of cohesiveness discussed in Chapter 11.

2. He taught lessons built around the prior knowledge and experiences of his learners. Because of his knowledge of his learners' background, he was familiar with their knowledge, skills, and attitudes toward the content. This knowledge allowed him to represent the subject matter in ways that encouraged his students to link it with what they already knew and felt.

3. He used instructional methods that allowed learners to actively participate in lessons, to use the language and soci-

olinguistic patterns of their culture, and the language and social interaction patterns both he and his learners were familiar with.

Dillon concludes that what teachers need to know in order to teach successfully in multicultural classrooms has more to do with knowing the values, socialization practices, interests, and concerns of their learners than with knowing about presumed learning style preferences and cognitive styles and the do's and don'ts of teaching learners with these traits. Rather, Dillon believes that the cultural knowledge teachers such as Appleby have about their learners allows them to represent subject matter content in ways that are meaningful to them, to develop lessons that gain their active participation, and to create social organizations in the classroom within which learners feel free to be themselves.

Summing Up

This chapter introduced you to some concepts and techniques for maintaining classroom order and discipline. Its main points were as follows:

1. Most classroom discipline problems are low intensity, continuous, and unconnected with any larger, more serious event.

2. The humanist tradition of classroom management focuses on the inner thoughts, feelings, psychological needs, and emotions of the individual learner. Humanist approaches emphasize the importance of allowing the student time to control his or her own behavior.

3. Ginott's "sane messages" communicate to students that their behavior is unacceptable but in a manner that does not blame, scold, or humiliate.

4. Glasser's cooperative learning emphasizes building a more friendly workplace that the learner would regret leaving for misbehavior, if told to do so.

5. The humanist tradition focuses on developing rules, getting support from school administrators, holding private conferences with students, and following through when students must be removed from the classroom.

6. The applied behavior analysis tradition of classroom management applies the techniques of operant conditioning to change socially important behaviors.

7. Behavior modification focuses on changing or modifying behavior by following a behavior with some type of reinforcement.

8. Positive reinforcement occurs when a desired stimuli or reward is provided after a desired behavior to increase its frequency.

9. Negative reinforcement occurs when a painful, uncomfortable, or aversive state is terminated to increase the frequency of a desired behavior.

10. *Antecedents* are events or stimuli present when you perform a behavior that elicit or set off the behavior, such as sounds, sights, or people.

11. The applied behavior analysis tradition focuses on identifying the appropriate and inappropriate behavior, identifying antecedents that could trigger these behaviors, the stu-

dent's goal for the misbehavior, and procedures for reinforcing the appropriate behavior.

12. The classroom management tradition frames the question of classroom order and discipline, not in terms of reaction, but in terms of prevention.

13. The classroom management tradition focuses on planning and organizing the classroom, teaching rules and routines, and informing students of the consequences of breaking the rules.

14. Low-profile classroom control refers to coping strategies used by effective teachers to stop misbehavior without disrupting the flow of a lesson.

15. Three ways to apply your authority in dealing with misbehavior are as follows:

- You alone judge what occurred and what the punishment should be.
- You provide some alternative forms of punishment from which the student must choose.
- You select a punishment from alternatives that the students provide.

16. The level of severity with which you respond to a misbehavior should match the misbehavior that has occurred.

17. The idea behind reinforcement theory is that any behavior can be controlled by the consequences that immediately follow it. When the consequences that follow a behavior change the probability of the behavior's recurrence, reinforcement has occurred.

18. Some misbehaviors that occur in classrooms are unintentionally increased through reinforcement, in which case the probability of the misbehavior increases because a consequence that follows the misbehavior is perceived as desirable by the student.

19. Both rewards and punishment can increase the probability of a behavior, although punishment without reward is rarely effective.

20. Punishment in the absence of rewards tends to be less effective in increasing the probability of a desired behavior for the following reasons:

- Punishment does not guarantee that the desirable response will occur.
- The effects of punishment are specific to a particular context.
- The effects of punishment can spread to undesirable behavior.
- Punishment can create hostile and aggressive responses.
- Punishment can become associated with the punisher.

21. After two or three warnings a punishment should be assigned.

22. Corporal punishment is rarely effective in deterring misbehavior.

23. One feature of the parent-teacher conference that accounts for its effectiveness is the involvement of the parent in eliminating the misbehavior.

For Discussion and Practice

*1. What are the six criteria of an effective classroom management plan? Which, in your opinion, will be the easiest to achieve in your classroom and which will be the most difficult?

*2. Describe what Ginott calls "sane messages" and give an example at your grade level?

*3. Using a realistic dialogue between teacher and student, provide an example of an "I message" to communicate your anger to a student.

*4. What are several specific recommendations Glasser would have you do as you begin to manage your classroom?

*5. How might you use both positive and negative reinforcement to stop a student from repeatedly talking out?

*6. Describe what is meant by "time out" and "response cost." Give an example of what you would do to implement each in your classroom?

*7. According to research studies of classroom management, what three broad classes of effective teaching behaviors do effective classroom managers possess?

8. Describe a low-profile anticipation-deflection-reaction sequence directed to a child who leaves a seat without permission.

*9. Identify three ways you can use your authority to assign consequences to a student for misbehaving.

10. Identify responses that reflect the severity of the offense for the following misbehaviors. Do not use the same response more than once.

> Talking back
>
> Cutting class
>
> Eating in class
>
> Jumping out of seat
>
> Smoking in class
>
> Sleeping in class
>
> Acting out
>
> Obscene gesturing

> Selling drugs
>
> Fighting

11. Give one reward that might be used to get a student to do each of the following:

> Do homework
>
> Stop talking
>
> Stop talking back
>
> Turn in assignments on time
>
> Be on time for class
>
> Remember to bring pen and pencil
>
> Not talk without raising hand

*12. Describe the steps you would take to transfer the control of an extrinsic reinforcer to that of a natural reinforcer.

*13. Identify five reasons why punishment is rarely effective in the absence of rewards.

*14. Under what two conditions is the use of punishment most effective?

*15. Identify two important objectives for having a parent-teacher conference.

16. In your own words, what is culturally responsive classroom management?

---

* Answers to asterisked questions (*) in this and the other chapters are in Appendix B.

Suggested Readings

Canter, L. (1989). *Assertive discipline for secondary teachers*. Santa Monica, CA: Canter & Associates.

> This book, geared primarily for the secondary classroom, presents classroom management from the applied behavior analysis tradition.

Glasser, W. (1990). *Quality school: Managing students without coercion*. New York: Harper Perennial.

> An introduction to the communication skills—or humanistic—approach to anticipatory classroom management.

Harcones, J. (1992). Natural reinforcement: A way to improve education. *Journal of Applied Behavior Analysis, 25* (1), 71–76.

> This article sets out the procedures for transferring the motivation for learning from external reinforcers to internal—or natural—reinforcers.

Jones, F. H. (1987). *Positive classroom discipline*. New York: McGraw-Hill.

> An up-to-date presentation of many useful techniques for managing your classroom during the first year of teaching.

Levin, J., & Nolan, J. (1991). *Principles of classroom management: A hierarchical approach*. Englewood Cliffs, NJ: Prentice-Hall.

An up-to-date classroom management book that covers the topics of low-profile classroom control and how to deal with "surface behaviors."

Rich, D. (1987). *Teachers and parents: An adult-to-adult approach*. Washington: National Education Association.

An up-to-date resource on the changing role of the family and the responsibility of teachers in creating ties between home and school.

Rotter, J., Robinson, E., & Fey, M. (1987). *Parent-teacher conferencing*. Washington: National Educational Association.

An extensive guide to planning and conducting parent-teacher conferences.

Sparzo, F. J., & Poteet, J. A. (1989). *Classroom behavior: Detecting and correcting special problems*. Boston, MA: Allyn & Bacon.

An excellent reference for the hard-to-manage classroom and the unengaged learner.

CHAPTER 13

Teaching Special Learners in the Regular Classroom

This chapter will help you answer the following questions:

1. Who is an "at-risk" learner?
2. With what strategies can I teach the at-risk learner?
3. Do at-risk learners benefit from tracked—or homogeneous—classes?
4. Who is a gifted and/or talented learner?
5. With what strategies can I teach the gifted and/or talented learner?
6. Do gifted and/or talented learners benefit from tracked—or homogeneous—classes?
7. What is bilingual education?
8. What are some types of bilingual programs in which I may be asked to participate?
9. With what strategies can I teach the bilingual learner?
10. Who are learners with disabilities?
11. In what ways might I be expected to participate in providing services to learners with disabilities?
12. With what strategies can I teach learners with disabilities?
13. What can I do to provide a positive, productive environment in my classroom for students with disabilities?

This chapter will also help you learn the meaning of the following:

at-risk learner
bilingual education
gifted and talented learner
heterogeneous grouping
individualized educational plan (IEP)
learners with disabilities
least restrictive environment
limited English proficient learners
magnet schools
mainstreamed learners
normalization
track systems

T he culture in which we live includes individuals who are both physically strong and weak, mentally able and less able, native and nonnative speakers, rich and poor, and well educated and undereducated. Unlike so many other cultures and educational systems throughout the world, we have welcomed this diversity in our communities and our schools. This cultural mix is illustrative of a nation based on democratic principles. These principles give equal rights to all learners irrespective of race, creed, intellect, language, or any other physical, cultural, or mental characteristic, and these rights have been interpreted in federal legislation to include the right to a free, public education in the least restrictive environment.

This policy and the federal and state laws that protect it make this chapter important to you. As a regular classroom teacher, you may expect to have a teaching career devoted to educating the "average" student. However, in the American school system "average" does not mean the absence of diversity; rather, it increasingly means that the diversity of people, cultures, and values represented in our communities and nation will be found in your classroom. The at-risk, gifted, and bilingual learner as well as learners with disabilities are a part of this diversity that is rapidly redefining the composition and character of the "regular" classroom. This means that as a regular classroom teacher you must be aware of the special learning needs of these students and be able to use teaching strategies that meet them. It also means you must be able to manage and teach in a classroom that is no less "average" than the community existing outside it.

We begin our study of special learners with several important observations:

1. The types of special learners we will study are not necessarily independent of one another. An at-risk, bilingual, or gifted learner may also have a physical disability. A learner can be average in one subject and gifted in another. It is even possible that a learner could be both at risk and gifted, when considering his or her accomplishments in widely different areas of the curriculum.

2. The variation in behavior within a group of learners (e.g., those "at risk") may be greater than the variation found between groups of learners. Even

A learner varies — may be gifted & home in one area & difficulty in another

when individuals are grouped by a common characteristic, they may differ in many other characteristics that also affect their behavior.

3. Classifications of special learners do not express general innate or unchangeable characteristics of individuals, but rather the unique instructional methods needed to remediate or enhance their learning abilities. Individuals who may be considered special learners may be more or less "special," depending on the content to be learned and the methods with which they must be taught.

4. Regardless of how learners may be grouped, categorized, or organized for instruction, every learner is capable of benefiting from the regular classroom. In other words, all learners are entitled to learn in an environment that allows them to experience the respect and dignity to which any person in our society is entitled.

So, why categorize learners at all? The advantages include the assistance that categorization provides in these areas:

1. Dispensing state and federal funds that often are earmarked for specific types of learners.
2. Developing and organizing instructional materials, texts, and media appropriate for and specifically targeted to certain types of learners.
3. Training and assigning the most qualified instructional staff to teach certain types of learners.

Now, let's use what we've learned in earlier chapters to examine the similarities and differences among four types of special learners and to suggest teaching methods specific to their learning needs.

>>> **THE AT-RISK LEARNER** <<<

Contrary to common belief, **at-risk learners** in the regular classroom are neither rare nor unique. Up to one-third of today's students will drop out of school before graduation, and of these, over

Who is an "at-risk" learner?

[handwritten margin note: Instructional methods change because they need special instruc. methods to learn.]

[handwritten margin note: All learners is capable of benefiting from the regular classroom.]

half have been described as "at-risk learners" (National Center for Education Statistics, 1993a, b). Your overall effectiveness as a teacher may well depend on your ability to recognize at-risk learners and to teach them appropriately. This section dispels common misconceptions about students who are at risk for their academic performance, explains who they really are, and suggests procedures for teaching this special group of learners.

One common misperception about at-risk learners is that they are mentally retarded or emotionally disturbed, or that they require continual disciplining. But "at-risk learner" refers to none of these characteristics. Nor does it refer to the student of average intelligence who may fail a subject due to difficulty with the language, lack of sufficient discipline to study, or lack of interest in school. Although such groups may include at-risk learners, these are not defining characteristics.

Students commonly called *at risk* for their academic performance are those who cannot learn at an average rate from the instructional resources, texts, workbooks, and learning materials that are designated for the majority of students in the classroom. These students need special instructional pacing, frequent feedback, remedial instruction, and/or modified materials, all administered under conditions sufficiently flexible for learning to occur.

Learners who are at risk for poor academic performance usually are taught in one of two possible instructional arrangements: (1) a class composed mostly of average students, or (2) a class specifically designated for below-average learners. The latter classes sometimes are part of a **track system** in which different sections of math, English, science, social studies, and so on are allocated for less able, average, and more able learners. It is estimated that 80 percent of secondary schools and 60 percent of elementary schools use some form of tracking (O'Neil, 1992).

The desirability and fairness of various tracking systems, however, is being extensively debated (Slavin, 1991a; Mansnerus, 1992; Gamoran, 1992). The argument typically offered in favor of tracking is that it allows schools to better differentiate instruction by giving high achievers the challenge and low achievers the support they need to learn. Opponents argue that (1) tracking is undemocratic in that it separates learners into homogeneous groups unrepresentative of the world outside the classroom, and (2) recent research has indicated that it fails to increase learner achievement beyond what can be expected to occur in heterogeneous classrooms (Slavin, 1987a, 1990a; Kavale, 1990; Skiritic, 1991).

Whether you meet at-risk learners in a regular class or in a tracked class, you will immediately feel the challenge of meeting their learning needs. One characteristic of this group of learners is their tendency to become disengaged from the learning process, placing them at risk of school failure and persistent behavioral problems. Keeping these learners actively engaged often requires more than the usual variation in presentation methods (e.g., direct, indirect), classroom climate (e.g., cooperative, competitive), and instructional materials (e.g., practice activities, learning centers). Other characteristics of these learners that place them at risk for school failure and/or behavioral problems are their deficiency in basic skills (reading, writing, mathematics), their difficulty in dealing with abstractions, and their sometimes unsystematic or careless work habits, which may require instruction in notetaking, listening, and organization skills. When these learning strategies are not provided as part of your instruction, the result is often a performance below the child's potential to learn, beginning a cycle of deficiencies that promotes poor self-concept, misbehavior, and disinterest in school—all of which have contributed to a particularly high dropout rate for this type of learner (Walker & Sylwester, 1991; Patterson, De Baryshe & Ramsey, 1989).

[handwritten margin note: ✳Characteristics — At Risk Learners]

Compensatory and Remedial Teaching

An important aspect of teaching at-risk learners is knowing the difference between *compensatory* teaching and *remedial* teaching (recall the discussion of these two approaches to *adaptive teaching* in Chapter 2).

Compensatory Teaching.   The term compensatory teaching originally referred to preschool programs of the 1960s, which were designed to *compensate* for the cultural deprivation of disadvantaged children (Dembo, 1981). Compensatory programs are based on the premise that enriching a child's environment can influence intellectual and academic development.

Compensatory teaching is an instructional approach that *alters the presentation* of content to circumvent a student's fundamental weakness or deficiency. Compensatory teaching reorganizes content, transmits it through alternate modalities (e.g., pictures vs. words), and supplements it with additional learning resources and activities (learning centers and simulations; group discussions and cooperative learning). This may involve modifying an instructional technique by including a visual representation of content, by using more flexible instructional presentations (e.g., films, pictures, illustrations), or by shifting to alternate instructional formats (e.g., self-paced texts, simulations, experience-oriented workbooks).

The objective of compensatory teaching is to deemphasize instructional stimuli that require the use of a child's weaker learning modalities (e.g., verbal, abstract) and to emphasize instructional stimuli and arrangements that require use of the child's stronger learning modalities (e.g., visual, concrete).

Remedial Teaching.   Remedial teaching is making use of activities, techniques, and practices to *eliminate* weaknesses or deficiencies that the learner is known to have. For example, deficiencies in basic math skills are reduced or eliminated by *reteaching* content not learned earlier. Instructional stimuli are not changed, as in the compensatory approach, but instead, conventional instructional techniques are employed, such as drill and practice or specifically designed programmed materials or computer software, to make up the deficiencies.

Comparing the Compensatory and Remedial Approaches.   For practical reasons, the compensatory approach is often favored because the remedial approach may require more instructional time reteaching basic skills, with no guarantee they will be learned. Since earlier attempts failed, subsequent efforts may meet the same fate. On the other hand, the compensatory approach represents the belief that many paths can be taken to acquire new knowledge. One path may emphasize one set of abilities, while another path may emphasize a different set. The teacher's role is to be flexible and seek a path to learning that works. Some remediation may still be needed, however, since some skills are so specific to subsequent learning that they must be acquired at almost any cost in instructional time.

Instructional Strategies for At-Risk Learners

With what strategies can I teach the at-risk learner?

While no single technique or set of techniques is sufficient for teaching this group of learners, the suggestions that follow are a starting point to help you develop instructional strategies that can uniquely address the learning needs of at-risk students.

Develop Lessons around Students' Interests, Needs, and Experiences.   This will help heighten the attention of at-risk learners and actively engage them in the learning process. To accomplish this, design some instructional lessons with their specific interests or experiences in mind. Oral or written autobiographies at the beginning of the year, or simple inventories (as shown in Chapter 11, Figure 11.4) in which students indicate their hobbies, jobs, and unusual trips or experiences can provide the basis for lesson plans, projects, and assignments that allow learners to construct their own meanings from direct experience and the interactions they have with others around them.

Encourage Oral as well as Written Expression.   For at-risk learners, many writing assignments go unattempted or are begun only half-heartedly because these learners recognize that their written product will not meet even minimal writing standards. You might consider a carefully organized audio- or videotaped assignment at the beginning of school; this has the advantage of avoiding at a crucial time spelling, syntax, and writing errors. Such errors can be so pervasive at the start of instruction as to destroy learners' hopes that they can ever achieve an acceptable level of performance, no matter how much effort they make.

Provide Study Aids.   Study aids alert students to the most important problems, content, or issues. They also eliminate irrelevant details that at-risk learners often laboriously study in the belief that they are important. The at-risk learner may have difficulty weighing the relative importance of competing instructional stimuli unless explicitly told or shown what is important and what is not. Example test questions or a list of source topics for possible questions can help focus student effort.

very helpful

Teach Learning Strategies.   Recall from Chapter 9 that learning strategies are general methods of thinking that improve learning across a variety of subject areas. They accomplish this by enhancing the way information is received, placed in memory, and activated when needed. You can increase your students' learning skills by teaching elaboration/organization (e.g., notetaking and outlining), comprehension and monitoring (e.g., setting goals, focusing attention, self-reinforcement), and problem-solving strategies (e.g., vocal and subvocal rehearsal). These strategies often are acquired through observation, but should be explicitly taught and modeled for the at-risk learner.

If you can help a child learn to organize elab. in work, they can increase learning skills.

All five of our key behaviors—lesson clarity, instructional variety, task orientation, engagement in the learning process, and student success—are relevant to the at-risk learner. But, the most important are instructional variety and student engagement at moderate-to-high rates of success. If you are unable to engage the attention of learners with a flexible and variable instructional style, you will accomplish little else in your classroom. You can achieve this level of engagement with at-risk learners if you *vary your instructional methods often and organize your lessons into small enough activities to ensure moderate-to-high rates of success.*

make lessons w/ small activities to insure better success.

Present Trends in Teaching the At-Risk Learner

Do at-risk learners benefit from tracked—or homogeneous—classes?

It has been estimated that 80 percent of secondary schools and 60 percent of elementary schools use some form of tracking that includes at-risk students (O'Neil, 1992). Recall that the argument in favor of tracking or *homogeneous grouping* is that it allows schools to better differentiate instruction by giving high achievers the challenges and low achievers the support they need to learn. But, important questions are, how representative of different cultures, ethnicities, and socioeconomic levels are the tracked or homogeneous groups, and do at-risk learners educationally benefit from tracked or homogeneous classes? Let's look at what the research has to say about the effects of tracking, with which many at-risk learners are taught.

Research data gathered from a national study involving 14,000 eighth-grade students in public schools (Mansnerus, 1992) has shed light on the relationship of tracking to race, ethnicity, and socioeconomic status. The data indicate that Asian and Anglo learners are more likely to be grouped into the upper track category in English and math classes, while the opposite is true for Hispanic, African American and Native American students. Also, learners in the top socioeconomic quarter are more likely to be in a high-ability group than learners in the bottom socioeconomic quarter. Thus, the argument of opponents of tracking that such a practice is biased against certain groups appears to rest on some evidence. There are some who feel that these data alone are reason enough to avoid grouping by tracks (Gamoran, 1992). Others agree. The National Governors Association endorsed detracking in its national education goals. The Carnegie Foundation task force report, "Turning Points," a 1988 report on the middle grades, came out strongly against tracking, as did the National Education Association. But, are there educational benefits to tracking that offset its inequality? Let's raise several questions to find out.

Has Tracking Improved Overall School Achievement? Studies by Slavin (1987a, 1991a), Fogelman (1983), and Kerchoff (1986) conclude that there is little evidence to support the claim that tracking increases overall school achievement relative to heterogeneous grouping. These studies have been conducted at the elementary level only. Few secondary schools do not use some form of tracking. Although Slavin (1987a) found that tracking fails to raise school achievement, he reports that subject-specific, within-class, flexible grouping for math and reading does have positive effects.

Has Tracking Narrowed the Achievement Gap between High- and Low-Ability Learners? Gamoran (1993) conducted a national survey that followed more than 20,000 learners in grades 10 through 12 who were academically tracked into higher-achieving and lower-achieving classes. His data show that in the progression through high school, high-track students gain while low-track learners fall further behind. In addition, he reports an even greater disparity in achievement between those assigned to different tracks than between learners who dropped out of school in the 10th grade and those who remained in school.

Will Untracking Increase Overall School Achievement? The research so far fails to make a strong case for the practice of tracking. Nevertheless, the research also does not make a case for abolishing tracking as a way to improve achievement. Moreover, if untracking simply results in untracked classes resembling low-tracked ones (for example, reduced content, overreliance on direct instruction, repetitive practice), an overall reduction in school achievement could result.

There are some lessons schools seeking to untrack may learn from those that have already done so. Since 1990, the Massachusetts Advocacy Center has made site visits to over 250 untracked middle schools and interviewed administrators, teachers, parents, and learners. Here is some of what they learned about successful alternatives to tracking (Wheelock, 1992):

- The motivation for untracking should be to improve education of all learners. All learners should experience more indirect and self-directed modes of instruction.
- Successful untracking springs from a belief that all students can learn. Schools that have successfully untracked are characterized by high expectations for all learners.
- Breaking down ability groups should proceed hand in hand with building up the curriculum for all learners. This includes making important reforms in curriculum development, instruction, assessment, and counseling. The overall learning environment should be levelled up, not scaled down.
- Parents should be involved in planning and implementing **heterogeneous grouping**. Principals of untracked schools report that parents can make or break the process.
- Teachers should be trained in instructional techniques suitable for at-risk learners. They should be allowed to learn and experiment with techniques such as cooperative learning, peer tutoring, and within-class flexible grouping.

>>> THE GIFTED AND/OR TALENTED LEARNER <<<

A student who reads rapidly, comprehends quickly, has an exceptional memory, is imaginative and creative, has a long attention span, and is comfortable with abstract ideas is described with words like *bright, exceptional, gifted*, and *talented*. Not all schools have programs for the learning needs of the gifted and talented. However, awareness is growing that **gifted and talented students** are an important natural resource that must be encouraged, activated, directed, and fully developed.

The size and scope of most specialized school programs, such as those for learners with disabilities or the disadvantaged, make programs for the gifted look pale by comparison. But teaching the gifted remains an important objective of virtually every school. Because of their importance to your school's objectives and the distribution of gifted and talented across every social class, community, and type of school, you should be aware of the learning needs of these special learners. This section explains some of the characteristics that make students gifted and talented and how you can meet their special learning needs.

When Will You Teach Gifted Students?

If you were to observe gifted and talented programs in different school districts, you would quickly see that the word *gifted* has many meanings. These different definitions of giftedness have created considerable diversity among both the students called gifted and the instructional programs designed to meet their needs. Gifted students are a population every bit as diverse as the at-risk learners just described.

You will meet the gifted in several instructional arrangements. One is a gifted class that is part of a districtwide gifted and talented program. Another is a tracked class specifically intended for the more able student. Still another is a so-called "average" or regular class composed mostly of average learners but including more able and gifted learners.

The number of gifted learners you might have depends largely on factors beyond your control, such as the availability of a special gifted program in your school, the existence of a formal tracking system for more able learners, and the proportion of gifted learners in the school community where you teach. But, whether you teach a gifted class, a more able class with some gifted learners, or a regular class with one

Gifted students may be in an "avg" or regular class.

or more gifted learners, you likely will be responsible for teaching some gifted learners *during your very first year of teaching*.

It is a mistaken notion that gifted learners are easy to teach. As most experienced teachers of the gifted will attest, nothing could be further from the truth! It is sometimes the case that the experienced teacher who has taught the gifted will prefer *not* to do so again, due to the extra work (e.g., preparing intellectually challenging exams, grading extended essays, dealing with parents' expectations) and special demands (e.g., knowing how to use specialized library resources, supplemental materials, and equipment). Hence, the assignment may be given to a beginning teacher, like yourself, who may have little choice in the matter.

The truth is that the job of teaching the gifted is as difficult and as challenging as teaching any other type of learner. There are important differences among learning types, but these are differences in kind, not degree. For example, preparation for teaching the gifted is different, but not measurably less, than for a class of less able learners. Likewise, discipline problems encountered with the gifted are different, but not measurably less, than for other types of learners. The time you spend teaching mastery of a concept does not vary measurably among types of learners, because the difficulty level also must vary with types of learners.

Therefore, when you teach the gifted, whether as an intact class in junior and senior high or as individuals in an average or regular elementary class, approach the task free of any illusion that something less will be required of you. On the contrary, it is likely to require something more.

Defining Gifted

Who is a gifted and/or talented learner?

Because the words *gifted* and *talented* often include considerable diversity among these learners, you should be aware of the different ways in which gifted students are identified. It is important to know that no single standard or definition of giftedness has ever been agreed on, or is likely to be. However, the *Congressional Record* of 10 October 1978 provides a broad definition:

> Gifted and talented children means children, and whenever applicable youth, who are identified at the preschool, elementary, or secondary level as possessing demonstrated or potential abilities that give evidence of high performance capability in areas such as intellectual, creative, specific academics, or leadership abilities, or in the performing and visual arts, and who by reason

[Handwritten margin notes: "Gifted learners are more difficult to teach because they constantly need to be challenged." and "— very challenging to teach this type of learner"]

thereof require services or activities not ordinarily provided by the school (H-12179).

While a consensus exists as to what general abilities and behaviors compose giftedness, there is considerable variation in how to measure both the degree of ability and the proper combination of sub-abilities that represent giftedness. The following are some of the most important behavioral ingredients from which an individual school district's definition of giftedness is likely to be composed.

Intelligence. Foremost among the characteristics of giftedness is general *intelligence*. We noted in Chapter 2 that aptitude in a specific area often is more predictive of future productivity and accomplishments (in that area) than is general intelligence, but nevertheless, most formulae for defining giftedness include general intelligence. This is particularly true in the elementary grades, where it is believed that learners are still developing their specialized intellectual capacities while their general intelligence was almost completely formed in the critical preschool years. The emphasis on general intelligence for aiding identification of giftedness at the elementary level also is a function of the difficulty of measuring specific aptitudes at that age, when many of the words and concepts required for accurately testing specific aptitudes have yet to be taught.

At the junior high and secondary levels, measures of specific intelligence are more likely to be substituted for general intelligence. The most common are verbal and mathematical aptitude, scores for which can be derived from most general IQ tests. For example, a sufficiently high score on verbal intelligence could qualify a learner for gifted English but not for gifted math, and vice versa; this gives greater flexibility to the definition of giftedness.

How high must a student score on tests of general or specific intelligence to be considered gifted? This depends on the school district's criteria. However, it is known how intelligence is distributed among individuals in the entire population. Recall that intelligence is distributed in a bell-shaped curve, with most individuals scoring around the middle of the curve, which represents an IQ score of 100. From the shape of this curve, we also know that less than 1 percent of the population scores 145 or higher, about 2 to 3 percent scores 130 or higher, and approximately 16 percent scores 115 or higher.

Although these percentages vary slightly depending on the test used, they are a useful guideline for selecting gifted learners. An IQ score of about 130 or higher generally makes one eligible for gifted instruction. However, in practice, because giftedness almost always is defined in conjunction with at least several other behaviors, admission to gifted programs and classes usually is far less restrictive. It is not uncommon to accept scores below 130 as eligible for gifted instruction. Sometimes IQ is not considered at all in determining giftedness, in which case the learner must exhibit unusual ability in one or more other areas.

Because IQ tests rely greatly on standard language usage that predominates in the middle class, a school district with a high concentration of disadvantaged students may not require a high level of tested intelligence (at least not as measured by standardized tests). In most cases, intelligence is one among several behaviors that constitute giftedness. Rarely is intelligence used as the only index of giftedness, nor should it be.

Achievement.   Among other behaviors frequently used to determine giftedness is the learner's *achievement*, usually in the areas for which gifted instruction is being considered. Achievement is measured by yearly standardized tests covering areas such as math, social studies, reading comprehension, vocabulary, and science. Cutoff scores in the form of percentile ranks are determined in each subject area, with a percentile score of 90 to 95 representing a typical cutoff. Although cutoff percentiles differ among school districts, a cutoff percentile of 90 means that a learner is eligible for gifted instruction if his or her score on the appropriate subscale of a standardized achievement test is higher than the scores of 90 percent of all those who took the test.

Creativity.   In addition to intelligence and achievement, indices of *creativity* often are considered in selecting gifted learners. Inclusion of this behavioral dimension has broadened the definition of this type of learner to include both the gifted and the talented. The significance of this addition is that not all gifted learners are talented, nor are all talented learners gifted. The phrase "gifted and talented," which is widely used, can mean talented but not gifted, gifted but not talented, mostly talented with some giftedness, mostly gifted with some talent, or both gifted and talented.

These alternative categorizations are made possible by inclusion of creativity indices in the eligibility standards. Because creative behaviors generally are considered in selecting gifted students, this type of learner more appropriately might be called "gifted and/or talented." Observable signs of creativity in a learner include the following:

- Applying abstract principles to the solution of problems
- Being curious and inquisitive
- Giving uncommon or unusual responses

- Showing imagination
- Posing original solutions to problems
- Discriminating between major and minor events
- Seeing relationships among dissimilar objects

In identifying the gifted and talented learner, the creative component usually is composed of recommendations from teachers based on these and other signs of creativity and any observable creative products (e.g., sculpture, painting, musical score, science fair project, short story). It is interesting to note that studies have shown only a modest relationship between intelligence and creativity, indicating that creativity is fairly independent of both IQ and achievement (Terman & Oder, 1959).

Task Persistence. A fourth behavior sometimes used in selecting gifted and talented learners involves recommendations from teachers and other knowledgeable sources concerning a learner's *task persistence*. This behavior is difficult to evaluate, but often is considered indispensable for satisfactory achievement in a gifted and talented program, because both the quantity and quality of the work are likely to be considerably above what is expected in the regular classroom. Obviously this trait alone would not be sufficient for qualifying a learner for gifted instruction, but if such instruction is indeed geared to the extremely able student, students will need unusual levels of task persistence to succeed. Behaviors teachers look for in determining task persistence include the following:

- Ability to devise organized approaches to learning
- Ability to concentrate on detail
- Self-imposed high standards
- Persistence in achieving personal goals
- Willing to evaluate own performance, and capable of doing so
- Sense of responsibility
- High level of energy, particularly in academic tasks

It is in evaluating these behaviors that parents play the greatest role in influencing their child's eligibility for gifted instruction. By providing testimony to the school about the ability of their child to work hard, to accept additional responsibility, and to live with increased performance and grading expectations, parents may convince the school that the learner can indeed profit from gifted instruction. Because prestige accrues to both parent and student from being in a gifted class, you can expect considerable pressure from parents to consider students who may not meet the standards of intelligence, achievement, and creativity. In some cases, you may need to point out why a particular learner would not benefit from gifted instruction and to help secure an alternative placement.

Instructional Strategies for Gifted and Talented Learners

You may consider one of your students gifted as a result of previously being assigned to gifted classes, or you may arrive at this conclusion from an independent assessment of the student's intelligence, achievement, creativity, and task persistence. In either case, there are several methods for teaching the gifted who must be taught among regular students. The following suggestions are starting points for managing and teaching the gifted and talented learner.

With what strategies can I teach the gifted and/or talented learner?

Choose Learning Activities to Allow Freedom and Include Interests.   This encourages independent thinking, while at the same time giving the student the extra motivation often required to pursue a topic in much greater depth than would be expected of an average student. Because gifted learners tend to take greater responsibility for their own learning than do average students, self-directed learning methods (Chapter 9) often predominate among teachers of the gifted.

Along with this, let students know that you are giving them a unique opportunity to, in a sense, create their own curriculum. Some gifted students become disenchanted with school, feeling that nothing there is relevant to their interests at their intellectual level. By letting them pursue and investigate some topics of their own choosing and construct their own meanings and interpretations, you will be making them participants in the design of their own learning.

Occasionally Plan Instruction Involving Group Activities.   Gifted students are among those most capable of picking up ideas from others and creating from them new and unusual variations. Brainstorming sessions, group discussion, panels, peer interviews, teams, and debates are among the ways you can start interactions among students. When carefully organized, this can create a "snowballing" of ideas that can turn initially rough ideas about a problem into polished and elegant solutions.

Include Real-Life Problems that Require Problem Solving.   Let your gifted students become actual investigators in solving real-world dilemmas in your content area. This will force them to place newly acquired knowledge and understandings in a practical perspective and to increase the problem-solving challenge. Ask them pointed questions

Gifted learners require flexibility of responding and independence of thought. This is most easily accomplished through self-directed learning methods that are relevant to the learner's interests and specialized abilities.

that do not have readily available answers: "How would you reduce world tensions among the superpowers?" "How would you eliminate acid rain?" "How could we harvest the seas?" "How could life be sustained on the moon?"

Be careful not to accept glib and superficial responses. Make clear that an inquiry must be conducted into the nature of the problem using methods of inquiry like those used by professionals—scientists, engineers, political scientists—in answering the question. Finally, require actual library or laboratory research that produces not just opinions, but objective evidence leading to a possible answer.

Pose Challenging Problems.   Perhaps more than any other learners, the gifted both are capable of and enjoy the freedom to independently explore issues and ideas that concern them. Give them this opportunity by posing a challenging problem and organizing data (e.g., references, materials, and documents) that they must screen for relevance. Focus the problem so the learner must make key decisions about what is important for a solution. This feeling of responsibility and control over the inquiry is essential if the learner is to see it as truly self-directed. Throughout the inquiry, students should feel your support, encouragement, and above all, availability to provide additional references and materials relevant to directions they wish to explore.

In Testing, Draw out Knowledge and Understanding. Because gifted students tend to be verbally fluent, it can be difficult to know whether an articulate response substitutes superficiality and glibness for an in-depth understanding. Fancy words at a high vocabulary level may hide a lack of hard work and investigation. Such responses may even be purposefully composed to intimidate the listener, whether teacher or classmate. Testing and questioning the gifted, therefore, should draw out the knowledge and understanding that lies within, to separate articulate superficiality from in-depth understanding.

Use tests and questions that make the student go beyond knowing and remembering facts. Asking your gifted students to explain, analyze, compare, contrast, hypothesize, infer, adopt, justify, judge, prove, criticize, and dispute are means of indicating that more than a verbally fluent response is required. Asking your students to explain the reasons behind their answers, to put together the known facts into something new, and to judge the outcome of their own inquiry are useful means of separating "slick" responses from meaningful answers.

Present Trends in Teaching the Gifted and Talented

Gifted and talented education has taken on added prominence in recent years as a result of the increase in alternatives by which the gifted learner can *accelerate*—or move through the traditional curriculum.

Do gifted and/or talented learners benefit from tracked—or homogeneous—classes?

Earlier, we learned that there is little evidence to support the claim that homogeneously grouped or tracked classes increase overall school achievement relative to heterogeneously grouped classes (Kerchoff, 1986; Slavin, 1991a; Gamoran, 1993). However, this research specifically excluded gifted learners, who represent approximately the top 3 to 5 percent of the school population. Research tends to support programs and classes specifically targeted to the gifted and talented when they are allowed to pursue *accelerated* programs, where a grade can be skipped and/or advanced courses taken, such as advanced placement (AP) courses for college credit (Slavin, 1991b). Those gifted and talented programs that simply *enrich* (add to) existing curriculum by allowing students to pursue games and simulations to promote creativity and problem solving, conduct individual investigations, or simply have the use of computers or other technology, tend to be less successful in increasing the achievement of these learners (Kulik & Kulik, 1984). Gifted and talented programs that are exclusively enrichment programs have been criticized for providing few activities that would not benefit all learners. Their primary advantage tends to be that they provide additional opportunities for learners who can master the regular curriculum rapidly enough to take advantage of them.

This has led to the increasing popularity of **magnet schools**, whose primary purpose is to provide curriculum in specialized areas, such as science, language arts, and the creative arts, to a broad range of students whose interest and sub-abilities qualify them. Some magnet schools are schools within a school, thereby promoting heterogeneous interactions among learners while providing advanced and accelerated coursework leading to college credit and/or early high school graduation to those who can master the curriculum more quickly. The magnet school concept, as well as other alternatives, such as early graduation, that move the gifted learner more rapidly through the school curriculum, increasingly are coming to define programs for the gifted and talented.

>>> THE BILINGUAL LEARNER <<<

Approximately five million students—about 10 percent of the entire schoolage population in this country—have a primary language other than English (Baca & Cervantes, 1989). Although their number varies with state and region, you can expect to meet some of them in your classroom. If you teach in some areas of the South, Southwest, and Northeast, as many as a third of your students may not speak English as their primary language.

 Predominant among this group are Mexican American, Puerto Rican, Caribbean, Central American, and South American students. They generally are considered *bilingual*, which implies proficiency in both their native Spanish and adopted English. In reality, however, many have **limited English proficiency** (LEP). This means they may range from being unable to express themselves at all in English to being marginally proficient, either orally or in writing. The vast—and increasing—numbers of these students in our school population presents a challenge to develop instructional materials and use techniques that meet their special learning needs.

Because Hispanics are the largest language minority in the United States, Spanish is used as an example in this chapter, but the information provided applies to all non-English speakers.

Although initially a regional concern, bilingual education is now a national issue of considerable importance. Our society's great mobility, plentiful transportation, and rapidly changing employment opportunities have integrated the bilingual learner into the schoolage population of almost every state. This has caused considerable financial and curriculum-development pressure on individual school districts where little if any planning existed for maximum development of the bilingual learner. The federal government and many state governments are providing funds for developing and operating bilingual programs. Although more than 30 states now make bilingual programs mandatory or encourage them through guidelines and statewide policies, only 29 percent of the bilingual programs use both native and English languages for instruction (Zakariya, 1987).

Laws and school district policies now require regular classroom teachers to assume some responsibility for teaching LEP bilingual students. Although special LEP programs exist in some areas, LEP students still spend at least part of their day **mainstreamed** in regular classrooms. This is in keeping with a general philosophy embodied in federal law that encourages use of the least restrictive instructional environment wherever it is deemed conducive to a child's education.

The more instruction that LEP students receive in a regular classroom, the less restrictive will be their instructional environment. This is because the regular classroom has a mix of learning types, personalities, and ethnicities that represents the community in which LEP students will live and work. Thus, many programs require LEP students to spend only part of the instructional day in a concentrated program of bilingual education and the remaining time in the regular classroom.

Bilingual education refers to a mix of instruction in two languages. This means teaching skills and words in English as well as in another language, which in the United States is predominately Spanish. The primary goal of bilingual education is not to teach English as a second language, but to teach concepts, knowledge, and skills through the language the learner knows best and then to reinforce this information through the second language (English), in which the learner is less proficient. This raises important related issues: Should the goal of bilingual education be to bring about a transition to the second language as quickly as possible? Or, should some emphasis be placed on maintaining and even improving the learner's proficiency in his or her native language?

What is bilingual education?

Such issues arise from the observation that *bilingual* or even *limited English proficiency* do not in reality mean that learners are proficient in their native language; experience shows that this very often is not the case. Essential skills in vocabulary, syntax, and reading comprehension may be lacking in both languages. This not only complicates instruction but also raises the issue of whether the bilingual program and schools have responsibility for nurturing and improving the native language in addition to English. Not surprisingly, the linguistic and cultural goals of bilingual education often differ from program to program. They also differ among states, which fund the majority of bilingual programs.

Four Approaches to Bilingual Education

What are some types of bilingual programs in which I may be asked to participate?

From the two basic philosophies—transition to a second language versus maintenance of the native language—four general approaches have emerged. These are defined by Baca and Cervantes (1989) as transition, maintenance, restoration, and enrichment.

Transition Approach.   The transition approach uses learners' native language and culture only to the extent necessary for them to learn English. Learners are not taught reading or writing in their native language. In the transition approach, the regular classroom teacher should encourage and sometimes expect LEP learners to respond, read, and write in English. The teacher using the transition approach first discerns the level of English proficiency of the learner and then expects the learner to function in English at or slightly above this level.

Maintenance Approach.   The maintenance approach, in addition to encouraging English language proficiency, endorses the idea that learners also should become proficient in their native language. The goal is to help learners become truly bilingual—to become fluent in both languages. Such learners have come to be called *balanced bilinguals* to emphasize that their proficiency is limited neither in English nor in Spanish.

Federal funding requirements favor transitional bilingual programs. But school districts, particularly in the South and Southwest where the Hispanic culture is most prominent, often supplement federal funds with local resources to meet the dual purposes of a maintenance approach. The implication for the regular classroom teacher is that alternative expressions in English and Spanish *must* be accepted as equally valid communication within the classroom.

That is not to say that a Spanish response can replace one in English, which clearly would be inappropriate if you are a non–Spanish speaking teacher. It means that, if the learner wishes, both languages can be used in articulating the same expression. This can be an important aid to the LEP student because thoughts can be organized, formulated, and even expressed in the comfort of the native language and then safely translated into English.

Those who have had to express themselves in a foreign language can attest to the helpfulness of this strategy. If they were not proficient in the language and were as yet unable to think in it, they invariably composed what they wanted to say in English and then replaced the English formulation word by word with its counterpart in the other language.

Restoration Approach.   The restoration approach attempts to restore the native language and culture of the bilingual student to its purest and most original form. As other languages have been assimilated into standard American culture, they have developed abbreviated forms in which words and phrases that mix both languages often compose regional dialects. These are like separate languages unto themselves. Even native speakers from other regions sometimes have difficulty deciphering these nonstandard, subcultural expressions.

Restoration's goal is to replace these nonstandard dialects with the original form of the language. From this perspective, the classroom teacher should discourage mixing Spanish and English phrases when they occur in the context of expressing the same idea or thought. In other words, expressions that are expressed alternatively and fully in both English and Spanish may be encouraged, but expressions that are half English and half Spanish are to be discouraged.

Enrichment Approach.   The fourth perspective is popularly called the enrichment approach. Like the transition approach, the goal of enrichment is movement from Spanish to English competence in the shortest time possible. However, in addition to this goal, Spanish culture and heritage also are emphasized. Avoided is any direct responsibility for maintaining and improving Spanish language proficiency.

The rationale for this approach comes from a desire to follow federal guidelines for the funding of bilingual education (they favor the transition approach) while maintaining a positive attitude and self-concept of the bilingual learner toward his or her native culture. Some argue that native language proficiency must be part of any such attempt, and so this approach sometimes is considered as giving only "lip service" to bilingual education. Regardless of this, it nevertheless strives, through classroom films, publications, clubs, and local cultural events, to create a warm and nurturing atmosphere that conveys acceptance of any minority culture in the school.

The implications for the regular classroom teacher following this approach are to convey respect for the cultural heritage of the bilingual student through the arrangement of bulletin boards, transmission of information about cultural events, and the teacher's own attitude.

Names of Bilingual Programs

A report by the U.S. General Accounting Office (1987) included a definition of the many different terms used to describe bilingual programs. This report categorized bilingual programs as shown in Table 13.1.

Instructional Strategies for Bilingual Learners

With what strategies can I teach the bilingual learner?

Because many regular classroom teachers will encounter bilingual learners either as full-time students or as part of a "pull-out" program in which part of the student's time is spent in the regular classroom, techniques for teaching bilingual learners can be an important adjunct to your list of teaching strategies. The suggestions that follow are starting points for developing instructional strategies for bilingual learners.

If You Don't Speak the Student's Language, Emphasize Other Communication. Other forms of communication include the visual, kinesthetic, and tactile modalities. You have seen the importance of the *visual mode* in teaching the at-risk learner, and it is no less important with the bilingual learner. Use pictures, graphs, and illustrations to supplement your teaching objectives wherever possible. Pictures cannot take the place of auditory cues, but they can place these cues in context, making them easier to recognize in relation to an illustration or picture.

Infrequently used but equally important are the kinesthetic and tactile modes of communication. The *kinesthetic mode* adds movement to the learning process by pointing or tracing so that the learner can feel the motion required to create a particular form, such as a word or letter. The *tactile mode* appeals to the sense of touch; in conjunction with auditory cues, it can be used to remember concepts and objects when some physical representation of them is available.

Thus, a multisensory approach is most appropriate for bilingual learners, using visual, kinesthetic, and tactile modalities wherever possible to reinforce and expand on auditory communication.

Use Direct Instruction. Many bilingual learners learn best from, and are most accustomed to, the direct presentation of instructional material. For example, the "look and say" approach to reading is more effective than the phonetic approach during the initial stages of reading instruction. Especially for those lacking almost any profi-

Table 13.1

Names of bilingual programs

Program Name	Description
English as a second language	Programs of bilingual education; instruction is based on a special curriculum typically involving little or no use of the native language and usually is taught only during certain periods of the school day. For the rest of the school day, the student may be placed in regular (or submersion) instruction or a bilingual program.
Immersion	General term for an approach to bilingual instruction not involving the child's native language. Two specific variations are *structured immersion* and *submersion.*
Structured immersion	Programs of bilingual education; taught in English, but (a) the teacher understands the native language and students may speak it to the teacher (although the teacher generally answers only in English) and (b) no knowledge of English is assumed and the curriculum vocabulary and pacing are modified so the content will be understood. Some programs include some language-arts teaching in the native language.
Submersion	Programs in which students having limited English proficiency are placed in ordinary classrooms where English is the language of instruction. Students receive no special program to overcome language problems, and their native language is not used in the classroom; also called "sink or swim." The Supreme Court found this type of submersion unconstitutional (Lau vs. Nichols, 414 U.S. 463 [1974])
Sheltered English	Programs which use a simplified vocabulary and sentence structure to teach school subjects to students who lack sufficient English-language skills to understand the regular curriculum.
Transitional bilingual	Programs of bilingual education with emphasis on developing English-language skills to enable students having limited English proficiency to shift to an all-English program of instruction. Some programs include English as a second language.

Learning materials that emphasize the visual, kinesthetic, and tactile modalities are often necessary for instructing the nonnative speaker. Supplement your teaching objectives with pictures, graphs, and illustrations when bilingual learners are present.

ciency in English, repetition of material (particularly recitation and practice) generally is superior to more conceptual presentations that emphasize perspective, justification, and rationale, which can be taught after the basics have been acquired.

Your first step should be to foster acquisition of basic skills and their retention in the most visual, concrete ways to provide building blocks for later conceptual presentations. You will find that bilingual Hispanic learners tend initially to respond better to direct instruction than independent seatwork or self-directed instruction for acquiring basic skills (Tharp, 1989); the structure and organization of the former supersede the advantages of the latter.

Be Sensitive to Cultural Differences. Your awareness of cultural differences will be important to successful communication. Throughout this text we note the importance of the cultural dimensions of learning. There is no substitute for understanding the culture of your students, even if you have little understanding of their language. For example, several cultural preferences have been noted among bilingual Hispanic learners. They often appreciate the cooperation of group achievement more than the competitive aspects of individual achievement. This means that sharing assignments and working as a team can be particularly useful instructional strategies for Hispanic students. This, in turn, suggests the value of a cooperative classroom climate for bilingual instruction.

Also, the acceptance, warmth, and nurturing of Hispanic culture are aspects that should not be lost in your classroom. Frequent meaningful praise and encouragement can set the stage for learning more efficiently than the repeated recitation of rules and warnings. Bilingual Hispanic learners, as well as most bilingual learners, initially learn best when physical demonstrations and experience activities supplement verbal presentations. This supports the multisensory approach that conveys information using various modalities, creating both alternate paths for learning and needed redundancy.

Carefully Evaluate Reading Level and Format of Materials.   When selecting or adapting materials, you may find a Spanish version of comparable content, but the reading level and format may not benefit your learners. If you are not fluent in Spanish, have someone who is fluent evaluate the difficulty level of the material. It is not unusual to initially select verbal material several grades below the level you are teaching. After a suitable trial, evaluate the materials again and adjust the reading level accordingly.

The format of materials is important, too. Material with illustrated text is better than concentrated prose. Notice whether the objects pictured will be familiar to the learners or whether they are specific to the Anglo audience for whom the materials may have been written.

Know Your Learners' Language Ability and Achievement Levels.   From school records or your school administrator, find out the following for each of your bilingual learners:

- Dominant language in the receptive mode (e.g., listening, reading)
- Dominant language in the expressive mode (e.g., talking, writing)
- Proficiency level in the dominant language
- Past achievement levels in the areas relevant to your instruction

This information is invaluable in selecting special materials and determining the best level and manner to begin instruction. For example, it is not unusual to find bilingual learners who choose Spanish as their dominant means of speaking but English as their dominant means of listening. Knowing this allows you to speak and be understood in English even though at least some of the learners' communications to you might be in Spanish. In this case, little adjustment is needed to your regular instructional plan, compared to what you would have to do if the opposite were true. Knowing your learners' ability and achievement levels makes your initial instructional contact far more effective, potentially avoiding weeks and even months of failing to communicate—and not knowing it!

Present Trends in Teaching the Bilingual Learner

Nearly three million schoolage children in the United States speak a language other than English at home (Berk, 1993). Many of these learners are considered to have limited English proficiency (LEP). Consequently, theoretical and practical questions are continually being asked about whether LEP students should be exposed to two languages during their preschool and early elementary years, whether bilingualism promotes or impedes language and cognitive development, and whether the best way for a child to acquire a second language is by total submersion in the second language or through bilingual education.

There are basically two ways for children to become bilingual: (1) by acquiring both languages simultaneously, or (2) by learning the second language after they have mastered the first. Research has shown that either method results in children acquiring normal language competence in both the language used at home and in the second language (Reich, 1986). Thus, parents and teachers need not fear that bilingualism adversely affects language competence.

Moreover, a growing body of research seems to suggest that bilingualism promotes overall cognitive development. Research by Hakuta, Ferdman, and Diaz (1987) indicates that bilingual children, in comparison to monolingual children, show superior performance on tests of analytical reasoning, concept formation, and cognitive flexibility. Other research shows that learners who are fluent in two or more languages have a better knowledge of language structure and detail, understand that words are arbitrary symbols for other words and actions, and can better detect grammatical errors in written and spoken communication (Galambos & Goldin-Meadow, 1990).

On how best to teach a second language, there seem to be some clear trends. Neither submersion in the second language nor immersion programs have been found as effective as maintenance and transition programs for teaching English to nonnative speakers (Padilla, et al., 1991; Willig, 1985). Submersion programs teach only the second language in the context of a regular, nonnative classroom, while immersion programs teach English as a second language in a regular classroom of mostly nonnative speakers with a teacher who speaks the native language. In maintenance and transition programs—sometimes called "true" bilingual programs—learners are given basic skills instruction in their native language during the first and second year of school, but are also exposed to the second language in the same classroom. Both languages are then maintained for several years before the child is expected to perform entirely in the second language.

Finally, it is important to note that some have suggested that children from economically impoverished areas who speak a non-standard form of English (for example, Black English) may suffer impaired cognitive development as a result (Hess & Shipman, 1965; Bereiter & Englemann, 1966). This hypothesis has been conclusively refuted (Dillard, 1972; Henderson, Swanson, & Zimmerman, 1974). We now know that *all* languages, including dialects and other forms of nonstandard English, are equally complex and equally capable of being used for learning and problem solving. Linguists have demonstrated that languages cannot be ranked in terms of intellectual sophistication. Consequently, intellectual impairment or slow cognitive development cannot result from the primary language a learner speaks, regardless of how "nonstandard" that language is.

>>> LEARNERS WITH DISABILITIES <<<

Since the enactment of Public Law 94–142 and subsequent legislation (PL 99–457, 1986; PL 101–336 and PL 101–476, 1990), "public education for all" has come to mean that every schoolage child has the basic constitutional right to be educated with programs and services appropriate to her or his educational needs. Further, PL 94–142 ensures that children with disabilities receive education in the **least restrictive environment** compatible with their needs. The special education profession and the public schools have interpreted this law as a mandate to provide minimally restrictive educational and supportive services to learners with disabilities, whenever possible, *in the context of the regular school program*. The significance of this law for the regular classroom teacher is that the regular classroom is the least restrictive alternative for meeting the educational needs of many learners with disabilities.

Over the past several decades, **learners with disabilities** have been classified and defined in a number of ways, while new definitions continue to evolve as more becomes known about these special learners. Before the significance of a disability for public school instruction can be discussed, however, we must determine the kind of disability. To do so, categories of disabilities have been identified

Who are learners with disabilities?

Public Law 94–142 states that "Schools have the responsibility to provide every child of school age with instruction in the least restricted environment compatible with his or her educational needs." In many instances, the regular classroom will be the least restricted learning environment for the handicapped learner.

to indicate the types of special services and instruction most appropriate. These categories usually include learners with a physical disability, auditory disability, visual disability, mental disability, emotional disability, learning disability, speech disability, learners who are autistic, and learners who have multiple disabilities, all described in Table 13.2.

In what ways might I be expected to participate in providing services to learners with disabilities?

The purpose of these categories is not to label the child with a disability but to identify specific students whose physical, emotional, and/or cognitive functions are so impaired from any cause that they can be educated adequately and safely only with the provision of special services. These special services are the direct responsibility of the special education program within a school. However, the regular classroom teacher is expected to help provide these services by assisting in child identification, individual assessment, Individualized Educational Plan (IEP) development, individualized instruction, and review of the IEP. Let's consider what the provision of each of these services means for you.

Child Identification

Child identification consists of a school's or district's procedures for identifying learners with disabilities who need special services. Students needing such services may never have entered school or could

Table 13.2

Categories of learners with disabilities

Physical disability	Students whose body functions or members are impaired by congenital anomaly and disease, or students with limited strength, vitality, or alertness due to chronic or acute health problems.
Auditory disability	Students who are hearing impaired (hard of hearing) or deaf.
Visual disability	Students who, after medical treatment and use of optical aids, remain legally blind or otherwise exhibit loss of critical sight functions.
Mental disability	Students with significantly subaverage general intellectual functioning existing concurrently with deficiencies in adaptive behavior. Severity of retardation is sometimes indicated with the terms profound, trainable, and educable. Not all of the students who are educable are placed in the regular classroom.
Emotional disability	Students who demonstrate an inability to build or maintain satisfactory interpersonal relationships, develop physical symptoms or fears associated with personal or school problems, exhibit a pervasive mood of unhappiness under normal circumstances, or show inappropriate types of behavior under normal circumstances.
Learning disability	Students who demonstrate a significant discrepancy, which is not the result of some other disability, between academic achievement and intellectual abilities in one or more of the areas of oral expression, listening comprehension, written expression, basic reading skills, reading comprehension, mathematical calculation, mathematics reasoning, or spelling.
Speech disability	Students whose speech is impaired to the extent that it limits the communicative functions.
Autistic	Students with severe disturbances of speech and language, relatedness, perception, development rate, or motion.
Multiple disabilities	Students who have any two or more of the conditions described above.

be among those who are attending school but who have not been identified as having a disability. The regular classroom teacher is expected to play an important role in identifying these students.

One stage of this identification is the referral process by which a child comes to be recommended for special services. Although referrals may be made by parents, physicians, community agencies, and school administrators as a result of districtwide testing or screening, you also may recommend students for special services. For students currently enrolled in regular education, you are the individual most likely to identify those needing special services. In such cases you will become a liaison between the child and the school's special education staff. In such a capacity you will be responsible for reporting data that accurately portray the following:

1. The student's current educational status, including attendance records, grades, achievement data, and written accounts of classroom observation.
2. Previous instructional efforts and strategies provided the student and the result of those efforts.
3. Data about the learner reported or provided to you by parents.

One classification of learner you may help to identify in your classroom is *learning disabled*. A discrepancy between a learner's intellectual ability and academic achievement qualifies a student as having a learning disability if either of the following is true:

1. The student's assessed *intellectual functioning* is above the mentally retarded range, but is significantly below the mean (usually one standard deviation) for the school district in one or more areas.
2. The student's assessed *educational functioning* is significantly below his or her intellectual functioning (usually one standard deviation).

When a learner's achievement level is significantly below the mean of the district, but is consistent with the student's intellectual functioning, he or she is not classified as learning disabled. Many measurement decisions are required in determining whether a learner has a learning disability. Although this designation is made cooperatively by a multidisciplinary team of regular teachers, special educators, counselors, and psychologists, the regular classroom teacher is expected to be sufficiently knowledgeable about the learner that discrepancies between achievement and academic aptitude can be accurately assessed.

Individual Child Assessment

A second process to which you may contribute is individual child assessment. This is the collecting and analyzing of information about a student to identify an educational need in terms of one or more of the following:

1. The presence or absence of a physical, mental, or emotional disability
2. The presence or absence of a significant educational need
3. Identification of the student's specific learning competencies together with specific instructional or related services that could improve and maintain the student's competencies

Although evaluation of a child's capabilities is the responsibility of certified professionals, you may be expected to corroborate the findings of these professionals with performance data from the classroom. Foremost among these data are formal and informal indications from workbooks, homework assignments, weekly and unit tests, and classroom observation of the student's language dominance and proficiency in both the expressive and receptive domains. Often, your observation and recording of these data will suggest that special educators evaluate the validity of any standardized tests the student took and whether they were in the child's dominant language.

Corroborative data on the student's physical attributes also can be recorded. You may be the only one to observe daily the learner's ability to manipulate objects necessary for learning, ability to remain alert and attentive during instruction, and ability to control bodily functions in a manner conducive to instruction. In some instances, you may provide the only available data source about the ability of the learner to benefit from regular class instruction.

You may be expected to provide data about sociological and environmental influences on the learner that might influence his or her classroom behavior. Such data often are obtained through communication with the family and knowledge of the circumstances leading to and/or contributing to the student's intellectual and emotional behavior. The extent to which the child's home life and out-of-school support and services contribute to the educative function can provide an important adjunct to in-school data.

Finally, there is the student's intellectual functioning, as demonstrated by both verbal and nonverbal performance. Although these behaviors usually are assessed by professionals certified in special education, you may be asked to provide corroborating data on the child's adaptive behavior, which indicates the degree to which the student meets standards of personal independence and social responsibility expected of his or her age and cultural group. Within the context of the regular classroom, you will have many opportunities to observe the social functioning of the child and to gain insights into the appropriateness of this functioning.

Individualized Educational Plan (IEP)

A third stage in which you may become involved in the implementation of PL 94–142 is in helping to develop an **individualized educational plan (IEP)** for a student in your classroom. A student receives special education services only after the multidisciplinary team mentioned previously has reviewed data from the comprehensive assessment. Data from this assessment are expected to address the language, physical, emotional/ behavioral, sociological, and intellectual functioning of the child. If this assessment determines that the student has a physical, mental, or emotional disability that establishes her or his eligibility to receive special education services, an IEP is written to state short-term and long-term objectives for instructional services and to specify the least restrictive environment where the instruction can occur.

The IEP developed for each student by the multidisciplinary team considers a statement of the student's present competencies taken from the overall assessment data, and includes the following:

1. Long-term (annual) and short-term (weekly, monthly) instructional objectives
2. The specific educational services to be provided the student within the least restrictive environment designated
3. The dates for the initiation of the services, the approximate amount of time to be spent providing each service, and a justification for the services and settings in which they will be provided
4. The criterion for and time of evaluating each long-term and short-term objective

Figure 13.1 illustrates the composition of a typical IEP.

Individualized Instruction

A fourth stage in which you may become involved in implementing PL 94–142 is in providing individualized instruction to the student.

INDIVIDUALIZED EDUCATIONAL PLAN

Student's Name: _Bob Miller_   School: _Oak Hill Elementary_   Grade: _4_   Date of Meeting: _2-25-95_

Date of Birth: _12-18-78_   Parent or Guardian: _Tom & Ann Miller_   Address: _25 Ruth Drive_   Phone: _443-2187_

Present Levels of Performance		COMMITTEE MEMBERS PRESENT:	
Word Recognition	1.5	Name: _Paula Scott_	Position: _Principal_
Reading Comprehension	2.0	Name: _Mary White_	Position: _Spec Ed Teacher_
Spelling	1.9	Name: _Anna Miller_	Position: _Parent_
Math	3.5	Name: _Terry Hull phd_	Position: _Psychologist_
Social Adaption	4th	Name: _Jackie Morgan_	Position: _Teacher_
Other(s) - _Speech below average_		Name: _Suzanne Martin_	Position: _Speech Therapist_

Learning Strengths	Learning Weaknesses
Good auditory learning skills	Short attention span in visual presentations & handwriting tasks
Knows all basic computation facts	Articulation
Positive social interaction	

From a review of pertinent data, the committee determined that this student DOES/DOES NOT meet eligibility criteria for: _Learning Disabled_

Speech Handicapped

Recommended Placement: 2 hrs. per day/week Special Education

4 hrs. per day/week Regular Education

1 hrs. per day/week Related Services

ANNUAL GOALS	SHORT TERM OBJECTIVES	EVALUATION CRITERIA	SPECIFIC SERVICES	DATE SERVICES BEGIN/END		SUGGESTED MATERIALS	STAFF RESPONSIBLE NAME	POSITION
Increase word recognition to 2.0	Complete Word Drill of Dolch Words Lists 1 and 2	Brigance Word Recognition Lists 2nd grade level completion	1/2 hr instruct in resource room	2/26/95	5/29/95	Dolch Word Cards Computer Game "Word Review"	Mary White	Resource Teacher
Increase reading comprehension to 2.5	Complete SRA series - 2nd level	Woodcock Johnson perform at 2nd grade level	1 hr instruct in resource room	2/26/95	5/29/95	SRA Series Scholastic Scope Magazine	Mary White	Resource teacher
Increase spelling level to 2.5	Complete 2nd level of "Spelling Sounds"	TOWL-Spell at 2.5 level on the Spelling section	1/2 hr instruct in resource room	2/26/95	5/29/95	Speak--- Write Spell Kit	Mary White	Resource Teacher
Articulate r-blends correctly	Articulate /Ar/ and /br/ correctly	Therapist and teacher observation of Daily Speech	1 hr/wk speech therapy	2/26/95	5/29/95		Suzanne Martin	Speech Therapist

Figure 13.1

Example individualized educational plan (IEP)

This is the day-to-day instruction provided according to the objectives set forth in the student's IEP. This program should be consistent with the student's needs and with your curriculum. Your activities may include providing any or all of the following:

- Specific instructional objectives, based on student needs as stated in the IEP
- Learning activities appropriate to each student's learning style, presented as specifically and sequentially as needed for the student to progress toward attainment of each instructional objective
- Instructional media and materials used for each learning activity, selected on the basis of the student's learning style
- An instructional setting that provides multiple arrangements for learning
- A schedule of teaching time ensuring the provision of instruction to each student in individual or group arrangements
- Procedures by which the teacher measures, records, and reports each student's progress

You also may be responsible for writing specific instructional objectives in accord with the student's IEP, and you may prepare and administer tests to record the student's progress toward these objectives.

Review of IEP

A fifth activity in which you may become involved is a review of the IEP. School districts usually have procedures or a system for reviewing each student's progress compared to the IEP objectives. This review determines not only the student's progress toward objectives, but also the need for modifying the plan and supplying further special services. A critical aspect of this review is documenting either the movement of a student to a more or less restrictive environment or the student's release from all special educational services.

Recommendations for major changes in the IEP, including placement (for example, to a more or less restrictive environment), is the multidisciplinary team's responsibility. However, all those involved in implementing the student's IEP are likely to be involved in this review. For example, the following are among the many pieces of information that must be gathered prior to a major change in a student's placement:

- The number of instructional options that have been attempted, including those within the regular classroom

- The appropriateness of the long-term and short-range educational objectives, including those written by the regular classroom teacher
- The reliability, validity, and accuracy of the testing that led or contributed to a review of the student's current placement, including testing completed within the regular classroom

In each of these areas, you may contribute critical data, because you may be in the most advantageous position to assess the student's everyday performance. Here, as elsewhere in implementing PL 94–142, your data will directly reflect your effectiveness in the regular classroom.

Instructional Strategies for Learners with Disabilities

Several of the previously described service responsibilities required by PL 94–142 (e.g., implementation of the IEP and provisions of individualized instruction) involve the direct instruction of the learner with a disability in the regular classroom. Many approaches to such instruction have been and currently are being used. Regular classroom teachers have found the following suggestions particularly useful.

With what strategies can I teach learners with disabilities?

Encourage Self-Management Skills.   One of the first things you will notice about some learners with disabilities is their lack of self-management skills. For example, many students with a learning disability consistently use poor organizational strategies; they may work impulsively and hurriedly, fail to accurately perceive and gauge time, and may not adequately judge and search for needed information. Part of your role as a teacher of a child with a disability in the regular classroom is to encourage self-management skills that can lead to greater independence and task completion. This can be accomplished through one or more of the following:

1. The use of study guides that present to the learner your instructional objectives, the specific assignment you want accomplished, and timelines for completion
2. Topical outlines that show the learner the sequence in which you will cover content in the workbook or class presentation
3. Technical vocabularies and glossaries that provide definitions for the more difficult words and concepts to be used
4. Brief summaries of the lesson that emphasize its most important points

Each of these teaching aids can assist the learner to better manage the learning task, making task completion more likely.

Have Students with and without Disabilities Learn from Each Other. A primary purpose of PL 94–142 is to bring regular and special learners together so they can learn from each other. The regular learner may discover just how "average" a special learner is, and the special learner may derive benefits from listening to and learning from somone having different experiences and perspectives.

These benefits are never more obvious than when heterogeneous groups of learners are formed explicitly on the basis of their differences in skill and ability level. These heterogeneous groups can lead to the regular students spontaneously taking responsibility for checking the work of special learners, correcting their errors, reviewing key concepts, and probing for additional responses. They also can provide the social and intellectual interaction conducive to cooperative learning. Also, you can select and train tutors from among your regular students, who may then be assigned to work on specific targeted skills with special learners.

Create Learning Centers. Learning centers can function much like peer tutoring and heterogeneous grouping when they are carefully thought out and made relevant to your instructional objectives. That is, they can provide valuable instruction to the learner with a disability without your having to neglect other learners in the classroom. Centers of instructional resources that include age- and ability-graded books, audiovisual aids, arts and crafts, graphic illustrations, exercises, study guides, topical outlines, and vocabulary lists allow students to work independently and at their own pace. These tools also give learners an opportunity to learn through different modalities (visual, auditory, tactile), and can be planned in ways that provide immediate feedback. These are all key elements to successfully teaching the learner with a disability.

Use a Less Formal Classroom Arrangement. The arrangement of the classroom itself is an important aspect of teaching special learners. You may either promote or restrict engagement in the learning process, one of the key teaching behaviors, by classroom arrangement and organization. Traditional arrangements place the teacher's desk at the front of the classroom and student desks in formal rows extending outward. This arrangement conveys a teacher-centered classroom in which lectures, supervision, control, and tests are the most predominant student expectations.

Unfortunately, this arrangement also suggests that all of your students will learn in the same way. When more than a few of your learners have a disability or depart from the norm in your classroom in any other way (e.g., are gifted or LEP), a more flexible use of classroom space may be called for. A less formal arrangement allows more freedom of movement for those who may wish to benefit from a learning center, independent study carrel, computer terminal, or audiovisual library. It also can more readily accommodate group projects, a heterogeneous grouping of students, and peer tutoring. However, because a less structured classroom arrangement can create more unwanted student talk and movement, make only one or two areas of your classroom into a less structured format as an initial first step.

Use Microcomputer Software.   By some estimates, well over two million microcomputers are actively being used in classrooms today, and this number is increasing each year. The microcomputer's capacity not only to ease your administrative burden but also to actually teach parts of the curriculum has been well demonstrated. To lessen the demands on you, considerable microcomputer software has been developed for individualizing instruction, developing IEPs, testing, and reporting the performance of learners with disabilities.

Use of the computer in the regular classroom can substantially lessen the sometimes overwhelming paperwork entailed in teaching heterogeneous ability groups. You may want to use the computer to provide remediation in critical skill areas, because this is where much of the available computer software is focused. There are programs that instruct in remedial mathematics and spelling, that teach verbs and how to use them in sentences, that correct misspelled words, and that even provide an analysis of common writing errors. You can become familiar with the most current versions of these and other software programs through your school's special education coordinator.

Present Trends in Teaching Learners with Disabilities

Underlying nearly a two-decade legal struggle to protect the rights of special learners is a principle called **normalization**, which addresses the standards for providing current services for learners with disabilities. In essence, this principle states that such learners are entitled to programs that allow them to experience the respect and dignity to which any person in our society is entitled.

What can I do to provide a positive, productive environment in my classroom for students with disabilities?

Normalization requires that programs for special learners reflect the culture of which these learners are a part. This applies both to what the program achieves for the learners (social skills, academic skills, personal appearance, etc.) and how it does it (physical setting, method of grouping learners, activities provided, staff serving the program, language used to describe the program). Five dimensions encompass the major themes of normalization as they apply to public school learners with disabilities (Gardner & Chapman, 1990): regular school participation, regular class participation, skill enhancement, image enhancement, and autonomy and empowerment. Here is how the principle of normalization applies to each:

- *Regular school participation*. According to the principle of normalization, all learners regardless of their disability should have the opportunity to participate in the routine life of their school. Learners in wheelchairs should be able to attend basketball games. Individuals with mental retardation should be able to attend school dances and other social events. Learners who are excluded from the regular classroom for severe disruptive behavior may still be allowed to have some access to their peers, for example, to eat in the cafeteria and attend assemblies.
- *Regular class participation*. This dimension emphasizes the importance of allowing learners with disabilities opportunities to develop normal social relationships within a regular classroom of peers.
- *Skill enhancement*. The focus of special education programs should be to teach individual skills that will make the lives of these learners as normal as possible. For example, it would violate the principle of normalization not to teach handwriting skills to a learner who finds this particularly difficult, assuming the learner had the physical capability to write. Likewise, individuals with mental retardation who lack skills in toileting, dressing, feeding, using public transportation, crossing streets, and so on should be taught these skills rather than making them dependent on others to handle these aspects of their life.
- *Image enhancement*. Special education programs violate the principle of normalization when they engage in practices that reinforce stereotypes about individuals with mental retardation, learning disabilities, or emotional disturbance, such as the following:
    1. Referring to special learners using stereotypic labeling, such as "MRs," "LDs," "EDs," or derogatory phrases.

2. Using signs in the school such as "alternative learning center," "remedial reading," "adaptive PE," which can stigmatize or psychologically separate one from his or her peers.

3. Using educational activities and materials inappropriate for the chronological age of the learner, for example, using toys and other materials that would normally be used exclusively with toddlers and preschoolers with older children with mental retardation.

- *Autonomy and empowerment*. Individuals with disabilities should be given as many of the same choices as possible as their nondisabled peers with respect to what they do, when and where they do it, with whom, for how long, and in what way. This dimension reminds educators, when practical, to transfer power and control to the person with the disability and encourage their participation in the regular classroom.

The principles of normalization have been embodied in what has come to be called the Regular Education Initiative, or *inclusion*. REI is an educational policy that advocates a partnership between regular and special educators in which learners with disabilities would receive individualized services in the regular classroom without the requirement of labeling or special classifications. Proponents of REI cite the following reasons for including most children with disabilities in the regular classroom for the full day:

1. Special education (whether for those labeled mentally retarded, learning disabled, or emotionally disturbed) has become a depository for learners who may be difficult to teach but who are not truly disabled.

2. Despite public laws requiring education in the "least restrictive environment," the present system of special education unintentionally imposes barriers to full integration in school and community life.

3. The criteria for being placed in a special education category are vague and as a result, sometimes, inconsistently applied. Often, the same learner could be declared eligible or ineligible for individualized services depending on the school attended or who did the assessment.

4. African American, Hispanic, Native American, and lower-SES (socioeconomic status) learners are often overrepresented in special education programs.

5. Typically, the curriculum of pull-out programs is poorly integrated with that of the regular classroom. Thus, students in

resource classrooms may not learn the academic or social skills needed to return to the regular classroom.

Many public schools across America are beginning to initiate or are being required to develop some form of REI. Since it is likely that you will become a part of the initiative, you will need to be informed about it and prepared to implement it.

Summing Up

This chapter introduced you to at-risk, gifted and talented, and bilingual learners, and learners with disabilities. Its main points were as follows:

1. The advantages of categorizing learners include the assistance they provide for the following:

- Dispensing state and federal funds that often are earmarked for specific types of learners.
- Developing and organizing instructional materials, texts, and media appropriate for certain types of learners.
- Training and assigning the most qualified instructional staff to teach certain types of learners.

2. The disadvantages of categorizing learners include the fact that variation within learner categories can exceed variation between categories, and the categories may not be independent of one another, i.e., a learner may reflect characteristics of more than one category.

3. A learner who is at risk for poor academic performance is a student who does not learn at the same pace as the majority of students using instructional methods and resources suitable for the average student.

4. It has been estimated that up to 20% of all students attending school today are at-risk learners in one subject or another.

5. At-risk learners require more than the usual variation in pacing, presentation method, classroom climate, and instructional materials to keep engaged in the learning process.

6. At-risk learners usually have deficiencies in the basic skills of reading, writing, and mathematics, difficulty comprehending abstract ideas, and unsystematic work habits. These deficiencies make instructional lessons geared to the average student difficult for the at-risk learner.

7. Compensatory teaching is an instructional approach that alters the presentation of content by reorganizing it, transmitting it by way of alternate modalities, and supplementing it with additional learning resources, with the aim of circumventing fundamental student weaknesses or deficiencies.

8. Remedial teaching is an instructional approach that uses techniques and practices specifically chosen to eliminate known deficiencies or weaknesses.

9. The following are instructional strategies for addressing the learning needs of at-risk learners:

- Developing lessons around the interests, needs, and experiences of the student.
- Encouraging oral expression, especially for those limited in writing ability.
- Providing study aids and advance organizers to alert students to important content or issues.
- Teaching notetaking, outlining, and listening skills.

10. The preparation and time required to teach the gifted may not be measurably less than for teaching any other type of learner—and may be more.

11. Among the behavioral characteristics for defining giftedness are intelligence, achievement, creativity, and task persistence.

12. Variations in the use of these behavioral characteristics to define giftedness have created considerable diversity, both among the types of students classified as gifted and in the instructional programs designed to meet their needs.

13. The following instructional strategies can address the learning needs of gifted learners:

- Allow students to investigate some topics of their own choosing, making them participants in the design of their own learning.
- Plan instructional activities that involve group work, such as brainstorming sessions, group discussions, panels, peer interviews, and debates.
- Plan instructional lessons that include individual and small group investigations of real-life problems.
- Pose challenging problems that allow the learner to make key decisions about what is important for a solution.
- Test and question in a manner that draws out knowledge and understanding and requires more than a verbally fluent response.

14. Approximately five million students—about 10% of the entire schoolage population in this country—have a primary language other than English.

15. Bilingual education refers to a mix of instruction through the medium of two languages. Although the word *bilingual* implies proficiency in two languages, it more often applies to students with limited English proficiency (LEP), who range between an inability to express themselves at all in English (either orally or in writing) to marginal proficiency in English.

16. Different approaches to bilingual education include the following:

- The transition approach, which uses the native language and culture of the learner only to the extent necessary to learn English.
- The maintenance approach, which in addition to encouraging English language proficiency endorses the idea that the learner should become proficient in his or her native language as well.
- The restoration approach, which attempts to restore the native language and culture of the bilingual student to its purest and most original form.
- The enrichment approach, which not only moves from native language to English competence in the shortest possible time but also emphasizes the student's native culture and heritage.

17. The following instructional strategies can address the learning needs of bilingual learners in the regular classroom:

- Emphasize forms of communication that use pictures, graphs, and illustrations to supplement teaching objectives.
- Emphasize the acquisition of facts and their retention in visual, concrete ways.
- Understand and use cultural awareness to enhance the overall learning environment and educational experience of the learner.
- Adapt instructional materials to the teaching level of your students.
- Know the language ability level and achievement level of your learners and select special materials accordingly.

18. Some of the special education functions mandated by PL 94–142 that may involve the regular classroom teacher include child identification, individual child assessment, development of the individualized educational plan (IEP), individualized instruction, and a review of the IEP.

19. The following instructional strategies can address the learning needs of students with disabilities in the regular classroom:

- Teaching of self-management skills that can increase the student's ability to learn independently.
- Use of peer tutoring to teach a specific list of targeted skills.
- Use of instructional resource (learning) centers to allow students to work independently at their own pace.

- Use of a less structured classroom arrangement to promote group projects, heterogeneous grouping, and peer tutoring.
- Use of the microcomputer to teach basic skills and content.

20. The principle of *normalization* requires providing instruction to learners with disabilities in a manner that allows them to experience the respect and dignity to which any person in our society is entitled.

For Discussion and Practice

1. Explain in your own words what is meant by the phrase "variation in behavior occurring within a category of learners may be greater than the variation found between categories of learners." Use the categories of "average" and "above average" to illustrate your point.

*2. Give three advantages of categorizing students by learning type.

*3. In your own words, give a practical definition of an at-risk learner in your grade or subject area.

4. What is one source of data a school district might use to assign a student to a class of at-risk learners?

*5. Identify the difference between compensatory and remedial teaching and give an example of each, using content from your teaching area.

*6. What are the four behaviors from which giftedness is most likely to be determined?

*7. What would be one argument against the exclusive use of IQ in selecting students for a gifted program?

*8. Give four different signs of creativity that might be used in determining a student's eligibility for a gifted and talented program.

*9. Give four different signs of task persistence that might be used in determining a student's eligibility for a gifted and talented program.

*10. Describe the language proficiency of a learner who has limited English proficiency (LEP).

*11. What is a balanced bilingual?

*12. Contrast the structured immersion method with the transitional method for teaching the bilingual student.

*13. In your own words, how do the requirements contained within PL 94–142 affect the regular classroom teacher?

*14. Identify nine categories of disabilities that make a student eligible for special education services.

15. Describe at least three ways a school might follow the principle of normalization.

---

* Answers to asterisked questions (*) in this and the other chapters are in Appendix B.

Suggested Readings

American Psychologist, 44, (2, February 1989). Published by the American Psychological Association.

This entire issue is devoted to children and their development. The articles on the social and behavioral problems of children present important information, theories, research, and implications for social policy.

Baca, L. M., & Cervantes, H. T. (1989). *The bilingual special education interface.* Santa Clara, CA: Times Mirror/Mosby.

An orientation to the historical background, legal basis, and practical implementation of bilingual services and bilingual teaching.

Colangelo, N., & Davis, G. (Eds.). (1991). *Handbook for gifted education.* Boston: Allyn & Bacon.

An extensive encyclopedia and excellent reference for teaching the gifted and talented.

Coleman, M. C. (1992). *Behavior disorder: Theory and practice.* Boston: Allyn & Bacon.

An introductory text on behavior disorders that presents a combination of theory and practical guidelines for classroom teachers.

Gearheart, B. R., Mullen, R. C., & Gearheart, C. J. (1993). *Exceptional individuals: An introduction.* Pacific Grove, CA: Brooks/Cole.

Introduces special services and teaching strategies for mainstreamed exceptional students.

Milgram, R. M. (Ed.). (1991). *Counseling gifted and talented children: A guide for teachers, counselors and parents.* Norwood, NJ: Ablex.

This book provides many helpful suggestions for teaching and counseling gifted and talented learners in the regular classroom.

Wang, M. C., & Walberg, H. J. (Eds.). (1985). *Adapting instruction to individual differences.* Berkeley, CA: McCutchan.

A collection of readings that covers the many unintended problems associated with categorizing and separating students into a variety of programs.

Wood, J. W. (1992). *Adapting instruction for mainstreamed and at-risk students* (2nd ed.). Englewood Cliffs, NJ: Merrill/Prentice Hall.

This book points to how schools can make mainstreaming a shared responsibility on the part of administrators, teachers, parents, and learners. It gives extensive advice to teachers on how to meet the learning and emotional needs of mainstreamed students.

CHAPTER 14

Assessing Learners:
Objective And Essay Tests

This chapter will help you answer the following questions:

1. What is the difference between a norm-referenced and a criterion-referenced test?
2. How can I be sure that my tests cover what I teach?
3. How can I write multiple-choice items that measure higher-level behaviors?
4. What are the advantages and disadvantages of different objective test formats?
5. How can I grade essay tests fairly?
6. How will I know if my tests measure what I say they measure?
7. How will I know if my tests are consistent in repeated administrations?
8. How do I assign grades or marks to my learners' test scores?
9. What does a percentile rank mean?
10. How is the nature of standardized tests likely to change in the future?

This chapter will also help you learn the meaning of the following:

criterion-referenced tests
extended response essay items
instructional validity
marks and grading systems
norm-referenced tests
objective test items
reliability
restricted response essay items
standardized tests
test accuracy
test blueprint
validity

S ome of your strongest childhood and adolescent memories probably include taking tests in school. For that matter, test taking probably is among the most vivid memories of your college experience. If you are like most people who have spent many years in school, you have strong or mixed feelings about tests. In this and the following chapter we will try to dispel some of the discomfort you might feel about them and show how they can be effective tools in your classroom.

Previous chapters focused on effectively bringing your learners to a greater understanding and comprehension of the material you teach. But, how do you know whether you have been effective? You will find out by constructing assessments that reliably and validly measure how well your students learn and perform. To accomplish this, you will need to know how to use tests and performance assessments to measure your learners' achievement and to evaluate their products and performances. In this chapter we will focus on how you can construct authentic classroom measures of your students' achievement. In Chapter 15 we will present ways to authentically measure your students products and performances, including student portfolios. Let's begin by introducing the key decisions you will need to make in order to evaluate and diagnose your learners' achievements.

>>> NORM-REFERENCED AND <<< CRITERION-REFERENCED TESTS

To evaluate your learners' progress, what type of information do you need? That depends on your purpose. Testing can provide two types of information:

1. A student's place or rank compared to other students is revealed by a **norm-referenced test** (NRT), so named because it compares a student's performance to that of a "norm group" (a large, representative sample of learners). Such information is useful when you need to compare a learner's performance to that of others at the same age or grade level.
2. A student's level of proficiency in or mastery of a skill or set of skills is revealed by a **criterion-referenced test** (CRT), so

named because it compares student performance with an absolute standard called a *criterion* (such as "75% correct"). Such information helps you decide whether a student needs more instruction to acquire a skill or set of skills.

Figure 14.1 illustrates when to use NRTs and CRTs. As the figure indicates, you always must identify the type of information needed *before* selecting a particular test.

Unfortunately, some teachers know little more about a student after testing than they did before. In our technically oriented society, test scores sometimes have become ends in themselves, without the interpretation of them that is essential for improvement of the learner. In such cases teachers, parents, and others may be quick to denounce a test, often suggesting that such abuse of testing "proves" that test data are useless. In reality, it may only indicate that the teacher who selected the test either failed to identify the specific information needed *before* administering the test or failed to carefully match the test to this purpose.

A similar situation can occur when existing test data are inappropriately used or interpreted. An example is the following situa-

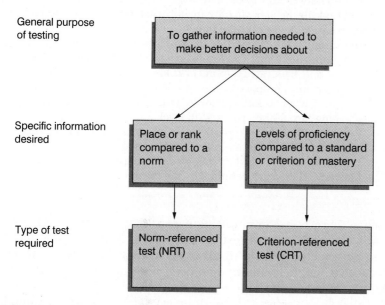

Figure 14.1

Relationships among the purpose of testing, information desired, and the type of test required

tion, in which counselor John is checking his records when sixth-grade teacher Mary taps on his door:

——

Mary: I just stopped by to see you about Danny. He's been in remedial classes for the last five years, and now he'll be in my class this year. Mrs. Rodrigues had him last year, and she said you have all the test information on him.

John: Yeah. In fact, I was just reviewing his folder. Danny's Math Cluster score on the Woodstock-Johnson is at the sixth percentile, and his Reading Cluster is at the first percentile. Good luck with him!

Mary: Boy, he sure is low. I guess that's why he's been in the remedial classroom for so long.

John: You've got it!

Mary: Well, really that's about what I was expecting. What about his skill levels?

John: What do you mean?

Mary: You know, his academic skill levels.

John: Oh, his grade levels! Umm, let's see . . . his math grade equivalent is 2.6, and his reading grade equivalent is even lower, 1.7.

Mary: Well . . . that's not really what I need to know. I know he's way below grade level, but I'm wondering about his skills—specific skills, that is. You know, like what words he can read, what phonetic skills he has, if he can subtract two-digit numbers with regrouping . . . things like that.

John: (becoming a bit irritated) Mary, what more do you need than what I've given you? Don't you know how to interpret these scores?

Mary: (stung and frustrated) John, I *do* know what those scores mean, but they only compare Danny to other students. I'm not interested in that. I want to know what he *can* and *can't* do, so I can begin teaching him at the proper skill level.

John: (shaking his head) Look, he's at first-grade level in reading and second-grade level in math. Isn't that enough?

Mary: But, what level of mastery has he demonstrated?

John: Mastery? He's years behind! He has mastered very little.

——

What is the difference between a norm-referenced and a criterion-referenced test?

It appears there is a communication gap between Mary and John. John has conveyed a lot of test information to Mary, yet she doesn't seem to get much out of it. John is frustrated, Mary is frustrated, and little that will help Danny has been accomplished. What is the problem?

The problem appears to be John's. Mary's questions refer to competencies or mastery of skills. Referring to Figure 14.1, we can conclude that she was interested in information about Danny's *level of proficiency*. But John's answers refer to test performance compared to other students, which means information about Danny's *rank compared to others*. Answers to Mary's questions can come only from a test designed to indicate whether Danny exceeded some standard of performance taken to indicate mastery of some skill.

If a test indicated that Danny could subtract two-digit numbers with regrouping, Mary would say that he had "mastered" this skill if, for example, "80 percent or more correct" was the criterion for mastery. In other words, he would have exceeded the standard of "80 percent mastery of subtraction of two-digit numbers with regrouping." Recall that a criterion-referenced test is designed to measure whether a student has mastered a skill, where the definition of mastery depends on an established level or criterion of performance.

But the information John provided was normative or comparative. Danny's grade-equivalent scores allow decisions only involving comparisons between his performance and that of the typical or average performance of learners in a "norm" group. Danny's grade-equivalent score of 1.7 in reading indicates that his reading ability equals that of the average first grader after seven months in the first grade. It says nothing about which words he knows, nor does it give any information about the process he uses to read new words or how long it takes him to comprehend what he reads or learn the meaning of new words. All this score indicates is that his ability to read is well below that of the average fifth grader and equivalent to that of an average first grader after seven months of school.

In short, grade-equivalent scores and other scores obtained from standardized, norm-referenced tests allow only general, comparative decisions, not decisions about mastery of specific skills.

Comparing Norm-Referenced and Criterion-Referenced Tests

As you may have guessed, criterion-referenced tests must be specific to yield information about individual skills. This is both an advantage and a disadvantage. With a specific test of individual skills you can be relatively certain that your students have either mastered or failed to master the skill in question. However, the major disadvantage is that many CRTs would be necessary to make decisions about the multitude of skills taught in the average classroom.

The norm-referenced test, on the other hand, tends to be general. It measures a variety of specific and general skills at once, but cannot measure them thoroughly. Thus, with NRT results, you are not as sure as you would be with CRT results that your students have mastered the individual skills in question. On the other hand, NRT results give you an estimate of ability in a variety of skills

The appropriateness of a given type of test depends on the purpose of testing. Criterion-referenced tests (CRTs) measure specific skills related to lesson objectives or unit content, while norm-referenced tests (NRTs) measure skills related to general categories of achievement and aptitude.

much faster than you could achieve with a large number of CRTs. Because of this tradeoff in the uses of criterion-referenced and norm-referenced measures, there are situations in which each is appropriate. Determining the appropriateness of a given type of test depends on your purpose in testing.

>>> THE TEST BLUEPRINT <<<

How can I be sure that my tests cover what I teach?

In Chapter 4 we discussed writing and analyzing instructional objectives, including the technique we call a *content-by-behavior blueprint* for writing objectives at different levels of behavioral complexity. In this chapter, we will use an extended version of this same technique (called a **test blueprint**) for matching test items to your objectives.

The test blueprint ensures that you do not overlook details essential to a good test. More specifically, it ensures that a test will sample learning across the range of (1) content areas covered by your instruction and (2) the cognitive and/or affective processes you consider important. It ensures that your test will include a variety of items that tap different levels of cognitive complexity. Figure 14.2 illustrates a test blueprint for a unit on elementary school mathematics.

A test blueprint is constructed according to the following procedure:

1. Determine the classification of each instructional objective from the categories in Chapter 4.

Content Outline	Knowledge	Comprehension	Application	Total	Percent
1. The student will discriminate the substraction sign from the addition sign.	1			1	4%
2. The student will discriminate addition problems from subtraction problems.	2			2	8%
3. The student will discriminate correctly solved subtraction problems from incorrectly solved subtraction problems.		4		4	16%
4. The student will solve correctly single-digit subtraction problems.			6	6	24%
5. The student will solve correctly subtraction problems with double-digit numerators and single-digit denominators.			6	6	24%
6. The student will solve correctly double-digit subtraction problems.			6	6	24%
Total	3	4	18	25	
Percent	12%	16%	72%		100%

Figure 14.2
Test blueprint for a unit on subtraction without borrowing

2. Record the number of items to be constructed for the objective in the cell corresponding to its category.
3. Repeat steps 1 and 2 for each objective in the outline.
4. Total the items for the instructional objective, and record the number in the *Total* row.
5. Repeat steps 1 through 4 for each topic.
6. Total the number of items falling into each category and record the number at the bottom of the table.
7. Compute the column and row percentages by dividing each total by the number of items in the test.

Constructing a test blueprint before preparing a test ensures that you have adequately sampled the content area and have accurately matched test items to your instructional objectives.

>>> OBJECTIVE TEST ITEMS <<<

Your test blueprint may call for objective test items. **Objective test items** have one of four formats: true-false, matching, multiple-choice, and completion (short answer). Stiggins (1994) prefers the term *selected response* for these formats to emphasize that it is the system by which these formats are *scored* that is "objective," not the selection of content that they measure. In this section we will consider characteristics of each format that can make your objective, or selected response, test items more effective.

Your first decision after completing the test blueprint will be to choose a format, or a combination of formats, for your test. The way you wrote the objectives may have predetermined the format, but in many instances you will have a choice among several item formats. For example, consider the following objectives and item formats.

True-False Items

True-false items are popular because they are quick and easy to write, or at least they seem to be. True-false items really do take less time to write than good objective items of any other format, but *good* true-false items are not so easy to prepare.

As you know from your own experience, every true-false item, regardless of how well or poorly written, gives the student a 50 percent chance of guessing correctly, even without reading the item! In other words, on a 50-item true-false test, we would expect individuals who were totally unfamiliar with the content being tested to answer about 25 items correctly. Fortunately, ways exist to reduce the effects of guessing:

1. Encourage *all* students to guess when they do not know the correct answer. Because it is virtually impossible to prevent certain students from guessing, encouraging all students to guess should equalize the effects of guessing. The test scores will then reflect a more or less equal "guessing factor" *plus* the actual level of each student's knowledge. This also will prevent test-wise students from having an unfair advantage over nontest-wise students.

2. Require revision of statements that are false. In this approach, provide space at the end of the item for students to alter false items to make them true. Usually the student first is asked to underline or circle the false part of the item and then to add the correct wording, as in these examples:

T (F) High-IQ children always get high grades in school.

                 tend to

T (F) Panama is north of Cuba.

                 south

T (F) September has an extra day during leap year.

                 February

With this strategy, full credit is awarded only if the revision is correct. The disadvantage of such an approach is that more test time is required for the same number of items and scoring time is increased.

Here are some suggestions to keep in mind when writing true-false test items:

1. Tell students clearly how to mark *true* or *false* (for example, circle or underline the T or F) before they begin the test. Write this instruction at the top of the test, too.
2. Construct statements that are definitely true or definitely false, without qualifications. If the item is true or false based on someone's opinion, then identify the opinion's source as part of the item—for example, "According to the head of the AFL-CIO, workers' compensation is below desired standards."
3. Keep true and false statements at approximately the same length, and be sure that there are approximately equal numbers of true and false items.
4. Avoid using double-negative statements. They take extra time to decipher and are difficult to interpret. For example, avoid statements such as, "It is not true that addition cannot precede subtraction in algebraic operations."
5. Avoid terms denoting indefinite degree (for example, *large, long time, regularly*), or absolutes (*never, only, always*).
6. Avoid placing items in a systematic pattern that some students might detect (for example, True-True-False-False, TFTF, and so on).

7. Don't take statements directly from the text without first making sure that you are not taking them out of context.

Matching Items

Like true-false, matching items are a popular and convenient testing format. Just like good true-false items, however, good matching items are not easy to write. Imagine you are back in your ninth-grade American history class and the following matching item shows up on your test:

DIRECTIONS: Match A and B

A	*B*
1. Lincoln	a. President during the twentieth century
2. Nixon	b. Invented the telephone
3. Whitney	c. Delivered the Emancipation Proclamation
4. Ford	d. Only president to resign from office
5. Bell	e. Black civil rights leader
6. King	f. Invented the cotton gin
7. Washington	g. Our first president
8. Roosevelt	h. Only president elected for more than two terms

See any problems? Compare the problems you identify with the descriptions of faults that follow.

Homogeneity. The lists are not homogeneous. Column A contains names of presidents, inventors, and a civil rights leader. Unless specifically taught as a set of related individuals or ideas, this is too wide a variety for a matching exercise.

Order of Lists. The lists are reversed—column A should be in place of column B, and column B should be in place of column A. As the exercise is now written, the student reads a name and then has to read through all or many of the more lengthy descriptions to find the answer, a much more time-consuming process. It also is a good idea to introduce some sort of order—chronological, numerical, or alphabetical—to your list of options. This saves the student time.

Easy Guessing. Notice that there are equal numbers of options and descriptions. This increases the chances of guessing correctly through elimination. If there are at least three more options than descriptions, the chance of guessing correctly is reduced to one in four.

Poor Directions.   The instructions are much too brief. Matching directions should specify the basis for matching:

> Column A contains brief descriptions of historical events. Column B contains the names of U.S. presidents. Indicate who was president when the historical event took place by placing the appropriate letter to the left of the number in column A.

Multiple Correct Responses.   The description "president during the twentieth century" has three defensible answers: Nixon, Ford, and Roosevelt. And, did you mean Henry Ford, inventor of the Model T automobile, or Gerald Ford? Always include first and last names to avoid ambiguities. Here is a corrected version of these matching items:

DIRECTIONS: Column A describes events associated with United States presidents. Indicate which name in Column B matches each event by placing the appropriate letter to the left of the number in column A. Each name may be used only once.

Column A

_____1. Only president not elected to office.

_____2. Delivered the Emancipation Proclamation.

_____3. Only president to resign from office.

_____4. Only president elected for more than two terms.

_____5. Our first president.

Column B

a. Abraham Lincoln

b. Richard Nixon

c. Gerald Ford

d. George Washington

e. Franklin Roosevelt

f. Theodore Roosevelt

g. Thomas Jefferson

h. Woodrow Wilson

Notice that we now have complete directions, more options than descriptions, homogeneous lists (all items in Column A are about U.S. presidents and all the items in Column B are names of presidents), and we have made the alternatives unambiguous.

Suggestions for Writing Matching Items.

1. Keep short and homogeneous both the descriptions list and the options list—they should fit together on the same page. Title the lists to ensure homogeneity (e.g., Column A, Column B).

2. Make sure that all the options are plausible *distractors* (wrong answer choices) for each description to ensure homogeneity of lists.

3. The descriptions list should contain the longer phrases or statements, while the options should consist of short phrases, words, or symbols.

4. Number each description (1, 2, 3, etc.) and letter each option (a, b, c, etc.).
5. Include more options than descriptions, or some that match more than one, or both.
6. In the directions, specify the basis for matching and whether options can be used more than once.

Multiple-Choice Items

Another popular item format is the multiple-choice question. Multiple-choice tests are more common in high school and college than in elementary school. Multiple-choice items are unique among objective test items because they enable you to measure higher-level cognitive objectives. When writing multiple-choice items, be careful not to give away answers by inadvertently providing students with clues in the following ways.

Stem Clue.   The statement portion of a multiple-choice item is called the *stem*, and the answer choices are called *options* or *response alternatives*. A stem clue occurs when the same word or a close derivative occurs in both the stem and an option, thereby cluing the test taker to the correct answer. For example:

> The free-floating structures within the cell that synthesize protein are called _____.
>> a. chromosomes
>> b. lysosomes
>> c. mitochondria
>> d. free ribosomes

In this item the word *free* in the option is identical to *free* in the stem. Thus, the wise test taker has a good chance of answering the item correctly without mastery of the content being measured.

Grammatical Clue.   Consider this item:

> U.S. Grant was an _____.
>> a. president
>> b. man
>> c. alcoholic
>> d. general

Most students would pick up on the easy grammatical clue in the stem. The article *an* eliminates options a, b, and d, because "*an* man," "*an* president," or "*an* general" are ungrammatical. Option c is the only one that forms a grammatical sentence. A way to eliminate the grammatical clue is to replace *an* with *a/an*. Similar examples are *is/are*, *was/were*, *his/her*, and so on. Alternatively, place the article (or verb, or pronoun) in the options list:

Christopher Columbus came to America in _____.
- a. a car
- b. a boat
- c. an airplane
- d. a balloon

Redundant Words/Unequal Length.   Two very common faults in multiple-choice construction are illustrated in this item:

When 53 Americans were held hostage in Iran, _____.
- a. the United States did nothing to free them
- b. the United States declared war on Iran
- c. the United States first attempted to free them by diplomatic means and later attempted a rescue
- d. the United States expelled all Iranian students

The phrase "the United States" is included in each option. To save space and time, add it to the stem: "When 53 Americans were held hostage in Iran, the United States _____." Second, the length of options could be a giveaway. Multiple-choice item writers have a tendency to include more information in the correct option than in the incorrect options. Test-wise students know that the longer option is the correct one more often than not. Avoid making correct answers more than one and one-half times the length of incorrect options.

All of the Above/None of the Above.   In general, use "none of the above" sparingly. Some item writers use "none of the above" only when there is no clearly correct option presented. However, students catch on to this practice and guess that "none of the above" is the correct answer without knowledge of the content being measured. Also, at times it may be justified to use multiple correct answers, such as "both a and c" or "both b and c." Again, use such options sparingly, because inconsistencies can easily exist among alternatives that logically eliminate some from consideration. Avoid using "all of the above," because test items should *encourage* discrimination, not discourage it.

Higher-Level Multiple-Choice Questions

How can I write multiple-choice items that measure higher-level behaviors?

A good multiple-choice item is the most time-consuming type of objective test item to write. Unfortunately, most multiple-choice items also are written at the knowledge level in the taxonomy of educational objectives. As a new item writer, you will tend to write items at this level, but you need to write some multiple-choice items to measure *higher*-level cognitive objectives as well.

First, write some of your *objectives* to measure comprehension, application, analysis, or evaluation. This ensures that your items will be at the higher-than-knowledge level. Following are some suggestions to make your higher-level multiple-choice questions more authentic.

Use Pictorial, Graphical, or Tabular Stimuli.   Pictures, drawings, graphs, and tables require the student to think at least at the application level in the taxonomy of educational objectives and may involve even higher cognitive processes. Also, such stimuli often can generate several higher-level multiple-choice items rather than just one.

Use Analogies to Show Relationships among Terms.   To answer analogies correctly, students must not only be familiar with the terms, but also be able to *understand* how the terms relate to each other. For example:

Physician is to humans as veterinarian is to _____.

   a. fruits
   b. animals
   c. minerals
   d. vegetables

Require Application of Principles or Procedures.   To test whether students comprehend the implications of a procedure or principle, have them use the principle or procedure with new information, or in a novel way. This requires them to do more than just follow the steps in solving a problem. It has them demonstrate an ability to go beyond the context within which they originally learned a principle or procedure. Consider this example, from a division lesson that relied on computation of grade-point averages as examples:

After filling his car's tank with 18 gallons of gasoline, Mr. Watts said to his son, "We've come 450 miles since the last fill up. What kind of gas mileage are we getting?" Which of the following is the best answer?

   a. 4 miles per gallon
   b. 25 miles per gallon

c. Between 30 and 35 miles per gallon

d. It can't be determined from the information given

Suggestions for Writing Multiple-Choice Items.

1. Be sure that there is one and only one correct or clearly best answer.
2. Be sure all wrong answer choices ("distractors") are plausible. Eliminate unintentional grammatical clues, and keep the length and form of all the answer choices equal. Rotate the position of the correct answer from item to item randomly.
3. Use negative questions or statements only if the knowledge being tested requires it. In most cases it is more important for the student to know what the correct answer *is* rather than what it is not.
4. Include three to five options (two to four distractors plus one correct answer) to optimize testing for knowledge rather than encouraging guessing. It is not necessary to provide additional distractors for an item simply to maintain the same number of distractors for each item.
5. Use the option "none of the above" sparingly and only when all the answers can be classified unequivocally as wrong.
6. Avoid using "all of the above." It usually is the correct answer and makes the item too easy for students who have only partial information.

Completion Items

Like true-false items, completion items are relatively easy to write. The first tests constructed by classroom teachers and taken by students often are completion tests. Like items of all other formats, there are good and poor completion items. Here are some suggestions for completion items:

1. Require a single-word answer or a brief, definite statement. Avoid items so indefinite that they may be logically answered by several terms:

   Poor Item: World War II ended in _____.

   Better Item: World War II ended in the year _____.

2. Be sure the item poses a problem. A direct question often is better than an incomplete statement because it provides more structure for an answer:

   Poor Item: What do you think about a main character in the story "Lilies of the Field?"

Better Item: The main character in the story "Lilies of the Field" was _____ .

3. Be sure the answer is factually correct. Precisely word the question in relation to the concept or fact being tested. For example, can the answer be found in the text, workbook, or class notes taken by students?

4. Omit only key words; don't eliminate so many elements that the sense of the content is impaired:

    Poor Item: The _____ type of test item usually is graded _____ than the _____ type.

    Better Item: The multiple-choice type of test item usually is graded more objectively than the _____ type.

5. Word the statement so the blank is near the end. This prevents awkward sentences.

6. If the problem requires a numerical answer, indicate the units in which it is to be expressed (for example, pounds, ounces, minutes).

Advantages and Disadvantages of Objective-Item Formats

What are the advantages and disadvantages of different objective test formats?

Table 14.1 summarizes the advantages and disadvantages of each of the preceding objective item formats.

>>> ESSAY TEST ITEMS <<<

In this section, we will explain what an essay item is, describe the two major types, and provide suggestions for writing them. In essay items, the student supplies, rather than selects, the correct answer. It demands that the student compose a response, often extensive, to a question for which no *single* response or pattern of responses can be cited as correct to the exclusion of all others. The accuracy and quality of such a response often can be judged only by a person skilled in the subject area.

Like objective test items, essay items may be well constructed or poorly constructed. The well-constructed essay item tests complex cognitive skills by requiring the student to organize, integrate, and synthesize knowledge, to use information to solve novel problems, or to be original and innovative in problem solving. The poorly constructed essay item may require the student to do no more than recall information as it was presented in the textbook or lecture.

Table 14.1
Advantages and disadvantages of various objective-item formats

True-False Tests	
Advantages	**Disadvantages**
Tend to be short, so more material can be covered than with any other item format; thus, use T–F items when extensive content has been covered.	Tend to emphasize rote memorization of knowledge (although complex questions sometimes can be asked using T–F items).
Faster to construct (but avoid creating an item by taking statements out of context or slightly modifying them).	They assume an unequivocally true or false answer (it is unfair to make students guess at your criteria for evaluating the truth of a statement).
Scoring is easier (tip: provide a "T" and "F" for them to circle, because a student's handwritten "T" or "F" can be hard to decipher).	Allow and may even encourage a high degree of guessing (generally, longer examinations compensate for this).

Matching Items	
Advantages	**Disadvantages**
Simple to construct and score.	Tend to ask trivial information.
Ideal for measuring associations between facts.	Emphasize memorization.
Can be more efficient than multiple-choice questions because they avoid repetition of options in measuring association.	Most commercial answer sheets can accommodate only five options, thus limiting the size of a matching item.
Reduce the effects of guessing.	

Worse, the poorly constructed essay item may not inform the learner what is required for a satisfactory response.

Extended Response Items

An essay item that allows the student to determine the length and complexity of a response is called an **extended response essay item**. This type of essay is most useful at the analysis, synthesis, or evaluation levels of cognitive complexity. Because of the length of this type of item and the time required to organize and express the

Table 14.1, *continued*

Multiple-Choice Tests	
Advantages	**Disadvantages**
Versatile in measuring objectives, from the knowledge level to the evaluation level.	Time consuming to write.
Since writing is minimal, considerable course material can be sampled quickly.	If not carefully written, can have more than one defensible correct answer.
Scoring is highly objective, requiring only a count of correct responses.	
Can be written so students must discriminate among options varying in correctness, avoiding the absolute judgments of T–F tests.	
Reduce effects of guessing.	
Amenable to statistical analysis, so you can determine which items are ambiguous or too difficult (see Kubiszyn & Borich, 1996, Chapter 8).	

Completion Tests	
Advantages	**Disadvantages**
Question construction is relatively easy.	Encourage a low level of response complexity.
Guessing is reduced because the question requires a specific response.	Can be difficult to score (the stem must be general enough to not communicate the answer, leading unintentionally to multiple defensible answers).
Less time is needed to complete than multiple-choice items, so more content can be covered.	Very short answers tend to measure recall of specific facts, names, places, and events instead of more complex behaviors.

response, the extended response item is sometimes better as a term-paper assignment or take-home test. The extended response essay often is of value in assessing communication ability as well as in assessing achievement. For example:

Compare and contrast the presidential administrations of George Bush and Ronald Reagan. Consider economic, social, and military policies. Avoid taking a position in support of either president. Your response will be graded on objectivity, accuracy, organization, and clarity.

Restricted Response Items

An essay item that poses a specific problem for which the student must recall proper information, organize it in a suitable manner, derive a defensible conclusion, and express it within the limits of the posed problem is called a **restricted response essay item**. The statement of the problem specifies response limitations to guide the student in responding and to provide evaluation criteria for scoring. For example:

> List the major similarities and differences between U.S. participation in the Korean War and World War II, being sure to consider political, military, economic, and social factors. Limit your answer to one page. Your score will depend on accuracy, organization, and conciseness.

When Should You Use Essay Questions?

Although each situation must be considered individually, some lend themselves to essay items. For example:

1. The instructional objectives specify high-level cognitive processes—they require supplying information rather than simply recognizing information. These processes often cannot be measured with objective items.
2. Only a few tests or items need to be graded. If you have 30 students and design a test with six extended response essays, you will spend a great deal of time scoring. Use essays when class size is small, or use only one or two essays in conjunction with objective items.
3. Test security is a consideration. If you are afraid test items will be passed on to future students, it is better to use an essay test. In general, a good essay test takes less time to construct than a good objective test.

Here are some learning outcomes for which essay items may be used:

Analyze relationships.

Arrange items in sequence.

Compare positions.

State necessary assumptions.

Identify appropriate conclusions.

Explain cause-and-effect relations.

Formulate hypotheses.

Organize data to support a viewpoint.

Point out strengths and weaknesses.

Produce a solution to a problem.

Integrate data from several sources.

Evaluate the quality or worth of an item, product, or action.

Create an original solution, arrangement, or procedure.

Suggestions for Writing and Using Essay Items

1. Have clearly in mind what mental processes you want the student to use before starting to write the question. Refer to the mental processes required at the various levels in the taxonomy of educational objectives for the cognitive domain (for example, compare and contrast, create alternatives, make choices among). If you want students to analyze, judge, or think critically, determine what mental processes involve analysis, judgment, or critical thinking.

   Poor item: Criticize the following speech by our President.

   Better Item: Consider the following presidential speech. Focus on the section dealing with economic policy and discriminate between factual statements and opinion. List these statements separately, label them, and indicate whether each statement is or is not consistent with the President's overall economic policy.

2. Write the question to clearly and unambiguously define the task to the student. Tasks should be explained (1) in the overall instructions preceding the test items and/or (2) in the test items themselves. Include instructions for the type of writing style desired (for example, scientific vs. prose), whether spelling and grammar will be counted, and whether organization of the response will be an important scoring element. Also, indicate the level of detail and supporting data required.

   Poor Item: Discuss the value of behavioral objectives.

   Better Item: Behavioral objectives have enjoyed increased popularity in education over the years. In your text and in class the advantages and disadvantages of behavioral objectives have been discussed. Take a position for or against the use of behavioral objectives in education and support your position with at least three of the arguments covered in class or in the text.

3. Start essay questions with such words or phrases as *compare, contrast, give reasons for, give original examples of, predict what would happen if,* and so on. Do not begin with such words as *what, who, when,* and *list,* because these words generally lead to tasks that require only recall of information.

    Poor Item: List three reasons behind America's withdrawal from Vietnam.

    Better Item: After more than 10 years of involvement, the United States withdrew from Vietnam in 1975. Speculate on what would have happened if America had *not* withdrawn at that time and had *not* increased significantly its military presence above 1972 levels.

4. A question dealing with a controversial issue should ask for, and be evaluated in terms of, the presentation of evidence for a position, rather than the position taken. It is not defensible to demand that a student accept a specific conclusion or solution, but it is reasonable to appraise how well he or she has learned to use the evidence upon which a specific conclusion is based.

    Poor Item: What laws should Congress pass to improve the medical care of all citizens in the United States?

    Better Item: Some feel that the cost of all medical care should be borne by the federal government. Do you agree or disagree? Support your position with at least three logical arguments.

5. Avoid using optional items. That is, require all students to complete the same items. Allowing students to select 3 of 5, 4 of 7, and so forth decreases the uniformity of the test across all students, which will decrease your basis for comparison among students.

6. Establish reasonable time and/or page limits for each essay item to help the student complete the entire test and to indicate the level of detail you have in mind. Indicate such limits either in the statement of the problem or close to the number of the question.

7. Restrict the use of essays to those learning outcomes that cannot be satisfactorily measured by objective items.

8. Be sure each question relates to an instructional objective. Check your test blueprint to see if the content of the essay item is represented.

Advantages and Disadvantages of the Essay Item

Here are several advantages:

- To the extent that instructional objectives require the student to organize information to solve a problem, analyze and evaluate information, or perform other high-level cognitive skills, the essay test is an appropriate assessment tool.
- Although essay tests are relatively easy to construct, do not construct the items haphazardly. Consult your behavioral objectives blueprint, identify only the topics and objectives that can best be assessed by essays, and build items around those—and only those.
- If developing communication skills is an instructional objective, you can test it with an essay item. However, this assumes that you have spent time teaching communication pertinent to the course area, including special vocabulary and writing styles, as well as providing practice with arguments for and against controversial points.
- Because no options are provided, the student must supply rather than select the proper response, reducing guessing.

Here are several disadvantages:

- It is tedious for you to wade through pages and pages of student handwriting. Also, it is difficult not to let spelling and grammatical mistakes influence grading or to let superior communication abilities cover up for incomplete comprehension of facts.
- It is difficult to maintain a common set of criteria for all students. Two persons may disagree on the correct answer for any essay item; even the same person will disagree on the correctness of one answer read on two separate occasions.
- Fewer essay items can be attempted than with objective items. Also, students become fatigued faster with essay items than with objective items.
- It is no secret that longer essays tend to be graded higher than short essays, regardless of content! As a result, students may bluff.

The first two limitations—time required for grading and maintaining consistent objectivity—are serious disadvantages. Fortunately, there are some ways to make the task of scoring essays more manageable and reliable.

Scoring Essays

As mentioned, essays are difficult to score consistently across individuals. That is, the *same* essay answer may be given an A by one scorer and a B or C by another scorer. Or, the same answer may be graded A on one occasion, but B or C on another occasion by the *same* scorer! As disturbing and surprising as this may seem, these conclusions are supported by research findings (Coffman, 1972). What can you do to avoid such scoring problems?

How can I grade essay tests fairly?

Write Good Essay Items.   Poorly written questions are one source of scorer inconsistency. Questions that do not specify response length are another. In general, long (for example, three-page) essay responses are more difficult to score consistently than restricted essay responses (say, one page). This is due to student fatigue and subsequent clerical errors, as well as a tendency for grading criteria to vary from response to response, or for that matter, from page to page, or even paragraph to paragraph within the same response.

Use Several Restricted Response Items.   Rather than a single extended response item, use several restricted response items. Writing good items and using restricted response essays will help improve essay scoring. However, as mentioned, extended response essays sometimes are desirable or necessary. When they are, use a predetermined scoring scheme.

Use a Predetermined Scoring Scheme.   All too often essays are graded without the scorer having specified in advance what he or she is looking for in a "good" answer. If you do not specify the criteria beforehand, your scoring consistency will be greatly reduced. If these criteria are not readily available (written down) for scoring each question, the criteria themselves may change (you may grade harder or easier after a number of papers, even if the answers do not change). Or, your ability to keep these criteria in mind will be influenced by fatigue, distractions, frame of mind, and so on. Because we all are human, we all are subject to these factors.

Some Criteria for Scoring Higher-Level Essay Items

Following are several criteria that are useful in scoring higher-level essay items.

Content. Although essays are used less to measure factual knowledge than thinking processes, the content of an essay can and should be scored specifically for its precision and accuracy, in addition to its organization and use (and tell your students if you are doing so).

Organization. Does the essay have an introduction, body, and conclusion? If you are looking for these characteristics, let the students know that you will be scoring for organization. Beyond these three general organizational criteria, you may want to develop specific criteria for your class. For example: Are recommendations, inferences, and hypotheses supported? Is it apparent which supporting statements go with which recommendation? Do progressions and sequences follow a logical or chronological development? You also should decide on a spelling and grammar policy and develop these criteria, alerting the students *before* they take the test.

Process. If your essay item tests at the application level or above, the most important criteria for scoring are those that reflect the extent to which the process has been carried out. Each process (application, analysis, synthesis, and evaluation) results in a solution, recommendation, or decision, or some reasons to justify or support the final decision, and so on. Thus, the process criteria should assess both the adequacy of the solution or decision and the reasons behind it.

Accuracy/Reasonableness. Will it work? Have the correct analytical dimensions been identified? You ultimately must decide what is accurate, but be prepared for unexpected, yet accurate, responses.

Completeness/Internal Consistency. Does the essay deal adequately with the problem presented? Again, your judgment will weigh heavily, but points should be logically related and cover the topics as fully as required.

Originality/Creativity. Again, it is up to you to recognize the unexpected and give credit for it. That is, expect some students to develop new ways of conceptualizing questions, and award credit for such conceptualizations when appropriate.

Tell students about any or all of the preceding criteria. Once they know how you are going to score the test, they can prepare better and more defensible responses.

>>> PACKAGING THE TEST <<<

After all the care and work you put into developing good test items, follow through and package the test properly for the sake of your learners and your own professionalism. As you study the following guidelines, you probably will recall seeing every one of them violated at some time on tests you have taken. Start off right by attending to these details.

Guidelines for Packaging

Here are guidelines for packaging your test:

- Group together items of similar format.
- Arrange test items from easy to hard.
- Properly space items.
- Keep items and options on the same page.
- Place illustrations near the descriptive material.
- Check for randomness in the answer key.
- Decide how students will record their answers.
- Provide space for the test taker's name and the date.
- Check test directions for clarity.
- Proofread the test.

Let's now briefly consider each of these.

Group Together All Items of Similar Format.   If you have all true-false items grouped together, all completion items together, and so on, then students will not have to "shift gears" and adjust to new formats. This enables them to cover more items than if item formats were mixed throughout the test. Also, by grouping items of a given format together, only one set of directions is necessary for each type of format—another timesaver.

Arrange Test Items from Easy to Hard.   Arranging test items according to level of difficulty will enable more students to answer the first few items correctly, thereby building confidence and hopefully reducing test anxiety.

Space the Items for Easy Reading.   Provide enough blank space between items so that each is distinctly separate from others. When items are crowded together, students may inadvertently perceive a word, phrase, or line from an adjacent item as being part of the item they are focused on.

Keep Items and Options on the Same Page.   Few things aggravate a test taker more than having to turn the page to read the options for multiple-choice or matching items, or to complete reading a true-false or completion item. To avoid this, do not begin an item at the bottom of the page unless you will have at least an inch left *after completing* the item. Not only does this eliminate carrying over items onto the next page, it also minimizes the likelihood that the last line or two of the item will be cut off when you photocopy the test.

Position Illustrations Near Descriptions.   Place diagrams, maps, or other supporting material immediately above the item or items to which they refer. In other words, if items 9, 10, and 11 refer to a map of South America, locate the map above items 9, 10, and 11—not between 9 and 10 or between 10 and 11 and not below them. Also, if possible, keep any such stimuli and related questions on the same page to save the test taker time.

Check Your Answer Key for Randomness.   Be sure the correct answers follow a random pattern. Avoid true-false patterns such as TFTF or TTFF and multiple-choice patterns such as DCBADCBA. At the same time, see that your correct answers are distributed about equally between true and false and among multiple-choice options.

Determine How Students Record Answers.   Decide whether your students will record their answers on the test paper or on a separate answer sheet. In the lower elementary grades, it is best for students to record answers on the test papers. In the upper elementary and secondary grades, separate answer sheets can facilitate scoring accuracy and reduce scoring time. Also, in the upper grades, learning to complete separate answer sheets familiarizes students with the process they will use when taking standardized tests.

Provide Space for Name and Date.   Be sure to include a blank on your test booklet and/or answer sheet for the student's name and the date. If you think this is unnecessary, you have never graded a pile of unsigned papers from young children, wondering who they belong to! It is *not* always evident to a nervous test taker that a name should be included on the test. Students are much more likely to put their names on tests if space is provided.

Check Test Directions. Check your directions for each item format to be sure they are clear. Directions should specify all of the following:

1. The numbers of the items to which the directions apply
2. How to record answers
3. The basis on which to select answers
4. Criteria for scoring

Proofread the Test. Proofread for typographical and grammatical errors and correct them before reproducing the test. Having to announce corrections to the class just before or during the test wastes time and will disturb the test takers' concentration.

Before reproducing the test, it's a good idea to check off these steps. The checklist in Figure 14.3 can be used for this purpose.

Test Assembly Checklist

Check each statement to see that it applies to your test.

	Yes	No
1. Are items of similar format grouped together?	❏	❏
2. Are items arranged in order of difficulty from easy to hard?	❏	❏
3. Are items properly spaced?	❏	❏
4. Are items and options on the same page?	❏	❏
5. Are diagrams, maps, and supporting material above designated items and on the same page with items?	❏	❏
6. Are answers random?	❏	❏
7. Have you decided whether an answer sheet will be used?	❏	❏
8. Are blanks for name and date included?	❏	❏
9. Have you checked the directions for clarity and completeness?	❏	❏
10. Have you proofread the test for errors?	❏	❏

Figure 14.3
Test assembly checklist

>>> VALIDITY, RELIABILITY, AND ACCURACY <<<

Test results are useful only if they are valid, reliable, and accurate. These terms are defined as follows:

1. *Validity*—does the test measure what it is supposed to?
2. *Reliability*—does the test yield the same or similar scores consistently?
3. *Accuracy*—does the test approximate an individual's true level of knowledge, skill, or ability?

Types of Validity

How will I know if my tests measure what I say they measure?

A test is **valid** if it measures what it says it is supposed to measure. For instance, if it is supposed to be a test of third-grade arithmetic ability, it should measure third-grade arithmetic skills, not fifth-grade arithmetic skills and not reading ability. If it is supposed to be a measure of ability to write behavioral objectives, it should measure that ability, not the ability to recognize poor objectives.

Clearly, if test results will be used to make any kind of decision and if the test information is to be useful, it is essential that the test be valid. There are several ways of deciding whether a test is sufficiently valid to be useful. The three methods most often used are *content validity, concurrent validity*, and *predictive validity*.

Content Validity. The content validity of a test is established by examining its contents. Test questions are inspected to see whether they correspond to what the teacher feels should be covered. This is easiest when the test is measuring achievement, where it may be fairly easy to specify what to include. It is more difficult if the concept being tested is a personality or aptitude trait, because it can be difficult to specify beforehand what a relevant question would look like.

A test sometimes can look valid but measure something different from what is intended, such as guessing ability, reading level, or skills that may have been acquired before the instruction. Content validity is, therefore, a minimum requirement for a useful test, but does not guarantee a valid test.

Concurrent Validity. Concurrent validity requires that an established test be administered at the same time as the new test you have designed. Unlike content validity, concurrent validity yields a numerical value in the form of a correlation coefficient, called a validity coefficient (see Kubiszyn & Borich, 1996, Chapter 14).

The concurrent validity of a test is determined by administering both the new test and the established test to a group of students and then finding the relationship—the correlation—between the two sets of test scores. If there exists an established test (criterion) with which the new test can be compared and in which people have confidence, concurrent validity provides a good method of estimating the validity of a test.

Predictive Validity.   Predictive validity refers to how well the test predicts some future behavior of the examinee that is representative of the test's content. This form of validity is particularly useful for aptitude tests, which attempt to predict how well the test taker will do in some future setting. Predictive validity also yields a numerical index, also in the form of a correlation coefficient. This time, however, it is the relationship between the test and some future behavior that is being measured.

All three methods for determining validity—content, concurrent, and predictive—assume that some criterion exists external to the test that can be used to anchor or validate it. In the case of content validity, it is the instructional objectives that provide the anchor or point of reference; in the case of concurrent validity, it is another well-accepted test measuring the same thing; and in the case of predictive validity, it is some future behavior or condition that we are attempting to predict.

Types of Reliability

The **reliability** of a test refers to the consistency with which it yields the same rank or score for an individual taking the test several times. In other words, a test is reliable if it consistently yields the same, or nearly the same, ranks among all individuals over repeated administrations during which we would not expect the trait being measured to have changed.

How will I know if my tests are consistent in repeated administrations?

There are several ways to estimate the reliability of a test. The three basic methods most often used are called *test-retest*, *alternative form*, and *internal consistency*.

Test-Retest.   Test-retest is a method of estimating reliability that is exactly what its name implies. The test is given twice to the same individuals and the relationship—or correlation—between the first set of scores and the second set of scores is determined.

Alternate Form.   If there are two equivalent forms of a test, both can be used to estimate the reliability of the test. Both are administered to a group of students, and the relationship (correlation) between the two sets of scores is determined. Because the two forms have different items but equivalent content, this estimate eliminates the problems of memory and practice involved in test-retest estimates of reliability. Large differences in a student's score on two forms of a test that supposedly measures the same behavior would indicate an unreliable test. To use this method of estimating reliability, there must be two equivalent forms of the test available, and they must be administered under conditions as nearly equivalent as possible and at approximately the same time.

Internal Consistency.   If the test measures a single basic concept, then it is reasonable to assume that people who get one item right will more likely get other, similar items right. In other words, items ought to be related or correlated with each other, and the test ought to be internally consistent. If this is the case, then the reliability of the test can be estimated by the internal-consistency method. (Specific numerical procedures for determining the internal consistency of a test and other methods of measuring reliability are in Kubiszyn & Borich, 1996.)

Here are some tips and cautions about interpreting reliability coefficients:

- Higher coefficients will result from heterogeneous groups than from homogeneous groups. Groups comprised of very different types of individuals (for example, at-risk and gifted, older and younger, motivated and unmotivated learners) will result in higher reliabilities than more homogeneous groups.
- Scoring reliability limits test reliability. If tests are scored unreliably, error is introduced that will limit the reliability of the test. A test cannot have reliability higher than the reliability of the scoring.
- All other factors being equal, the more items included in a test, the higher the test's reliability.
- Reliability tends to decrease as tests become too easy or too difficult.

Typically, validity coefficients for a test are lower than reliability coefficients. Acceptable validity coefficients for a test generally range between .60 and .80 or higher, while acceptable reliability coefficients generally range from .80 to .90 or higher. 1.0 is the maximum coefficient obtainable for either validity or reliability. **Test accuracy** is in part a combined measure of validity and reliability, and in part determined by how well the test content matches the prevailing general educational curriculum.

Marks and Marking Systems

After you have administered your test, you will have to score it and assign marks. Often the type of symbol a teacher uses to represent a mark is determined at the school or district level—for example: A–F, E–G–S–P–U (Excellent–Good–Satisfactory–Poor–Unsatisfactory), or a numerical marking system. However, the classroom teacher often has considerable flexibility in determining how to assign these marks to learners. You may have considerable control over *how* you decide who gets an A or B or 75 or 80. **Marks and grading systems** are based on comparisons, usually comparisons of students with one or more of the following:

How do I assign grades or marks to my learners' test scores?

- Other students
- Established standards
- Aptitude
- Actual vs. potential effort
- Actual vs. potential improvement

Comparison with Other Students.   The expression "grading on the curve" means that your grade or mark depends on how your achievement compares with the achievement of other students in your class. Sometimes districts or schools encourage grading on the curve by specifying the percentages of students who will be assigned various grades.

The main advantage of such a system is that it simplifies marking decisions. The student either is in the top 10 percent or doesn't get an A. There is no deliberation or agonizing over what cutoff scores should determine whether students get this grade or that. However, this type of marking system fails to consider differences in the overall ability level of the class. Regardless of achievement, in such a system some students always will get As, and some always will get Fs.

Comparison with Established Standards.   In this marking system, it is possible for any student to get an A or F or any grade between. Achievements of individual students are unrelated to other individual students. All that is relevant is whether a student attains a defined standard of achievement or performance. We labeled this approach

Comparisons with other students, established standards, aptitude, effort, and improvement all can be the basis for assigning grades. Ultimately, you must decide the balance of approaches to use that best fits the goals of the classroom and school.

criterion-referenced earlier in this chapter. In such a system, letter grades may be assigned, based on the percentage of test items answered correctly, as this distribution illustrates:

Grade	Percentage of Items Answered Correctly
A	85
B	75
C	65
D	55
F	less than 55

In theory, this system makes it possible for all students to obtain high grades if they put forth sufficient effort (assuming that the percentage cutoffs are not unreasonably high). Also, grade assignment is simplified; a student either has correctly answered 75 percent of the items or has not. As with the comparison with other students method, there is no deliberating or agonizing over assigning grades. Also, teachers who work to improve their teaching effectiveness can observe improvement in grades with the passage of time.

As you might expect, such a system also has its drawbacks. Establishing a standard for each grade attained is no small task, and what is reasonable for an A may vary from school to school and from time to time, as a result of ability levels, the content being taught, and curriculum changes.

Comparison with Aptitude.   *Aptitude* is another name for potential or ability. In such systems, students are compared neither to other students nor to established standards. Instead, they are compared to themselves. That is, marks are assigned depending on how closely to their potential they are achieving. Thus, students with high aptitude or potential who are achieving at high levels would get high grades, because they would be achieving at their potential. Those with high aptitude and average achievement would get lower grades, because they would be achieving below their potential.

But students with average aptitude and average achievement also would get high grades, because they would be considered to be achieving at their potential. Thus, the same grade could mean very different things in terms of absolute achievement.

Comparison of Achievement with Effort.   Systems that compare achievement with effort are similar to those that compare achievement with aptitude. Students who get average test scores but have to work hard to get them are given high marks. Students who get average scores but do not have to work hard to get them are given lower grades. The advantage cited for grading on effort is that it motivates slower or turned-off students. However, it also may turn off brighter students, who quickly see such a system as unfair.

Comparison of Achievement with Improvement.   Such systems compare the amount of improvement between the beginning and end of instruction. Students who show the most progress get the highest grades. An obvious problem occurs for the student who does well on a test at the beginning of the instruction, called the *pretest*, because improvement for this student is likely to be less than for a student who does poorly on the pretest.

Which marking system should you choose? Most now agree that comparisons with established standards would best suit the primary function of marking, which is to provide feedback about academic achievement. Once standards are established, comparisons among schools and students may be more easily made. In reality, many schools and districts have adopted multiple marking systems, such as assigning separate grades for achievement and effort or achievement, effort, and improvement. As long as the achievement portion of the grade reflects *only* achievement, such systems are appropriate.

>>> STANDARDIZED TESTS <<<

So far, we have limited our discussion to teacher-constructed tests. However, many teachers also are required at least once a year to administer *standardized* tests, evaluate their results, and interpret them to curious and sometimes concerned parents.

Standardized tests are developed by test-construction specialists, usually with the assistance of curriculum experts, teachers, and school administrators, to determine a student's performance level relative to others of similar age and grade. These tests are *standardized* because they are administered and scored according to *specific* and *uniform* (standard) procedures.

When standardized tests are employed, test results from different students, classes, schools, and districts can be more easily and confidently *compared* than is the case with different teacher-made tests. For the most part, standardized tests are used for comparative purposes. This is quite different from the purposes of teacher-made tests, which are to determine pupil mastery or skill levels, to assign grades, and to provide specific feedback to students and parents. Table 14.2 compares standardized and teacher-made tests on several important dimensions.

What does a percentile rank mean?

The results of standardized tests are reported as percentile ranks. Percentile ranks enable you to determine how a student's performance compares with others of the same grade or age. Keep in mind two points when interpreting percentile ranks:

1. Percentile ranks often are confused with *percentage correct*. In using percentile ranks, be sure you communicate that a percentile rank of 62 (for example) means that the individual's score was *higher* than 62 percent of all the people who took the test (called the *norming sample*). Or, you can say that 62 percent of those who took the test scored *lower* than this individual. (Commonly, a score at the 62nd percentile is misinterpreted to mean that the student answered only 62 percent of the items correctly. But realize that a score at the 62nd percentile might be equivalent to a B or a C, whereas a score of 62 percent likely would be an F.)

2. Equal differences between percentile ranks do *not* necessarily indicate equal differences in achievement. In a grade of 100 pupils, the difference *in achievement* between the 2nd percentile and 5th percentile is substantial, whereas the difference between the 47th and 50th percentile is negligible. Interpretation of percentile ranks must take into consideration that percentiles toward the extreme or end points of the

Table 14.2

A comparison of standardized and teacher-made achievement tests

	Standardized Achievement Tests	Teacher-Made Achievement Tests
Learning outcomes and content measured	Measures general outcomes and content appropriate to the majority of U.S. schools. These tests of general skills and understanding tend not to reflect specific or unique emphasis of local curricula.	Well adapted to the specific and unique outcomes and content of a local curriculum; adaptable to various sizes of work units, but tend to neglect complex learning outcomes.
Quality of test items	Quality of items generally is high. Items are written by specialists, pretested, and selected on the basis of results from quantitative item analysis.	Quality of items is often unknown. Quality is typically lower than standardized tests due to limited time available to the teacher.
Reliability	Reliability is high, commonly between .80 and .95, and frequently above .90 (highest possible is 1.0).	Reliability is usually unknown, but can be high if items are carefully constructed.
Administration and scoring	Procedures are standardized; specific instructions are provided.	Uniform procedures are possible, but usually are flexible and unwritten.
Interpretation of scores	Scores can be compared to norm groups. Test manual and other guides aid interpretation and use.	Score comparisons and interpretation are limited to local class or school situation. Few if any guidelines are available for interpretation and use.

distribution tend to be spread out (like a rubber band), while percentiles toward the center tend to be compressed.

>>> NEW TRENDS IN STANDARDIZED TESTING <<<

Standardized testing has undergone criticism in recent years (Stiggins, 1994; Ysseldyke & Marston, 1990; Elliott & Shapiro, 1990). This criticism has centered on three questions concerning the relevance of standardized tests:

1. How much does classroom learning depend on the skills measured by a standardized test?
2. Are these tests fair to learners from diverse cultures and ethnic backgrounds?
3. Do such tests provide information useful for making instructional decisions in the classroom?

How is the nature of standardized tests likely to change in the future?

Consideration of these questions has led to alternative approaches to and revisions in the way in which standardized tests are constructed. Underlying these alternative approaches and revisions are four assumptions that are likely to guide the development of standardized tests in the future. Let's look at them briefly.

Learning Is a Process

The standardized testing tradition sought to measure the outcomes of learning (facts, concepts, principles, generalizations, etc.) by making assumptions about, but not actually measuring, the processes involved in achieving these outcomes. For example, the standardized approach assumed that learning could be measured by systematically recording its effects, that repeated measurement of the effects would overcome any imprecision in the measures themselves, and that the amount of learning acquired could be known through relative (comparison with other students) rather than absolute measurement. New approaches to standardized tests are likely to record both the *effect* (what was learned) and the *process* (how it was learned). In other words, the cognitive processes employed to attain the effect will be as important as the test scores themselves.

Learning Ability Can Be Improved

The standardized testing approach originated at a period in our history when we believed that ability to learn was inherited, fixed, and largely immutable. These beliefs exerted strong influence on the manner in which standardized tests were constructed and interpreted. We now know that some types of learning ability can be enhanced and that there are many skills that can be instrumental in doing so. New approaches to standardized testing are likely to be based on the modifiability of learning ability and the identification of specific learning abilities that can be changed through instruction.

Learning Occurs in a Social Context

Many tests derived from the standardized approach view learning as a largely private act. The results of such tests have been used to place learners in programs emphasizing homogeneous groups or tracks, or into instructional programs emphasizing self-paced, mastery learning. But, classrooms by their very nature are social settings and most learning takes place in a social context. Consequently, since learning is an inherently social act, new approaches to standardized testing are likely to take into account that teachers and groups of peers interact to affect the process of learning. One goal of standardized testing in the future may be to include the measurement of children's learning in cooperative groups or the naturally occurring social dialogue of the classroom.

Learning Assessment Should Have Instructional Validity

One of the fundamental problems with the use of standardized tests in the classroom has been that they do not identify the instructional processes that can help learners remove learning deficits. This has been called the **instructional validity** of a test (Bergan & Dunn, 1976). The assessment of learning should not only reliably identify learning deficits, but also point the way to resolving them. To meet this standard of test validity, standardized tests in the future may have to do more than present evidence of content, concurrent, and predictive validity. They would have to show evidence that school-based programs can remediate the learning deficits they uncover.

Summing Up

This chapter introduced you to some techniques for evaluating student learning. Its main points were as follows:

1. A test that determines a student's place or rank among other students is called norm-referenced. This type of test conveys information about how a student performed compared to a large sample of pupils at the same age or grade.

2. A test that compares a student's performance to a standard of mastery is called criterion-referenced. This type of test conveys information about whether a student needs additional instruction on some skill or set of skills.

3. The major advantage of a norm-referenced test is that it covers many different content areas in a single test; its major disadvantage is that it is too general to be useful in identifying specific strengths and weaknesses tied to individual texts or workbooks.

4. The major advantage of a criterion-referenced test is that it can yield highly specific

information about individual skills or behaviors. Its major disadvantage is that many such tests would be needed to make decisions about the many skills or behaviors typically taught in school.

5. A test blueprint is a graphic device that matches the test items to be written with the content areas and levels of behavioral complexity taught. The test blueprint helps to ensure that a test samples learning across (1) the range of content areas covered and (2) the cognitive and/or affective processes considered important.

6. Objective test item formats include the following:

- True-false
- Matching
- Multiple choice
- Completion or short answer

7. Two methods for reducing the effects of guessing in true-false items are to (1) encourage all students to guess when they do not know the answer and (2) require revision of statements that are false.

8. In constructing matching items:

- Make lists homogeneous, representing the same kind of events, people, or circumstances.
- Place the shorter list first and list options in chronological, numbered, or alphabetical order.
- Provide approximately three more options than descriptions to reduce the chance of guessing correctly.
- Write directions to identify what the lists contain, and specify the basis for matching.
- Closely check the options for multiple correct answers.

9. Avoid the following flaws when writing multiple-choice items:

- Stem clues in which the same word or a close derivative appears in both the stem and an option.
- Grammatical clues in which an article, verb, or pronoun eliminates one or more options from being grammatically correct.
- Same words are repeated across options that could have been provided only once in the stem.
- Response options are of unequal length, indicating that the longer option may be correct.
- Use of "all of the above," which discourages response discrimination, or "none of the above," which encourages guessing.

10. Suggestions for writing higher-level multiple-choice items include use of the following:

- Pictorial, graphical, or tabular stimuli.
- Analogies that demonstrate relationships among items.
- Previously learned principles or procedures.

11. The following are suggestions for writing completion items:

- Require a single-word answer.
- Pose the question or problem in a brief, definite statement.
- Check to be sure that an accurate response can be found in the text, workbook, or class notes.
- Omit only one or two key words.
- Word the statement so the blank is near the end.
- If the question requires a numerical answer, indicate the units in which the answer is to be expressed.

12. An *extended response* essay item allows the student to determine the length and complexity of a response.

13. A *restricted response* essay item poses a specific problem for which the student must recall and organize the proper information, derive a defensible conclusion, and express it within a stated time or length.

14. Essay items are most appropriate when (1) the instructional objectives specify high-level cognitive processes, (2) relatively few test items (students) need to be graded, and (3) test security is a consideration.

15. Suggestions for writing essay items include the following:

- Identify beforehand the mental processes that you want to measure (for example, application, analysis, decision making).
- Identify clearly and unambiguously the task to be accomplished by the student.
- Begin the essay question with key words, such as *compare, give reasons for, predict*.
- Require presentation of evidence for controversial questions.
- Avoid optional items.
- Establish reasonable time and/or page limits.
- Restrict the use of essay items to those that cannot easily be measured by multiple-choice items.
- Relate each essay question to an objective on the test blueprint.

16. The following are suggestions for increasing consistency and accuracy when scoring essay items:

- Specifying the response length.
- Use several restricted response essay items instead of one extended response item.
- Prepare a scoring scheme in which you specify beforehand all ingredients necessary to achieve each of the grades that could be assigned.

17. Some suggestions for packaging the test are as follows:

- Group together all items of similar format.
- Arrange test items from easy to hard.
- Space items for easy reading.
- Keep items and options on the same page.
- Position illustrations near descriptions.
- Check the answer key.
- Determine beforehand how students are to record the answers.
- Provide space for name and date.
- Check test directions for clarity.
- Proofread the test.

18. Validity refers to whether a test measures what it says it measures. Three types of validity are content, concurrent, and predictive.

19. *Content* validity is established by examining a test's contents. *Concurrent* validity is established by correlating the scores on a new test with the scores on an established test given to the same set of individuals. *Predictive* validity is established by correlating the scores on a new test with some future behavior of the examinee that is representative of the test's content.

20. Reliability refers to whether a test yields the same or similar scores consistently. Three types of reliability are test-retest, alternative form, and internal consistency.

21. *Test-retest* reliability is established by giving the test twice to the same individuals and correlating the first set of scores with the second. *Alternative form* reliability is established by giving two parallel but different forms of the test to the same individuals and correlating the two sets of scores. *Internal consistency* reliability is established by determining the extent to which the test measures a single basic concept.

22. Accuracy refers to whether a test approximates an individual's true level of knowledge, skill, or ability.

23. Marks are based on comparisons, usually comparisons of students with one or more of the following:

- Other students
- Established standards
- Aptitude
- Actual versus potential effort
- Actual versus potential improvement

24. Standardized tests are developed by test-construction specialists to determine a student's performance level relative to others of similar age and grade. They are *standardized* because they are administered and scored according to specific and uniform procedures.

25. The following assumptions are likely to guide the development of standardized tests in the future:

- Learning is a process.
- Learning ability can be improved.
- Learning occurs in a social context.
- Learning assessment should have instructional validity.

*1. Identify the characteristics of a norm-referenced and criterion-referenced test and the decisions for which each is best suited.

*2. What two instructional dimensions are measured by a test blueprint?

*3. Identify four formats for objective test items and give two advantages and two disadvantages of each.

*4. Identify four impediments to writing good multiple-choice test items.

*5. What three devices may be used to prepare multiple-choice questions at higher levels of cognitive complexity?

*6. Contrast the characteristics of extended response and restricted response essay items. Prepare an example of each in your teaching field.

*7. Identify three reasons for preparing an essay as opposed to objective test.

*8. Describe three advantages and three disadvantages of essay items.

*9. What is a "scoring scheme" for an essay item? Construct a scoring scheme for each of the essay items you prepared in question 6.

*10. Identify six possible criteria for scoring higher-level essay items.

*11. Identify ten guidelines for packaging a test.

*12. Define the concepts of validity, reliability, and accuracy.

*13. What three methods may be used to determine the validity of a test? Give an example of what information each would provide for a test given in your classroom.

*14. What three methods may be used for determining the reliability of a test? Give an example of what information each would provide for a test given in your classroom.

*15. Provide an approximate range for an acceptable validity and acceptable reliability coefficient. What is the maximum possible size of a validity or reliability coefficient?

*16. Identify five procedures for assigning marks and one advantage and one disadvantage of each.

*17. What is a standardized test?

*18. What does a percentile rank indicate for a given individual? What two points should be kept in mind in interpreting a percentile rank?

---

* Answers to asterisked questions (*) in this and the other chapters are in Appendix B.

Suggested Readings

Coker, D. (1988). Improving essay tests: Structuring the items and scoring responses. *Clearing House, 61*(6), 253–255.

   Some well-proven tips for writing effective essay items.

Gronlund, N., & Linn, R. (1995). *Measurement and assessment in teaching (7th ed.).* Englewood Cliffs, NJ: Merrill/Prentice Hall.

   A comprehensive guide for constructing classroom tests, including extensive coverage of both multiple-choice and essay items.

Kubiszyn, T., & Borich, G. (1996). *Educational testing and measurement: Classroom applications and practice* (5th ed.). New York: HarperCollins.

   A practical introductory text on testing and measurement in the classroom prepared especially for the beginning teacher.

Lyman, H. (1991). *Test scores and what they mean.* Englewood Cliffs, NJ: Prentice Hall.

   Emphasizes the practical use and interpretation of test scores from the teacher's perspective.

Mehrens, W., & Lehmann, I. (1987). *Using standardized tests in education* (4th ed.). New York: Holt, Rinehart & Winston.

   Covers the basic issues of proper use and interpretation of standardized tests that are of primary concern to teachers, parents, and administrators.

Popham, W. (1990). *Modern educational measurement*. Englewood Cliffs, NJ: Prentice Hall.

A thorough discussion of criterion-referenced tests and how to use them in your classroom.

Thorndike, R. M., Cunningham, G. K., Thorndike, R. L., & Hagen, E. P. (1991). *Measurement and evaluation in psychology and education (5th ed.)*. Englewood Cliffs, NJ: Merrill/Prentice Hall.

This text devotes extensive coverage to planning, classroom tests, and rules for writing a variety of test items. It also has a thorough treatment of standardized tests.

CHAPTER 15

Assessing Learners:
Performance Assessment

1. What is a performance test?
2. How are some teachers conducting performance assessments?
3. Can performance tests measure noncognitive outcomes?
4. What are some examples of performance objectives?
5. What types of tasks should I select for a performance test?
6. How do I score a performance test reliably?
7. What limitations should I place on learners during a performance test?
8. What is a student portfolio?
9. How can I combine performance test grades with other classroom grades?

This chapter will also help you learn the meaning of the following:

complex cognitive processes
habits of mind
holistic scoring
multimodal assessment
observable performance
performance objectives
performance testing
portfolio assessment
primary trait scoring
rubrics
testing constraints

I n Chapter 4 (Instructional Objectives), you learned of a variety of skills that children acquire in school. Some of these require learners to acquire information by memorizing vocabulary, multiplication tables, dates of historical events, and so on. Other skills involve learning action sequences or procedures to follow when performing mathematical computations, dissecting a frog, focusing a microscope, handwriting, or typing. In addition, you learned that students must acquire concepts, rules, and generalizations that allow them to understand what they read, to analyze and solve problems, carry out experiments, write poems and essays, and design projects to study historical, political, or economic problems.

Some of these skills are best assessed with paper and pencil tests. But, other skills—particularly those involving independent judgment, critical thinking, and decision making—are best assessed with performance tests. Although paper and pencil tests currently represent the principal means of assessing these more complex cognitive outcomes, in this chapter we will study other ways of measuring them in more authentic contexts.

>>> PERFORMANCE TESTS: <<< DIRECT MEASURES OF COMPETENCE

What is a performance test?

In Chapter 14 you learned that many educational tests measure learning indirectly. That is, they ask questions whose responses *indicate* that something has been learned or mastered. **Performance tests**, on the other hand, use direct measures of learning, rather than indicators that simply suggest cognitive, affective, or psychomotor processes have taken place. In the field of athletics, diving and gymnastics are examples of performances judges rate directly. Their scores are pooled and used to decide who, for example, earns a medal, who wins first, second, third, and so on, or who qualifies for district or regional competition. Likewise, at band contests judges directly see and hear the competence of trombone or

---

This chapter was prepared with Martin L. Tombari. Portions appear in G. Borich & M. Tombari, *Educational Psychology: A Contemporary Approach*, New York: HarperCollins, 1995.

violin players and pool their ratings to decide who makes the state or district band and who gets the leading chairs.

Teachers can use performance tests to assess **complex cognitive processes**, as well as attitudes and social skills in academic areas such as science, social studies, or math. When doing so, they establish situations that allow them directly to observe and to rate learners as they analyze, problem-solve, experiment, make decisions, measure, cooperate with others, present orally, or produce a product. These situations simulate real-world activities, as might be expected in a job, in the community, or in various forms of advanced training, for example, in the military, a technical institute, on the job training, or college.

Performance tests also allow teachers to observe achievements, habits of mind, ways of working, and behaviors of value in the real world that conventional tests may miss, and do so in ways that an outside observer would be unaware that a "test" is going on. Performance tests can include observing and rating learners as they carry out a dialogue in a foreign language, conduct a science experiment, edit a composition, present an exhibit, work with a group of other learners to design a student attitude survey, or use equipment. In other words, the teacher observes and evaluates student abilities to carry out complex activities that also are used and valued outside the immediate confines of the classroom.

Performance Tests Can Assess Processes and Products

Performance tests can be assessments of processes, products, or both. For example, at the Darwin School in Winnipeg, Manitoba, teachers assess the reading processes of each student by noting the percentage of words read accurately during oral reading, the number of sentences read by the learner that are meaningful within the context of the story, and the percentage of story elements the learner can talk about in his or her own words after reading.

How are some teachers conducting performance assessments?

At the West Orient school in Gresham, Oregon, fourth-grade learners assemble a portfolio of their writing products. These portfolios include rough as well as final drafts of poetry, essays, biographies, and self-reflections. Several math teachers at Twin Peaks Middle School in Poway, California, require their students to assemble math portfolios, which include the following products of their problem-solving efforts: long-term projects, daily notes, journal entries about troublesome test problems, written explanations of how they solved problems, and the problem solutions themselves.

Teachers at the Darwin School in Winnepeg, Canada, assess the reading processes of each student by noting the percentage of words read accurately during oral reading, the number of sentences the learner reads that are meaningful within the context of the story, and the percentage of story elements the learner can talk about in her or his own words after reading.

Social studies learning processes and products are assessed in the Aurora, Colorado, Public Schools by having learners engage in a variety of projects built around the following question: "Based on your study of Colorado history, what current issues in Colorado do you believe are the most important to address, what are your ideas about the resolutions of those issues, and what contributions will you make toward the resolutions?" (Pollock, 1992). Learners answer these questions in a variety of ways involving individual and group writing assignments, oral presentations, and exhibits.

Performance Tests can be Embedded in Lessons

The preceding examples of performance tests involved performances that occurred outside the context of a lesson and that were completed at the end of a term or during an examination period. Many teachers use performance tests as part of their lessons. In fact, some proponents of performance tests hold that the ideal performance test is a good teaching activity (Shavelson & Baxter, 1992). Viewed from this perspective, a well-constructed performance test can serve as a student learning experience as well as an assessment.

For example, Figure 15.1 illustrates a performance activity and assessment that was embedded in a unit on electricity in a general science class (Shavelson & Baxter, 1992). During the activity, the teacher observes and rates the learners on the method they used to solve the problem, the care with which they measured, the manner

HANDS-ON ELECTRIC MYSTERIES INVESTIGATION

Find out what is in the six mystery boxes A, B, C, D, E, and F. They have five different things inside, shown below. Two of the boxes will have the same thing. All of the others will have something different inside.

Two batteries:

A wire:

A bulb:

A battery and a bulb:

Nothing at all:

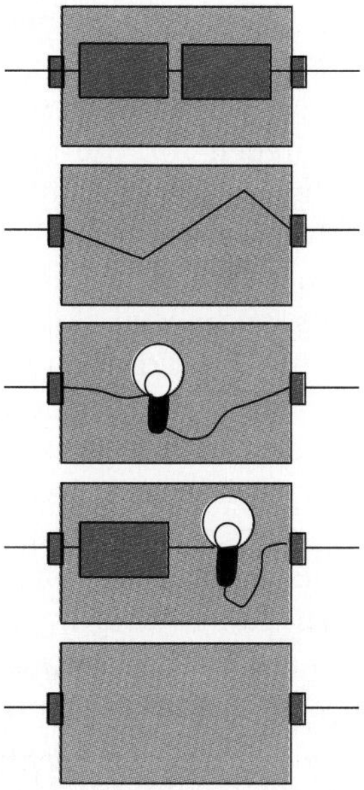

You can use your bulbs, batteries, and wires any way you like. Connect them in a circuit to help you figure out what is inside.

When you find out what is in the box, fill in the spaces on the following pages.

Box A: Has _____ inside.

Draw a picture of the circuit that told you what was inside **Box A**.

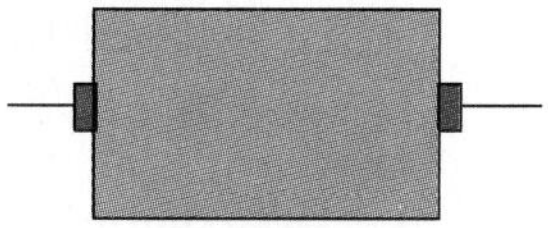

How could you tell from your circuit what was inside **Box A.**

_____

_____

_____

Do the same for Boxes B, C, D, E, and F.

_____

_____

Figure 15.1

Sample performance activity and assessment

From Shavelson, R. J., & Baxter, G. P. What we've learned about assessing hands-on science. *Educational Leadership*, 1992, 49(8), p. 22. Alexandria, VA: Association for Supervision and Curriculum Development. Copyright © 1992 by ASCD. Used with permission.

of recording results, and the correctness of the final solution. This type of assessment provides immediate feedback on how learners are performing, reinforces hands-on teaching and learning, and underscores for learners the important link between teaching and testing. In this manner, it moves the instruction toward higher-order and more authentic behavior.

Other examples of lesson-embedded performance tests might include observing and rating the following as they actually happen: typing, preparing a microscope slide, reading out loud, programming a calculator, giving an oral presentation, determining how plants react to certain substances, designing a questionnaire or survey, solving a math problem, developing an original math problem and a solution for it, critiquing the logic of an editorial, or graphing information.

Performance Tests Can Assess Affective and Social Skills

Can performance tests measure noncognitive outcomes?

Teachers across the country are using performance tests not only to assess higher-level cognitive skills but also noncognitive outcomes such as self-direction, ability to work with others, and social awareness (Redding, 1992). This concern for the affective domain of learning reflects an awareness by educators that the skilled performance of complex tasks involves more than the ability to recall information, form concepts, generalize, and problem-solve. It also involves habits of mind, attitudes, and social skills.

The Aurora Public Schools in Colorado has developed a list of learning outcomes and their indicators for learners in kindergarten through 12th grade. These are shown in Figure 15.2. For each of these 19 indicators a four-category rating scale has been developed to serve as a guide for teachers who are unsure of how to define "assumes responsibility" or "demonstrates consideration." While observing learners during performance tests in social studies, science, art, or economics, teachers are alert to recognize and rate those behaviors that suggest learners have acquired the outcomes.

Teachers in the Aurora Public Schools are encouraged to use this list of outcomes when planning their courses. They first ask themselves, What key facts, concepts, and principles should all learners remember? In addition, they try to fuse this subject area content with the five district outcomes by designing special performance tests. For example, a third-grade language arts teacher who is planning a writing unit might choose to focus on indicators 8 and 9 to address district outcomes related to "collaborative worker," indicator 1 for the outcome of "self-directed learner," and 13 for the outcome, "quality producer." She would then design a performance assessment that allows learners

Figure 15.2

Learning outcomes of Aurora Public Schools

From *Curriculum Report*, Aurora Public Schools, Aurora, Colorado, 1993, p. 11.

A Self-Directed Learner

1. Sets priorities and achievable goals.
2. Monitors and evaluates progress.
3. Creates options for self.
4. Assumes responsibility for actions.
5. Creates a positive vision for self and future.

A Collaborative Worker

6. Monitors own behavior as a group member.
7. Assesses and manages group functioning.
8. Demonstrates interactive communication.
9. Demonstrates consideration for individual differences.

A Complex Thinker

10. Uses a wide variety of strategies for managing complex issues.
11. Selects strategies appropriate to the resolution of complex issues and applies the strategies with accuracy and thoroughness.
12. Accesses and uses topic-relevant knowledge.

A Quality Producer

13. Creates products that achieve their purpose.
14. Creates products appropriate to the intended audience.
15. Creates products that reflect craftsmanship.
16. Uses appropriate resources/technology.

A Community Contributor

17. Demonstrates knowledge about his or her diverse communities.
18. Takes action.
19. Reflects on his or her role as a community contributor.

to demonstrate learning in these areas. She might select other indicators and outcomes for subsequent units and performance tests.

Performance tests represent an addition to the testing practices reviewed in the previous chapter. Paper and pencil tests are the most efficient, reliable, and valid instruments available for assessing knowledge, comprehension, and some types of application. But, when it comes to assessing complex thinking skills, attitudes, and social skills, performance tests can, if properly constructed, do a better job. On the other hand, if not properly constructed, performance assessments can have some of the same problems with authenticity, scoring efficiency, reliability, and validity as traditional approaches to testing.

Stiggins (1994) emphasizes that performance assessments of affect must adhere to the same standards of evaluation and scoring as assessments of achievement, or the results may prove too subjective and inferential to be of value. This chapter will guide you through a process that will allow you to properly construct performance tests in your classroom.

>>> DEVELOPING PERFORMANCE <<< TESTS FOR YOUR LEARNERS

As we learned in the previous section, performance assessment has the potential to improve both instruction and learning. But, as we have also learned, there are both conceptual and technical issues associated with the use of performance tests that teachers must resolve before performance assessments can be effectively and efficiently used. In this section we will discuss four steps to consider in planning and designing a performance test, shown in Figure 15.3. We will identify the tasks around which you may base performance tests, and how to score these tasks. Also, we will suggest how to improve the reliability of performance test scoring, including evaluation of portfolios.

Step 1. Deciding What to Test

The first step in developing a performance test is to create a list of **performance objectives** that specifies the knowledge, skills, attitudes, and indicators of the outcomes that will be the focus of your instruction.

There are three general questions to ask when deciding what to teach:

- What knowledge or content (i.e., facts, concepts, principles, rules) is essential for learner understanding of the subject matter?
- What intellectual skills are necessary for the learner to use this knowledge or content?
- What habits of mind or attitudes are important for the learner to successfully perform with this knowledge or content?

What are some examples of performance objectives?

Instructional objectives that come from answering question one are usually measured by paper and pencil tests (discussed in Chapter 14). Objectives derived from answering questions two and three, although often assessed with objective or essay-type questions, can be more authentically assessed with performance tests. Thus, your

Figure 15.3
Steps for developing a performance test

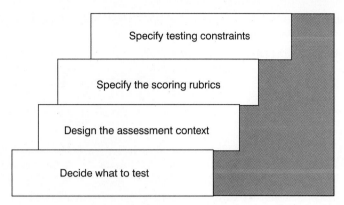

Specify testing constraints

Specify the scoring rubrics

Design the assessment context

Decide what to test

assessment plan for a unit should include both paper and pencil tests to measure mastery of content and performance tests to assess skills and attitudes. Let's see what objectives for these latter outcomes might look like.

Performance Objectives in the Cognitive Domain. Designers of performance tests usually ask the following questions to help guide their initial selection of objectives:

- What kinds of essential tasks, achievements, or other valued competencies am I missing with paper and pencil tests?
- What accomplishments of those who practice my discipline (historians, writers, scientists, mathematicians) are valued but left unmeasured by conventional tests?

Typically two categories of performance skills are identified from such questions:

1. Skills related to acquiring information
2. Skills related to organizing and using information

Figure 15.4 presents a list of skills useful for acquiring, organizing, and using information. As you study this list, consider which you might use as a basis for a performance test in your area of expertise.

The following are sample objectives for performance tests derived from a consideration of the performance skills described in Figure 15.4.

1. Write a summary of a current controversy drawn from school life and tell how a courageous and civic-minded American you have studied might decide to act on the issue.

Figure 15.4
Skills for acquiring, organizing, and using information

Skills in acquiring information	Skills in organizing and using information
Communicating explaining modeling demonstrating graphing displaying writing advising programming proposing drawing **Measuring** counting calibrating rationing appraising weighing balancing guessing estimating forecasting **Investigating** gathering references interviewing using references experimenting hypothesizing	**Organizing** classifying categorizing sorting ordering ranking arranging **Problem Solving** stating questions identifying problems developing hypotheses interpreting assessing risks monitoring **Decision Making** weighing alternatives evaluating choosing supporting defending electing adopting

2. Draw a physical map of North America from memory and locate 10 cities.
3. Prepare an exhibit showing how your community responds to an important social problem of your choosing.
4. Construct an electrical circuit using wires, a switch, a bulb, resistors, and a battery.
5. Describe two alternative ways to solve a mathematics word problem.
6. Identify the important variables that accounted for recent events in our state, and forecast the direction they might take.

7. Design a freestanding structure in which the size of one leg of a triangular structure must be determined from the other two sides.
8. Program a calculator to solve an equation with one unknown.
9. Design an exhibit showing the best ways to clean up an oil spill.
10. Prepare a presentation to the city council using visuals requesting increased funding to deal with a selected problem in our community.

Performance Objectives in the Affective and Social Domains.   Performance assessments not only require curriculum to teach thinking skills but also to develop positive dispositions and "habits of mind." **Habits of mind** include such behaviors as constructive criticism, tolerance of ambiguity, respect for reason, and appreciation for the significance of the past. Performance tests are ideal vehicles for assessing positive attitudes toward learning, habits of mind, and social skills (for example, cooperation, sharing, and negotiation). The following are key questions to ask when including affective and social skills in your list of performance objectives:

- What dispositions, attitudes, or values characterize successful individuals in the community who work in my academic discipline?
- What are some of the qualities of mind or character traits of good scientists, writers, reporters, historians, mathematicians, musicians, and others?
- What will I accept as evidence that my learners have or are developing these qualities?
- What social skills for getting along with others are necessary for being successful as a journalist, weather forecaster, park ranger, historian, economist, mechanic, and so on?
- What evidence will convince my learners' parents that their children are developing these skills?

Following are examples of attitudes, or habits of mind, which could be the focus of a performance assessment in science, social studies, and mathematics.

In science (from Loucks-Horsley et al., 1990, *Elementary School Science for the '90's*, p. 41):

□ Desiring knowledge. Viewing science as a way of knowing and understanding.

☐ Being skeptical. Recognizing the appropriate time and place to question authoritarian statements and "self-evident truths."

☐ Relying on data. Explaining natural occurrences by collecting and ordering information, testing ideas, and respecting the facts that are revealed.

☐ Accepting ambiguity. Recognizing that data are rarely clear and compelling, and appreciating the new questions and problems that arise.

☐ Willingness to modify explanations. Seeing new possibilities in the data.

☐ Cooperating in answering questions and solving problems. Working together to pool ideas, explanations, and solutions.

☐ Respecting reason. Valuing patterns of thought that lead from data to conclusions and, eventually, to the construction of theories.

☐ Being honest, Viewing information objectively, without bias.

In social studies (from Parker, 1991, *Renewing the Social Studies Curriculum*, p. 74):

☐ Understanding the significance of the past to their own lives, both private and public, and to their society.

☐ Distinguishing between the important and inconsequential to develop the "discriminating memory" needed for a discerning judgment in public and personal life.

☐ Preparing to live with uncertainties and exasperating, even perilous, unfinished business, realizing that not all problems have solutions.

☐ Appreciating the often tentative nature of judgments about the past, and thereby avoiding the temptation to seize on particular "lessons" of history as cures for present ills.

In mathematics (from Willoughby, 1990, *Mathematics Education for a Changing World*, p. 62):

☐ Appreciating that mathematics is a discipline that helps solve real-world problems.

☐ Seeing mathematics as a tool or servant rather than something mysterious or mystical to be afraid of.

☐ Recognizing that there is more than one way to solve a problem.

Once you have completed step one, you will have identified the important knowledge, skills, and attitudes that will be the focus of your instruction and assessment. The next step is to design the task or context in which you will assess these outcomes.

Step 2. Designing the Assessment Context

First, and most obviously, you must identify and define the specific directly **observable performance** that will tell you whether you have achieved your instructional objectives. The purpose of step two is to create an authentic task, simulation, or situation that will allow learners to demonstrate their acquired knowledge, skills, and attitudes. Ideas for these tasks may come from newspapers, reading popular books, or interviews with professionals as reported in the media (for example, an oil tanker runs aground and creates an environmental crisis, a drought occurs in an underdeveloped country causing famine, a technological breakthrough presents a moral dilemma). The tasks should center on issues, concepts, or problems important to your subject matter. In other words, they should be the same issues, concepts, and problems that professionals in the field face everyday.

Here are some questions to get you started on step two, suggested by Wiggins (1992):

- What does the doing of mathematics, history, science, art, writing, and so forth look and feel like to professionals who make their living working in these fields in the real world?
- What are the projects and tasks performed by these professionals that can be adapted to school instruction?
- What are the roles—or habits of mind—that these professionals acquire that learners can recreate in the classroom?

The tasks you create may involve debates, mock trials, presentations to a city commission, re-enactments of historical events, science experiments, job responsibilities (for example, a travel agent, weather forecaster, park ranger), or other scenarios. Regardless of the specific context, they should present the learner with an authentic challenge.

For example, consider the following social studies performance test item (adapted from Wiggins, 1992).

> You and several travel agent colleagues have been assigned the responsibility of designing a trip to China for 12- to 14-year-olds. Prepare an extensive brochure for a monthlong cultural exchange trip. Include itinerary, modes of transportation, costs, suggested budget, clothing, health considerations, areas of cultural sensitivity, language considerations, and other information necessary for a family to decide if they want their child to participate.

Notice that this example presents learners with (1) a hands-on exercise or problem to solve that produces (2) an observable outcome or product (typed business letter, a map, graph, piece of clothing, multi-media presentation, poem, etc.), such that the teacher (3) can observe and assess not only the product but also the process used to get there.

What types of tasks should I select for a performance test?

Designing the content for a performance test involves equal parts inspiration and perspiration. While there is no formula or recipe to follow that guarantees a valid performance test, the following criteria can help you in revising and refining the task (Wiggins, 1992; Resnick & Resnick, 1991).

Make clear the requirements for task mastery, but not the solution itself. While your tasks should be complex, learners should not have to question whether they are finished, or whether they have provided what you want. They should, however, have to think long and hard about how to complete the task. As you refine the task, make sure you can visualize what mastery of the task looks like and identify the skills you can infer from it.

The task should represent a valid sample from which you can make generalizations about the learner's knowledge, thinking ability, and attitudes. What performance tests lack in breadth of coverage, they make up in depth. In other words, they get you to observe a lot of behavior in a narrow domain or skill. Thus, the type of tasks you choose should be complex enough and rich enough in detail to allow you to draw conclusions about transfer and generalization to other tasks. Ideally, you should be able to identify about 8 to 10 important performance tasks for an entire course of study (one or two a unit) that assess the essential performance outcomes you wish your learners to achieve (Shavelson & Baxter, 1992).

The task should be complex enough to allow for multimodal assessment. Most assessment tends to depend on the written word. Performance tests, however, are designed to allow learners to demonstrate learning through a variety of modalities. In science, for example, you could make direct observations of students while they investigate a problem using laboratory equipment, have students give oral explanations of what they did, require them to record procedures and conclusions in notebooks, prepare an exhibit of their project, and solve short-answer paper and pencil problems. This **multimodal assessment** will be more time consuming than a multiple-choice test only, but will provide unique information about your learners' achievement untapped by other assessment methods. Shavelson and Baxter (1992) have shown that performance tests allow teachers to draw different conclusions about a learner's problem-solving ability than do higher-order multiple-choice tests or restricted response essay tests that ask learners to analyze, interpret, and evaluate information.

The task should yield multiple solutions where possible, each with costs and benefits. Performance testing is not a form of practice or drill. It should involve more than simple tasks for which there is one solution. Performance tests should be, in the words of Resnick (1987), nonalgorithmic (the path of action is not fully specified in advance), and complex (the total solution cannot be seen from any one vantage point), and should involve judgment and interpretation.

The task should require self-regulated learning. Performance tests should require considerable mental effort and place high demands on the persistence and determination of the individual learner. The learner should be required to use cognitive strategies to arrive at a solution rather than depend on coaching at various points in the assessment process.

Figures 15.5, 15.6, and 15.7 illustrate performance assessments containing most of these design considerations.

Step 3. Specifying the Scoring Rubrics

One of the principal limitations of performance tests is the time required to score them reliably. Just as these tests require time and effort on the part of the learner, they demand similar commitment from teachers when scoring them. True-false, multiple-choice, and fill-in tests are significantly easier to score than projects, portfolios, or performances. In addition, these latter accomplishments force teachers to make difficult choices over how to weigh in the final score affective qualities such as effort, participation, and attitude.

Given the challenges confronting teachers who use performance tests, there is a temptation to limit the scoring criteria to those performance qualities that are easiest to rate, rather than those most important for doing an effective job. Wiggins (1992) cautions teachers that resorting to scoring what is easiest or least controversial can turn a well-thought-out and authentic performance test into a bogus one. Thus, your goal when scoring performance tests is to do justice to the time spent developing them and the effort expended by students taking them. You can accomplish this by developing carefully articulated scoring systems, called **rubrics**.

By giving careful consideration to rubrics, you can develop a scoring system that minimizes the arbitrariness of your judgments while holding learners to high standards of achievement. Let's look at some important considerations for developing rubrics for a performance test.

How do I score a performance test reliably?

Joe, Sarah, José, Zabi, and Kim decided to hold their own Olympics after watching the Olympics on TV. They needed to decide what events to have at their Olympics. Joe and José wanted a weightlifting and frisbee toss event. Sarah, Zabi, and Kim thought a running event would be fun. The children decided to have all three events. They also decided to make each event of the same importance.

One day after school they held their Olympics. The children's mothers were the judges. The mothers kept the children's scores on each of the events.

The children's scores and rankings for each of the events are listed below:

Child's Name	Frisbee Toss	Weightlifting	50-Yard Dash
Joe	40 yards (3)	205 pounds (1)	9–5 seconds (5)
José	30 yards (4)	170 pounds (2)	8–0 seconds (2)
Kim	45 yards (2)	130 pounds (4)	9–0 seconds (4)
Sarah	28 yards (5)	120 pounds (5)	7–6 seconds (1)
Zabi	48 yards (1)	140 pounds (3)	8–3 seconds (3)

Answer the question, "Who Won the Olympics?" and give an explanation of how you arrived at your answer (4 points). Sample responses:

Student A

Who would be the all-round winner?

Zabi

Explain how you decided who would be the all-round winner. Be sure to show all your work.

I decided by how each person came in and that's who won   2

Student B

Who would be the all-round winner?

Zabi

Explain how you decided who would be the all-round winner. Be sure to show all your work.

I wrote in order all the rankings from first place to fifth place. Then I averaged them, and whoever had the least amount, won.   3

Student C

Who would be the all-round winner?

Zabi

Explain how you decided who would be the all-round winner. Be sure to show all your work.

Zabi got one first and 2 thirds. I counted 3 points for every first place they got and 2 points for second place and 1 point for third place. Zabi got the most points.   4

Figure 15.5
Performance assessment: Math

Adapted from Blumberg, E., Epstein, M., MacDonald, W., & Mullis, I., 1986. *A pilot study of higher-order thinking skills assessment techniques in science and mathematics (Final Report)*. Princeton, NJ: National Assessment of Educational Process.

Figure 15.6
Performance assessment: Communication

From Redding, N. Assessing the Big Outcomes, *Educational Leadership*, May, 1992, p. 49. Alexandria, VA: Association for Supervision and Curriculum Development. Copyright © 1992 by ASCD. Used with permission.

1. You are representing an ad agency. Your job is to find a client in the school who needs photos to promote his/her program. (Examples: the Team Mothers' program, the fine arts program, Student Congress.)

2. Your job is to research all the possibilities, select a program, learn about that program, and then record on film the excitement and unique characteristics that make up the program you have selected. Your photos will be used to advertise and stimulate interest in that area.

3. Previsualize how you will illustrate your ideas by either writing descriptions or by drawing six of your proposed frames. Present these six ideas to your instructor (the director of the ad agency) before you shoot.

Figure 15.7
Performance Assessment: History

From Wiggins. G. Creating Tests Worth Taking, In *Educational Leadership*, May, 1992, p. 28. Alexandria, VA: Association for Supervision and Curriculum Development. Used with permission.

You and your colleagues (groups of 3 or 4) have been asked to submit a proposal to write a U.S. history textbook for middle school students. The publishers demand two things: that the book hit the most important things, and that it be interesting to students. Because of your expertise in 18th-century American history, you will provide them a draft chapter on the 18th century, up to but not including the Revolution, and "field-tested" on some middle school students. They also ask that you fill in an "importance" chart with your response to these questions:

1. Which event, person, or idea is more important in this time period, and why?

2. Which of three sources of history—ideas, people, events—is most important?

You will be expected to justify your choices of "most important" and to demonstrate that the target population will likely be interested in your book.

Develop rubrics for a variety of accomplishments. In general, performance tests require four types of accomplishments from learners:

Products:	Poems, essays, charts, graphs, exhibits, drawings, maps, etc.
Complex cognitive processes:	Skills in acquiring, organizing, and using information (see Figure 15.4)

Observable performance:	Physical movements as in dance, gymnastics, or typing; oral presentations; use of specialized equipment as in focusing a microscope; following a set of procedures as when dissecting a frog, bisecting an angle, or following a recipe
Attitudes and social skills:	Habits of mind; group work and recognition skills

As this list suggests, the effect of your teaching may be realized in a variety of ways. The difficulty in scoring some of these accomplishments should not be a deterrent to your attempts to measure them. Kubiszyn and Borich (1996), Shavelson and Baxter (1992), Stiggins (1994), and Sax (1989) have shown that performance measures can be scored reliably, depending on the care with which they are developed and the training of those doing the scoring.

Choose a scoring system best suited for the type of accomplishment you want to measure. In general, there are three categories of rubrics to use when scoring performance tests: checklists, rating scales, and holistic scoring. Each has certain strengths and limitations and each is more or less suitable for scoring products, cognitive processes, performances, or attitudes and social skills.

Checklists.   Checklists contain lists of behaviors, traits, or characteristics that can be scored as either present or absent. They are best suited for complex behaviors or performances divisible into a series of clearly defined, specific actions. Dissecting a frog, bisecting an angle, balancing a scale, making an audiotape recording, or tying a shoe are behaviors requiring sequences of actions that may be clearly identified and listed on a checklist. Checklists are scored on a yes/no, present or absent, 0 or 1 point basis, and also should provide the opportunity for observers to indicate that they had no opportunity to observe the performance. Some checklists also include frequent mistakes that learners make when performing the task. In such cases, a score of +1 may be given for each positive behavior, –1 for each mistake, and 0 for no opportunity to observe. Figure 15.8 shows a checklist for using a microscope.

Rating Scales.   Rating scales are typically used for those aspects of a complex performance that do not lend themselves to yes/no or present/absent type judgments. The most common form of rating scale assigns numbers to categories of performance. Figure 15.9 shows a rating scale for judging elements of writing in a term paper. This

Figure 15.8

Checklist for using a microscope

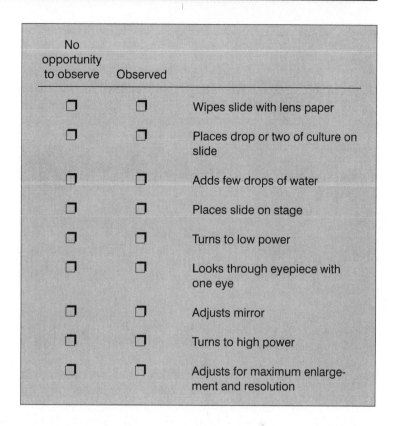

No opportunity to observe	Observed	
☐	☐	Wipes slide with lens paper
☐	☐	Places drop or two of culture on slide
☐	☐	Adds few drops of water
☐	☐	Places slide on stage
☐	☐	Turns to low power
☐	☐	Looks through eyepiece with one eye
☐	☐	Adjusts mirror
☐	☐	Turns to high power
☐	☐	Adjusts for maximum enlargement and resolution

scale focuses the rater's observations on certain aspects of the performance (accuracy, logic, organization, style, etc.) and assigns numbers to five degrees of performance.

Most numeric rating scales use an analytical scoring technique called **primary trait scoring** (Sax, 1989). This type of rating requires that the test developer first identify the salient characteristics or primary traits of greatest importance when observing the product, process, or performance. Then, for each trait, the developer assigns numbers (usually 1–5) representing degrees of performance.

Figure 15.10 displays a numerical rating scale using primary trait scoring to rate problem solving (Szetela & Nicol, 1992). In this system, problem solving is subdivided into the three primary traits of understanding, solving, and answering the problem. Points are assigned to certain aspects or qualities of each trait. Notice how the designer of this rating scale identified characteristics of both effective and ineffective problem solving.

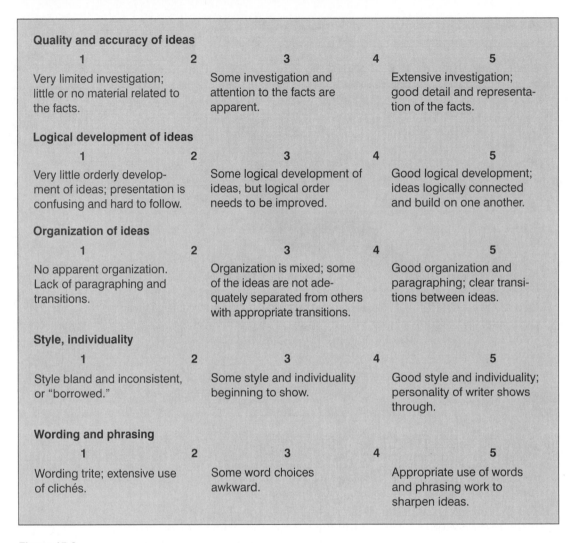

Figure 15.9
Rating scale for themes and term papers that emphasizes interpretation and organization

Usually, two key questions are addressed when planning scoring systems for rating scales using primary trait scoring (Wiggins, 1992):

1. What are the most important characteristics that show a high degree of the trait?
2. What errors most justify achieving a lower score?

Figure 15.10

Analytic scale for problem solving

From Szetela, W., & Nicol, C. Evaluating problem solving in mathematics. *Educational Leadership,* 1992, 49(8), p. 42. Alexandria, VA: Association for Supervision and Curriculum Development. Copyright © 1992 by ASCD. Used with permission.

Understanding the problem

0 — No attempt
1 — Completely misinterprets the problem
2 — Misinterprets major part of the problem
3 — Misinterprets minor part of the problem
4 — Complete understanding of the problem

Solving the problem

0 — No attempt
1 — Totally inappropriate plan
2 — Partially correct procedure but with major fault
3 — Substantially correct procedure with major omission or procedural error
4 — A plan that could lead to a correct solution with no arithmetic errors

Answering the problem

0 — No answer or wrong answer based upon an inappropriate plan
1 — Copying error, computational error, partial answer for problem with multiple answers; no answer statement; answer labeled incorrectly
2 — Correct solution

Answering these questions can prevent raters from assigning higher or lower scores on the basis of performance that may be trivial or unrelated to the purpose of the performance test, such as the quantity rather than quality of a performance. One advantage of rating scales is that they focus the scorer on specific and relevant aspects of a performance. Without the breakdown of important traits, successes, and relevant errors provided by these scales, a scorer's attention may be diverted to aspects of performance unrelated to the purpose of the performance test.

Holistic Scoring.   **Holistic scoring** is used when the rater is more interested in estimating the overall quality of the performance and assigning a numerical value to that quality than in assigning points for including or omitting a specific aspect of performance. Holistic scoring is typically used in evaluating extended essays, term papers, and some artistic performances, such as dance or musical creations.

For example, a rater might decide to score an extended essay question or term paper on an A to F rating scale, in which case it would be important for the rater to have a model paper that exemplifies each score category. After having created or selected these models from the set to be scored, the rater again reads each paper and then assigns it to one of the categories. A model for each category (A–F) helps to ensure that all the papers assigned to a given category are of comparable quality.

Holistic scoring systems can be more difficult to use for performances than for products. For the former, some experience in rating the performance, for example, dramatic rendition, oral interpretations, debate, etc. may be required. In these cases, audio- or videotapes from past classes can be helpful as models representing different categories of performance.

Combining Scoring Systems. As suggested above, good performance tests require learners to demonstrate their achievements through a variety of primary traits, for example, cooperation, research, and delivery. You may therefore need to combine several ratings from checklists, rating scales, and holistic impressions to arrive at a total assessment. Figure 15.11 shows how scores across several traits for a current events project might combine to provide a single performance score.

Comparing the Three Scoring Systems. Each of the three scoring systems has its particular strengths and weaknesses. Table 15.1 evaluates each scoring system as suitable for a given type of performance, according to the following criteria:

1. *Ease of construction.* Refers to the time involved in coming up with a comprehensive list of the important aspects or traits of successful and unsuccessful performance. Checklists, for example, are particularly time consuming, while holistic scoring is not.
2. *Scoring efficiency.* Refers to the amount of time required to score various aspects of the performance and sum these scores into an overall score.
3. *Reliability.* The likelihood of two raters independently coming up with a similar score; or the likelihood of the same rater coming up with a similar score on two separate occasions.
4. *Defensibility.* Refers to the ease with which you can explain your score to a student or parent who challenges it.
5. *Quality of feedback.* Refers to the amount of information the scoring system gives to learners or parents about the strengths and weaknesses of the performance.

Limit the number of points the assessment or component is worth to what can be reliably discriminated. For example, 25 points

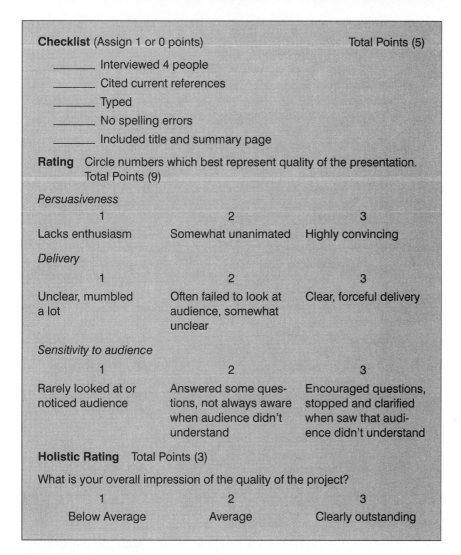

Figure 15.11
Combined scoring rubric for current events project (17 total points)

assigned to a particular product or procedure assumes that the rater can discriminate 25 degrees of quality. When faced with more degrees of quality than can be detected, a typical rater may assign some points arbitrarily, reducing the reliability of the assessment.

On what basis should you assign points to a response on a performance test? On the one hand, you want a response to be worth enough points to allow you to subtly differentiate response quality. On

Table 15.1
The strength of three performance-based scoring systems according to five measurement criteria

	Ease of Construction	Scoring Efficiency	Reliability	Defensibility	Feedback	Performance Most Suitable For
Checklists	low	moderate	high	high	high	procedures
Rating Scales	moderate	moderate	moderate	moderate	moderate	attitudes, products, social skills
Holistic Scoring	high	high	low	low	low	products and processes

the other hand, you want to avoid assigning too many points to a response that does not lend itself to complex discriminations. Thus, assigning one or two points to a math question requiring complex problem solving would not allow you to differentiate among outstanding, above average, average, and poor responses. On the other hand, assigning 30 points to this same answer would seriously challenge your ability to distinguish a rating of 15 from a rating of 18. Two considerations can help you make decisions about the size and complexity of a rating scale.

The first is that you may prepare a scoring model wherein the rater specifies the exact performance—or examples of acceptable performance—that corresponds with each scale point. The ability to successfully define distinct criteria, then, can determine the number of scale points that are defensible. The second consideration is that, although it is customary for homework, paper and pencil tests, and report cards to use a 100-point (percent) scale, scale points derived from performance assessments do not need to add up to 100. In a following section we will indicate how to assign marks to performance tests and how to integrate them with other aspects of an overall grading system (for example, homework, paper and pencil tests, classwork, etc.), including portfolios.

Step 4. Specifying Testing Constraints

Should performance tests have time limits? Should learners be allowed to correct their mistakes? Can they consult references or ask for help from other learners? Were these questions asked of a multiple-choice test, most test developers would respond negatively without much hesitation. But, performance tests confront the designer with the following dilemma: If performance tests are designed to confront learners with real-world challenges, why shouldn't they be allowed to tackle these challenges as real-world people do?

In the world outside of the classroom, mathematicians make mistakes and correct them, journalists write first drafts and revise them, weather forecasters make predictions and change them. Each of these workers can consult references to help them solve problems and consult with colleagues. Why, then, shouldn't learners who are working on performance tests that simulate similar problems be allowed the same working (or testing) conditions? But, even outside the classroom professionals have constraints on their performance, such as deadlines, limited office space, outmoded equipment, and so on. So, how does a teacher decide which conditions to impose during a performance test? Before examining this question, let's look at some of the typical conditions imposed on learners during tests. Wiggins (1992) includes the following among the most common forms of **testing constraints**:

What limitations should I place on learners during a performance test?

1. *Time*. How much time should a learner have to prepare, rethink, revise, and finish a test?
2. *Reference material*. Should learners be able to consult dictionaries, textbooks, notes, etc. as they take a test?
3. *Other people*. May learners ask for help from peers, teachers, experts, etc. as they take a test or complete a project?
4. *Equipment*. May learners use computers, calculators, etc. to help them solve problems?
5. *Prior knowledge of the task*. How much information on what they will be tested should learners receive in advance?
6. *Scoring criteria*. Should learners know the standards by which the teacher will score the assessment?

Wiggins recommends that teachers take an "authenticity test" to decide which of the above constraints to impose on a performance assessment. His authenticity test involves answering the following questions:

1. What kinds of constraints authentically replicate the constraints and opportunities facing the performer in the real world?
2. What kinds of constraints tend to bring out the best in apprentice performers and producers?

3. What are the appropriate or authentic limits one should impose on the availability of the six resources listed above?

Indirect forms of assessment, by the nature of the questions asked, require numerous constraints during the testing conditions. Allowing learners to consult reference materials or ask peers for help during multiple-choice tests would significantly reduce their validity. Performance tests, on the other hand, are direct forms of assessment in which real-world conditions and constraints play an important role in demonstrating the competencies desired.

>>> PORTFOLIO ASSESSMENT <<<

What is a student portfolio?

According to Paulson and Paulson (1991), portfolios tell a story. The theme of the story is determined from answering the student question, "What have I learned during this period of instruction and how have I put it into practice?" Some portfolios represent the student's own selection of products—scripts, musical scores, sculpture, videotapes, research reports, narratives, models, and photographs—that represent the learner's attempt to construct her or his own meaning out of what has been taught. Other portfolios are preorganized by the teacher to include the results of specific products and projects, the exact nature of which may be determined by the student.

Whether portfolio entries are preorganized or left to the student's discretion, several questions must be answered prior to the portfolio assignment:

- What are the criteria for selecting the samples that go into the portfolio?
- Will individual pieces of work be evaluated as they go into the portfolio or will all the entries be evaluated collectively at the end of a period of time—or both?
- Will the amount of student growth, progress, or improvement over time be graded?
- How will different entries, such as videos, essays, artworks, and reports, be compared and weighted?
- What role will peers, parents, other teachers, and the student herself or himself have in the evaluation of the portfolio?

Shavelson, Gao, and Baxter (1991) suggest that at least eight products or tasks over different topic areas may be needed to obtain a reliable estimate of performance from portfolios. Therefore, portfo-

Portfolios tell a story. They answer the student question, "What have I learned during this period of instruction and how have I put it into practice?"

lios are usually built and assessed cumulatively over a period of time. These **portfolio assessments** determine the quality of individual contributions to the larger portfolio at various intervals throughout a period of instruction and of the entire portfolio at the end of instruction. Various schemes have been devised for evaluating portfolios (Paulson & Paulson, 1991). Most involve a recording form in which (1) the specific entries representing student performance are cumulatively rated over a course of instruction, (2) the criteria used to evaluate each entry is identified beforehand, and (3) an overall rating scale is provided for rating each entry against the criteria given.

Frazier and Paulson (1992) and Hebert (1992) report successful ways in which peers, parents, and the students themselves have participated in portfolio evaluations. Figure 15.12 represents one example of a portfolio assessment intended for use as a cumulative record of accomplishment over an extended course of study in mathematics.

Mathematics Problem Solving Criteria
Vermont Portfolio Scoring Guide: Mathematics Rev. 6/94

	Level 1	Level 2	Level 3	Level 4
PS1 Understanding the Problem	*. . . misunderstood the problem __or__ didn't understand enough to get started or make progress.*	*. . . understood enough to solve part of the problem __or__ to reach a partial solution.*	*. . . understood the problem, including identifying and using any information minimally required to solve the problem.*	*. . . identified special factors beyond those minimally required to solve the problem __and__ applied the factors consistently and correctly.*
	Part of a Problem: For multi-part problems, if all the parts of the problem are not addressed, then the student only "understood enough to solve part of the problem." **Solution:** A solution includes: all of the work that was done to complete the problem, an explanation of the decisions made along the way, and an answer. **Special Factors:** Factors beyond minimal information required to solve the problem which add to the complexity of the problem and affect student's solution. **Special Considerations:** For Level 4, student must identify factors (explicitly or implicitly) at the start of solution.			
PS2 How Student Solved the Problem	*. . . approach didn't work __or__ no approach evident.*	*. . . approach would lead to solving only part of the problem __or__ reaching a partial solution.*	*. . . approach worked __or__ would work for the problem.*	*. . . approach worked __and__ was efficient or sophisticated.*
	Approach: The strategy or skill used to solve the problem. **Would:** An approach that would work for a problem even if computation errors or an incomplete response prevented a solution is credited as a Level 3. **Efficient:** Efficiency is determined by the directness of the approach. Use of an algorithm to solve a problem suggests this was just an application of knowledge, not a real problem. If finding the least common multiple, the use of prime factorization is efficient; listing all multiples is not. **Sophisticated:** A sophisticated approach shows evidence of applying concepts and skills in a novel way to solve the problem (not the standard, or usual approach). **Special Considerations:** A piece scored 1 or 2 on PS1 can not score more than 2 on PS2.			
PS3 Why — Decisions Along the Way	*. . . no reasoning evident from the work __or__ reasoning is incorrect.*	*. . . only partially correct reasoning __or__ correct reasoning used for only part of the problem.*	*. . . work __suggests__ correct reasoning used in making decisions throughout the problem.*	*. . . work __clearly exhibits__ correct reasoning used in making decisions throughout the problem.*
	Suggests: Look for evidence in the student's understanding of the task, appropriateness of the strategy, and reasonableness of solution. Support for reasoning is not clearly explicated and/or is incomplete but decisions made by student are evident in work and decisions are correct. Evidence may include a change in approach, but no support given for the change; having more than one approach but no comparisons to show this was done as verification; work of other approaches given but without explanation of their part in reaching solution. **Clearly exhibits:** support present for key decisions made in form of comments on approach, explanation of decisions, annotations, justification for path followed, or use of multiple approaches with comparison and verification.			

Figure 15.12
Mathematics portfolio criteria: Problem solving and communication

From *Vermont Portfolio Scoring Guide: Mathematics,* 1994, Vermont Department of Education. Used with permission.

PS4 So What—Outcomes of Activities	. . . *solved the problem and stopped or made an observation that is inappropriate or irrelevant with respect to his/her solution.*	. . . *solved the problem and made a mathematically relevant comment or observation about some aspect of his/her solution.*	. . . *solved the problem and made a mathematical connection between solution and other mathematics or the "real world."*	. . . *solved the problem and made a general rule about the solution or extended the solution to a more complicated situation.*

Connections can be: between mathematical ideas; between problems; to other classes or content areas; or to real-life applications or examples. There must be sufficient evidence to demonstrate that the application, example, or connection is relevant to the student's solution.

General Rule: a rule that can be used no matter what the numbers in the problem are. Need not be an algebraic rule, it can also be a generalization of the problem to a more complicated situation. Student need not "prove" the rule works but must demonstrate understanding either through explanation of the derivation or application of the generalization to a specific case.

Prompted Response: Specific prompts within the problem statement (e.g., What does this problem have to do with factors?, How is this similar to pricing items at a grocery store?) limit scoring to a Level 1.

Special Consideration: Score Level 4 if a generalization was made at any point in the problem, whether a requirement of the problem or not, as long as an explanation showing understanding or derivation of the generalization is included.

Mathematics Communication Criteria
Vermont Portfolio Scoring Guide: Mathematics Rev. 6/94

	Level 1	Level 2	Level 3	Level 4
C1 Mathematical Language	. . . *used no mathematical language beyond problem statement or consistently used inappropriate or inaccurate math language to communicate his/her solution.*	. . . *used appropriate mathematical language to communicate his/her solution, may have some errors in accuracy and lack variety.*	. . . *used mathematical language accurately and appropriately throughout to communicate his/her solution, and exhibited variety.*	. . . *used mathematical language accurately and appropriately throughout, exhibited variety, and used sophisticated math language to communicate some aspect(s) of his/her solution.*

Variety: Refers to use of variety of terms, notation, and symbols beyond those used in the task statement. For example, a response using the terms "add" and "subtract" with one operation is most likely a Level 2, if those terms and notation do not appear in the problem statement.

Sophisticated Mathematical Language: Includes language not commonly used at this student's grade level. For example, words like exponent or sequence, or notation like $x<6$ or 2^7.

Special Considerations: Don't consider math language that is included in the problem statement. Simply repeating words in the problem earns only Level 1. Use of a single term rarely merits a Level 2.

C2 Mathematical Representation	. . . *used inappropriate mathematical representation* or *didn't use any mathematical representation to communicate the solution.*	. . . *attempted to use appropriate mathematical representation to communicate solution.*	. . . *used appropriate mathematical representation accurately to communicate the solution.*	. . . *used sophisticated mathematical representation(s) accurately to communicate the solution.*
	Mathematical Representations include graphs, charts, tables, models, diagrams, and equations that are linked to representations. Lists of numbers in columns without any labeling are not considered charts or tables and receive Level 1. **Appropriate Representation:** One that is related to the student's solution, regardless of the correctness of the student's approach and solution. **Accurate:** Accurate mathematical representations are those that are technically correct and executed properly. Accurate graphs, tables, charts and diagrams are appropriately labeled and have titles and/or keys, when necessary. Graphs must also include correctly scaled axes. **Sophisticated** representations are those that are perceptive and/or complex and stand alone. They must be appropriate and technically accurate. OR The use of representation may be sophisticated. Evidence of sophisticated use may include combinations of many graphs, charts, and tables to organize, display, and link data; or representations that were relied upon to obtain a solution. **Special Considerations:** A table or graph which is appropriate but not technically accurate receives a Level 2. Completion of a structured chart at grade 4 receives Level 2, at Grade 8 receives Level 1.			
C3 Presentation	. . . *presentation of solution is unclear.*	. . . *presentation of solution contains some clear parts.*	. . . *presentation of solution is clear, but reader must fill in some details to understand the solution.*	. . . *presentation of solution is clear throughout, well-organized and detailed.*
	Unclear suggests the reader has little or no idea what was done to solve the problem. **Some clear parts** suggests the reader understood some of the work but is uncertain about what the student did to solve the problem, must fill in major gaps and try to guess at what the student was thinking in parts of the solution. **Fill in some details** means that although most of the presentation is clear it may be missing some details which the reader is required to fill in, or it is detailed but lacks organization and the reader is required to fill in. **Clear throughout:** Student's presentation contains sufficient detail for reader to understand solution without having to make interpretations or inferences. **Well organized** pieces of work have all the parts connected to each other (e.g., any representation used is consistent with the student's solution).			

Figure 15.12, *continued*

Many teachers are using portfolios as a means of increasing student reflections about their own work and encouraging the continuous refinement of portfolio entries. Portfolios have the advantage of containing multiple samples of student work completed over time that can represent finished as well as works in progress. Entries designated "works in progress" are cumulatively assessed at regular intervals on the basis of student growth or improvement and the extent to which the entry increasingly matches the criteria given.

>>> PERFORMANCE TESTS AND <<<
REPORT CARD GRADES

Performance tests require a substantial commitment of teacher time and learner engagement. Consequently, a teacher who decides to use them should ensure that the performance test grade has substantial weight in the six-week or final report card grade. Here are two approaches to designing a grading system that includes performance assessments.

How can I combine performance test grades with other classroom grades?

The first approach to scoring quizzes, tests, homework assignments, performance assessments, and so on is to score each on the basis of 100 points. Computing the final grade, then, simply involves averaging the grades for each component, multiplying these averages by the weight assigned, and adding these products to determine the total grade. Figure 15.13 provides examples of three formulae for accomplishing this. These methods require that you assign 0 to 100 points to everything you grade.

The second approach is to use a "percentage of total points" system. With this system, you decide individually how many points each component of your grading system is worth. You may want some tests to be worth 40 points, some 75, and so on, depending on the complexity of the questions and the performance desired. Likewise, some of your homework assignments may be worth 10 points, some 5 points, and some 15 points. With such a system there is no need to have every homework assignment, test, or class assignment worth 100 points or the same number of points. Following are the procedures involved in setting up such a grading scheme for a six-week grading period.

Step 1: Identify the components of your grading system and assign each component a weight. A *weight* is the percentage of total points a particular component carries. Components and example weights for a six-week grading plan are shown here:

Component	Weight (%)
Homework	15
Objective Tests	20
Performance Tests	20
Portfolio	20
Classwork	15
Notebook	10
	100

Step 2: Record in your grade book the actual points earned out of the possible points. Leave a column for totals (see Figure

Grading Formula Example #1:

This formula is known as the "One, Two, Three Times Plan."

Homework and Classwork:

All grades for homework and classwork are totaled and averaged. The average grade will count once.

Homework and classwork grades followed by the average: 84, 81, 88, 92, 96, 85, 78, 83, 91, 79, 89, 94 = 1040 ÷ 12 = 86.6 = 87 average

Quizzes:

All of the quizzes are totaled and averaged. This average grade will count two times.

Quiz grades followed by the average: 82, 88, 80, 91, 78, 86 = 505 ÷ 6 = 84.2 = 84 average

Tests and Major Projects:

All of the tests and major projects are totaled and averaged. This average grade will count three times.

Test and major project grade followed by the average: 81, 91, 86 = 258 ÷ 3 = 86 average

The six weeks grade would be computed as follows: 87 (one time) + 84 + 84 (two times) + 86 + 86 + 86 (three times) = 513 ÷ 6 = 85.5 = 86 as the grade

Grading Formula Example #2:

This formula is known as the "Percentages Plan."

A teacher determines a percentage for each area. For example, homework and classwork will count 20% of the grade; quizzes will count 40% of the grade; and tests and major projects will count 40% of the grade.

Using the same scores as listed above, a student's grade would be computed as follows:

20% of the 86.6 for homework and classwork is 17.3; 40% of the 84.2 for quizzes is 33.7; and 40% of the 86 for tests and major projects is 34.4. 17.3 + 33.7 + 34.4 = 85.4 = 85 as the six weeks grade. (The average is different because the "weight" put on each area varies in the two examples.)

Figure 15.13

Three examples of different ways to compute and weight grades

Grading Formula Example #3:

This formula is known as the "Language Arts Plan."

A language arts teacher determines that the publishing, goal meeting, journal, and daily process grades each count one fourth (25%) of the six weeks grade.

A language arts grade will be computed as follows:

The publishing grade is issued only at the end of the six weeks = 88

The goal meeting grade is issued only at the end of the six weeks = 86

The journal grades are: $82 + 92 + 94 + 90 + 88 + 86 = 532 \div 6 = 88.7 = 89$

The daily process grades are : $78 + 82 + 86 + 94 + 94 + 91 = 525 \div 6 = 87.5 = 88$

The six weeks grade would be: $88 + 86 + 89 + 88 = 351 \div 4 = 87.75 = 88$

15.14). As you can see, each component and each separate assignment has varying numbers of points possible to be earned. Assign possible points for the components based on the complexity of the required performance, the length of the assignment, your perception of your ability to assign reliable ratings, and so on.

Step 3: Total the actual points earned for each component and divide this by the possible points. The results represent the percentage of points earned for each particular component. Thus, in our example from Figure 15.14, Cornell and Rosie earned the following total points:

	Cornell	Rosie
Homework	50/70 = 71%	55/70 = 79%
Objective Tests	45/60 = 75%	35/60 = 58%
Performance Tests	33/40 = 83%	39/40 = 98%
Portfolio	18/20 = 90%	15/20 = 75%
Classwork	39/50 = 78%	37/50 = 74%
Notebook	5/10 = 50%	8/10 = 80%

Step 4: Multiply each of these percentages by the weights assigned, as shown below and in Figure 15.14. Then, sum these products.

Component	Homework							Objective Tests			Performance Tests			Portfolio	Classwork						Notebook
Dates	8/20	9/7	9/14	9/20	9/28	10/6	Total	9/17	10/7	Total	9/23	10/8	Total	10/7	9/2	9/6	9/14	9/23	10/5	Total	10/8
Cornell	10/10	8/10	14/15	10/10	8/15	0/10	50/70	20/30	25/30	45/60	15/20	18/20	33/40	18/20	9/10	7/15	10/10	9/10	4/5	39/50	5/10
Rosie	10/10	5/10	12/15	8/10	12/15	8/10	55/70	15/30	20/30	35/60	20/20	19/20	39/40	15/20	8/10	14/15	0/10	10/10	5/5	37/50	8/10

Figure 15.14
Sample grade recording sheet, first six weeks

	Cornell	Rosie
Homework	71 x .15 = 10.6	79 x .15 = 11.8
Objective Tests	75 x .20 = 15	58 x .20 = 11.6
Performance Tests	83 x .20 = 16.6	98 x .20 = 19.6
Portfolio	90 x .20 = 18	75 x .20 = 15
Classwork	78 x .15 = 11.7	74 x .15 = 11.1
Notebook	50 x .10 = 5	80 x .10 = 8
Sum Totals	76.9	77.1

Step 5: Record the six-week grade either as a letter grade (A = 90–100%, B = 80–89%, C = 70–79%, etc.) or as the percentage itself, depending on your school's marking system.

>>> A FINAL WORD <<<

Performance assessments create challenges that differ from those of objective and essay tests. Performance grading requires greater use of judgment than do true-false or multiple-choice questions. These judgments can become more reliable if (1) the performance to be judged (process and product) is clearly specified, (2) the ratings or criteria used in making the judgments are determined beforehand, and (3) two or more raters independently grade the performance and an average taken.

Using video- or audiotapes can enhance the validity of performance assessments when direct observation of performance is required. Furthermore, performance assessments need not take place at one time for the whole class. Learners can be assessed at different times, individually or in small groups. For example, learners can rotate through classroom learning centers (Shalaway, 1989) and you may assess them when you feel they are acquiring mastery.

Finally, don't lose sight of the fact that performance assessments are meant to serve and enhance instruction rather than being simply an after-the-fact test given to assign a grade. When tests serve instruction, they can be given at a variety of times and in as many settings and contexts as instruction requires. Some performance assessments can sample the behavior of learners as they receive instruction, and some may occur within ongoing classroom activities rather than consume extra time during the day.

This chapter introduced you to performance-based assessment. Its main points were as follows:

1. Performance tests use direct measures of learning that require learners to analyze, problem solve, experiment, make decisions, measure, cooperate with others, present orally, or produce a product. Performance tests not only can assess higher-level cognitive skills but also noncognitive outcomes, such as self-direction, ability to work with others, and social awareness.

2. Paper and pencil tests are most efficient, reliable, and valid for assessing knowledge, comprehension, and some types of application. When properly constructed, performance tests are most efficient, reliable, and valid for assessing complex thinking, attitudes, and social skills.

3. Three questions to ask when deciding what to test with a performance assessment are the following:

- What knowledge or content is essential for learner understanding?
- What intellectual skills are used?
- What habits of mind or attitudes are important?

4. Two categories of performance skills in the cognitive domain are (1) skills related to acquiring information and (2) skills related to organizing and using information.

5. The four steps to constructing a performance assessment are (1) deciding what to test, (2) designing the assessment context, (3) specifying the scoring rubrics, and (4) specifying the testing constraints.

6. Some questions to ask in designing the performance assessment context are (1) what does the "doing of math, history . . . " etc. look and feel like to professionals, (2) what projects and tasks are performed by these professionals, and (3) what roles—or habits of mind—do professionals assume?

7. A good performance assessment includes a hands-on exercise or problem, an observable outcome, and a process that can be observed.

8. *Rubrics* are scoring standards composed of model answers, which are used to score performance tests. They are samples of acceptable responses against which the rater compares a student's performance.

9. Primary trait scoring is a type of rating that requires that the test developer first identify the most relevant characteristics or primary traits of importance.

10. A performance test can require four types of accomplishments from learners: Products, complex cognitive processes, observable performance, and attitudes and social skills. These performances can be scored with checklists, rating scales, or holistic scales.

11. Checklists contain lists of behaviors, traits, or characteristics that can be scored as either present or absent. They are best suited for complex behaviors or performances that are divisible into a series of clearly defined, specific actions.

12. Rating scales assign numbers to categories representing different degrees of performance. They are typically used for those aspects of a complex performance, such as attitudes, products, and social skills, that do not lend themselves to yes/no or present/absent type judgments.

13. Holistic scoring estimates the overall quality of a performance by assigning a single numerical value to represent a specific category of accomplishment. It is used for measuring both products and processes.

14. Constraints to decide on when constructing and administering a performance test are amount of time allowed, use of reference material, help from others, use of specialized equipment, prior knowledge of the task, and scoring criteria.

15. Student portfolios tell a story with the students' own contributions of what was learned during a period of instruction.

16. Two approaches to combining performance grades with other grades are (1) to assign 100 total points to each assignment that is graded and average the results, and (2) begin with an arbitrary total and then determine the percentage of points each component is worth.

For Discussion and Practice

*1. Compare and contrast some of the reasons given to explain why we give conventional tests with those given to explain why we give performance assessments.

*2. In your own words, explain how performance assessment can be a tool for instruction.

*3. Using an example from your teaching area, explain the difference between a direct and an indirect measure of behavior.

4. Describe some "habits of mind" that might be required by a performance test in your teaching area. How did you learn about the importance of these attitudes, social skills, and ways of working?

*5. Describe how at least two school districts have implemented performance assessments. Indicate the behaviors they assess and by what means they are measured.

6. Would you agree or disagree with the statement that "an ideal performance test is a good teaching activity?" With a specific example in your teaching area, illustrate why you believe as you do.

7. State at least two learning outcomes and how you would measure them in your classroom to indicate that a learner is (1) self-directed, (2) a collaborative worker, (3) a complex thinker, (4) a quality producer, and (5) a community contributor.

*8. Describe what is meant by a "scoring rubric."

9. In your own words, how would you answer a critic of performance tests who says

they do not measure generalizable thinking skills outside the classroom and can't be scored reliably?

10. Identify for a unit you will be teaching several attitudes, habits of mind, and/or social skills that would be important when using the content taught in the real world.

11. Create a performance test of your own choosing that (1) requires a hands-on problem to solve, (2) results in an observable outcome, and (3) involves observable processes used by learners to achieve the outcome. Use the five criteria by Wiggins (1992) and Resnick and Resnick (1989) as a guide.

12. For the performance assessment in question 11, describe and give an example of the accomplishments—or rubrics—you would look for in scoring the assessment.

13. For this same assessment, compose a checklist, rating scale, holistic scoring method, or a combination, by which you could evaluate a learner's performance. Explain why you chose the scoring system you did.

14. For the performance assessment in question 11, describe the constraints you would place on your learners pertaining to time to prepare for and complete the activity; references they may use; people they may consult, including other students; equipment allowed; prior knowledge about what is expected; and points or percentages you would assign to various degrees of their performance.

15. Imagine you have to arrive at a final grade composed of homework, objective tests, performance tests, portfolio, classwork and notebook, which together you want to add up to 100 points. Using Figures 15.13 and 15.14 as a guide, compose a grading scheme that indicates the weight, number, individual points, and total points assigned to each component. Indicate the percent and total number of points required for the grades A through F.

---

* Answers to asterisked questions (*) in this and the other chapters are in Appendix B.

Suggested Readings

Educational Leadership. (May, 1992). ASCD special issue on using performance assessment, Vol. 49, No. 8. Alexandria, VA.

This special issue contains clear, detailed examples of what teachers around the country are doing to give performance tests a try.

Linn, R. L., Baker, F. L., and Dunbar, S. B. (1991). Complex performance based assessment: Expectations and validative criteria. *Educational Researcher, 20*(8), 15–21.

A clear, concise review of the strengths and limitations of performance tests. Also discusses research that needs to be done to improve their validity and reliability.

Loucks-Horsley, S., Kapiton, R., Carlson, M. D., Kuerbis, P. J., Clark, P. C., Melle, G. M., Sachse, T. P., & Wolten, E. (1990). *Elementary school science for the 90's.* Alexandria, VA: Association for Supervision and Curriculum Development.

This book illustrates the importance of measuring attitudes or habits of mind in performance assessment as well as understanding and application.

Mitchell, Ruth. (1992). *Testing for learning: How new approaches to evaluation can improve American schools.* New York: Free Press.

The first comprehensive treatment of alternative approaches to traditional testing. Includes excellent discussions of the problems of current testing practice and the advantages of performance tests. The examples of performance tests are especially helpful.

Stiggins, R. J. (1994). *Student-centered classroom assessment.* Englewood Cliffs, NJ: Merrill/Prentice Hall.

This text comprehensively surveys the various types of assessment. It provides detailed information on constructing and evaluating different assessment formats, with the goal of creating instruments that accurately and thoroughly assess the desired learnings.

Wiggins, G. (1992). Creating tests worth taking. *Educational Leadership, 49*(8), May, 26–34.

This article provides excellent examples of teacher-made performance tests in a number of different areas.

Teacher Concerns Checklist

Francis F. Fuller   Gary D. Borich
The University of Texas at Austin

(See description of this questionnaire in the section "A Hierarchy of Planning Needs" in Chapter 3.)

DIRECTIONS: This checklist explores what teachers are concerned about at different stages of their careers. There are no right or wrong answers, because each teacher has his or her own concerns.

On the following page are statements of concerns you might have. Read each statement and ask yourself: WHEN I THINK ABOUT TEACHING, AM I CONCERNED ABOUT THIS?

- If you are *not concerned*, or the statement does not apply, write *1* in the box.
- If you are *a little concerned*, write *2* in the box.
- If you are *moderately concerned*, write *3* in the box.
- If you are *very concerned*, write *4* in the box.
- And if you are *totally preoccupied* with the concern, write *5* in the box.

Be sure to answer every item. Begin by completing the following:

1. Name _____ Male _____ Female _____
   Age _____ Date _____
2. Circle the number of the statement that best describes your teaching experience:

(1) No education courses and no formal classroom observation or teaching experience.

(2) Education courses but no formal observation or teaching experience.

(3) Education courses and observation experience but no teaching.

(4) Presently student teaching.

(5) Presently an inservice teacher.

3. If you are a student: Freshman _____ Sophomore _____ Junior _____ Senior _____ Graduate _____

4. The grade level you plan to teach (if student) or are now teaching (if inservice):
Preschool _____ Elementary _____ Junior High _____ Senior High _____ College _____ Other _____

5. Years of teaching experience (if inservice) _____

For each statement below, decide which of the five responses best applies to you now. Place the number of the answer in the box at the left of the statement. Please be as accurate as you can.

① Not concerned   ② A little concerned   ③ Moderately concerned
④ Very concerned   ⑤ Totally preoccupied

○ 1. Insufficient clerical help for teachers.
○ 2. Whether the students respect me.
○ 3. Too many extra duties and responsibilities.
○ 4. Doing well when I'm observed.
○ 5. Helping students to value learning.
○ 6. Insufficient time for rest and class preparation.
○ 7. Not enough assistance from specialized teachers.
○ 8. Managing my time efficiently.
○ 9. Losing the respect of my peers.
○ 10. Not enough time for grading and testing.
○ 11. The inflexibility of the curriculum.
○ 12. Too many standards and regulations set for teachers.
○ 13. My ability to prepare adequate lesson plans.
○ 14. Having my inadequacies become known to other teachers.
○ 15. Increasing students' feelings of accomplishment.
○ 16. The rigid instructional routine.
○ 17. Diagnosing student learning problems.

○ 18. What the principal may think if there is too much noise in my classroom.
○ 19. Whether each student is reaching his or her potential.
○ 20. Obtaining a favorable evaluation of my teaching.
○ 21. Having too many students in a class.
○ 22. Recognizing the social and emotional needs of students.
○ 23. Challenging unmotivated students.
○ 24. Losing the respect of my students.
○ 25. Lack of public support for schools.
○ 26. My ability to maintain the appropriate degree of class control.
○ 27. Not having sufficient time to plan.
○ 28. Getting students to behave.
○ 29. Understanding why certain students make slow progress.
○ 30. Having an embarrassing incident occur in my classroom for which I might be judged responsible.
○ 31. Not being able to cope with troublemakers in my classes.
○ 32. That my peers may think I'm not doing an adequate job.

○ 33. My ability to work with disruptive students.

○ 34. Understanding ways in which student health and nutrition problems can affect learning.

○ 35. Appearing competent to parents.

○ 36. Meeting the needs of different kinds of students.

○ 37. Seeking alternative ways to ensure that students learn the subject matter.

○ 38. Understanding the psychological and cultural differences that can affect my students' behavior.

○ 39. Adapting myself to the needs of different students.

○ 40. The large number of administrative interruptions.

○ 41. Guiding students toward intellectual and emotional growth.

○ 42. Working with too many students each day.

○ 43. Whether students can apply what they learn.

○ 44. Teaching effectively when another teacher is present.

○ 45. Understanding what factors motivate students to learn.

The following items on the Teacher Concerns Checklist represent the dimensions of Self, Task, and Impact:

Self	*Task*	*Impact*
2	1	5
4	3	15
8	6	17
9	7	19
13	10	22
14	11	23
18	12	29
20	16	34
24	21	36
26	25	37
28	27	38
30	31	39
32	33	41
35	40	43
44	42	45

You can complete the concerns instrument at the beginning and again at the end of your student teaching or field observation experience, noting any changes in the three areas of concern over time.

To determine your score, total the number of responses in each of the three categories of concern—self, task, and impact. The higher your score in a category (out of a maximum 75 per category), the more you are identi-

---

Teacher Concerns Checklist by Francis F. Fuller and Gary D. Borich, The University of Texas at Austin, from Gary D. Borich, *Effective Teaching Methods* (2nd ed.), Merrill/Prentice Hall. This instrument was revised with the assistance of John Rogan, Western Montana University.

fied with that stage of concern. Also, by summing responses to items in each category and dividing by the number of items completed, you may compute an average rating for each of the three areas.

The sum of the scores for each of the three areas of concern (maximum = 75) can be recorded in the format below, shown here with some example data:

Stage	Beginning	End	Change
Self	60	45	−15
Task	45	60	+15
Impact	15	30	+15

This example profile indicates a shift of concern from self to task and from self to impact. This is typical of student teachers who spend about a semester in a field experience. Smaller shifts following this same pattern are not uncommon, however, after a semester of in-school observation without practice teaching. Larger shifts, particularly from task to impact, are frequently noted for beginning inservice teachers during their first two to three years of teaching.

References

Borich, G. (1995). *Becoming a teacher: An inquiring dialogue for the beginning teacher*. Bristol, PA: Falmer Press Ltd.

Borich, G. (1994). *Observation skills for effective teaching*: 2nd edition. Columbus: Merrill/Prentice Hall (Chapter 4).

Borich, G. (1992). *Clearly outstanding: Making each day count in your classroom*. Boston: Allyn & Bacon (Chapter 8).

Fuller, F. F. (1969). Concerns of teachers: A developmental conceptualization. *American Educational Research Journal, 6*, 207–226.

Fuller, F., Brown, O., & Peck, R. (1966). *Creating climates for growth*. Austin: University of Texas, Research and Development Center for Teacher Education, ERIC Document Reproduction Service, ED 013 989.

Fuller, F., Pilgrim, G., & Freeland, A. (1967). *Intensive individualization of teacher preparation*. Austin: University of Texas, Research and Development Center for

Teacher Education. ERIC Document Reproduction Service, ED 011 603.

Hall, G.E., & Hord, S.M. (1987). *Change in schools: Facilitating the process*. Ithaca: State University of New York Press.

Hord, S.M., Rutherford, W.L., Huling-Austin, L., & Hall, G.E. (1987). *Taking charge of change*. Alexandria: Association for Supervision and Curriculum Development.

Rogan, J., Borich, G., & Taylor, H. (1992). Validation of the stages of concern questionnaire. *Action in Teacher Education, 14*(2), 43–49.

Rutherford, W.L., & Hall, G.E. (1990). *Concerns of teachers: Revisiting the original theory after twenty years*. Paper presented at the annual meeting of the American Educational Research Association, Boston. (Available from W. Rutherford, College of Education, The University of Texas at Austin, Austin, TX 78712.)

Answers to Chapter Questions

These are answers to questions marked (*) in the "For Discussion and Practice" sections of the text chapters. Answers are not supplied for questions that lack the asterisk.

Chapter 1

1. 1, 2, 1 (or 2), 1 (or 2), 2, 3, 2, 3, 2 (or 1), 3, 2, 3, 3.

3.

	Lower SES
Individualization:	Supplement standard curriculum with media and specialized material.
Teacher affect:	Provide warm and encouraging climate.

	High SES
Thinking and decision making:	Pose and require questions that encourage associations, generalizations, and inferences.
Classroom interaction:	Encourage interactions in which students take responsibility for their own learning.

Chapter 2

1. a. Match instructional methods to individual learning needs.

b. Understand the reasons behind the school performance of individual learners.

2. Environmentalists believe that differences in IQ scores among groups can be attributed to social class or environmental differences. Hereditarians believe that heredity rather than the environment is the major factor determining intelligence.

3. By some estimates "social competence" may account for about 75% of school learning, leaving only about 25% to the influence of intelligence. If the influence of socioeconomic status on learning could be removed, differences in IQ among learners could be expected to become smaller.

4. Factors that would be more predictive of school learning than general IQ would be specialized abilities such as those suggested by Thurstone and Gardner and Hatch, which may include verbal intelligence (English), spatial intelligence (Art), and interpersonal intelligence (Social Studies, Drama).

8. Get students to talk about themselves; reward unique talents.

9. a. state
b. trait
c. trait
d. trait
e. state
f. trait
g. trait
h. state but also trait
i. trait
j. trait but also state

11. Form heterogeneous groups composed of members of different peer groups. Conduct a group discussion of class norms.

Chapter 3

1. a, g, a, g, a, g, a, g, g, g.

5. (1) Strengthening of the curriculum in the areas of math, science, English, foreign language, and social studies.

(2) Renewed effort to teach higher-order thinking skills.

(3) Raising school grading standards.

(4) Raising college admission standards.

(5) More work in core subjects.

6. To teach students how to think.

9. (1) Aims and goals (texts, curriculum guides, policy reports).

(2) Learner needs (student achievement, workbook exercises, class performance).

(3) Knowledge of academic discipline (subject matter texts).

(4) Knowledge of teaching methods (key and catalytic behaviors).

(5) Tacitly acquired knowledge from day-to-day experience in the classroom.

13. ● Front half/back half
● Girls/boys
● More able/less able
● Nonminority/minority

14. ● Spreading interactions across categories of students.
● Selecting students randomly.
● Pairing students.
● Coding class notes.

15. Self, task, impact.

17. First teacher has profile B, second teacher has profile A, third teacher has profile C, fourth teacher has profile D.

Chapter 4

1. a. To tie general aims and goals to specific classroom strategies that will achieve those aims and goals.

b. To express teaching strategies in a format that allows you to measure their effects upon your learners.

2. The behavior is observable, it is measurable, and it occurs in a specifiable period of time.

3. The observable behavior, conditions under which it is to be observed, and level of proficiency at which it is to be displayed.

4. Teachers tended to focus their concerns on self and task, sometimes to the exclusion of their impact on students.

5. Because action verbs truly point toward the goal of achieving the desired behavior and observing its attainment.

6. A, O, A, A, A, O, O, O.

7. The circumstances under which the behavior is to be displayed.

8. By establishing the setting under which the behavior will be tested, which guides them in how and what to study.

9. The extent to which the conditions are similar to those under which the behavior will have to be performed in the real world.

10. The level of proficiency at which the behavior must be displayed.

12. (1) b
(2) a
(3) b
(4) e
(5) f

Chapter 5

1. Knowledge of aims and goals, knowledge of learners, knowledge of subject matter content and organization, knowledge of teaching methods, and tacit knowledge.

2. By the way in which individual lessons are sequenced and build upon one another to produce a unified whole.

3. • Hierarchy helps us see the relationship between individual lesson outcomes and the unit outcome. It also helps us identify lessons that are not too big or too small, but that are just right.

• Task-relevant prior learning is used to identify the proper sequence of lessons needed to teach the unit outcome.

4. Both help us picture the flow and sequence of a lesson plan.

5. • Cognitive: analysis, synthesis, evaluation.

• Affective: valuing, organization, characterization.

• Psychomotor: precision, articulation, naturalization.

6. They represent smaller, more detailed portions of content.

8. The former must show hierarchy and sequence; the latter does not.

9. Ability grouping, peer tutoring, learning centers, review, and followup materials.

10. Mastery learning is when each student displays a high level, if not complete proficiency, of each intended outcome.

11. Gaining attention, informing the learner of the objective, stimulating recall of prerequisite learning, presenting the stimulus material, eliciting the desired behavior, providing feedback, assessing the behavior.

12. Presenting the stimulus material.

13. Assessing the behavior.

14. Eliciting the desired behavior.

15. Providing feedback: immediate and nonevaluative. Assessing the behavior: delayed and evaluative.

Chapter 6

1. ● Type 1: facts, rules, action sequences.

● Type 2: concepts, patterns, abstractions.

● Type 1 outcomes generally apply to the knowledge, comprehension, and application levels, while Type 2 outcomes generally apply to the analysis, synthesis, and evaluation levels.

2. ● Knowledge acquisition: facts, rules, action sequences.

● Inquiry or problem solving: concepts, patterns, and abstractions.

3. Full class instruction; questions posed by the teacher; detailed and redundant practice; one new fact, rule, or sequence mastered before the next is presented; arrangement of classroom to maximize drill and practice.

4. ● Cognitive: to recall, to describe, to list.

● Affective: to listen, to attend, to be aware.

● Psychomotor: to repeat, to follow, to place.

5. (1) To disseminate information that is not readily available from texts or workbooks in appropriately sized pieces.

(2) To arouse or heighten student interest.

(3) To achieve content mastery.

6. (1) Having students correct each other's work.

(2) Having students identify difficult homework problems.

(3) Sampling the understanding of a few students who represent the range of students in the class.

(4) Explicitly reviewing the task-relevant information necessary for the day's lesson.

7. Part–whole, sequential, combinatorial, comparative.

8. Rule–Example–Rule.

9. To create a response, however crude, that can become the basis for learning.

10. It is used to help convert wrong or partially correct answers to right answers by encouraging the student to use some aspects of the answer given in formulating the correct response.

11. (1) Correct, quick, and firm: acknowledge correctness and either ask another question or move on.

(2) Correct but hesitant: acknowledge correctness and review steps for attaining correct answer.

(3) Incorrect but careless: acknowledge incorrectness and immediately move on.

(4) Incorrect due to lack of knowledge: acknowledge incorrectness and then, without actually giving the student the answer, channel student's thoughts in ways that result in a correct answer.

14. Review key facts, explain steps required, prompt with clues or hints, walk student through a similar problem.

15. 60–80%. Reduce content coverage, increase opportunities for practice and feedback.

16. To form action sequences. They should increasingly resemble applications in the real world.

17. Keep contacts to a minimum, on the average of 30 seconds; spread contacts across most students, avoiding concentrating on a few students.

18. About 95%.

19. Gradually increase the coverage and depth of weekly reviews until time for a comprehensive monthly review arrives.

Chapter 7

1. Inquiry, discovery, and a problem.

2. ● Type 1: facts, rules, and action sequences.

● Type 2: concepts, patterns, and abstractions.

3. The learner indirectly acquires a behavior by transforming stimulus material into a response or behavior that differs (1) from the stimulus used to present the learning and (2) from any previous response emitted by the learner.

4. It is not generally efficient or effective for attaining outcomes at the higher levels of complexity involving concepts, patterns, and abstractions.

5. ● Unitization: the learning of individual facts or rules.

● Automaticity: putting the facts or rules together in an action sequence and being able to execute the sequence rapidly and automatically.

● Example: learning to read.

6. ● Generalization: classifying apparently different stimuli into the same category on the basis of criterial attributes.

● Discrimination: distinguishing examples of a concept from nonexamples.

● Example: learning the meaning of *democracy*.

7. (1) 1
(2) 2
(3) 1
(4) 2
(5) 2
(6) 1
(7) 2
(8) 2
(9) 1
(10) 2

8. Our memories would become overburdened trying to remember all possible instances of the concept; also, instances of the concept could easily be confused with noninstances.

11. ● Induction: the process of thinking in which a set of specific data is presented or observed and a generalization or unifying pattern is drawn from the data.

● Deduction: the process of thinking in which the truth or validity of a theory is tested in a specific instance.

12. Stating a theory, forming a hypothesis, observing or collecting data, analyzing and interpreting the data, making a conclusion.

14. ● Criterial: lesson clarity, instructional variety, task orientation, engagement in the learning process, moderate-to-high success rate.

● Noncriterial: number of credit hours attained, degree held, number of inservice workshops attended, college grades, years of teaching experience.

15. (1) Provide more than a single example.

(2) Use examples that vary in ways that are unimportant to the concept.

(3) Include nonexamples of the concept that also include important dimensions of the concept.

(4) Explain why nonexamples are nonexamples, even though they have some of the same characteristics as examples.

16. ● Direct instruction: to elicit a single right answer or reveal level of understanding.

● Indirect instruction: to help the student search for and discover an appropriate answer with a minimum of assistance.

17. Questions that present contradictions, probe for deeper responses, extend the discussion, and pass responsibility back to the class.

18. Student-centered or unguided discovery learning. In indirect instruction, student ideas are used as means of accomplishing the goals of the prescribed curriculum.

19. (1) Encouraging students to use examples and references from their experience; (2) asking students to draw parallels and associations from things they already know; (3) relating ideas to students' interests, concerns, and problems.

20. In direct instruction, nearly all instances of the facts, rules, and sequences are likely to be encountered during instruction. This is not true during indirect instruction, so student self-evaluation is essential.

21. Orienting students, providing new or more accurate information, reviewing and summarizing, adjusting the flow of information to more productive areas, and combining ideas and promoting compromise.

22. (1) direct
(2) direct
(3) indirect
(4) indirect
(5) direct
(6) direct
(7) direct
(8) indirect
(9) indirect
(10) indirect

Both models might be used for topics 3, 4, 8, and 10.

Chapter 8

1. A question that actively engages a student in the learning process.

2. Structuring, soliciting, reacting.

3. 80%.

4. As high as 80%; as low as 20%.

5. Interest- and attention-getting, diagnosing and checking, recall of specific facts or information, managerial, encourage higher-level thought processes, structure and redirect learning, allow expression of affect.

6. • A convergent question has only a single or small number of correct responses.

• A divergent question has no single best answer and generally has multiple answers; however, divergent questions can have wrong answers.

8. If the learner previously has seen and memorized an answer to this question.

9. If the learner arrived at the solution by other than simple recall and memorization, perhaps by reasoning $2 + 2 + 2 + 2 = 8$, which is the same as 2 multiplied by 4.

10. Such questions are unlikely to affect standardized achievement but are likely to increase the learner's analysis, synthesis, and evaluation skills.

16. The time the teacher waits for a student to respond to a question. Generally, beginning teachers should work to increase their wait time.

17. Raising overly complex questions, not being prepared for unusual answers, not knowing the behavioral complexity of the response desired from a question, providing answers to questions before students can respond, using questions as a form of punishment.

Chapter 9

1. (1) To actively engage them in the learning process.

(2) To help them acquire reasoning, critical thinking, and problem-solving skills.

2. (1) Providing when and how to use mental strategies.

(2) Illustrating how the strategies are to be used.

(3) Encouraging learners to go beyond the information given.

(4) Gradually shifting the responsibility for learning to the student.

3. Metacognition refers to the mental processes used by the learner to understand the content being taught. Metacognitive strategies are procedures that assist learners in internalizing, understanding, and recalling the content to be learned.

4. (1) Illustrating the reasoning involved.

(2) Making students conscious of it.

(3) Focusing learners on the application of the reasoning illustrated.

6. Mental modeling can help students internalize, recall, and generalize problem solutions to different content at a later time.

7. During mediation, the teacher helps students restructure what they are learning to move them closer to the intended outcome.

8. The "zone of maximum response opportunity" is the content difficulty and behavioral complexity from which the student can most benefit at the moment.

10. Reciprocal teaching provides opportunities to explore the content to be learned via group discussion.

11. ● Asking what students think they will learn from the text.

● Reading from text.

● Choosing a discussion leader to ask questions regarding text.

● Asking the discussion leader to summarize text, and invite comments.

● Discussing points that remain unclear, inviting more predictions, and rereading text if needed.

12. To gradually shift the responsibility for learning to the student through scaffolded discussion.

13. To model the same line of reasoning and the same types of questions, prompts, and cues used by the teacher at an earlier stage.

15. Declarative knowledge is intended only for oral and verbal regurgitation. Procedural knowledge is used in some problem-solving or decision-making task.

17. ● Provide a new learning task.

● Ask the student to explain how he or she will complete the task (for example, learn the content).

● Provide another learning task on which the student can try out the new approach.

● Model self-questioning behavior for the student as the new material is being learned.

● Provide a third opportunity for practice, decreasing your role as monitor.

● Check the result by questioning for comprehension.

18. (1) Jingles or trigger sentences

(2) Narrative chaining

(3) Number rhyme or peg word

(4) Chunking

Chapter 10

1. (1) Engaging students in the learning process.

(2) Promoting higher—more complex—patterns of thought.

2. (1) Attitudes and values.

(2) Prosocial behavior.

(3) Alternative perspectives and viewpoints.

(4) Integrated identity.

(5) Higher thought processes.

3. (1) Improved collaborative skills.

(2) Better self-esteem.

(3) Increased achievement.

4. (1) Teacher–student interaction.

(2) Student–student interaction.

(3) Task specialization and materials.

(4) Role expectations and responsibilities.

5. (1) Specifying the goal.

(2) Structuring the task.

(3) Teaching the collaborative process.

(4) Monitoring group performance.

(5) Debriefing.

6. ● Written group reports

● Test achievement

● Oral performance

● Enumeration of issues

● Critique

● Reference list

7. 4 or 5 members.

8. (1) Ask students to list peers.

(2) Randomly assign students.

(3) Purposefully form groups heterogeneously.

(4) Share with students the selection process.

9. (1) Request a product that requires a clearly defined division of labor.

(2) Form pairs within groups which have the responsibility of looking over and correcting each other's work.

(3) Visually chart group's progress on individually assigned tasks.

10. (1) Summarizer

(2) Checker

(3) Researcher

(4) Runner

(5) Recorder

(6) Supporter

(7) Observer/Troubleshooter

11. (1) Grades—individual and group

(2) Bonus points

(3) Social responsibilities

(4) Tokens or privileges

(5) Group contingencies

12. Forming a ratio, with a score for individual effort on top and a score for the group to which the individual belongs on the bottom.

13. (1) Communicating one's own ideas and feelings.

(2) Making messages complete and specific.

(3) Making verbal and nonverbal messages congruent.

(4) Conveying an atmosphere of respect and support.

(5) Assessing if the message was properly received.

(6) Paraphrasing another's point of view.

(7) Negotiating meanings and understandings.

(8) Participating and leading.

14. (1) Repeat or remind group of its assigned role.

(2) Redirect group's effort to more productive area.

(3) Provide emotional support and encouragement.

15. (1) Openly talking about how the groups functioned.

(2) Soliciting suggestions for how the process could be improved.

(3) Getting viewpoints of predesignated observers.

16. (1) Not enough time for group debriefing.

(2) Debriefing stays vague.

(3) Students stay uninvolved.

(4) Written reports are incomplete or messy.

(5) Students exhibit poor collaborative skills.

Chapter 11

1. Expert and referent power. By keeping up with developments in your field and giving your students a sense of belonging and acceptance.

2. Forming, storming, norming, and performing.

4. Diffusion occurs when different academic and social expectations held by different members are spread throughout the group. Crystallization occurs when expectations converge and crystallize into a shared experience. Diffusion precedes crystallization.

5. Sole provider of information (commander-in-chief), translator or summarizer of student ideas, and equal partner with students in creating ideas and problem solutions; student opinion, student talk, and spontaneity will increase from the former to the latter.

6. (a) drill and practice

(b) group discussion

(c) seatwork

9. Visitor at the door; safety concerning equipment.

10. Make rules consistent with your classroom climate.

Make rules that can be enforced.

State rules generally enough to include specific behaviors.

11. When the rule cannot be consistently reinforced over a reasonable period of time.

13. (1) Allow no talking.

(2) Allow no more time than is absolutely necessary.

(3) Make arrangements according to time to be spent, not exercises to be completed.

(4) Give a five-minute and a two-minute warning.

14. Give reasons for the assignment and give assignment immediately following the content presentation to which it is related.

15. (1) Restating highest-level generalization.

(2) Summarizing key aspects of content taught.

(3) Providing codes or symbols for remembering the content.

17. Establish an open risk-free climate.

Plan lessons that match student interests and needs.

Allow for activities and responsibilities congruent with the learners' cultures.

Chapter 12

1. (1) Establish positive relationships.

(2) Prevent attention seeking and work avoidance.

(3) Quickly and unobtrusively redirect misbehavior.

(4) Stop persistent and chronic misbehavior.

(5) Teach self-control.

(6) Respect cultural differences.

2. Sane messages communicate to students that their behavior is unacceptable in a manner that does not blame, scold, or humiliate.

3. "I messages" focus on your feelings about the behavior or situation that angered you.

4. (1) Develop classroom rules.

(2) Get support from school administrators for an area to which disruptive students can be moved temporarily.

(3) Hold private conferences with disruptive students.

(4) Follow through by giving students an opportunity to return to the classroom.

5. Positive: give a reward immediately following a desirable behavior.

Negative: end an uncomfortable state when a desirable behavior occurs.

6. Time out: removing a student to an area in which he or she can receive no reinforcement.

Response cost: removing a reinforcer or privilege contingent on disruptive or inappropriate behavior.

7. (1) They devote extensive time to organizing their classroom to minimize disruption and enhance work engagement.

(2) They methodically teach rules and routines and monitor their compliance.

(3) They inform students of the consequences for breaking the rules and enforce the consequences.

9. (1) You alone can be the judge of what occurred, what the proper punishment is, and whether the punishment has been met.

(2) You provide alternative forms of punishment from which the student must choose.

(3) You select a punishment from alternatives provided by the student.

12. (1) Select the target behavior.

(2) Identify natural consequences of the target behavior.

(3) Choose from among the natural consequences those most likely to be reinforcing.

(4) Identify from these the natural consequences most easily noticed by the learner.

(5) Design lessons that make the natural consequence conspicuous to the learner.

(6) Select appropriate backup reinforcers.

(7) Condition the natural reinforcer by having learners engage in the behavior.

13. Punishment does not guarantee that the desirable behavior will occur; the effects of punishment are specific to a particular context and behavior; the effects of punishment can spread to desirable behaviors; punishment can elicit hostile and aggressive responses; punishment can become associated with the punisher.

14. When the desired behavior is made clear at the time of the punishment and when used in conjunction with rewards.

15. (1) To gain support of the parent for assuming some of the responsibility for the discipline management process.

(2) To design a plan of action for addressing the problem at home and at school.

Chapter 13

2. (1) Dispensing state and federal funds.

(2) Efficient development and organization of instructional materials, texts, and media.

(3) Training and assignment of instructional staff.

3. A student who cannot learn from the instructional resources designated for the majority of students.

5. ● Compensatory: transmitting content by way of alternate modalities to circumvent a fundamental weakness.

● Remedial: using conventional techniques and practices to repeat instruction to eliminate the weakness.

6. Intelligence, achievement, creativity, and task persistence.

7. It might eliminate gifted students whose tested IQs may not reflect their true intelligence.

8. Applying abstract principles, being curious, giving uncommon responses, showing imagination.

9. Ability to devise organizational approaches; ability to concentrate on detail; self-imposed high standards; persistence in achieving personal goals.

10. Anywhere from being unable to express themselves in English to being marginally proficient in English.

11. A learner who is equally proficient in two languages.

12. Structured immersion allows the student to respond in her or his native language, whereas the transitional method encourages the student to shift to English as soon as possible.

13. Because of the requirement that learners with disabilities be educated in the least restrictive environment, some learners must be taught in the regular classroom, at least part of the time.

14. Physical disability, auditory disability, visual disability, mental disability, emotional disability, learning disability, speech disability, autistic, and multiple disabilities.

Chapter 14

1. ● NRTs compare a student's performance to the performance of a large sample of pupils (called the norm group) representative of those being tested. It is useful when you need to compare a learner's performance to that of others of the same age or grade level.

● CRTs compare a student's performance to a standard of mastery called a criterion. It is useful when we wish to decide if a student needs more instruction in a certain skill or area of content.

2. (1) Level of cognitive complexity.

(2) Area of instructional content.

3. (1) True-False

(2) Matching

(3) Multiple-choice

(4) Completion or short answer

4. (1) Stem clues.

(2) Grammatical clues.

(3) Redundant words/unequal response length.

(4) Use of "all of the above"/"none of the above."

5. (1) Pictorial, graphical, or tabular stimuli.

(2) Analogues that demonstrate relationships among terms.

(3) Application of previously learned principles or procedures.

6. ● Extended response: Allows student to determine the length and complexity of a response. It is most useful when the problem provides little or no structure and outcomes at the synthesis and evaluation levels are desired.

● Restricted response: poses a specific problem for which the student must recall proper information, organize it, derive a defensible conclusion, and express it within the limits of the problem. It is most useful when the problem posed is structured and outcomes at the application and analysis levels are desired.

7. (1) Higher-level cognitive processes have been taught and are to be tested.

(2) Only a few tests need be graded.

(3) Test security is a consideration.

8. ● Advantages: they require students to utilize higher-level cognitive processes, some topics and objectives are best suited for them, and they can measure communication skills pertinent to a subject area.

● Disadvantages: they are tedious to read and score, may be influenced by communication skills of the learner, and may involve some degree of subjectivity on the part of the scorer.

9. A guide written in advance, indicating the criteria or components of an acceptable answer.

10. (1) Content

(2) Organization

(3) Process

(4) Accuracy/reasonableness

(5) Completeness/internal consistency

(6) Originality/creativity

11. (1) Group similar items together.

(2) Arrange items from easy to hard.

(3) Properly space items.

(4) Keep items and options on same page.

(5) Place illustrations near descriptive material.

(6) Check for randomness.

(7) Decide how students will record answers.

(8) Provide space for name.

(9) Check directions for clarity.

(10) Proofread the test.

12. ● Validity—does the test measure what it is supposed to measure?

● Reliability—does the test yield the same or similar scores consistently?

● Accuracy—does the test approximate an individual's true level of knowledge, skill, or ability?

13. (1) Content

(2) Concurrent

(3) Predictive

14. (1) Test-retest

(2) Alternate form

(3) Internal consistency

15. ● Validity, approximately .60–.80 or higher

● Reliability, approximately .80–.90 or higher

● 1.0

16. Comparisons with:

(1) Other students

(2) Established standards

(3) Aptitude

(4) Actual versus potential effort

(5) Actual versus potential improvement

17. A test constructed by specialists to determine a student's level of performance relative to other students of similar age and grade.

18. That the student's score associated with the percentile rank was higher than the scores of that percentage of individuals in the norming sample—or that in the norming sample the percent indicated scored lower than this individual.

(1) It is not the percent of correct answers.

(2) The extreme or end points of a percentile distribution tend to be spread out, while percentiles toward the center tend to be compressed, making comparisons between the same number of points at different portions of the scale difficult.

Chapter 15

1. Conventional tests are given to provide data on which to base grades, indicate how much has been learned, make decisions about instructional placement, talk to parents about, and help others make employment decisions. Performance assessments are given to stimulate higher-order thinking in the classroom and simulate real-world activities.

2. By refocusing the curriculum on thinking, problem solving, and student responsibility for learning.

3. An indirect measure, such as knowledge shown in a multiple-choice test, will only suggest that something has been learned. A direct measure, such as a problem-solving activity, requires that what has been learned can be applied and exhibited in the context of a real-world problem.

5. For example, the Darwin School records percentage of words read accurately during oral reading, number of sentences read with understanding, and number of story elements learners can talk about on their own. The West Orient School requires portfolios of poetry, essays, biographies, and self-reflections.

8. Scoring rubrics are model answers against which a learner's performance is compared. They can be a detailed list of what an acceptable answer must contain or a sample of typical responses that would be acceptable.

Formative Observation of Effective Teaching Practices Instrument

(See reference to the behaviors in this instrument in Chapter 1, "The Effective Teacher," Tables 1.2–1.4, 1.6, and 1.7.)

The instrument (Figure C.1) contains 28 behaviors alongside which you can place a checkmark when you observe a particular effectiveness or ineffectiveness indicator. Your observations may lead you to check an *ineffective* practice, an *effective* practice, or *both*, in which case a teacher may have exhibited behaviors associated with both effective *and* ineffective teaching. When the lesson does not provide the opportunity to observe a particular teaching effectiveness indicator, write the code "N/A" for not applicable beside it.

The purpose of observing and recording your observations is to reflect upon what you see for *your own self-improvement*. (The purpose is not to make conclusions about individual teachers, for which your brief period and frequency of observation would be inadequate.) We call this a "formative" observation instrument to underscore its use in helping to *form* or mold effective teaching behaviors instead of to grade, test, or evaluate.

Following are three classroom dialogues with which you can practice "seeing" some of the behaviors identified on the instrument and discussed in Chapter 1. Additional practice dialogues and observation instruments appear in the companion text to this volume, *Observation Skills for Effective Teaching*, 2nd edition (Borich, 1994).

Key Behavior	Indicators of Effectiveness	Observed* (✓)	Observed* (✓)	Indicators of Lack of Effectiveness
Clarity	1. Informs learners of skills or understandings expected at end of lesson			Fails to link lesson content to how and at what level of complexity the content will be used
	2. Provides learners with an advance organizer with which to place lesson content in perspective			Starts presenting content without first introducing the topic in some larger context
	3. Checks for task-relevant prior learning at beginning of lesson and reteaches when necessary			Moves to new content without checking understanding of prerequisite facts or concepts
	4. Gives directives slowly and distinctly; checks for understanding along the way			Presents too many directives at once or too quickly
	5. Knows learners' ability levels and teaches at or slightly above their current level of functioning			Fails to recognize that the instruction is under or over the heads of students
	6. Uses examples, illustrations, or demonstrations to explain and to clarify content in text and workbooks			Restricts presentation to oral reproduction of text or workbook
	7. Ends lesson with review or summary			Fails to restate or review main ideas at the end of the lesson
Variety	8. Uses attention-getting devices			Begins lesson without full attention of most learners
	9. Shows enthusiasm and animation through variation in eye contact, voice, and gestures			Speaks in monotone and/or is motionless; lacks external signs of emotion

*Checkmarks may be tallied over reported observations to accumulate frequencies. Use the code "N/A" for not applicable, where appropriate.

Figure C.1
Formative Observation of Effective Teaching Practices instrument

Key Behavior	Indicators of Effectiveness		Observed* (✓)	Observed* (✓)	Indicators of Lack of Effectiveness
Variety, *continued*	10. Varies activities with which the instructional stimuli are presented (e.g., lecturing, questioning, discussion, practice [daily])				Uses single instructional activity for long periods at a time and/or infrequently alters the modality through which learning is to occur (seeing, listening, doing)
	11. Uses mix of rewards and reinforcers (weekly, monthly)				Fails to provide rewards and reinforcements that are timely and meaningful to the student
	12. Uses student ideas and participation to foster lesson objectives when appropriate (weekly)				Assumes role of sole authority and provider of information; ignores student input and diversity
	13. Varies types of questions and probes	Q convergent divergent			Repeatedly uses only one type of question or probe
		P to clarify to solicit to redirect			
Task Orientation	14. Develops unit and lesson plans in accordance with text and curriculum guide				Teaches topics tangential to curriculum guide and adopted text; easily gets side-tracked by student or personal interests
	15. Handles administrative and clerical interruptions efficiently				Uses large amounts of instructional time to complete administrative and clerical tasks
	16. Stops misbehavior with a minimum of disruption to the class				Focuses at length on individual instances of misbehavior during instructional time

Key Behavior	Indicators of Effectiveness	Observed* (✓)	Observed* (✓)	Indicators of Lack of Effectiveness
Task Orientation, *continued*	17. Generally, uses direct instruction strategies for teaching Type 1 behaviors and indirect instruction strategies for teaching Type 2 behaviors			Uses ineffective instructional methods for achieving lesson objectives (e.g., confuses drill and practice content with group discussion content)
	18. Establishes end products (e.g., reviews, tests) that are clearly visible to students			Fails to establish clearly identifiable weekly and monthly milestones (e.g., tests and reviews toward which the class works)
Engagement	19. Provides for guided practice			Fails to ask learners to attempt the desired behavior or skill after instruction has been given
	20. Provides correctives for guided practice in a nonevaluative atmosphere			Calls attention to the inadequacy of initial responses
	21. Uses individualized or attention-getting strategies to promote interest among special types of learners when appropriate			Does not attempt to match instructional methods to the learning needs of special students
	22. Uses meaningful verbal praise			Always uses same verbal clichés, (e.g., "OK") or fails to praise when opportunity occurs
	23. Monitors seatwork by circulating and frequently checking progress			Fails to monitor seatwork or monitors unevenly

Figure C.1, *continued*

Following are three classroom dialogues with which to practice "seeing" and discussing some of the behaviors identified on the Formative Observation of Effective Teaching Practices Instrument and discussed in Chapter 1 and throughout the text. Additional practice dialogues and observation instruments appear in a companion text to this volume, *Observation Skills for Effective Teaching*, 2nd Edition (Borich, 1994, Merrill/Prentice Hall).

Key Behavior	Indicators of Effectiveness	Observed* (✓)	Observed* (✓)	Indicators of Lack of Effectiveness
Moderate-to-high success rates	24. Unit and lesson organization reflects task-relevant prior learning			Fails to sequence lessons based on task-relevant prior learning
	25. Administers correctives immediately after initial response			Delays in checking and correcting wrong responses after initial practice is completed
	26. Divides lessons into small, easily digestible pieces			Prepares lessons with more content or complexity than can be taught in the allotted time
	27. Plans transitions to new content in small, easy-to-grasp steps			Makes abrupt changes between lesson topics; no sign of "dovetailing"
	28. Establishes momentum (e.g., pacing and intensity gradually build toward major milestones)			Lessons lack changes in pacing (e.g., slower pace after a major event building to a faster pace just before a major event); intensity and tempo are static

Dialogue 1

The scene is a hard-to-handle, lower-track junior high life science class in which the teacher is presenting a lesson on reproductive systems. Her goal is to teach the biological foundations of sexual reproduction required by the curriculum guide. This class is designed as an introduction to a unit on sex education to be taught the following semester. The teacher has taught for a year and a half and is certified in social studies (major) and biology (minor). The dialogue begins on page 000.

_ . _ . _ . _ . _ . _ . _ . _ . _ . _ . _ . _ . _ . _

Teacher: I know everyone will be attentive to today's lesson, because it's about the reproductive cycle. (Some snickering can be heard in the back of the room.) Now this is serious stuff, and I don't want any laughing or fooling around. Who knows some ways by which lower forms of animal life reproduce?

Tim: Well, one way we studied last year is by dividing in half.

Teacher: OK. That is reproduction by fission, in which the parent organism splits into two or more organisms, thereby losing its original identity. It is the way most single-celled animals reproduce. Can anyone think of any other means of reproduction?

Tracy: Sometimes an egg—or something like an egg—gets fertilized.

Teacher: We're just talking about *lower* forms of animal life.

Bill: Isn't there a way that new life can be created by parts of other things coming together?

Teacher: Good. You must be talking about the process called conjugation. This occurs when two similar organisms fuse, exchange nuclear material, and then break apart, taking on two different identities. This is the most primitive method of reproduction. Does anyone know of any other ways in which animal life can reproduce?

Rick: You mean like dogs and cats?

Teacher: No! We're not at that point yet. Well, there is one other—and you should know this, because it's in the text. Many multicellular animals reproduce by having male and female reproductive cells, which unite to form a single cell called a zygote—which then divides to form a new organism. The word that describes the union of male and female cells is *fertilization*. In this form of reproduction, half the genes in the zygote come from one parent and half from the other.

Mark: That's what sex is all about.

Teacher: OK . . . speaking out without raising your hand means an extra assignment for tonight. If it happens again, you will have one day in detention. If that doesn't cure you, we will make it two days. Answer all the questions under A, B, and C at the end of Chapter 7. Have you learned your lesson?

Mark: I suppose so.

Teacher: Now, where were we?

Barbara: We were talking about zions.

Teacher: They're called zygotes. Now in higher animals—including humans—single species are either male or female, according to whether they produce male reproductive cells or female reproductive cells. Somewhere there's a picture of this in your text. The typical male reproductive cell is a sperm, and the typical female reproductive cell is an egg or ovum.

Unidentified student: We know all that!

Teacher: That's enough! I don't want to hear anyone . . .

Principal: (Breaking in over the P.A. system) Teachers, I'm sorry to interrupt, but I have an important announcement. Orders for individual and class pictures must be in no later than 3:00 P.M. today. Failure to place your order by that time means you will not receive pictures for this year. While I have your attention, I would like to tell students to remind their parents that tonight is parent-teacher night, and we would like a good turnout, so be sure to remind mom and dad. Thank you. (During the announcement, some students begin leaving their seats and talking with their neighbors.)

Teacher: Class isn't over yet, so be quiet and let's get back to work. Open your books to the questions at the end of Chapter 7. Mark, you take the first one. What is reproduction by fission?

Mark: Fission. Well . . . I'm not sure.

Teacher: But I just told you. How could you forget so soon? Debbie?

Debbie: It's reproducing by cellular division or the splitting of an organism into two parts.

Teacher: Next, Robert. What's reproduction by fusion?

Robert: It's . . . it's when things come together.

Teacher: Mary, could you give us a better answer?

Mary: It's when two similar organisms fuse, exchange nuclear material, and then divide again, producing new identities.

Teacher: That's a perfect answer. OK, class, now let's change our focus to how plant life reproduces, because that's in Chapter 7 too. Does anyone know how plant reproduction differs from animal reproduction? (There is silence for a few seconds.) OK, then, I'll tell you.

Dialogue 2

For this example we observe the beginning of an elementary school lesson in arithmetic. Today's lesson is about ratios and proportions and is taught by a teacher who has been at this school for two years and at another school in the same district for three years before that. Math ability does not seem high for most class members, and they have been noticeably anxious about an upcoming unit test. Moreover, some may not have grasped all that they should from earlier lessons in this unit.

Teacher: Today our goal will be to study ratios and proportions, but using more real-life problems than in previous lessons. Some of you have had trouble learning how to calculate a ratio, so let's back up and review our skills in division. Who can tell me why division is so important in computing a ratio?

Marc: It's because ratios are nothing but division problems.

Teacher: Yes, that's right, in the sense that ratios can be expressed as one number over another, like this (writes $4/8$ on board). Now, let's look at this cereal box I have here. Sue, take the box in your hands and tell me how full it is.

Sue: Well, I don't exactly know. It feels pretty heavy—I mean it's kind of full.

Teacher: What if I asked you to tell me how much *kind of full is*?

Sue: I'd say *kind of* means almost full—well, maybe a little less than almost full (class laughs).

Teacher: I think the class may have thought your answer was humorous because they would like to know what "a little less than almost full" means. Now, because this is a very typical problem—like the kind people face every day at home and at work—it would be nice to express some things more accurately without the use of words, which tend to be very imprecise when used to describe amounts of things. How might we be more precise, John?

John: Let's form a ratio.

Teacher: OK. But how do we go about forming a ratio to describe the amount of cereal in this box? Can you tell us some more?

John: Well, we need to know how much the box holds.

Teacher: That's right. You've got the first step. Now, Tim, what's the next step?

Tim: I don't know.

Teacher: Mary?

Mary: (silence)

Teacher: Betty? (after 10 seconds)

Betty: (silence)

Teacher: Come on, class. You were all doing so well. Somebody make a guess.

Betty: (without raising her hand) I think we should compare how much the box holds to how much it has in it.

Teacher: Never speak out without raising your hand, Betty. So, our second step, Betty, is . . .

Betty: To measure how much is in the box.

Teacher: That's right. You have just given us the form of a ratio, maybe without even knowing it. That form is (writes on board):

$$\frac{\text{what is}}{\text{what could be}} = \frac{\text{a little less than half full}}{\text{full}}$$

Now comes the hard part. How will we find numbers to put in the top and the bottom of this division problem? Any suggestions?

Danny: I have an idea. Let's see how many glasses of water the box holds and then see how many glasses of water it takes to fill the box to where the cereal is.

Teacher: That's a pretty clever idea, but it may have a few problems as well. Bobby, you have your hand up.

Bobby: The box isn't going to hold water long enough to do the counting.

Teacher: Right. And what if the box doesn't fill up exactly at a full glass? We'd have to measure in parts or fractions of glasses, and we haven't come to that yet. Let's look on the box and read how the manufacturer measured what's inside (hands box to Terri).

Terri: It says, "This box contains six 8-ounce servings measured by volume."

Teacher: So how many ounces does the whole box contain? Let's review (writes on board). You supply the answers as I go down the list.

$$1 \times 8 = 8$$
$$2 \times 8 = 16$$
$$3 \times 8 = 24$$
$$4 \times 8 = 32$$
$$5 \times 8 = 40$$
$$6 \times 8 = 48$$

So 48 ounces is our total. Now, let's go back to Danny's original idea with the water, but let's measure the contents of the box using ounces. I happen to have an 8-ounce measuring cup. Marc, you pour while the rest of us count.

Class: One.

Marc: Where do I empty it?

Teacher: Let's put it here in the shoe box.

Class: Two . . . three . . . four . . . five

Marc: The sixth one's not full.

Teacher: OK. Read on the side of the cup how full it is.

Marc: It's right at 2 on the cup.

Teacher: That means 2 ounces. Let's do a little arithmetic. What's our total? Now, who wants to do this problem? (Mary raises her hand)

Mary: Well, we had five full cups, so that's
$$8 + 8 = 16 + 8 = 24 + 8 = 32.$$

Class: One more.

Mary: Yea, I guess that's only four, so $32 + 8 = 40$ and then the 2 at the end makes 42.

Teacher: OK. Now we have all that we need to create a ratio to describe exactly how full the box was. What does this ratio look like, class?

Class: 42 over 48 (teacher writes):

$$\frac{42}{48} = \frac{\text{what is}}{\text{what could be}}$$

Teacher: Because you've learned this so well, we will move on to our next topic. But first, I need to get some overheads from my drawer. No talking, except in a soft voice.

━ ・ ━ ・ ━ ・ ━ ・ ━ ・ ━ ・ ━ ・ ━ ・ ━ ・ ━ ・ ━ ・ ━ ・ ━ ・ ━ ・ ━

Dialogue 3

This dialogue is from a high school English class for which the curriculum guide specifies a unit on poetry appreciation. Because the curriculum guide is vague about how to achieve this outcome, the teacher decides the best way to appreciate poetry is first to learn its fundamentals. To accomplish this he decides to introduce the unit with a lesson on poetic meter. This teacher has taught 11 years but has been at this school only one year after being transferred from another school to fill a midyear vacancy.

Teacher: I want you to listen to a brief excerpt of two popular songs being played on the radio. I think you'll recognize them. Here they are—listen carefully. (Turns tape recorder on until about half of each song is played.) How many like the first song better than the second? (counts 12 hands) Now, how many like the second better? (counts 18 hands) Who can tell me what they like about the first song?

Diana: I like the beat . . . I guess it's the rhythm.

Teacher: Anyone care to say why they like the second song?

Tom: Well, I like its beat . . . the way it gets you stirred up inside . . . maybe its rhythm . . . just what Diana said, I guess.

Teacher: I chose these two songs not only because they are both very popular right now and I knew you would recognize them, but because they have two very different beats or tempos. Because a good number of you chose each one, both tempos seemed to work—but in very different ways. Now: If you were to exchange the words of these two songs but keep the original tempos, do you think the songs would still be as popular as they are? Joan, you have your hand up.

Joan: It just wouldn't work. The songs would sound silly. The words wouldn't match the rhythm, in my opinion.

Teacher: Well, I think there would be quite a few who might agree with you. These songwriters had to find the right beat to match the words. Although today we will be talking about poetry and not your favorite songs (class groans in jest), the two have much in common. Poets, like songwriters, must find the right rhythm to match the words. In poetry, concepts such as *beat, tempo*, and *rhythm* are represented by a poem's meter.

To appreciate a poem—and especially to gain the full emotional impact intended by its author—you must be able to recognize its meter, or rhythm. Today I will describe the different meters used by poets. Listen carefully, because toward the end of the period we're going to have a little fun. Because you all groaned, and I knew you would, I plan to play parts of some of the other popular songs—some of your favorites—and then ask if you see any resemblance between their rhythms and the four types of poetic meter I will now describe. Let's begin by examining what meter is. Anyone care to venture a guess? (Debby raises her hand)

Debby: Well, meter is a form of measurement, like in millimeter or kilometer.

Teacher: That's a good beginning. You've gone right to the root of the word itself. And, surprising to some people, it also is a form of measurement in poetry. So we're off to a good start. Because I don't think anyone would be interested in the length and width of a poem, how is meter used in poetry?

Ruth: Well, could it be to measure its rhythm, or what Diana meant when she used the word *beat*?

Teacher: Correct. You've made the transfer from measuring something physical with the concept of meter to measuring what we will call *verse*. But maybe we should define verse. Any ideas?

Roland: It's like the lyrics in a song . . . the words, kind of . . . but they wouldn't look right if you saw them written out, only if they're sung or read out loud.

Teacher: Yes. The lyrics in a song have much in common with verse in a poem, because both are the vehicles that convey the author's message. Now, *how* a poet communicates his or her message is just as important as *what* is communicated—just as you pointed out in the two songs I played, when you said the words wouldn't work if sung to the other song's rhythm. The poet has to get the rhythm right, otherwise the words—or verse—might not convey the message. To do this, the poet must choose an appropriate meter, which requires making a number of decisions; it's not as simple as it looks.

Today we will look at just one of these, called the foot. In the next few lessons we will cover the others, which will lead us to an appreciation of how the poet arranges the number of syllables to a line, creates a pattern among various lines by the use of rhyme, and forms groups of two or sometimes three lines, which are called *stanzas*. So—what's a foot?

Rich: It's what you put your socks over (class snickers).

Teacher: No talking out without raising your hand. This is a warning, Richard. A foot is the way in which syllables in a line of poetry are accented. A foot consists of one accented syllable accompanied by one or two unaccented syllables. The accented syllable may precede or follow either one or two unaccented syllables in a regularly recurring sequence throughout the line. Let's look at this line on the transparency to actually see what I mean (switches on overhead).

Bŭt tár/riĕs yét / thĕ caúse / fŏr whích / hĕ díed. (writing on board) This symbol "˘" means an unaccented syllable and this "´" means an accented syllable. What kind of consistent pattern do you see and hear? (reads line)

Toby: Well, it's kind of singsong.

Teacher: What do you mean by singsong?

Toby: One unaccented syllable always precedes one accented syllable.

Teacher: That's right. And, in fact, the poet wanted this line to vary, just as you said, in a down-up or singsong-type pattern, because that's the rhythm he felt would best convey his message. We will look at the rest of the lines of this poem later to get its full meaning, but for now you've gotten the idea of a foot and of meter. By the way, how many feet are in this line, Toby?

Toby: Four.

Teacher: No! You're not being careful. Mary, how many are there?

Mary: Five.

Teacher: Very good. The pattern repeats itself five times. This type of pattern is called an *iamb* or an *iambic foot*. It is only the first of four different ways of accenting syllables that we will study. Before looking at some examples of these, let's practice recognizing the iambic foot. On the next four lines of poetry, place the accents where you think they should go to create an iambic foot. When you're finished, look up and I'll give you my answers. Oops, someone's at the door. Sue, would you take a message, please?

Sue: (whispering) It's a counselor.

Teacher: When you've finished with these four, go on to the iambic exercise marked *D* at the end of Chapter 11. Check your work with the answer key in the appendix. I'll give bonus discussion points for those who get them all right. (Goes to door.)

Alberto, P., & Troutman, A. (1986). *Applied behavior analysis for teachers: Influencing student performance* (2nd ed.). Englewood Cliffs, NJ: Merrill/Prentice Hall.

Anderson, J. R. (1990). *Cognitive psychology and its implications* (4th ed.). San Francisco: W. H. Freeman.

Anderson, L., & Block, J. (1987). Mastery learning models. In M. J. Dunkin (Ed.), *International encyclopedia of teaching and teacher education* (pp. 58–67). New York: Pergamon.

Anderson, L., Evertson, C., & Brophy, J. (1982). *Principles of small group instruction in elementary reading.* East Lansing, MI: Michigan State University, Institute for Research on Teaching.

Anderson, L., Stevens, D., Prawat, R., & Nickerson, J. (1988). Classroom task environments and students' risk-related beliefs. *The Elementary School Journal, 88,* 181–296.

Anderson, M. G. (1992). The use of selected theater rehearsal technique activities with African-American adolescents labeled "Behaviorally Disordered." *Exceptional Children, 59,* 132–140.

Aschlbacher, P. R. (1991). Humanitas: A thematic curriculum. *Educational Leadership, 49*(2), 9–16.

Atkinson, M. L. (1984). Computer-assisted instruction: Current state of the art. *Computers in the Schools, 1,* 91–99.

Ausubel, D. P. (1968). *Educational psychology: A cognitive view.* New York: Holt, Rinehart & Winston.

Baca, L., & Cervantes, H. (1989). *The bilingual special education interface.* Santa Clara, CA: Times Mirror/Mosby.

Baer, D. M., Wolf, M. M., & Risley, T. R. (1968). Some current dimensions of applied behavior analysis. *Journal of Applied Behavior Analysis, 1,* 91–97.

Bandura, A. (1977). Self-efficacy: Toward a unified theory of behavioral change. *Psychology Review, 84,* 191–215.

Bandura, A. (1986). *Social foundations of thought and action: A social cognitive theory.* Englewood Cliffs, NJ: Prentice Hall.

Bangert, R., Kulik, J., & Kulik, C. (1983). Individualized systems of instruction in secondary schools. *Review of Educational Research, 53,* 143–158.

Barnes, J. (1987). Teaching experience. In M. J. Dunkin (Ed.), *International encyclopedia of teaching and teacher education* (pp. 608–611). New York: Pergamon.

Bartz, K., & Levine, E. (1978). Child rearing by black parents: A description and comparison to Anglo and Chicano parents. *Journal of Marriage and the Family, 40,* 709–719.

Beane, J. A. (1991). Sorting out the self-esteem controversy. *Educational Leadership, 49,* 25–30.

Bee, H. (1992). *The developing child.* New York: HarperCollins.

Bellack, A., Kliebard, H., Hyman, R., & Smith, F. (1966). *The language of the classroom.* New York: Teachers College Press.

Bennett, C. (1990). *Comprehensive multicultural education: Theory and practice* (2nd ed.). Boston: Allyn & Bacon.

Bennett, N., & Desforges, C. (1988). Matching classroom tasks to students' attainments. *The Elementary School Journal, 88,* 221–224.

Bennett, N., Desforges, C., Cockburn, A., & Wilkinson, B. (1981). *The quality of pupil learning experiences: Interim report.* Lancaster, England: University of Lancaster, Centre for Educational Research and Development.

Bereiter, C., & Engelmann, S. (1966). *Teaching disadvantaged children in the preschool.* Englewood Cliffs, NJ: Prentice Hall.

Bergan, J. R., & Dunn, J. A. (1976). *Psychology and education: A science for instruction.* New York: Wiley.

Berk, L. E. (1993). *Infants, children and adolescents.* Boston: Allyn & Bacon.

Bettencourt, E., Gillett, M., Gall, M., & Hull, R. (1983). Effects of teacher enthusiasm training on student on-task behavior and achievement. *American Educational Research Journal, 20,* 435–450.

Block, J. (1987). Mastery learning models. In M. J. Dunkin (Ed.), *International encyclopedia of teaching and teacher education.* New York: Pergamon.

Bloom, B. (1981). *All our children learning.* New York: McGraw-Hill.

Bloom, B., Englehart, M., Hill, W., Furst, E., & Krathwohl, D. (1984). *Taxonomy of educational objectives: The classification of educational goals. Handbook I: Cognitive domain.* New York: Longman Green.

Blumenfeld, P. C., Soloway, E., Marx, R. W., Krajcik, J. S., Guzdial, M., & Palinscar, A. (1991). Motivation project-based learning: Sustaining the doing, supporting the learning. *Educational Psychologist, 26,* 369–398.

Bombeck, E. (1984). *At wits' end.* Thorndike, ME: Thorndike Press.

Borich, G. (1993). *Clearly outstanding: Making each day count in your classroom.* Boston: Allyn & Bacon.

Borich, G. (1994). *Observation skills for effective teaching* (2nd ed.). Englewood Cliffs, NJ: Merrill/Prentice Hall.

Borich, G. (1995). *Becoming a teacher: An inquiring dialogue for the beginning teacher.* Bristol, PA; Falmer Press.

Borich, G., & Tombari, M. (1995). *Educational psychology: A contemporary approach.* New York: HarperCollins.

Bowers, C., & Flinders, D. (1991). *Culturally responsive teaching and supervision: A handbook for staff development.* New York: Teachers College Press.

Boyer, E. (1993, March). *Making the connections.* Address presented to the meeting of the Association for Supervision and Curriculum Development, Washington, DC.

Bradstad, B., & Stumph, S. (1982). *A guidebook for teaching study skills and motivation.* Boston: Allyn & Bacon.

Bransford, J. D., & Steen, B. (1984). *The IDEAL problem solver.* New York: Freeman.

Bronfenbrenner, V. (1979). *The ecology of human development.* Cambridge, MA: Harvard University Press.

Bronfenbrenner, V. (1989). Ecological systems theory. In R. Vasta (Ed.), *Annals of child development* (Vol. 6, pp. 187–251). Greenwich, CT: JAI Press.

Brophy, J. (1981). Teacher praise: A functional analysis. *Review of Educational Research, 51,* 5–32.

Brophy, J. (Ed.). (1989). *Advances in research on teaching* (Vol. 1). Greenwich, CT: JAI Press.

Brophy, J. (1992). Probing the subtleties of subject-matter teaching. *Educational Leadership, 49* (7), 4–8.

Brophy, J., & Evertson, C. (1976a). *Learning from teaching: A developmental perspective.* Boston: Allyn & Bacon.

Brophy, J., & Evertson, C. (1976b). *Process-product correlations in the Texas Teacher Effectiveness Study: Final report* (Research Report 74–4). Austin: University of Texas, Research and Development Center for Teacher Education. (ERIC Document Reproduction Service No. ED 091 094.)

Brophy, J., & Good, T. (1974). *Teacher-student relationships: Causes and consequences.* New York: Holt, Rinehart & Winston.

Brophy, J., & Good, T. (1986). Teacher behavior and student achievement. In M. C. Wittrock (Ed.), *Handbook of research on teaching* (3rd ed.) (pp. 328–375). Englewood Cliffs, NJ: Merrill/Prentice Hall.

Brown, A. L. (1980). Metacognitive development and reading. In R. J. Spiro, B. C. Bruce, & W. F. Brewer (Eds.), *Theoretical issues in reading comprehension: Perspectives from cognitive psychology, linguistics, artificial intelligence, and education* (pp. 453–481). Hillsdale, NJ: Erlbaum.

Brown, G., & Edmondson, R. (1984). Asking questions. In E. Wragg (Ed.), *Classroom teaching skills* (pp. 97–119). New York: Nichols.

Brown, G., & Wragg, E. (1993). *Questioning.* London: Routledge.

Browne, D. A. (1984). WISC-R scoring patterns among Native Americans of the northern plains. *White Cloud Journal, 3,* 3–16.

Bruner, J. (1978). The role of dialogue in langage acquisition. In A. Sinclair, R. Jarvella,

& W. Levelt (Eds.), *The child's conception of language* (pp. 241–256). New York: Springer-Verlag.

Bruner, J. S. (1966). *Toward a theory of instruction*. New York: W. W. Norton.

Bullough, R. V. (1989). *First-year teacher: A case study*. New York: Teachers College Press.

Burden, P. (1986). Teacher development: Implications for teacher education. In J. Raths and L. Katz (Eds.), *Advances in teacher education* (Vol. 2). Norwood, NJ: Ablex.

Calfee, R. (1986, April). *Those who can explain teach*. Paper presented at the annual meeting of the American Educational Research Association, San Francisco.

Canter, L. (1976). *Assertive discipline: A take-charge approach for today's educator*. Seal Beach, CA: Canter and Associates.

Canter, L. (1989). Assertive discipline. More than names on the board and marbles in a jar. *Phi Delta Kappan*, September, 1989, 57–61.

Carlson, C. (1992). Single parenting and step-parenting: Problems, issues and interventions. In M. J. Fine & C. Carlson (Eds.), *The handbook of family–school intervention: A systems perspective* (pp. 188–214). Boston: Allyn & Bacon.

Cassidy, J., & Asher, S. R. (1992). Loneliness and peer relations in young children. *Child Development, 63*, 350–365.

Christenson, S. L., Rounds, T., & Franklin, M. J. (1992). Home–school collaboration: Effects, issues and opportunities. In S. L. Christenson & J. C. Conoley (Eds.), *Home-school collaboration: Enhancing children's academic and social competence*. Silver Spring, MD: National Association of School Psychologists.

Civil Rights Commission. (1973). *Teachers and students. Report V: Differences in teacher intervention with Mexican-American and Anglo students*. Washington, DC: U.S. Government Printing Office.

Clark, C., & Peterson, P. (1986). Teachers' thought processes. In M. R. Wittrock (Ed.), *Handbook of research on teaching* (3rd ed.) (pp. 255–296). Englewood Cliffs, NJ: Merrill/Prentice Hall.

Clark C., & Yinger, R. (1979). *Three studies of teacher planning* (Research Series No. 55). East Lansing, MI: Michigan State University, Institute for Research on Teaching.

Cochran, M., & Dean, C. (1991). Home–school relations and the empowerment process. *American Journal of Education*.

Coffman, W. E. (1972). On the reliability of ratings of essay examinations. *NCME Reports on Measurment in Education, 3* (3).

Cohen, H. G. (1985). A comparison of the development of spatial conceptual abilities of students from two cultures. *Journal of Research in Science Teaching, 22*, 491–501.

Cohen, R. A. (1969). Conceptual styles, cultural conflict and nonverbal tests of intelligence. *American Anthropologist, 71*, 828–856.

Congressional Record. 89th Cong., 2nd sess., 1978. P.H—12179.

Cooper, J. O., Heron, T. E., & Heward, W. L. (1987). *Applied behavior analysis*. Englewood Cliffs, NJ: Merrill/Prentice Hall.

Corey, S. (1940). The teachers out-talk the pupils. *School Review, 48*, 745–752.

Corno, L., & Snow, R. (1986). Adapting teaching to individual differences among learners. In M. C. Wittrock (Ed.), *Handbook of research on teaching* (3d ed.) (pp. 605–629). Englewood Cliffs, NJ: Merrill/Prentice Hall.

Costa, A., & Lowery, L. (1989). *Techniques for teaching thinking*. Pacific Grove, CA: Midwest Publications.

Covington, M., & Omelich, C. (1987). "I knew it cold before the exam": A test of the anxiety blockage hypothesis. *Journal of Psychology, 79*, 393–400.

Crawford, J., Gage, N. L., Corno, L., Stayrouk, N., Mitman, A., Schunk, D., & Stallings, J. (1978). *An experiment on teacher effectiveness and parent-assisted instruction in the third grade* (3 vols.). Stanford, CA: Center for Educational Research, Stanford University.

Cronbach, L., & Snow, R. (1977). *Aptitudes and instructional methods*. New York: Irvington/Naiburg.

Cushner, K., McClelland, A., & Safford, P. (1992). *Human diversity in education: An integrative approach.* New York: McGraw-Hill.

Dahllof, U., & Lundgren, U. P. (1970). *Macro- and micro-approaches combined for curriculum process analysis: A Swedish educational field project.* Goteborg, Sweden: University of Goteborg, Institute of Education.

de Charms, R. (1976). *Enhancing motivation: Change in the classroom.* New York: Irvington.

Delgado-Gaitan, C. (1991). Involving parents in the schools: A process of empowerment. *American Journal of Education, 100* (1), 20–46.

Delgado-Gaitan, C. (1992). School matters in the Mexican-American home: Socializing children to education. *American Educational Research Journal, 29* (3), 495–516.

Dembo, M. (1981). *Teaching for learning: Applying educational psychology in the classroom* (2nd ed.). Glenview, IL: Scott, Foresman.

Devin-Sheehan, L., Feldman, R. S., & Allen, V. L. (1976). Research on children tutoring children: A critical review. *Review of Educational Research, 46,* 355–385.

Dillard, J. L. (1972). *Black English: Its history and usage in the United States.* New York: Random House.

Dillon, D. (1989). Showing them that I want them to learn and that I care about who they are: A microethnography of the social organization of a secondary low-track English reading classroom. *American Educational Research Journal, 26,* 227–259.

Dillon, J. T. (1988a). *Questioning and discussion: A multidisciplinary study.* Norwood, NJ: Ablex.

Dillon, J. T. (1988b). *Questioning and teaching: A manual of practice.* New York: Teachers College Press.

Dishon, D., & O'Leary, P. (1984). *A guidebook for cooperative learning.* Kalamazoo, MI: Learning Publications.

Dishon, T. J., Patterson, G. R., Stoolmiller, M., & Skinner, M. L. (1991). Family, school and behavioral antecedents to early adolescent involvement with antisocial peers. *Developmental Psychology, 27,* 172–180.

Doneau, S. (1987). Structuring. In M. J. Dunkin (Ed.), *International encyclopedia of teaching and teacher education* (pp. 398–406). New York: Pergamon.

Donnellan, A. M., & LaVigna, G. W. (1990). Myths about punishment. In A. C. Repp & N. N. Singh (Eds.), *Perspectives on the use of non-aversive and aversive interventions for persons with developmental disabilities* (pp. 33–58). Sycamore, IL: Sycamore.

Douglas, M. (1975). *Implicit meaning.* London: Routledge and Kegan Paul.

Dowaliby, F., & Schumer, H. (1973). Teacher-centered versus student-centered mode of college classroom instruction as related to manifest anxiety. *Journal of Educational Psychology, 64,* 125–132.

Doyle, W. (1983). Academic work. *Review of Educational Research, 53,* 159–200.

Doyle, W. (1986). Classroom organization and management. In M. Wittrock (Ed.), *Handbook of research on teaching* (3rd ed.) (pp. 392–431). Englewood Cliffs, NJ: Merrill/Prentice Hall.

Duffy, G., & Roehler, L. (1989). The tension between information-giving and mediation: Perspectives on instructional explanation and teacher change. In J. Brophy (Ed.), *Advances in research on teaching* (Vol. 1) (pp. 1–33). Greenwich, CT: JAI Press.

Duffy, G., Roehler, L., & Herrman, B. (1988). Modeling mental processes helps poor readers become strategic readers. *The Reading Teacher, 41* (8), 762–767.

Dunkin, M., & Biddle, B. (1974). *The study of teaching.* New York: Holt, Rinehart & Winston.

Eisner, E. (1969). Instructional and expressive educational objectives: Their formulation and use in curriculum. In W. Popham, E. Eisner, H. Sullivan, & L. Tyler (Eds.), *Instructional Objectives: AERA Monograph Series on Curriculum Evaluation,* No. 3 (pp. 1–18). Chicago: Rand McNally.

Elbaz, A. (1983). *Teacher thinking: A study of practical knowledge.* New York: Nichols.

Elliot, S. N., & Shapiro, E. S. (1990). Intervention techniques and programs for academic performance problems. In T. B. Gutkin & C. R. Reynolds (Eds.), *The handbook of school psychology* (2nd ed.) (pp. 637–662). New York: Wiley.

Emmer, E., Evertson, C., & Anderson, L. (1980). Effective classroom management at the beginning of the school year. *The Elementary School Journal, 80* (5), 219–231.

Emmer, E., Evertson, C., Clements, B., & Worsham, M. (1994). *Classroom management for secondary teachers*. Englewood Cliffs, NJ: Prentice Hall.

Englemann, S. (1991). Teachers, schemata, and instruction. In M. M. Kennedy (Ed.), *Teaching academic subjects to diverse learners*, 218–234. New York: Teachers College Press.

Englemann, S., & Carnine, D. (1982). *Theory of instruction: Principles and applications*. New York: Irvington.

Epstein, J. L. (1987). Toward a theory of family–school connections: Teacher practices and parent involvement. In K. Hurrelmann, F. Kauffman & F. Losel (Eds.), *Social interventions: Potential and constraints* (pp. 121–136). New York: De Gruyter.

Erikson, E. (1968). *Identity, youth and crises*. New York: W. W. Norton.

Evertson, C., & Emmer, E. (1982). Effective management at the beginning of the school year in junior high classes. *Journal of Educational Psychology, 74*, 485–498.

Fielding, G., Kameenui, E., & Gerstein, R. (1983). A comparison of an inquiry and a direct instruction approach to teaching legal concepts and applications to secondary school students. *Journal of Educational Research, 76*, 243–250.

Flanders, N. (1970). *Analyzing teacher behavior*. Reading, MA: Addison-Wesley.

Floden, R. (1991). What teachers need to know about learning. In Kennedy, M. (Ed.), *Teaching academic subjects to diverse learners*, 189–216. New York: Teachers College Press.

Fogelman, K. (1983). Ability grouping in the secondary school. In K. Fogelman (Ed.), *Growing up in Britain: Papers from the National Child Development Study*. London: Macmillan.

Franklin, M. E. (1992). Culturally sensitive instructional practices for African-American learners with disabilities. *Exceptional Children, 59*, 115–122.

Frazier, D. M., & Paulson, F. L. (1992). How portfolios motivate reluctant learners. *Educational Leadership, 49* (8), 62–65.

French, J. Jr., & Raven, B. (1959). The bases of social power. In D. Cartwright (Ed.), *Studies in social power* (pp. 150–168). Ann Arbor: University of Michigan Press.

Froyen, L. A. (1993). *Classroom management: The reflective teacher-leader* (2nd ed.). Englewood Cliffs, NJ: Merrill/Prentice Hall.

Fuller, F. (1969). Concerns of teachers: A developmental conceptualization. *American Educational Research Journal, 6*, 207–226.

Gage, N. (1976). A factorially designed experiment on teacher structuring, soliciting and reacting. *Journal of Teacher Education, 16*, 35–38.

Gage, N., & Berliner, D. (1992). *Educational psychology* (5th ed.). Chicago: Rand McNally.

Gagné, E., Yekovich, C., & Yekovich, F. (1993). *The cognitive psychology of school learning*. Boston: Little, Brown.

Gagné, R. M. (1985). *The conditions of learning* (3rd ed.). New York: Holt, Rinehart & Winston.

Gagné, R., & Briggs, L. (1979). *Principles of instructional design*. New York: Holt, Rinehart & Winston.

Gagné, R., & Briggs, L. (1992). *Principles of instructional design*. New York: Holt, Rinehart & Winston.

Galambos, S. J., & Goldin-Meadow, S. (1990). The effects of learning two languages on levels of metalinguistic awareness. *Cognition, 34*, 1–56.

Gall, M. (1984). Synthesis of research on questioning in recitation. *Educational Leadership, 42* (3), 40–49.

Gallimore, R., Tharp, R. G., Sloat, K., Klein, T., & Troy, M. E. (1982). *Analysis of reading* achievement test results for the Kamehameha Early Education Project: 1972–1979. (Tech. Rep. No. 102). Honolulu: Kamahameha Schools/Bishop Estate.

Gamoran, A. (1992). Synthesis of research: Is ability grouping equitable? *Educational Leadership, 50* (2), 11–13.

Gamoran, A. (1993). Alternative uses of ability grouping in secondary schools: Can we bring high-quality instruction to low-ability classes? *American Journal of Education, 102,* 1–22.

Garcia, R. L. (1991). *Teaching in a pluralistic society: Concepts, models, strategies* (2nd ed.). New York: HarperCollins.

Gardner, H., & Hatch, T. (1989). Multiple intelligences go to school. *Educational Researcher, 18* (8), 4–10.

Gardner, J. F., & Chapman, M. S. (1990). *Program issues in developmental disabilities* (2nd ed.). 39–57, Baltimore: Paul H. Brookes.

Garger, S., & Guild, P. (1984). Learning styles: The crucial differences. *Curriculum Review, 23,* 9–12.

Ginott, H. G. (1972). *Teacher and child: A book for parents and teachers.* Englewood Cliffs, NJ: Merrill/Prentice Hall.

Glasser, W. (1986). *Control theory in the classroom.* New York: Harper & Row.

Glasser, W. (1990). *Quality school: Managing students without coercion.* New York: Harper & Row.

Goetz, E. T., Alexander, P. A., & Ash, M. J. (1992). *Educational psychology: A classroom perspective.* Englewood Cliffs, NJ: Merrill/Prentice Hall.

Good, T. (1979). Teacher effectiveness in the elementary school. *Journal of Teacher Education, 30,* 52–64.

Good, T., & Brophy, J. (1987a). *Educational psychology: A realistic approach.* New York: Longman.

Good, T., & Brophy, J. (1987b). *Looking in classrooms* (4th ed.). New York: Harper & Row.

Good, T., & Brophy, J. (1990). *Looking in classrooms* (5th ed.). New York: Harper & Row.

Good, T., & Grouws, D. (1979). Teaching effects: A process-product study in fourth-grade mathematics classrooms. *Journal of Teacher Education, 28,* 49–54.

Good, T., & Stipek, D. (1983). Individual differences in the classroom: A psychological perspective. In G. D. Fenstermacher & J. I. Goodlad (Eds.), *Individual differences and the common curriculum* (82nd yearbook of the National Society for the Study of Education, Part 2) (pp. 9–43). Chicago: University of Chicago Press.

Goodlad, J. (1984). *A place called school.* New York: McGraw-Hill.

Gordon, T. (1974). *Teacher effectiveness training.* New York: Peter H. Wyden.

Grant, C. A. (1991). Culture and teaching: What do teachers need to know? In M. M. Kennedy (Ed.), *Teaching academic subjects to diverse learners* (pp. 237–256). New York: Teachers College Press.

Grave, M. E., Weinstein, T., & Walberg, H. J. (1983). School-based home instruction and learning: A quantitative analysis. *Journal of Educational Research, 76* (6), 351–360.

Greenwood, C. R., Delguardi, J. C., & Hall, R. V. (1984). Opportunity to respond and student academic achivement. In W. L. Heward, T. E. Heron, D. S. Hill, & J. Trap-Porter (Eds.), *Focus on behavior analysis in education* (pp. 58–88) Englewood Cliffs, NJ: Merrill/Prentice Hall.

Gullickson, A. R., & Ellwein, M. C. (1985). Post-hoc analysis of teacher-made tests: The goodness of fit between prescription and practice. *Educational Measurement: Issues and Practice, 4* (1), 15–18.

Hakuta, K., Ferdman, B. M., & Diaz, R. M. (1987). Bilingualism and cognitive development: Three perspectives. In S. Rosenberg (Ed.), *Advances in applied psycholinguistics: Volume 2. Reading, writing, and language learning* (pp. 284–319). New York: Cambridge University Press.

Hall, E. (1977). *Beyond culture.* Garden City, NY: Anchor.

Hall, R. V., Delguardi, J., Greenwood, C. R., & Thurston, L. (1982). The importance of opportunity to respond in children's academic success. In E. B. Edgar, N. G. Haring, J. R. Jenkins, & C. G. Pious (Eds.), *Mentally* handicapped children: Education and training (pp. 107–140). Austin, TX: PRO-ED.

Hansford, B., & Hattie, J. (1982). The relationship between self and achievement/performance measures. *Review of Educational Research, 52*, 123–142.

Harrow, A. (1972). *A taxonomy of the psychomotor domain: A guide for developing behavioral objectives*. New York: David McKay.

Hartup, W. W. (1989). Social relationships and their developmental significance. *American Psychologist, 44*, 120–126.

Haynes, H. (1935). *The relation of teacher intelligence, teacher experience and type of school to type of questions*. Unpublished doctoral dissertation, George Peabody College for Teachers, Nashville, TN.

Hebert, E. A. (1992). Portfolios invite reflection from students and staff. *Educational Leadership, 49* (8), 58–61.

Henderson, R. W. (1980). Social and emotional needs of culturally diverse children. *Exceptional Children, 46*, 598–605.

Henderson, R. W., Swanson, R. A., & Zimmerman, B. J. (1974). Inquiry response induction in preschool children through televised modeling. *Developmental Psychology, 11* (4), 523–524.

Herrnstein, R. & Murray, C. (1994). *The bell curve: Intelligence and class structure in America*. NY: Free Press.

Hess, R. D., & Shipman, V. C. (1965). Early experience and the socialization of cognitive modes in children. *Child Development, 36*, 869–886.

Hill, H. (1989). *Effective stategies for teaching minority students*. Bloomington, IN: National Educational Service.

Hilliard, A. G. (1976). *Alternatives to IQ testing: An approach to the identification of gifted minority children*. Final report, Sacramento Division of Special Education, California State Department of Education. (ERIC Document Reproduction Service No. ED 147009)

Hilliard, A. G. (1992). The pitfalls and promises of special education practice. *Exceptional Children, 59*(2), 162–172.

Hodgkinson, H. (1988). *All one system: Demographics of education, kindergarten through graduate school*. Washington: The Institute for Educational Leadership.

Holmes Group. (1990). *Tomorrow's schools: Principles for the design of professional development schools*. East Lansing, MI: Author.

Horcones, J. (1991). Walden Two in real life: Behavior analysis in the design of the culture. In W. Ishag (Ed.), *Human behavior in today's world*. New York: Praeger.

Horcones, J. (1992). Natural reinforcement: A way to improve education. *Journal of Applied Behavior Analysis, 25* (1), 71–76.

Hunkins, F. (1989). *Teaching thinking through effective questioning*. Boston: Christopher-Gordon.

Hunt, D. (1979). Learning style and student needs: An introduction to conceptual level. In *Student learning styles: Diagnosing and prescribing programs*. Reston, VA: National Association of Secondary School Principals.

Hunter, M. (1982). *Mastery teaching*. El Segundo, CA: Instructional Dynamics, Inc.

Iwata, B. A. (1987). Negative reinforcement in applied behavior analysis: An emerging technology. *Journal of Applied Behavior Analysis, 20*, 361–387.

Jackson, P. (1968). *Life in classrooms*. New York: Holt, Rinehart & Winston.

Jensen, A. (1969). How much can we boost IQ and scholastic achievement? *Harvard Educational Review, 39* (1), 1–123.

Johnson, D., & Johnson, R. (1987). *Learning together and alone* (2nd ed.). Englewood Cliffs, NJ: Prentice Hall.

Johnson, D., & Johnson, R. (1991). *Learning together and alone* (3rd ed.). Englewood Cliffs, NJ: Prentice Hall.

Jones, F. C. (1987). *Positive classroom discipline*. New York: McGraw-Hill.

Kaplan, A. (1964). *The conduct of inquiry*. San Francisco: Chandler.

Kavale, K. A. (1990). Effectiveness of special education. In T. B. Gutkin & C. R. Reynolds (Eds.), *The handbook of school psychology* (2nd ed.) (pp. 870–900). New York: Wiley.

Kendall, F. E. (1983). *Diversity in the classroom: A multicultural approach to the education of young children.* New York: Teachers College Press.

Kendon, A. (1981). *Nonverbal communication, interaction, and gesture.* The Hague: Mouton.

Kennedy, M. (Ed.). (1991). *Teaching academic subjects to diverse learners.* New York: Teachers College Press.

Kerchoff, A. C. (1986). Effects of ability grouping in British secondary schools. *American Sociological Review, 51,* 842–858.

Knight, G. P., & Kagan, S. (1977). Acculturation of prosocial and competitive behaviors among second- and third-generation Mexican-American children. *Journal of Cross-Cultural Psychology, 8,* 273–284.

Kounin, J. (1970). *Discipline and group management in the classroom.* New York: Holt, Rinehart & Winston.

Kozulin, A. (1990). *Vygotsky's psychology: A biography of ideas.* Cambridge: Harvard University Press.

Krabbe, M., & Polivka, J. (1990, April). *An analysis of students' perceptions of effective teaching behaviors during discussion activity.* Paper presented at the annual meeting of the American Educational Research Association, Boston.

Krathwohl, D., Bloom, B., & Masia, B. (1964). *Taxonomy of educational objectives. The classification of educational goals. Handbook II: Affective domain.* New York: David McKay.

Kubiszyn, T., & Borich, G. (1996). *Educational testing and measurement: Classroom application and practice* (5th ed.). New York: HarperCollins.

Kulick, J. A., & Kulick, C. C. (1984). Effects of accelerated instruction on students. *Review of Educational Research, 54,* 409–425.

La Berge, D., & Samuels, S. (1974). Toward a theory of automatic information processing in reading. *Cognitive Psychology, 6,* 293–323.

Lambert, N. M. (1991). Partnerships of psychologists, educators, community-based agency personnel, and parents in school redesign. *Educational Psychologist, 26,* 185–198.

Lein, L. (1975). "You were talkin' though, oh yes, you was." Black American migrant children: Their speech at home and school. *Council on Anthropology and Education Quarterly, 6* (4), 1–11.

Leler, H. (1983). Parent education and involvement in relation to the schools and to parents of school-aged children. In R. Hoskins & D. Adamson (Eds.), *Parent education and public policy* (pp. 141–180). Norwood, NJ: Ablex.

Levin, H. (1986). *Educational reform for disadvantaged students: An emerging crisis.* Washington: National Education Association.

Levin, J., & Nolan, J. F. (1991). *Principles of classroom management: A hierarchical approach.* Englewood Cliffs, NJ: Prentice Hall.

Levine, D., & Havinghurst, R. (1984). *Society and education* (6th ed.). Boston: Allyn & Bacon.

Levis, D. S. (1987). Teachers' personality. In M. J. Dunkin (Ed.), *Encyclopedia of teaching and teacher education* (pp. 585–588). New York: Pergamon.

Lightfoot, S. (1983). *The good high school.* New York: Basic Books.

Lindsley, O. R. (1991). Precision teaching's unique legacy from B. F. Skinner. *Journal of Behavioral Education, 1,* 253–266.

Lindsley, O. R. (1992). Why aren't effective teaching tools widely adopted? *Journal of Applied Behavior Analysis, 25* (1), 21–26.

Linney, J. A., & Vernberg, E. (1983). Changing patterns of parental employment and the family-school relationship. In C. D. Hayes & S. Kamerman (Eds.), *Children of working parents: Experiences and outcomes* (pp. 73–99). Washington, DC: National Academy Press.

Lippitt, R., & Gold, M. (1959). Classroom social structure as a mental health problem. *Journal of Social Issues, 15,* 40–58.

Loucks-Horsley, S., Kapiton, R., Carlson, M. D., Kuerbis, P. J., Clark, P. C., Melle, G. M., Sachse, T. P., & Wolten, E. (1990). *Elementary school science for the '90s.*

Alexandria, VA: Association for Supervision and Curriculum Development.

Luiten, J., Ames, W., & Aerson, G. (1980). A meta-analysis of advance organizers on learning and retention. *American Educational Research Journal, 17*, 211–218.

Lysakowski, R., & Walberg H. (1981). Classroom reinforcement and learning: A quantitative synthesis. *Journal of Educational Research, 75*, 69–77.

Mansnerus, L. (1992, November 1). Should tracking be derailed? *Education Life.* New York Times Magazine, 14–16.

Marx, R., & Peterson, P. (1981). The nature of teacher decision-making. In B. Joyce, C. Brown, & L. Peck (Eds.), *Flexibility in teaching: An excursion into the nature of teaching and training.* New York: Longman.

Marx, R., & Walsh, J. (1988). Learning from academic tasks. *The Elementary School Journal, 88* (3), 207–219.

Mauer, R. E. (1985). *Elementary discipline handbook: Solutions for the K–8 teacher.* West Nyack, NY: The Center for Applied Research in Education.

Mayer, R. E. (1987). *Educational psychology: A cognitive approach.* Boston: Little, Brown.

McKenzie, R. (1979). Effects of questions and testlike events on achievement and on-task behavior in a classroom concept learning persentation. *Journal of Educational Research, 72*, 348–350.

Medrich, E. A., Roizen, J. A., Rubin, V., & Burkley, S. (1982). *The serious business of growing up: A study of children's lives outside school.* Berkeley: University of California Press.

Michaels, S., & Collins, J. (1984). Oral discourse styles: Classroom interaction and the acquisition of literacy. In D. Tannen (Ed.), *Coherence in spoken and written discourse.* Norwood, NJ: Ablex.

Mitchell, R. (1992). *Testing for learning: How new approaches to evaluation can improve American schools.* New York: Free Press.

National Center for Education Statistics. (1993a). *The condition of education 1993.* Washington, DC: U.S. Department of Education, Office of Educational Research and Improvement.

National Center for Education Statistics. (1993b). *Youth indicators 1993: Trends in the well-being of American youth.* Washington, DC: U.S. Department of Education, Office of Educational Research and Improvement.

National Commission on Excellence in Education (1983). *A nation at risk: The imperative for educational reform.* Washington, DC: U.S. Department of Education.

O'Neil, J. (1992). On tracking and individual differences: A conversation with Jeannie Oakes. *Educational Leadership, 50* (2), 18–21.

Oser, F. (1986). Moral education and values education: The discourse perspective. In M. Wittrock (Ed.), *Handbook of research on teaching* (3rd ed.) (pp. 917–941). Englewood Cliffs, NJ: Merrill/Prentice Hall.

Padilla, A. M., Lindholm, K. J., Chen, A., Duran, R., Hakuta, K., Lambert, W., & Tucker, G. R. (1991). The English-only movement: Myths, reality, and implications for psychology. *American Psychologist, 46*, 120–130.

Palincsar, A. (1987). *Discourse for learning about comprehending text.* Paper presented at the National Reading Conference, St. Petersburg Beach, FL.

Palincsar, A., & Brown, A. (1989). Classroom dialogues to promote self-regulated comprehension. In J. Brophy (Ed.), *Advances in research on teaching* (Vol. 1) (pp. 35–71). Greenwich, CT: JAI Press.

Parker, W. C. (1991). *Renewing the social studies curriculum.* Alexandria, VA: Association for Supervision and Curriculum Development.

Patterson, G. R., DeBarsyshe, B. D., & Ramsey, E. (1989). A developmental perspective on anti-social behavior. *American Psychologist, 44*, 329–335.

Paul, R. (1990). *Critical thinking.* Rohnert Park, CA: Center for Critical Thinking and Moral Critique, Sonoma State University.

Paulson, P. R., & Paulson, F. L. (1991). Portfolio: Stories of knowing. In P. H. Dryer (Ed.), *Claremont Reading Conference 55th yearbook 1991. Knowing: The power of stories* (pp. 294–303). Claremont, CA: Center for Developmental Studies of the Claremont Graduate School.

Piaget, J. (1977). Problems in equilibration. In M. Appel & L. Goldberg (Eds.), *Topics in cognitive development: Vol. 1. Equilibration: Theory, research and application* (pp. 3–13). New York: Plenum.

Piestrup, A. (1973). *Black dialect interference and accommodation of reading instruction in first grade* (Monograph No. 4). Berkeley, CA: University of California, Language Behavior Research Laboratory.

Polanyi, M. (1958). *Personal knowledge.* Chicago: University of Chicago Press.

Pollock, J. E. (1992). Blueprints for social studies. *Educational Leadership, 49* (8), 52–53.

Posner, G. (1987). Pacing and sequencing. In M. J. Dunkin (Ed.), *Encyclopedia of teaching and teacher education* (pp. 266–271). New York: Pergamon.

Public Law 94–142. The Education for All Handicapped Children Act, 20 U.S.C. 1401 et seq., 89 Stat. 773 (29 November 1975).

Putnam, J., & Burke, J. B. (1992). *Organizing and managing classroom learning communities.* New York: McGraw-Hill.

Ramirez, M., & Castaneda, A. (1974). *Cultural democracy: Biocognitive development and education.* New York: Academic Press.

Raven, B. H. (1974). The comparative analysis of power and power preference. In J. T. Tedeschi (Ed.), *Perspectives on social power* (pp. 172–198). Chicago: Aldine.

Redding, N. (1992). Assessing the big outcomes. *Educational Leadership, 49* (8), 49–53.

Redfield, D., & Rousseau, E. (1981). A meta-analysis of experimental research on teacher questioning behavior. *Review of Educational Research, 51,* 237–245.

Reich, P. A. (1986). *Language development.* Englewood Cliffs, NJ: Prentice Hall.

Resnick, L. B. (1987). *Education and learning to think.* Washington, DC: National Academy Press.

Resnick, L. B., & Resnick, D. P. (1991). Assessing the thinking curriculum: New tools for educational reform. In B. R. Gifford and M. C. O'Connor (Eds.), *Future assessments: Changing views of aptitude, achievement and instruction.* Boston: Kluwer.

Reynolds, M. C. (Ed.). (1989). *Knowledge base for the beginning teacher.* New York: Pergamon.

Rich, D. (1987). *Teachers and parents: An adult-to-adult approach.* Washington: National Education Association.

Richmond, G., & Striley, J. (1994). An integrated approach. *The Science Teacher, 61* (7), 42–45.

Rinne, C. (1984). *Attention: The fundamentals of classroom control.* Englewood Cliffs, NJ: Merrill/Prentice Hall.

Rist, R. (1970). Student social class and teaching expectations: The self-fulfilling prophecy in ghetto education. *Harvard Educational Review, 40,* 411–451.

Roberts, P., & Kellough, R. (1996). *A guide for developing interdisciplinary thematic units.* Englewood Cliffs, NJ: Merrill/Prentice Hall.

Rogan, J., Borich, G., & Taylor, H. P. (1992). Validation of the stages of concern questionnaire. *Action in Teacher Education, 14* (2), 43–49.

Rohrkemper, M., & Corno, L. (1988). Success and failure on classroom tasks: Adaptive learning and classroom teaching. *The Elementary School Journal, 88* (3), 298–312.

Rosenshine, B. (1971a). Objectively measured behavioral predictors of effectiveness in explaining. In I. D. Westbury & A. A. Bellock (Eds.), *Research into classroom processes* (pp. 51–100). New York: Teachers College Press.

Rosenshine, B. (1971b). *Teaching behaviors and student achievement.* London: National Foundation for Educational Research in England and Wales.

Rosenshine, B. (1983). Teaching functions in instructional programs. *The Elementary School Journal, 83,* 335–351.

Rosenshine, B. (1986). Synthesis of research on explicit teaching. *Educational Leadership, 43* (7), 60–69.

Rosenshine, B., & Stevens, R. (1986). Teaching functions. In M. C. Wittrock (Ed.), *Handbook of research on teaching* (3rd ed.) (pp. 376–391). Englewood Cliffs, NJ: Merrill/Prentice Hall.

Rotter, J., Robinson, E., & Fey M. (1987). *Parent-teacher conferencing*. Washington: National Education Association.

Rowe, M. B. (1974). Wait-time and rewards as instructional variables, their influence on language, logic, and fate control: Part one—wait-time. *Journal of Research in Science Teaching, 11*, 81–94.

Rowe, M. B. (1986). Wait time: Slowing down may be a way of speeding up. *Journal of Teacher Education, 23*, (January–February), 43–49.

Rowe, M. B. (1987). Wait time: Slowing down may be a way of speeding up. *American Educator, 11* (1), 38–43, 47.

Ryan, K. (1992). *The roller coaster year: Essays by and for beginning teachers*. New York: HarperCollins.

Sacks, S. R., & Harrington, C. N. (1982, March). *Student to teacher: The process of role transition*. Paper presented at the meeting of the American Educational Research Association, New York.

Samuels, S. (1981). Some essentials of decoding. *Exceptional Education Quarterly, 2*, 11–25.

Savage, T. (1991). *Discipline for self-control*. Englewood Cliffs, NJ: Prentice Hall.

Sax, G. (1989). *Principles of educational and psychological measurement and evaluation* (3rd ed.). Belmont, CA: Wadsworth.

Scarr, S. (1981). Testing for children: Assessment and the many determinants of intellectual competence. *American Psychologist, 36* (10), 1159–1166.

Schmuck, R., & Schmuck, P. (1992). *Group processes in the classroom* (6th ed.). Dubuque, IA: William C. Brown.

Schutz, W. (1958). *FIRO: A three-dimensional theory of interpersonal behavior*. New York: Holt, Rinehart & Winston.

Scollon, R. (1985). The machine stops: Silence in the metaphor of malfunction. In D. Tannen & M. Saville-Troike (Eds.), *Perspectives on silence*. Norwood, NJ: Ablex.

Shade, B. J. (1982). Afro-American cognitive style: A variable in school success. *Review of Educational Research, 52*, 219–244.

Shalaway, L. (1989). *Learning to teach*. Cleveland, OH: Edgell Communications.

Shavelson, R. J., & Baxter, G. P. (1992). What we've learned about assessing hands-on science. *Educational Leadership, 49* (8), 20–25.

Shavelson, R. J., Gao, X., & Baxter, G. (1991). *Design theory and psychometrics for complex performance assessment*. Los Angeles: UCLA Center for Research on Evaluation, Standards and Student Testing.

Shulman, L. S. (1992). Toward a pedagogy of cases. In J. H. Shulman (Ed.), *Case methods in teacher education* (pp. 72–92). New York: Teachers College Press.

Singer, H., & Donlon, D. (1982). Active comprehension problem-solving schema with question generation for comprehension of complex short stories. *Reading Research Quarterly, 17*, 116–186.

Sizer, T. (1985). *Horace's compromise: The dilemma of the American high school*. Boston: Houghton & Mifflin.

Skinner, B. F. (1953). *Science and human behavior*. Englewood Cliffs, NJ: Merrill/Prentice Hall.

Skrtic, T. M. (1991). The special education paradox: Equity as the way to excellence. *Harvard Educational Review, 61* (2), 148–206.

Slavin, R. (1984). Students motivating students to excel: Cooperative incentives, cooperative tasks and student achievement. *Elementary School Journal, 85*, 53–64.

Slavin, R. (1985). Team-assisted individualization: A cooperative learning solution for adaptive instruction in mathematics. In M. Wang & H. Walberg (Eds.), *Adapting instruction to individual differences*. Berkeley: McCutchan.

Slavin, R. (1987a). Ability grouping and student achievement in elementary schools: A best evidence synthesis. *Review of Educational Research, 57,* 273–336.

Slavin, R. (1987b). *Cooperative learning: Student teams* (2nd ed.). Washington: National Education Association.

Slavin, R. (1990a). Achievement effects of ability grouping in secondary schools: A best evidence synthesis. *Review of Educational Research, 60,* 471–499.

Slavin, R. (1990b). *Cooperative learning.* Englewood Cliffs, NJ: Prentice Hall.

Slavin, R. (1991a). Are cooperative learning and untracking harmful to the gifted? *Educational Leadership, 48,* 68–71.

Slavin, R. (1991b). *Educational psychology: Theory into practice.* Englewood Cliffs, NJ: Prentice Hall.

Slavin, R. (1993). *Student team learning: An overview and practical guide.* Washington, DC: National Education Association.

Slavin, R., Sharan, S., Kagan, S., Hertz-Lazarowitz, R., Webb, C., & Schmuck, R. (1985). *Learning to cooperate, cooperating to learn.* New York: Plenum.

Sleeter, C., & Grant, C. (1991). *Race, class, gender, and disability in current textbooks.* New York: Routledge & Chapman.

Smilansky, M. (1979). *Priorities in education: Preschool, evidence and conclusions.* Washington, DC: World Bank.

Smith, B., & Meux, M. (1970). *A study of the logic of teaching.* Champaign, IL: University of Illinois.

Smith, H. (1984). State of the art of nonverbal behavior in teaching. In A. Wolfgang (Ed.), *Nonverbal behavior: Perspectives, applications, intercultural insights.* New York: Hogrefe.

Soar, R., & Soar, R. (1983). Context effects in the learning process. In D. C. Smith (Ed.), *Essential knowledge for beginning educators* (pp. 156–192). Washington, DC: American Association of Colleges of Teacher Education.

Sparzo, F., & Poteet, J. (1989). *Classroom behavior: Detecting and correcting special problems.* Boston, MA: Allyn & Bacon.

Spielberger, C. (Ed.) (1966). *Anxiety and behavior.* New York: Academic Press.

Stallings, J., & Keepes, B. (1970). *Student aptitudes and methods for teaching beginning reading: A predictive instrument for determining interaction patterns. Final report* (Project No. 9-1-099, Report OEG-9-70-0005). Washington, DC: U.S. Department of Health, Education and Welfare, Office of Education, Bureau of Research.

Sternberg, R. (1989). *The triarchic mind: A new theory of human intelligence.* New York: Penguin.

Stevenson, C., & Carr, J. (Eds.). (1993). *Integrated studies in the middle grades.* New York: Teachers College Press.

Stiggins, R. J. (1994). *Student-centered classroom assessment.* Englewood Cliffs, NJ: Merrill/Prentice Hall.

Swap, S. (1987). *Enhancing parental involvement in schools.* New York: Teachers College Press.

Szetela, W., & Nicol, C. (1992). Evaluating problem solving in mathematics. *Educational Leadership, 49* (8), 42–45.

Tannen, D. (1986). *That's not what I meant!* New York: Morrow.

Terman, L., & Oden, M. (1959). The gifted group in mid-life. In L. Terman (Ed.), *Genetic studies of genius* (Vol. 4). Stanford, CA: Stanford University Press.

Tharp, R. G. (1987, August). *Culture, cognition and education: A culturogenetic analysis of the wholistic complex.* Paper presented at the Conference of the Institute on Literacy and Learning. University of California, Santa Barbara.

Tharp, R. G. (1989). Psychocultural variables and constants: Effects on teaching and learning in schools. *American Psychologist, 44,* 349–359.

Tharp, R. G., & Gallimore, R. (1989). *Rousing minds to life: Teaching, learning and schooling in social context.* New York: Cambridge University Press.

Thorndike, R. L. (1913). *The psychology of learning (Educational Psychology II).* New York: Teachers College Press.

Thurstone, L. (1947). *Primary mental abilities, Form AH*. Chicago: Science Research Associates.

Turnbull, A. P., & Turnbull, H. R. (1986). *Families, professionals and exceptionality*. Englewood Cliffs, NJ: Merrill/Prentice Hall.

Tyler, R. W. (1934). *Constructing achievement tests*. Columbus, OH: Ohio State University Press.

Tyler, R. W. (1974). Considerations in selecting objectives. In D. A. Payne (Ed.), *Curriculum evaluation: Commentaries on purpose, process, product*. Lexington, MA: D. C. Heath.

U.S. General Accounting Office. (1987). *Bilingual education: A new look at the research evidence* (GAO/PEMD—87—12BR). Gaithersburg, MD: Author.

Vasta, R. (1976). Feedback and fidelity: Effects of contingent consequences on accuracy of imitation. *Journal of Experimental Child Psychology, 21*, 98–108.

Vygotsky, L. (1962). *Thought and language*. Cambridge, MA: MIT Press.

Walberg, H. (1986). Syntheses of research on teaching. In M. C. Wittrock (Ed.), *Handbook of research on teaching* (3rd ed.) (pp. 214–229). Englewood Cliffs, NJ: Merrill/Prentice Hall.

Walker, H., & Sylwester, R. (1991). Where is school along the path to prison? *Educational Leadership*, 14–16.

Watson-Gegeo, K. A., & Boggs, S. T. (1977). From verbal play to talk story: The role of routines in speech events among Hawaiian children. In S. Ervin-Tripp & C. Mitchell-Kernan (Eds.), *Child discourse*, 67–90. New York: Academic Press.

Weisner, T., Gallimore, R., & Jordan C. (1988). Unpackaging cultural effects on classroom learning: Native Hawaiian peer assistance and child-generated activity. *Anthropology and Education Quarterly, 19*, 327–353.

Wheelock, A. (1992). The case for untracking. *Educational Leadership, 50* (2), 6–10.

Wiertsch, J. (1980). The significance of dialogue in Vygotsky's account of social, egocentric, and inner speech. *Contemporary Educational Psychology, 5*, 150–162.

Wiggins, G. (1992). Creating tests worth taking. *Educational Leadership, 49* (8), 26–34.

Wilen, W. (1991). *Questioning skills for teachers* (3rd ed.). Washington, DC: NEA.

Willoughby, S. S. (1990). *Mathematics education for a changing world*. Alexandria, VA: Association for Supervision and Curriculum Development.

Wyne, M., & Stuck, G. (1982). Time and learning: Implications for the classroom teacher. *The Elementary School Journal, 83*, 67–75.

Young, V. H. (1970). Family and childhood in a Southern Georgia community. *American Anthropologist, 72*, 269–288.

Ysseldyke, J. E., & Marston, D. (1990). The use of assessment information to plan instructional interventions: A review of the research. In T. B. Gutkin & C. R. Reynolds (Eds.), *The handbook of school psychology* (2nd ed.) (pp. 663–684). New York: Wiley.

Zahorik, J. (1987). Reacting. In M. J. Dunkin (Ed.), *Encyclopedia of teaching and teacher education* (pp. 416–423). New York: Pergamon.

Zakariya, S. (1987). How to keep your balance when it comes to bilingual education. *The American School Board Journal, 6*, 21–26.

Zimbardo, P. G. (1992). *Psychology and life*. New York: HarperCollins.

Zimmerman, B. (1989). A social cognitive view of self-regulated academic learning. *Journal of Educational Psychology, 81*, 329–339.

Zimmerman, B., & Kleefeld, C. (1977). Toward a theory of teaching: A social learning view. *Contemporary Educational Psychology, 2*, 158–171.

Gary Borich grew up on the south side of Chicago, where he attended Mendel High School and later taught in the public school system of Niles, Illinois. He received his Ph.D. from Indiana University, where he was director of evaluation at the Institute for Child Study under Nicholas J. Anastasiow. Dr. Borich is presently a member of the College of Education faculty at the University of Texas at Austin and a past member of the Board of Examiners of the National Council for the Accreditation of Teacher Education.

Dr. Borich's other books include *Clearly Outstanding: Making Each Day Count in Your Classroom, Becoming a Teacher: An Inquiring Dialogue for the Beginning Teacher, Observation Skills for Effective Teaching, Educational Testing and Measurement* (with T. Kubiszyn), and *Educational Psychology: A Contemporary Approach* (with M. Tombari).

Dr. Borich lives in Austin, Texas with his wife, Kathy (a school teacher) and his two children, Brandy and Damon. His interests include training and riding Arabian horses, and pottery.